Cognition

Fully revised and updated for the fifth edition, *Cognition* offers an approachable yet deep introduction to the science of the mind. Avoiding the pitfall of a grab bag of phenomena, Willingham and Riener survey key mental processes such as memory, language, and problem-solving and connect them to experimental process. This new edition has been fully revised and updated with new references, figures, and experiments, with particular attention to the intersection of cognition and culture. Written in a down-to-earth narrative prose that avoids jargon, addresses the reader directly, and cracks a few jokes, *Cognition* offers an accessible introduction that is ideal for students of all levels.

Daniel T. Willingham is Professor of Psychology at the University of Virginia, where he has taught since 1992. He has won multiple department and university teaching awards. His research focuses on the application of cognitive principles to K-16 education, and his work on that subject has appeared in twenty-three languages. In 2017, he was appointed by President Obama to serve as a Member of the National Board for Education Sciences.

Cedar Riener is Professor of Psychology at Randolph-Macon College, where he was awarded the college's highest teaching award in 2021. His primary area of research focuses on our perception of the natural world and how the state of our body influences our perception. He has also written about applying research in cognitive science to education. He teaches courses in Cognition, Perception, Introduction to Psychology, History of Psychology, and several unique seminar courses.

Cognition

The Thinking Animal

Fifth Edition

DANIEL T. WILLINGHAM
University of Virginia

CEDAR RIENER
Randolph-Macon College

CAMBRIDGE
UNIVERSITY PRESS

CAMBRIDGE
UNIVERSITY PRESS

Shaftesbury Road, Cambridge CB2 8EA, United Kingdom

One Liberty Plaza, 20th Floor, New York, NY 10006, USA

477 Williamstown Road, Port Melbourne, VIC 3207, Australia

314–321, 3rd Floor, Plot 3, Splendor Forum, Jasola District Centre, New Delhi – 110025, India

103 Penang Road, #05–06/07, Visioncrest Commercial, Singapore 238467

Cambridge University Press is part of Cambridge University Press & Assessment,
a department of the University of Cambridge.

We share the University's mission to contribute to society through the pursuit of
education, learning and research at the highest international levels of excellence.

www.cambridge.org
Information on this title: www.cambridge.org/highereducation/isbn/9781009244374

DOI: 10.1017/9781009244367

First, Second and Third editions published by Pearson Education, Inc., 2001, 2004, and 2007 respectively.
Fourth edition published by Cambridge University Press 2019.
Reprinted 2020
Fifth edition published by Cambridge University Press 2025.

A catalog record for this publication is available from the British Library.

Library of Congress Cataloging-in-Publication Data
Names: Willingham, Daniel T., author. | Riener, Cedar, 1976- author.
Title: Cognition : the thinking animal / Daniel T. Willingham, University of Virginia, Cedar Riener,
    Randolph-Macon College.
Description: Fifth edition. | Cambridge, United Kingdom ; New York, NY, USA : Cambridge University Press,
    2024. | Includes bibliographical references and index.
Identifiers: LCCN 2024012509 | ISBN 9781009244374 (hardback) | ISBN 9781009244398 (paperback) |
    ISBN 9781009244367 (ebook)
Subjects: LCSH: Cognitive psychology.
Classification: LCC BF201 .W56 2024 | DDC 153–dc23/eng/20240424
LC record available at https://lccn.loc.gov/2024012509

ISBN 978-1-009-24437-4 Hardback
ISBN 978-1-009-24439-8 Paperback

Additional resources for this publication at www.cambridge.org/willingham-riener

Brief Contents

Contents

Preface

Many instructors believe that cognitive psychology does not have the intrinsic interest of some other areas in the field. Textbook authors try to overcome this problem by including "real-world" examples and many demonstrations, usually found in little boxes that appear every few pages. We believe that the basic research into how we think is interesting in itself, and we've done three things in this book to communicate this interest to the reader:

- We begin with the basic questions that people find interesting, phrased in a plain and straightforward way. In addition, these questions are posed so that they can be answered by empirical research in cognitive psychology, for example, "In what way is attention a limited resource?" and "Is language special?" Each chapter in this book is organized around two or three such questions that are easy to appreciate and the importance of which is explained in detail.

- We use a narrative structure. There are links within and across chapter sections so that it is clear why you are reading something. The models of memory presented in Chapter 8 explain memory performance on many laboratory tests but don't allow for complicated relationships among ideas. The concept of a structured mental representation, which does help to relate different ideas, is introduced in Chapter 9. Then, research on structured mental representations is expanded upon in Chapters 10 and 11 with linguistic representations.

- We write in an approachable style that is not overly academic. When we discuss whether brain localization informs cognitive function, we ask, "Where is the damage?" and "Where is the activation?" We address whether neuroscience alone will describe how we think with "Do we really need cognitive psychology?"

Pedagogical Features

Readability is fine, but the goal of a textbook is, after all, that students learn the material. Different students like and use different pedagogical features, so we've included a few different ones to help them learn.

- Brief previews of each section pose the broad questions and provide the broad answers contained in the section.

- Key terms are identified by boldface type and are defined immediately thereafter. They are also collected in a glossary.

- Each section closes with two types of review questions.

- The first type gets the reader to pause for a moment and make sure they understood the major points by summarizing what they have just read.

- The second type requires the student to apply what they have just learned to new situations or to go beyond the material in some way.

We believe this text will make students enthusiastic about this field and will make them curious to learn more than they can find within the covers of this book. In short, we hope that this book will serve as a starting point from which students will want to learn still more about the field.

Changes in This Edition

There are two major changes in this edition, in addition to updated references.

First, the chapter on visual imagery has been moved into an appendix. While the concepts in this chapter are interesting to both authors and many teachers of cognitive psychology, it is our judgment that getting the book to thirteen chapters to complement the number of weeks in a typical semester is an improvement and that visual imagery is not currently an active enough area of research in cognitive psychology to merit an entire chapter.

Second, we have added far more inclusion of the role of culture in cognition throughout the book as well as citations and references from research and perspectives across the world. A new subsection in Chapter 9 asks, "How does culture shape concepts and categories?" The section on history and development of psychology now includes expanded discussion of the importance of the Islamic Golden Age in preserving and advancing scientific and intellectual traditions in between classical Greek philosophers and the Renaissance in Western Europe. The examples used to describe spreading activation models now include cultural variation in breakfast foods. This new emphasis shows how valuable it can be for student knowledge to be inclusive of a wide variety of cultural perspectives to show that there are both interesting variations across the world in how we think and universal principles of mental processes.

1 Cognitive Psychologists' Approach to Research

Introduction

When you are driving and your mind wanders from the song on the radio to the next left turn to what's for dinner, do you pause in the middle to wonder what makes your mind wander? Probably not. Many people only contemplate how the mind works when their minds let them down. They contemplate memory ("Why can't I remember the answer to this test question?"), attention ("I want to understand this material, so why can't I keep my focus on my book and not on my phone?"), and vision ("How could someone think those two colors go well together?"). Questions such as "How does vision work?" seem somewhat interesting, but no more interesting than thousands of other questions about how the world works (How do viruses work? How do cell phones work? How do your lungs work?). These questions become interesting to most people when they consider how the answers might help their own lives. For example, if we understood how vision worked, maybe we could build cars that can see (see Figure 1.1).

To scientists, these questions are the fascinating entry into a world of other questions. Once we start looking a little closer and more systematically (by using the methods of science), we can

Figure 1.1. As it turns out, engineers designing self-driving cars gave up on making cars see as well as people (solving "human vision") and added a bunch of useful sensors, such as GPS, lidar (which sends out pulses of light and measures how they bounce back), radar, and infrared and ultrasonic sensors, all unavailable to human vision. (Source: JasonDoiy/ iStock Unreleased/Getty Images.)

uncover answers to these vital questions, but we also discover new layers of questions. Viruses have parts, but how are these parts related, and what are their functions? How do viruses reproduce? What are the steps in the process, and what happens if we interfere?

Cognitive psychology is a science of mental processes. This book is therefore an introduction to the scientific study of your own mind. We will provide some answers you didn't know you wanted and a world of fascinating questions you didn't know you had about something we all too often take for granted: our own minds.

The first thing we have to decide, then, is which questions to ask – how to get more specific than "How do we see?" You'll find that the questions we ask are deeply influenced by assumptions we make about the mind and, indeed, assumptions about what it is to be human.

It seems obvious that it would be better not to make assumptions when we are just starting to study the mind. After all, shouldn't we have an open mind about what we might find before we begin our investigation? The first question to take up is, **Why make assumptions?** As we'll see, the answer is that it is often impossible to avoid making assumptions. If that's true, we should at least be clear about the assumptions cognitive psychologists make. If you know the assumptions, it will be clearer why cognitive psychologists ask the questions they do, and if you understand why they ask a particular question, it will be much easier to understand the answer.

As with any set of questions and assumptions, the approach cognitive psychologists take has developed over time, in response both to other approaches that people had tried in the past and to other historical contexts, such as technology and culture. Thus, our second question is, **How did**

philosophers and early psychologists study the mind? As we'll see, several different approaches have been tried in the last 2,000 years, but it was only about 150 years ago that scientists began a serious, systematic effort to apply the scientific method to human thought. That date is some 200 years or more after the scientific method had been used in other domains of knowledge. Furthermore, cognitive psychology was not the first scientific approach to studying the mind; it arose in response to flaws in other methods.

Finally, our third question is, **How do cognitive psychologists study the mind?** As we'll see, the cognitive approach began with an analogy of the mind to a computer. Like a computer, the mind takes in information, manipulates it, and then produces responses. The truth is more complicated than that, of course, and we elaborate on this metaphor later.

Why Make Assumptions?

Preview

People make two types of assumptions when they study the mind. The first assumption concerns the questions we ask. Our mental processes are not obviously composed of parts, or based on foundations, so breaking the big questions into parts or foundations involves assumptions about what those big questions are and how they can be divided. We can't study everything at once, so we must pick some aspect of the mind as a starting point for study. The second assumption is that the way the mind works will be related to our experiences of how it works. In other words, as we study the mind, we are guided by a set of general, vague beliefs about vision, attention, or memory based on how it feels to see, attend, and remember. In this section, we look at examples of these assumptions in the study of vision.

Psychologists typically make two types of assumptions in studying the mind. First, we make assumptions about what aspects of the mind are important enough to explain. We can't say, for example, "This study will explain everything about vision." Of course, we want to do that eventually, but we have to start somewhere. So what question about vision will we pose first? Maybe, "How do we perceive colors?" Or "How do we perceive space? Or objects? Or motion?" All of these are possible starting points, but they also represent an assumption, namely, that they are separate questions. Are perceiving an object's color and perceiving that object's motion separate psychological processes? Does recognizing an object require a different mental process than knowing its location so you can grab it? Is it best to separate our study into perception of object features (such as color, motion, location) or separate types of objects (such as faces, people, cars, food)?

The second type of assumption is that beliefs about mental processes are often based on our own experience of them. For example, we assume that our eyes are active agents in perception, that they *do* something to help us see; indeed, as we move our heads, point our eyes in different directions, and focus on objects, we perceive different parts of the world. But a faulty assumption also stems from this experience. Some people today (and many people years ago) thought that we perceive the world by emitting something from our eyes. In antiquity, many believed that the mechanism for vision was some sort of invisible ray shooting out of our eyes, rebounding off the world, and returning to tell us its characteristics (see Figure 1.2). Such an assumption might lead us

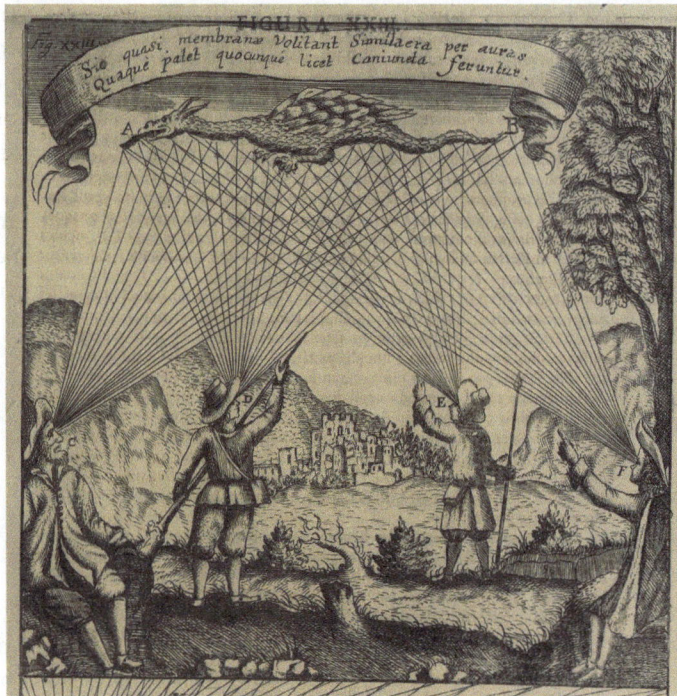

Figure 1.2. Many ancient philosophers thought that vision was dependent on rays emitted from the eyes. The Muslim polymath Ibn al-Haytham (or the Latinized version of Alhazen) was one of the first to propose a purely intromission theory (only rays coming in), in the tenth century, but such beliefs persisted. Even Leonardo da Vinci remained convinced that our eyes emitted rays. (Source: Johann Zahn's *Oculus Artificialis* [1685], https://publicdomainreview .org/collections/images-from-johann-zahns-oculus-artificialis-1685/.)

to investigate the nature of those rays. Interestingly, many young children (Winer & Cottrell, 1996) and some adults (Winer et al., 2002) still believe something like this.

Here's another example of each type of assumption (the first, what's to be explained, and the second, how our experience of a mental process is a good guide to how it works). For most of the last 2,000 years, people interested in vision have wanted to explain the conscious experience of visual perception, asking, "How do we consciously perceive the qualities of an object – its shape, size, and distance?" In assuming that the conscious experience of perception was what needed explaining, unconscious processes involved in vision were not considered. For the second type of assumption, in seeking to explain conscious perception, most investigators have assumed that what seem like distinct and separable qualities in our conscious visual experience are processed separately and therefore can be investigated separately. For example, color, shape, and motion feel like different conscious visual properties and are therefore (we assume) supported by different mental processes. This is a pretty useful assumption, but it is not always true, as the illusion in Figure 1.3 shows.

Cognitive psychologists also seek to explain conscious visual perception, but they are more interested in the unconscious processes that eventually lead to conscious perception. In some ways, visual information in consciousness is the end point of vision; we need to explain the many steps that lead to this end point. Indeed, it has recently become obvious that some types of vision never become conscious. For example, some parts of the visual system help you maintain your balance, but you are never aware of any aspect of this type of vision.

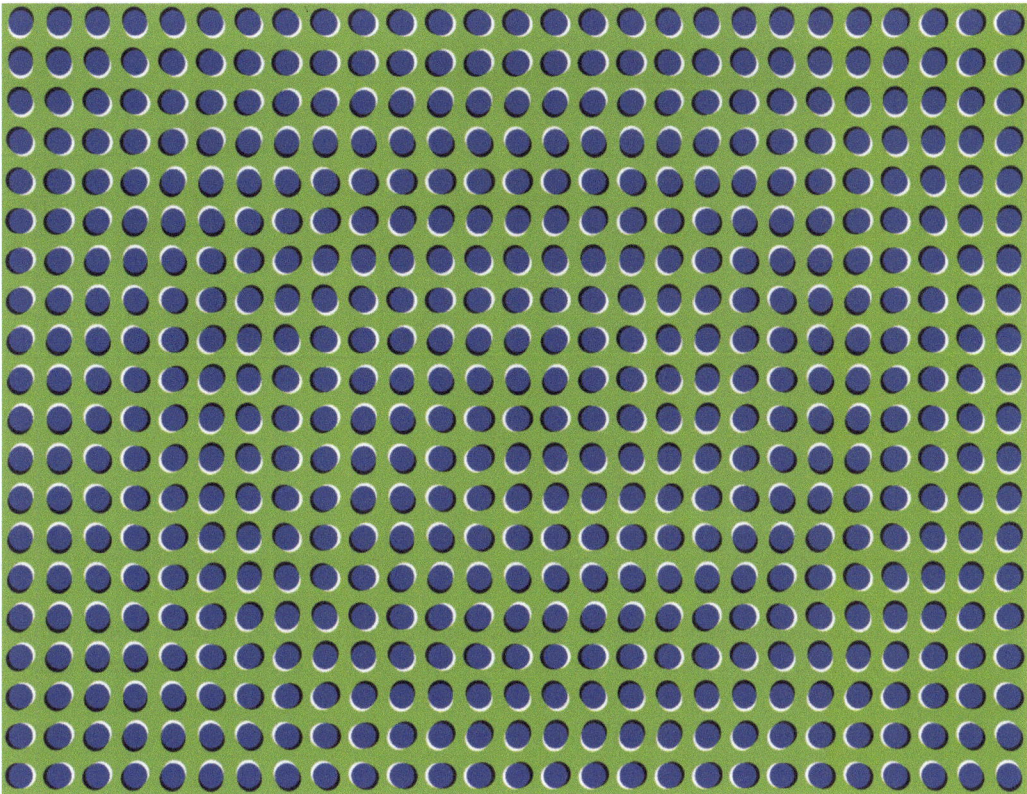

Figure 1.3. Color, shape, and motion seem like they should be independent and separate mental processes, but it turns out that certain colors and shapes can cause us to see motion. (Source: Akiyoshi Kitaoka.)

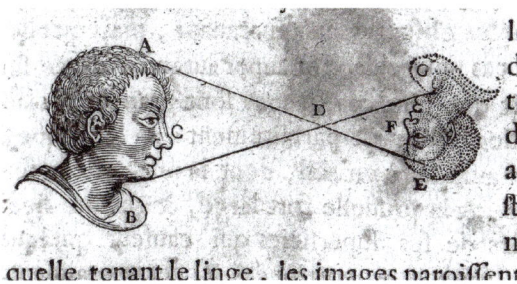

quelle tenant le linge , les images paroiſſent

Figure 1.4. Light falling on the eye is inverted by the lens. Descartes depicted this in a drawing for his *Discourse on the Methods*. Therefore, the image on the retina is upside down compared with objects in the real world. (Source: Wellcome Collection. Reproduced under Creative Commons License Attribution 4.0 International [CC BY 4.0].)

The second type of assumption, about the characteristics of mental processes, includes beliefs that influence the questions we pose when we study something. For example, one dilemma about vision was this: Light enters the opening at the front of the eye so that the image is projected onto the back of the eye upside down. We obviously don't see the world upside down, so how does the image get turned right side up? (See Figure 1.4.)

This question was posed in 1604 after Johannes Kepler speculated that the crystalline body of the eye functions as a lens and therefore inverts the image. (René Descartes put the idea to the test

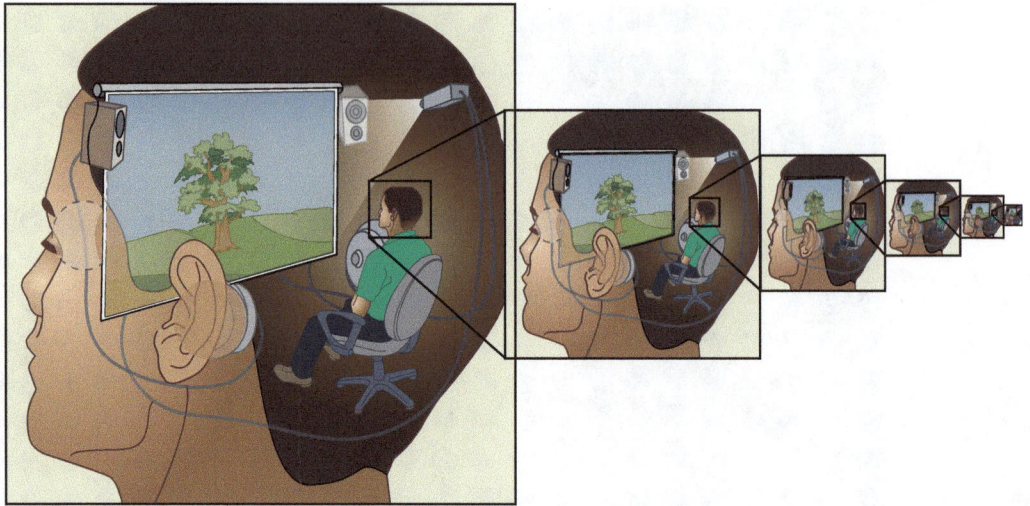

Figure 1.5. If there is a little person in your head, watching the image on the back of your eye, like a movie screen, what is inside the head of that little person that enables them to perceive the world? (Source: Illustration by Jennifer Garcia.)

some twenty years thereafter, conducting an experiment with the eye of a bull.) This question bothered philosophers until the early nineteenth century, even though William Molyneux, writing in 1692, gave the correct answer to this problem: It's not really a problem. It doesn't matter that the top of the world is represented on the bottom of the **retina** (the layer that contains the light-sensitive cells at the back of the eye).

Why was the inversion of the retinal image so perplexing? Because of a background assumption about vision everyone was making. It seemed reasonable to assume that the conscious perception of the visual world was not in the retina but in some part of the brain. The assumption was that the retina presents an image to the part of the brain that handles conscious perception. You might think of the back of the eye as a screen on which another part of the brain watches the world go by – upside down. So the natural question to ask is, "How does the mind perceive the world right side up?" But this assumption is wrongheaded, because the conscious visual part of the brain is not a little person watching the retina. Who would watch that little person? And what happens to their eyes? (See Figure 1.5.)

Here's another way of thinking about it: The way that your visual system translates the pattern of light into brain signal (which then leads to your conscious experience of seeing) is when the pigment inside your rod and cone photoreceptors undergoes a chemical change in response to light. In addition, your ability to change your focus from near to far objects depends on muscles flexing and relaxing inside your eyeball. So moving your eyes to focus from this well-lit page to a darker object in the distance involves both muscles moving and a chemical change in cell pigments. Your conscious experience, however, does not feel like either muscle relaxation or chemical bleaching. Our experience does not necessarily give us insight into the biology of our eye; it also does not necessarily give us insight into the mechanisms of our mind.

Johannes Müller, a German physiologist, proposed instead that everything the mind perceives is a function of the state of the nerves coming into the brain. He called it the "theory of specific nerve energies" (Müller, 1840). The pattern of neural activity is perception; perception is not the product of a little person in your brain watching an image that your eye makes. Therefore, it doesn't matter whether the top of the world is represented in the top or the bottom of the retina, as

(a)

(b)

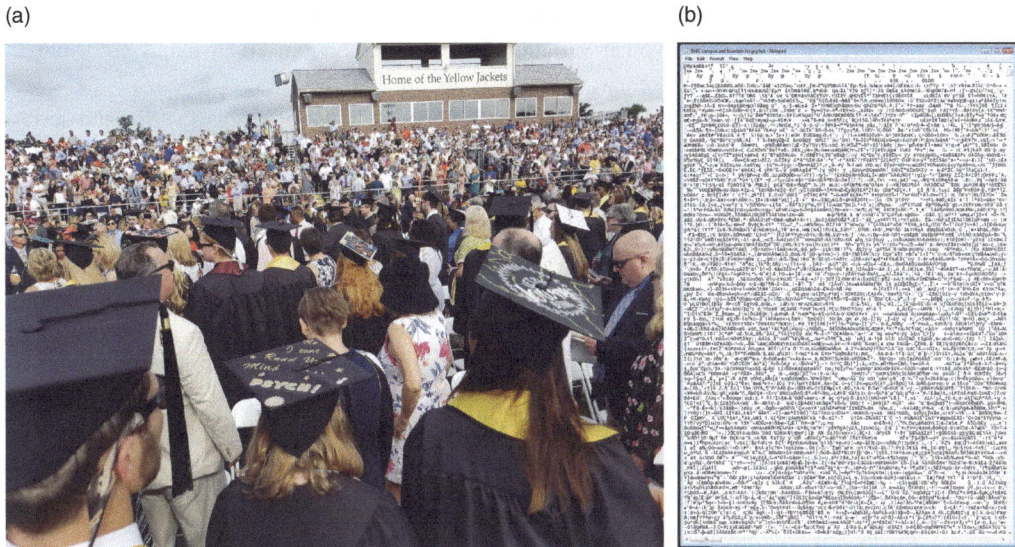

Figure 1.6. A computer can represent (a) the image of a happy college graduation (b) in a format that looks nothing like the image. The representation is interpreted by software in the computer and displayed as an image on the screen. The cells in our eye and brain could do the same thing, representing the light, dark, and color of a scene without being "image-like" at each step. This is why the "upside-down problem" is not really a problem. (Source: (b) Photograph by Cedar Riener.)

long as there is a consistent relationship between what is in the world and the overall pattern of neural activity to which it leads. If the top of the world could be represented anywhere in the retina, that would be a problem, but with the top of the world consistently in the bottom of the retina, we understand what we are seeing.

Here's another way to think about it. As you might know, a computer graphic file is stored as a series of 1s and 0s. You might have discovered this fact if you tried to open an image file with a word processor. When they are interpreted by the (correct) software in your computer, the 1s and 0s form an image of . . . let's say a lovely view of a college graduation. You would not expect that if you printed out the 1s and 0s on a piece of paper, they would form the image of the graduation; the 1s and 0s are a different representation of the image of the view (see Figure 1.6). If you were transmitting that information, information from the top of the image wouldn't have to be transmitted first. In the same way, the pattern of neural activity on the retina doesn't have to look like the thing it's representing. Once you drop the belief that the pattern of neural activity on the retina must look like what is out in the world, you realize the inverted image is not a problem. The way that information about the light gets from the retina to the brain is not as an image but as a code. And codes aren't upside down or right side up.

If making assumptions prompts you to ask pointless questions, it seems obvious enough that we should avoid making assumptions. But it's much harder than you might think not to assume anything. Many of our assumptions are hard to spot because we take them for granted. Had the authors of this book lived in the seventeenth century, we don't think we would have been smarter than everyone else about the lens-inverting-the-image problem. We would have been scratching our heads with the rest of them.

One important assumption that cognitive psychologists make concerns the similarity of mental processes across people. We each have unique experiences and therefore different memories, and different views on the world, but how different are the basic *processes* used to sense and think about the world? What's more, within the range of human differences, what is "typical" and what is "atypical"? What is typical variation in color perception, and what is color-blindness? What is typical variation in memory, and what is an amnesic disorder?

Cognitive psychologists are generally more interested in discovering and describing commonalities in mental processes across people, rather than in how these processes differ. For example, there are important debates about the line between neurotypical and neurodivergent individuals, whether in memory, attention, or social expressions and communication. Cognitive psychologists acknowledge these differences and this complicated debate, but we try to understand the universal elements of mental processes, which don't require us to resolve those issues first.

Let's take an example. All human eyes have a hole (the pupil) in the front, a light-sensitive surface in back, and photoreceptors that have different wavelength sensitivities to help us see color. Human beings, across many boundaries of diversity, use visual perception to help us navigate, communicate, and recognize objects, as well as each other. Cognitive psychologists, while acknowledging the vast diversity in human navigation, communication, and recognition, seek to understand the universals in these mental processes, just as a biologist might seek to understand the biological universals in the structures of the eye.

We did say cognitive psychologists are "generally" more interested in universals, but we will also present cases where exceptional people have helped to reveal universal patterns in mental processes. Sometimes people with unusual and tragic damage to their brains, such as the case of Henry Molaison, help illustrate the nature of memory processes, as we'll see in Chapter 5. Some people with unusual language experiences, such as deaf children in Nicaragua we'll read more about in Chapter 12, help reveal universal patterns of language learning and processing. Informative exceptions can reveal general rules.

So we need to ask what assumptions cognitive psychologists make. How do they view the mind? What questions seem natural to ask if you're a cognitive psychologist? We get to that later in the chapter. In fact, we're going to step back before continuing our discussion of studying the mind with cognitive psychology. The field of cognitive psychology is only about sixty years old, yet people have been thinking about how the mind works for more than 2,400 years. It is misleading to wrench cognitive psychology out of that historical context. Many of the ideas in cognitive psychology grew out of older ideas or, in some cases, in direct opposition to older ideas. So we start with the older ideas, which set the stage for cognitive psychology. We will follow a similar pattern in many future chapters, understanding how older ideas (which are often the first that come to mind) have changed our assumptions about the mind.

Stand-on-One-Foot Questions

1.1.   What two types of assumptions are usually made when we study the mind?

Question That Requires Two Feet

1.2.   When we study the mind, we can't observe it directly. We can observe what people do, and we can observe the environment around them, but we can't observe thought directly. What do you think this fact will mean for theories of the mind?

1.3.   Why isn't it a problem that the the image on the back of our eye is inverted?

How Did Philosophers and Early Psychologists Study the Mind?

Preview

We can identify three waves in the history of the study of the mind before the advent of cognitive psychology. In the first wave, philosophers considered the workings of the mind. They were interested primarily in the acquisition of knowledge in all its forms. The second wave occurred in the late nineteenth century, when researchers applied the scientific method (which stresses observation, not reason alone) to the study of the mind. Although the scientific method had been developed during the Renaissance and applied to other domains, it had not been applied to the mind, mostly because of assumptions people held about how the mind was likely to work. Initially, psychology was largely the study of conscious experience, but it took a radical turn between 1910 and the 1920s, when consciousness was expunged and psychology became the science of overt behavior. This movement, called behaviorism, was the third wave. Behaviorism was ascendant until the late 1950s, when mental life reasserted itself as an important part of any explanation of human behavior.

In this section, we cover three broad trends in the history of the study of the mind before the development of cognitive psychology. The first trend concerns the philosophical background of the study of the mind. We discuss mainly Western philosophy because that is the philosophical tradition that influenced early psychologists and, eventually, cognitive psychologists. Other thinkers certainly thought about the mind, such as Ibn al-Haytham (mentioned earlier) understanding vision as receiving light, not emitting anything (Falco, 2017), or ancient Indian philosophers of Samkhya-Yoga (Sedlmeier & Srinivas, 2016), but many of their ideas did not have as direct an influence on modern thought, even if they were closer to the truth than many of their Western counterparts.

More recently, some cognitive psychologists are wondering how assumptions modern cognitive psychologists have inherited from their predominantly Western tradition can limit the generality of current findings: Is how the mind works in our studies really how all minds work? The historical development of modern psychology was mostly guided by educated rich white men in Western industrialized countries. One of the limits of this guidance was that the minds being studied were also this same group of people, recently described by the acronym **WEIRD**: Western, educated, industrialized, rich, and democratic (Henrich, 2020). Even today, this legacy of WEIRD experimental participants in psychology continues, though there are efforts to remedy it (Silan et al., 2021). Has the narrow group of people who have historically guided the field led it to narrow conclusions, leaving gaps and flaws in the knowledge of how the mind works? As we cover domains of cognition later in the book, we will consider this question, as well as including global voices, as cognitive psychology is now actively studied across the entire world.

The second trend concerns the application of the scientific method to the study of the mind. Even if the scientific method was applied to much of the physical world in the eighteenth century, it wasn't until much later that it was used to study the human mind. The third concerns the abandonment of the study of the mind in favor of the study of behavior. Studying mental processes proved quite difficult for early scientific psychologists, and focusing on behavior, instead of mental processes, dominated psychology in the early twentieth century.

Philosophical Underpinnings

ANCIENT GREECE   Approximately 2,400 years ago, the philosophers of ancient Greece left the first written record displaying consistent curiosity about the mind and speculation about how it works (although there are bits and pieces scattered through earlier documents).

Philosophy is the pursuit of knowledge in all its forms, although over time many philosophical questions have been co-opted by the sciences. Because knowledge is central to philosophy, philosophers have been especially interested in how knowledge is acquired. There are three ways of asking how knowledge is acquired, and these three questions were later asked by cognitive psychologists:

- **Perception.** How do we gain access to knowledge about the world immediately around us?
- **Memory.** How do we retain knowledge about the world for later use?
- **Nature and nurture.** What is the origin of knowledge? Is knowledge gained through experience, or is it largely innate, with experience serving to release or activate knowledge we are born with?

The Greek philosophers posed questions about the mind that were relevant to their broader interests about knowledge. How accurate were their answers? They weren't even close. In fact, the Greeks were usually incorrect both in outlook and in detail. For example, Plato proposed that visual perception occurs when the eye emits some sort of beam, which combines with an essence of the object and then projects back to the eye, an idea we've already mentioned held sway for a long time.

Maybe the answers that Greek philosophers produced were not accurate, but were they at least asking good questions? Many books will tell you that the Greeks' lasting contribution lies in the questions they raised, which set the agenda for future philosophers and eventually for cognitive psychology. We don't think that's quite accurate, though. Their real contribution lay not in their specific questions but in three assumptions they made that allowed them to pose those questions:

- **The world is predictable.** The world can be understood and predicted because it works in systematic ways. If events occurred randomly or at the whim of capricious gods, trying to predict events would be hopeless.
- **Humans are physical objects.** Humans are part of the physical world, and as is true for other entities in the world, we can potentially understand and predict how they will operate. If humans were completely different from physical objects and animals, we could never hope to predict what people might do or think.
- **Explanations of phenomena should consist of other physical events.** Explanations of events in this world should rely on other events within this world instead of invoking magical or mystical happenings. For example, Hippocrates proposed that epilepsy was a disease of the body (as other diseases were understood to be), thereby rejecting earlier views that it resulted from the direct intervention of a god.

These beliefs seem so natural to us today that it is hard to remember that they are assumptions. Indeed, these three assumptions are critical to all the sciences. Experience tells us that these assumptions are helpful in trying to explain things around us; at the time the Greeks first made them, however, they were quite bold. Once you assume that the world is predictable, that you can understand it, and that humans have no special place in this world (meaning that human behavior can be explained just like anything else), it is natural to take the next step and ask a few questions about how the human mind works, such as how it perceives and remembers things. Again, it's the assumptions of the ancient Greeks that are most impressive rather than the questions or the answers they posed.

Figure 1.7. The Romans, who built amazing ways to move water through their cities, were not as concerned with figuring out how thoughts moved throughout their minds. (Source: David Soanes Photography/Moment/Getty Images.)

THE DARK AGES AND THE MIDDLE AGES   Few lasting influences were added to the philosophy of mind between the time of Aristotle, who died in 322 BCE, and the birth of Descartes at the end of the sixteenth century. How is this possible?

Several factors contributed to this turn of focus away from the mind. By 146 BCE Greece was dominated by the Romans, who had a more practical mind-set than the Greeks. Pursuit of knowledge for its own sake was not especially esteemed, so no one was asking where knowledge comes from, as the Greeks had (see Figure 1.7). After the fall of the Roman Empire in 476 CE, Western Europe was dominated by various Germanic peoples, usually called barbarians. Although *barbarian* has unpleasant connotations that aren't fairly applied to these folks, they also had other things on their minds besides, well, minds. In addition, feudalism and the decline of urbanism did little to help intellectual life. Nor did the ascendance of the Christian Church around the year 400 make for a favorable climate for philosophy of mind. The Church was interested in the soul, not in scholarly pursuits unrelated to theology.

While Western Europe may have turned away from the philosophy of mind of the Greeks, the Islamic world had a flourishing intellectual, scientific, and philosophical period, called the Islamic Golden Age, roughly dated from the eighth century to the fourteenth century. Islamic scholars translated many classical Greek texts and continued developing these ideas and combining them with Islamic theology. (See Figure 1.8.) Abu-Ali al-Husayn ibn Abdalah ibn-Sina (known to the Western world as Avicenna) (980–1030) made many contributions across the sciences, including describing many mental illnesses and proposing memory as one of five internal senses (Müller, 2015). Abu Zayd al-Baleki (850–934) was a physician who emphasized the connection of the mind, body, and spirit (Mitha, 2020). The Renaissance in Western Europe was thereby influenced both by

عمر كثير البوحيد ... والشرب ...
... الرياضة ...
... المنطق ...

Figure 1.8. Islamic scholars during the Islamic Golden Age (roughly eighth to fourteenth centuries) translated and commented on classical Greek texts. Here a thirteenth-century text depicts Sughrat (or Socrates) teaching his pupils.

the preservation of the classical texts through translation from Islamic scholars and by unique contributions and intellectual developments of the Islamic Golden Age.

THE RENAISSANCE THROUGH THE NINETEENTH CENTURY

The Advent of the Scientific Method. The **Renaissance** refers to a time in Europe (the thirteenth through seventeenth centuries, very broadly) marked by the rise of humanism, a subsequent flowering of literature and the arts, and the beginnings of modern science. Humanism emphasizes secular concerns and the individual (as opposed to religious concerns and the religious community). From the viewpoint of a cognitive psychologist, a critical feature of the Renaissance was the return of one of the assumptions characteristic of ancient Greece (and sustained through the translation, maintenance, and expansion of science in the Islamic Golden Age): that the world can be understood and predicted, and even more, that trying to understand the world is a worthwhile pursuit. Thus, the literal meaning of *renaissance* ("rebirth") is appropriate. The Renaissance also saw a birth: the birth of modern science.

What makes something scientific? We often think of science as being associated with white coats and antiseptic laboratory equipment. In fact, science is not characterized by the people who do it or by subject matter. Science is simply a *method* of finding out new things. The scientific method is well suited to some questions ("What does the heart do?") and poorly suited to other questions ("What makes a song great?").

What made the scientific method new in the Renaissance was its emphasis on observation as a route to knowledge. How do you know something is true? There are two possible roads to the truth: You can sit in your armchair and reason about what you think must be true, or you can go out and observe what happens in the world. For example, you might reason that planetary orbits must be circles because a circle is a perfect shape, and it would make sense for the Universe to be organized

(a)

Figure 1.9. The two main methods of inquiry: reasoning and observation. (a) In Raphael's *School of Athens*, the Renaissance artist depicts influential philosophers from throughout history engaged in reasoning about the world through debate, contemplation, and consulting texts. (Source: Universal History Archive/Getty Images.)

in terms of perfect shapes. Or you might get a telescope and make observations of the planets and try to determine what orbital shape is consistent with your observations. Before the Renaissance, people did some observation, but contemplation and logic were more often considered the best routes to knowledge. (See Figure 1.9.)

Here is Galileo complaining to Kepler about philosophers who refused to look through his telescope:

> My dear Kepler, I wish that we might laugh at the remarkable stupidity of the common herd. What do you have to say about the principal philosophers of this academy who are filled with the stubbornness of an asp and do not want to look at either the planets, the moon or the telescope, even though I have freely and deliberately offered them the opportunity a thousand times? Truly, just as the asp stops its ears, so do these philosophers shut their eyes to the light of truth.
>
> Verily, just as serpents close their ears, so do these men close their eyes to the light of truth. These are great matters; yet they do not occasion any surprise. People of this sort think that philosophy is a kind of book like the *Æneid* or the *Odyssey*, and that the truth is to be sought, not in the universe, not in nature, but (I use their own words) by comparing texts! (Bethune, 1830, p. 29)

(b)

Figure 1.9. *(cont.)* (b) In the second painting – *Galileo Demonstrating His Telescope* by Henry-Julien Detouche – Galileo seems to be saying, "If you just turn your head and put your eye at the end of that metal pipe, you can see the stars; you don't have to reason about them, you can see them with your own eyes." (Source: Universal History Archive/Getty Images.)

There are two things to bear in mind. First, scientists have always used both methods. After you've made your observations, you still go back to your armchair to try to make sense of them, using reason. But the key is that then you go back out into the world again, armed with new predictions (the product of your reasoning), which you will test with new observations. Galileo wants the stubborn philosophers to look into his telescope, then confront what those observations tell them about their theory of astronomy (maybe Jupiter has moons, and if Jupiter has moons, then Earth isn't the only heavenly object with something else orbiting around it). Overreliance on armchair reasoning as the only method, without directly observing (whether moons, planets, or mental processes), limits scientific progress.

The second thing to bear in mind is just because you're observing doesn't mean that you won't make (occasionally colossal) mistakes. Aristotle's observations led him to conclude that the mind must be located in the heart, not the brain, because people sometimes survived severe injury to the brain, but they never survived serious injury to the heart. Many seasoned observers concluded that flies spontaneously came into being on rotting flesh, after seeing maggots appear with seemingly no precursor.

Renaissance scientists made mistakes of interpretation (like Aristotle and even scientists today), but they were sound in their emphasis on observation. The attempt to understand nature through observation had a number of dramatic successes during the Renaissance. Copernicus asserted that Earth revolves around the Sun and not vice versa; Galileo formulated the law relating distance, time, and the speed of free-falling bodies; Isaac Newton discovered that gravity rules both heavenly bodies and the humble apple; and William Harvey learned that blood circulates and that the heart functions as a pump. All these advances were triumphs of the observational method as a path to knowledge. Such emphasis on observation wasn't unique to this time and place. For example, Muḥammad ibn Mūsā al-Khwārizmī (whose latinized name, Algoritmi de numero Indorum, became the word *algorithm* and whose widely used textbook became *algebra*) made important astronomical observations and introduced the Indian decimal system of numbers to European mathematicians around 820 CE. But the Renaissance saw an acceleration of this approach to gaining knowledge.

Why Didn't Psychology Start until 1879?   The pace of science picked up in the seventeenth century as advances were made in astronomy, physics, chemistry, and biology. So why did it take another 200 years for scientists to apply the scientific method to the study of the mind? You might imagine that it was an equipment problem – scientists needed computers, sophisticated timing devices, and so forth. Forget it. Revealing experiments on the workings of the mind can be done with a deck of playing cards (invented in about the tenth century). Indeed, there are still interesting experiments conducted with playing cards or similar stimuli (Craig et al., 2016).

No, the problem was still one of assumptions. The Renaissance brought back two of the assumptions the Greek philosophers made: that the world can be understood and predicted and that explanations should be of this world (i.e., we can't invoke ghosts or gods in our explanations). But the third assumption – that humans have no special status – was difficult to resurrect. Renaissance thinkers could accept that the human body was like the bodies of other animals, but the human mind remained special in their view. Whatever it was that made decisions and guided the human body was unique (and uniquely blessed).

Suppose we assume that humans have no special status in the world, so our behavior is as predictable as the behavior of physical bodies (e.g., a falling apple). Humans are more complex, obviously, but they are still predictable. What does being predictable imply? It implies that the mind follows a set of rules. When you're in situation A, your mind follows rule 1; when you're in situation B, it follows rule 2; and so on. In saying that behavior is predictable, we are essentially saying, "It is possible to have a complete understanding of human behavior such that I can know what a person will do before they do it." This view is called **deterministic**.

The alternative is a **nondeterministic** view. This view says, "No, there is something else that guides our thoughts and determines our actions. Call it a soul, if you like. It's the working of this other agent that gives us free will. We are free to act as we please, so you will never be able to predict another person's behavior accurately."

Under the nondeterministic view – accepting the belief that people have free will – studying the mind seems futile. Psychology tries to understand why people act as they do. But if they act as they do because of the vagaries of free will, which is by definition not bound by rules, how will psychologists ever understand human behavior? They won't.

During the Renaissance, most people probably assumed that free will existed. They would have recognized that the scientific method could analyze the behavior of inanimate bodies such as planets and falling rocks, but they would have believed that humans are wholly different. The idea of applying the scientific method to studying the mind probably would have seemed as ridiculous to them as it would seem to you if we suggested that we apply the scientific method to deciding who you should marry.

The foregoing discussion does not mean that scientists believe that there is no such thing as a soul or that there is no such thing as free will. Whether you have a soul is a question that science is not well suited to answer. Many scientists believe that humans have a soul and have free will. Yet we cannot use these concepts in scientific theories and explanations of human behavior. Even if they exist, they are not understood in a scientific sense, so they don't mesh well with other scientific concepts.

Many psychological scientists therefore choose a middle path. They avoid explaining *individual* thought and behavior in a purely deterministic manner ("He remembered eighteen out of twenty words on that test because he studied for 2.7 hours using spaced repetition study technique"). Instead scientists recognize that while each person experiences individual free will, when scientists look at behavior across many people in the same situation, or the same person across different situations, they see patterns of predictability and the limits on free will. Individuals may be free to devote their attention anywhere they please when watching TV, but the attention of the average person is guided by sudden motion or a flash of color. Individuals are free to buy what food they please at the grocery store, but companies pay millions to have their products placed in high-visibility areas because on average, physical convenience powerfully influences purchasing decisions.

The great philosopher Immanuel Kant raised a different objection to a science of the mind. He concluded that mental processes take place in time, but they don't take up any space and therefore can't be measured. Thus, the scientific method could not be applied to mental processes. Many people were persuaded by this argument and concluded that there was no point in trying to use the scientific method to understand mental processes.

During the Renaissance, then, there was no science of the mind because of a background assumption that the scientific method would not work on the mind because the mind was inherently unpredictable. But smart people were still contemplating the workings of the human mind. In the 300 years or so between the time of Descartes and the beginnings of scientific psychology, many topics were debated that were rooted in one question: Where does knowledge come from? Like the Greeks, Renaissance philosophers were interested in memory and perception, but these interests often developed from the question of the origin of knowledge.

On the Origin of Knowledge.   Descartes, shown in Figure 1.10, is usually credited with the first modern extended treatment of philosophy of mind, written in the early seventeenth century. He set forth a fairly moderate view on the origin of knowledge, saying that there are ideas that come from experience as well as innate ideas that everyone is born with. The position that ideas are innate came to be known as **nativist** because ideas were seen as native to every human. Another group of philosophers (Thomas Hobbes, John Locke, George Berkeley) who came to be known as **empiricists** argued that all our knowledge comes from experience which changes an impressionable mind. Later empiricists (David Hume, James Mill, John Stuart Mill) argued that the mind is more active in learning from experience, whereas the earlier empiricists had painted a picture of a rather passive mind being shaped by experience.

Gottfried Leibniz, in a direct response to Locke (but published much later), wrote that innate ideas are very important. He believed that experience serves only to liberate ideas that were in the mind already, presumably because one is born with such knowledge.

Immanuel Kant offered a compromise between nativist and empiricist views that was similar in spirit to Descartes' view, arguing that experience is the teacher, but *how* people experience

Figure 1.10. René Descartes. (Source: traveler1116/DigitalVision Vectors/Getty Images.)

things depends on native categories. Experience fills the boxes of the mind, so to speak, but native categories define the number of boxes, and their shapes. For example, your perception of time and space does not depend on experience. You are born with the ability to perceive them; you don't need to be exposed to time and space the way you *do* need to be exposed to a language to learn it. Furthermore, how you perceive time and space does not depend on your experience. All humans experience time and space because they are human.

Nativist and empiricist views had been set forth by the Greeks, most forcefully by Plato and Epicurus, respectively, but philosophers in the Renaissance and beyond furthered these views, considered new arguments, and formulated compromise positions.

Perception. If knowledge comes from experience of the world, then that experience is rooted in the way we interface with the world: our senses. Descartes discussed perception for the same reason as the Greeks – to understand where knowledge comes from. Other philosophers, notably George Berkeley, discussed perception as part of the empiricist versus nativist argument. Berkeley was an extreme empiricist. In *An Essay towards a New Theory of Vision*, he set out to show that even basic perceptual experience is learned (Berkeley, 1709/1948–1957). Berkeley argued that even something that feels as natural as the perception of distance actually requires experience. He discussed some cues to the perception of distance that are still recognized as important, but he emphasized that there are no native, inborn ideas and that everything must be learned.

Memory. The empiricists were also associationists. **Associationism** holds that knowledge originates when simple information from the senses is combined into more complex ideas. Perception therefore makes the "atoms" that combine to make all of our complicated knowledge. You know what an apple looks like because you have seen an apple before. But some complex ideas, such as the concept of democracy, clearly are not sensations. So where does this sort of knowledge come from? A complex idea such as democracy is the product of a number of simpler ideas that are joined together (associated). Things become associated if they occur at the same time.

Aristotle described the process of association, proposing several principles or rules by which associations are formed: Ideas would be associated if they were similar, or if they were very dissimilar, or if they happened in the same place or at the same time. All empiricists (Hobbes, Locke, Berkeley, Hume, James Mill, and John Stuart Mill, to name the best known) agreed that an association in time or place was important. If a clown appears every time you go to a particular coffee shop, you'll come to expect to see the clown when you enter. Experimental work in the twentieth century showed that the empiricists were correct in stressing time as a critical factor in associations. Locke and Hobbes were also correct when they stressed that repeating an association would make it easier to learn, and Locke added the (mostly correct) idea that learning associations also depends on whether they lead to pleasure or pain.

SUMMARY   This discussion has introduced the ideas of Renaissance and post-Renaissance philosophers. What's important to know is what they were trying to do. For the most part, they were arguing about the origin of knowledge. Renaissance philosophers also made observation part of their method, although the observations they included were more like "use your senses" than "conduct a careful scientific observation in an experiment." We might infer that they began to include more observation in their arguments about cognition because of the success of the scientific method in other fields. Many Renaissance philosophers borrowed metaphors from other sciences in discussing the mind. Locke talked about consciousness as a chemical compound, perhaps because he had been at Oxford University, where Robert Boyle had demonstrated that chemical compounds are composed of elements. Mill also used the chemistry analogy. Hobbes was influenced by Galileo's movement studies and believed that thought was motion of the nervous system. Hume also discussed Newton and the possibility of finding basic laws of thought that would correspond to the laws of motion. Thus, in their use of scientific metaphors and their increasing use of observation in the world to support their ideas, we can see the creeping influence of the scientific method on Renaissance philosophers.

The Beginnings of Modern Psychology

In the last section, we saw that the intellectual foundation was in place to start a science of the human mind as early as the seventeenth or eighteenth century, but background assumptions about the nature of thought led people to conclude that it would not be worthwhile to apply the scientific method to this field. The first investigators who made the attempt would launch a new science.

Wilhelm Wundt, shown in Figure 1.11, usually gets credit for founding modern psychology in 1879, although he was not the first to publish a scientific psychological work. Gustav Fechner and Ernst Weber had performed landmark experiments years earlier. Why, then, aren't Fechner and Weber called the first psychologists? The reason you usually hear is that Wundt was the

Figure 1.11. Wilhelm Wundt (standing, center) in his laboratory with psychological laboratory equipment. (Source: Archives of the History of American Psychology, The Drs. Nicholas and Dorothy Cummings Center for the History of Psychology, University of Akron.)

first to establish a laboratory devoted to psychology. It's not actually true. Wundt started his lab in 1879 at the University of Leipzig. William James started a lab in 1875 at Harvard. But James apparently used it only for demonstrations in teaching, so that lab is deemed not to count. Actually, the year doesn't matter so much. Wundt founded the discipline of psychology not because he started a lab but because he did what was necessary to make scientific psychology an institution.

Imagine for a moment that you have invented a new scientific field. You note that there is little agreement about what is ethical and what isn't, and you think that the scientific method could be used to discover the one true set of ethical principles that all humans should use to guide their concepts of right and wrong. How will you launch your new science of ethicology? Here are some things you might do:

- Start journals devoted to ethicology to show that the field is making progress.
- Train students who can go out and teach ethicology.
- Write a textbook of ethicology to make it easier to teach others.
- Organize symposia on ethicology to gain publicity.
- Encourage universities to organize departments of ethicology.
- Spend a fair amount of time persuading people that the whole enterprise is possible, because initially they'll think it's a crock.

Wundt did all these things for psychology. Over his sixty-five-year career, he wrote twenty-two volumes of textbooks totaling 53,000 pages, and he supervised 184 PhD students (Wong, 2009).

Another important thing you must do if you are starting a science is define its domain. What does the science seek to explain? There were two slightly different answers to this question around the turn of the twentieth century. Wundt was inspired by the success of chemistry. The periodic table had just been worked out, and Wundt believed it was a realistic and worthwhile goal to try to work out a periodic table of the mind. What are the basic elements of consciousness, out of which more complex thoughts are constructed? Although Wundt later denied the chemistry analogy, his writings are suffused with the idea. This viewpoint came to be known as **structuralism** because the goal was to describe the structures that compose thought. (We can recognize the associationism of Locke and others in this approach of combining simple concepts.) Many of Wundt's studies used very simple stimuli of sensation and perception, such as colored lights or the sound of a metronome. His strategy was to study what he assumed were basic building blocks of consciousness and eventually work toward a more complete view of human thought.

Meanwhile, William James, the guy who started the laboratory that didn't count, was inspired by developments in evolutionary theory. A guiding principle for James was that mental processes must have a purpose; they must be *for* something. This viewpoint came to be known as **functionalism** because the emphasis was not on mental structures but on the function of mental processes.

The emphasis on what was to be explained differed between Wundt and James, but there was a common thread. Both sought to explain how thought worked, and for them, thought was nearly synonymous with consciousness. Structuralism and functionalism had different ways of framing this question, however, and they had different methods of gathering evidence. Wundt championed **introspectionism**, a method of study in which people tried to follow their own thought processes, usually as they performed some simple task such as listening to a metronome. Such introspection was said to require training. A person couldn't just listen to the metronome; someone more experienced had to teach the "right" way to listen, telling the trainee what they should be experiencing. If that sounds odd to you, it should. This method turned out to be a big problem. Five people may have had five different experiences when they looked at an apple, but after they had been trained they would all report the same experience, which was pretty much whatever the trainer believed they should say.

James also used introspection, but of a different sort. He followed his own mental processes as a way of learning about them, but he was much less dogmatic about how introspection should be done. He frowned on dogma in psychology, and he had a healthy respect for objective experiments, which do not rely on introspection, although he disliked doing them himself. Perhaps because James later lost interest in psychology or because his distaste for dogma was not conducive to starting a movement in the field, functionalism never became a prominent school of psychology. Still, James had a more lasting impact on the ideas in experimental psychology than any other nineteenth-century figure. His *Principles of Psychology* (James, 1890) is still a source of ideas for cognitive psychologists.

Wundt's legacy is quite different. Although he worked out a detailed theory of psychology and published prolifically, little of his thinking remains influential. Still, he is duly credited with starting the field, and because he trained so many students, many of today's psychologists can trace their academic lineage to Wundt. (See Figure 1.12 for how the academic family tree of Wundt spreads down to the authors of this text.)

The Response: Behaviorism

There was one big problem with Wundt's introspectionism: It didn't work. There was the problem of training people to introspect – a problem of the method they used – and there were other methodological problems. A more basic problem was that the introspectionists didn't come up with any interesting results. In the end, you can make all the arguments you want for why your method is the best, but if you don't learn something using the method, the whole enterprise begins to look silly. Between 1879 and 1913, the introspectionists had few results to which they could point.

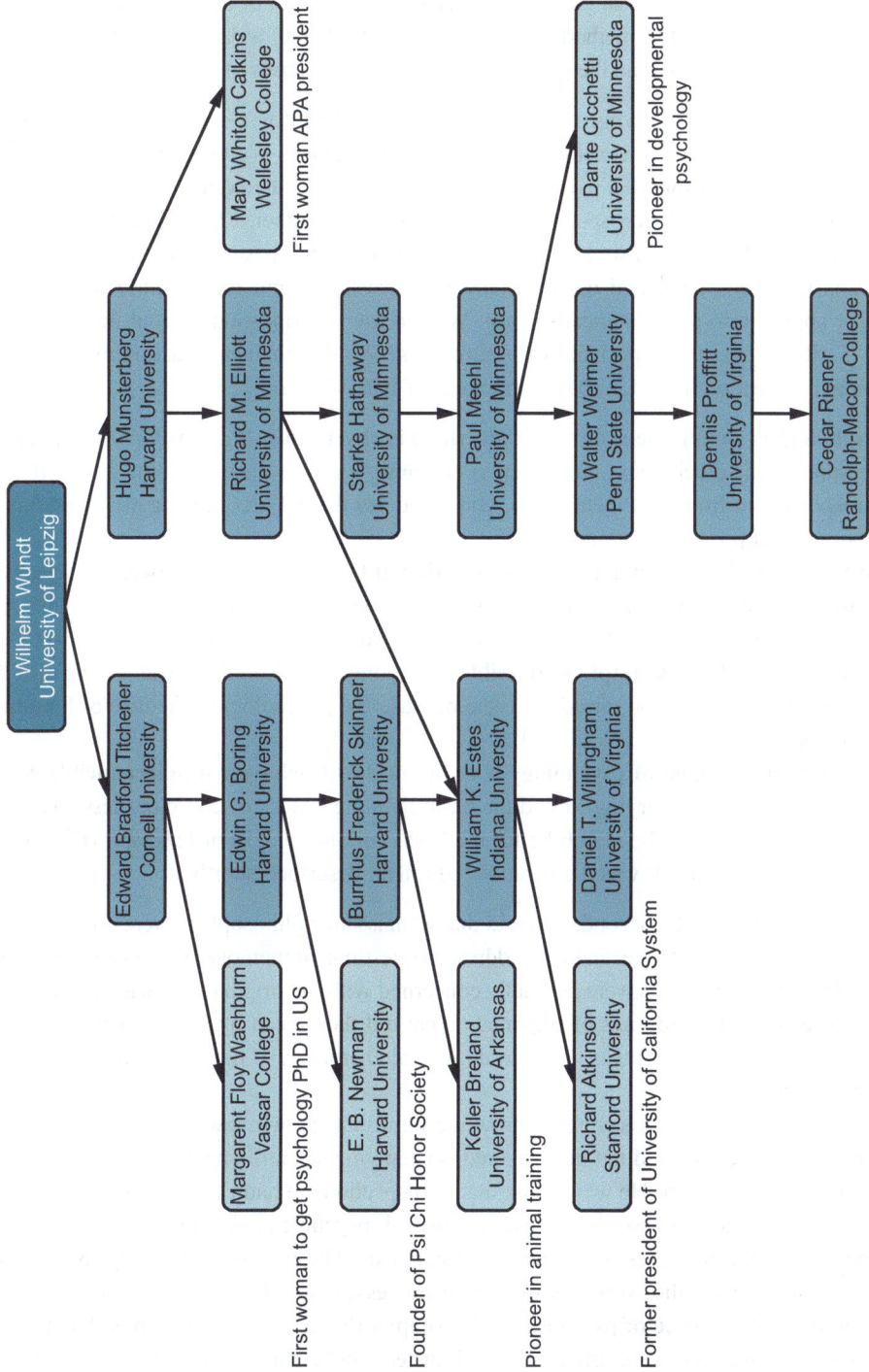

Figure 1.12. A partial academic family tree for the authors, showing how they are related to Wundt (as well as some other notable psychologists). Notice how there are more Williams than women, as our family tree is representative of a highly gender-imbalanced history of psychology. Modern cognitive psychology does not have the same gender imbalance, and our modern references attest to the contributions of women to the study of cognition.

In 1913, John Watson published a paper titled "Psychology as the Behaviorist Views It." In the first paragraph of that paper, Watson made it clear he sought to replace the introspectionist approach to psychology with a new model:

> Psychology as the behaviorist views it is a purely objective experimental branch of natural science. Its theoretical goal is the prediction and control of behavior. Introspection forms no essential part of its methods, nor is the scientific value of its data dependent upon the readiness with which they lend themselves to interpretation in terms of consciousness. (p. 158)

Watson was throwing down the gauntlet, calling for a complete shift in psychology. By 1913, psychology was considered a full-fledged science. Wundt had trained many students, and they in turn had founded psychology departments in academic institutions around the world. Most of them remained introspectionists of one sort or another. They were the establishment of psychology in 1913, but as we said earlier, these introspectionists couldn't turn to any one finding that was both rock solid and useful. Many were frustrated and needed little nudging to turn to another approach to psychological science. Watson found a ripe environment for change.

Remember the importance of assumptions? Watson challenged assumptions of Wundt and the establishment with his four basic principles of **behaviorism**:

- **Psychologists should focus only on that which is observable.** Watson emphasized that objective measurement is crucial, and introspection obviously can't be measured objectively. If you were introspecting in front of a metronome, you could say that you're thinking about anything and nobody could prove you wrong.
- **Psychologists should explain behavior, not thought or consciousness.** Because objective measurement was so important, Watson maintained that consciousness was not a suitable subject for psychology. In other words, Watson was saying that the subject matter of the science should change.
- **Theories should be as simple as possible.** Everyone agreed on this basic principle of the scientific method; Watson raised the issue because the psychological theories of the time were becoming convoluted.
- **The overarching goal of psychology is to break down behavior into irreducible constructs.** Structuralists had been trying to find the basic building blocks of consciousness. Watson suggested instead that the search be for the basic building blocks of *behavior*. (His candidate for the basic building block was the conditioned reflex, described shortly.)

Backtrack just a second. We said that Renaissance philosophers were concerned primarily with the origin of knowledge, and they addressed questions of memory and perception as part of that issue. The introspectionists were not really concerned with the origin of knowledge but instead were trying to explain the workings of the mind. What did they mean by *mind*? They meant *conscious thought*. Recall that Wundt was trying to do mental chemistry, to figure out the basic elements that compose consciousness.

Now Watson was saying, "Throw the mind out the window." Remember Kant's position that mental processes could not be measured, so applying scientific methods to them is impossible? Watson agreed with him! He was saying that introspectionism hadn't made progress because trying to deal with mental processes was hopeless. Instead, psychology should be redefined. It was not a science of mental processes but a science of behavior. The impasse psychologists faced was this: How can we explain the workings of mental processes, which are so complicated and elusive? Watson made the science of psychology a lot simpler (he might have said "possible") by declaring that mental processes were irrelevant, and instead behavior should be the subject matter of psychology. This point of view had to be tempting. Many of the problems that stumped researchers of the mind for centuries would simply disappear if instead of thought they studied behavior.

And psychologists went for behaviorism. It's fair to say that behaviorism was the dominant point of view in the United States from the 1920s through the 1950s (Gardner, 1985). It wasn't just a matter of expedience. Behaviorism worked – researchers using these methods obtained interesting experimental results. In the end, however, behaviorism was found lacking and was replaced by cognitive psychology. This doesn't mean that many insights of behaviorism haven't had lasting influence – for example, if something can be explained with a simple stimulus and response mechanism, then claiming a complicated mental process needs more experimental evidence. Before we explain what went wrong with behaviorism, let us tell you why it looked good for a while.

Behaviorism's Success

The philosophy underlying behaviorism was appealing because it was so straightforward. Psychologists could feel they were being scientific when they emphasized behavior because it is observable. Everyone can agree on what a person does, but it is much more difficult to say anything about a person's mental processes (see Figure 1.13). Everyone can agree that Joe hit Bill, but it's much harder to agree on what Joe's thoughts were when he hit Bill: Was Joe angry or frustrated, or was he just having a bad day?

Behaviorism also seemed to offer a promising start on the framework of a grand theory of behavior. Behaviorism, like almost every other science, sought to simplify complex subject matter by finding basic, irreducible, observable units. Chemistry has the element, biology has the cell, physics has the atom, and psychology has … what? Behaviorists proposed that the basic unit of behavior is the **reflex**, an automatic action by the body that occurs when a particular stimulus is perceived in the environment.

You are born with many reflexes. If you touch something hot, you will pull your hand away. If you place something in a baby's hand, that baby will close its hand to grasp it (Figure 1.14). You don't need to learn that reflex; you're born with it. Other reflexes are learned. For example, if every day we ring a bell and then give you a sour ball, in time the sound of the bell will elicit the responses usually elicited by the sour ball (e.g., salivation).

Figure 1.13. It is difficult to agree on what a rat is doing if you try to guess the rat's internal states; it's much easier to agree on the rat's behavior. The same is true of humans.

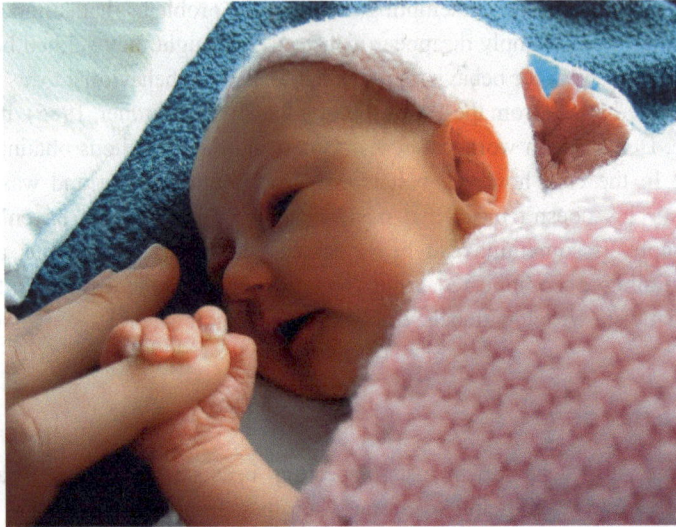

Figure 1.14. Babies are born with a reflex to close their hands when you touch their palms but have to learn how to open them voluntarily. (Source: Photograph by Cedar Riener.)

Does that example make you think of Pavlov's dogs? Watson proposed that the basic unit of behavior might be the conditioned reflex, as described by Pavlov. You are born with some innate reflexes (e.g., withdrawing your hand from pain), and others are the product of experience (e.g., salivating when you hear a bell). These learned reflexes are called **conditioned reflexes**. The training procedure (and the resultant learning) that produces conditioned reflexes is called **classical conditioning**.

Classical conditioning begins with an **unconditioned stimulus** which elicits an **unconditioned response**. *Unconditioned* means that the animal comes to the experiment with the predisposition to respond in a particular way. Food is an unconditioned stimulus leading to the unconditioned response of salivation because before the experiment is conducted, the unconditioned stimulus (food) leads to the unconditioned response (salivation). A **conditioned stimulus** evokes little or no response. If you ring a bell, a dog might turn toward the sound; if you ring the bell several times, the dog stops turning its head.

If you pair the conditioned stimulus (bell) with the unconditioned stimulus (food) enough times, the conditioned stimulus (bell) comes to elicit a **conditioned response**. The conditioned response is often similar to (but not always identical to) the unconditioned response. In this case, the conditioned response would be salivation, but the animal might not salivate as much.

The idea that the conditioned reflex might be the building block of all thought and behavior sounds reminiscent of the empiricist philosophers: Simple associations build up to produce more complex thoughts. Indeed, the basic idea was very old. Aristotle noted that if two things happen at the same time often enough, they become associated.

So why is Pavlov famous? The difference between Pavlov's work and previous observations is that Pavlov was specific about how the learning takes place and therefore could speculate about the mechanism. Pavlov performed a simple operation to relocate one of the dog's salivary glands on the outside of its cheek so the number of drops of saliva it secreted could be measured accurately. Thus, he could get a precise measure of how much the dog salivated, which in this case is essentially a measure of the dog's expectation of being fed. Having this good experimental setup allowed Pavlov to ask other questions: How many times must the bell and food be paired for the animal to learn? What happens if we ring a different bell? What happens if sometimes we ring the bell and don't provide food? What happens if we ring the bell and give the dog a different type of food? Being able to ask (and answer) such specific questions allowed behaviorists to start thinking about a general theory of behavior, with the conditioned reflex at its center. (For a modern review of classical conditioning, see Honey and Dwyer [2022].)

It wasn't long before people noticed that the conditioned reflex can't account for all behavior. In the conditioned reflex, two stimuli are presented to the animal, and the animal responds to stimuli, but animals can also actively do things (that aren't reflexes) that have important consequences. For example, suppose you try a new restaurant in town, and the food is awful. You figure that the cook may have had a bad night or you ordered something that happened to be bad, so you try again. Again, it's awful. So you don't go back. This experience obviously entails learning, but it is not classical conditioning. Going to a restaurant is not a reflex; you actively made a choice. That choice had consequences: That mushroom avocado turkey burger with mango salsa tasted gross. The consequences of your choice influence the likelihood that you will make the same choice again. This type of learning is called **operant conditioning**. It occurs when the animal actively makes a response (the operant) and the probability of making that response in the future changes depending on the consequences the animal encounters. Operant conditioning was seen as different from classical conditioning. In classical conditioning, a neutral stimulus (e.g., a bell) comes to have meaning. In operant conditioning, an initially neutral response (e.g., selecting a particular restaurant) comes to have meaning.

Edward Thorndike (1911) did some work in this vein in the early twentieth century. He put a cat in a slatted box that had a door operated by a lever inside (Figure 1.15). Thorndike timed how long it took the cat to make its escape over a number of trials and discovered a systematic learning curve. On the basis of this and other experiments, Thorndike proposed the law of effect, which basically said that if you do something and good consequences follow, you're more likely to do it

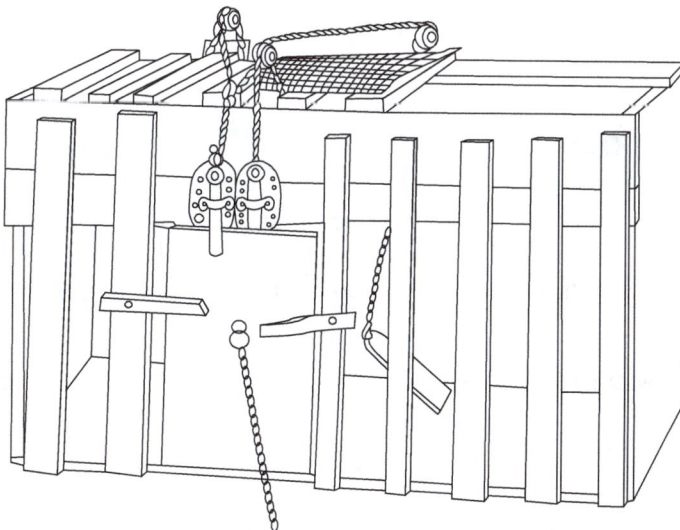

Figure 1.15. Thorndike puzzle boxes. Edward Thorndike was able to conduct pioneering experiments observing cat learning. Despite their crude construction, these boxes showed how cats learn the behaviors necessary to escape. (Source: E. Thorndike [1898], *Animal Intelligence: An Experimental Study of the Associative Processes in Animals* [New York: Macmillan].)

again, whereas if bad consequences follow, you're less likely to do it again. It seems obvious, but Thorndike's puzzle boxes offered a new way to study the learning process by observing behavior (Chance, 1999). Still, it wasn't until the 1930s that the importance of this type of learning was fully appreciated, largely through the work of B. F. Skinner (1938).

Instead of following the story of behaviorism, let's push ahead to cognitive psychology. (For a review of more recent work in operant conditioning, see Murphy and Lupfer [2014] and Thompson and Wolpaw [2014].) Suffice it to say that from the 1920s to the early 1960s, virtually all experimental psychologists in the United States were behaviorists. Behaviorism dominated American psychology because it worked. Behaviorists could make many accurate predictions about behavior. Most of their experiments were with animals, but there was a good reason for that choice. From the behaviorist perspective, behavior was mostly the product of what had happened to you, meaning what sorts of conditioned reflexes you had acquired through the environment and what sorts of behaviors had been rewarded or punished over the course of your lifetime. It was therefore difficult to conduct experiments on humans because the experimenter had no way of knowing what their history was and therefore what they already knew coming into the experiment. Investigators could raise an animal from birth and know exactly what its history was, so they used animals.

But were animals really like people? Behaviorists figured that humans were much more complex, but the basic laws of learning probably were the same. They also noted that every science starts with simple situations. The fundamental chemistry principles and elements isolated in the lab are the same as those that make a fine wine. When Galileo wanted to investigate how objects move, he started with spheres rolling down planes, not leaves blowing in a high wind. Once you understand the simple situation, you can move on to more complex situations. Indeed, skilled behaviorists could train animals to do a great number of complex behaviors (see Figure 1.16).

Despite many successes, in the late 1950s, behaviorism began to crumble. There were a number of reasons, but they fall into two categories: (1) People started to doubt that behaviorism could do what it had promised, and (2) it became obvious that eliminating any discussion of mental processes from psychology was hurting more than it was helping. The replacement for behaviorism was cognitive psychology, and so our story begins.

Stand-on-One-Foot Questions

1.3.   Why was the scientific method not applied to the human mind before the nineteenth century?
1.4.   What psychological questions did philosophers address during the Renaissance?
1.5.   What change did scientific psychology undergo in terms of what it sought to explain?

Questions That Require Two Feet

1.6.   One of the assumptions that the Greeks made was that explanations for events in the world should be "of this world." In other words, there is not much point in proposing explanations of observable events in terms of unobservable forces. To what extent do you think people you know hold this assumption?
1.7.   Behaviorism swept away the introspective method, but should people's introspections be of any interest to psychology?

Figure 1.16. The IQ zoo, set up by Marian and Keller Breland, featured animals trained through operant conditioning to engage in complex behaviors. (Source: Archives of the History of American Psychology, The Drs. Nicholas and Dorothy Cummings Center for the History of Psychology, University of Akron.)

How Do Cognitive Psychologists Study the Mind?

Preview

The impetus for a new way to study the mind came from several sources. Among psychologists, there was increasing dissatisfaction with the behaviorist position because it seemed unable to account for some important human behaviors, such as language. Scientists in other fields (including artificial intelligence and neuroscience) made great use of abstract constructs – hypothetical representations and processes – in accounting for intelligent behavior, although these were anathema to behaviorists. In moving away from behaviorism, cognitive psychologists needed to move toward something, and artificial intelligence offered a ready model. One could conceive of the human mind as similar in some respects to a computer. Both manipulated information as a way of generating intelligent behavior. This computer metaphor has remained influential, although it shouldn't be taken too literally. In the last part of this section, we show how a cognitive psychologist would analyze one simple bit of behavior – answering the question "Where are you from?"

What Behaviorism Couldn't Do

Serious problems for behaviorism were raised in the 1950s. Behaviorism was perceived by psychologists as proposing that the experiences of an animal during its lifetime completely determined its behavior – in other words, that the animal's genetic inheritance counted for nothing and that what the animal did was a function of what it had been rewarded and punished for doing.

Strictly speaking, that is not what behaviorism proposed, and indeed, such a proposal could only be called silly. Obviously, it is easy to train a pigeon to peck something and very difficult to train a rat to peck something; the predisposition to peck or not to peck is a product of the animal's genetic inheritance. But it is true that behaviorists did not emphasize the possibility of important genetic contributions to behavior. Almost everything they studied was the learning that took place during the lifetime of the animal, and so it seemed as though they were saying that when an animal is born it is a clean slate, a blank tablet, waiting to be written on by the environment.

Early evidence against the blank slate came from studies of wild animals, outside of psychology. In the 1950s, a number of important papers were published in ethology showing that the clean slate idea could not be true. Ethologists do not study animals in laboratory settings; they go into the wild and study animals in their natural habitat. Ethologists described **fixed-action patterns**, complex behaviors in which animals engage even though they have little opportunity for **practice** or reward. For example, the male stickleback fish performs a series of stereotyped mating behaviors, including establishing a territory, building a nest, luring a female into the nest with seductive wagging motions, and inducing the female to lay eggs in the nest by prodding her tail (Tinbergen, 1952). Behaviorist accounts do not offer a ready explanation for such stereotyped, complex behaviors. According to behaviorist principles, these actions should require more practice, and their performance should require reward.

Another dramatic finding from ethology was that of a **critical period**, a window of time during which an organism is primed to learn some particular information. If the organism doesn't learn the information within the critical period, later it may be unable to acquire the information. For

Figure 1.17. Konrad Lorenz with goslings who follow him. (Source: Nina Leen/The LIFE Picture Collection/Getty Images.)

example, there is a critical period during which chicks learn who their mother is (Hess, 1958). The first large object a chick sees during this time period is taken to be its mother, and the chick follows the object thereafter. If a few days pass before chicks see a large object, the learning is more difficult to obtain. If the first object that chicks see is a large ethologist – for example, Konrad Lorenz – then the ethologist is taken to be Mom (Figure 1.17). (For a review of this work, see Bolhuis and Honey [1998]; see also Rosa Salva et al. [2015].)

As with fixed-action patterns, the results supporting critical periods indicate that the nervous system is not a learning machine that responds only to reward or punishment following an action. Rather, organisms seem to come into the world with a nervous system that is primed to learn particular things; it is part of their genetic heritage. This explanation sounds obvious, but it did not fit into the behaviorist theory in any obvious way. If some tasks are easier to learn than others, and if some actions come "preprogrammed," the blank slate doesn't seem so blank anymore.

The first problem with behaviorism, then, was that it could not account for some elements of animal behavior. The second problem was that people became uneasy about whether behaviorism could account for all varieties of human behavior.

Failures of Behaviorism in Accounting for Human Behavior

The study of language was a dark cloud looming on the behaviorist horizon almost from the beginning. Keep in mind that behaviorists conducted almost all their experiments on animals. They were essentially offering a promise: "Don't worry, all our work with animals will apply to humans." Some people did worry, and their chief worry was that behaviorist principles derived from experiments with animals would not be able to account for human language. Skinner (1984) recounts in his autobiography that as a newly minted PhD in the mid 1930s, he had such a discussion with the great philosopher Alfred North Whitehead:

> Here was an opportunity which I could not overlook to strike a blow for the cause, and I began to set forth the principal arguments of behaviorism with enthusiasm. Professor Whitehead was equally in earnest – not in defending his own position, but in trying to understand what I was saying and (I suppose) to discover how I could possibly bring myself to say it. Eventually we took the following stand. He agreed that science might be successful in accounting for human behavior provided one made an exception of *verbal* behavior. Here, he insisted, something else must be at work. He brought the discussion to a close with a friendly challenge: "Let me see you," he said "account for my behavior as I sit here saying, 'No black scorpion is falling upon this table.'"
>
> The next morning I drew up the outline of a book on verbal behavior. (pp. 149–150)

Skinner may have outlined the book the next morning, but it was not until 1957 that he published *Verbal Behavior*. His analysis of language was straightforward behaviorism. How does a child learn language? Through reward in the environment. That is, the infant learns that saying "da" elicits excitement from the parents, which is very rewarding. But the parents get used to the child saying "da," and soon the child must produce a more complex utterance, such as "Dad," to be rewarded. Through reward, the child learns ever more complex utterances. The analysis was more sophisticated than that, but it did not stray far from the behaviorist line (Skinner, 1957).

Two years after Skinner's book was published, a review appeared that soon attracted more attention than the book, although the review was not published in a major journal. It was written by a young linguist named Noam Chomsky (1959) and can be summarized this way: "Not only is Skinner's account wrong but a behaviorist explanation cannot, in principle, ever account for language." Chomsky argued that Skinner had grossly underestimated the complexity of language. First, he attacked Skinner's account of the "scorpion on the table" problem. To account for why a person utters a remark at any given time, Skinner could only say that the behavior was under stimulus control, meaning that some subtle property of the stimulus (combined with the individual's history) had elicited this verbal response. Chomsky pointed out that this explanation is really not an explanation. If you see a painting and say "Dutch," it is presumably due to some subtle property of the painting. But you might just as well have said "Stinks," "Nice," or "Too much red." In each case, Skinner could only say that, because of the comment you made, he must infer that that particular aspect of the stimulus (stinkiness, niceness, redness) was controlling your behavior. That is no explanation.

A second important point Chomsky made was that language is **generative**, meaning that people can create novel sentences. Behaviorism can explain why you might repeat a behavior (you were rewarded last time), but it's not nearly as good at describing why you do something novel, such as utter a sentence you've never said before. After all, the ability to generate novel utterances is the heart of language. We seldom say the same thing twice in just the same way.

Indeed, how is it that you can say or comprehend a series of words you've never said or heard before, such as "Banana peels have nothing to do with success as a cab driver"? How do you get the grammar right? It's tempting to say,

> There are *rules* for what makes a sentence grammatical. It's like the formula for a line: $y = mx + b$. You put in values for m, which is the slope, and for b, which is where the line

runs into the *y*-axis, and you have described a line. In the same way, there might be abstract formulas you use to construct a sentence. You plug in the ideas for the things you want to say, and the formulas turn your ideas into a grammatical sentence.

This idea was a big blow to behaviorism. Starting in the 1950s and 1960s, psychologists of language proposed such sets of rules (called grammars) and left behaviorist accounts behind.

Convinced that the results of animal experiments did *not* extend to human linguistic abilities, many psychologists, not just those who studied language, were shaken by Chomsky's argument. If behaviorism can't account for language, who knows how else it will fail?

The impression that behaviorist principles couldn't give a complete account of human behavior was reinforced by studies of memory. Here's an example from a study by Weston Bousfield (1953). Suppose we give you this list of words to remember:

lion, onion, Bill, firefighter, carrot, zebra, John, clerk, Tim, nurse, cow

Ten minutes later, we ask you to recall the words. Most people do not recall the words in the order they heard them. They recall one category, such as animals, then another category, and so on. How can this result be explained? When participants are asked what they are doing in such studies, they say they are using a strategy. They know that one animal will make them think of other animals, so it's easiest to remember all the animals at once. A behaviorist would shrink from the term *strategy* because a strategy is not observable. But people clearly reorder the words, and they say they are doing so to help them remember better. Can we ignore what the people say they are doing? We can't ignore the fact that people reorganize the word order and that people are more likely to remember certain words than others – that's observable behavior – so how can we account for it? Behaviorism dictated that psychologists shouldn't consider a person's inner mental states in accounting for what they do. But the idea of strategy seemed to be a major component of what people did in memory studies such as this one.

Behaviorism did not provide a framework in which to use constructs such as grammars or strategies. But if behaviorism were abandoned, what would take its place? A replacement was found through analogy of the human mind to a computer.

The Computer Metaphor and Information Processing

Metaphors are very important in the study of the mind (Daugman, 1990). No one knows what the mind is or how it works, so people often say, "I think the mind is like . . ." For example, Descartes was impressed by animated statues in the gardens at the chateau of Saint-Germain-en-Laye, outside Paris. As a visitor strolled through the gardens, they stepped on hidden plates that set the statues in motion. In one, Perseus descended from the ceiling of a grotto and slew a dragon that rose from the water. The system animating the statues was based on hydraulics – water moving through hidden pipes – and Descartes (1664/1972) proposed a hydraulic system of nerve function. You can see a similar hydraulic fountain in Figure 1.18, this one using a waterwheel to move statues, designed by Salomon de Caus.

While Descartes imagined the brain as a series of tubes, many of his contemporaries imagined that the mind was based on the same mechanical principles as the most amazing machine at the time: a clock. With new technologies came new amazement, and new metaphors for the mind. In the nineteenth century, many researchers likened the brain to a telephone switchboard; the crisscrossing pattern of connectivity of neurons is reminiscent of an enormous switching station

Figure 1.18. The garden designer and hydraulic engineer Salomon de Caus (1576–1626) designed statues in gardens that could move through hidden pipes, valves, and water. Descartes was inspired by such displays and thought similar mechanisms might be at work in the human nervous system. (Source: The Elisha Whittelsey Collection, The Elisha Whittelsey Fund, 1949.)

(von Helmholtz, 1910/1962). Donald Hebb (1949) proposed a model of neural functioning in the late 1940s that invoked solenoids and capacitors.

In the 1950s, a new metaphor became available. Artificial intelligence researchers realized that early computers solved number-crunching problems with symbols. The number 6 was not physically realized with six pieces of something in the computer, the way an abacus represents 6 with six beads. The computer uses a binary code in which the sequence 0 1 1 0 might mean "6," but 0 1 1 0 is just a symbol, one that could just as easily represent "bird" or "twiddling thumbs." So artificial intelligence researchers began speculating on what a computer might be capable of if the symbols it used represented something other than numbers.

Naturally, when 0 1 1 0 means "6" and the goal is to get a computer to manipulate numbers, we have certain expectations. We want to be able to add numbers, subtract them, and so forth, and we expect that the basic laws of addition will be built into the computer. For example, the order in which numbers are added by the computer shouldn't matter: 6 + 3 = 9 is equivalent to 3 + 6 = 9. Thus, a computer uses representations (e.g., 0 1 1 0) and processes that do things to the representations (e.g., addition and subtraction). A **representation** is a symbol (0 1 1 0) for an entity in the real world ("6"). A representation, therefore, is like a code, a symbol that translates a real-world object or event into the "language" of the mind and brain. A **process** manipulates representations in some way.

That's clear enough for computers. What if we can approach human thought that way? Suppose that humans, like computers, use representations and processes. If we think of humans as processors of information, we can set up new questions for the study of the mind. What we want to know about humans is (1) what kind of symbols or representations humans use and (2) what processes humans use to manipulate those representations.

Here's another way to use the computer metaphor. Computers have hardware and software. The hardware is the actual physical piece of machinery (the central processing unit, the hard drive, the memory chips, and so on). The software is the set of instructions that tells the hardware what to do. Why not think of humans that way? This approach has been fruitful for neuroanatomists studying the hardware and cognitive psychologists studying the software of the brain. You could say that behaviorists wanted to talk only about what was observable – what was seen on the screen of the computer and what was typed on the keyboard – and therefore were missing most of the interesting information.

This metaphor proved very powerful and became known as the **information processing** model. This approach to studying the human mind is characterized by three assumptions:

- Humans are processors of information, just as computers are processors of information. The processing of information supports human thought and behavior.
- Representations (of objects and events) and processes that operate on these representations underlie information processing.
- Information processing typically occurs within largely isolated modules, which are organized in stages of processing. Thus, one module receives information from another module, performs an operation on the information, and passes on the information to another module.

We provide an example of this information processing perspective toward the end of this chapter. For now, keep in mind that humans take in information from the environment (e.g., through sight and hearing), transform that information (e.g., by comparing it to memories), and then output more information (e.g., through speech or action).

The idea that psychologists could propose hypothetical representations used by the mind is powerful. We've already mentioned the case of language, in which sentence grammar seemed necessary to account for the ability to generate novel sentences. Memory is another domain of behavior in which hypothetical processes and representations are potentially useful.

It is easy to keep a small amount of information in mind for a short time (about thirty seconds). You might ask friends what they want on their pizza and what kind of drinks they want, repeating their orders to yourself as you find your phone to order the food. If you are interrupted as you cross the room so that you stop repeating the order, you may have to ask them again. Clearly, you usually remember things for longer than thirty seconds. Why do you remember their order only for that long?

Here's an account you might give. You might say that there are two types of memory: long-term memory, which can keep memories for years, and short-term memory, which is used to maintain information for thirty seconds or so. Short-term memory is useful because it is hard to get material into long-term memory, and you don't always need to remember things for years.

Short-term memory could be said to contain representations. Just as a computer has a representation (0 1 1 0) for the concept "6," your mind has a way to represent "olives and anchovies and a Diet Coke." Furthermore, short-term memory uses processes that manipulate representations. For example, if you wanted to remember "pizza with olives and anchovies and a Diet Coke" for several minutes, a process would continually refresh this representation so that it remains accessible.

A behaviorist would object, "Where, exactly, is this mystical representation of 'pizza'? I don't see it." The response is that short-term memory is an **abstract construct** – a theoretical set of processes (e.g., refresh) and representations (e.g., "olives and anchovies") that are useful in explaining some data. Any abstract construct you propose is therefore a mini-theory. It is a proposal about the way the mind operates. A behaviorist would argue that proposing the abstract construct of short-term memory is wrong for these reasons:

- **The construct is circular.** The behavior that people easily recall information for thirty seconds is said to be "explained" by stating that it occurs because we have a memory system designed to remember things for thirty seconds.
- **The concept diverts attention from the important issues.** Remember, psychology is a science of behavior, not of thought.
- **The proposition is impossible to verify because it is not observable.** There is no way to confirm whether short-term memory exists, because it can't be seen, touched, or measured in any way.

It was difficult for psychologists to abandon the idea that if they talked about representations and processes, then they were not being scientific. Indeed, while the dominance of behaviorism faded, their criticisms of abstract constructs, representations and emphasis on observable behaviors continues to be relevant. Cognitive psychologists also valued studying observable behaviors, but have expanded the definition of what is observable and also found support for abstract constructs such as mental representations. In other words, these mini-theories of abstract constructs became the full-fledged theories we'll be discussing in this book, even if they remain challenging to study and observe. Studies of human memory helped show that abstract constructs such as "category" or "strategy" had potential to explain memory performance where conditioning could not. There were even studies of rat behavior in which it seemed quite clear that they were not simply developing responses to stimuli. For example, in one study (Krechevsky, 1932), rats had to navigate a maze with a series of choices between left and right doors. Krechevsky found that rats tested "hypotheses": choosing all the left doors, then choosing all the right doors, then picking another quality (they were different colors). In an influential paper summarizing these findings in rats, Tolman (1948) argued that rather than a set of stimulus–response pairings, the rats instead developed something akin to "cognitive maps" as they solved mazes. But even more persuasive support came from the importance (and success) of abstract constructs in two fields outside of psychology: computer science and neuroscience.

Abstract Constructs in Other Fields

It looked as if the information processing perspective might be useful in accounting for human thought, but there was still the issue of whether investigators were being scientific if they used abstract constructs. In both computer science and neuroscience, however, researchers used abstract constructs freely with no apparent loss of rigor.

ARTIFICIAL INTELLIGENCE   Artificial intelligence is the pursuit of intelligent behavior by a computer. The idea is to get a computer to produce output that would be considered intelligent if a person were to produce it. Most researchers think that a program that gets a computer to complete a task can be considered a theory of how the human mind completes the task. These theories rely completely on abstract constructs. These researchers propose that certain information is contained in memory – that this information can be combined or used in specific ways, according to a set of rules, and that these rules and the information in memory drive behavior.

Here's an example. In the mid 1950s, Allen Newell and Herb Simon (1956) developed a program that proved theorems in formal logic. It ran on a computer called JOHNNIAC, which used vacuum tubes. The program worked by starting with a list of axioms – statements that it could take as true – and a list of rules for how the axioms could be combined. The program also remembered proofs that it had already discovered so they could be used as needed. The program had a number of strategies it used to discover proofs; for example, sometimes it tried working backward by starting with the conclusion and trying to get back to the initial premises.

Three things are critical about this program and what it represents. First, the behavior the program produced was quite impressive. Until that time, behaviorists could more easily ignore artificial intelligence because the artificial intelligence programs didn't do anything sophisticated. Behaviorists could say, "Computers are nothing but fancy adding machines. What they are capable of is not comparable to human behavior." But here was a program constructing logical proofs; this certainly sounds like sophisticated behavior.

Second, Newell and Simon were not simply saying, "Look, we can get a computer to do something that looks like thought. Cool, huh?" To this, a behaviorist might reply, "So what? You programmed the computer to solve proofs, and it solves proofs. *You* are the intelligent agent because you programmed the computer." But Newell and Simon were saying that the method the computer used to solve the problem was like the method humans used. They provided evidence for this by asking people to prove the theorems and to describe what they were doing as they did it. People reported strategies similar to those the program used (e.g., working backward).

The third important thing about the program is that it used abstract constructs. You can't see or touch the strategies that the program used. The usual response of behaviorists to a theory that entailed strategies was, "That's not scientific. You can't observe strategies." But there was nothing unscientific or mystical about the program. The artificial intelligence researcher could say, "I'm being quite specific about what I mean by 'strategy.' Look, there's the strategy right there in the program, and here are the rules describing when the strategy is invoked." In the usage of the artificial intelligence researcher, *strategy* was not like our common usage of a vague plan but more like the specific and precise grammar rules of the linguist.

NEUROSCIENCE   Another way to be specific about an abstract construct is to tie it to a brain structure. It's one thing to propose the existence of a short-term memory system. It's something else again to find a short-term memory system located in the dorsolateral frontal cortex of the brain.

The links between brain structure and function have been pursued since the nineteenth century. One way to do this is by examining people with brain damage caused by stroke, tumor, or disease. Some of these people have specific cognitive problems. For example, suppose you find a patient with brain damage whose cognitive functioning appears completely normal in every other respect but who has no short-term memory – he can't keep a food order in mind for thirty seconds. If you know the location of the brain damage, you might infer that you know the location of short-term memory. If this patient has damage to brain area X and no longer has short-term memory, then brain area X must support short-term memory.

This inference is correct up to a point. The problem is, how do we know which part of the brain is damaged? In the 1950s, the main way to know where brain damage had occurred was as a consequence of surgery. If a surgeon must go in and remove some tissue (e.g., to remove a tumor), we know the exact location of the brain damage because the surgeon caused it. In the late 1950s and early 1960s, there were a few cases in which dramatic and important things were learned about cognition from such patients.

Perhaps the most famous patient of this sort is Henry Molaison (Corkin, 2013). Known only by his initials, H.M., until his death in 2008, Molaison had epilepsy that was unresponsive to even very high dosages of medication. His seizures were frequent, severe, and so debilitating that he could not continue in school. Seizures usually have a focus, meaning that they start in one part of the brain and then spread. If a surgeon can take out the part of the brain that is the focus, the seizures may stop.

In 1953, at the age of twenty-seven, Molaison underwent surgery in which a number of structures near the center of his brain were removed. A photograph of his brain (Figure 1.19) shows which parts of his brain were removed. At that time, the best knowledge about the function of these structures was that they were important to the sense of smell, so it was thought that Molaison probably would lose his sense of smell. That seemed a small price to pay to eliminate the seizures.

Unfortunately, however, Henry Molaison lost his ability to form new memories. His short-term memory remained normal. He could remember a phone number for thirty seconds just like anyone else. His long-term memory was mostly fine, too, if you asked him about events that happened before the surgery. He could remember his friends in high school, what was happening in the world in the early 1950s, and so on. What he couldn't do is form new long-term memories. Thus, from 1957 until his death, Molaison learned almost nothing new. He couldn't name the sitting president or tell you the year. He didn't know that Apple is a computer maker and not just a kind of pie.

The point here is that data from Molaison provided dramatic evidence in favor of using an abstract construct such as short-term memory in a theory of how memory works. We know that the

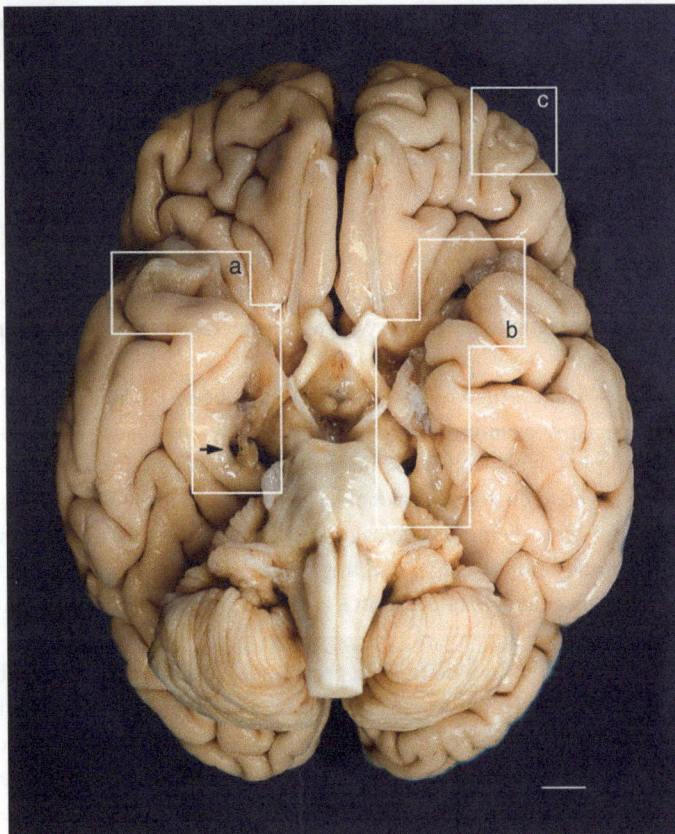

Figure 1.19. The underside of Henry Molaison's brain, showing evidence of surgical lesions and a mark produced by the surgical clips (black arrow) (Annese et al., 2014). (Source: Reprinted by permission from Springer Nature, Nature Communications, Natalie M. Schenker-Ahmed, Hauke Bartsch, Paul Maechler, Colleen Sheh et al. [2014], Postmortem examination of patient H.M.'s brain based on histological sectioning and digital 3D reconstruction, *Jacopo Annese*, p. 3)

hippocampus and other structures that he lost are important for transferring information from short-term memory into long-term memory. But we know that those structures don't support short-term or long-term memory themselves because Molaison was able to accomplish tasks using these types of memory just fine.

Suppose now that you're not a neurologist but an experimental psychologist interested in learning and memory. On one hand, the behaviorists are saying, "You can't use terms such as *short-term memory*. They are not rigorous because they refer to things that cannot be observed." On the other hand, findings such as those from Henry Molaison strongly suggest that the concept of short-term memory would be useful. What would you do?

So What, Finally, Is the Cognitive Perspective?

We have discussed some of the developments that have influenced cognitive psychology:

- Behaviorism could not account for all the experimental data, especially in studies of language and memory.
- It looked as if abstract constructs could help account for the complexity of human behavior where behaviorist reflexes could not.
- Neuroscientists and artificial intelligence researchers provided examples of how abstract constructs could be used effectively in a scientific way.
- The interaction of representations and the processes that manipulate them can be likened to the workings of a computer.

This brief overview also makes the assumptions of the cognitive perspective seem obvious. The chief assumption is that there are representations as well as processes that operate on them. Another assumption is that we can discover these processes and representations. There is currently no way to observe these processes directly. We infer the existence of these processes based on people's behavior. For the moment, let's just say that the assumptions of the cognitive perspective appear reasonable, but we should never forget that they are assumptions. (For a recent perspective on the use of representations in cognition and neuroscience, see Gilead et al. [2020].)

So that's the approach and the assumptions behind it. How is it applied? Here's the way a cognitive psychologist would think about a problem. Suppose you and I meet and you ask me where I am from. It takes me less than a second to say "DC." But an amazing amount of cognition (unconscious, of course) had to happen in that brief second. I perceived what you said, not just as sounds but as words in a language we share; looked up the answer in my memory; made a decision about how much background knowledge you have (I didn't need to say Washington, DC, United States of America); and so on. Each of these processes looks pretty remarkable just on its own.

This example outlines how cognitive psychologists think about problems. They look at cognitive tasks and try to figure out which processes are absolutely necessary to getting the task accomplished. Cognitive psychologists tend to think of mental work as being performed in stages (in our example, speech perception, language, memory, decision-making), and a psychologist usually studies just one of these stages. Each stage is so complex that it's enough of a challenge to understand just one. In trying to characterize these stages, cognitive psychologists devise theories in terms of abstract constructs: hypothetical representations and processes that operate on those representations.

That's the overview of the cognitive perspective. Cognitive psychologists think in terms of stages of information processing. Information from the environment is perceived, then memory is contacted, and so on. This book follows that stage theory in presenting one cognitive process in each chapter.

But the process probably still seems a little strange to you. How exactly can one conduct experiments that tell us about mental processes? We consider that question in more detail in Chapter 2.

Stand-on-One-Foot Questions

1.8.   What problems led to a decline in the influence of behaviorism?
1.9.   What is information processing?
1.10.   How did cognitive psychologists respond to the protests of behaviorists that references to abstract representations and processes were not scientific?

Questions That Require Two Feet

1.11.   Do you think some of the things humans learn might be subject to critical periods?
1.12.   At the start of this chapter, we mentioned that most of the people we know tend to notice the workings of their minds only when they fail. How often do you think that your mind fails, relative to the number of times it succeeds in carrying out a cognitive process?
1.13.   The "Where are you from?" example in the last paragraphs of the chapter suggested that many cognitive processes are involved in performing what seems to be a simple cognitive task. What are some of those processes?

2 Methods of Cognitive Psychology

In Chapter 1, we discussed the objections the behaviorists raised to the cognitive program. One of their concerns was the use of nonobservables in theory, for example, creating a theory of how memory works that includes representations such as short-term and long-term memory. No one can actually *see* or otherwise directly observe short-term memory, so how can we use it to explain human behavior? Cognitivists replied that they were going to use human behavior to test their models. But if so, it seems inevitable that their reasoning would end up being circular. They want to explain how humans behave, yet they plan to test whether the model is right using that same behavior.

In this chapter, we will consider how we can use experimental data to form good explanations, but we should first pause a moment and ask ourselves, What makes an explanation for behavior good? And who should do the explaining? Take just about any interesting behavior and we quickly find a range of explanations. For example, why are you able to read this sentence? An economist might point to the circumstances of your upbringing that sent you to a school where you learned to read and a set of choices that led to your choice of college and perhaps even your professor's (perfectly rational) choice of textbook. A sociologist might explain cultural and institutional factors that have shaped your education up to this point, or perhaps the sociological factors that separate English readers from others in the world. A biologist, however, might consider that human reading depends on light-sensitive cells, packed in a certain density to allow us to distinguish a *C* from an *O*, and a transparent, light-bending lens to bring the pattern of light into focus. A physicist might be more interested in the physics of the light hitting the page (or emanating from the screen). Each of these explanations of "why can you read this sentence?" contains valid insights, and indeed each contributes to understanding the phenomenon of human behavior.

This cataloging of explanations helps us situate cognitive psychology within the sciences by delimiting the kinds of explanations that cognitive psychology will not provide, as well as picking which phenomena need explaining and how they will be explained. A cognitive psychologist sees "Why can I read this sentence?" as a question about the mental processes necessary to translate the patterns of ink on the page into meaning. The physicists can describe the light, the biologists can describe the light-sensitive cells in your eyes, but the cognitive psychologists seek to explain reading by describing how we can recognize the individual letters, know what the letters $R - E - A - D$ spell (and that it is the "read" pronounced like *reed*, not *red*), look up in a kind of "mental dictionary" what this word means, and choose which meaning applies to this context. This chapter describes how scientists have investigated the nature of these mental processes, using both behavioral and neuroscientific data.

Can we use behavioral data to test cognitive theories? Cognitive psychology seems to confront an impossible problem. We can't directly observe a mental process, so how can we observe behavior to explain behavior? A biologist seeking to understand the function of some tissue might use a microscope to examine the cells that make up the tissue, but the boundaries and components of behavior are not nearly as clear. How can psychologists explain mental processes when there is no microscope for the mind?

Measuring behavior, not mental processes, is the answer, and we can avoid the circularity problem if we do two things. First, we can create theories that are detailed enough to make specific predictions about what the pattern of behavior should look like if the theory is correct and what the data will look like if it is not correct. Second, we must create experiments that carefully control and manipulate behavior. In other words, for behavioral data to test cognitive theories, we need theories that generate specific predictions and experimental conditions that will test these predictions.

Can we use neuroscientific data to test cognitive theories? You may be wondering, "Well, what about the brain?" You have likely heard or read about brain imaging techniques whereby scientists can locate the part of the brain that is active when a particular cognitive activity like reading takes place. Can't we just use that technology to eavesdrop on the brain while it is reading, then base our cognitive theories on which areas light up? Different ways of imaging and depicting brain activity are shown in Figure 2.1. If the mind is what the brain does, observations of the brain should shape our theories of mental processes.

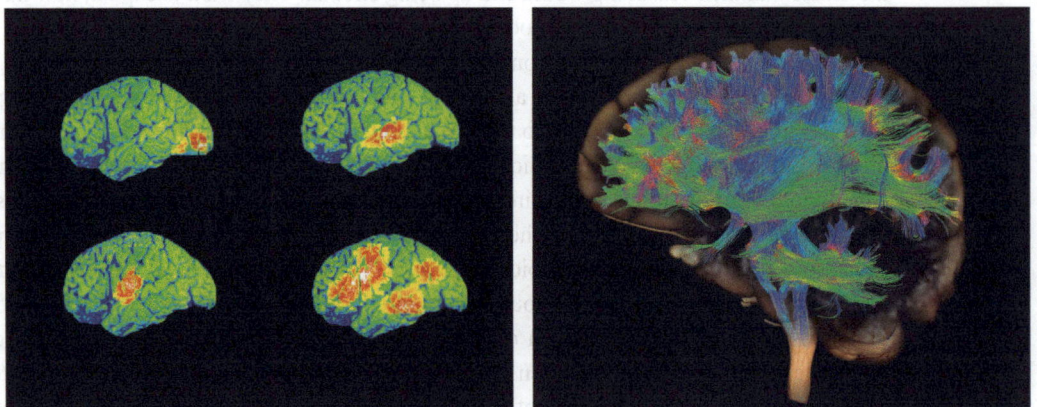

Figure 2.1. Pretty pictures of brain activity, such as those provided by (left) functional MRI and (right) diffusion tensor imaging, don't tell us much about the brain unless they are accompanied by specific theoretical predications and carefully controlled experiments.

That strategy turns out to be more complicated than we would initially guess. For example, suppose we determine that the temporal lobe is more active when people read than when they watch a movie. Now what? "Why can I read?" "Because temporal lobe" is not an explanation.

And we can't assume that the temporal lobe is the "reading area" of the brain. Maybe it's important for attention, or for remembering words, or for appreciating humor (if the story was funny). This sort of information – the apparent brain location of cognitive activity – *can* be useful, but the simple existence of the information is not proof that we understand cognitive function. In this chapter, we discuss in more detail what you need to know for neuroscientific data to be useful to cognitive theory and how cognitive psychologists have used such data.

Can We Use Behavioral Data to Test Cognitive Theories?

Preview

As we described in Chapter 1, many cognitive theories propose abstract mental constructs, such as "memory" or "attention," to explain behavior. Although testing theories that use abstract constructs seems daunting, it can be done. The critical job is to specify how these constructs, which are unobservable, will change behavior, which is observable. Three broad classes of behavioral research contribute to this goal. Descriptive research simply describes the world. Relational research describes how different factors change together (e.g., people who have more general knowledge about the world score better on reading comprehension tests, and people who have less general knowledge score worse). Cognitive psychologists most often use experimental research, in which the researcher changes one factor and observes the other (e.g., changing the ink color of printed words to see if that affects memory for the words).

To better understand why behaviorists thought that psychology had to be rooted in observable behavior, consider the definition of science. We said in Chapter 1 that science is not defined by its subject matter but by its method. Definitions of this method vary, but they usually include three properties: empiricism, public verifiability, and solvable problems. Empiricism in this sense is different than the seventeenth-century philosophical movement mentioned in Chapter 1. In science, **empiricism** means that we are dedicated to learning about the world by trying things out and observing: We develop a hypothesis about the world, and then we test it. This method can be contrasted with learning about the world through logic and reason without experimentation, or with learning about the world by studying sacred texts such as the Bible.

Public verifiability means that we must make our hypotheses and our experiments available to everyone to examine, to critique and be able to conduct again themselves, in a process called *replication*. Imagine your reaction if I said that I had scientific proof that ingestion of chocolate led to small but consistent increases in intelligence, but when you asked to see this proof, I refused to show it to you or showed you only a limited summary of my results. You wouldn't think that my claim was worth the time of day, and you'd be right.

A final characteristic of science is that it deals with **solvable problems**. This principle recognizes that science is well suited to studying some problems (how do planets move?) and ill suited to studying other problems (is it moral for someone who is starving to steal food?).

Scientists continually revisit these principles to consider whether we are living up to them. For example, what exactly do we mean by public verifiability? How public is public? What counts as verification? In recent years, many scientists have expressed concern that professional incentives such as publishing novel and exciting findings, getting grants, and jobs make it tempting to cut corners on public verifiability. Several institutions and reforms have sought to address these concerns (see callout box).

Scientists have identified two methods to improve public verifiability in science. There need to be professional incentives to adhere to these values and tools to enable sharing. The Center for Open Science was founded in 2013 to address both. The center has worked with the professional journals that publish scientific studies to support openness by encouraging scientists to make their data and materials available to all, instead of publishing just summaries of results. One such incentive is the use of badges attached to published articles that advertise researchers' publicly verifiable practices. See Figure 2.2 for examples of these badges and how they will appear next to journal articles.

Behaviorists argued that the cognitive approach was unscientific because it was not empirical; one couldn't conduct studies to confirm or disconfirm cognitive theories. For that reason, they also believed the cognitive program failed the "solvable problems" criterion; one couldn't use the scientific method to explain thought, they argued, any more than one could use the scientific method to explain morality.

Behaviorists had a point. Unobservable mental processes are very powerful as theoretical devices because there is no limit to what they can do; the theorist is free to invent any process or representation they choose with any desired properties. Let's make this concrete. Suppose Willingham is at a large party with his wife, Trisha, making small talk with friends. He goes to the drink table and notes that Coke, Sprite, Irn-Bru (the most popular soft drink in Scotland), lemonade, iced tea, and ginger ale are being served. He keeps the offerings in mind so he can tell Trisha her choices. When he returns, Trisha asks, "Do they have Irn-Bru?" and he immediately replies, "Yes."

Dan kept the six types of drinks available in memory. When Trisha asked about Irn-Bru, he had to search the contents of his short-term memory and determine that Irn-Bru was among the choices. How did this search take place? Three relatively simple alternatives come to mind (see Figure 2.3), although we could likely list more.

First, he might have searched through the list in his short-term memory, one item at a time, halting the search when he came to Irn-Bru because he had found the item she asked about. Second, he might have searched through all items in the list, continuing the search even if he found the item. It may seem odd to continue searching once he had found the target (Irn-Bru), but doing so makes the search simple in another way; he always searches the same way (i.e., the entire list) each time he does the task. A third possibility is that he doesn't search through the list one item at a time but rather is able to compare the target Trisha asks about – Irn-Bru – to all items in the list simultaneously, effectively searching through the entire list at once.

So which of these three possibilities is correct? We can't directly observe short-term memory to find out. We could ask the **participant** – a participant is anyone who provides data for psychological research – "How did you search short-term memory?" But psychologists generally

Research Article

Mugs and Plants: Object Semantic Knowledge Alters Perceptual Processing With Behavioral Ramifications

Psychological Science
1–13
© The Author(s) 2022
Article reuse guidelines:
sagepub.com/journals-permissions
DOI: 10.1177/09567976221097497
www.psychologicalscience.org/PS
SAGE

Dick Dubbelde and Sarah Shomstein
Department of Psychological and Brain Sciences, The George Washington University

Research Article

The Social Effects of an Awesome Solar Eclipse

Psychological Science
1–11
© The Author(s) 2022
Article reuse guidelines:
sagepub.com/journals-permissions
DOI: 10.1177/09567976221085501
www.psychologicalscience.org/PS
SAGE

Sean P. Goldy, Nickolas M. Jones, and Paul K. Piff
Department of Psychological Science, University of California, Irvine

Figure 2.2. The Center for Open Science seeks to improve openness and transparency at each step of the scientific process. Open data and open materials badges proclaim that data or materials are publicly available, often on the web platform created by the Center for Open Science called Open Science Framework (https://osf.io/). Another badge indicates that the study was preregistered, in which the authors preregister their hypotheses with a journal in which they seek to publish before running the experiment, preventing them from hypothesizing after the results are known (or HARKing), a practice that can lead to misinterpretation of results.

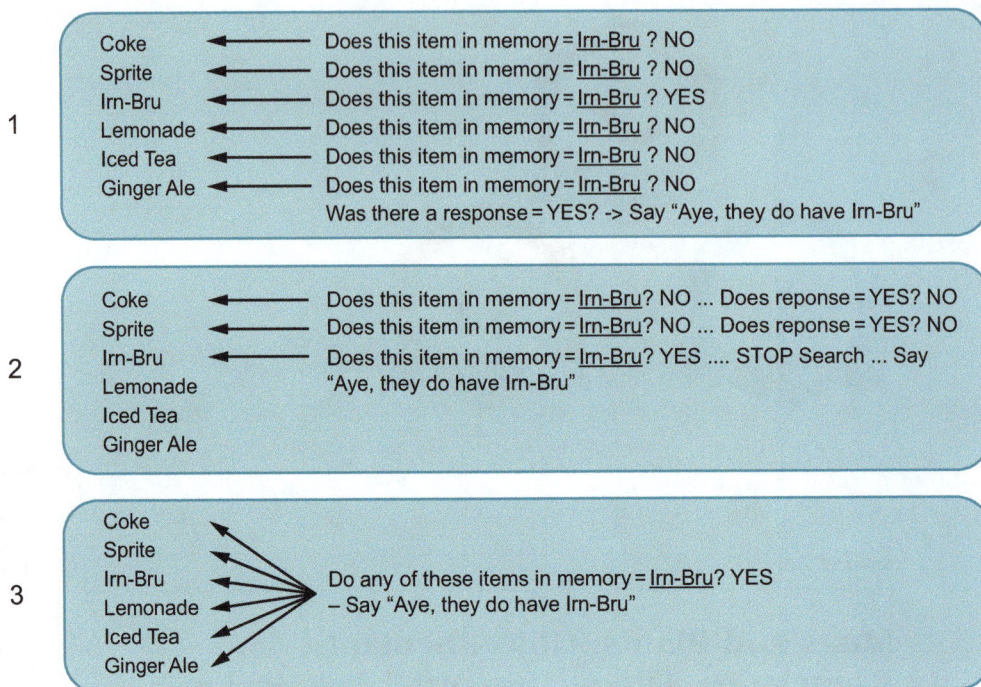

Figure 2.3. Three possible mental processes for keeping a list in memory to report later whether an item is on that list.

don't have a lot of confidence in people's ability to introspect about this kind of process, and even if we did ask, participants' introspections would have all the problems we discussed in Chapter 1. So how do you make this theory testable?

Testing Cognitive Theories

Cognitive psychologists solved this problem by articulating not only their theories of mental processes but also how different unobservable mental processes might produce different behaviors. Thus, they didn't create theories of behavior, but they specified the behavior that could be expected if their cognitive theory were right. We can derive predictions of overt behavior that differentiate the three theories of short-term memory if we make the simple assumption that the search process takes time.

The first theory says that you stop the search when you find the target. Therefore, it predicts that the search will be faster when the target is present than when it is not. Irn-Bru was third on the list, so Dan would stop the search after the third item. We'd predict that if Trisha had asked about cranberry juice, the search would have taken longer because Dan would have had to search through the whole list to determine it wasn't there. The second theory, however, says that you always search through all items in short-term memory. Therefore, it predicts that these two searches (target present, target absent) will take the same amount of time. The last model, in which all drinks in short-term memory are evaluated simultaneously, makes a different type of prediction. According to the first two theories, the search takes longer, on average, as items are added to the list – Dan would be quicker to answer Trisha's question if two drinks were available at the party instead of six. According to the third theory, the number of items in short-term memory does *not* affect how long

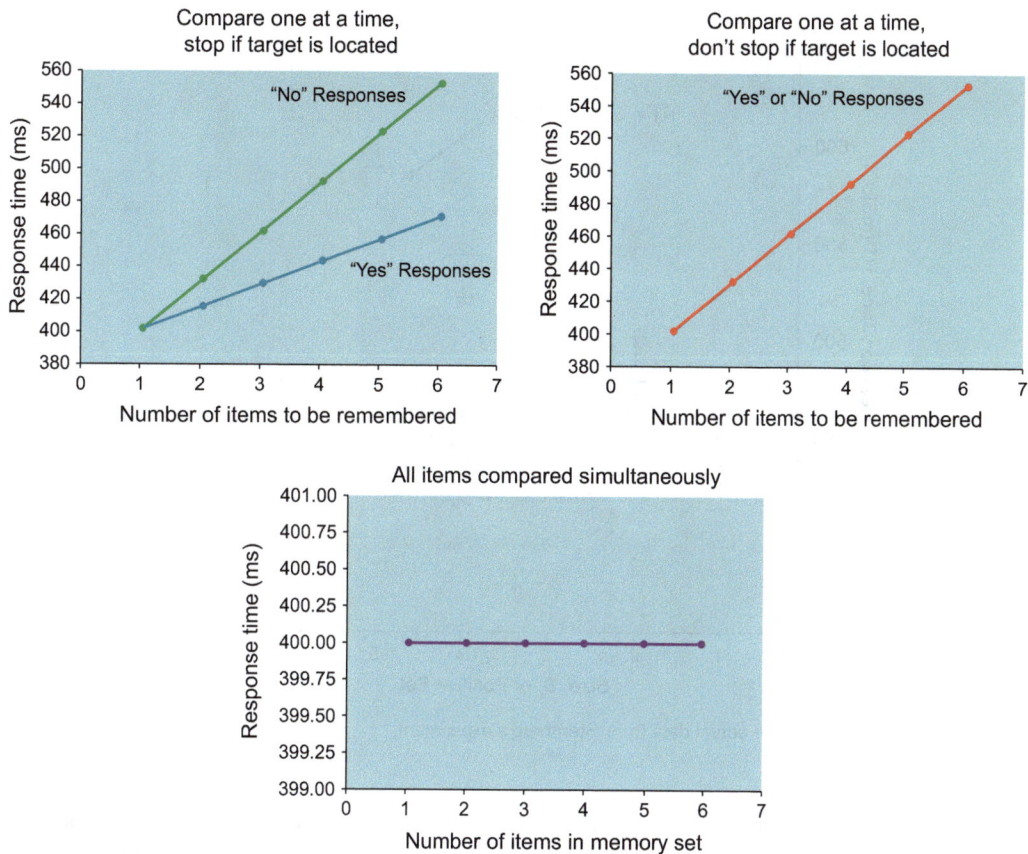

Figure 2.4. Different predictions of the data outcome for three theories of searching short-term memory.

the search should take. Because they are all searched simultaneously, Dan can search through two items as quickly as he searches through six items. It's easiest to appreciate these different predictions graphically, as shown in Figure 2.4.

We're obviously not going to set up a party to test this theory (more's the pity). A more efficient experimental setup would be to have the participant sit in front of a computer. On each trial, some letters (instead of drink names) appear on the screen to be held in short-term memory, and after a brief pause, a new letter appears. It's better to use letters rather than drinks because in our example, Scottish people might have an advantage due to their familiarity with Irn-Bru. The participant presses one button if the new letter was in the first set and another button if it was not. The experiment I've just described is similar to one conducted by Saul Sternberg (1966). The results of Sternberg's experiment were quite clear-cut. As shown in Figure 2.5, the data were consistent with the second theory but not with the other two; you scan short-term memory one item at a time, and you don't stop if you find that target.

Thus, it is possible to experimentally test cognitive theories, even though they use unobservable abstract constructs. We can summarize the necessary steps in the following way:

Develop alternative theories. Our understanding is much deeper if we have at least two possibilities in mind and try to choose among them, rather than having one model that we try to confirm or disconfirm. For example, suppose that I developed the hypothesis that we

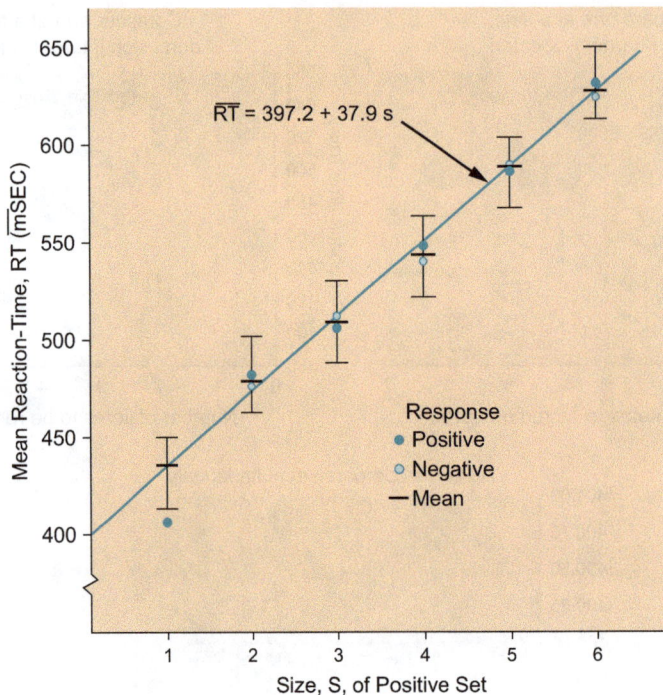

Figure 2.5. The actual data from Sternberg's experiment.

scan lists in our memory all at once. I conduct my experiment and I find that the data don't support the theory, but I don't know what theory the data *do* support.

Derive signature predictions for each theory. We can't choose among different theories if they all make the same prediction. For example, I may develop two theories of **forgetting**. In one, forgetting occurs because memories decay over time. In the other, new learning interferes with old learning. My planned experiment is to read a list of words to participants in the morning and then test their memory in the afternoon. But both theories make the same prediction – forgetting will have occurred – due to either decay (theory 1) or interference (theory 2).

This step – deriving predictions – entails solving the key problem with which we started. The problem was that the theories to be compared used unobservable abstract constructs (different methods of searching short-term memory). In developing predictions for each theory, we specify how these search processes interact with the observable environment. Does each possible search process use the same input differently? We specified observable things that the experimenter can change (number of items to be remembered, presence or absence of the searched item in the list), and we specified observable behaviors that would result from the workings of the unobservable search process (changes in time to respond). Thus, a key part of our theory is that it predicts exactly how our abstract mental processes interact with the objective, observable world.

Obtain data to compare the theories. The need for this step is self-evident. The real concern is to ensure that the experiment is designed and conducted properly. That is the subject matter of a course in experimental methods, but we review here some of the basic approaches to research.

Descriptive Research

In **descriptive research**, one simply describes some behavior as one finds it in the world. Three commonly used methods are descriptive: naturalistic observation, case studies, and self-report. These methods never provide decisive data for cognitive psychologists – that is, they do not tell us which candidate theory is correct – but they can provide inspiration for other types of work or highlight behavioral phenomena that had been ignored. Also, it's sometimes useful to have a systematic description of some aspect of the world, even if it's not directly applicable to a theory. The US census is one such description, and it's an example of descriptive research. A political poll is another. This type of research is not as common in cognitive psychology, but there are still some good examples. How many words do people know? Which words do people use most frequently? A researcher might want to compare memory for words that are equally common because people might find it more difficult to remember rare words (*apples* and *oranges*, rather than *pumelos* and *kumquats*), but this would need to start with descriptive research on how frequently words are used. (For a recent review of the word frequency effect in word processing, see Brysbaert et al. [2018].)

Naturalistic observation refers to observing behavior in its natural setting. For example, if you wanted to know how good people are at mental calculation, you could sit in a restaurant for several hours and surreptitiously record how people calculated the amount to tip: mentally, with paper and pencil, or with a calculator. We encountered an example of naturalistic observation in Chapter 1 – ethologists who observe animals in the wild and carefully record their behavior.

Recent examples of naturalistic observation can be found in research on social media and online communities. In one study, playfully titled "You Are What You Tweet," researchers measured the personalities of 142 participants and then observed their tweets for a period of one month (Qiu et al., 2012). In another study, researchers analyzed the language in tweets of nearly 3 million users before, during, and after the solar eclipse of 2017, finding that more statements of awe were written by those in the path of the eclipse but also that those who used elevated awe-language also used other language that was more humble, collective, and prosocial after the eclipse than before (Goldy et al., 2022). Notice how "naturalistic" doesn't mean that the behavior has to be out in nature but that the behavior occurs without the expectation of being observed or in an experiment (Figure 2.6).

Naturalistic observation usually involves observation of more than one participant. In a **case study**, the researcher observes an individual on a number of occasions. Case studies are seldom naturalistic. The researcher usually interacts with the participant of the study, sometimes asking

Figure 2.6. Naturalistic observation is observing behavior in natural settings, whether animals in the wild or virtual behavior on social media.

them to perform tasks of interest. Case studies are often used when a group of similar participants is unavailable so intense study of an individual is the only method one can use. For example, neurological patients with rare brain disorders are often the subject of case studies. One of the best-known case studies is "Victor," a boy found living on his own in the forest in southern France. What would the cognitive abilities be of a human who grew up only in the presence of animals, without observing other people? This question was addressed in the case study *The Wild Boy of Aveyron* (Itard, 1962). A more recent case study was a patient who received an anesthetic at the dentist and somehow lost the ability to form new memories, but unlike Henry Molaison described in the last chapter, this patient could retain memories from the previous ninety minutes, rather than just the past one or two minutes (Burgess & Chadalavada, 2016).

Cognitive psychologists usually consider descriptive research a starting point, a source of ideas, rather than definitive data. Consider the impact of smartphones and multitasking on memory and attention. Cognitive psychologists are aware of descriptive data showing that more automobile accidents occur when drivers are using their phones, but this pattern must be tied to specific mental processes through controlled experiments. Some have used realistic driving simulators to investigate questions such as, Is a phone conversation less distracting if it is hands-free? No, both are distracting and result in longer latency to brake (Strayer et al., 2003). Does a phone conversation disrupt memory for irrelevant objects (like advertising billboards) and relevant objects (like pedestrians) differently? No, memories for high- and low-relevance objects were each worsened by a phone conversation (Strayer & Drews, 2007). Do the attentional costs of multitasking while driving stop immediately when you put down the phone? No, the effects of intermittent multitasking persist even after the multitasking stops (Strayer et al., 2022). Such experiments might use descriptive research as an inspiration, but well-designed experiments are the source of evidence for settling empirical questions. Figure 2.7 shows an example of a futuristic display on a car windshield that the research on attention you just read would suggest is ill advised.

Relational Research

Descriptive research seeks to describe some aspect of the world. **Relational research** examines two or more aspects of the world with an eye to seeing whether they are related. For example, I might measure people's memory ability and measure their age, and then determine whether one is related to the other. Many studies have shown that, as we age, our memory abilities decline (Park & Festini, 2017). Or I might measure relationships between people's mask-wearing behavior and their judgments of risks and dangers of the SARS-CoV-2 virus in 2020 as the COVID-19 pandemic spread across the globe. Note that in relational research, one takes two measures from each individual, in this case a measure of mask-wearing behavior and a measure of their judgments of risk. Other associations relevant to the psychology of the pandemic might be vaccination (a behavior) and overall trust in the medical system (a mental construct).

Relational research sounds like it's a step closer to finding the causes and mental mechanisms that cognitive psychologists seek, and indeed, that's true. Saying "the 45 percent of people who report wearing masks indoors are more likely to rate their own risk of getting the virus as very high" is certainly more suggestive of the causal relationships between thought and behavior than "45 percent of people report wearing masks indoors." In the last section, we said that the key to evaluating cognitive theories is to test predictions that they make about behavior. In relational research, the data provided and the predictions made describe associations of factors. For example, we might find that people who rated their own risk of contracting COVID-19 as "very high" were more likely to wear masks.

Figure 2.7. It might seem exciting and futuristic to use a car windshield as a computer display, but research on attention suggests we should be very careful with driving and distraction.

Relational research is still not decisive, however. The problem is that knowing that factors are associated doesn't tell us why they are associated, and the *why* is usually critical to evaluating theories. A science of mental processes, just like any science, doesn't care only about a pattern or relationships but about what is causing what. We might be tempted to say that in the case of masks and perceived risk of COVID-19, a high perceived risk is causing the behavior of more mask wearing. However, it may also be the case that a third variable is causing each of these: Perhaps a vigorous public health educational program is both convincing people of the danger of COVID-19 and encouraging people to wear masks. Free mask availability at pharmacies in a certain neighborhood or country might both encourage mask wearing and cause people to see themselves as more at risk. While it seems sort of backward, it could also be that mask wearing (or perhaps the social signal of seeing many in your community wear masks) is causing the higher beliefs of risk, rather than a higher judgment of risk causing more mask wearing. Relational research tells you that changes in factor A (e.g., mask wearing) tend to go with changes in factor B (e.g., judgments of COVID-19 risk), but it doesn't tell you whether A causes B, or B causes A, or whether factor C (e.g., peer pressure, public health education, mask availability) causes changes in both A and B. As you can probably tell from the preceding example, working out the causal relationships (what is the cause and what is the effect) can be especially tricky in the science of mental processes.

Experimental Research

Relational research tells us that two things go together, but it doesn't tell us whether changes in one cause changes in the other, which is usually important for evaluating theories. How can we gain information about causality? We need to eliminate the problem described previously – third factors (C) that are associated with the factors that interest us (A and B) and the direction of the causality between A and B. The problem was that we were taking people as they came to us – the people who tended to choose to wear masks at the beginning of the pandemic might also have been more likely to have access to masks through their profession, be it health or construction; they might have been more educated about infectious diseases; they might have had more experience with epidemics in the past. In these cases, it isn't really their judgments of risk that are causing their mask wearing but something else. But suppose we randomly select 1,000 people, then randomly assign them to two groups. For one group, we intervene to *make* their judgment of COVID-19 risk higher (perhaps through a public health educational campaign) and compare them to another group whose judgments we don't change (perhaps through a generic "be healthy and well" message not specific to infectious disease or COVID-19). Then, at some point in the future, we follow up and observe mask-wearing behavior. Because we selected them randomly, and then randomly assigned them to a group, there is no reason to think these people are any different than other people and no reason to think our increased risk-judgment group is different than the control group in any other way. When we measure any differences in mask wearing, we are more sure that the reason for this difference is the change that we caused.

That is the core of experimental research. Just like relational research, we measure whether two things are related, but in **experimental research**, we change one factor (while holding other factors equal) and observe the effect of the change on the other. In psychology, it might be seeking to change a thought or belief and observing some change in behavior. It might even be the opposite, getting people to change behavior and observing whether that changes their thoughts or beliefs. In an experiment, the **independent variable** is the one that the researcher manipulates. The **dependent variable** is the other factor the researcher measures – it's the one that they think will vary, depending on how the independent variable is manipulated. Usually, the independent variable is something that the researcher believes will influence cognition, such as how many items must be scanned in a short-term memory experiment or the color of the background in a perception experiment. The dependent variable is often some measure of behavior that reflects cognitive performance (e.g., how accurately the participant responds, how quickly the participant responds). Note that there is not an independent or dependent variable in relational research because the researcher doesn't manipulate anything.

The great advantage of an experiment is that we can be much more confident that we understand the relationship between two factors when they have been evaluated in an experiment, rather than in a case study or in relational research. Still, a single experiment does not decisively settle an issue. Suppose, for example, that making people count backward by three seconds in their head disrupts their ability to answer trivia questions, while making people imagine rotating shapes in their heads does not disrupt trivia performance. We might want to conclude that counting backward is a verbal task that disrupts another verbal task, using limited cognitive resources for that purpose, whereas imagined spatial rotation is not verbal and perhaps uses another set of cognitive resources. This sounds plausible, but we would need several other experiments, with other tasks and measures, as well as confirmation that it wasn't some other property of the tasks that differed – for example, perhaps one is more difficult than the other, and *that* explains the difference in answering trivia questions. We would need to conduct another experiment to eliminate alternative accounts. In general, clear answers to complex questions emerge only after systematic work, sometimes taking years.

Such work is, however, essential to avoiding mistakes, some of which might be costly. For example, expert video game players (see Figure 2.8) seem to be better at a variety of basic processes of visual perception and attention (Castel et al., 2005; McDermott et al., 2014). This relationship (found

Figure 2.8. Expert video game players might tend to be better at certain other cognitive functions, but we should be careful about concluding that it is the games that are responsible.

through relational research) could be because playing video games improves cognitive function, it could be because individuals of higher cognitive function are drawn to playing more video games, or it could be a third variable that causes each (Boot et al., 2008). Careful experiments have documented that, at least in some instances, video game experience can have a causal role in, for example, faster reaction times in certain situations (Dye et al., 2009). Such evidence has been part of the inspiration for brain training or "brain games": video games specifically designed for improving cognition. However, despite millions of dollars spent by companies marketing these programs, and millions of dollars spent by customers looking to improve or maintain cognitive function, a recent review found that while these programs improve performance on the tasks people practiced (and very similar tasks), there is little evidence of more general cognitive improvement (Simons et al., 2016; Sala & Gobet, 2019).

Students often raise two objections to cognitive experiments. The first is that the vast majority of them are conducted on college students, who tend to be young, wealthy, and of European descent. Can researchers draw conclusions about the "human mind" when they have in fact tested just a small, nonrepresentative segment of humanity? One review labeled the participants of most behavioral science experiments WEIRD: Western, educated, industrialized, rich, and democratic (Henrich et al., 2010). The researchers argued that while this doesn't invalidate the experiments themselves, we should be more cautious in concluding that we are discovering universal psychological principles.

Until the 1990s, cognitive psychologists weren't all that worried about this point. They reasoned that the basic architecture of the cognitive system probably *was* the same in Europeans, Asians, Africans, and so on. Although culture would shape social interactions, the basic cognitive system is part of our genetic inheritance and is unlikely to vary much. While there are cultural variations in language and communication, rituals and traditions, and many other thoughts and behaviors, cognitive psychologists assumed that there were some universal patterns and rules that described all of human perception, memory, and attention, for example. More recently, researchers have begun to appreciate that culture can shape some cognitive processes (Ojalehto & Medin, 2015; Majid & Burenhult, 2014; Wang, 2021).

To show that the differences between WEIRD populations and the rest of the world aren't restricted to cultural values and social conventions, Henrich and colleagues begin with an interesting example from perception. In the Müller–Lyer illusion (Figure 2.9), the perceived length of a line is affected by the context of arrows around it. While this illusion seemingly reflects a basic process of visual perception immune to cultural factors, the degree to which people are susceptible to this illusion actually varies across cultures (Segall et al., 1966). It would seem that we should be much more cautious about generalizing the results of our studies to all humans.

This result (Figure 2.9) doesn't mean that the Müller–Lyer illusion is "wrong." A closer look at the results helps support one proposed explanation of the illusion (and many other similar illusions) rather than casting doubt on it. One common interpretation for many such illusions is that they reflect how the mind has learned (over countless experiences with blocks, buildings, rooms, doors, windows, etc.) to take our two-dimensional views of right angles and translate those into an interpretation of the three-dimensional world (Gregory, 2015). The presumption in this theory is that seeing is *not* wholly a function of our genetic inheritance. We *learn* to see. When we learn in a world that has a lot more right angles than other angles, this experience leads us to be biased to see right angles when the visual conditions support such an interpretation. For example, see the two views of the same book in Figure 2.10. Testing people in societies that offer fewer visual experiences with right angles (circular buildings; fewer manufactured items like books, blocks, frames, and windows) affords a way to test this theory. (We noted that cognitive psychologists usually deal with experimental data; here's an instance when relational data prove useful.)

Let's take another example to see how expanding the view of cognitive psychology across the globe can show how cultural differences can affect cognition, revealing some processes to be universal and others to be dependent on culture.

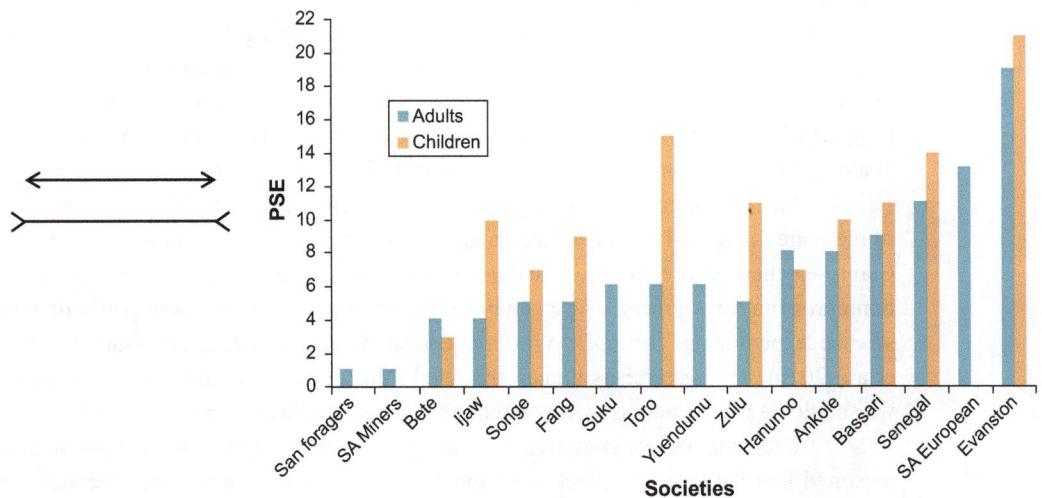

Figure 2.9. Results of tests of the level of illusion in the Müller–Lyer illusion; 0 would be accurately seeing the lines as equal, whereas higher numbers (PSE = point of subjective equality) indicate higher susceptibility to the illusion. Note that residents of Evanston (the city in Illinois, USA) had the highest levels of susceptibility to the illusion.

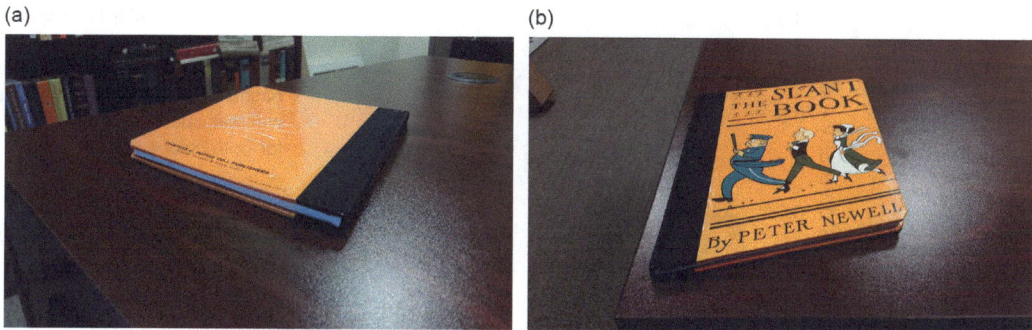

Figure 2.10. (a) This view looks like a normal book with four right angles, but (b) here it is revealed to be a weird book with four angles that are not ninety degrees. The desk on which it is placed is rectangular.

Asifa Majid and colleagues have investigated the connection between language and thought in different cultures, one interesting case being the connection between smell and language (Majid & Burenhult, 2014). Many previous studies found that people's language for smells is often limited and specific to an item ("this smells like a banana") and that their ability to name smells is poor, especially compared to rich and abstract language in visual and auditory domains (this banana is curved, shiny and a sickly yellow-green shade). However, now reading the "many previous studies found that people's language" should give you brief pause. Is it "people's language for smells" or is it "WEIRD people's language for smells"? Majid and Burenhult (2014) compared speakers of American English in Austin, Texas, to speakers of Jahai from the Malay Peninsula in Malaysia on a previously used Brief Smell Identification Test (B-SIT) (Doty et al., 1984). Each group named and described smells as well as standard colors using Munsell color chips. Speakers of Jahai used abstract language equally with smells ("roasted" or "bloody like raw meat or fish") and with colors ("red"), whereas English speakers were much more likely to use abstract language for colors ("red") than for smells ("like Big Red gum") and were also more hesitant and uncertain about smells than about colors (see Figure 2.11). While this was a relational study, it does show that the connection between language and smell is not universal.

The second common objection to experimental work in cognitive psychology is that the experiments don't seem very much like real life. That is, they are low in **ecological validity**. A participant sits alone in a dim room trying to remember nonwords, such as *lum* and *wik*. What can such an exercise tell us about how the mind works? Again, this criticism makes some sense. Psychologists must be mindful of the relationship between what happens in the laboratory and the world that the laboratory is meant to model. But the history of scientific discovery has shown that scientific experiments might create strange little worlds and still be informative. Biologists use petri dishes and physicists use supercolliders because they provide controlled environments that make it possible to examine parts of our world that are too complex to investigate in their natural state. Similarly, psychologists attempt to strip down the complex world into its essential components.

An example of a class of experiments that is low in ecological validity yet an interesting test of a psychological theory is testing perceptual learning using Greebles, a set of three-dimensional figures designed to be unfamiliar (Gauthier & Tarr, 1997, 2002; Bukach et al., 2012). (See Figure 2.12.) The fact that they are unlike things we encounter in real life is an experimental strength, in that the hope is that all observers are equally unfamiliar with these figures.

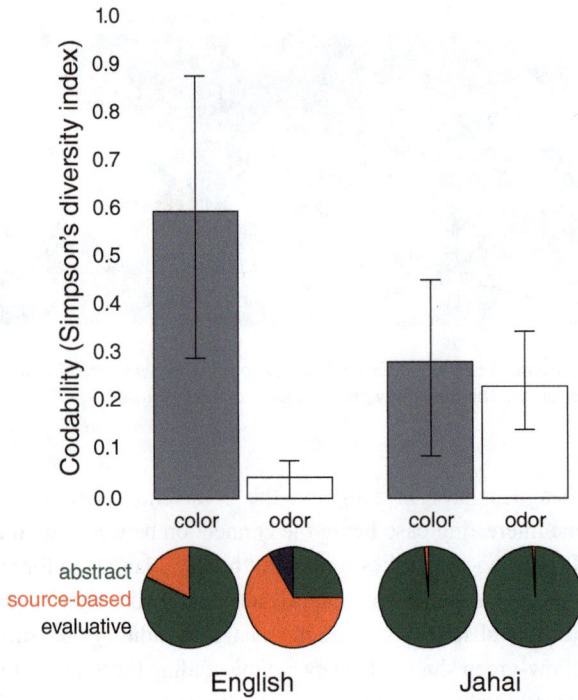

Figure 2.11. In Majid and Burenhult's (2014) study, English speakers tended to use more abstract words for color (like yellow) but source-based words for odor (smells like a banana), whereas speakers of Jahai used abstract terms for both color and odor.

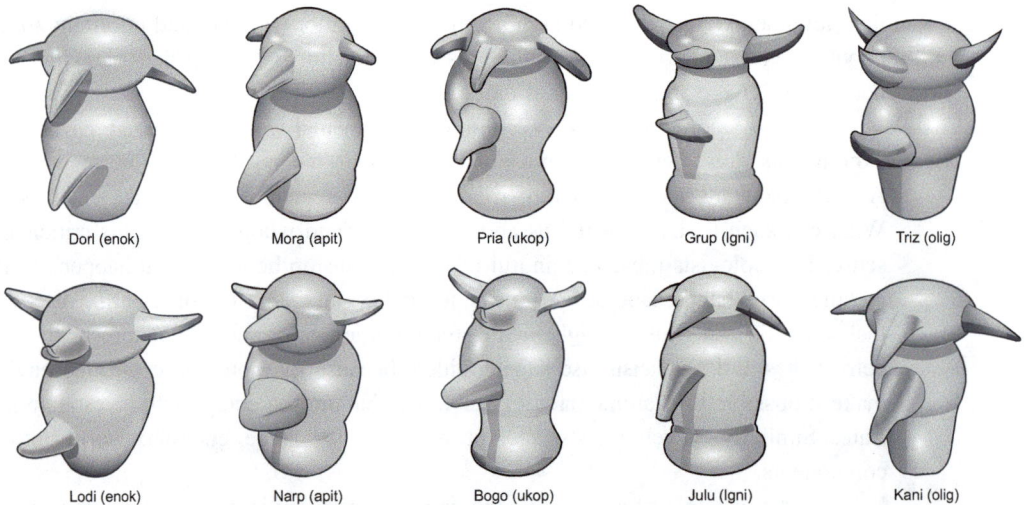

Figure 2.12. Different kinds of Greebles, an artificial three-dimensional figure intended to be unfamiliar to new viewers. They each have individual names as well as family groups (in parentheses), allowing researchers to study not only individual identification but also categorization. (Source: C. Rezlescu, J. J. Barton, D. Pitcher, and B. Duchaine, B. [2014], Normal acquisition of expertise with greebles in two cases of acquired prosopagnosia, *Proceedings of the National Academy of Sciences of the USA*, 111[14], 5123–5128.)

We've given an overview of the steps in the scientific process as relevant for cognitive psychology, with different examples in each section (reading, masks and risk judgment, language and smell, etc.). For a review of the concepts using a single example throughout (visual mental imagery), see Appendix A.

In summary, cognitive psychologists can use behavioral data to test cognitive theories. To do so, they must specify how the unobservable abstract constructs in the theory are influenced by observable manipulations and express this influence in observable behavior. Psychologists use experiments to evaluate whether the predicted relationships between these variables hold true.

Stand-on-One-Foot Questions

2.1.   What are the three characteristics of the scientific method?
2.2.   What are the three steps in doing behavioral research?
2.3.   What are the three broad classes of behavioral research, and how do they differ?

Questions That Require Two Feet

2.4.   Scientific journals use a process called peer review whereby two or more experts in the discipline read and critique an article before it is published in the journal to ensure that the science is sound. On occasion, you will hear one scientist criticize another for publicizing a scientific result (e.g., in a press conference) before the article has undergone the peer review process. Why the criticism? Isn't the scientist living up to the public verifiability ideal?

2.5.   You may have heard that Freud's psychoanalytic theories were not very scientific (although they did contain many ideas that proved useful). A key criticism of his theory was that it could account for everything. If someone with a very strict father grew up to be shy, the theory had an explanation, but if someone with a very strict father grew up to be outgoing, the theory could account for that as well. It would seem that success in accounting for data would be considered a strength. What's the problem? (Think of the three steps of behavioral research.)

2.6.   Is it possible to conduct experiments examining the differences between genders?

Can We Use Neuroscientific Data to Test Cognitive Theories?

Preview

Neuroscience can inform cognitive theories in two ways. First, the most common method is through localization, which refers to finding the location in the brain that supports a cognitive function. Localization requires tools to identify locations in the brain. These are of three types: Some tools record the activity of small groups of brain cells, some localize where brain damage has occurred, and some record the activity of brain systems that include millions of cells. The second method is to directly test some aspect of the cognitive theory – not just where it is but how it works. Neuroscientific data that offer this kind of information is rare. The take-home message of this section is that applying neuroscience to test cognitive theories is much more difficult than it might seem and that neuroscience is, at best, a complement to, rather than a replacement for, behavioral evidence.

It would seem self-evident that if you're interested in the mind, you ought to be interested in the brain. After all, the mind is what the brain does. Until the mid 1980s, however, most cognitive psychology textbooks contained little information about the brain, and that choice accurately reflected the research strategy of the field. Cognitive psychologists used the behavioral measures described in the first part of this chapter.

Today, cognitive psychology is informed by neuroscience. This change was accelerated in the mid 1970s, when better tools to examine the human brain became available, but our understanding of cognitive processes has been informed by the brain since the beginnings of cognitive psychology itself. The case of Henry Molaison that we discussed in Chapter 1 is a good example of how biological understanding of the brain can inform cognitive theories. The information about the brain that has proved most useful to cognitive psychologists is **localization**, which means finding a location in the brain that supports a particular cognitive process or function. For example, if we propose that people use visual images to solve certain problems, we should be able to find a location in the brain that stores images or part of the brain that supports a process to manipulate them, perhaps by rotating them or making them larger or smaller.

How can we find evidence of localization? Two families of methods have been used:

- If brain area *X* supports cognitive function *Y,* then *damage* to area *X* will lead to an impairment in tasks that require function *Y.* For example, if the temporal cortex of the brain supports the storage of mental images, then damage to the temporal cortex should lead to impairment in the use of mental images.
- If brain area *X* supports cognitive function *Y,* then area *X* will be *active* when function *Y* is engaged. For example, if the temporal cortex of the brain supports the storage of mental images, then the temporal cortex should be active when people use visual images.

These principles seem straightforward enough, and the principles dictate the tools we need.

For the first method, we need some method of knowing where the brain is damaged. For the second method, we need some way of measuring brain activity. We examine each in turn. Before we begin, however, it is important to keep in mind that brain localization is useful only if the behavioral tasks are rigorously designed. For example, in the two preceding points, designing a task that tests the "storage of mental images" is just as important as properly calibrating the brain scanning device. We'll consider that problem later in the chapter.

Where Is the Damage?

Damage to the brain can result from many causes, such as a stroke, an infection, an operation to relieve epilepsy or remove a tumor, or a degenerative disease such as Alzheimer's disease, to name a few. Examining patients who have some damage to the brain and using that information to infer the function of different parts of the brain has a long history of success. In the early 1860s, Paul Broca reported the case of a patient who had damage to the left frontal lobe and had a problem producing speech. The patient could understand language, as long as the grammar was simple, but could produce speech only poorly. A few years later, Carl Wernicke reported the case of a patient who had damage to a different part of the brain; this patient could not understand speech, and although he could speak fluently, what he said did not make sense. These observations caused a sensation because they clearly indicated that different functions could be assigned to different parts of the brain. People inferred that these areas handled production and perception of speech, respectively. Note that the inference takes this form:

> If the patient cannot understand language, and the patient has damage to ventral lateral frontal cortex, then the ventral lateral frontal cortex supports language understanding.
>
> If the patient cannot produce language, and the patient has damage to the superior temporal gyrus, then the superior temporal gyrus supports language production.

To make that conclusion, psychologists needed to know the location of the damage, but there were few ways to determine this in the late nineteenth century. One method was to wait until the patient died and then physically inspect the brain to see the location of the damage, but it might be decades until the patient died. (Broca's patient died young because of an infection.) Another method was to focus on the small population of cases in which the location of the damage was known because it was the result of brain surgery, but most brain damage is the consequence of stroke or injury, not surgery, so the investigator won't get to examine many people.

Much better would be a method by which one could see the brain damage without opening the patient's skull. Why not take an X-ray picture of the brain? X-ray images show internal structure, but they compress the three-dimensional brain into a two-dimensional image. Look, for example, at the two X-ray images of people who had swallowed foreign objects in Figure 2.13. Because the images are a flat collapsing of three-dimensional objects, it is difficult to tell that the child in Figure 2.13a swallowed a ring, while it is easier to tell that the child in Figure 2.13b swallowed a SpongeBob figurine since the figurine is luckily facing a direction where the X-ray image is identifiable. The resulting images provide some information about location, but not enough.

A better solution is a type of scan that retains volumetric information by measuring thin slices of the brain, rather than squashing them together. A **computed tomography** scan (commonly called a **CT** scan) uses X-ray technology to show three-dimensional structure. The patient lies on a gurney with their head in the center of a large, doughnut-shaped structure. Around the perimeter of the doughnut are X-ray sources and X-ray detectors. As the X-rays are directed through the patient's head, some are absorbed by various structures (the skull, blood, the brain itself), and some pass all the way through the head to the X-ray detector on the other side. The denser a structure is, the more X-ray energy it absorbs.

The detector on the other side of the X-ray source can tell you how much of the X-ray has gotten through the head, but what absorbed some of the X-rays along the way, and where was it? It can only measure the average density of everything the X-ray passed through, be it skull, brain, or blood. Figure 2.14 shows a simple model for how this information can be made useful, using visible light and tinted glass. Imagine we had a three-dimensional cube made up of many small cubes, sort of like a Rubik's Cube made out of glass. If one of the cubes were green, but we could take a picture only from one angle, we would see only one of the views, and we would know only that the green cube was one of three cubes. But if we get multiple views, we have a better guess of where the colored cube is.

That is what a CT scan does. It uses multiple X-ray values, as shown in Figure 2.14. Each detector gives the density of the tissue in a single line, but if we combine the densities along intersecting lines, we can derive the density for a single point.

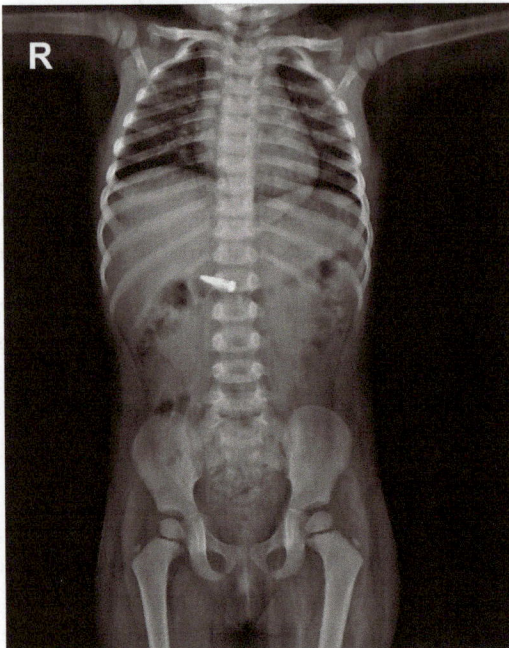

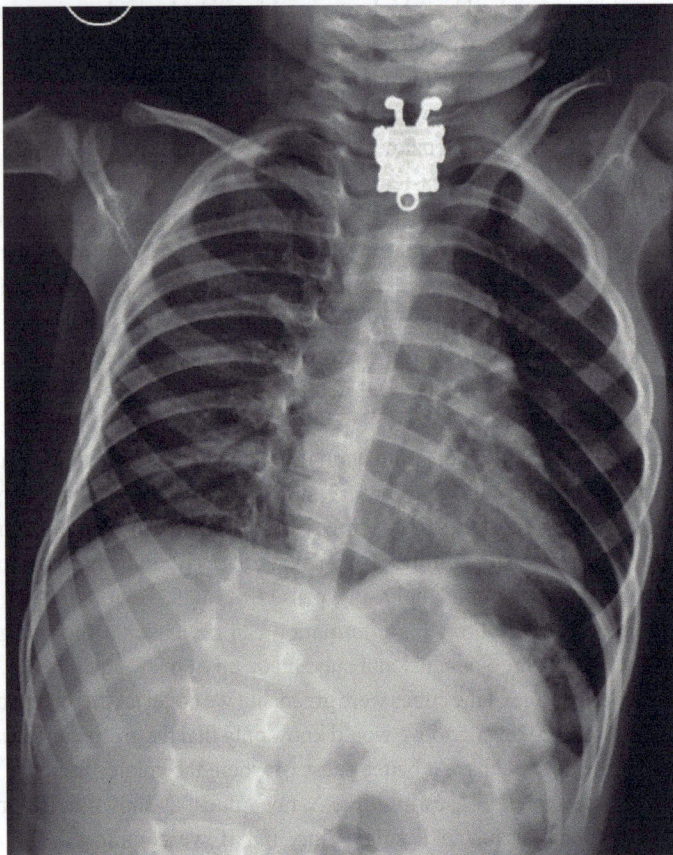

Figure 2.13. X-ray images do not always make clear the three-dimensional structure of the foreign objects that children accidentally ingest.

Top view   plus   Side view   =   Likely 3-D arrangement

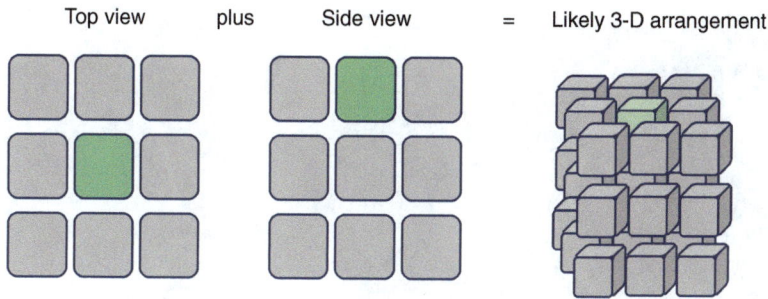

Figure 2.14. If we are given only one view, it is hard to tell the three-dimensional variations in density (where is the green cube if we are given only the top view?). But if we are given several views, we can estimate where the density is.

A CT scan compares thousands of values, so the calculations are performed by a computer. The resulting values represent the average density of a cube of tissue; if there are density differences within that tissue, you won't see them. A CT scan provides a three-dimensional map of values, a sculpture of density values, usually presented in two-dimensional slices.

How do we use these density values? The tissues of interest vary in density. Bone is very dense, blood is not dense at all, and brain cells (the part we care about) are of intermediate density. This technique allows us to see tumors, which differ from surrounding healthy tissue in density, and to see lesions (areas of tissue damage, usually the consequence of a stroke). So, we can localize some types of damage to the brain without opening the patient's head.

A second method using similar logic, **magnetic resonance imaging (MRI)**, provides much better resolution. MRI also yields a tissue density map, but the principle is not X-ray detection. Instead, MRI exploits the magnetic properties of hydrogen atoms, which are plentiful in organic matter. In their normal state, hydrogen atoms spin around an axis, and these axes are oriented randomly. The MRI machine generates a strong magnetic field that causes hydrogen atoms to orient their axes in parallel. A second magnetic wave is then applied to make only certain atoms spin or resonate (just as sound waves of the correct frequency make a tuning fork resonate). The concentration of the hydrogen can be read from the intensity of the resonance. (Localizing these intensity values actually requires a third signal, but you get the idea.) An example of an MRI image can be seen in Figure 2.15. Note that an MRI image is a slice, like a CT image.

Broca and Wernicke could not know where their patients suffered brain damage while they lived. These scanning technologies now make this possible. These methods are of interest because we want to localize function in the brain. One way to do that is to apply the principle that if brain area X is damaged and cognitive function Y is lost, we can infer that area X supports function Y. These methods allow us to make confident statements about which part of the brain is damaged.

Where Is the Activation?

A different approach to localization measures ongoing activity in the brain while an organism engages in a behavior. If brain area X supports function Y, then neural activity should be observed in area X when function Y is engaged. This logic is based not on physical brain damage impairing a

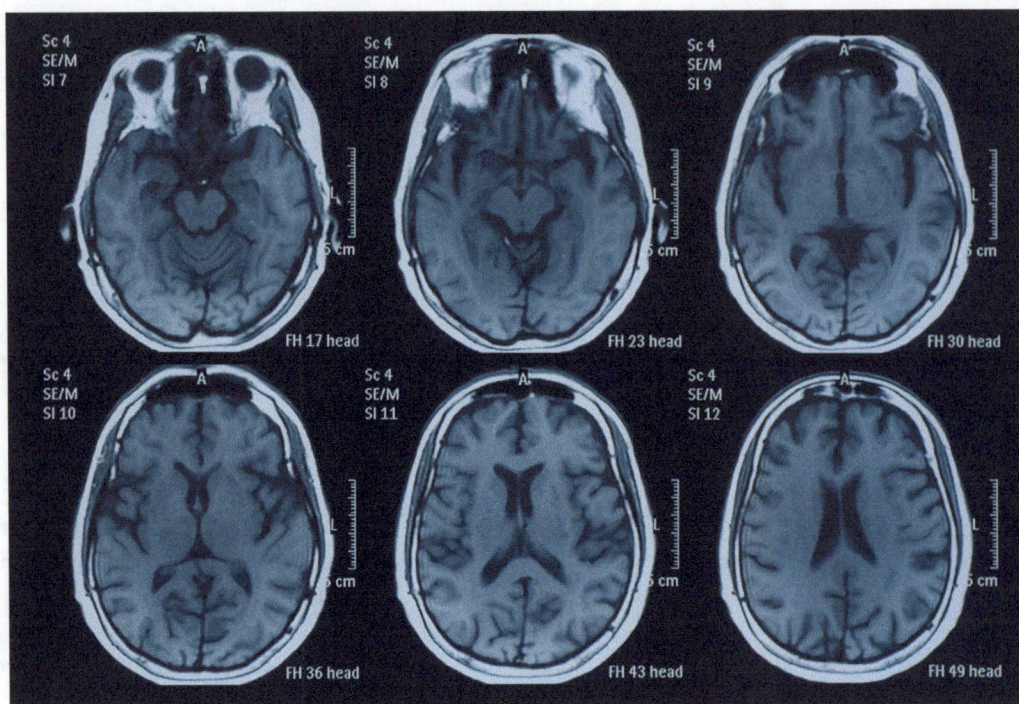

Figure 2.15. MRI images of a brain, showing six slices.

behavioral task but on physical brain activity facilitating a behavioral task. In other words, instead of "brain area is inactive and behavioral task is disrupted," the logic is "when person does behavioral task, brain area is active." This approach requires us to know a bit more about the basics of brain activity.

As you may know, the cells in the brain that support cognition are called **neurons**. There are approximately 85 billion neurons in the human brain (Azevedo et al., 2009). Neurons are interconnected, and one neuron can "tell" another neuron that it is active. If enough of a neuron's neighbors are active, that indicates to an individual neuron that it, too, should be active, and it will, in turn, communicate this activity to its neighbors.

Neural communication is both chemical and electrical. (See Figure 2.16.) Neurons release chemicals that influence their neighbors. The effect of the chemicals is to change the neighboring neurons' membranes so electrically charged ions can pass through them. Under normal circumstances, there are more negative ions inside a neuron's membrane than in the fluid surrounding the neural membrane; the charge across the membrane – its membrane potential – is about -70 megavolts. Surrounding neurons can alter the chemicals outside of that membrane, allowing positively charged ions to rush into the neuron, changing the membrane potential to 140 megavolts. Thus, the chemical influence of neighboring neurons causes a chemical change in the neural membrane, which results in an electrical change in the neuron, which propagates down the axon, leading to a release of chemicals (called neurotransmitters) starting the process again in another neuron. Influenced as we are by the metaphor of the computer (and even before that, other

(a)

Resting

Absolute refractory period

Relative refractory period

Resting

40-

3 Sodium channels close

2 Potassium channels open; K⁺ starts to leave cell

Action potential

0-

mV

1 Sodium channels open; Na⁺ rushes in

4 Potassium channels close

Depolarization

Threshold

-55

Resting potential

-70

Hyperpolarization

0   1   2   3

Time (ms)

Depolarizing stimulus applied

(b)

3. Glial cell degradation

1. Reuptake

4. Autoreceptors

5. Diffusion

■● = ■ + ● 2. Enzymatic deactivation

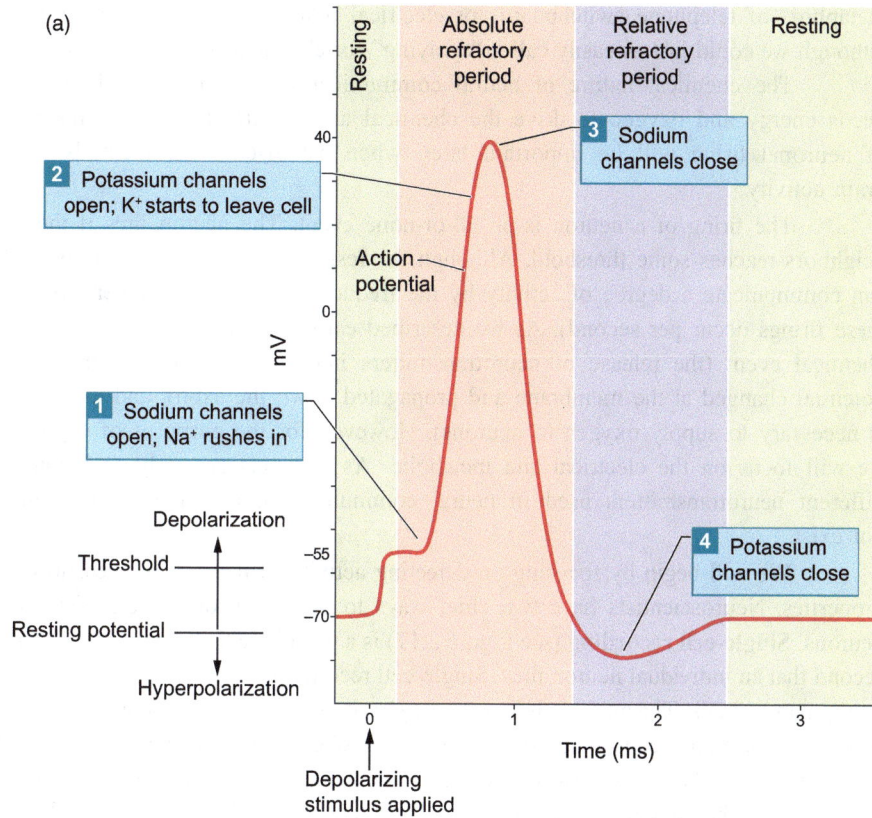

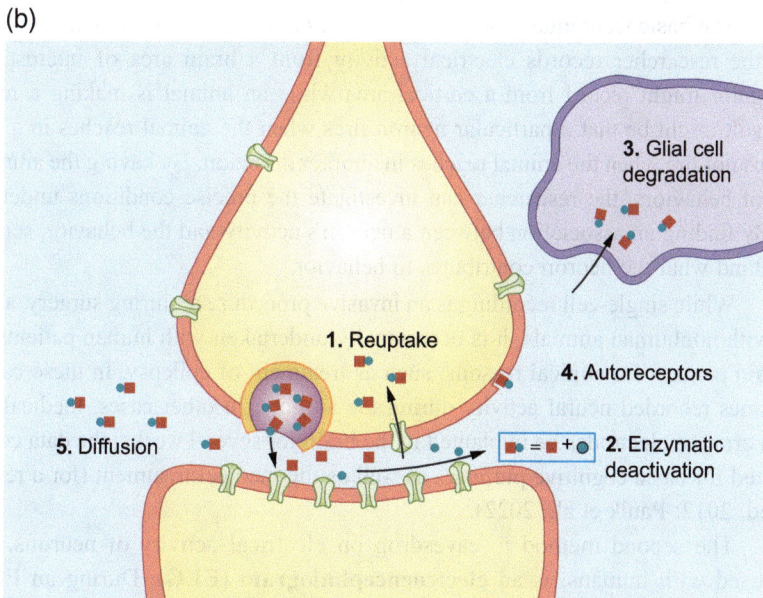

Figure 2.16. (a) Neural communication is electrical; the electrical signal is propagated down the axon, which leads to a message to the next neuron. (b) Neural communication is chemical.

metaphors of telephone switchboards or electrical relays), we call this process "neural firing," although we could just as easily call it "spraying" for chemicals being released.

The chemical nature of neural communication is also a metabolic event; a neuron needs energy and oxygen to drive the chemical and electrical activity. This metabolic nature of neuronal firing will be important later, when we discuss the methods we use to detect brain activity.

The firing of a neuron is an all-or-none event. The neuron fires if the influence of its neighbors reaches some threshold. Although the response seems to be "on" or "off," the neuron can communicate a degree of activity by the frequency of firing (in other words, how many of these firings occur per second). As we described earlier, we can see neural communication as a chemical event (the release of neurotransmitters into the synapse), electrical event (electrical potential changed at the membrane and propagated down the axon), and metabolic event (blood is necessary to supply oxygen to neurons). However, for the purposes of cognitive psychology, we will focus on the electrical and metabolic. As it stands currently, techniques to detect the different neurotransmitters used in neural communication associated with cognitive tasks do not exist.

We will begin by focusing on detecting activity of neurons by measuring their electrical properties. Neuroscientists have two chief ways to eavesdrop on the electrical conversations of neurons. **Single-cell recording** (see Figure 2.17) is a technique that records the number of times per second that an individual neuron fires. Single-cell recording studies are almost always performed on nonhuman animals. The animal undergoes surgery in which a small hole is drilled in the skull and a plastic anchoring device is attached. An electrode probe can be placed through the anchoring device and directly into the desired part of the brain. The brain does not have pain receptors, so the probe does not hurt the animal. The probe is insulated, except for the tip, so the probe's tip can record electrical activity, specifically, neural firings.

The basic technique in single-cell recording is to have the animal engage in some behavior while the researcher records electrical activity from a brain area of interest. For example, the investigator might record from a cortical area while an animal is making a reaching movement. The result might be that a particular neuron fires when the animal reaches in a particular direction but does not fire when the animal reaches in another direction. By having the animal engage in many different behaviors, the researcher can investigate the precise conditions under which the neuron fires. By finding an association between a neuron's activity and the behavior, scientists can begin to understand what the neuron contributes to behavior.

While single-cell recording is an invasive procedure requiring surgery, and therefore mostly done with nonhuman animals, it is occasionally undertaken with human patients who are undergoing brain surgery for clinical reasons, such as treatment of epilepsy. In these cases, scientists have sometimes recorded neural activity during the surgery. In other cases, medical treatment requires that an array of electrodes be implanted in the brain for several weeks; the data collected can later be evaluated for basic cognitive purposes as well as the medical treatment (for a review, see Mukamel & Fried, 2012; Paulk et al., 2022).

The second method to eavesdrop on electrical activity of neurons, and the one most often used with humans, is an **electroencephalogram (EEG)**. During an EEG, electrodes are placed over the participant's scalp (see Figure 2.18). Each electrode reads the electrical activity of the neurons below it. An EEG does not localize activity as well as other methods. The electrical activity is very weak, of course, so the signal must be greatly amplified. Usually twelve

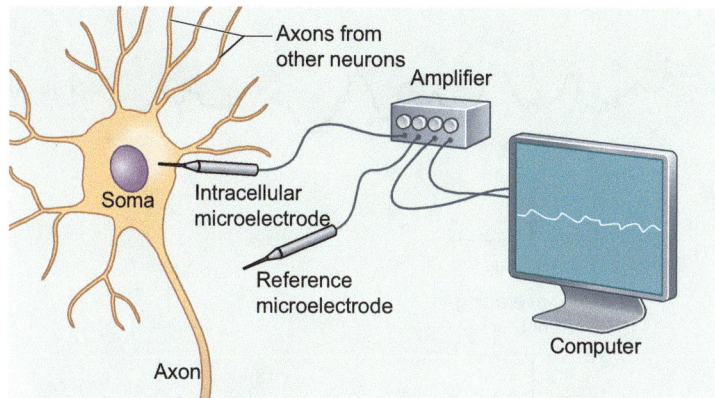

Figure 2.17. Single-cell recording uses an electrode probe to test a small and very specific area of the brain.

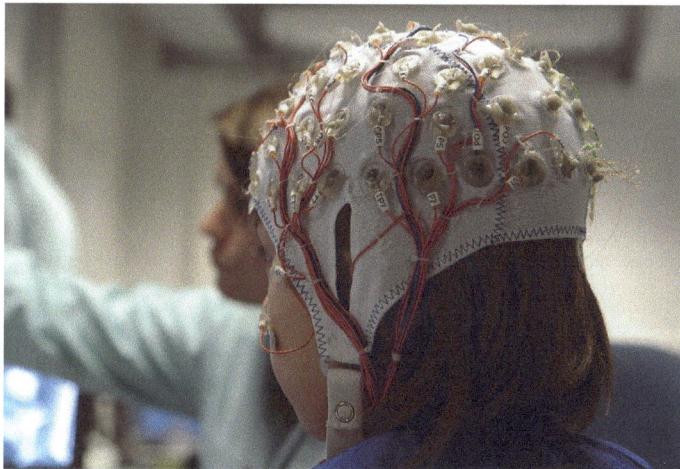

Figure 2.18. This child is wearing a set of EEG electrodes to monitor brain activity.

to sixty-four electrodes are used, so each electrode records the summed activity of millions of neurons. Furthermore, the skull and protective tissue covering the brain are fairly good insulators that diffuse the electrical signal. One advantage of EEG, however, is that it can provide precise information about when neural activity takes place (temporal information). In fact, EEG can measure this summed neural activity with an accuracy of a thousandth of a second, or one millisecond.

If you were simply to put electrodes on a person's head, what you would see would not be a flat line (representing no electrical activity) and then some activity once they do some task. Instead, you would see a wavy line all the time, representing continuous brain activity. Neurons have resting potentials, which means that they are always firing at a rather slow pace (just how quickly or slowly depends on the type of neuron). Thus, each electrode summarizes millions of neurons, each of which is always slightly active. To get around this problem, researchers measure **event-related potentials (ERPs)**. In this technique, the researcher administers tens or

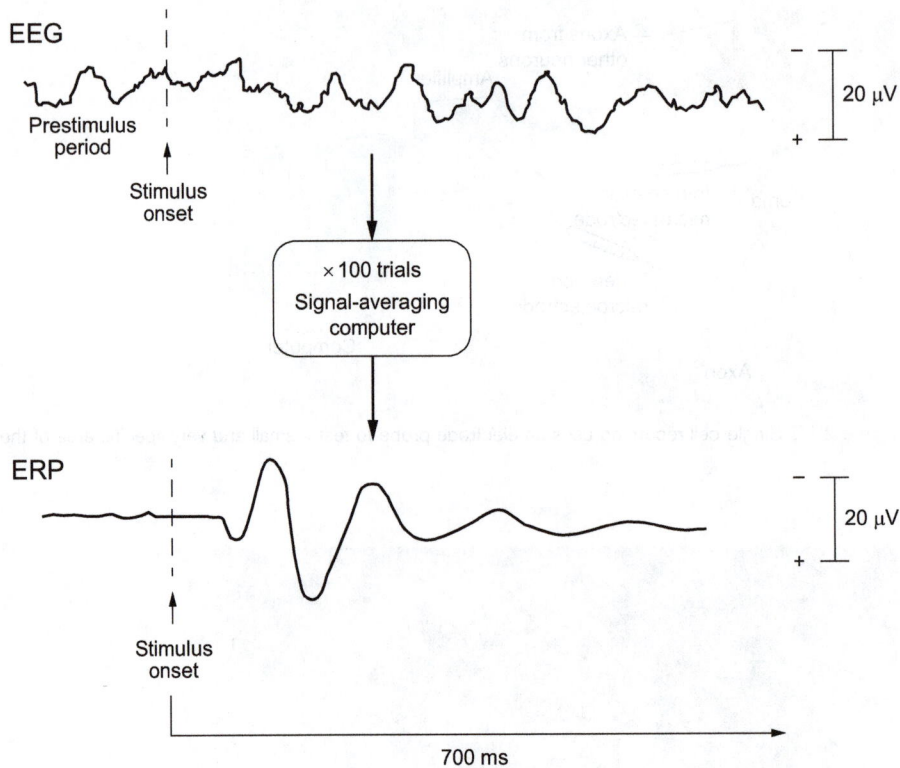

Figure 2.19. Comparison of electroencephalogram (EEG) and event-related potential (ERP) waves.

hundreds of trials that are similar to one another, then averages all squiggly EEG waves from these trials (see Figure 2.19).

The resulting average wave is smooth. Researchers often compare two types of ERPs that are similar but vary on one dimension. For example, a researcher studying memory might compare ERPs when the participant successfully recalled a word with ERPs when the participant couldn't recall a word (recall vs. no recall) at each of the sixty-four electrodes. There probably will be no difference in the ERPs of these two types of trials at most of the electrodes, but any electrode sites that do show a difference will show the researcher when and where activity associated with successful recall occurs in the brain.

Again, EEG is not a very good technique for spatial localization (exactly where the brain activity happens), but it is good for temporal resolution (exactly when brain activity happens). EEG may tell you only that a difference in successful and unsuccessful retrieval appears in the ERP of the right frontal lobe, which is pretty vague, but the technique could tell you very precisely at what time you start to see a difference in brain activity between successful and unsuccessful recall. Researchers can also use EEG in combination with other techniques so they can get information about activity that is precise in terms of both when it occurs and where it occurs (Huster et al., 2012; Cichy & Oliva, 2020).

The most important method of localizing human brain activity is **functional magnetic resonance imaging (fMRI)**. Early studies in localizing brain activity used a technology called PET (positron emission tomography), but that technology required an injection with a small dose of radioactive dye to track brain activity and has been mostly replaced by fMRI, which does not require injection of any kind. Studies using these methods have had a significant impact on cognitive psychology since the mid 1990s (Poldrack, 2012). Single-cell recording and EEG are both electrical measures and therefore measure a direct product of neural activity. fMRI measures brain activity indirectly by detecting changes in blood flow in the brain. One assumption, which appears to be well founded, is that blood flow follows brain activity; when the brain is more active, it demands more glucose (the sugar the brain uses for energy). Remember when we talked about how neural firing is a metabolic event? The chemical reaction needs metabolic energy in the form of glucose. If a particular part of the brain needs more glucose, the vascular system will shunt more blood to that part of the brain to satisfy the need. It is pretty amazing to imagine so much action taking place in your brain, even as you sit quietly reading this book: blood sloshing from place to place, electrical signals zapping back and forth, and chemicals bursting into gaps and gobbled up by receptors and enzymes. Equally amazing is our ability to detect slices of this action by putting people in a giant magnet. An example of an fMRI image may be seen in Figure 2.20.

The technique of fMRI works much like the type of MRI we've already discussed (which is sometimes called structural MRI to emphasize that it reveals neural structure but not activity). fMRI takes advantage of the magnetic properties of blood hemoglobin, the protein that carries oxygen to all cells of the body. Blood from which the oxygen has been absorbed is deoxygenated. Oxygenated and deoxygenated blood have different magnetic properties. fMRI techniques calculate the ratio of oxygenated to deoxygenated blood in a local area. You would think that an active area would have mostly deoxygenated blood because the brain has absorbed all the oxygen. Actually, the opposite is true; the vascular system floods the active part of the brain with oxygenated blood, and there is momentarily extra blood "hanging around" in the active spot. fMRI works by detecting that extra blood.

The Behavioral Side of the Equation

Recall that there are two inferences we want to make that will help us localize cognitive function in the brain:

- If brain area X supports cognitive function Y, then damage to area X will lead to an impairment in tasks that require function Y.
- If brain area X supports cognitive function Y, then area X will be active when function Y is engaged.

We have discussed ways of figuring out whether area X is damaged and whether area X is active, but we have not yet discussed how to isolate cognitive function Y. How do we isolate a cognitive function when most human behaviors depend on a combination of them? A similar problem arises in neuroscientific studies. For example, in Chapter 1, we mentioned patient Henry Molaison, who cannot learn new information. Suppose you read a list of words aloud to him and asked him a few minutes later to recall the list, but he was unable to remember any of the words. You are tempted to conclude that Molaison's memory is impaired. But how do you know it's his memory that is causing the problem? What if he has an attention problem and ignored the words you read? What if his memory is fine, but he didn't understand the words? To test these possibilities, you could ask him to immediately repeat the words so you know he's

A Pictures

10^{-15}

10^{-3}

Figure 2.20. **Figure 2.20.** An fMRI image

B Sounds

10^{-8}

10^{-3}

C Spoken words

10^{-15}

10^{-3}

D Written words

10^{-7}

10^{-2}

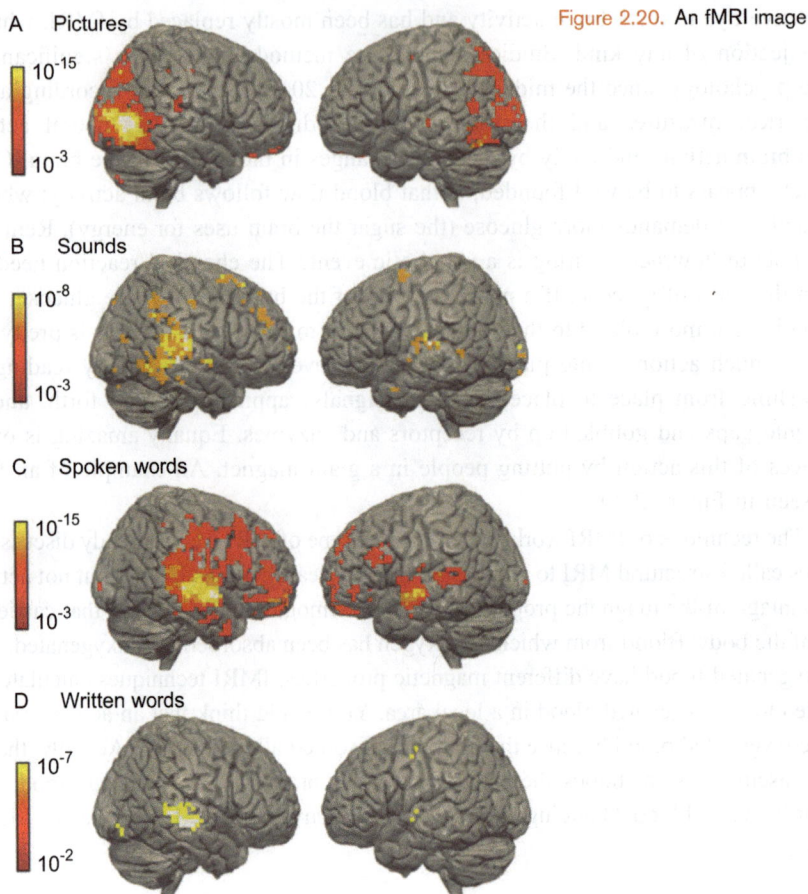

paying attention, and you could test his language ability in other ways to make sure he can understand the words in the memory task. Basically, that's what you do in all experiments when you test someone with damage to the brain. Usually, there are many potential reasons someone could be impaired on a task, so you have to administer several other tasks to determine the cause.

A good metaphor for thinking about this problem and its solution is the evaluation of an injury to another part of your body. Have you ever injured your knee or ankle? The doctor didn't just ask "where does it hurt?" then put a brace or cast on that part. The pain is a clue to the source of the injury but doesn't guarantee accurate diagnosis. For example, you could have a muscular injury from above or below the knee that causes knee pain. Orthopedists and physical therapists use a set of tasks and positions that isolate different parts of the knee ("when I hold this part of your leg in this position, are you able to push here?") to test the relationship between knee anatomy and our everyday functions, like walking and jumping and turning. Even a familiar and easy activity such as walking is a remarkably complex and coordinated action of many muscles, not only in your legs but also your back, core, and arms, so to diagnose an injury, doctors must carefully control to isolate the source of the problem.

Mental activity is similar, in that fMRI studies measure brain activity, but most of the brain is active most of the time. If you wanted to know which part of the brain is involved in reading a word, for example, you couldn't simply put people in a scanner and have them read aloud, since they would be using eye muscles to move their eyes across the screen, vision to identify the letters, prior knowledge to identify their meaning, and so on. Instead, you must administer at least two similar tasks that differ in the particular function you want to study. We hinted at this technique when we mentioned ERPs, and we said you might compare trials where participants succeeded or failed in recalling a word. Just as we can't understand the disrupted function of a muscle (in the injury example) by observing walking (we need a set of controlled and isolating movements), we can't understand mental functions by asking people to read in a scanner. We need a set of controlled tasks that isolate cognitive functions.

For reading, you might conduct a study like this one using four conditions:

Condition	Task description	Hypothetical processes involved
1	See fixation point	Attention
2	See random letter strings	Attention + vision
3	Read words	Attention + vision + reading
4	Say related word	Attention + vision + reading + memory

For each task, we have a set of cognitive processes that we think are needed to accomplish the task. We can take a fMRI scan showing the brain areas that are active for condition 2 and subtract the activation from condition 1, and that should subtract out the activations caused by attention, leaving us with just the activations caused by the visual processes engaged when the participant looks at letters. We can do similar subtractions to isolate other cognitive processes because each successive condition adds one cognitive process. Other techniques in fMRI do not use subtractions per se, but they still make use of task comparisons like this one.

Problems and Limitations of Localization Studies

Let's summarize what we've said so far. Our ultimate goal is to gain support for hypothetical cognitive processes and representations. One way to do that is to localize these processes or representations in the brain. We do that by two inferences:

- If brain area X is damaged and cognitive function Y is impaired, then X supports Y.
- If brain area X is active while cognitive function Y is performed, then X supports Y.

So far, we have discussed how we know when brain area X is damaged (localizing the lesion) and how we know when X is active (using single-cell recordings and imaging techniques). We've also discussed how to isolate function Y. Unfortunately, these inferences are not as straightforward as we would like.

People who have suffered brain damage may not show cognitive impairment; the brain may have found a new way to support the behavior, or the patient may consciously adopt new strategies for these tasks to minimize their reliance on the missing cognitive process. Area X may support function Y, there can be damage to area X, and yet you don't observe any deficit.

By analogy, someone with an injured leg muscle could still walk by compensating and changing their gait style. If we are just measuring walking speed, the person with the adjusted gait may walk just as fast.

A second possible problem is that area X may be damaged and function Y compromised, yet area X doesn't directly support Y. Rather, other brain areas support cognitive process Y, but they must communicate to do so, and the fibers connecting them pass through area X. The brain damage severed the connection. Another problem lies at the very heart of the logic of interpreting brain damage studies. Consider this metaphor. Suppose you remove a spark plug from a car, with the result that the engine coughs. You cannot conclude that the spark plug was a cough suppressor. Damage to area X leading to loss of function Y does not allow the conclusion that X supports Y. Just as the interactions among the components of a car are complex and loss does not provide a clear window to function, we can expect the interactions of the components of the brain to be complex.

Functional imaging studies have different problems of interpretation. One potential problem is that of correlated activity. Functional scans show all the brain activity associated with a particular cognitive function. Some of that activity may be reliably associated with the function – every time you perform the function, you get the activity – even if the brain area showing the activity is not crucial to getting the function done. For example, the **medial** prefrontal cortex (mPFC) reliably shows robust activation in memory studies, but if that cortex is damaged or missing, patients do not necessarily show a devastating loss of memory. One proposal is that this area supports associations between events and adaptive or emotional responses (Euston et al., 2012). That is, to accurately and precisely describe the localization of memory and the mPFC requires a more precise and sophisticated model of different memory systems.

Another problem in interpreting imaging studies lies in the task analysis. Recall that each participant would perform several tasks, each task adding one cognitive process. If the tasks are not analyzed correctly, the whole enterprise falls apart.

BEYOND LOCALIZATION   Localization can be useful but clearly has its limits, even with more powerful technology that is able to "zoom in" ever closer on the active brain. Recent neuroscience has tried to move beyond localization to get more insight into the relationship between brain and cognition.

For example, Lisman (2015) describes how a series of techniques have enabled scientists to observe and manipulate the process of memories being "replayed" in the rat hippocampus. Researchers identified cells that responded to the place (in the environment) when a rat learned a path through a maze. Those same cells fired in the same sequence during rest or sleep – the memory was "replayed" (Wikenheiser & Redish, 2013; Foster, 2017). Furthermore, memory-guided behavior was disrupted if the "replaying" was disrupted through targeted electrical stimulation (Girardeau et al., 2009; Jadhav et al., 2012; Schmidt et al., 2019). In other words, memory of the path through a maze is supported not only by a location in the brain (the hippocampus) but by a specific pattern of firing, a pattern that is replayed during rest or sleep. Furthermore, by selectively disrupting that replay, later memory is disrupted. Replay is still an active area of research, as investigators expand it to humans (Higgins et al., 2021) and discover more specific mechanisms.

Certainly, such invasive recording and manipulation of the brain and such a basic conception of memory (the path through a maze) may limit the generalizability of this set of studies, but they do offer a recipe for how to move beyond localization in helping neuroscientific methods inform cognitive theories. A somewhat analogous technique appropriate for humans examines *patterns and timing* of activity in fMRI. In other words, instead of localizing just the peak of activation, the broader pattern of activation – the peak, but also smaller blips of activity – is taken to be important. Imagine if, rather than the brain as a machine in which different parts accomplish different functions, the brain was more a piano, whereby different combinations of keys (and notes) played with different timing and patterns represented different mental processes. This approach has been applied to the cognitive task of identifying faces and shows that the pattern of activity across a broad area of the brain, not the location of activity within a single area, is what seems to represent a certain type of stimulus (Haxby, 2013; see also O'Toole et al., 2007; Norman et al., 2013; Naselaris & Kay, 2015).

We've seen an array of tools that can bring together cognitive and neural approaches to understanding the mind. But none is foolproof – each can lead to misinterpretation. So what do we do about these problems? The answer is that we cannot rely on any one method; we must try to use all methods simultaneously. If they all point to the same answer, we have more confidence that we have successfully localized a cognitive process. Notice that the methods have different drawbacks. For example, patients with a lesion might find another way to perform a task, and functional imaging might indicate activity in a brain area that is not crucial for a cognitive process. These drawbacks are mirror images of one another; lesion studies might tell you which brain areas are essential for a cognitive process but might miss areas typically associated with a process, whereas imaging studies show you all areas associated with a cognitive process but not which areas are crucial for getting the job done. The strengths and weaknesses of different techniques complement one another. The strategy of employing multiple techniques to address the same question is usually called using **converging operations**. If different methods converge on one answer, our confidence that the answer is correct greatly increases.

Do We Really Need Cognitive Psychology?

In this chapter, we've gone over the approach that cognitive psychologists use to study the mind. Part of that approach has been to use the physical structure of the mind – that is, the brain – to help us determine how the mind works. We might ask, therefore, whether we might not be better off studying the brain. If we believe that the workings of the mind depend on what happens in the brain, why not study the brain to start with?

We should recognize that there are often different, but equally valid, ways of describing the same thing. It is sometimes useful to think of *levels* of description. A common example is the relationship of chemistry and physics. Both physicists and chemists agree that most or all of chemistry is reducible to physics. That doesn't mean that chemistry is pointless or that chemists are merely biding their time until the physicists come along and finish the job. In the same way, we might say that cognitive events are, of course, reducible to brain events, but that doesn't devalue the cognitive level of description.

These different levels of description are particularly important when we're talking about the brain. The reason is that even a simple behavior – for example, seeing and recognizing a friend – calls on many different brain regions. So if we study brain region X, we might understand what it does, but to understand how we recognize a friend, we need to know about brain regions X, B, R, O, and C, and in addition, we need to learn how they communicate and interact. Studying the brain alone will not lead us to examine the interaction of brain areas X, B, R, O, and C. Actually, it is quite the opposite – it is studying the cognitive level of description that will reveal the importance of a function such as recognizing a friend, and that in turn will motivate us to study complex brain interactions.

Finally, there are important practical results of studying a cognitive level of description of what the brain does. For example, consider cochlear implants (Rauschecker & Shannon, 2002). These are microelectrode arrays implanted in the inner ear to directly stimulate the auditory nerve of the brain. These arrays of twenty or fewer electrodes had no hope of directly replicating the precision of 100 inner ear hair cells communicating to 30,000 auditory neurons (Rubinstein, 2004), so they filter some elements of the sound, selecting for sounds that would be informative for speech. Newer versions provide both more and less information by adding more electrodes in the array but focusing more narrowly on speech sounds. For example, designers omit both low and high sound frequencies from a cochlear implant – simplifying the job the implant must perform – at no cost to the perception of important sounds, such as speech. Thus, if we are trying to develop electronic devices to replace faulty brain parts, we need to know more than the anatomy and physiology of the brain. It is also useful to have a cognitive description of how the brain works because that can suggest more efficient designs for such devices.

In sum, although neuroscience informs cognitive psychology and, indeed, cognitive psychology informs neuroscience, one is not a replacement for the other.

Stand-on-One-Foot Questions

2.7.   What information must be known for localization to be helpful, and why do we need this information?

2.8.   Why is it important to use converging operations in localization?

Questions That Require Two Feet

2.9.   It seems that brain imaging has a huge impact on the public, especially on their view of a phenomenon as scientific. Why do you suppose that's true?

2.10.   Studies of human patients with lesions are not true experiments because we cannot induce lesions for the sake of an experiment. If we wanted to conduct a true experiment that investigates the consequence of a brain lesion, what might we do?

3 Visual Perception

What Makes Visual Perception Hard?

- Shape

- Color

- Size

How Are Visual Ambiguities Resolved?

- Shape

- Brightness

- Distance and Size

- Top-Down Influences in Vision

- An Alternative: The Ecological Approach

What Is Vision For?

- Identifying Objects

- Navigation and Visually Guided Action

Of all the cognitive functions your brain performs, vision is both the most remarkable and the most difficult to appreciate. It is difficult to appreciate vision precisely because it is so marvelous; your visual system works so efficiently, so effortlessly, that you have no clue what it is doing or how difficult its task is. Consider this: For decades we've had calculators that can perform long division far more quickly and accurately than any human. We also have computer programs that can beat 99 percent of the population in chess. Now, after years of work and millions of dollars spent, we are finally beginning to have computers that are able to recognize faces and drive a car. Why was it so much easier to program a computer to play chess than it was to get one to recognize a face? As you look at Figure 3.1, consider how a computer might recognize that all four pictures include the same person, one of the authors of this textbook.

For a computer, making the judgment that these four pictures have the same person in them is a more difficult problem than playing grandmaster-level chess. This example should tell you one thing: Vision is hard. The first question we'll take up is, **What makes visual perception hard?** We can't simply ask "How do humans see?" That question is not specific enough. We need to know why it's hard to see – what specific problems must be solved for vision to work – before we can start to think about how the human visual system might solve those problems. As we'll see, vision is hard because the pattern of light that falls on your eye could be the result of light bouncing off many

Figure 3.1. These four photographs all depict one of the authors. It has taken millions of hours and billions of dollars of research to develop computer programs that are able to accomplish a task that most humans find relatively easy. (Source: Photographs by Cedar Riener.)

Figure 3.2. This object appears to be a square, but it could be a cube or any other three-dimensional object with one square face that happens to be oriented toward you.

different objects or scenes. The light itself is not enough to specify all the objects, scenes, and visual events. For example, what is the object depicted in Figure 3.2?

You probably said that this object is a red square, but it could be a cube, the bottom of a pyramid, or a number of other solids. And the object itself may not be red – it may be a white object bathed in red light. Thus, even this simple picture is consistent with more than one object in the world, and knowing with certainty the object's identity is impossible. You may well be protesting, "We're all very impressed by your square, but the fact is that we do see, and we usually see accurately." That's true, and we might add that vision happens quickly, and its product (your conscious visual perception) is consistent. When you walk into a room, you immediately perceive the objects that are in the room, their relative positions, their colors, their textures, whether they are moving, and so on. Indeed, everyone would agree on these properties, just as everyone agrees that Figure 3.2 depicts a square.

If knowing the identity of the object is impossible, why does everyone agree? This agreement indicates that our perceptual systems are all finding the same way to solve the problem.

Figure 3.3. When #TheDress appeared on social media, it caused quite a sensation when some people saw it as white/gold, others as blue/black. This xkcd comic shows the two possibilities and a slice of the dress itself in the middle. (Source: www.xkcd.com/1492. Image reproduced under Creative Commons Attribution-NonCommercial 2.5 License.)

In other words, just because we all resolve the ambiguities present in Figure 3.2 doesn't mean that there aren't fundamental ambiguities in how we translate the light that hits our eye into our perceptual experience. Just because we all guess the same doesn't mean that we aren't guessing. The second question we will take up is, **How are visual ambiguities resolved?** The answer is that the perceptual system uses multiple sources of information – not just light but also clues such as the muscle movements in our eyes or the different perspectives we get from each eye. Our visual system also makes assumptions about the way objects in the world usually look so we can resolve the ambiguity of figures such as the square. For example, one assumption the visual system makes is that objects are unlikely to be oriented at improbable angles. There are many ways a cube could be oriented in space, but very few of those orientations leave just one face of the cube visible to the observer. It would be like seeing a coin that just happens to be edge-on so it looks like a line. Such orientations are so rare that your visual system assumes that they don't happen. Figure 3.2 is much more likely to be a square than a just-happens-to-be-oriented-that-way cube, so the visual system gambles that it's a square.

Users of social media got an excellent reminder of perceptual ambiguity with #TheDress (Figure 3.3), in which a dress in a photograph appeared to be different colors to different people. We will be returning to #TheDress later in the chapter, but at this point, it illustrates the ambiguity of the pattern of light on our eyes. In most cases we all resolve this ambiguity the same way, but the dress provides a remarkable instance of when we don't.

OK, we can see. But why? **What is vision for?** Broadly speaking, vision serves two purposes. First, it allows us to know the qualities of an object at a distance (e.g., how big it is, whether it is moving, whether it has large, pointy teeth?). This knowledge helps us behave in appropriate ways (attack small, edible-looking things, flee from large, aggressive-looking things). The "at-a-distance" feature is helpful because we can evaluate what something is without having to walk up and touch it. The second function of vision is that it serves action, meaning that we know where things are so we can move around effectively (pounce with accuracy on the small, edible-looking thing, skirt immovable objects while fleeing the aggressive-looking thing). So, briefly put, the function of visual perception is to (1) identify objects and (2) help us navigate in the world. How do we identify objects, and how does vision help us navigate? As we'll see, these two functions are separable, with different mental processes and representations, and are supported by separate parts of the brain.

What Makes Visual Perception Hard?

Preview

As we've just discussed, visual perception is complicated, but it's not easy to appreciate that fact because our cognitive systems are so good at analyzing visual stimuli. In this section, we examine more closely what makes visual perception difficult. The crucial point is that the image falling on the retina does not fully determine what is in the world. For example, size and distance are indeterminate; if the image of something is small, the object in the world might be either small or far away. Other indeterminisms we'll discuss include shape and orientation (if you see what looks like an ellipse, what's in the world might really be an ellipse, or it might be a circle that is turned slightly to the side), as well as light source, reflectance, and shadow.

The limited information of the pattern on your retina results in three kinds of indeterminacy or trade-offs, in terms of the objects and properties in the world. Think of it this way: If I told you I have three coins in my hand that add up to thirty cents, you know which coins they must be; the answer is determined by the information I have given you. However, if I tell you that I have thirty cents but I do not tell you how many coins, the answer is undetermined. I could have a quarter and a nickel, thirty pennies, three dimes, or another combination. The light on the retina is more similar to the second case than the first; there is not enough information to solve the problems your visual system wants to solve. In other words, the light on your retina does not determine the shape, size, or color of the objects you observe.

Shape

The chief problem the visual system faces is the **inverse projection problem**, which relates to the way that light from the world falls on the **retina** (the layer of light-sensitive cells on the back of the eye). How do we recover the three-dimensional shape of a real-world object from a two-dimensional projection on the retina? An infinite number of three-dimensional objects could give rise to a single two-dimensional projection. We cannot know what is out in the world solely on the basis of the information source available to us – neural impulses from the retina of the eye – because the world is three-dimensional and the image projected on the retina is two-dimensional (Figure 3.4).

The first trade-off is **shape and orientation indeterminacy**. For example, when we look at a roll of tape, most of the time the shape of the image on the retina is an ellipse. However, we are familiar with rolls of tape and know that they are in fact circular, so we assume that we are seeing a circle *shape* at an oblique *orientation*, which results in an elliptical retinal image. This indeterminacy is shown in Figure 3.5, in which all four tape rolls are circular, but as can be seen from the blue outlines in Figure 3.5b, only one of them is projecting a (nearly) circular image on the retina.

Color

A second thing we want to know about an object is the color of its surfaces. What we call "color" is actually three different perceptual dimensions of a surface. These dimensions are hue (red vs. blue),

Figure 3.4. A three-dimensional object seen from a single perspective creates a unique two-dimensional projection. However, this two-dimensional projection is consistent with an infinite number of three-dimensional objects. The problem we are faced with is similar to viewing the silhouette of these dancers from the company Pilobolus, reconstructing the exact three-dimensional shapes and positions that made that silhouette. That "woolly mammoth" is in fact several other dancers arranging themselves so that they make a compelling shadow on the screen. (Source: Frank Hoensch/Getty Images Entertainment/Getty Images.)

(a)

(b)

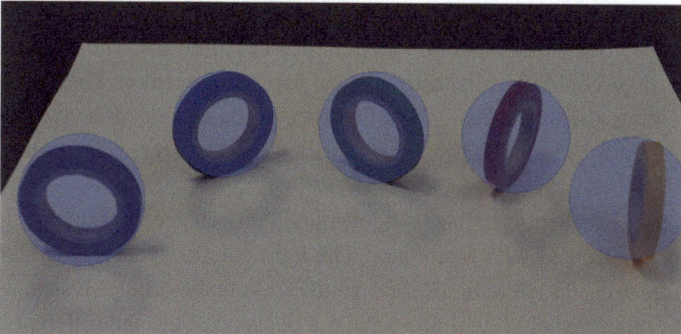

Figure 3.5. (a) These rolls of tape are all circular, but most views of the rolls do not project a circular image on the retina; just as in these photographs, their images are not circular on the page. (b) Blue outlines showing only one projecting a near-circular image.

Figure 3.6. Antarctica. Is all the ice the same color but with different light and shadow? Or is some ice a different shade? (Source: Fiona McAllister Photography/Moment/Getty Images.)

saturation (how much color relative to white, like red vs. pink), and brightness (the intensity of light reflected from the surface, so red paint might have the same hue and saturation of a red lamp but will of course be less intense light). Each of these dimensions has the problem of ambiguity at the eye, which we will describe in more detail later. For the purposes of introducing the concept of indeterminacy, we are going to focus on just one dimension for now: brightness.

We run into a problem in trying to determine an object's brightness because the only source of information we have is the amount of light that enters the eye. The technical term for the amount of light the eye receives is **luminance**. Three factors contribute to luminance: the amount of illumination (a 100-watt lightbulb, a twenty-five-watt lightbulb, and the Sun all illuminate a surface with different amounts of light), the reflectance of the object (white, black, and gray surfaces all reflect different amounts of light), and whether the object is in shadow. A piece of coal viewed in bright sunlight actually has greater luminance than a snowball viewed in candlelight: More light is getting to your eye from the coal because it is so strongly illuminated, even though it is a less reflective colored surface. Nevertheless, the coal looks black, and the snowball looks white. How does the visual system unravel the three factors that contribute to luminance so it gets the reflectance of objects right?

For an example, look at the photo of Antarctic ice in Figure 3.6. The darker sections could indicate shadows, or they could also indicate ice that is a darker color. The color of the ice is determined by the lighting, the shadow, and the reflectance of the surface of the ice itself (how much light the surface itself tends to reflect). Thus, this is called **light source, reflectance, and shadow indeterminacy**.

#TheDress is an excellent example of light source, reflectance, and shadow indeterminacy. Your visual system is confronted with a problem: The light entering your eye is blue, but are you seeing a blue dress under bright white light? Or a white dress under a blueish shadow? To "solve" the color of the dress, your visual system must make a decision about the different sources of the light hitting your eyes. The decision about the light source (or the prevailing color of the light) then leads to a decision about the color of the fabric of the dress. How much is due to the illumination? How much is due to the reflectance of the fabric of the dress (Gegenfurtner et al., 2015)? You can't see one without deciding on the other.

The differing perceptions are due to the different ways we interpret ambiguity in lighting conditions. Many cameras are able to automatically correct for bright light that may overexpose the image. In the case of #TheDress, the combination of bright light in the background and shaded foreground limited the camera's ability to correct for uniformly bright light. However, that doesn't explain why some people see it as white/gold and others as blue/black. People who see the dress as white/gold perceive the color of light hitting the dress as more blueish, a more cool illuminant. People who see it as blue/black assume a warmer hue of illuminating light. Lafer-Sousa et al. (2015) describe these biases (toward warm or cool illuminants) as the reason that older people and women are more likely to see the dress as white/gold (with cool illuminant): They are more likely to have a daytime chronotype (i.e., to be early morning people) (Adan et al., 2012; Wallisch, 2017). Younger people and men are more likely to be night owls, thereby adapting to the slightly warmer light scheme typical of artificial light and thereby seeing the dress as blue/black.

Size

The second indeterminacy or trade-off is between object size and distance from the eye. A two-dimensional image does not tell you the size of the object or its distance from the viewer. Bear in mind that everything you know about objects in the world comes from the images that the objects project onto the retina. In general, larger objects do project larger images onto the retina, but the size of the retinal projection also depends on the distance between the object and the observer. If you see a square that appears small, is it truly a small square, or is it actually a large square that is far away? Thus, this is called **size and distance indeterminacy**.

One real-world example of the relationship between object size and distance involves the Sun and the Moon (Figure 3.7). Although the Moon is much smaller than the Sun, it is also much closer. It so happens that these two factors balance out nearly perfectly; the Sun and the Moon project same-size images on the retina and thus appear to be the same size when viewed from Earth. That's why the Moon just covers the Sun during a total eclipse. The Moon would not appear to be the same size as the Sun from a vantage point nearer or farther than Earth.

Figure 3.7. A supermoon over the Propylaea, the main entrance to the Acropolis in Athens. A supermoon occurs when the Moon is closest to Earth in its orbit. While the Moon may appear similar sized to the Sun in the sky, the Sun is in fact 400 times larger, but (thankfully) much farther away. (Source: George Pachantouris/Moment/Getty Images.)

The main things you would want to know about an object – its shape, the color and brightness of its surface, its size, its distance – are indeterminate from the information that is available to the retina, so that's why vision is hard. How, then, are we able to see?

Stand-on-One-Foot Question

3.1.   Name the three indeterminacies that make visual perception difficult.

Questions That Require Two Feet

3.2.   Size and distance are indeterminate, so if you see a car that appears small, you can't know whether it is a big car far away or a small car close by. Yet, you seem to have no problem figuring that out. Why?

3.3.   The apparent size of the tip of your thumb when held at arm's length is about the same size as the Moon viewed from Earth. Would it work the same way if you stood on the Moon and looked at Earth? That is, would the tip of your thumb appear about the same size as Earth?

How Are Visual Ambiguities Resolved?

Preview

How do our cognitive systems resolve the ambiguities inherent in visual perception so we can accurately interpret what we see? The answer is that we make unconscious assumptions that resolve the ambiguities. Shape and orientation are resolved by assuming that objects are not in unusual orientations. Shape perception is also influenced by the frame of reference in which the object is viewed. Light source, reflectance, and shadow are resolved by making assumptions about the color of objects and typical ambient lighting. Size and distance are usually resolved by using cues to distance in the environment (e.g., an object that partially covers another must be closer to the observer).

Ecological psychologists propose that all these problems and ambiguities may be more in the minds of psychologists than in the visual fields of observers. They propose that the environment actually provides a variety of cues that make the job of vision much simpler than it first appears. We examine the sorts of cues they claim that people use.

The short answer to the question of how visual ambiguities are resolved is that these insoluble problems become solvable if you are willing to make assumptions. Your visual system makes assumptions about the nature of objects in the world and how they are illuminated. The visual system also takes into account information beyond simply the two-dimensional image of light on the retina. We use the muscles in the eyes and the different perspectives we get from each of our two eyes as extra clues to resolve ambiguities. We also use information provided by our own motion. One approach to perception, discussed at the end of this section, proposes that this information provided in motion should entirely replace our concept of a two-dimensional retinal image: The pattern of moving lights is the information for vision, not the still image on the retina. You should note that these assumptions and extra information are not made by some extra decision process, external to the visual system. Rather, they are built in to the way the visual system itself is engineered, the same way many older cameras were designed with the assumption that pictures will be shot in daylight.

Yet the assumptions built in to the visual system do not guarantee a correct solution. Indeed, if you know these assumptions, you can create two-dimensional paintings that look compellingly three-dimensional, or you can induce the visual system to make errors as the creators of visual illusions do. The main point is that vision is not a representation of exactly what is in the world; it is a representation of what is probably in the world. It's a construction based on wise gambles. We'll go through the key visual properties of objects – shape, brightness, and size – one by one.

Shape

Let's start with the square shown in Figure 3.2. Why do you call the figure a square and not a cube? Your visual system is sensitive to what sorts of objects are likely to have projected a particular image onto your retina. Yes, the object could be a cube, but think of all the different angles at which a cube could be positioned. Only a few views of a cube look like a square, so your visual system assumes that what you're seeing is actually a square. Hermann von Helmholtz (1910/1962), one of the first giants of vision research, called this the **likelihood principle**. This principle has been important in many modern theories of vision, although as some researchers have pointed out, it's hard to distinguish whether the visual system interprets stimuli using likelihood or simplicity as the guide (Chater, 1996; Feldman, 2009; van der Helm, 2000).

We can state generally that the likelihood principle implies that a two-dimensional straight line will be interpreted as being straight in three dimensions, and lines that appear parallel in two dimensions will be interpreted as parallel in three dimensions. Our visual system is also biased to see corners as right angles. This is especially true for some objects that we know have right angles, such as books. For example, take a look at the photo of the book in Figure 3.8. (You may remember it from Chapter 2.) We assume that this book has a shape (rectangular) similar to the shapes of

(a)   (b)

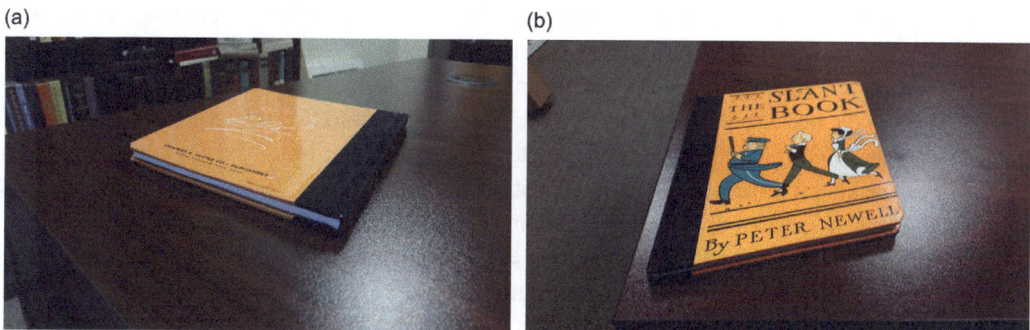

Figure 3.8. The book is lying flat on the desk in both photographs. (a) We assume that it is a rectangular book due to the likelihood principle, but (b) we are mistaken, as is shown when the book is next to the corner of the rectangular desk.

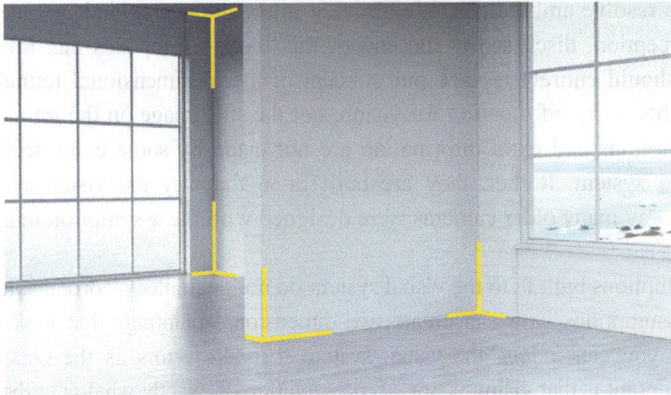

Figure 3.9. An empty room. The fork junctions shown in yellow are interpreted as right angles using Perkins' laws. (Source: Huber & Starke/Corbis/Getty Images.)

thousands of other books we have seen. While that use of the likelihood principle usually leads to an accurate perception, in this case, the book is not rectangular.

We use more than the likelihood principle to resolve shape indeterminacy. For example, to decide which angles are right angles, we can also use Perkins' (1972, 1973) laws, a set of mathematical relationships between the three angles that make up a corner in two dimensions. When three lines meet and no angle is greater than 180 degrees, we call that a fork junction. If all three angles in a fork junction are greater than ninety degrees, we will see that as a meeting of three rectangular surfaces in three dimensions, as you can see in Figure 3.9. Each of those four angles could be a view of a cube (an object with right angles). So we can use Perkins' laws to disambiguate shape, even when the objects aren't as familiar as books.

Brightness

A change in luminance (the amount of light hitting the retina) can result from a number of factors. For example, the cylinder in Figure 3.10 appears to be uniformly colored, and there is a light shining on it from the right. However, it is possible that the cylinder is illuminated evenly but is colored lighter green on the right and darker on the left. The visual system makes three simple assumptions to choose between these alternatives.

First, the visual system assumes that surfaces are uniformly colored. That's why shading makes such a difference in the three-dimensional quality of a painting. Changes in shading are assumed by the visual system to reflect shadows caused by hills and valleys in the surface of an object, not variations in how different parts of the object's surface reflect light. The full Moon looks so flat because it is uniformly bright. When the light of the Sun strikes the many craters and hills of the Moon, it reflects at many angles. Thus, the brightness is even across the entire full Moon, making it appear to be a disk and not a sphere. The same is true of surfaces that are uniformly black. When surfaces are coated with Vantablack, the blackest paint in the world (actually a forest of millions of carbon nanotubes), they are uniformly dark, so they also appear flat, such as the sphere that the scientists are holding in Figure 3.11.

The second assumption is that gradual changes in brightness are caused by shadows. Shadows have fuzzy edges, but changes in the reflectance of a surface (color of the paint or the surface material itself) typically do not (Casati, 2004). Hence, it is easy to distinguish the change in

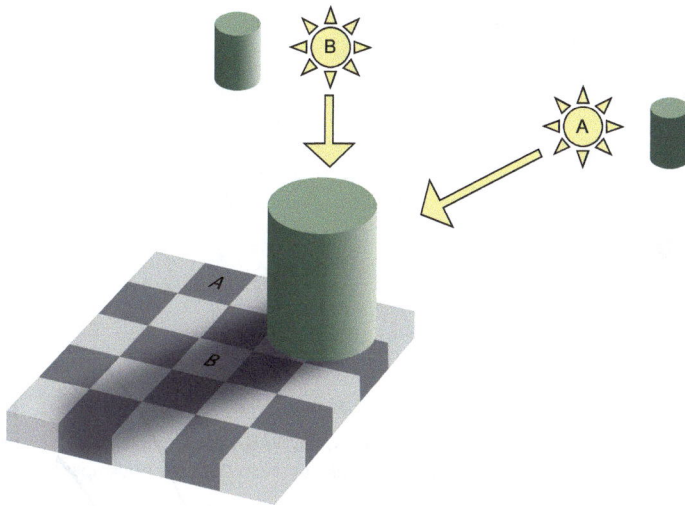

Figure 3.10. Three factors contribute to luminance: light source, shading, and shadow. How you see the color of the cylinder as well as the shade of the squares depends on your visual system's calculation of the relative contributions of illumination, reflectance, and shadow to luminance. (a) If the illumination is from the right, the cylinder is a single color and brightly illuminated on the right. (b) But the appearance of the cylinder is also consistent with the illumination coming from above and the cylinder colored multiple shades of green. But notice how the shadowed checkerboard is consistent with situation (a), since the uniformly colored cylinder illuminated from one side would put part of the checkerboard in shadow.

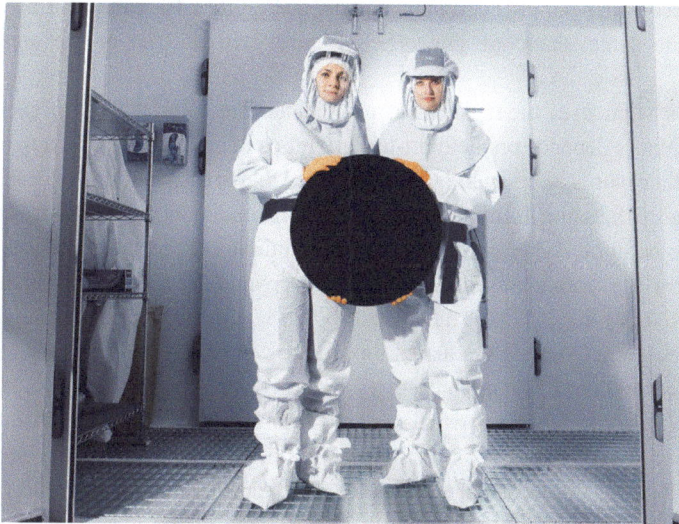

Figure 3.11. These two scientists are carrying a large sphere coated with Vantablack. Vantablack is a coating that causes the surface to be not only a perfectly uniform single color (and therefore seen as flat) but also incredibly dark, absorbing all visible light and so showing no texture at all. (Source: Copyright Surrey Nanosystems.)

brightness caused by the cylinder's shadow from the change in brightness caused by the light and dark square of the checkerboard; the shadow has fuzzy borders. Another important cue to shadows comes from movement: If an object moves, its shadow moves in association with the object.

Nevertheless, there is still ambiguity in decoding information that comes from shape. Look at Figure 3.12, of the Giordano Bruno crater on the Moon. In interpreting shading information, the

Figure 3.12. Light sources are assumed to come from above, so the NASA photograph appears to be a crater. The exact same photograph turned upside down looks to be a plateau or mesa (turn the book upside down). (Source: NASA/Goddard/Arizona State University.)

visual system assumes that light comes from above an object – a sensible assumption because vision evolved in a world where light almost always comes from the Sun. The third assumption is that light comes from above. That assumption is what makes the crater in Figure 3.12 look concave; turn this book upside down and see what happens when the pattern of shading changes. Even when we can clearly see that the light source is not from above, we cannot adjust the visual system to the violation of this assumption.

Now let's reconsider the checkerboard pattern in Figure 3.10. Believe it or not, square A and square B are the same shade of gray. (See Figure 3.10 and cover the area in between for proof.)

The visual system uses **local contrast** to evaluate the likely shade of each square; the perceived surface lightness depends on the light-to-dark ratios of areas that are next to one another in the same plane. In other words, the visual system assumes that areas right next to each other in the same plane have roughly the same illumination. Squares surrounded by darker squares (in shadow or not) are considered to be light. As we noted, the sharp boundaries of the squares also help the visual system determine that the boundaries are likely to be created by paint, not shadows, because shadows usually have fuzzy edges. Thus, the checkerboard is easy to interpret as being a field with light and dark squares. Hence, the light squares look light even when they are in shadow.

Does the checkerboard illusion represent a failing of your visual system? No. As its designer, Edward Adelson (1995), points out, your visual system does not need to assess the absolute brightness of regions of space. It needs to analyze complex scenes to find simple, meaningful components, such as "checkerboard with dark and light patches, partly in shadow." Another example of your visual system analyzing a complex scene into meaningful components is the images of the chess pieces shown in Figure 3.13. The chess pieces themselves are exactly the same, but the visual system is able to decompose the image into object (white chess pieces), background (black background), and the foggy air we are seeing them through (Anderson & Winawer, 2005).

Distance and Size

SIZE AND DISTANCE TRADE-OFF   When an object is far away, it appears small, and when it is near, it seems large. How can we determine the true size and distance of the object? Yes, we could

Figure 3.13. The chess pieces are exactly the same shades of gray. (Source: Adapted from B. L. Anderson and J. Winawer [2005], Image segmentation and lightness perception, *Nature*, 434[7029], 80.)

make assumptions, but since we move around the world, getting closer and farther from objects, an assumption like "light comes from above" for distance is not as helpful since we are often different distances from an object. Here we need other information, so we take in a variety of clues about size and distance and unconsciously combine them. We call these clues **depth cues**, and we divide them into four classes: **Oculomotor depth cues** are based on the movements of muscles in your visual system; **binocular disparity** is based on the different perspectives of your two eyes; and cues derived from images on the retinas we call **pictorial depth cues**. The final type of depth cues, called **motion cues**, are those provided when either we or an object moves.

OCULOMOTOR CUES   Oculomotor depth cues use the state of the muscles which control our eyes to inform our visual system about depth. The first oculomotor depth cue is **accommodation** (Figure 3.14). When objects get closer to the eye, the lens of the eye must change shape to focus an image on the retina. Believe it or not, you have small muscles inside your eyeball that control the shape of the lens. When we contract those ciliary muscles, the lens becomes thicker, allowing us to focus on closer objects (and therefore this contraction informs our visual system that the object must be close). This cue is important only at relatively close ranges (less than one meter or so), when the muscles must work quite hard.

The other oculomotor cue to depth is called **convergence**. As an object gets closer, your eyes cross increasingly more to gaze at it. The relevant muscles here are those that turn your eyes inward and outward. You point your eyes at an object so the light reflecting from it falls on the center of the retina, which is called the **fovea**. This part of the retina is the most accurate at seeing small details. Because your eyes are some distance apart, when objects are fairly close to you, your eyes start to cross to keep the image on the fovea of each eye. Your brain can sense where the eyes

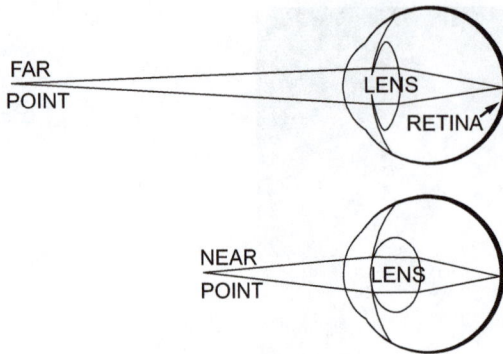

Figure 3.14. Accommodation is when the muscles connected to the lens change shape to focus on more distant objects.

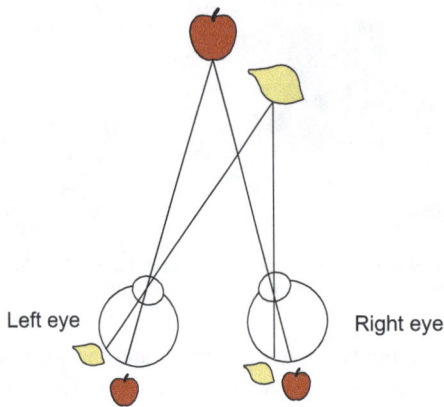

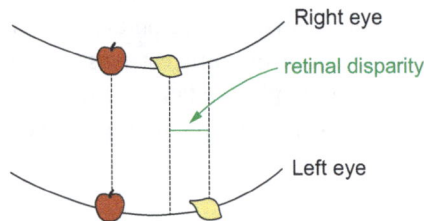

Figure 3.15. The process of using retinal disparity to calculate distances to objects is called stereopsis.

are positioned; from that, it can estimate the distance of the object you're focusing on. However, convergence helps only when objects are fairly close. For objects that are moderately far away (say, more than twenty feet), the eyes are nearly parallel.

BINOCULAR DISPARITY   In addition to cues from the movement of muscles in our eyes, we also use cues from the fact that we have two eyes in different places and therefore two slightly different views of the world. Hold one finger in front of your face, and rapidly open and close your left and right eyes, alternately. Does your finger seem to change positions? This difference in view of the left and right eye is called *binocular disparity* (*bi* = two, *ocular* = eyes).

Now look at Figure 3.15. When both eyes are rotated to point at the lemon, but they can see the apple as well, they receive different views of this scene. The difference in views between the eyes of the apple is an important piece of information that the apple is closer than the lemon. If the apple was much farther away, its image would not be in drastically different places on the retina. Thus, the disparity between the views of the left and right eyes is larger for nearby objects. The visual system uses the difference between the left and right eye to figure out how far away an object must be. This process of using **retinal disparity** to calculate distance is called **stereopsis**. If a lemon appears in roughly the same place on the left and right retinas, it is quite distant. If its position is very different in each eye, the visual system would know the lemon is nearby.

PICTORIAL DEPTH CUES   There are also depth cues that we can use with only one retinal image. These are called monocular depth cues because we can appreciate them with one eye. Monocular cues in the environment concern distance and are often called **pictorial cues**. They are called pictorial because they can be drawn (or painted) in pictures but also more generally are patterns in the picture plane: surfaces oriented facing our line of sight like pictures are.

Familiar size is one such cue. As the name implies, it's the use of experience to estimate the size (and therefore distance) of objects. When we see a car, we might assume it is the size of a typical car, even if it is far away and appears small. Similarly, people should be people sized, houses house sized, and so forth. We don't often see an object that we've never encountered before, which would give us no clue as to its likely size.

Bill Epstein (1965; see also Marotta & Goodale, 2001) showed the limits of familiar size as a cue to distance. He took photographs of a dime, a quarter, and a half-dollar and then printed each coin as the size of a quarter. Epstein mounted the photographs on black rods and placed them an equal distance from the observer. The room was darkened, and the photographs were illuminated with a spotlight. The participants had to view them monocularly (i.e., with one eye only). The participants believed the photographs were real coins, and because they appeared to be the same size, participants judged them to be different distances away (e.g., a real dime would have to be closer than the half-dollar for the coins to look the same size).

Thus, familiar size can influence the perception of size and distance. But Epstein's results changed completely when people viewed the stimuli binocularly (i.e., using both eyes), seeing the coin photos as they actually were – equidistant and of equal size. Binocular viewing made a difference because participants could use stereopsis, and pitted against familiar size, stereopsis was the clear winner.

Familiar size solves the size–distance trade-off by providing information about object size. Other pictorial cues offer information about size and distance in other ways. Perhaps the most well known of these pictorial cues can be seen in the simple picture of a house in Figure 3.16. Lines that are parallel in three dimensions, such as the top and bottom of the walls and the top line of the roof, converge on a point when such a scene is depicted in two dimensions (drawn or painted on a flat surface). This cue is called **linear perspective**, or perspective convergence.

One of the most iconic paintings of Western art, Leonardo da Vinci's *The Last Supper*, is shown in Figure 3.17. This painting used many pictorial cues to give the illusion of depth. One is occlusion. An object that is in front of another will partly overlap it. In the painting, each image of a person is covered by the table, but their depth order is also shown by how their clothes are covered by the person in front of them.

The **relative height** of objects also is a cue to distance. Objects that are lower in the picture plane are assumed to be closer to the viewer, whereas objects higher up are assumed to be farther away. So, for example, the food lower in the painting appears to be closer to the viewer than that

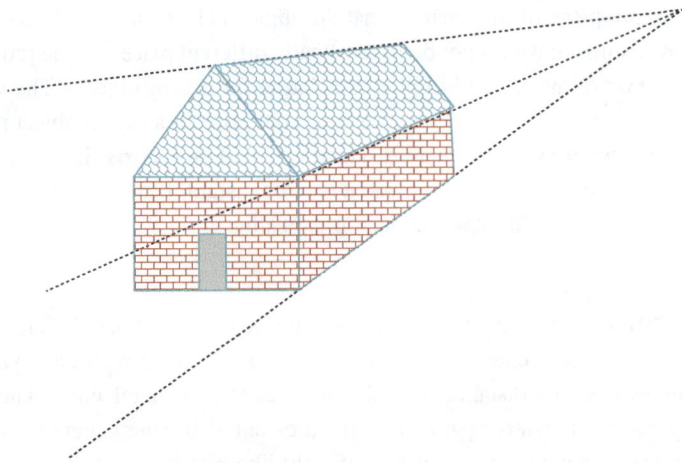

Figure 3.16. A simple drawing of a house in three dimensions, using the pictorial depth cue of linear perspective.

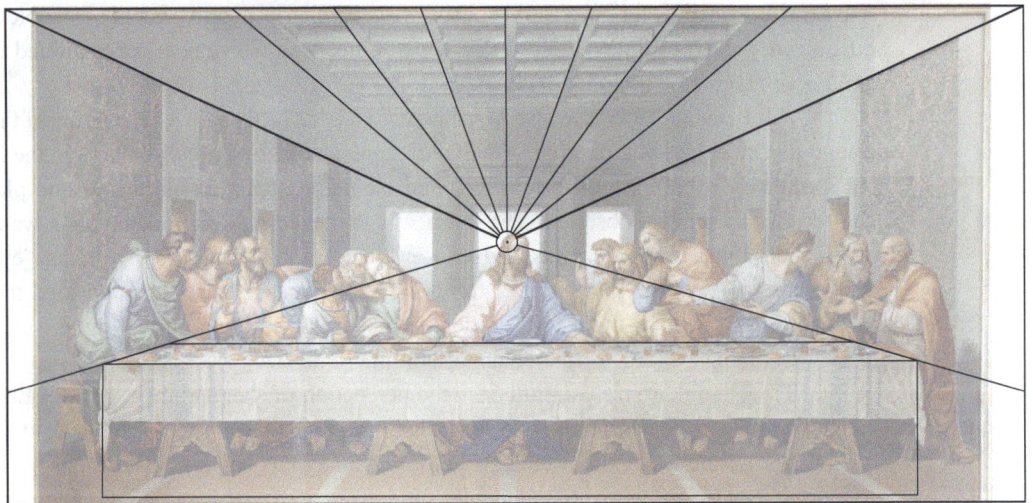

Figure 3.17. Da Vinci's *The Last Supper*. (Source: sedmak/iStock/Getty Images Plus.)

higher up. In addition, the top of the doorway is higher up in the picture than the human figures and is therefore seen as farther away.

The Last Supper also provides an example of linear perspective. Lines that are parallel in three-dimensional space converge in two-dimensional space if you extend them far enough. (Recall we said before that they still look parallel if they are short.) The farther the distance is, the closer they are to converging. If we look through the figures seated at the table, we see the parallel lines of the alcoves as well as the ceiling tiles all converging at a point.

Another pictorial cue to distance is called **texture gradient**. In the real world, we can make out more detail when things are nearby, so objects lower in the picture plane that are more detailed look closer. In *Paris Street; Rainy Day* by Gustave Caillebotte (Figure 3.18), we can make out individual stones in the street toward the bottom of the picture, presumably closer to the viewer, whereas further up in the image (or, as perceptual psychologists call it, the picture plane), the stones are much smaller

Figure 3.18. The stones on the street in *Paris Street; Rainy Day* by Gustave Caillebotte illustrate the depth cue of texture gradient. (Source: Art Institute of Chicago; Barney Burstein/Corbis/VCG via Getty Images.)

and denser, and still further up, the stones blend into a dense mass. It is possible, of course, that the background is not farther away, and there happen to be no individual stones in those regions; but again, just as the visual system assumes that surfaces are uniformly colored, so it, too, assumes uniform texture, so the lack of detail higher in the picture plane is interpreted as indicating distance.

The final pictorial cue to distance is **atmospheric perspective**. Objects in the distance look indistinct and often have a hazy, bluish appearance. The air is full of dust and water particles that scatter light of shorter wavelengths (what we see as blue), so if you view a distant object, more of the light reflected from the object is scattered by the time it hits your eye. The image of these distant objects is blurred because much of the light has been scattered, and the light looks blueish because shorter wavelengths are more likely to be scattered. If you look closely at *The Last Supper*, you might notice a blueish tinge to the mountains in the background. Both authors of this book live in Virginia, where we enjoy views of the Blue Ridge Mountains (see Figure 3.19). These mountains are not actually blue but appear so from far away due to atmospheric perspective, enhanced by the thick pine vegetation which scatters even more short wavelengths than other vegetation (Cocke, 2004). But the "Atmospheric Perspective Mountains" doesn't have quite the same ring to it, does it?

MOTION DEPTH CUES   The final set of cues to depth are based on motion: whether an object moves, or we do. Imagine you are a passenger in a car on a highway, looking out of the window. Signs that are closer to you move past your window a lot faster than distant trees and buildings. The

Figure 3.19. The Blue Ridge Mountains appear blue because of the depth cue of atmospheric perspective. (Source: Photograph by Ken Thomas.)

same is true of your retinal image; objects that are closer to you move very quickly through your retinal image, whereas more distant objects move much more slowly. The Moon, since it is so far, seems not to be moving at all, which contributes to the illusion that it is following you as you move. When movement of our body creates different relative motion of objects on your retinal image (some move faster than others), we call that cue **motion parallax** (Figure 3.20).

Why are there so many cues to distance? The reason is that they are useful for locating objects at different distances. It's true that size and distance trade off, but distance is usually discernible from one of these cues, and knowing distance helps us determine size.

Top-Down Influences in Vision

We've seen that visual processing is complicated because the two-dimensional image on the retina underspecifies what the three-dimensional world looks like. You can't tell what the shape of an object is from the retinal projection because shape and orientation trade off; you can't tell the size or distance of an object because these two factors trade off; and you can't tell whether an object is white, gray, or black because differences in luminance could result from shading, lighting, or shadows. Yet these problems can be solved if you're willing to make a few assumptions, taking advantage of cues in the environment and your eye muscle movements.

So far in our discussion, information seems to flow in one direction. This **bottom-up processing** begins with raw, unprocessed sensory information (the pattern of light on the retina, or cues from the eyes) and builds up from the basic characteristics of that object (such as size, color, and textures of its surfaces) to the identity of that object. The conceptual representation or meaning of that object ("it's a microphone") therefore comes after the processing of all of its basic features.

Figure 3.20. While motion blur is not quite the same thing as motion parallax (you don't move your eyes like you move a camera, and you don't "take pictures"), this photograph gives you an idea of motion parallax from the blurrier close pedestrians, the less-blurry farther pedestrians, and the more in-focus buildings and trees in the background. (Source: Jacques LOIC/Photononstop/Getty Images.)

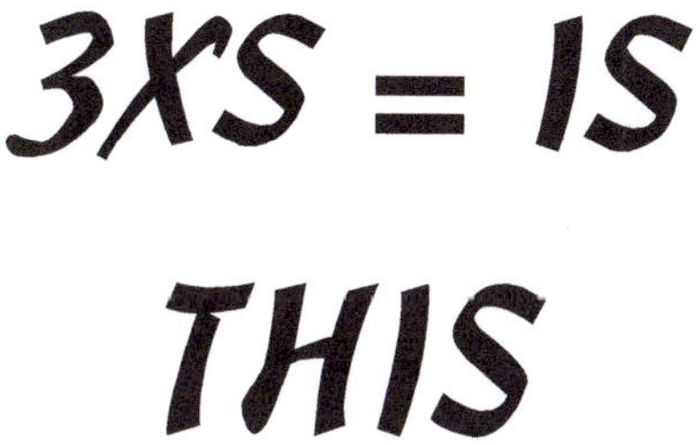

3XS = IS

THIS

Figure 3.21. The final two characters are identical, in the first line and the second line, but they are interpreted differently because of the surrounding context.

But bottom-up processing can't handle all vision alone (Kayser et al., 2004); sometimes our conceptual knowledge helps resolve basic ambiguities.

For example, how can the mind arrive at different interpretations of the last two characters in each line of Figure 3.21? This demonstration seems to argue for **top-down processing** in which conceptual knowledge influences the processing or interpretation of lower-level perceptual processes. In the first line, the last two characters seem like 15 since you interpret the line as a math equation. If you're reading the second line in the figure, the conceptual knowledge that you are reading letters leads you to interpret the ambiguous characters as the letters that complete the word "THIS." People do use conceptual information when they see, up to a point.

In a classic experiment showing the effects of conceptual information on vision, Stephen Palmer (1975) presented participants with complex scenes. They were given two seconds to look at the scene – plenty of time to figure out that it was a kitchen, for example. Next, one of three objects was flashed within the scene very briefly: either a contextually appropriate object (bread), a similarly shaped contextually inappropriate object (a mailbox), or an object that didn't fit the context and wasn't shaped like the target object. The objects were flashed for just sixty-five milliseconds. Participants correctly identified the contextually appropriate object 80 percent of the time but were right only 40 percent of the time for the other objects. Similar effects have been demonstrated by Irving Biederman (1981). More recent studies have managed to detect this perceptual expectation in the brain, identifying the neural signals that predict a particular object or sensory stimuli before the stimulus appears (Kok et al., 2017).

Of course, you would recognize the mailbox if it were presented longer, even when it is out of context. However, there are some instances in which you can't identify an object without the context. For example, take a look at four shapes in Figure 3.22.

Figure 3.22.   (a–c) The eye, nose, and mouth shown here form (d) one of the most iconic American faces. But we have a difficult time identifying the parts when they are not in the context of the whole. (Source: CSA Images/Archive/Getty Images.)

We've been assuming that processing is mostly bottom-up. In that case, you would look at the eye, nose, and mouth of Figure 3.22 and identify that they come together to complete a face. When all the pieces are together, not only is the figure instantly recognizable as a face but it is also recognizable as a particularly famous face – that of Abraham Lincoln. What's odd about this demonstration is this: You can't identify the eye or nose or mouth as Lincoln's when it is isolated. But how can you recognize Lincoln's face if you don't recognize the eyes, the nose, and all the rest? Palmer called this situation the **parsing paradox**. (*Parsing* means figuring out the pieces of a larger whole.) Palmer suggested that the resolution to the parsing paradox is that we do both top-down and bottom-up processing simultaneously and that each type of processing helps the other.

There is obviously a role for top-down processes in visual perception: Vision operates more quickly when contextually consistent information is perceived and ambiguous stimuli are perceived in a way that is consistent with context. But top-down processes must take a back seat to bottom-up processes. When something truly unusual appears in the environment (say, a chimp typing at a computer in an office), you may be slower to perceive it because it is out of context, but you do perceive it.

An Alternative: The Ecological Approach

A second point of view on the whole problem of vision contends that the model posed at the beginning of the chapter is flat-out wrong. (Please don't sigh.) Up until now, we have been discussing what is often called the **inferential approach**, which assumes that the information in the environment is impoverished – all the retina has to work with is ambiguous, two-dimensional images – and therefore the visual system must make educated guesses, or **inferences**, to recover the three-dimensional shapes and movements of the environment.

J. J. Gibson (1979) is considered to be the founder of an alternative to the inferential approach: the **ecological approach** to visual perception. Gibson believed vision looks so hard because psychologists have done a terrible job of describing visual cues and the environment that creates them. According to Gibson, the environment contains not just a variety of patchy cues that merely hint at the state of the world, instead the pattern of light has rich and complete information to specify exactly what is out in the world. The problem is that previous perceptual researchers acted as though the information our visual system gets is mostly composed of flat lines on nonmoving flat retinal images. Gibson believed that there is much more information in the world we can take advantage of; the pattern of light that bounces off the world and gets into our eyes is not arbitrary but far more structured than previously acknowledged. Not only that but Gibson argued that the visual information available to an animal is the result of active exploration by that animal, which has a particular mode of navigation. Earlier, we briefly mentioned motion cues provided when we move or when an object moves, giving the example of how when we are driving, the Moon barely moves at all, whereas signs near the road race by. Gibson says that we are not fully describing the rich information that motion provides and also that driving is a poor example of behavior, because human vision evolved paired with the dominant form of human navigation: walking. Therefore, all perceptual information is a combination of information about the world and about our own state and motion within it. The visual system need not make assumptions and perform elaborate computations because the information in the visual environment (information we create by moving rather than merely receive) is quite rich. Let's go through two examples of these sorts of information sources.

OBJECT SIZE   If we see an unfamiliar object (or a familiar object that can take many different sizes, such as a tree), how can we determine its size? According to the inferential approach, we'd

Figure 3.23. An example of how eye height provides information about object size. Objects meet the horizon at the eye height of the observer (outlined in gray). If the observer's eye height is five feet from the ground, the horizon intersects the telephone pole at five feet. The horizon intersects a little less than halfway up the pole, so the pole is somewhat more than ten feet tall. (Source: Adapted from J. J. Gibson et al. [1979], *The Ecological Approach to Visual Perception* [Boston: Houghton Mifflin], figure 9.6, p. 165.)

have to first figure out about how far away it is, because it's an unfamiliar object. We could do that using a combination of some of the pictorial cues (oculomotor cues aren't that useful beyond arm's length). Then, we'd note how big the retinal image is (i.e., how big it looks) and work back to how big the actual object is, based on its distance.

Researchers from the ecological perspective pointed out that better size information was already in the environment (Mark, 1987; Rogers, 1996; Warren, 1984). The horizon line intersects with an object at the **eye height** of the observer (at the height of the observer's eyes). Figure 3.23 shows the gray outline of an observer's head – let's say a man about six feet tall, so his eye height would be around five feet six inches. Therefore, the horizon intersects with the object at five feet six inches. Notice that the horizon intersects with the telephone poles a little below the middle of the pole; the spot where the horizon intersects the pole is five feet six inches (the eye height of the observer). Therefore, the pole is a little more than twice five feet six inches, or around eleven feet tall. Notice that even though the poles get smaller and smaller from our perspective, the horizon always intersects the pole a little less than halfway up the pole because each pole is the same size.

There is evidence that people use this eye height metric. Maryjane Wraga (1999a, 1999b) showed people different-sized steps, and they were to judge the height of each step relative to a standard rod (was the step taller or shorter than the rod?). The tricky part of the experiment was how she manipulated eye height. The participants viewed the steps from another room through a small window. On some of the trials, the floor of this other room was about 6.5 inches higher than the floor on which they were standing. This difference is small enough that participants didn't notice anything unusual about the floor in the other room. Still, participants judge their eye height relative to where they think the floor is, so the false floor effectively changed their eye height. (The manner in which Wraga and others hypothesized the eye height information is used is actually more complicated than this, but the principle is the same.) The results showed that the false floor did affect size judgments: Participants judged steps to be about an inch shorter when the floor was raised.

(a)

(b)

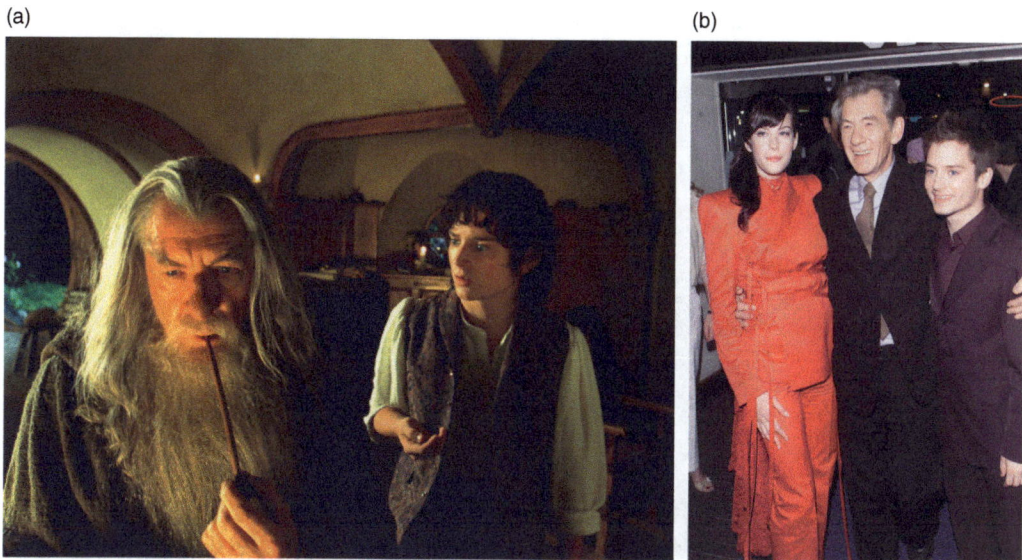

Figure 3.24. The actors Ian McKellen and Elijah Wood are somewhat different in height, but not nearly as different as they appear in the movie. (Source: (a) New Line/WireImage/Getty Images; (b) Dave Hogan/Getty Images.)

Eye height information is used in the entertainment industry. Things look bigger when your eye height is made artificially lower. You might note this next time you are at the movies. A director who wants to make an actor look taller or more impressive will film that actor with the camera held not at eye level, but at perhaps waist level, effectively lowering the eye height of the moviegoer and thereby making the actor seem taller. *The Lord of the Rings* movies used many of these types of simple camera tricks to make the actors playing the hobbits seem much smaller than the actors playing the humans, when in fact they are very similar in height (Figure 3.24).

MOTION AND OPTIC FLOW Remember when we said that size and shape are indeterminate given a two-dimensional projection? The ecological approach has it that the two-dimensional projection is not the information for perception. Gibson argues that in our rush to simplify perception into its basic elements, we have destroyed tremendously useful information. For example, researchers taking the inferential view consider how we identify objects and *separately* consider how we know about the motion of those objects. A researcher taking the ecological perspective would point out that motion information can help resolve object identity *and* that the motion of images is not arbitrary but corresponds to our own movement through the world. We are not watching a movie; we cause the motion of the pattern of light on our retinas by navigating through the world.

Gibson argued that we should focus on how lines and points of light move relative to each other over time in what he called a **vector flow field**. A vector is a point or a line with a direction of motion, and the field is all of the vectors put together. When we take into account that we have two legs and we walk on the ground, often toward the objects we are interested in, that flow field becomes very informative as to the actual three-dimensional structure of the world. While it is hard to see in a still image in a book (the whole point is that the world moves as we do), one can get an idea of what Gibson meant by seeing the pattern of motion shown when spaceships fly through the stars (Figure 3.25). All of the lights, instead of being still points, are lines showing how the stars have moved as the ship moved. How these points move relative to the viewer and relative to each

(a)

(b)

Figure 3.25. When you move through space (not just outer space but any movement on Earth too), the pattern of light hitting your eyes moves as a flow of vectors. (a) This image is the pattern you would see if you were flying through space. (b) This is the image you would see driving down a street. As you pass green lights, your movement would make the dot of a green light become a line, moving above you as you pass beneath it. (Source: (a) filo/DigitalVision Vectors/Getty Images; (b) Tom Winstead/Moment/Getty Images.)

other provides information about the speed and direction of the ship. This analysis of the vector flow field for a moving point of observation is very useful in studying visually guided actions, such as catching fly balls or braking a car (Rogers et al., 2005).

DISTANCE FOR NAVIGATION   Suppose you're playing left field in a baseball game and someone hits a ball your way. How do you get to the right position to catch it? Well, maybe you calculate the trajectory of the ball, judge where it is going to land, and run to that spot. That's what the inferential approach would dictate, and it would take a fair amount of calculation. But a simple cue in the environment can be used instead.

Michael McBeath et al. (1995) provided evidence that people actually catch a fly ball by running so the trajectory of the ball looks like a straight line. Imagine a two-dimensional picture in which the baseball goes upward and to the left. If you run in a direction that makes the ball appear to travel in a straight line, you will go directly to the spot where the ball will land. The details of the geometry are complex, but the basic point is quite simple. There is even evidence that Frisbee-catching dogs use this principle (Shaffer et al., 2004). It's a beautiful example of the ecological approach.

The ecological approach holds that most vision researchers make the problem of visual perception more difficult than it actually is. Once we have fully described all the rich sources of information available in the environment, they argue, many of the problems of visual perception disappear. Are they right?

To a point, we think the answer must be yes. Ecological psychologists have made this point in the experiments described previously and in others. Still, it is not difficult to find common ground between the two perspectives; even the most determined ecological researchers admit that the perceptual system must do some additional processing on the information in the environment, and even the most determined inferential researchers admit that moving through the environment and assuming stable eye height reduces the need for the visual system to make inferences. Thus, the difference between the perspectives may best be thought of as one of emphasis.

Stand-on-One-Foot Questions

3.4. What assumptions does the visual system make about luminance?
3.5. What's the difference between top-down and bottom-up processing?
3.6. Summarize the differences between the inferential and the ecological points of view.

Questions That Require Two Feet

3.7. I once stood on a hill overlooking San Francisco on a brilliantly clear day, and the city looked like a small model seen at about thirty feet rather than like a full-size city seen at a distance. Why?
3.8. Can you think of a way to use what you know about perceived size and eye height to improve your relationship with a young child?

What Is Vision For?

Preview

Vision helps you know what objects are in the world and helps you navigate (move around). For objects to be recognized, there must be some representation in memory of what they look like. But an object like a car looks very different from the front, back, and side. Does that mean you need three mental representations to be sure you can recognize it from each perspective? One group of theories holds that you have a single mental representation of an object that supports recognition from any angle. Another group of theories proposes that you keep several representations of each object in memory. We discuss the merits of each of these ideas. We also discuss navigation and focus on the difference between conscious visual perception and visual perception that supports navigation. One set of visual processes supports our conscious perception of where things are and what objects are out in the world. Another set of processes, privileged to the motor system, helps you move, but you can't get conscious access to their contents.

In this section, we describe two of the basic tasks of perception: identifying objects and visually guided action and navigation. Knowing an object's identity helps us know what to do to it. If it's an apple, eat it; if it's a stapler, squeeze it; if it's a clump of poison ivy, avoid it. Knowing an object's location is helpful so you will know where it is relative to you, the best place to grasp it, whether there are obstacles in the way if you decide to grasp it, and so on.

One role of the perceptual system is to figure out what an object is. Another is responsible for figuring out properties of the object (size, orientation, etc.) that are important for interacting with it. Object identity has been much more thoroughly studied, so we can say more about how that might work. Only recently was it concluded that the visual action system is separate from the object identity system; most of our discussion focuses on how researchers drew that conclusion.

Identifying Objects

We have discussed how the visual system determines the attributes of objects (their distance, size, and brightness). But how does it identify what those objects are? Shape is the most obvious characteristic we use to identify objects – for example, a banana is easy to recognize because of its shape – but other properties can be helpful too. For example, you can identify the handle on a chest of drawers by its location, even if it has a very unusual shape. A piece of cheese and a brick may have similar shapes, but they are distinguishable by their color and texture. Thus, the first thing we should realize is that many cues contribute to visual object recognition. Most researchers have focused on shape, however, probably because it is the most reliable cue to object identity (but see Figure 3.26).

The core task of object identification is to match our perception with some representation of the object stored in memory. In Chapter 1, we emphasized the importance of representation in cognitive psychology. For object identification, we have to have something in our memory to compare to what we see. The key question is this: What does the memory representation that supports object identification look like? Suppose you recognize that an animal is a cat. Some information in memory must enable you to identify that animal. You have to have some information stored about what cats look like. What kind of information is it?

There are two families of answers to this question. First, the representation in memory could be specific to your viewpoint; you store how the object looks to you, not its actual structure. This is called a **viewer-centered representation** because the representation of the object depends on how the viewer sees it. The second family of theories claims that you store how the object looks independent of any particular viewpoint. In **object-centered representation**, the locations of the

Figure 3.26. Notice how hard it is to recognize some of these foods when the cue of shape has been removed. Color and pattern then become the only clues to identity. (Source: Martin Kreppel/EyeEm/Getty Images.)

object's parts are defined relative to the object itself, not relative to the viewer. A viewer-centered representation of an airplane might contain the information that its nose is to the left of its tail. That representation won't work, however, if the plane is turned around or if the viewer is looking at the plane from the front. The object-centered representation locates an object's parts relative to its other parts; thus, it would contain the information that the plane's nose is attached to the fuselage.

For both families of theories, a key problem is dealing with objects at different orientations. You never know in what orientation you'll see a cat; it might be running, climbing a tree, or curled up by a fire. Think of what an odd profile a cat has when it is curled up by a fire. According to object-centered theories, the representation in memory can't be specific to one viewpoint because an object can appear in different orientations. This claim seems self-evident, yet the viewer-centered theories have a response, as we'll see. /

Viewer-centered theories work pretty well for objects like letters and numbers. Using a viewer-centered picture (or a set of pictures) of what an *R* looks like and checking for a match is a pretty good way of identifying *R*s. This approach also works fine for identifying dollar bills in vending machines or deposited checks via a photo app.

But viewer-centered theories don't work so well for rotated letters. Why is it harder to recognize an upside-down *R* than *R*? Couldn't we just store an upside-down *R* too? When we see and recognize objects out in the world instead of in our books, we see them at a wide variety of orientations and still have little problem identifying them.

The object-centered answer to recognizing a rotated *R* starts by noting that the parts of the *R* are *not* rotated relative to one another. If your frame of reference is the object, then all parts are where they are supposed to be relative to one another. Likewise, when you are looking at a natural object like a dog, you shouldn't look for a head at the top and feet at the bottom. You should look for a head connected to a neck, feet connected to legs, a tail connected to the back, and so on (Biederman & Gerhardstein, 1993). The relationships between the parts do not change depending on whether the dog is facing left or right, running, or curled up. But once we are able to identify a set of parts connected in roughly the way these parts are often connected, we can identify the whole object.

But using this representation of parts relative to each other relies on your being able to recognize the parts themselves. How do you do that? How do you "decompose" a dog into parts?

Several object-centered theories propose that we identify parts of objects as geometric solids. An influential theory was proposed by Irving Biederman (1987), who argued that object recognition is supported by a set of thirty-six shapes he called geons (simple shapes that look like bricks, cylinders, etc.) that operate like letters of the alphabet. Complex objects can be built from them, as shown in the left column of Figure 3.27. So the memory representation that helps you identify, say, a cat consists of a set of simple geometric shapes *and* the locations of those shapes relative to one another.

A strength of Biederman's theory is that geons are easy to distinguish from one another. For example, from most viewing angles, the geon called a brick has three parallel edges and intersections that look like arrows, and a cylinder has two parallel edges, two curved edges, and two line intersections that look like a *Y*.

To test his theory, Biederman showed participants pictures of objects constructed from geons, similar to those in Figure 3.27. The pictures were degraded in one of two ways. In each case, he deleted the same total length of line segments. In the center column, the line vertices have been left intact, and in the right column many have been removed or changed. Biederman showed participants the incomplete drawings for varying amounts of time (as short as 100 milliseconds or as long as five seconds) and asked them to name the objects depicted. If the vertices were present, people were pretty good at this task. They named 90 percent of the pictures they could see for 750 milliseconds. With the vertices removed, however, participants only got 30 percent correct, even if they saw the pictures for five seconds. These data support Biederman's contention that vertices are crucial for correctly interpreting geometric solids, and other data indicate that geons may be important in visual memory (Cleary et al., 2004). These geometric solids, according to Biederman, are the building blocks of visual object identification (Figure 3.28).

It seems that object-centered theories would almost have to be right. If the representation of an object is based on views specific to your perspective, you would need a different representation each time you or the object moved. Seen from different angles, common objects can look radically different, as shown in Figure 3.29.

But perhaps we could solve the problems of multiple views not with object-centered representations but with a series of viewpoint-specific representations. If you have multiple viewpoints, then you can mentally rotate your representation to match the particular view of the object you are now seeing. There is some evidence in support of this theory; when people view an object from a new angle, they take longer to recognize it, consistent with the idea that they mentally rotate an image of the object (Tarr, 1995).

So which type of theory is correct – decomposition in parts (object centered) or viewer centered? Researchers have tried to collect definitive neuroscientific evidence and have discovered that the brain appears to use both types of representation. Single-cell recording studies in nonhuman primates show that some neurons code objects from a specific viewpoint (e.g., Epstein et al., 2003; Logothetis et al., 1995), whereas others do not (e.g., Booth & Rolls, 1998; Murty & Arun, 2015). Brain imaging data from humans also show evidence for both types of representation. These clever studies examined adaptation. The brain activation caused by seeing an object drops if you see the same object repeatedly. But what happens if you see the same object from different views? The viewer-centered theory predicts that the brain activation will drop, whereas the object-centered theory predicts

Figure 3.27. Examples of common objects that can be constructed with the geons proposed in Biederman's theory. The center and right columns show two ways of decomposing the figures: by either (center) retaining line vertices or (right) omitting them. In accordance with Biederman's theory, it is easier to identify objects when the vertices are still present. (Source: I. Biederman [1987], Recognition-by-components: A theory of human image understanding, *Psychological Review*, 94[2], figure 16, p. 135.)

that it will not. Data from different studies support both theories (Burgund & Marsolek, 2000; Fang & He, 2005; Grill-Spector & Malach, 2001; Kourtzi et al., 2003; Nishimura et al., 2015).

These data support earlier theoretical suggestions that the mind may use two methods of recognition, each serving different functions (Barenholtz & Tarr, 2011; Cooper et al., 1992; Farah, 1990; Jolicoeur, 1990; Tarr & Pinker, 1990). The decomposition-into-parts approach may work well to distinguish between a car and a truck, for example, but it can't make finer-grained distinctions

Figure 3.28. Artists can build amazing sculptures using just basic geometric shapes, such as this entry in a snow sculpture contest in Japan. (Source: Glowimages/Getty Images.)

between a Ford and a Chrysler (Davitt et al., 2014). The decomposition-into-parts idea seems to work well for objects that have some telltale geons that make it easy to identify the object at many different orientations, like a car or a coffee mug. The multiple-view approach seems to retain more information about details and thus may be effective for recognizing objects that don't have telltale parts and for distinguishing between closely related objects, such as different varieties of cars.

Our Ford-versus-Chrysler example might have gotten you thinking about whether research in object perception suffers from the WEIRD problem we mentioned in Chapter 1. How universal are the rules of object perception and identification? One very clever recent study (Kemp et al., 2022) examined how twenty-seven different cultures across the world have perceived the objects that all Earthlings can see: the stars. They found that the same universal geometric principles explained how different cultures chose which stars came together into constellations. They did not catalog and compare the meanings of all the constellations in different cultures, but previous work has noted striking similarities between interpretations. For example, Greek traditions and several Australian Aboriginal cultures interpret the same set of stars as being a hunter (Johnson, 2011; Leaman & Hamacher, 2019).

ARE SOME OBJECTS SPECIAL?   Look at the objects in Figure 3.30. Could you recognize them without turning the book upside down? Martin Yin (1969) was the first to report that people are greatly impaired in recognizing upside-down faces, but the cost to perceiving other objects did not seem as great. Perhaps you've had this experience when you're seated across from a friend who is looking at photos. It's difficult to recognize the faces of people in the photos – even of yourself! The impairment indicates that faces might be perceptually special in some sense. Some data support that interpretation, but as we'll see, this conclusion is controversial.

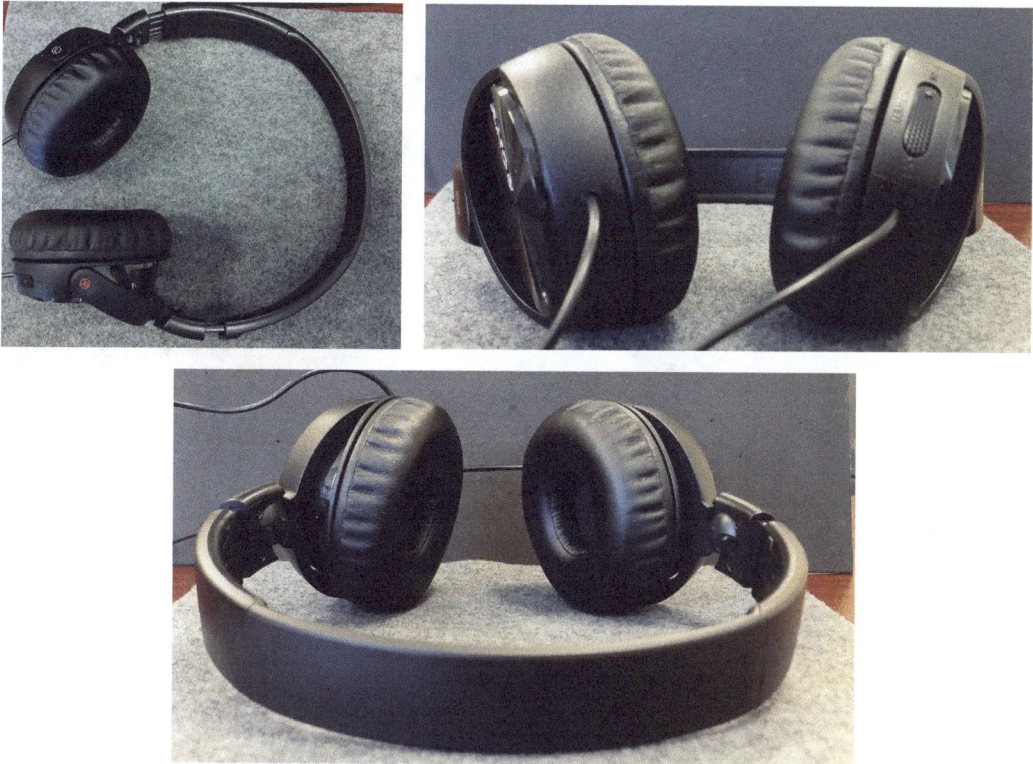

Figure 3.29. Seen from different perspectives, common objects like headphones can look quite different, but we can still recognize them as headphones. (Source: Photograph by Cedar Riener.)

The "specialness" of face processing is supported by a neuropsychological deficit called **prosopagnosia**, which is a selective deficit in recognizing faces. A patient with prosopagnosia can recognize objects – a radio, a glove, a car – but cannot visually recognize faces, even that of a spouse. However, the patient can recognize people by the sounds of their voices or by other nonvisual information, so the deficit appears to be specific to the visual processing of faces (Hécaen & Angelergues, 1962; Richler & Gauthier, 2014). Because face processing can be damaged selectively, this might be taken to imply that there is a face-processing module that is separate from other types of visual processing.

Brain imaging data appear to be consistent with that hypothesis. Face recognition is strongly associated with activation in the **fusiform gyrus** of the brain, which is located on the ventral part of the temporal lobe (Kanwisher, 2010; Kanwisher et al., 1997). This area seems so specific for face processing that some have called it the fusiform face area. For example, Galit Yovel and Nancy Kanwisher (2004) showed people houses and faces (either upright or inverted) and asked them to do one of two tasks. One task required focusing on the specific shape of the parts (e.g., the windows or the eyes), and the other task asked them to focus on the distance between the parts. They found that the fusiform face area was always active for the faces and never the houses, and the task performed on the stimuli didn't matter much. The importance of processing faces seems plausible in light of evolution. Because we evolved as a social species, recognizing other individuals is important.

(a)

(b)

(c)

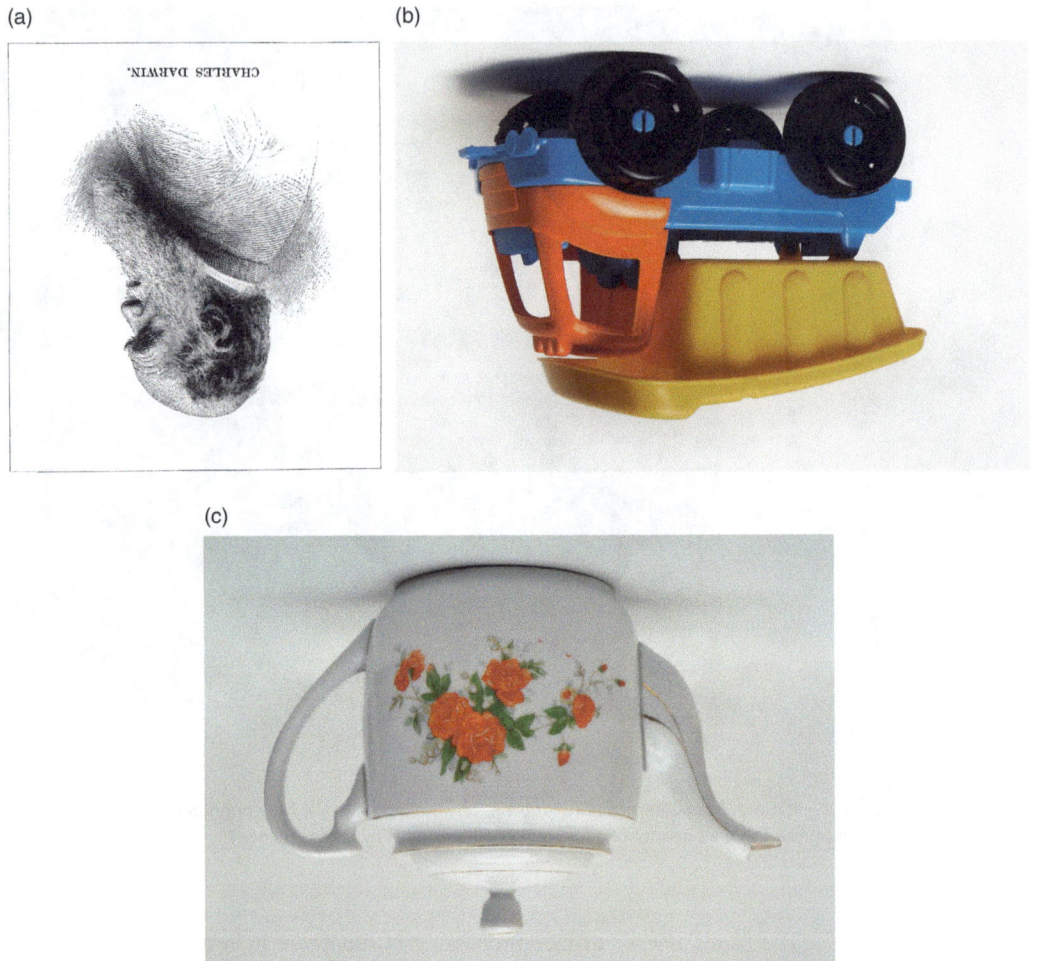

Figure 3.30. Can you identify each of these three objects, even though they are upside down? (Source: (a) benoitb/DigitalVision Vectors/Getty Images; (b) Andy Crawford/Getty Images; (c) Dani Daniar/EyeEm/Getty Images.)

Another explanation of these data is possible. Note that the task of identifying a face is different than identifying an object because you not only want to identify it as a face but also specify exactly whose face you see. For an object, you just need to know it's a teapot, not which teapot. Identifying an individual is difficult because all faces share a lot of features in common: two eyes, a nose, a mouth, and so on. It's the distance between the parts that seems to be very important for identifying individual faces. (Of course, some faces have a single identifiable feature – e.g., Hitler's mustache – but not many.) Thus, perhaps the fusiform face area is really specialized to identify individuals, and that requires different processing than identifying a broad object category (Tarr & Gauthier, 2000). In this sense, the fusiform face area supports perceptual expertise (Gauthier et al., 2003; McKeeff et al., 2010; Tarr & Cheng, 2003). The same area might support the car enthusiast's ability to distinguish a 1972 Ford Mustang from the 1973 model (McGugin et al., 2012), the chess expert distinguishing positions of chess pieces (Bilalić et al., 2011), or a bird watcher distinguishing an African from a European swallow (Gauthier et al., 2000; Gilliam & Jones, 1975). It might appear to researchers that the fusiform face area supports face processing only because all of us are face-processing experts – we must differentiate faces all the time.

Jim Haxby and his colleagues (Chao et al., 1999; Haxby et al., 2001; Haxby et al., 2004; O'Toole et al., 2005) offered a third account of these data. They acknowledge that perceiving faces leads to activation in the fusiform gyrus but point out that brain imaging techniques emphasize the areas of greatest activation. A lot of other areas also show lower levels of activation, but researchers tend to ignore those areas. The peaks of activation for faces may be localized, but large, overlapping areas of the temporal lobe may actually be contributing to the recognition of faces and other objects. In one important demonstration of this idea, Haxby et al. (2001) measured brain activation in fMRI as participants viewed faces, cats, bottles, scissors, shoes, houses, and chairs. The researchers showed that even a brain area that responded maximally to just one type of stimulus still showed identifiable patterns of response to the other categories of objects. Thus, they argue, an area might respond maximally to faces, but it's not just a face area because it still responds to other types of stimuli and seems to be helping to identify them. A great deal of research has been conducted since the year 2000 (for a review of new techniques, see Haxby et al., 2014) to address these three possibilities: localized representation that depends on object type (e.g., faces in one part of the brain); localized processing (e.g., visual expertise in one part of the brain); or **distributed representation** (e.g., localized peaks of activation for faces, but contribution from large areas of cortex). The topic is so actively researched because it's so important. Researchers are really trying to figure out the principle by which perceptual representations are organized in the brain. Are representations clustered together in the brain so faces are all in the same place? Or are processes clustered together in the brain so all perceptual expertise is in the same place? Or perhaps nothing is clustered together and both processes and representations are distributed.

Researchers have tried to pit one theory against the other. For example, would someone with prosopagnosia be able to gain expertise with other stimuli? A recent case of a woman with congenital prosopagnosia *was* able to acquire visual expertise for horses (Weiss et al., 2016). Other experiments have examined brain activations when butterfly experts or car experts look at butterflies or cars and activations when these same experts look at faces. Some studies report that activation is in the fusiform face area for faces but in a separate area for these visually expert perceptions (Grill-Spector et al., 2004; Rhodes et al., 2004). Other studies, however, report that the brain activation for faces and for expertise is largely overlapping (Gauthier et al., 2000).

In the end, definitive data to choose among these three theories (a face area specialized for faces, a visual expertise area specialized for any other objects one is an expert at identifying, or there is distributed representation) are not yet available. Given the importance of the question and the potential complexity of the answer, it is not surprising that the issue has not yet been settled. The prolonged debate does suggest that there is some functional organization in that area of the brain, such that certain areas are specialized for certain functions of conscious visual object recognition (Kanwisher & Dilks, 2013), but there is still disagreement over the boundaries and over the best way to describe the function (McGugin et al., 2012; Salehi et al., 2020).

Navigation and Visually Guided Action

The second function of vision is to help us act in the world. When you reach out to grab a coffee cup, how do you know the location of the cup? Most people have the intuition that you are conscious of the cup's location and guide your hand to that location. Strangely enough, the evidence indicates that your conscious awareness of the cup's location is not important in guiding your hand. There is another part of your visual system of which you are mostly unaware that operates in parallel with the conscious one and that drives movements.

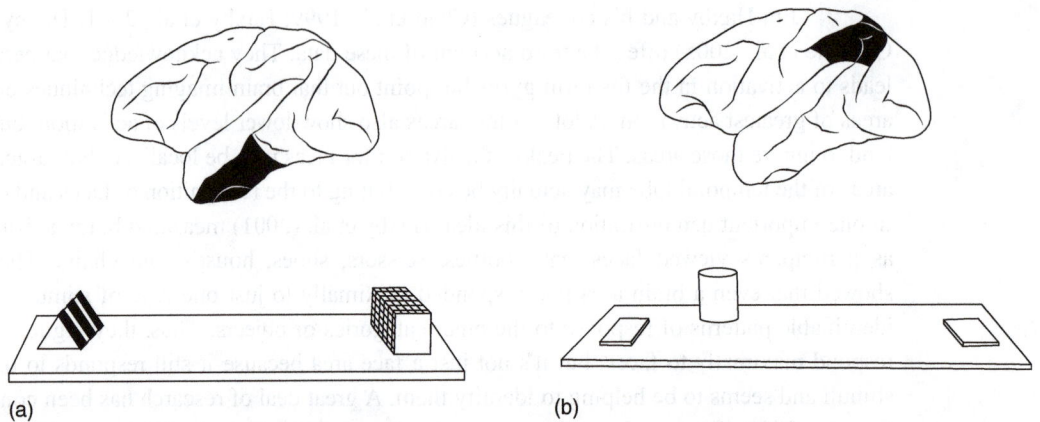

Figure 3.31. Representation of the tasks used by Ungerleider and Mishkin (1982), as well as the brain areas that support them. (a) Nonmatching to sample – the monkey would have just seen one of the two objects and must pick the novel one. A lesion to the ventral pathway (shaded on the figure) compromises performance on this task. (b) Landmark task – the monkey simply chooses the trap door closer to the cylinder. Damage to the dorsal pathway impairs performance on this task. (Source: M. Mishkin, L. G. Ungerleider, and K. A. Macko [1983], Object vision and spatial vision: Two cortical pathways, *Trends in Neurosciences*, 6[10], figure 2, p. 415. *Trends in Neurosciences* is published by Elsevier.)

A key finding came from visual researchers examining the primate brain. Leslie Ungerleider and Mortimer Mishkin (1982; see also Ungerleider & Haxby, 1994) proposed that there are two visual pathways in the brain. One pathway identifies objects, and the other determines the location of objects. They proposed this hypothesis after studying brain anatomy and then tested it in monkeys. They had two tests: one for object identity and one for object location, depicted in Figure 3.31. The object identity test is called nonmatching to sample. Here's what happens. A sliding door rises, and the monkey sees an object. The monkey knocks the object aside to find a reward, such as a peanut. The door then goes down and comes back up, and the monkey sees two objects: the one it just saw and a new object. If the monkey knocks aside the new object, it will find another peanut reward. If it knocks aside the object it just saw, it gets nothing. That's how the task got its name; the first object is the sample, and the monkey is supposed to pick the nonmatching object. Note that the monkey doesn't need to know anything about object location to perform the task well; all it needs to do is recognize the object it just saw.

The object location task is called the landmark task. In this task, the monkey sees two trapdoors. Under each trapdoor is a well containing either a peanut reward or nothing. A landmark (usually a cylinder) lies closer to one trapdoor than the other, and the monkey should simply choose the trapdoor closer to the cylinder. Thus, for this task object identity is irrelevant; the monkey needs to know the location of the trapdoors and the cylinder.

Ungerleider and Mishkin (1982) trained some monkeys until they were very good at each task. Next, the researchers removed part of the monkeys' brains: For one group of monkeys, it was part of the temporal lobe, and for the other, it was part of the parietal lobe. The results were dramatic. The group with the temporal lobe lesion performed well on the landmark task but could no longer succeed at nonmatching to sample. The group with the parietal lesion showed the opposite pattern of results. Ungerleider and Mishkin interpreted this experiment as showing that there are two streams of processing in the visual system: a "what" stream that identifies objects and a "where" stream that determines where objects are located. This model can be called the **what/where hypothesis** (see also Kravitz et al., 2013; Ungerleider & Haxby, 1994). There are also data indicating separation of "what" and "where" processing in other senses, such as touch (Reed et al., 2005) and audition (Lomber & Malhotra, 2008), and even in the multisensory integration of sound and touch (Renier et al., 2009).

This result was very influential in vision research, but there have always been one or two oddities in this interpretation. For example, how can the spatial information be separate from the processes that identify objects? Don't you need to know where an object's parts are to identify it?

Ungerleider and Mishkin's findings were later reinterpreted in an interesting and convincing way. Melvyn Goodale and David Milner and colleagues (Goodale & Milner, 1992, 2004; Goodale & Westwood, 2004; Whitwell et al., 2014) suggested that it is better to think of them as "what" and "how" streams (which we'll call the **what/how hypothesis**). They argue that spatial information is present in both streams, but its function differs. The "what" stream in the temporal lobe identifies objects and is associated with consciousness. The end product of this processing stream is the conscious perception of where objects are, what they are, their colors, and so on. The "how" stream handles information that helps us move. Thus, the "how" stream knows the shape and location of objects so we can grasp them effectively and reach to the right spot.

There are convincing data for the separation of two streams of visual processing in the human brain. For example, either stream can be selectively damaged, leaving the other intact. Patients with **visual agnosia** typically suffer damage to the border of the temporal and occipital lobes and have difficulty recognizing objects using vision but can do so using other senses. Some of these patients, however, are able to accurately direct movements using vision. One of the more dramatic examples is patient D.F. described by Milner and Goodale (1995). Even though she could see colors and textures, she had a great deal of difficulty visually recognizing objects, so much so that even recognizing *properties* of objects was tough – when shown a cylinder with a slot cut into it, D.F. could not describe the orientation of the slot (as horizontal or vertical, for example). Yet, when handed a card and instructed to put the card in the slot, she was able to do so effortlessly (Figure 3.32). The interpretation is that the dorsal system (which supports perception for movement) can use visual information to guide action on the slot, but the ventral system (which supports object recognition and conscious perception) cannot use visual information to describe the slot.

The opposite pattern of results has also been observed. Patients with **optic ataxia** usually suffer damage to the superior parietal cortex (dorsal system), and they are impaired in using visual guidance for movement (Perenin & Vighetto, 1988; see also Himmelbach & Karnath, 2005). When reaching for an object, they grope about unsurely, like a person seeking a light switch in the dark, but they can identify objects by sight without problem.

Brain imaging evidence also supports the separation of the **dorsal** and **ventral** visual streams. For example, Geoff Aguirre and Mark D'Esposito (1997) had their participants spend several sessions exploring a small town in virtual reality. Then, the researchers administered a test of their knowledge. Participants saw a landmark (e.g., a building) and were asked to make one of two judgments – a judgment whether the landmark looked accurate (or had been changed slightly) or a judgment about the relative position of another landmark. When participants judged what landmarks looked like, the ventral system was active. When they judged the locations of landmarks, the dorsal system was active (see also Faillenot et al., 1997; Kohler et al., 1995).

Recent research has expanded on this finding, showing that the degree of connectivity between different areas of the hippocampus and these dorsal and ventral networks is associated with higher memory performance on those tasks. For example, better topographical memory (such as location of landmarks) was associated with stronger hippocampal connection to the right **anterior** hippocampus (the area of the hippocampus closer to the dorsal visual stream) (Sormaz et al., 2017).

(a) Preception condition

Task instruction: turn the card so it matches the slot

Figure 3.32. Patient D.F. is able to place the card in the slot but is not able to match the orientation of the card to the orientation of the slot.

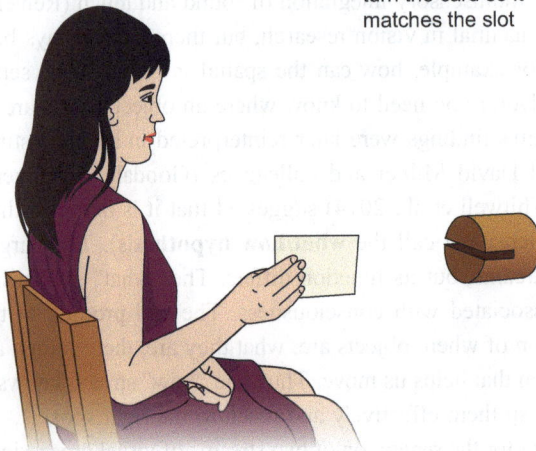

(b) Action condition

Task instruction: put the card in the slot

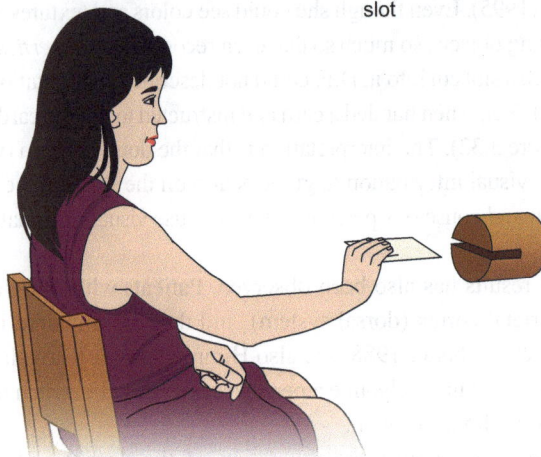

Most of the time, you would have no reason to know that there are two visual streams because they are in agreement: You feel that the visual experience of seeing (ventral system) supports reaching (dorsal system) because the two systems concur. However, there are times the systems are misaligned. For example, visual illusions fool one system more than the other. Ganel et al. (2008) found that for a series of visual illusions, the "what" system misjudged the size of certain parts of the illusions, whereas visually guided action (the "how" system) accurately judged these same parts (Figure 3.33). (Researchers measured how far apart people placed their fingers when they reached to pick up the objects that were a part of the illusion.)

a

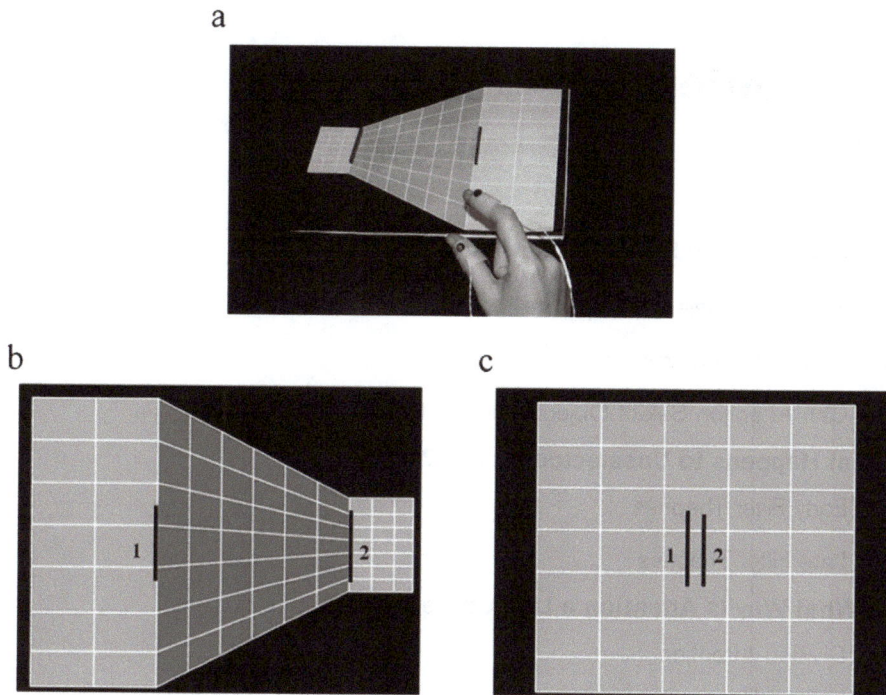

b

c

Figure 3.33. A version of the Ponzo illusion in which study participants either matched the length of one of the lines or reached to grasp one of the lines. They were less affected by the illusion when they reached to grasp. (Source: T. Ganel, M. Tanzer, and M. A. Goodale [2008], A double dissociation between action and perception in the context of visual illusions: Opposite effects of real and illusory size, *Psychological Science*, 19[3], 222. https://doi.org/10.1111/j.1467-9280.2008.02071.x.)

In this chapter, we've discussed the basics of visual perception. But we've discussed it as though the mere presence of a visual stimulus were enough for it to be processed. That is inaccurate. It is quite possible not to see a large object that is right in front of you ... if you're not paying attention to it (Mack, 2003). Attention is vital for all kinds of cognitive processing, not just vision, and we will discuss attention in Chapter 4.

Stand-on-One-Foot Questions

3.9.   What are the two basic ideas about how objects are represented?

3.10.   Name two types of evidence indicating that "what" and "how" are represented separately by the visual system.

Questions That Require Two Feet

3.11.   Are there some objects that you almost always see in the same orientation? Do you think that your mental representation of those objects might reflect that select experience?

3.12.   How might your perception of cars be different from your perception of faces?

3.13.   Think of a sport with which you are familiar. Which parts of performance in the sport are due to the what system? Which are due to the how system?

4 Attention

The last chapter explored how we interpret the raw data from our eyes to perceive meaningful objects and events. In this chapter we explore attention. Like perception, attention seems to be a straightforward mental concept used in everyday life. Just as you could ask someone "did you see that?" without bothering to define "see," you can ask someone to "pay attention" and expect them to know what you were talking about.

Despite intuitive familiarity, cognitive psychologists have struggled to define attention as a mental concept – a recent article titled "No One Knows What Attention Is" attests to the ongoing challenge (Hommel et al., 2019). William James (Figure 4.1) said trying to observe one's mind at work was "like seizing a spinning top to catch its motion, or trying to turn up the [lights] quickly enough to see how the darkness looks" (James, 1890, p. 244). James neverthe-less included attention in his definition of conscious experience: "My experience is what I agree to attend to."

But what, then, is **attention**? While cognitive psychologists haven't succeeded in pinning it down, a common provisional definition is that attention is further cognitive processing; whatever attention *is*, we define it by what it *does* – it ensures more cognitive processing on its target. In that spirit, researchers have focused their attention on investigating a few key operations of attention as a process (how it works). Attention "chooses" some stimuli and does not choose others: It is **selective**. Because there is not an infinite amount of attention to devote, attention is **limited**. Even though we can select one object and not another, can we *divide* attention? If we can divide attention, how does that influence our ability to multitask?

Figure 4.1. William James, paying attention to something other than the camera. (Source: CORBIS/Corbis via Getty Images.)

Let's start by imagining a very simple and commonplace set of events. You are sitting in your room studying. A friend comes in and tells you there is free pizza downstairs. You go down and eat some pizza. How do processes of attention guide you through these events?

First, as you study, you *select* the words on the page to pay attention to, not the sounds in your room nor the pressure on your bottom as you sit. How do we choose which items get cognitive processing? **How is attention selective, and what is selected?** How do you select the words on the page for processing and avoid selecting the other sensory stimuli?

Next, even though you have selected some stimuli, the others are not completely ignored. Even as you dedicate your mind to studying, the unselected stimuli – other things in the room to see and hear, for example – still do get some cognitive processing. That's why you say that attention prompts *continued* cognitive processing; everything gets at least some processing. You can appreciate that by imagining that a friend enters the room you're in right now and says with urgency, "Free pizza downstairs!" You would not be oblivious to that sound because you were attending to this book. Your friend's voice would seem to have hijacked your attention. But that's actually not quite right. Shifting attention would be *your* act, not your friend's. Some quiet decision maker in your unconscious concluded that attention should be moved from the book to the voice. What's the basis of this decision? **What happens to unselected stimuli?**

Now suppose you begin to talk with your friend about what kind of pizza is being offered. You don't need to look at him to hear him, so suppose you keep your eyes on your book. Are you able to keep studying while you have your conversation? You might feel as if you don't have the mental resources to do both at once. Cognitive psychologists are also interested in this question: **In what way is attention a limited resource?**

Now suppose you've gone downstairs to partake of the free meal. You're chatting with another friend while eating, and simultaneously checking your phone, and also ruminating on the fact that you need to read this chapter by tomorrow. You are confident in your ability to multitask until you realize your friend asked you something but you didn't fully hear it. Can we effectively divide attention, and what are the costs to multitasking?

How Is Attention Selective and What Is Selected?

Preview

At any given moment, there are countless things in the world we could process further, that is, pay attention to. We attend to only a subset of the available stimuli. How do we decide what gets "in" to attention? How does selection operate? And what is selected – does attention focus on objects or regions of space? The most current theory proposes that the process of selection happens as we bind features together to form objects, and we are able to direct this process and so decide what gets "in" to attention. Although that makes it sound like attention selects objects, not space, there are actually aspects of both types of selection in contemporary theories.

While attention seems familiar, and the idea of selecting some stimuli for further processing makes sense, it has proven difficult to observe the process of attentional selection in experiments. One problem is that the process of selection ("found it!") is incredibly fast and difficult to isolate from perceptual processes and from responses. Another problem is that attentional selection is difficult to manipulate experimentally. Despite these difficulties, researchers have devised some tasks that illuminate the selective nature of attention.

How Does Selection Operate?

The Transportation Security Administration (TSA) officer looking for contraband in luggage, the radiologist looking for abnormalities on an X-ray, and you searching for your car when you exit a concert are all engaged in a similar task. You want your attention directed to a particular object (contraband, a tumor, your car), and your attention is not currently directed at the object. So you sweep attention around the visual field, with the idea that attention will stop when and if you find the desired object. Cognitive psychologists call this a **visual search task**. By varying characteristics of the **target** and the nontargets (usually called **distractors**), we can figure out how it works. To get a feel for it, look for the red letter *Q* in the three arrays in Figure 4.2.

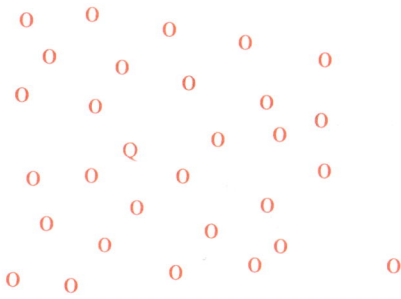

Figure 4.2. Stimulus arrays used in typical visual search tasks (such as Treisman & Gelade, 1980). In each array, the target is a small red Q. In the top and center arrays, the target is easy to find because a single dimension differentiates the targets from the distractors (Q-ness in the top, color in the middle). In the bottom array, more than one dimension is necessary to distinguish the target from distractors. The targets in the top and center arrays can be found using a disjunctive search, whereas the bottom requires conjunctive search.

You probably found this task easy for the first two arrays and more difficult in the third. In the first array, a single feature of the *Q* – the diagonal line – differentiates it from the other letters present. In the second array, again, a single feature – its color – makes the target different from the other letters. In the third array, however, no single feature differentiates the targets and the distractors.

These two types of searches are called disjunctive and conjunctive. In a **disjunctive search**, the target differs from the distractors by just one feature, as in the two top arrays. In a **conjunctive**

search, a particular combination of features differentiates the target from the distractors. There are shapes that match the target and sizes that match the target, but there is only one combination (or conjunction) of shape and size that match the target. Visual search experiments showing similar results have been conducted with many different features, such as different shapes, sizes, colors, textures, and spatial orientations (Buetti et al., 2016; for a review, see Wolfe, 2020).

Laboratory experiments confirm the feeling that some searches are easier than others. Increasing the number of elements in the array does not affect the reaction time to find the target in the disjunctive search – when you're searching for a small *Q*, it doesn't matter whether there are three large *Q*s or thirty large *Q*s. But the number of elements in the array *does* affect search time in conjunctive searches. This pattern indicates that a disjunctive search is conducted in *parallel* – all elements are evaluated simultaneously – so increasing the number of items to be evaluated does not increase the total search time. On the other hand, the process of conducting a conjunctive search is *serial* – elements are checked one by one – so increasing the number of items increases the search time. The participant will locate the target, on average, after checking half the items in the array.

The importance of the difference between disjunctive and conjunctive searches was emphasized by Anne Treisman and Garry Gelade (1980). They proposed that individual features (e.g., color and shape) are processed **preattentively**; that is, attention is not needed to know if one of these features is present somewhere in the environment. A conjunctive search, however, requires knowing that more than one feature belongs to an individual object; you're not just looking for a circle, or something red, but a red circle. Redness and circleness must belong to the same object, or to put it another way, redness and circleness must be in the same spatial location. Localizing features in space (rather than just knowing redness is out there, somewhere) requires attention, according to Treisman and Gelade. So in this view, the purpose of attention is to bind features together to assign them to an object. And space is intrinsic to the selection process of attention. We figure out that we've found the small red *Q* in a conjunctive search because two features (smallness and the diagonal line) are *in the same place*. This theory of attention in which attention binds together features into objects in space is called **feature integration theory** (for a recent review, see Hochstein, 2020).

One prediction of feature integration theory is that if the process of binding features is interrupted, they would remain free floating or the attentional binding wouldn't be complete so there would be guesses or errors in which features belonged together; a blue *Q* and a red *P* might be misidentified as a blue *P* and a red *Q*. These guesses or errors are called **illusory conjunctions**. As the theory predicts, when a display of colored shapes is flashed for only 250 milliseconds (one-fifth of a second) and followed by a random dot mask, observers reported incorrect features (e.g., a green triangle when the triangle was red) in nearly 20 percent of the trials (Treisman & Schmidt, 1982).

Whether a target differs from the distractors in one dimension or several is an important element of visual search. An altogether different aspect of search concerns the frequency with which the target is present at all. That's an important practical consideration, because outside of laboratories – for example, when inspectors search for guns in luggage – visual search usually turns up nothing. Jeremy Wolfe and colleagues concluded that "if you don't find it often, you don't often find it" (Evans et al., 2013). People are much less likely to find targets that appear only once every few hundred trials. Strange as it sounds, it may make sense to insert fake guns and bombs into the images of luggage to improve the ability of TSA officers to find the real thing (Wolfe et al., 2013) (see Figure 4.3).

Two other examples of real-world visual search tasks show the importance of understanding basic processes of scanning a visual scene looking for a target, while also recognizing that each

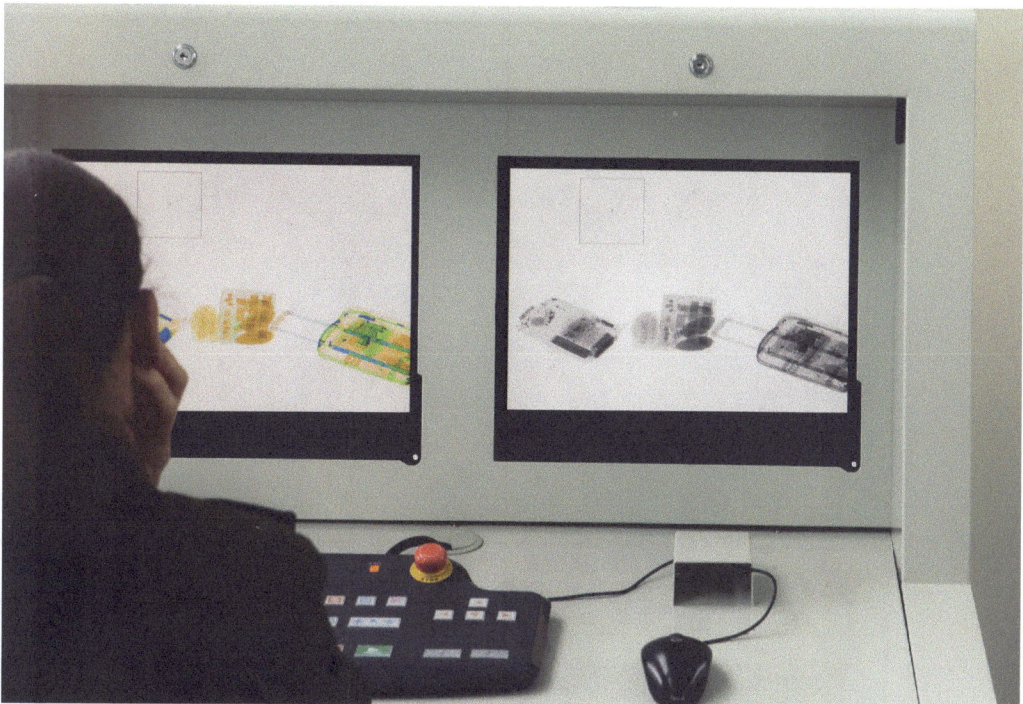

Figure 4.3. The rarity of weapons in carry-on luggage means that there are thousands of distractors for every one target. Such a pattern makes it more difficult for TSA officers' attention to select the target when it does appear. (Source: MediaProduction/Getty Images.)

task has unique characteristics. Doctors scan medical images looking for evidence of disease or damage. Recent advances in imaging technology allow for volumetric (three-dimensional) data so that this process of visual search is not merely searching a single flat image for a dark spot but doing that at the same time as "drilling" up and down between images in depth (for a review of visual search in medical imaging, see Wu & Wolfe, 2019).

A lifeguard at a busy beach or pool offers a second example (see Figure 4.4). Looking for swimmers in distress is a visual search problem as well, but the lifeguard must identify a particular kind of movement in a sea of similar movement, rather than a target that differs in color, shape, or texture. A recent study comparing experienced lifeguards to novices on a drowning detection task found that lifeguards were faster in drowning detection but did not differ in the paths of their eye movements (Laxton et al., 2021), suggesting that their training improved some other element of their search ability.

What Is Selected?

Treisman's model of visual search likens attention to glue – it binds features together. And it's spatial, because features are bound if and only if they are at the same location. Another useful metaphor – also spatial – likens attention to a flashlight beam (Norman, 1968; Posner et al., 1980). According to this metaphor, attention acts similarly to eye movements and selects spatial locations as it moves around a scene; anything that is in the "beam" of attention is selected for further processing.

Figure 4.4. A lifeguard at a crowded beach and a doctor evaluating a set of medical images each has difficult visual search tasks that demand finding rare targets among many similar distractors.

A conjunctive visual search task is an obvious case where we seem to move an attentional spotlight around a scene. Other studies used a cueing paradigm. The subject's task was simple: push a button as quickly as possible when a GO signal appeared somewhere on the screen. Sometimes a cue indicated where the GO signal would appear, and predictably, people were faster on those trials – they could have attention locked on the right location before the GO signal appeared. More interesting, the cue still helped even when subjects were instructed to keep their eyes locked on a crosshair at the center of the screen. (An eye tracker measured whether they really did so.) The cue nonetheless helped people respond faster, indicating that attention could be moved independently of eye movements (for a review, see Carrasco & Barbot, 2019).

Variations of the cueing paradigm have been deployed to investigate other questions about the spotlight. Can the spotlight be made smaller? Yes (Eriksen & St. James, 1986). Can it be spread out so that attentional resources are not simply on or off but spread in a gradient? Yes (Downing & Pinker, 1985). Is the spotlight continuously active, or does it seem as if it "blinks" periodically? It blinks (VanRullen et al., 2007). We will address the question of whether it can be divided in a later section.

Can Attention Select Objects, Not Just Space?

There is no doubt that attention selects locations, but does it always select locations? The spotlight metaphor does not seem useful in thinking about other studies in which attention seems to select an object or a feature of an object. Consider this: Have you ever used a pane of glass – perhaps a shop window or the glass in front of a framed picture – as a mirror? Doing so requires ignoring the contents of the shop window or picture and focusing on your reflection. But your reflection overlaps with the picture; they occupy the same spatial location, so both should fall in the attention "beam." You shouldn't be able to attend to one without the other.

In a laboratory demonstration of this phenomenon, Ulric Neisser and Robert Becklen (1975) had participants watch a monitor with two different video images superimposed. One video showed two people playing a hand-slapping game, and the other showed three people playing a ball-catching game. Participants were to attend to one video or the other, and they had to indicate when certain key events, such as the ball being thrown, happened in the video they were watching. Neisser and Becklen found that participants knew very little about the unattended video. Participants find it easy to attend to just one object of two, even if they are in overlapping spatial locations. If attention were directed by spatial location, that should not be possible.

One of the most famous studies in modern cognitive psychology further confirms that attention is not a simple spotlight. In fact, you may not perceive something that is *right in front of you* if you are not attending to it. In a dramatic study of this phenomenon, Daniel Simons and Chris Chabris (1999) asked people to watch a video of six people playing a ball-catching game. Three wore black shirts, and three wore white. Participants were to count the passes between the white team. The players moved constantly so that the task was quite attention demanding. In the middle of the video, a person in a gorilla suit walked right in the middle of the six people, thumped his chest, and sauntered off. As long as participants were engaged in the task that required close attention to the players, they did not perceive the gorilla, even though it was among the players; surely if attention is a spatial beam, the gorilla should have been attended to. This demonstration also shows that without attention, there is no perception, even for a stimulus we would think ought to be quite obvious. (For a review of such phenomena, see Matias et al. [2022].)

Figure 4.5. Stimuli of the sort used in Baylis and Driver's (1993) experiment.

Another more recent confirmation of the limits of a location-based account of visual attention came with a study of X-ray technicians evaluating an image for a possible tumor. A small image of a gorilla was embedded in the X-ray. Despite moving their eyes all around the image, twenty of the twenty-four radiologists did not notice the gorilla (Drew et al., 2013). Another more recent study (Williams et al., 2021) assessed whether radiologists would detect an unexpected abnormality (breast cancer) when they were looking for lung cancer. While their attention was focused on searching for lung cancer, 66 percent of radiologists did not detect the breast cancer, but only 3 percent missed it when instructed to search for a broad range of abnormalities. These results show that there is more to attention than simply moving one's attention around the scene like a spotlight (Wolfe et al., 2021; Wu & Wolfe, 2019).

Here's another example of how attention can be object based. If attention were directed to space, we would expect that the farther an object is from the location where attention is directed, the less attention it will get. If two object parts are equidistant from the location, they should get equal amounts of attention. For example, if your attention is focused on Judy's face, each of her hands would get the same amount of attention if they are equidistant from her face. Now, suppose that Judy has one hand behind her back, Sherry is standing next to her, and Sherry's left hand is the same distance from Judy's face as Judy's right hand. The spatial theory of attention would predict that Sherry's hand and Judy's hand will get equal amounts of attention because they are equidistant from Judy's face, the focus of attention. The object view of attention would predict that Judy's hand will get more attention. By looking at Judy's face, you select an object (Judy) for attention, and all parts of the object therefore get more attention.

Gordon Baylis and Jon Driver (1993) tested this prediction. They showed that it is harder to judge the relative distance of two corners when the corners are parts of different objects than when they are parts of the same object. In other words, they compared two tasks that should be identical for a purely location-based account but different for an object-based account.

On each trial, participants saw a picture similar to Figure 4.5. They were asked which angle was higher, the one on the left or the one on the right. Some participants were told to examine the white parts of the figure to make these judgments. For these participants, the figure on the left would require comparing parts (the angles) of a single object, but the figure on the right would require comparing parts of two separate objects. Other participants were told to compare the angles of the black parts of the figure; for these participants, the figure on the left required comparing parts of two objects, the figure on the right just one. Thus, Baylis and Driver were able to use the same stimulus for each condition; they got participants to interpret the figure as depicting one or two objects by using different instructions. The results showed that participants were reliably slower in making the judgment (by about thirty milliseconds) when the instruction led them to compare the angles of two objects rather than one object. Again, this result is consistent with the idea of attention being focused on objects, not regions of space.

The current consensus holds that we have two forms of visual attention (Jans et al., 2010), one that selects spatial locations and another that selects objects or object features (Berggren & Eimer, 2018; Chen, 2012; Maunsell & Treue, 2006). Evidence for this dissociation comes from the behavioral studies we've described but also from neuroscience studies in both humans (Hopf et al., 2004) and monkeys (Bichot et al., 2005; Bichot et al., 2015; Motter, 1993) in which feature-based attention relies on neural networks distinct from those that support spatial attention tasks. We are capable of engaging each of these forms of attention, depending on the task.

Stand-on-One-Foot Questions

4.1. What does selective visual attention select?
4.2. Summarize when a visual search is easy and when it's hard.

Questions That Require Two Feet

4.3. In many horror movies, the heroine calmly takes a shower and doesn't notice the scuffling sounds made by the clodhopper shoes of the zombie carrying the ax. How can this be explained as a problem of attention?
4.4. After reading this discussion, can you think of a situation from your own experience indicating that attention is directed to objects, not spatial locations?

What Happens to Unselected Stimuli?

Preview

As discussed, there are many stimuli in the world, but only some are selected for continued cognitive processing. In this section, we turn to those that are not selected. Do they pass entirely unnoticed, or do they somehow receive minimal processing to make sure they aren't worth redirecting attention to? When we are driving, we keep our eyes (and attention) on the road in front of us, but what if something important happens outside of our attention, like a child running into the street, chasing a ball? Many important real-world situations require us to notice an unattended object or feature and quickly redirect our attention. Because of this type of problem, researchers have investigated the cognitive fate of unselected stimuli.

Let us again consider the many perceptual stimuli that are currently bombarding your senses. Light is illuminating the book you are reading, but your eyes are also receiving the light reflected from whatever is in the background, behind the book. It appears that the unselected stimuli, although they activate your perceptual systems, are processed no further. This is probably what William James meant when he referred to attention as "withdrawal from some things" in his book more than 100 years ago (James, 1890):

> Everyone knows what attention is. It is the taking possession by the mind, in clear and
> vivid form, of one out of what seem several simultaneously possible objects or trains of

Figure 4.6. Even when your attention is focused on a task like looking at your phone, you are simultaneously monitoring sensory input to see if your attention should be redirected. These four people are looking at their own phones but probably monitoring what they are hearing in case any of their friends find something interesting, which should trigger a quick switch of attentional resources.

thought. Focalization, concentration, of consciousness are of its essence. It implies withdrawal from some things in order to deal effectively with others. (pp. 403–404)

What happens to those things we "withdraw from"? That question may initially strike you as odd – why should anything happen to unattended stimuli? Don't we just fail to perceive them? Wasn't that the point of the gorilla experiments? No attention, no perception, right? (See Figure 4.6.)

But that can't be quite right; if we simply missed everything we didn't pay attention to, we'd never notice anything we weren't paying attention to. That was the point of the "Free pizza downstairs!" example – even though you were attending to the book, surely you would perceive your friend entering the room and saying "free pizza!" Indeed, if there were absolutely no processing of stimuli that you were ignoring, you would have to periodically make a conscious decision to

Stimuli from environment

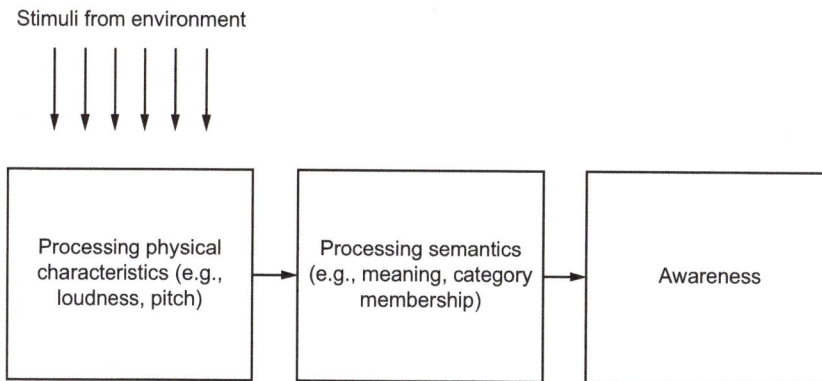

Figure 4.7. Simple diagram showing the assumed order in which sensory stimuli are processed.

monitor your environment to see if anything important was happening: "Let's see, is anyone shouting 'fire'? Is someone tapping me on the shoulder? Is water dripping on my head?" But what is it about your friend entering the room, or about your attention, that allows you to detect whether unselected stimuli should get more processing (your friend's voice) or are unimportant distractors from your current attentional focus (gorilla thumping its chest)?

We have to start our discussion of this problem by outlining an assumption. The assumption is that perception follows a processing course like that in Figure 4.7. It is assumed that the physical characteristics of a stimulus are processed first. For visual information, these would be shape, color, spatial location, and so on. For auditory information, they would be loudness, pitch, spatial location, and so on. After we know the physical characteristics of the stimulus, more processing is necessary to determine what the object is and its meaning; that shiny red globe is an apple, which means that it is edible, it has seeds, it is a member of the category *fruit*, and so on. As it turns out, this assumption (first physical, then meaning) is not quite right, which we will discuss later, but it is useful as a rough approximation as we consider what happens to unselected stimuli.

An early hypothesis held that attention acts as a filter, stopping most of the information before it reaches awareness. More recently, as we've come to think of attention as a set of processes or functions with different qualities, we've shifted away from a filter metaphor. We've gotten better at detecting what Chun and Marois (2002) call the dark side of visual attention (stimuli or features which receive minimal processing and are often ignored), but we've also come to realize that it's too simple to treat incoming information as a single processing stream that can be stopped or allowed through, as a filter might. Let's follow the scientific story so we can see how attention researchers have come to this conclusion.

One way to separate filter theories is according to what they let in and what they keep out. A window screen lets a summer breeze through but keeps bugs out. A water filter lets fresh water through but keeps particles and impurities out. For filter theories of attention, the location of the filter is crucial. In **early filter** theories, the sensory characteristics of all stimuli are processed, and then they hit the filter. Most stimuli are not processed past that point, but the filter allows through attended stimuli for processing to determine their semantic characteristics (their meaning), whereupon they enter awareness.

In **late filter** models, all stimuli are processed to determine both their physical and semantic characteristics, and only then do the stimuli hit the filter; the stimuli that are attended to pass the filter and are allowed to enter awareness. You can see that the key difference between these theories is the location of the filter – either before or after the meaning of the stimuli is processed.

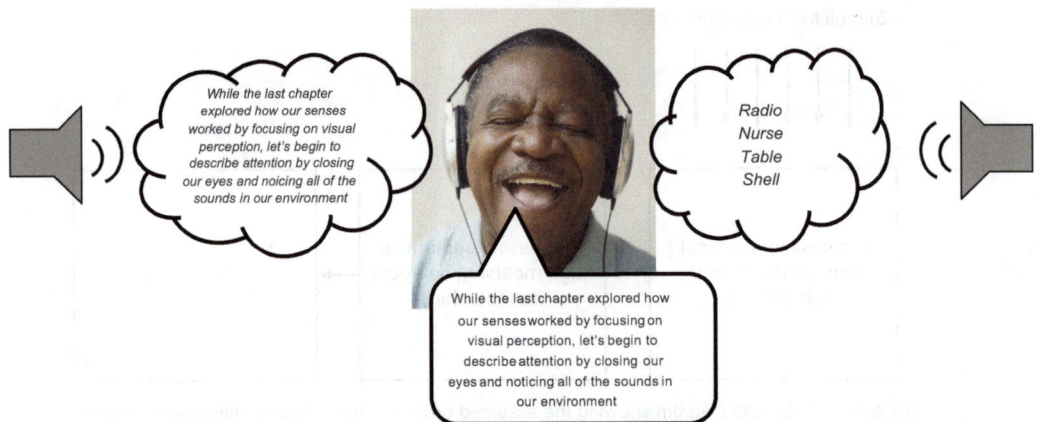

Figure 4.8. The dichotic listening procedure. (Source: Jose Luis Pelaez Inc./Blend Images/Getty Images.)

Early Filter Theories

What evidence supports early filter theories? One of the first studies relevant to this question was performed by Cherry (1953) using the **dichotic listening task**, depicted in Figure 4.8. Participants listened to material on headphones. Each earpiece played a different message, and participants were asked to pay attention to just one of the messages. To ensure they were attending as instructed, they had to **shadow** the message, meaning they had to repeat the message aloud. Thus, as they were shadowing what they heard over the right earpiece, another message was playing in the left earpiece. Later, participants were asked to report what they could about the message from the unattended ear. Performance was terrible. Cherry found that participants didn't even notice if the unattended message switched into another language or if the message was played backward. Participants did notice if a pure tone replaced the unattended speech or if the gender of the speaker changed.

Cherry concluded that unattended speech is not analyzed to a semantic level; that is, it is not analyzed for meaning. Instead, it is analyzed for physical characteristics, such as pitch and loudness. Thus, if you're focusing attention on the message in the left ear, you won't know anything about the meaning of what's coming in the right ear, but you can tell when it becomes physically different from speech, as when pitch changes (because the gender of the speaker has changed). A dramatic example of the extent to which people don't know the meaning of unattended speech was provided by Moray (1959), who played the same word list for participants in the unattended ear thirty-five times. On a later test, participants didn't recognize any of them. This lack of recognition despite extreme repetition would certainly suggest that those items are filtered out before the meaning is determined.

Let's focus on the idea that all stimuli are analyzed for their physical characteristics, but only a limited number (those to which you attend) are also analyzed for their semantic content. Recall that unattended stimuli must be processed in case something important requires your attention. If you are in a crowd and someone shouts "Fire!" the loudness of the unattended message will make you shift your attention to the source of the sound. But presumably if someone merely said "Fire," you wouldn't hear it because the word doesn't stand out from any other stimuli.

An interesting variation of the dichotic listening procedure has been applied recently not just to investigate how people use attention as a filter but to apply the fact that some stimuli always get through the filter and use that to "jam" the system. When we speak, we not only produce sound

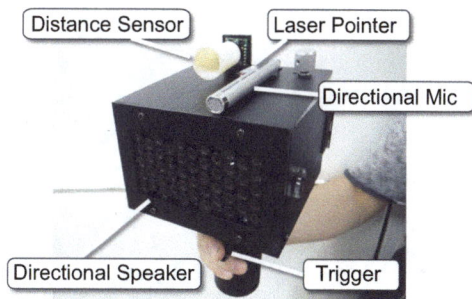

Figure 4.9. The SpeechJammer uses our inability to filter out our own voices (slightly delayed) when we are speaking to stop us from speaking. (Source: K. Kurihara and K. Tsukada (2012), SpeechJammer: A system utilizing artificial speech disturbance with delayed auditory feedback, http://arxiv.org/abs/1202.6106.)

but also pay attention to the sound our voice makes. Think of this auditory feedback as speech we can't "unattend." If our speech is recorded and played back at a very small delay (just a few hundred milliseconds), it is often quite difficult to separate the two streams of our voice, the one we are generating and the one played to us. The result is that we stop speaking altogether. The inventors of a device called the SpeechJammer (Kurihara & Tsukada, 2012; Figure 4.9) paired a directional microphone with a directional speaker to disturb the speech of a single individual at a distance. They propose that this device could be used to stop people from speaking in contexts such as libraries or facilitate turn-taking in meetings. I'm sure you could come up with your own uses for such a speech-jamming gun.

Late Filter Theories

Late filter theories, in contrast to early filter theories, suggest that all stimuli are evaluated not just for their physical characteristics but for their meaning (Deutsch & Deutsch, 1963; Norman, 1968). If the meaning is important, the stimulus might break into ongoing processing and demand attention. It turns out that this theory is not correct. But if it's wrong, why is it that when you're talking to a friend and a second friend says your name, your name attracts your attention? This phenomenon is called the **cocktail party effect** (for a review, see Bronkhorst, 2015; Figure 4.10). Isn't it the meaning (not the loudness or pitch) of what your second friend said that attracted your attention? This phenomenon works not just for your name but for other topics of importance to you. For example, if you have been thinking about *Star Wars* and someone at the next table in a restaurant starts talking about it, you might notice.

This effect has been tested in the laboratory using the dichotic listening task (Moray, 1959; Wood & Cowan, 1995; Röer & Cowan, 2021). While the participant shadowed a message in one ear, the other earpiece played something in the unattended ear and then added a message with the participant's name. Participants sometimes (but not always) noticed their own name on the unattended channel; about 33 percent showed the effect. Case closed? Our own name is processed, even when unattended, showing that the filter can be late (i.e., items processed for meaning before being filtered?).

Not so fast. Another way to interpret this result is that about one-third of the participants don't follow the instructions; they switch their attention to the unattended channel every now and then. This possibility seems likely because when Wood and Cowan told people that they should be ready for new instructions during the task, 80 percent detected their name. The increase probably resulted from more participants sampling the channel they were not supposed to attend to because

Figure 4.10. Noticing one's own name amid a sea of noise is also called the cocktail party effect. (Source: skynesher/E +/Getty Images.)

they were listening for the new instructions. Another experiment in which the task was a search through visual stimuli showed that one's name (and other emotional targets) don't seem effective in grabbing attention (Harris et al., 2004).

Other studies (e.g., Dupoux et al., 2003; Franconeri et al., 2005) have indicated that effects of the unattended channel are observed when that information is especially salient due to its physical characteristics, which causes participants to switch attention to the unattended channel; for example, your name might be said on the unattended channel in a slightly louder voice. Still other studies put safeguards in to ensure that participants *weren't* switching attention, for example, by examining their shadowing performance; if participants stumbled when they were saying aloud the content they were supposed to attend to, researchers reasoned that error might reflect a moment the participant directed attention to the other channel. When researchers cut those data out of the analysis, there was very little evidence for semantic processing of unattended information (e.g., Lachter et al., 2004). In other words, what looked like a late filter was in fact switching attention.

Researchers in this area all face a significant challenge: People have difficulty sustaining attention *only* to one thing. The experimenter tells the subject to attend only to the voice coming from the left earpiece, and the subject gives it an honest try . . . but it seems almost impossible not to take brief acoustic "peeks" at the right earpiece.

This insight – that it's really hard to keep attention in just one place in these experiments – helps answer our original question: Is the filter early or late? The current consensus is that rather than one linear system of input in which a filter is inserted at some point in the line, it's instead useful to imagine several forms of attention operating at the same time (Chun et al., 2011), each of which is capable of selection and facilitating further processing. The first line is active and sustained, like your attention to these words in this space on the page right now. This type of attention is often called **endogenous**, in that it is driven by an internal goal and controlled by the observer. The second is more passive and transient, flicking around a scene to check for anything that needs noticing. This type of attention is called **exogenous**, as it is driven by environmental cues. The exogenous system is on the lookout for any stimuli that might merit a switch of attention (that friend with the free pizza announcement), while the endogenous is focused on the task at hand.

Imagine you are walking two dogs. The first is a Great Dane that slowly and regally walks down the path, obediently taking your directions (endogenous). The second is a yippy, distractible terrier puppy, flitting around, barking at every leaf and bird (exogenous). You mostly ignore your puppy's little yips, but if there is sustained and focused barking, you might take a closer look (and direct the Great Dane to do the same). This two-systems approach explains how people can voluntarily allocate attention to an area of space when told it is likely to contain a target (using their endogenous system), but they are unable to ignore distracting or uninformative cues (Barbot et al., 2011; Yeshurun & Rashal, 2010; McCormick et al., 2018) because these cues alert the exogenous system.

The systems view is now the modern consensus (Carrasco, 2011, 2014) as it captures a few points of agreement about attention. First, attention is not a single unitary and linear construct such that it could be described as stimuli going through a filter. Second, separate systems of attention, each with their own characteristics, better describes both modern studies of visual attention, which precisely vary the timing of visual cues and precisely measure responses, and older dichotic listening tasks in auditory attention, whereas the filter metaphor only works better with the older tasks. Finally, while attention is clearly selective, the systems view of exogenous and endogenous better explains experiments in which performance is not simply unselected stimuli and selected ones but suggests that these different forms of attention are limited not by a filter on a type of stimuli but by more general cognitive resources (Lavie, 2005; Donovan et al., 2020). In other words, exogenous and endogenous attention may be different types of attention, but they seem to share the same pool of processing resources. This notion of attentional resources leads us to our next section.

Stand-on-One-Foot Questions

4.5. What is some evidence that the attentional filter is early, and what is some evidence that it is late?

4.6. What is the difference between endogenous and exogenous attention?

Questions That Require Two Feet

4.7. What are the unselected stimuli in your environment right now? What is an environmental change that could drive your exogenous attention?

4.8. Describe your attention when you are listening to music while doing your homework in terms of endogenous and exogenous attention. Do the type of music and type of homework matter?

In What Way Is Attention a Limited Resource?

Preview

As we described in the previous section, older theories described unattended stimuli as caught by a filter, and so they undergo no further processing. Newer theories describe attention as a set of processes that are separate but dependent. Unselected stimuli are processed (or not) depending on the attention demanded by the selected stimuli. Attention is not a filter but fuel for deeper thought. Assuming attention can behave like a fuel raises several questions. First, how do mental processes compete for limited attentional resources when we divide our attention between tasks? Second, can we improve our use of attentional resources through practice so that some tasks become automatic and so require less or perhaps no fuel? Finally, given that people do switch attention back and forth between tasks, how does task switching apply to situations where we multitask? As we'll see, although it *feels* like we divide attention when we do two tasks simultaneously, we are probably rapidly switching attention rather than truly dividing it. Your intuition about attention is more accurate when it comes to automaticity; we really can, with practice, reduce the attentional demands of a task. Finally, we'll see that switching between multiple tasks always carries a cost to performance.

Let's introduce the next metaphor of attention with another thought experiment. You are driving to an unfamiliar place using GPS. You are also chatting with a friend in the passenger seat and listening to the radio. As you get closer to your destination, you might feel the need to turn off your radio and pause your conversation so as to concentrate your attention on the directions. It's as if you had a limited amount of attention, and you detected that as one task became more demanding (i.e., used more attention), the three tasks would now cumulatively use more attention than you have, disrupting one of the tasks. By turning off the radio and pausing the conversation, you save that attention so that you can use it on the task you most care about: navigating successfully to your destination (Figure 4.11). In this section, we consider attention as a limited resource. We consider three ways to investigate this feature of attention. First, when we divide attention, we can observe how two tasks can compete for limited attentional resources. Second, we can ask which conditions reduce attentional demands for certain tasks and when tasks become automatic. Finally, given what we know about divided attention and automaticity, how do we multitask?

Psychologists have likened attention to mental fuel that makes continued cognitive processing possible. This definition is close to the way researchers thought about attention when they first started considering its limited nature more than 100 years ago (Bryan & Harter, 1897) and has been central to formulations since (Kahneman, 1973; Moray, 1967). In our everyday use of the word, we often refer to attention as being limited.

What can we say about the particular way in which attention is limited? We can make a few predictions consistent with a limited capacity for attention and with our own experience:

Attention can be divided and distributed to more than one task at a time. We can drive while listening to the radio. We can walk while talking to friends and deciding how many slices of pizza we want.

With sufficient practice, a task will require fewer attentional resources. Although mentally taxing to beginners, driving becomes automatic when they are experienced. Even walking was once an attentionally demanding task (see Figure 4.12).

Figure 4.11. If attention is a resource, this driver has to be using up his limited capacity. (Source: TommL/E+/Getty Images.)

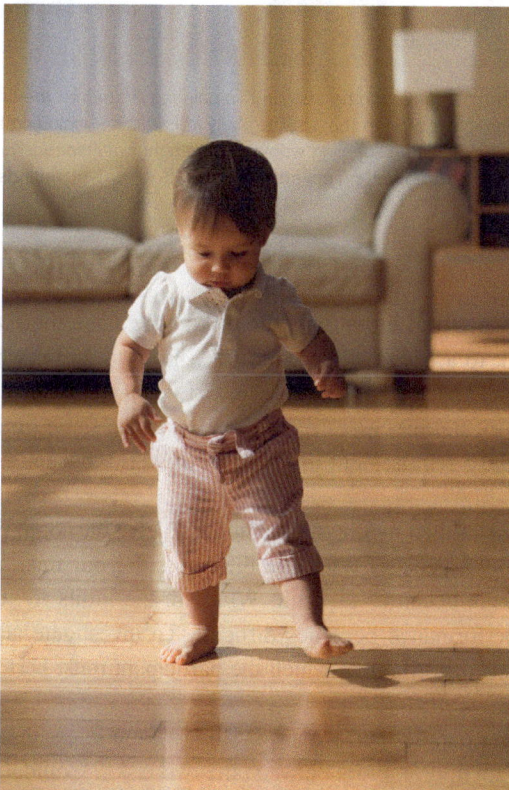

Figure 4.12. Karen Adolph and colleagues (2012) have investigated how toddlers learn to walk. Infants just beginning to walk fall an average of thirty-two times an hour even as they are often concentrating on staying upright. At the beginning, walking is quite a challenging task. (Source: Jose Luis Pelaez Inc./Blend Images/Getty Images.)

These two assumptions sound reasonable and fit with our everyday experience, but we cannot be sure they are true. As cognitive psychologists have studied them, it seems that the second is true, but the first turns out to be tricky to test.

Figure 4.13. Multitasking is not a recent phenomenon; it can be seen in this painting *Alexander the Great Looking on Apelles Painting Campaspe* by Willem van Haecht, dated to the 1630s. Many individuals – including those in the paintings! – are engaged in multitasking. For example, the kneeling woman to the right simultaneously reaches into the cabinet, offers something to her friend, and tries to avoid getting poked in the eye. (Source: Netherlands Institute for Art History.)

Divided Attention

It seems obvious that it is possible to perform more than one task at the same time. After all, you frequently do two things at once: talk to a friend while you drive, listen to music while you read, walk and chew gum, look at your phone and . . . do everything else. Even if we feel like we are doing these tasks at the same time, are the mental processes really running at the same time, in parallel? Dividing our attention might seem like a requirement of the modern world, but multitasking has a long history (see Figure 4.13).

A good way to learn about the limited nature of attention is to give the cognitive system too much to do and then observe the consequences. What are the limits to your muscles? Let's add weights and observe when performance becomes difficult. What are the limits to your attention? Let's add tasks and observe when performance becomes difficult. To investigate attention in the laboratory, researchers use a **dual task paradigm** in which the participant must perform two tasks at once.

Here's the key question about parallel performance: How do you know that you're really dividing attention and not switching attention rapidly between the two tasks? Couldn't you listen to the GPS, drive the car, and talk to your friend one task at a time, but switch among them so rapidly and seamlessly that it seems as if you're doing them simultaneously?

Researchers have tried to get around this problem by using continuous tasks rather than discrete tasks. A **discrete task** has an identifiable beginning and ending, and there is usually a pause

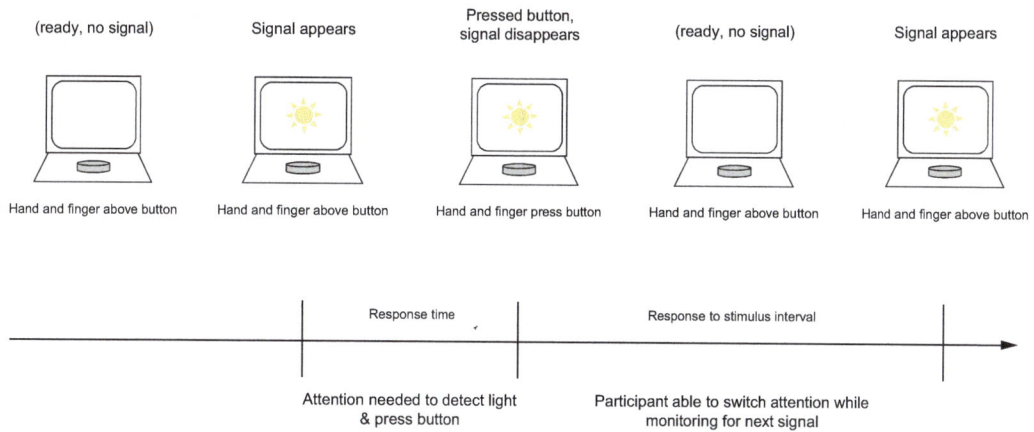

(ready, no signal)	Signal appears	Pressed button, signal disappears	(ready, no signal)	Signal appears
Hand and finger above button	Hand and finger above button	Hand and finger press button	Hand and finger above button	Hand and finger above button

Response time — Attention needed to detect light & press button

Response to stimulus interval — Participant able to switch attention while monitoring for next signal

Figure 4.14. Simple response time task with a visual signal and a button-press response.

between the end of one trial and the beginning of the next. For example, in a simple response time task, a stimulus is presented (a light appears on a computer monitor or a tone sounds), and the participant responds by pressing a button as quickly as possible when the stimulus occurs. Figure 4.14 shows a **response to stimulus interval**, which is the period of time after the participant has responded but before the next stimulus appears. During this period, the participant waits for the next stimulus to appear and could easily switch attention to some other task. Even if the researcher makes the next stimulus appear immediately after a response, the participant can simply switch attention to the other task at this point, effectively taking a break from this task.

A **continuous task** (Figure 4.15), in contrast, uses a continuous stream of stimuli and often demands a continuous stream of responses. For example, in a pursuit tracking task, a target moves on a computer screen, and the participant must chase the target with a cursor controlled by a joystick. Performance is measured as the distance between the cursor and the target. The target is always moving, so it would seem that even a momentary lapse of attention would make performance suffer. Another continuous task is touch typing. In one experiment, a skilled typist could recite nursery rhymes aloud while typing with only a 10 percent loss of typing speed (Shaffer, 1975). This study was meant to show that typing required little attention for a highly skilled typist.

The problem with such evidence, as noted when we discussed filter theories, is that nothing guarantees that participants will treat continuous tasks as continuous (Broadbent, 1982; Welford, 1980). For example, experienced typists often report that once they've seen a word, they don't really need to think about the word as they type it, and a number of studies indicate that this is true (Salthouse, 1984). Just because the hands are typing at a steady rate doesn't mean that attentional resources are needed at a steady rate. In the case of typing, it seems likely that attention is needed in bursts; a burst of attention might be needed to read a word, and then very little attention would be needed to type the word.

Thus, using dual task paradigms does not seem to guarantee that people can share attentional resources between tasks. No matter how much it looks as if the participant is dividing attention between two tasks, it will remain possible that the participant is rapidly switching attention between the tasks. Thus, we wouldn't say that people *can't* divide attention between two tasks but rather that it's hard to be certain that they can. (Note that we've said nothing about how *well* you perform multiple tasks at once – we'll get to that question later.)

Follow traget

Hand and finger around joystick

Figure 4.15. A sample continuous task, called a pursuit tracking task, requires a participant to move a joystick to control a circle so that it keeps a moving star inside the circle.

Automaticity

Another strong assumption we make is that the attentional demand of a task is reduced with practice. Driving a car may have taxed your attentional resources when you were first learning, as you watched for oncoming cars, made sure to stay in the center of your lane, checked your mirrors and speed, monitored the pressure you applied to the gas pedal, read the road signs, and so on. With enough practice, however, these tasks became **automatic**. Cognitive psychologists define automaticity as having two signature characteristics: A process is automatic if it requires few attentional resources and if it happens without intention (Shiffrin & Schneider, 1977). Indeed, simple tasks that you now take for granted because they are automatic once took great concentration, as shown in Figure 4.16.

If a task takes few attentional resources, you should be able to perform several automatic tasks at once. As we noted, an experienced driver might drive while talking on a cell phone, listening to the radio, and eating French fries – an accomplished task, if not attractive to watch. In addition, an automatic process that happens without intention occurs regardless of whether you want it to: If certain conditions are present in the environment, the automatic process occurs. For example, on occasion, a passenger in Willingham's car will slam their foot against the floorboard in a vain effort to stop the car, due to some trifling matter such as an oncoming truck. Willingham always informs such passengers that their foot motion is perfectly understandable; the proper stimulus was present in the environment (danger) to bring about an action (braking), even though the action was futile. How do we know that automaticity has these characteristics (it requires little or no attention, and it happens without intention)?

First, let's consider whether automatic processes really require no attention at all. How would we determine if a task uses no attention? One way is to give people more of the automatic task to do; if it really doesn't require attention, the extra burden will pose no problem. Early studies on automaticity used a visual search task (Shiffrin & Schneider, 1977) similar to the types of tasks you saw early in this chapter when you searched for the small letter Q. Shiffrin and Schneider used conjunctive (and,

Figure 4.16. This girl recently learned to tie her shoes, and it still requires some attentional resources. With daily practice, it will soon become automatic, just like other tasks that once required a lot of attentional resources, like riding a bike.

therefore, serial) searches. The "extra burden" was the number of nontargets in the display. As those increased, search times increased, because subjects had to check each character one by one. But with lots of practice (around 2,000 trials), the search became automatic, and that extra burden didn't affect performance. Response time didn't increase when the figure included more distractors.

Another type of experiment asks participants to perform some *other* task and then add the one we think is automatic; if it's truly automatic, it shouldn't affect performance on the first task. If walking is automatic, you should walk just as well if we add another task, say, reciting a poem from memory. If a task is not automatic (like studying for an exam), it will be disrupted by adding another attentionally demanding task (like reciting a poem). This experimental test of automaticity allows us to take a candidate mental task that may feel like it requires no attention and test whether that is the case in the controlled conditions of the laboratory. For example, letter identification (Pashler & Johnston, 1989) seems to be automatic, but judging facial attractiveness (Jung et al., 2012) and identifying familiar faces (Jung et al., 2013) do not appear to be automatic.

The second criterion for automaticity is that it happens without intention. An automatic mental process occurs without you meaning to do it, if the conditions that trigger the process are in the environment. As we mentioned earlier, letter identification is automatic. You have practiced the mental task of seeing a letter and identifying it so much that it is impossible to see the letter R and refuse to identify it as an R. One way to experience this phenomenon is via one of the most famous demonstrations in psychology, called the Stroop (1935) task. Your job is to name the ink color of printed letters. People are typically able to do this task much faster with Figure 4.17a than with Figure 4.17b. The reason is that reading the names of the colors happens without intention and conflicts with their attempt to name the ink colors.

Why, if this task is automatic, does it then interfere with the task of identifying the color of the ink, when in the previous section, we suggest that if a task is automatic, it will not interfere with other tasks? In this case, the automatic task does not interfere by using attention. Rather, it interferes because a similar response is needed for each task. Both the assigned task (name the ink color) and the automatic task (read the printed color name) prompt a response of reporting a color name. The interference happens via response selection, a process we'll take up in the next section, on multitasking and switching attention.

(a) Read the printed words:

red blue orange purple

orange blue green red

blue purple green red

orange blue red green

purple orange red blue

green red blue purple

(b)

Say the <u>COLOR</u>, not the word:

PURPLE	ORANGE	BLUE
BLUE	RED	PURPLE
BLACK	GREEN	YELLOW
GREEN	BLUE	RED
ORANGE	YELLOW	GREEN

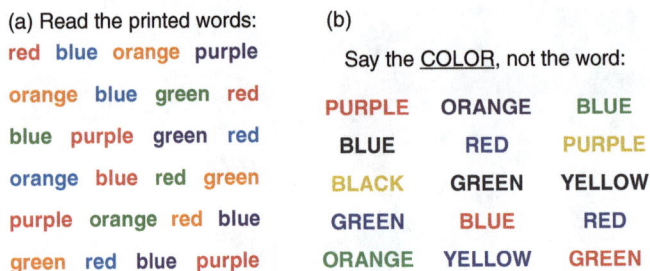

Figure 4.17. The Stroop task is when observers are asked to name the color of the ink for the following lists of words. Since reading the word takes place without intention, it interferes with the correct response. For example, when the word BLUE is printed in red ink, as in (b), it is difficult to read BLUE and say "red."

Thus, there is good evidence that with practice, some tasks use less of our limited attention. The exact mechanism by which this happens is still under debate. Some researchers have suggested that some of the intermediate steps in a complex series of processes are eventually eliminated (Anderson, 1993; Newell & Rosenbloom, 1981), whereas others suggest that a second process that does not demand attention develops more slowly and finally takes over the task (Willingham, 1998b). The differences between gaining automaticity in different types of tasks suggest that attention is not the only process that changes as tasks become automatic.

Gordon Logan (1988, 2002; see also Chun, 2011) suggested a different account of automaticity: Increasing facility with well-practiced tasks may reflect an increasing role of memory. For example, if we asked you how many letters are in the word *quotidian*, you would have to spell it to yourself and count the letters. If we asked you the same question a few minutes later, you wouldn't go through the same process; you'd remember what you had said earlier and say it again. Logan suggested that memory may play just such a role in automaticity. In every task, memory competes with slower processes that calculate an answer to the task at hand. As you practice, you have more answers in memory, making it increasingly likely that on any given trial, you can use an answer from memory and not need to do the calculation. Attention and memory definitely have a close relationship (for a recent review, see Oberauer, 2019), as anyone trying to remember something they learned when they weren't paying attention can attest. We'll return to the question of how they are related as we describe short-term memory in the next chapter.

Multitasking and Switching Attention

The previous section investigated whether we can divide attention or practice tasks so that they do not require attention. In this section, rather than treating task switching as due to unruly people not following instructions, we will study the switching itself. When we study multitasking, we acknowledge that task switching is either unavoidable or something people want to do, and we study its characteristics. How do we successfully multitask, and what are the costs to performance? How much control do we have over each of these tasks?

We'll focus on two questions:

- Can people perform multiple tasks at once without changing how well they do each task and how much attention each task requires?
- Can people efficiently switch their attention between tasks as they choose?

As it turns out, the answer to each of these questions is mostly no.

The first bit of evidence that we can't multitask without a cost is that even if one task passes our tests for automaticity, we can't select a response for two different tasks at once. Whenever we need to select a response, we must switch attention to that task. For example, while you can drive and operate the car radio at the same time, you cannot decide whether to change the station away from ABBA while you decide whether to stop at the yellow light; you must pick one task. It's also worth noting that interference is observed not only with relatively complex tasks like choosing a song on the radio. Even if the tasks are as simple as "push a button when you see a light" and "push another button when you hear a tone," you still observe interference, and the interference is still due to **response selection**, even though the choices are as simple as "push" or "don't push" (Pashler, 1994).

This conclusion might seem counterintuitive to those of us who are habitual multitaskers (i.e., all of us), so it is worth describing the experiments in some detail. Here's a typical experiment to test whether we can multitask (based on a series of experiments by Pashler, e.g., Pashler, 1994). Here are your two tasks: If a light turns on, you are to press a button. If you hear a tone, you depress a foot pedal. The tasks come in little bursts. You see the light, and then you hear the tone. You don't know how much time will separate the light and the tone, however. That delay is called the **stimulus onset asynchrony**, or the time between when one task's stimulus appears (its onset) and another task's stimulus in a dual task experiment. We want to know whether we truly multitask, doing both of these mental tasks at once. It turns out that we can multitask with some parts of tasks, but not with others.

What do we mean by "parts of tasks"? As simple as these tasks are, they still have three components: You must perceive the stimulus (is the light on?), select the response (what do I do when the light is on?), and execute the response (what movement will depress the button?). By varying the stimulus onset asynchrony, the authors can vary the overlap in the stages of the light–button and tone–pedal tasks. In other words, we might illuminate the light and sound the tone simultaneously, in which case you must do the perception part of both tasks at once. But suppose we illuminate the light then wait a bit before sounding the tone. You've finished perceiving the light and you're selecting the response to the light as the tone comes on (and you must perceive it). So by varying stimulus onset asynchrony, researchers can examine interference among different stages of these simple tasks.

As depicted in Figure 4.18, a common finding across these studies is that while we may be able to perceive two things at once, and we may be able to generate two actions (e.g., button presses), we are unable to *select responses* for two different tasks at the same time. This leads to a delay, or a **psychological refractory period**, of a given task to allow response selection in another task.

It's especially important to note how simple these tasks are. If we observed a cost during simultaneous response selection of two really complicated tasks – say, writing an essay and reciting Christmas carols by heart – one might argue that the problem is not response selection. The problem is working memory – we're seeing interference because the participants just have too much to do. But the light–button and tone–pedal tasks are each so simple that it would seem participants ought to be able to keep both tasks in working memory at the same time. Hence, the interference we observe is not due to working memory being overwhelmed. It's because the cognitive system simply can't select more than one task at a time.

It may be that you push buttons a little slower in the lab task described, and maybe you're a little slower to switch radio stations if you're coming up to a light. But how big a deal is that, really? For example, how dangerous is it to text and drive? And what about divided attention for academic work? Does it matter if you're switching between X (formerly Twitter), Snapchat, and the teacher or switching between looking out the window and reading this textbook? Is texting in class really that

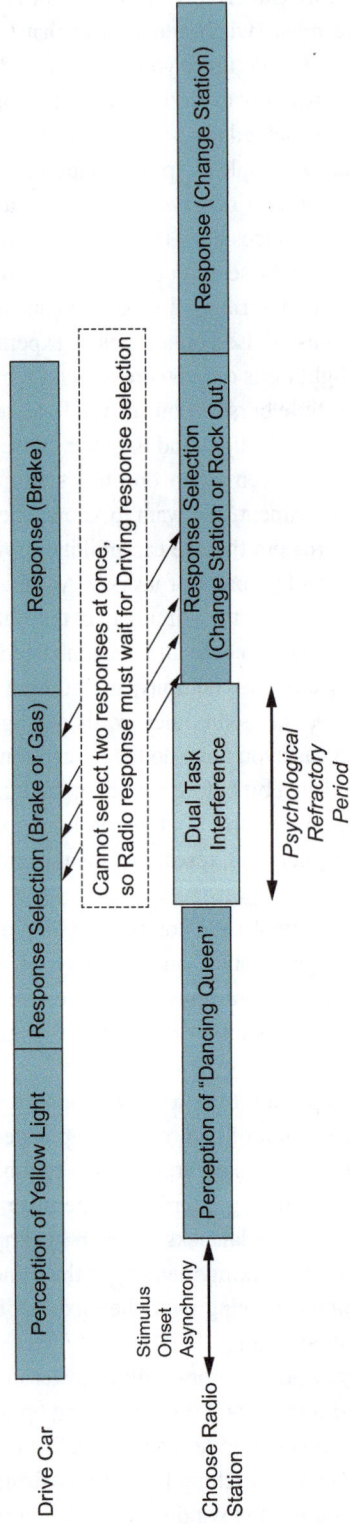

Figure 4.18. A schematic of how someone might be driving and listening to the radio but cannot decide whether to stop or go for a yellow light at the same time as deciding whether to change the radio station.

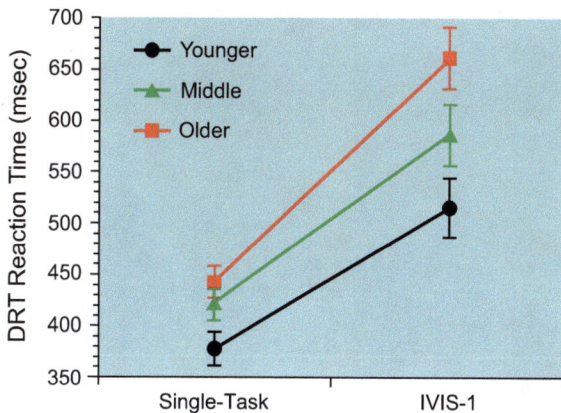

Figure 4.19. Detection response task reaction time. Participants were monitored when a red light was illuminated and clicked a button that was attached to their thumbs when they saw the light. The single task reflects performance when subjects were just driving. Dual tasks show reaction times when subjects were using the voice-activated system (IVIS) to complete a task, such as dialing a number from their contacts or tuning their radio. Notice that younger participants are faster than older ones, but everyone's performance is reduced (they are slower) when using the voice-activated system, even after five days of practice. (Source: D. L. Strayer, J. M. Cooper, J. Turrill, J. R. Coleman, and R. J. Hopman [2016], Talking to your car can drive you to distraction, *Cognitive Research: Principles and Implications*, 1[1], 16.)

much worse than daydreaming? To answer these questions, we look to studies that are more similar to these real-world tasks than the lights-and-buttons variety but still offer some control over the stimuli participants see and the opportunity to measure performance precisely. Driving simulators offer one such environment. Another is a typical classroom lecture under different multitasking conditions. Let's consider each.

Strayer and colleagues (2016) investigated the effects of interacting with a vehicle through voice commands (see Figure 4.19). This type of system has the benefit of being "hands-free" – you are not fussing with texting on a small phone screen, and you don't need to move your eyes to issue voice commands or listen. But as you've learned from reading this chapter, attention isn't determined solely by where your eyes are, and tasks can be attentionally demanding without being physically demanding. People in the study were trained to use voice commands to interact with a vehicle information system (tuning the radio, calling a contact, etc.). Participants in this study were trained and familiarized with the vehicle and the tasks one day (and baseline performance measures were collected) and then given the vehicles to drive around for five days, during which they practiced using the voice-activated in-vehicle information system. Then they returned to the lot to be tested again. To examine whether using voice commands while driving was subject to the typical costs of multitasking, subjects were asked to monitor a red light and click a button when they noticed it illuminated. After five days of training with the voice commands, they were faster at noticing the light than they were at the beginning of training. However, when they were interacting with the voice commands, they were still much slower than they were when not using voice commands.

What about switching attention in the classroom? Sana et al. (2013) conducted a study in which students attended a university-style lecture (a forty-five-minute lecture on meteorology) and took notes on a laptop (see Figure 4.20). Half of the participants were given a series of other tasks designed to mimic typical student web browsing, such as checking TV schedules. Those who multitasked scored 11 percent lower on a comprehension test given immediately following the lecture. Certainly one reason for this lower performance is distraction: You're paying attention to the internet instead of the lecture. We also know that switching attention from one task (lecture) to another (evaluating a shoe sale on Amazon) slows the response to either. Whether the psychological refractory period and multitasking switch costs are academically meaningful and outweigh the

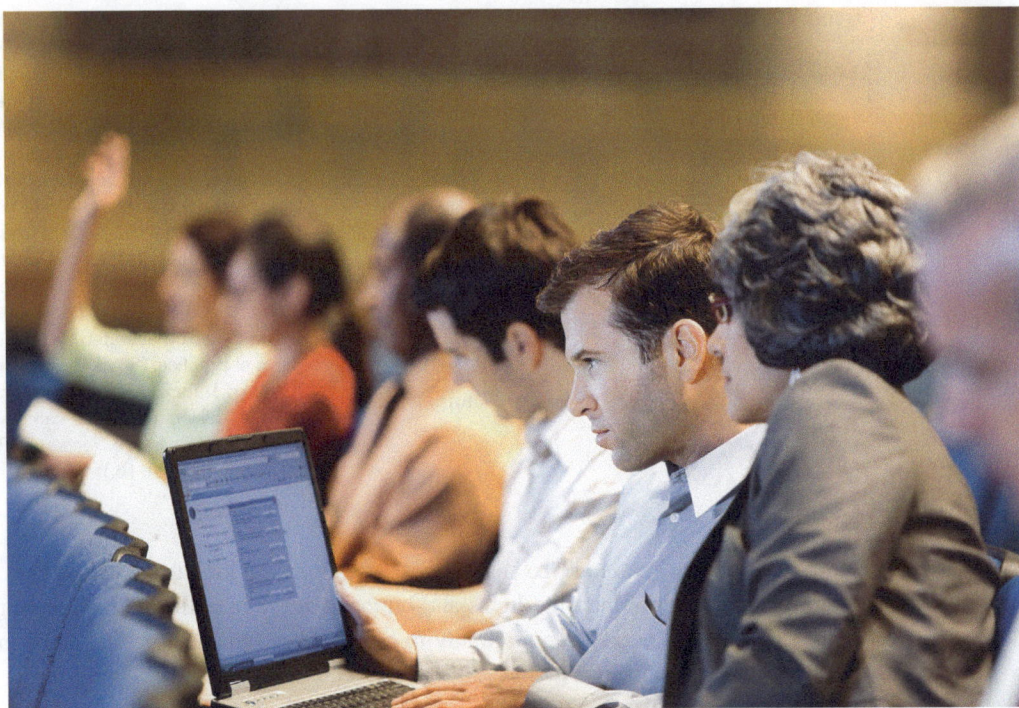

Figure 4.20. Laptops can be a great tool for taking notes, but they can also be distracting, not only for the user but for nearby peers as well. (Source: Robert Nicholas/OJO Images/Getty Images.)

possible benefits of laptops in the classroom, however, remains an open question (Gaudreau et al., 2014; Ravizza et al., 2017).

Translating the basic research from the cognitive psychology laboratory to the classroom can be difficult and suffers from many of the methodological difficulties we mentioned in Chapter 2. Certainly nonacademic use of a laptop during a class is associated with lower academic performance, but is that due to laptop use or some third variable, such as motivation, preparation, or academic ability? Initial research does indicate that greater internet use during class reduces exam grades regardless of academic ability or motivation (Ravizza et al., 2014; Jamet et al., 2020), but weighing the costs and the benefits of laptop use in classrooms depends on how they are used (Day et al., 2021).

In addition, isolating the cognitive elements of the process of multitasking in a real-world learning situation might miss out on some of the important social elements of attention. For example, as many students engaged in remote learning on Zoom during parts of the COVID-19 pandemic, they were learning on laptops instead of in person and therefore likely engaged in more multitasking than they might have done in a classroom. But they were also in a state of heightened anxiety as a global pandemic disrupted many other family routines and raised thoughts of illness and concern over vulnerable loved ones. The cognitive elements are only one part of the puzzle of understanding multitasking in real-world learning environments.

To conclude, attention is continued cognitive processing. It is selective in that it selects some stimuli for further cognitive processing while leaving other stimuli unselected. However, those unselected stimuli still get some processing, both based on their basic sensory characteristics (early filter theories) and based on their meaning (late filter theories). We can also treat attention as limited, although we can do more within those limits by practicing attentionally demanding tasks until they become mostly automatic. Finally, we would love to be able to divide attention, but the evidence points to the reality that we don't divide attention but instead switch between tasks, and there are costs of trying to do so in real-world situations, such as driving and in the classroom.

Stand-on-One-Foot Questions

4.9.   Can people divide attention between more than one task? How is this known?

4.10.   What is the key condition for automaticity to develop?

4.11.   Is driving a discrete task or a continuous task? Whichever way you answer, what would have to change about the task of driving to turn it into the other kind of task?

Questions That Require Two Feet

4.12.   I once heard a comic remark that he thought it was funny that people turn the radio off when they are looking for a house number in a strange neighborhood. What theory of attention does this comedian favor?

4.13.   Do you think it's safe to talk on a cell phone while driving?

4.14.   Why might listening to music while doing something else (driving, doing homework, cooking) not be considered multitasking, as described in this chapter?

5 Sensory and Working Memory

What Is Sensory Memory?

- Early Span of Apprehension Studies
- Characteristics of Iconic Memory
- Echoic Memory

What Are the Characteristics of Working Memory?

- Early Studies of a Short-Term Information Buffer
- Capacity
- Forgetting
- Representation

How Does Working Memory Work?

- Early Models
- Working Memory Model
- Working Memory as a Workspace

We began the last chapter by defining attention as continued cognitive processing or continued thought. For the next few chapters, we follow that continued thought in the form of memory. We usually think of "memory" as something we're aware of, as when you remember which friend is allergic to shellfish or where you parked your car. But we're going to expand what we think of as memory by imagining a few cases where the time between the event and the memory of the event is so short that we use it without realizing it.

Suppose that as you prepare to walk across a busy street (Figure 5.1), your view is obscured by a parked car. You look to the left and to the right of the parked car, and you get several obscured views of another car moving down the street. Were they different views of one car or parts of several cars? Even though your views of the car are separated only by a fraction of a second, the car is out of view and time has passed, so cognitive psychologists consider it a kind of memory that you use to link these brief views.

Another example: A friend describes an amazing night at the theater, and she mumbles, "We had vestibule in thous." You say, "What?" but even as you're saying it you replay her words in your head and are able to decide that she said "We had the best view in the house." Your memory played back that spoken statement and so offered a second chance to understand it. If a friend leans in to you during a loud concert and yells something above the din, you may not understand it the first time, but again, replaying the words in your head might help you understand (see Figure 5.2).

Figure 5.1. At a busy intersection in Kuala Lumpur, Malaysia, cars, bicycles, and pedestrians are moving and occasionally obscured by each other. Alert pedestrians need to use their memory of currently unseen objects to cross safely. (Source: @Didier Marti/Moment/Getty Images.)

Figure 5.2. Loud concerts make it difficult to hold conversations. But you can use a kind of short-term memory to repeat a voice in your head a second time to understand. (Source: Hollie Fernando/DigitalVision/Getty Images.)

The kind of memory called for in these examples seems different than that invoked when someone says "remember that time a few days ago when you laughed at that joke in chapter 1?" or "remember that weird clown you had at your seventh birthday party?" Putting together several views of a car or mentally rehearsing a mumble shows a need for a holding place, a short-term, temporary buffer to keep information active while some cognitive process – vision, for example, or language comprehension – uses it. In this chapter, we will consider this short-term buffer memory.

Metaphors can be useful in cognitive psychology in that they suggest dimensions to test and experiments to test them. For example, if we think of our short-term memory as a temporary holding area or buffer, that metaphor naturally leads to certain questions. Is there a single buffer or several nested ones? How long can we keep stuff in the buffer? How big is it? Are the sides of the buffer solid or permeable? What sort of stuff fits inside?

The first question, "Is there one buffer or several?" has been answered. Cognitive psychologists agree that there are at least two distinct holding stages for memories that last just seconds. The first is sensory memory, a brief and immediate memory stemming directly from our senses. Our first question, therefore, is, **What is sensory memory?** We'll start by describing the history and characteristics of sensory memory. In our description of sensory memory, we will consider questions of capacity (how much fits?), representation (what kind of information is stored?), and forgetting (how does it go away?). In brief, **sensory memory** is capable of storing a great many items, but it is fragile and transitory, lasting just fractions of a second.

The second type of buffer also holds information briefly, but not as fleetingly as sensory memory. Researchers have adopted the term *working memory* to denote the fact that this type of memory is not merely a buffer to hold things but is more like a desktop because work happens there. Our second question is, **What are the characteristics of working memory?** Just as we did for sensory memory, we will address questions of capacity, representation, and forgetting. Working memory initially seemed easy to characterize on these dimensions, but it turned out to be more complex than researchers had first appreciated.

In the final section, we ask, **How does working memory work?** We discuss two models: the modal memory model and the working memory model. The modal memory model is considered outdated, but it continues to be so important to cognitive psychology that some familiarity with it is necessary. The working memory model has been quite successful in accounting for a great deal of data. We close this chapter with some examples of how working memory contributes to cognitive processing.

What Is Sensory Memory?

Preview

The seeds of the study of sensory memory were planted by the introspectionists. Recall that they were interested in the contents of consciousness, and they were therefore interested in the amount of information that could rush into consciousness simultaneously. They determined that people could perceive four or five complex stimuli (e.g., letters) in a very brief exposure. Participants in their experiments often reported that they felt as though they had perceived more letters but forgot some of them even as they were reporting the others. It was not until 1960 that psychologist

George Sperling showed conclusively that many more stimuli are actually perceived, but only four or five are reported because the remainder are forgotten. Sperling proposed the existence of a memory system that can hold a large number of items, but only for a second or so. In this section, we consider the characteristics of sensory memory: how much information it can hold, the type of information it holds, and how forgetting occurs.

How much information can you take in simultaneously? In other words, how much can you perceive in an instant? This question has been of interest since psychology's earliest days, and if you think back to Chapter 1 and recall the program of the introspectionists, you'll realize their interest is predictable. Remember that they were concerned almost exclusively with conscious processes. Thus, it was important to them to know how much information could get into consciousness at once. William James begins his chapter on memory in his 1890 *Principles of Psychology* with the following:

> The stream of thought flows on; but most of its segments fall into the bottomless abyss of oblivion. Of some, no memory survives the instant of their passage. Of others, it is confined to a few moments, hours or days. Others, again, leave vestiges which are indestructible, and by means of which they may be recalled as long as life endures.
>
> Our consciousness of these transitive states is shut up to their own moment – hence one difficulty in introspective psychologizing. (p. 643)

Despite the obvious difficulty in observing the most fragile elements of your own consciousness in the moment, as their "segments fall into the bottomless abyss of oblivion" (see Figure 5.3), some early investigators were able to devise studies to test just how much could fit into the momentary memory. They called this measure the **span of apprehension**. Studies of the span of apprehension paved the way for the study of sensory memory because even though researchers were trying to study a purely perceptual process – how much information could be perceived in a very brief exposure – it seemed that memory processes nevertheless were involved in the tasks they used.

Early Span of Apprehension Studies

The basic approach to studying memory that only lasts an instant was pioneered nearly 150 years ago by Stanley Jevons (1871), a logician. While not looking, Jevons tossed black beans from a bowl so that some landed inside a small white box while most landed outside the box on a black tray. Then, he briefly glanced at the box and immediately estimated how many beans it held. Then he counted them to see how close his guess was. He did this 1,027 times, and he found that if there were three or four beans, his instant estimate was always correct. With five beans, he was still very good, but not perfect (about 95 percent). His accuracy dropped as the number of beans increased, so if there were fifteen beans, he was correct a little less than 20 percent of the time (see Figure 5.4). This is why, for decades, we considered that the capacity of sensory memory was approximately nine beans. (He was still more than half right at nine. That was picked as an arbitrary cutoff, because "approximately nine" is simpler than "perfect at four, near perfect at five, still mostly right at nine, but more wrong than right at ten and above.")

Figure 5.3. Most moments in a dance flow on, as each movement, and moment, falls into the next. Dance is a good representation of those segments of consciousness that "fall into the bottomless abyss of oblivion." Photography, on the other hand, is able to capture the vestiges and make them indestructible. (Source: Photograph by Phillip Wolak.)

Jevons' estimate	Actual numbers												
	3	4	5	6	7	8	9	10	11	12	13	14	15
3	23												
4		65											
5			102	7									
6			4	120	17								
7			1	20	113	30	2						
8					25	76	24	6	1				
9						28	76	37	11	1			
10						1	18	46	19	4			
11							2	16	26	17	7	2	
12								2	12	19	11	3	2
13										3	6	3	2
14										1	1	4	6
15											1	2	2
% correct	100%	100%	95%	82%	73%	56%	62%	43%	38%	42%	23%	29%	17%

Figure 5.4. Results of Jevons' experiment. (Source: W. S. Jevons [1871], The power of numerical discrimination, *Nature*, 3, 281.)

Obviously, Jevons' "momentary glance" was not a precise measurement in an experiment in which the length of a moment probably matters a fair amount. More sophisticated equipment became available by the 1920s that allowed precise timing of the exposure of visual stimuli. One such device is a **tachistoscope**, which used a variety of methods to allow the participant to see the stimulus for a precise amount of time (see Figure 5.5). A number of experimenters conducted span-

(a)

(b)

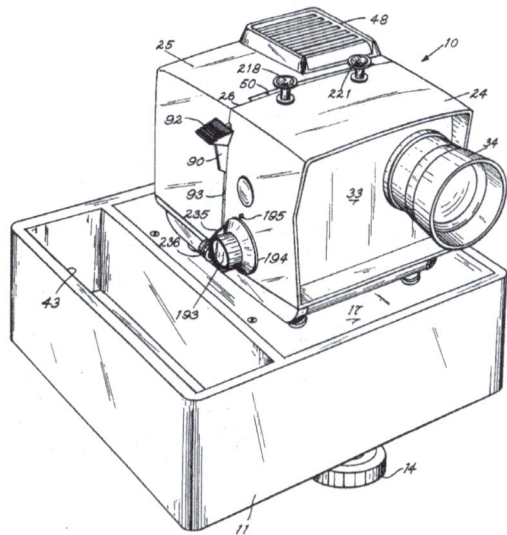

Jan. 30, 1962

K. F. KURZ
TACHISTOSCOPE

3,018,686

Filed Jan. 10, 1961

6 Sheets-Sheet 1

Fig.1

INVENTOR.
KARL KURZ
BY
BUCKHORN, CHEATHAM + BLORE
ATTORNEYS

Figure 5.5. (a) The simplest form of tachistoscope was a drop tachistoscope, in which a door fell at a controlled rate, exposing the stimulus for a brief amount of time. (b) Later versions, like this first patent application for a tachistoscope using a projector, used precise camera shutters. (Source: Cummings Library for History of Psychology.)

of-apprehension experiments with better-controlled exposure durations (and substituting black dots on a white card for the beans). Their estimates of the span of apprehension were close to Jevons'; they averaged around 8.4 (Fernberger, 1921; Glanville & Dallenbach, 1929; Oberly, 1924).

These experimenters controlled the duration of stimulus presentation, but there was another problem they could not solve. They were not measuring the span of apprehension directly; instead, they were measuring the span of what participants could apprehend *and report*. For example, A. Douglas Glanville and Karl Dallenbach (1929) reported that some of their participants said that as they were reporting some stimuli, they were forgetting the others.

It wasn't until 1960 that a better method of testing the span of apprehension was devised, based not on new technology but on a clever experimental paradigm. George Sperling (1960) flashed arrays of numbers and letters like those in Figure 5.6. Participants saw a display of four to twelve items for fifty milliseconds (one-twentieth of a second). When asked to remember as many as they could, participants reported about four items, or 33 percent, of a twelve-item array (Figure 5.6, top). As in earlier experiments, Sperling's participants said they felt that they could see more items but forgot them quickly. Sperling's innovation was called the **partial-report procedure**. In this

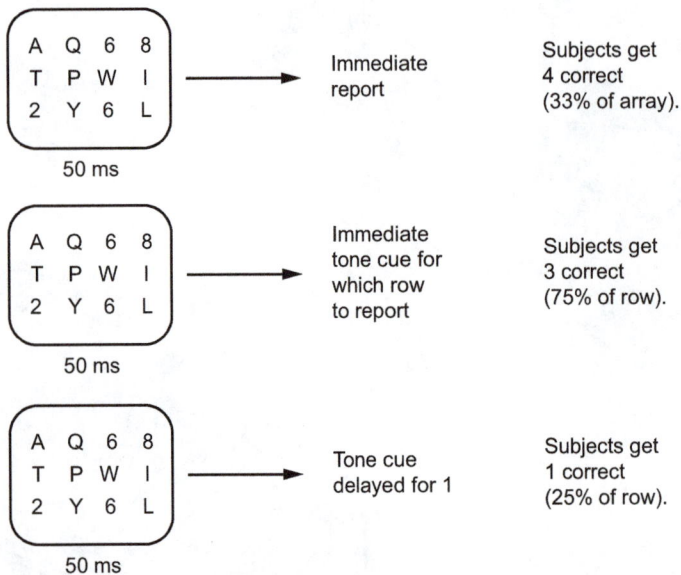

Figure 5.6. The design and representative results of Sperling's experiment. Note that (center) the partial-report procedure indicates that much of the array is perceived, but (bottom) if the cue in the partial-report procedure is delayed one second, much of the information from the array is lost. (Source: G. Sperling [1960], The information available in brief visual presentation, *Psychological Monographs*, 74[11, Whole no. 498], 1–26.)

condition, participants saw the array quickly flashed, then they heard a tone that signaled (through a high, medium, or low pitch) which row they should report. Now, instead of the whole array, they reported just one row. When this partial-report procedure was used, participants got, on average, three items from the desired row correct (Figure 5.6, middle). This result doesn't seem so exciting, but keep in mind that participants did not know which row they would have to report because the tone was random each time and presented after the array had disappeared. Participants must have been equally prepared to report any of the three rows because they couldn't know which row they would have to report. Sperling (1960) reasoned that the percentage of the row participants got correct was a good indicator of their knowledge of the entire array. Participants reported an average of three items correctly (75 percent of the row) when the partial-report procedure was used, so Sperling inferred that they knew 75 percent of the full array, or nine items. Thus, while the full report procedure indicates that the span of apprehension is four items, Sperling found a way to measure what many had previously suspected, that this apparent limited capacity of the span of apprehension was more a limit of how long it took to report than a limit of the true capacity.

A great analogy to this is a typical exam in a class. Let's say you study a study guide with 100 possible exam questions on it. Then your exam has twenty items, of which you get eighteen correct (90 percent – nice job!). A reasonable assumption would be that your memory has ninety of the 100 items, not just the eighteen that you were able to report. The exam only gave you an opportunity to show your knowledge of those twenty. Sperling was making the same claim about the capacity of sensory memory, except in this case, it wasn't that the exam itself had only twenty items but that by the time you reported the eighteen items you knew, you forgot the remaining seventy-two of the ninety you had studied.

Sperling (1960) argued that when the array of stimuli is presented, it enters a large-capacity **iconic memory** from which the contents decay rapidly. The participant therefore rushes to report the contents of iconic memory, but by the time they have reported four letters, the contents have faded. (Sperling actually used the term *sensory memory*, which later came to refer to any of a number of sensory buffers, including a visual buffer, an auditory buffer, and possibly others. The term *iconic memory* came to refer to the visual buffer, and we follow that terminology here.)

Characteristics of Iconic Memory

LARGE CAPACITY   It's possible that iconic memory maintains most of what the perceptual system encounters. It seems that the capacity of iconic memory can vary with the conditions of the stimulus. For example, Emanuel Averbach and George Sperling (1961) found that the brightness of the field presented before and after a flashed stimulus affected how many items were recalled. That the capacity of iconic memory depends on what comes before and after indicates that this type of memory is closely related to basic sensory qualities. The bottom line is that the capacity of iconic memory can be large – it holds seventeen letters at the briefest delay with the dark fields – but the size and duration depend heavily on the details of the experimental situation.

FORGETTING   As has been emphasized in our description of these experiments, iconic memory can hold a lot of information, but the memory is short-lived, perhaps as short as 500 milliseconds and typically no longer than one second, depending on the experimental situation. We haven't specified how information is lost from iconic memory, but we've made it sound like information spontaneously decays. Even if the participant does nothing but look at a simple white (or black) field, the contents of iconic memory will degrade. That finding is clear enough from Sperling's original experiments. Researchers later followed up with discoveries that although iconic memory does spontaneously decay, the decay begins not when the stimulus disappears but very soon after it appears (Di Lollo, 1980) and it seems to decay quite suddenly (Pratte, 2018). Imagine you are in dark woods with your camera and see a deer. You point the camera and take a picture. The flash illuminates the deer, which then runs off, whereupon the flash quickly fades. Iconic memory starts fading immediately after its onset, like the flashbulb fading, not when the stimulus disappears (the deer running off). To continue the metaphor, the flash would fade even if the deer did not run (i.e., if the stimulus did not disappear).

In addition to spontaneous decay, there is a second way that information can be lost from iconic memory; the icon can be actively erased. The technical term is to **mask** the icon, which means to present some random visual stimuli that replace the material currently in iconic memory. In the early 1960s, a number of studies showed that the partial-report advantage disappears if the stimulus array is followed by a mask, consistent with the idea that the mask erases the contents of iconic memory (for reviews, see Breitmeyer & Ganz, 1976; Turvey, 1973). More recent studies have shown that characteristics of the mask affect the masking process (Jannati et al., 2013; Pilling et al., 2019; Spalek & Di Lollo, 2022).

REPRESENTATION   Remember that William James said of these memories, "Our consciousness of these transitive states is shut up to their own moment." Researchers have continued the attempt to break open and peer into the moment before it quickly fades into the bottomless pit of oblivion. Iconic memory initially was believed to be a rather literal representation of the physical characteristics of the stimuli: an image, a literal picture of shapes and colors, but with no semantic information of what they depict (Coltheart et al., 1974; Neisser, 1967; Sperling, 1960). In other words, if the stimulus *A* is in iconic memory, there is no information about whether *A* is a number or a letter; iconic memory stores the physical shape of the stimulus but nothing about what it means. Researchers drew this conclusion because only physical characteristics were effective partial-report cues. For example, Sperling's initial experiments used the physical location of the stimulus (top, middle, or bottom row) as the cueing characteristic, which yielded a partial-report advantage over full report. Other physical characteristics also yielded cueing effects, such as the size of stimuli when participants were directed to report either large or small stimuli (Von Wright, 1968). But when information about stimulus category was used ("Report only the letters, not the digits"), a partial-report effect was not observed (e.g., see Sperling, 1960). Researchers concluded that iconic memory must not include categorical information.

However, recent studies have challenged this purely image-like view of what is represented in iconic memory. These studies have shown that in addition to basic individual physical character-istics, iconic memory also represents what Coltheart (1980) called "postcategorical" information (or information related to semantic categories). For example, observers have been successful in quickly representing overall patterns of a group of stimuli based on features that are not simple sensory qualities. When researchers flash not an array of letters, but a crowd of faces, observers can accurately judge the average emotion of faces in the crowd, or the proportion of genders (Haberman & Whitney, 2007), or gaze direction (Sweeny & Whitney, 2014), although they would not be able to enumerate those characteristics for individual faces. In addition, this averaging happens more for own-gender faces than other-gender faces (de Fockert & Gautrey, 2013). That is, even if an observer is unable to accurately represent the individual semantic elements in quickly decaying iconic memory, they are still often able to represent averages of these features (for a review, see Whitney & Leib, 2018). Sensory memory may not be purely sensory after all. Indeed, there is even recent evidence that ensemble coding for faces may vary by culture, with Chinese observers showing the same level of averaging for both genders, not demonstrating the own-gender effect mentioned earlier (Peng et al., 2020).

Echoic Memory

Echoic memory is the auditory version of iconic memory. Again, *sensory memory* is a more general term. Iconic and echoic memory are both forms of sensory memory.

CAPACITY   There is good evidence for some storage of sound in the very short term. Unlike iconic memory, where visual input allows us to take in more than one stimulus at the same time, echoic memory's capacity is an instant of time. How long is this instant? One source of evidence comes from masking experiments conceptually similar to those we discussed for vision. For example, Dominic Massaro (1970) had participants listen to a tone and identify it as high or low in pitch. The task was made difficult by the presence of a masking tone of random pitch that followed the target tone. If the delay between the target and mask was rather long (350 millisec-onds), participants averaged about 90 percent correct, but if the mask followed the target without delay, participants averaged just 60 percent correct.

Presumably, the negative effect of the mask decreases with delay because the auditory system has had more time to get the stimulus into a more stable state (perhaps to transfer it to working memory). Once the delay between the stimulus and the tone reaches 250 milliseconds, the mask doesn't matter, presumably because 250 milliseconds is how long it takes to get the target safely out of echoic memory and into working memory. We can tentatively place the duration of echoic memory at 250 milliseconds (Cowan, 1987; see Kaernbach, 2004 for a review of echoic memory).

FORGETTING   As the Massaro (1970) example shows, information is lost from echoic memory, either through decay (if the second tone interferes with transfer to a more stable memory store) or through masking (in which the second tone actively erases the echoic memory). More recent efforts have used white noise (Soemer & Saito, 2015) or a composite of all tones (Li et al., 2013) to mask echoic memory, but evidence for interference (rather than decay) has been inconclusive. This ambiguity is in part due to that fact that unlike visual sensory memory, it is trickier to study memory for sounds: "produce that tone" is a much harder task than "write that number." Recent efforts to use cortical signals through EEG have confirmed earlier behavioral results that information in echoic memory is lost through decay and have also found support of interference through masking (Kinukawa et al., 2019).

REPRESENTATION   Echoic memory is represented in a sensory code (like an echo) rather than a semantic one. Nees (2016) refers to this type of sensory memory as "a set of acoustic features organized in time" – that is, not categories or meaning, but simply raw sensory data.

Studying sensory memory in other sensory modalities besides vision and audition has proved even more difficult, but the consensus is that we do have sensory memories associated with all of our senses. Researchers have confirmed that tactile iconic memory can be studied with the partial-report procedure (Gallace et al., 2008), whereas studying the momentary storage and decay of taste sensations cannot be done with that same display techniques as vision and audition. (How could you only quickly stimulate and then remove a taste or smell stimulation? And then only partially report taste or smell sensations?)

Sensory memory is the first, fastest, and most fleeting type of memory representation. While certainly our memories wouldn't be very good if they lasted less than a second, understanding the challenges and successes of how cognitive psychologists have studied sensory memory (with Sperling's partial-report procedure, for example) is good preparation for understanding other, more familiar memory processes. We will move on to one of these, working memory, in the next section.

Stand-on-One-Foot Questions

5.1.   What is the point of the partial-report procedure?

5.2.   What are the characteristics of sensory memory?

Questions That Require Two Feet

5.3.   Sensory memory is certainly a real phenomenon, but it doesn't seem that we would use it very often. Ralph Haber commented that it would be useful only for reading, at night, during a lightning storm. Can you think of a time when you use iconic memory, however briefly? Hint: Think of the movies.

5.4.   Most people have noticed that if they stare at something for thirty seconds or more and then look at something blank (a wall or sheet of paper), they see an afterimage of what they stared at. Is that a demonstration of iconic memory?

What Are the Characteristics of Working Memory?

Preview

It has long been noted that information may be held in mind for a brief period of time. As a simple example, if a friend mentions five things she needs from the grocery store, you can repeat them back immediately. In the late 1950s, researchers began to think that such brief memories might be supported by a memory system separate from the one that supports more enduring memories. We discuss three characteristics of working memory: its capacity, the nature of forgetting, and the format in which the information is coded.

Let's begin by thinking of a buffer that lasts longer than the flash of sensory memory but shorter than a minute. When your GPS says "stay right at the fork, then in 500 feet, go left onto Magnolia St," you must maintain these three facts in memory (stay right for the next few seconds, then wait until the car goes 500 feet, then take a left). When your friend says "my coworker Dave's sister's best friend went backstage at a Drake concert and learned that he really liked mustard," you have to maintain in your head your own possible relationship to someone who can somehow get backstage passes to a Drake concert as well as update your knowledge of Drake ("likes mustard"). In addition to these situations, such a short-term buffer is valuable in cases in which we need to mentally simulate something and consider the outcome. If we move this piece of furniture, what will the room look like? If you tell this person you like their atrocious new haircut, will they believe you?

In the following section, mirroring our discussion of sensory memory, we will first address some early studies on this buffer, then its capacity, then describe how forgetting occurs, and finally discuss representation.

Early Studies of a Short-Term Information Buffer

The first theory of working memory was published by Donald Broadbent (1958). Broadbent likened the human mind to an information processing system, and he's famous for a diagram through which one could trace the flow of information from the environment to various components of the mind. Information first entered a large-capacity sensory memory, then went through an attentional filter that filtered out most of the information (we saw something similar in Chapter 4), and finally entered working memory. Information could enter working memory not only from sensory memory but also from long-term memory. Broadbent's particular formulation was less important than his distinction between working and long-term memory. There was a buffer beyond sensory memory, and this buffer had a limited capacity.

A second influential article (Miller, 1956) proposed not just that the short-term buffer was limited but that that limit had a number. Miller noted that across a number of tasks, the number seven often pops up as a limit on human performance: People can reliably distinguish between sounds of approximately seven different pitches or loudness, but when there were more, people sometimes confuse them. People can remember about seven bits of information, whether they are digits, letters, or black dots flashed on a screen. The article was really about a limit to information processing, but it is almost always cited for its inclusion of the working memory limit of seven items (plus or minus two). Indeed, it was as much a proposal for a "cognitive revolution" in psychology (Miller, 2003) as it was for a specific limit on working memory. However, Miller's "The Magical Number Seven, Plus or Minus Two" remains one of the most cited papers in all of psychology and has wide influence, from the length of telephone numbers (seven digits) to the amount of information recommended for a billboard or for one PowerPoint slide (many business guides to effective presentations include a "Rule of Six": six bullet points on a slide and six words per bullet point [Halpern, 1998]). Unfortunately, Miller's findings are often misinterpreted (as they were for the billboards and the PowerPoint rules), as the limits on working memory capacity are far more complicated than "about seven items." Let's have a look at that issue.

When Miller said the capacity of working memory is seven, he meant seven items of any sort, but many researchers used numbers as the typical item. Since the turn of the twentieth century, researchers had used a **digit span task** to measure the capacity of working memory. In this task, the experimenter reads aloud a series of digits at a rate of one digit per second. The participant must repeat back the digits in the correct order. The experimenter increases the number of digits until the participant cannot repeat them back without error. Most adults can reproduce about seven digits. Average digit span is often described as "seven plus or minus two" to reflect the fact that people's performance varies, but most of us can recall between five and nine digits. Notice that this approach to measuring capacity assumes random digits are a good example of something that needs to be maintained in memory. But wouldn't the stuff we want to keep in working memory usually be meaningful?

Herb Simon (1974) investigated the capacity of working memory for information that is not arbitrary but can be grouped and organized by meaning. Simon tested his own working memory using stimulus materials of different lengths. He found he could remember about seven one- or two-syllable words but only six three-syllable words. He then tested his working memory capacity using brief phrases with which he was familiar, such as "Milky Way" and "Lincoln's Gettysburg Address." Simon found he could remember about four of these phrases on average. Finally, he tried some long phrases, such as "Four score and seven years ago" or "To be or not to be, that is the question," and found he could remember three long phrases. These data are summarized in Table 5.1.

Simon tested just one participant (himself), but the results are typical of what you'd see in most anyone. There are two important points to note. First, the capacity of working memory when measured in syllables or words varies quite a lot, but it varies much less when measured in chunks, indicating that chunks are the right way to measure memory. Second, the amount of information per chunk makes a difference in capacity; as the number of syllables per chunk increases, the number of chunks recalled decreases. What do these results tell us about the capacity of working memory? Simon could recall fewer three-syllable words than one-syllable words. This result suggests that information has a capacity limited by time, rather than a discrete number of slots. An important clue to the capacity of auditory information comes from the **word length effect**. Participants can remember more short words than long ones in a working memory task. This effect was demonstrated by Baddeley, Thomson et al. (1975). They gave participants a simple task – listen to country names and repeat them back – and found that participants averaged 83 percent correct if the names were short (Chad, Cuba) but only 56 percent if the names were long (Somaliland, Australia). The word length effect suggests that the capacity for auditory information is limited to a few seconds, rather than a few slots.

Returning to Simon's result, it seems in line with the word length effect reported by Baddeley, Thomson et al. (1975). But when words were knit into familiar phrases, Simon could maintain twenty-two words in working memory. This is obviously many more than could fit if words

Size of item	Syllables	Words	Chunks	Syllables per chunk
1	7	7	7	1.0
2	14	7	7	2.0
3	18	6	6	3.0
2 words	22	9	4	5.5
8 words	26	22	3	8.7

Table 5.1 Results from Simon's (1974) investigation into the capacity of working memory

Source: H. A. Simon (1974), How big is a chunk?, *Science*, 183, 482–488.

were random, so these phrases must have been represented in terms of their meaning, their semantic content, rather than number of digits or seconds of auditory information.

Simon therefore emphasized the importance of chunking in the capacity of working memory: A **chunk** is a unit of knowledge that is decomposable into smaller units. Chunking is finding a way to combine several units, such as treating the letters *B, L, U,* and *E* not as four separate letters but as one word. Simon noted that he could maintain more syllables in working memory if they were organized into chunks of greater size and held together through the semantic relationships between their parts. This is easy to appreciate in the stimuli that Simon used. The two-word idioms and the eight-word phrases have coherence as chunks because of the semantic relationship of the words, recalled from long-term memory. Simon was able to treat "Four score and seven years ago" as an effective chunk because he was familiar with that phrase; it was already in his long-term memory. "Arise with strength! For we have raised our flag" (the first line of the Djibouti national anthem, in English) would not work as well. Thus, the capacity of working memory for information grouped by meaning depends on the stimuli, specifically, how easily they can be chunked, which depends in part on what is already in long-term memory. For example, you might remember the string of numbers 83020033072007 as an arbitrary set of digits (well beyond the digit span discussed earlier), but for one of the authors of this textbook, it is two important birthdates (8/30/2003 and 3/07/2007).

Capacity

The early studies of Broadbent, Miller, and Simon established that capacity of working memory is limited, but defining that limit is not a simple matter, because the size of the buffer seems to change as we change the units of measurement (digits? items? chunks?). The complexity of the question of capacity is also apparent in modern investigations of visual working memory. While auditory working memory clearly has a capacity limited mostly by time (as shown by the word length effect studies discussed previously), the capacity of visual working memory is much less clear. For example, does working memory represent visual information in terms of object features (lines, colors, and so on) or in terms of unified objects? Or does working memory capacity depend on an object's visual complexity, such that when an object has many different features, it requires more working memory than a simple one? One can see an analogy here to the chunking discussed earlier. For example, the two shapes in Figure 5.7 show the same nine lines, but those in Figure 5.7a form an object.

Initial studies found that complexity didn't seem to matter: Visual working memory held the same number of stimuli, whether those stimuli were simple (colored squares, lines at different

(a)

(b)

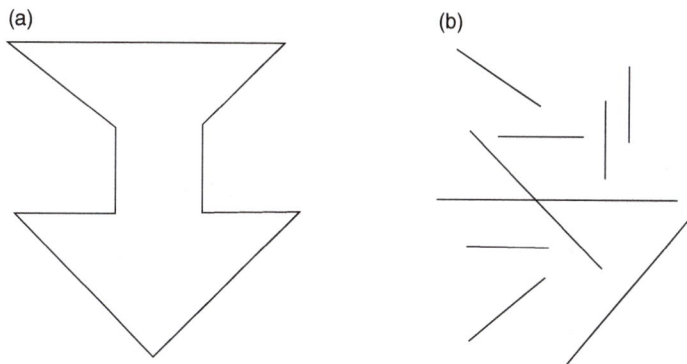

Figure 5.7. Two figures containing the same nine line segments. Clearly, the shape in (a) would be easier to remember than the lines in (b) because the lines in (a) can be chunked on the basis of their spatial relationships.

orientations) or more complex (squares with multiple colors, colored lines at different orientations) (Luck & Vogel, 1997; see also Lee & Chun, 2001; Vogel et al., 2001).

Recent reports, however, indicate that the complexity of the figures may play some role – that is, one can remember fewer complex stimuli compared to simple stimuli. George Alvarez and colleagues compared memories for items such as cubes with differently shaded sides to memory for more simple stimuli such as colored squares or letters (Alvarez & Cavanagh, 2004; Brady & Alvarez, 2015; Davis & Holmes, 2005). In these types of studies with visual stimuli, the test is not free recall but detecting a change. These tasks remind us that complexity need not only be defined by the object itself but by the task demands: It might not take a lot of visual working memory to remember a soccer ball to distinguish it from a basketball, but it takes more to remember a certain orientation of a soccer ball. See Figure 5.8 for stimuli and sample trials.

These recent experiments suggest that visual working memory does not have a fixed capacity but that the "size" of visual working memory is dependent on the complexity of the features of those items. If the size of memory changes depending on what it stores, is it right to describe working memory as having a capacity at all? Some researchers have suggested an altogether different understanding of "capacity." Maybe the limit is not in a *structure* (a limited number of slots, a limited amount of time) but a limitation of a *process*. Perhaps it is better to think of working memory as a mental resource that we can spread across different stimuli (Ma et al., 2014) or something akin to "fidelity": how many features of complex stimuli we can *accurately* represent (Brady & Alvarez, 2015). You might think of this as similar to the capacity of a memory card on a digital camera: It can store 1,000 images with high fidelity but 5,000 with low fidelity.

In previous experiments, participants were instructed to devote equal resources across stimuli. In such a case, the resource view (working memory is a process) and the structure view (working memory is a place with slots to put things) would make equivalent predictions. However, we might also be able to devote unequal resources to stimuli or represent features of stimuli at different fidelity depending on the situation. Indeed, Smith et al. (2018) note that the quality and precision of visual working memory representations are systematically related to attentional engagement. As attentional demands of the task increase, it is not just that working memory capacity is lesser but that working memory resources allow for less overall fidelity.

Neuroscientific investigations of working memory seem also to support the resource view rather than the slots view (Bays, 2015). Earlier research suggested that working memory was "stored" in the area of the brain that perceived it, so that continued activity in visual areas in the

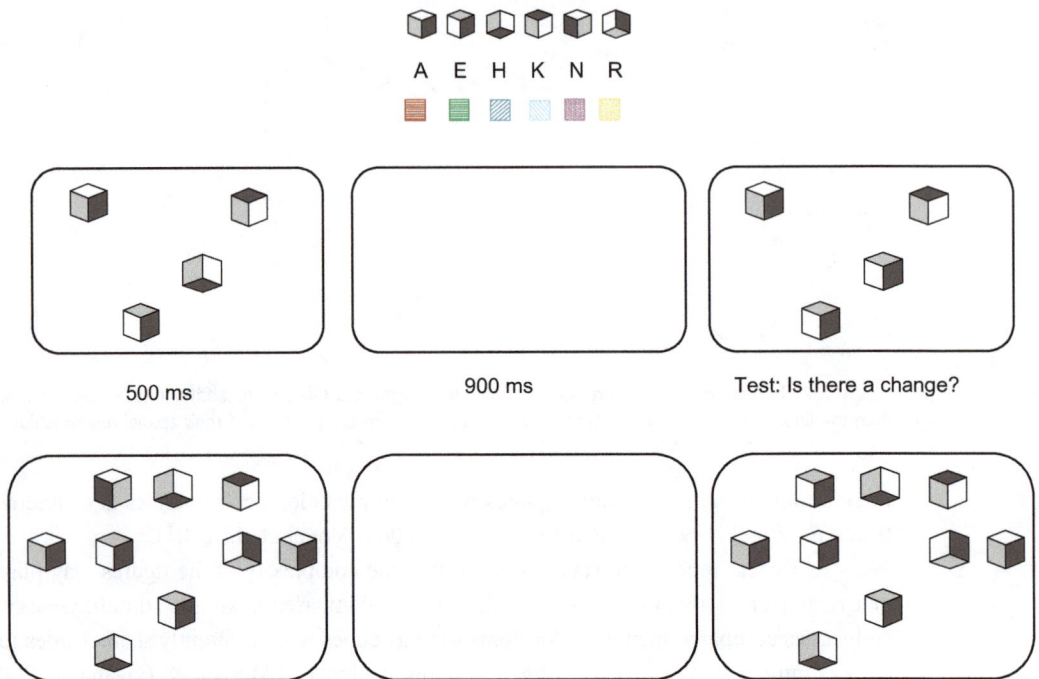

Figure 5.8. Sample stimuli and two trials from Alvarez and Cavanagh (2004). You might notice that the second trial (with nine items) is considerably harder than the trial with four items, even when you have a chance to look back and forth to compare. (Source: G. A. Alvarez and P. Cavanagh [2004], The capacity of visual short-term memory is set both by visual information load and by number of objects, *Psychological Science*, 15, 107.)

occipital lobe would support storing visual information in working memory, while continued activity in auditory areas in the temporal lobe would support auditory working memory (Vallar & Baddeley, 1984; Vallar & Papagno, 2002). However, recently, researchers have also found evidence of modality independent working memory in the brain: a set of neurons that uses the same code of activity for information across two modalities. Vergara et al. (2016) trained a monkey to compare the frequency of two series of stimuli across a small delay of a few seconds. On some trials, the first stimulus was a tactile flutter (think of a machine that taps your finger) and the comparison stimulus was an auditory series of tones. The task could only be completed if the monkey could compare frequency across modalities – touch and hearing. The researchers found that individual neurons in the presupplementary motor area were active during the delay period and were active in the same way regardless of whether the first stimulus was tactile or auditory. These individual neurons are encoding a simple but abstract element of an episode (frequency) across sensory modalities.

A recent review argued that working memory storage in the brain is not isolated in a single area but distributed across a network of areas, with the contributions of each area best understood not as representing different features of objects but as different stages of processing responsible for combining features into objects (Christophel et al., 2017). In other words, the limits on working memory are better understood as limits on processing, rather than limits on capacity.

To conclude, the investigation of working memory capacity may have begun with seven plus or minus two, but it did not converge over time on a more exact number. Rather, further research has revealed that the question of capacity depends on what is being represented. If it is a simple item, such as a digit, you can fit a lot in your working memory (where "a lot" is still fewer than ten items). If it is a complex item, like a cube with multicolored sides or an unfamiliar character, then the capacity of working memory seems to collapse to a single item. While much of the history of this research has been conducted with WEIRD samples, recent studies have confirmed the generalizability of this basic summary (Cockcroft, 2022; Cook et al., 2019). Even as consensus has formed on this characterization of capacity, work is ongoing on this complex issue (Oberauer et al., 2018).

Forgetting

Forgetting means loss of information. In the sensory memory section, we noted that sensory memory fades away quickly but can also be actively erased with a mask. Something similar seems to be true in working memory. If we wait too long, things in working memory seem to disappear on their own. Cognitive psychologists term this *decay*, a spontaneous forgetting of information. We can also lose information when new and old information compete and one of them loses out and is forgotten. This type of process is known as **interference**. In this section, we will explore those two possibilities more carefully. Cognitive psychologists have investigated several possible mechanisms by which information in working memory is lost and whether it is recoverable.

Decay is certainly an intuitive mechanism by which forgetting happens in working memory. Imagine one of those times when you walk into your kitchen from your living room and then can't remember what you needed to do in the kitchen. It feels like this memory just disappeared. While it exists, decay doesn't seem to match our introspections. Early experiments investigated how information in working memory decays by trying to observe memory when it is isolated from the processes that rehearse and maintain it. Similar findings were published nearly simultaneously by two different laboratories: John Brown's (1958) in England and Lloyd Peterson and Margaret Jean Peterson's (1959) in the United States. Brown and the Petersons showed that participants forget even a very small amount of information over a very short delay if they are distracted. The task they used is somewhat similar, so it is called the Brown–Peterson task. It worked like this. The participant heard a trigram of three consonants, such as *TPW*, and then a three-digit number, such as 529. The participant's task was to immediately start counting backward by threes, beginning with the three-digit number (529, 526, 523, and so on). After some delay (between zero and eighteen seconds), the experimenter stopped the participant's counting and asked them to report what the three consonants were. The point of the backward counting was to prevent the participant from rehearsing the letters.

Three letters are well within the working memory capacity of most participants, so when the delay was zero seconds, participants were nearly 100 percent correct. But if the participant counted backward for eighteen seconds, recall dropped to around 10 percent (see Figure 5.9). If these letters were well within the capacity of working memory, why were they lost so quickly? Brown and the Petersons argued that interfering with a maintenance process allowed the information to decay. That is, without a rehearsal process to keep the memory active, it fades away. It seemed that some mental processing must be devoted to maintaining information in working memory; counting backward represents a competing mental process that interfered with the maintenance process.

But studying decay might not be as straightforward as it seems. Time is not a cause in itself. For example, iron rusts, not due to time, but due to oxidation (exposure to oxygen), a process that *occurs in time* (McGeoch, 1932). Likewise, there must be a mechanism that causes decay that occurs in time. Isolating metal (perhaps by spraying it with wax) from oxygen will prevent rust. Isolating food (with vacuumed sealing) from moisture and bacteria will prevent it from decaying.

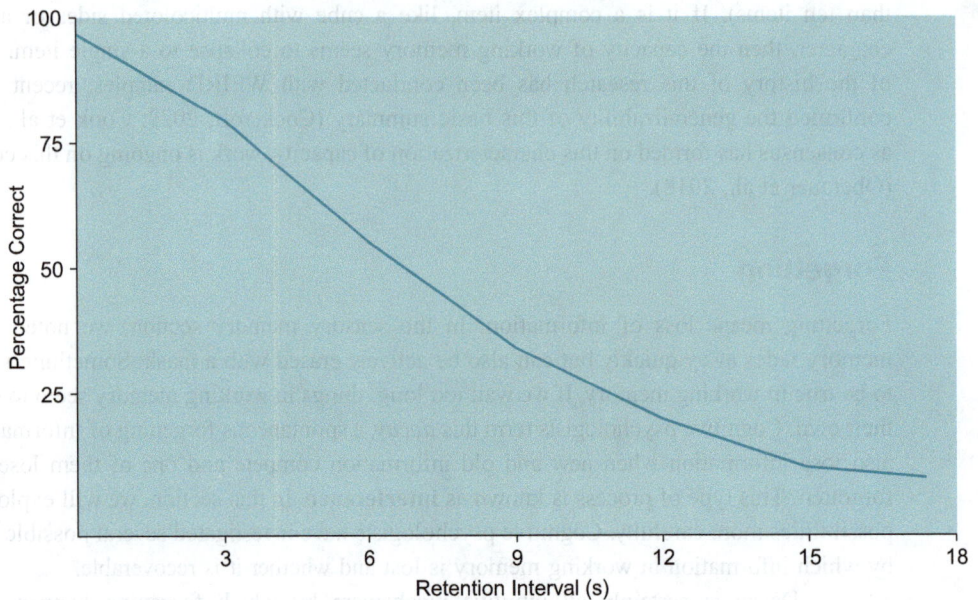

Figure 5.9. Results from Peterson and Peterson's (1959) study showing forgetting of very little information (three letters) after a brief delay (eighteen seconds) if participants are distracted. (Source: L. Peterson and M. J. Peterson [1959], Short-term retention of individual verbal items, *Journal of Experimental Psychology*, 58, 195.)

In these other contexts, we can isolate a possible decay process and note the lack of decay. Working memory, however, is quite resistant to efforts to "isolate" decay. It's very hard to "seal off" a thought process from any external influence.

Perhaps the best attempt at such isolation comes from Stephen Lewandowsky and colleagues (Lewandowsky et al., 2004; Oberauer & Lewandowsky, 2008). They asked people to remember lists of the letters *H, J, M, Q, R,* and *V* in random order. In one experiment, participants recalled the lists verbally, but in between each response, they had to repeat the word *super* either once, twice, or three times. If working memory naturally decays, then we would expect that performance in these conditions would be different, because having to *repeat* super three times allows more time for the later items to decay. But that is not what they found. Instead, there was no additional time-based decay in the repeat-*super*-three-times condition than in the just-say-*super*-once condition. So as much as forgetting by decay seems to match our experience, there's little evidence that it is responsible for much forgetting in working memory.

There is, however, good evidence that interference causes forgetting from working memory. We can see two kinds of effects of interference on working memory. **Proactive interference** occurs when older learning interferes with new learning. For example, suppose that you're trying to learn some French vocabulary words. Look at the two study schedules in Table 5.2. In both cases, you study French vocabulary for an hour and then take a test, but in one case, you've just finished studying Spanish. You are likely to remember less French if you've just finished studying Spanish. That is proactive interference: Earlier learning interferes with new learning.

Geoffrey Keppel and Benton Underwood (1962) examined performance on the Brown–Peterson paradigm and found that even with an eighteen-second delay, participants averaged 95 percent correct on the first trial. On the second trial, they averaged about 70 percent correct, on the third they were down to 55 percent, and by the sixth, it was 40 percent correct. This rapid

Table 5.2 If we compare performance on the French test, the people in the top row should show proactive interference compared with the people in the bottom row

8 a.m.	9 a.m.	10 a.m.
Study Spanish vocabulary	Study French vocabulary	Take French test
Sleep	Study French vocabulary	Take French test

Table 5.3 If we compare performance on the French test, the people in the top row should show retroactive interference compared with the people in the bottom row

8 a.m.	9 a.m.	10 a.m.
Study French vocabulary	Study Spanish vocabulary	Take French test
Study French vocabulary	Sleep	Take French test

decline in performance across trials strongly indicates proactive interference. The first trial was easy, even with a long delay, but by the fifth, they had difficulty remembering the stimulus (or rather, remembering the one they are supposed to remember) due to proactive interference.

In **retroactive interference**, later learning interferes with earlier learning, as shown in Table 5.3. In this case, studying Spanish comes after the learning we are concerned with (French), so we would say that there is retroactive interference from learning Spanish. (Naturally, there is also proactive interference from the French learning on the Spanish learning in this case.)

Judith Reitman (1971) found a clever way to demonstrate that working memory in the Brown–Peterson paradigm is also susceptible to retroactive interference. She reasoned that retroactive interference increases as the new material becomes more similar to the old material. For example, there would be considerable retroactive interference if you first studied baseball statistics and then studied football statistics, but there would be much less if you first studied baseball statistics and then studied dance steps. Reitman varied what people did during the delay period of the Brown–Peterson paradigm: either they listened to a humming sound or they listened to syllables, searching for a target. Because the target material was nouns, if working memory is susceptible to interference, the second task should interfere more because it's verbal. That's exactly what Reitman found.

As a student reading our examples of studying, you might be thinking, "There's proactive interference before! Retroactive interference after! Interference everywhere! What's a student to do?!" You're right that interference is a common feature of memory (it's just a kind of forgetting). For studying, your full goal is getting information from working memory into long-term memory and then getting it back into working memory for the exam. We'll have more to say about this in the next few chapters, but for now, avoiding studying content with a high degree of similarity close together (that you want to be able to distinguish) is a good idea, and studying across multiple sessions is a good way to do that.

Representation

As the preceding description of capacity suggests, it appears that how much information can fit in working memory depends on the type of information (and how it is organized). While the early studies focused on the span of working memory as some sort of fixed capacity irrespective of content, modern understandings suggest that capacity depends on content. So let's look at the different ways that working memories can be represented.

Material can be coded in working memory in at least three ways: visuospatially, acoustically (in terms of sound), and semantically (in terms of meaning). There is also evidence for a working memory component that can store tactile memories – that is, how things feel on the skin – but not much research has been directed toward that representation (Harris et al., 2002; Kaas et al., 2013; Romo & Salinas, 2003).

The earliest research indicated that everything in working memory was coded acoustically, and the type of coding was pointed to as a difference between working and long-term memory: Working memory was thought to use an acoustic code, whereas long-term memory used a semantic code. As we'll see, that conclusion that these codes are unique to each memory system was premature, but the early work did establish that working memory used an acoustic code at least some of the time. Alan Baddeley (1986) conducted a convincing experiment on this point. To get a feel for how it worked, read the following list aloud, look away from the page, and see whether you can recall the words:

mad, man, mat, cap, cad, can, cat, cap

That probably seemed pretty difficult. Now try to do the same thing with a second set of words:

big, long, broad, great, high, tall, large, wide

Finally, try it with a third list of words:

cow, day, bar, few, hot, pen, sup, pit

As you probably noticed, the first list contained words that sounded the same. Baddeley asked participants to remember five words drawn from the lists shown here; twenty-four five-word lists were compiled from each master list. When the words all sounded the same, participants could produce only 9.6 percent of the sequences perfectly. When the words were semantically related, as in the second list, they could produce an average of 71.0 percent of the lists perfectly. When the words were neither acoustically nor semantically related, as in the third list, participants could produce 82.1 percent of the lists perfectly. Thus, there is a huge cost to performance when the words sound the same, as well as a smaller cost when the words are semantically related. Baddeley concluded from this result that the words had been coded acoustically in working memory (see also Mueller et al., 2003); it wouldn't be so difficult to remember similar-sounding words if subjects weren't coding them in terms of sound.

The conclusion that an acoustic code was important in working memory was strengthened by findings showing that if the experimenter presented words visually, participants recoded them into sound. Conrad (1964) showed this in an ingenious experiment. He presented a series of letters on a screen at a rate of one per 0.75 seconds. After six letters appeared, participants were to write them down on an answer sheet, guessing if necessary. One twist was that only a subset of the letters of the alphabet were used: *B, C, P, T, V, F, M, N, S*, and *X*. Conrad was interested in what sorts of errors people made. If they didn't remember *B*, for example, would they just randomly put in one of the other nine letters? No. Participants made systematic errors based on the sound of the letters. Making such errors is called the **acoustic confusion effect**.

For example, when *M* was presented in the stimulus, if people made an error, they were very likely to recall the letter as *N*, which sounds like *M*, rather than recalling *X* or *V*, which look a bit like *M* but don't sound like it. Notice how this conclusion isn't based only on the level of correct performance, like Baddeley's, but also on the pattern of incorrect responses.

Nevertheless, we do not rely only on an acoustic code in working memory. What do we do with spatial information, for example? Suppose we said to you,

> We'd like you to imagine a 4 × 4 matrix of squares because that might help you in this next task. Suppose the upper right-hand cell is the starting square, and in that square, we'd like you to put a 1. In the next square down, put a 2. In the next square to the left, put a 3. In the next square to the left, put a 4.

Then, we ask you to reproduce our instructions – what we said – to you. Almost everyone reports attempting this working memory task using a spatial code. In another similar set of tasks, people remember numbers either presented one at a time at the center of a screen or placed at the positions they would be on a telephone keypad. Working memory performance is greater in the keypad condition (Darling & Havelka, 2010; Darling et al., 2017).

Another source of evidence that people code this type of information spatially comes from interference experiments. What would happen if you asked a participant to perform a spatial task at the same time as the matrix task? Alan Baddeley is a British psychologist who became a fan of American football while studying in the United States. Once, while driving on a California freeway, he tried listening to a football game on the radio and noticed it was difficult to track the spatial relations from the game and steer effectively at the same time (see Figure 5.10). He was inspired to study this interference in the lab (definitely safer that way) (Baddeley, 1986).

Baddeley and his colleagues asked participants to do the above working memory matrix task while performing a pursuit tracking task in which they had to follow a little spot of light with a handheld stylus (Baddeley, Grant et al., 1975). As you might expect, having to do this spatial tracking task played havoc with their working memory in the matrix task. Performance went from an average of a little over two errors without the tracking task to about nine errors with the tracking task. But how do we know that it was the *spatial* nature of each task that interfered and not just that it's hard to do two tasks at once? The experimenters administered a second version of the matrix task that was not spatial. They replaced the words *left*, *right*, *up*, and *down* with *good*, *bad*, *slow*, and *quick*. The sentences became a little odd ("In the next square to the *quick*, put a 2"), but that didn't matter, because the participants' job was to report back the sentences, regardless of whether they were sensible. In this version of the task, participants didn't code the sentences spatially, and the tracking task had no effect on their performance. Again, the point of these experiments is to show that there is a spatial medium in which to maintain information for short periods of time.

We also use a third type of code in working memory: a semantic code that can maintain information about what things mean. A particular task paradigm that has been used frequently to investigate semantic codes in working memory is called **release from proactive interference**. We noted that proactive interference occurs when information learned earlier interferes with the learning of new information; it is observed in the Brown–Peterson task when performance in remembering the letter trigrams decreases over trials. Release from proactive interference refers to the fact that the proactive interference dissipates if the stimulus materials are changed. For example, Delos Wickens and his associates (1976) used the standard Brown–Peterson paradigm, but instead of consonant trigrams (e.g., *WRJ*), participants were to remember the names of fruits, such as *apple*, *pear*, and *orange*. After three trials, different groups of participants heard different stimuli. One group (the control group) heard the names of fruits again; another group heard the names of

(a)

(b)

Figure 5.10. (a) You've probably noticed that there are some things you can listen to in the car and other things that you save for other tasks. While some of this might be personal preference, it might also be related to interference between processes using spatial representations in working memory. (b) Imagine trying to figure out which of these cubes in the fourth column could be a rotation of another cube in the rest of the figure while also trying to hear directions and help a driver navigate. Some mental tasks can be done at once because they don't interfere with each other, and some use the same spatial processes in working memory and are tremendously difficult to do at the same time.

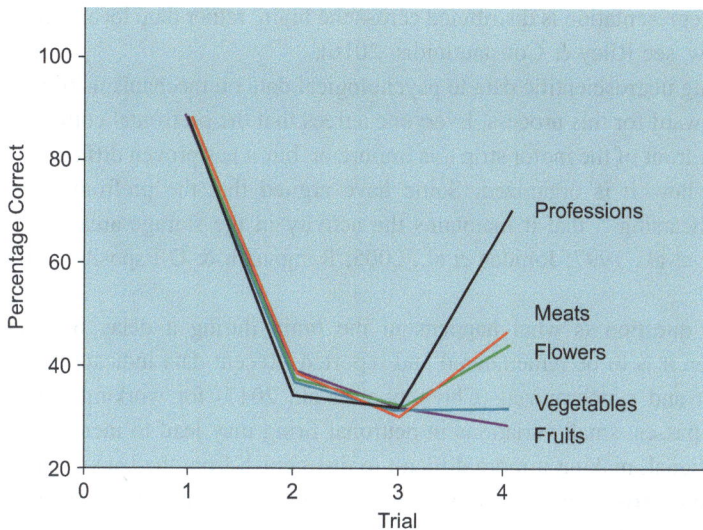

Figure 5.11. Results from Wickens et al. (1976). All five groups used the Brown–Peterson paradigm for the first three trials with fruits as stimuli. Notice how performance declined because of proactive interference. On the fourth trial, the stimuli changed for four of the groups. Notice that performance increased when the meaning of the stimuli changed. The reduction in proactive interference with the change in stimuli is called release from proactive interference. (Source: D. Wickens, R. Dalezman, E. Eggemeier, and F. Thomas [1976], Multiple encoding of word attributes in memory, *Memory and Cognition*, 4, 307–310.)

vegetables, another flowers, another meats, and a final group the names of professions. As shown in Figure 5.11, there was considerable difference in the performance on this fourth trial.

Notice that the group that continued to hear the names of fruits performed the worst; they continued on the downward trend caused by proactive interference. The other groups showed varying amounts of release from proactive interference; the most dramatic improvement came from participants whose stimuli were professions, which are arguably the most different in meaning from fruits. This experiment constitutes evidence that working memory codes semantics or meaning; if it did not, the change in semantic content on the fourth trial would make no difference in performance.

Neuroscientific studies confirm the conclusions of the behavioral research that working memory represents information by its basic perceptual characteristics (acoustically and visually in sensory areas) as well as by its meaning (semantically supported by prefrontal areas). As you might imagine, nailing down how the brain supports semantic representation has been a difficult issue. Recent studies have suggested that working memory processes extend beyond the prefrontal cortex and are more distributed than previously thought (Christophel et al., 2017). Although brain imaging studies consistently show a lot of prefrontal activation during working memory tasks, patients with prefrontal damage are not reliably impaired on the tasks (D'Esposito & Postle, 1999). Recent fMRI techniques that tie specific content (rather than tasks) to specific areas of the brain have also shown how working memory representations involve both sensory areas (in the occipital cortex) and areas in the parietal and frontal cortices. This pattern of data has led some researchers to suggest that the prefrontal cortex serves some other function that happens to be part of most working memory tasks (and so the prefrontal cortex is active in imaging studies) but is not crucial to getting the working memory task done (and so damage doesn't affect the task). In summary, we know that the prefrontal cortex is somehow related to regulating mental activity, but the more we look, the more we see that working memory representation is distributed across the brain, rather than localized in the prefrontal cortex (for a review, see Riley & Constantinidis, 2016).

Connecting neuroscientific data to psychological data on mechanisms of forgetting has not been as straightforward for this process. Everyone agrees that the prefrontal cortex – that portion of the frontal lobes in front of the motor strip – is important, but it has proven difficult to be certain just what it does and how it is organized. Some have argued that the prefrontal cortex is indeed responsible for rehearsing – that it maintains the activity in the storage areas in the back of the brain (e.g., Cohen et al., 1997; Jonides et al., 2005; Ranganath & D'Esposito, 2005; Sreenivasan et al., 2014).

One key question is what happens in the brain during a delay between information presented and when it is to be remembered and reported. Recent data indicate that neuronal firing must be persistent and synchronized (Christophel et al., 2017) for working memory to operate properly. As time passes, small variations in neuronal firing may lead to increasing disruptions in this synchronous signal, making it more difficult to distinguish from the background noise of other neurons. While the neuroscience of working memory processes is an active area of research, it has supported many of the behavioral findings: that interference is a robust reason for forgetting and that decay is still difficult to isolate.

The picture of working memory representation presented earlier suggests that working memory may not be a single, simple system or process but a network of related processes, perhaps operating under similar constraints. But how is this network organized? In the next section, we will explore different models of working memory. How do all these parts fit together and fit in with the rest of cognition? How does working memory work?

Stand-on-One-Foot Questions

5.5.   What are the three representations in which working memory may code material?

5.6.   Is it accurate to say that the capacity of working memory is seven plus or minus two items?

Questions That Require Two Feet

5.7.   Some researchers have tried to examine working memory without any possibility of proactive interference by administering only one trial to each participant. Can you argue that proactive interference may have been at work in such experiments nevertheless?

5.8.   In this section, we discussed proactive and retroactive interference using the example of studying French or Spanish. Given that you must study more than one subject, it seems as though there is always going to be proactive or retroactive interference. What is the best way to minimize the effects of interference?

5.9.   Languages use different sounds to represent numbers. Would you therefore expect that the digit spans of people who speak different languages would be different? How about the digit span of an individual who speaks two languages?

How Does Working Memory Work?

Preview

In this section, we discuss two models of working memory, and we describe how working memory contributes to cognition. The modal model, an amalgam of many closely related models proposed in the 1960s, remains influential, although it is now known to be incorrect in its details. A second model, simply called the working memory model, is much more successful in accounting for the enormous range of relevant data collected in the last half century. We also discuss its brain basis as well as investigations into how working memory contributes to cognitive functions like intelligence and reading.

We have discussed the characteristics of sensory memory and working memory. Before moving on to long-term memory, we will describe two important models of working memory's structure and how information flows through it.

Baddeley's **working memory** model (Baddeley, 1986, 2003; Baddeley & Hitch, 1974) accounts well for the data we've discussed thus far – representation, the nature of forgetting, and so on. Indeed, these data were collected to test the model. We begin, however, with the **modal model**. It was so important in the late 1960s and early 1970s that every cognitive psychologist must be familiar with it. For that matter, the model was so important that the terms for the distinction between *short-term memory* and *long-term memory* seeped into popular culture.

Early Models

From the mid 1960s through the early 1970s, psychologists proposed a number of models of human memory that drew a distinction between sensory, short-term, and long-term systems. The models had so many features in common that Bennet Murdock (1967) pointed out that one could construct a modal model of memory simply by listing the properties that these models shared (see Figure 5.12). He intended it as a pun, based on a statistical measure, the mode, which is the number that occurs most often in a group of numbers, and the name stuck. This was not a criticism of memory theory at the time; Murdock was pointing out that there was general agreement among many researchers on the basic architecture of memory. Some other similar models were proposed by Waugh and Norman (1965) and Atkinson and Shiffrin (1968).

The modal model emphasizes the flow of information through the cognitive system. Information enters from the senses to sensory memory. There may not be sensory memory for each sense, such as smell and taste, but we know that iconic and echoic memory exist. Some of the information is lost from sensory memory, and some is passed on to short-term memory. Whatever you pay attention to in iconic memory is passed on to sensory memory.

Information in short-term memory decays after approximately thirty seconds, unless it is rehearsed. To **rehearse** means to practice material in an effort to remember it. If it is rehearsed, it can be maintained indefinitely. The amount of processing in **short-term memory** determines the

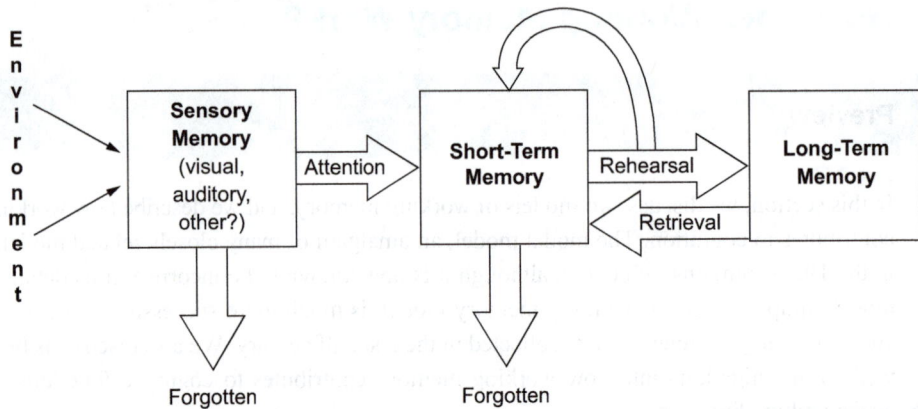

Figure 5.12. The modal model, showing sensory, short-term, and long-term memories and their interactions. This model has been superseded by newer research.

likelihood that information will enter long-term memory; information that is processed longer in short-term memory is more likely to be encoded (passed on) to long-term memory. Individual models varied in terms of exactly what sort of processing in short-term memory was likely to lead to entry into long-term memory.

Information can also enter short-term memory from long-term memory. Because short-term memory is the site of consciousness, this makes sense. The fact that you like maple syrup on pancakes but prefer lingonberry jam on toast is in long-term memory but not short-term memory. When we ask, "What do you like on pancakes?" you retrieve the answer from long-term memory and enter it into short-term memory.

Finally, note that Figure 5.12 shows no arrow that indicates forgetting from long-term memory. That's because forgetting from long-term memory was believed to occur via interference, not decay. Nothing is irretrievably lost from long-term memory, according to the model. Forgetting is a problem of access.

The modal model was shown to be incomplete or inaccurate in several respects (for a discussion, see Nairne, 2002). For example, the description of rehearsal (the process by which material is transferred from short-term to long-term memory) was incomplete because it proposed that short-term memory used only an acoustic code and long-term memory only a semantic code. The model also proposed that forgetting in short-term memory occurred primarily through decay.

Despite these inaccuracies and deficiencies, the broad architecture of the modal model – sensory memory feeding into working memory, which feeds into long-term memory – remains influential today (Malmberg et al., 2019).

Working Memory Model

The basic architecture of working memory is fairly simple (Baddeley, 2000, 2001, 2003; Baddeley & Hitch, 1974; for a review, see Baddeley, 2012). It includes a central executive and three subsystems, as shown in Figure 5.13. The three storage buffers are called subsystems because they do the central executive's bidding. Each stores a different type of information. The **phonological loop** stores auditory information, the **visuospatial sketch pad** stores visual information, and the **episodic buffer** stores information in a multimodal code, that is, a code that can represent visual,

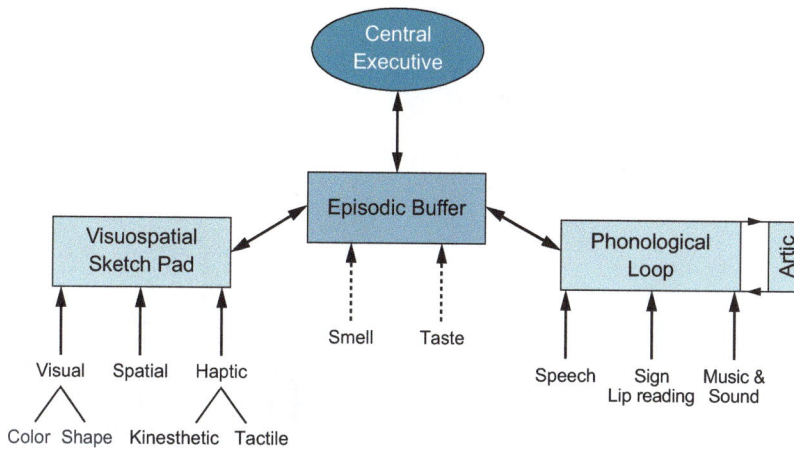

Figure 5.13. The basic components of working memory. The central executive communicates with the other components, which do not communicate with one another. The central executive controls the activity of the other components. (Source: A. D. Baddeley, R. J. Allen, and G. J. Hitch [2011], Binding in visual working memory: The role of the episodic buffer, *Neuropsychologia*, 49[6], 1399.)

auditory, or semantic information and possibly other kinds. The **central executive** doesn't store anything – rather, it directs the activities of the other components. We examine each in turn.

The phonological loop has two components: the **phonological store** and the **articulatory control process**. The phonological store holds about two seconds of auditory information. It is like a short tape loop on which you can copy auditory information. Information can enter the phonological store from the environment; for example, we could say a list of words aloud that we want you to remember. Information can also enter via the articulatory control process, which literally means talking to yourself (articulation). You might use the articulatory control process by repeating a grocery list to yourself. The articulatory control process can also be used to refresh information that is already in the phonological store to keep it from fading.

Evidence for the nature of the phonological loop comes from **articulatory suppression** studies. The articulatory control process that writes material to the phonological loop is proposed to be similar to speech. Therefore, you shouldn't be able to use it while you're speaking. If you're talking out loud, you can't put anything on your tape loop because the articulatory process is already busy. So, suppose an experimenter asked a participant to talk while they performed a standard working memory task. The experimenter wouldn't want the participant to have to think of what to say, because that would require attention, so the participant might just say "blahblahblah" aloud while viewing words on a screen to be remembered. What strategy would the participant bring to this memory task if the words can't be coded acoustically because the articulatory control process is busy? They would have to find some other way to code the words.

If the participant is not coding the words in terms of sound, the acoustic confusion effect should disappear. You'll recall that it's hard to remember a list of words that sound alike (*mad, man, mat*). That effect does indeed disappear if participants say "blahblahblah" while they hear the words: Participants remember words that sound alike (*man, mad, mat*) as well as they remember words that don't (*pit, sup, bar*). That's because speaking aloud occupies the articulatory control process, forcing them to code the words in some way other than acoustically, so they are not susceptible to the acoustic confusion effect (Baddeley et al., 1984). You might wonder whether the effect is caused by the attentional requirements of saying "blahblahblah," even though it might seem that saying such a

Figure 5.14. You might notice obligatory access to the phonological store if you are taking notes or writing while listening to music with words. You'll be in the middle of writing a great sentence in your cognitive psychology paper and insert song lyrics. The song lyrics gained obligatory access to your phonological store, which then got mixed with what you were typing.

simple syllable repetitively would not demand much attention. The experimenters compared articulatory suppression with finger tapping, another simple task that did not require articulation. With that secondary task, the acoustic confusion effect was still present.

Even though articulation will get material into the phonological store, simply listening to something (even if you are not trying to remember it) guarantees that it will get into the phonological store through **obligatory access**. (See Figure 5.14.) For example, Herbert Colle and Alan Welsh (1976) looked at participants' memories for strings of letters presented visually with a short delay, tested either in silence or while listening to a tape of a foreign language they did not know. (It was a passage from "A Hunger Artist" by Franz Kafka, in the original German.) Colle and Welsh found that there was significant interference from the speech; errors increased an average of 12 percent. The interpretation is that speech sounds gain obligatory access to the phonological store, even if you're trying to ignore them, and interfere with memory for target consonant strings.

The visuospatial sketch pad is conceived of as a visual analog to the phonological loop. It is a medium in which to keep visual or spatial information active. Earlier in this chapter, we discussed evidence that people maintain spatial information in working memory. (Remember the matrix task with sentences such as "In the next square to the left, put a 3.")

Baddeley proposed that spatial information (where things are) and visual information (what they look like) are separable in the visuospatial sketch pad. We noted in Chapter 3 that visual and spatial information might be handled separately in perception; it might well be that they are also separate in the visuospatial sketch pad.

Many studies have examined whether visual and spatial aspects of stimuli are remembered separately in working memory (e.g., Baddeley & Lieberman, 1980; Logie & Marchetti, 1991; Quinn & McConnell, 1996). The most thorough study was a series by Karl Klauer and Zengmei Zhao (2004), who used an interference procedure. Participants had to remember either the location of a dot on a computer screen (spatial task) or a Chinese ideograph (visual task). There was a ten-second retention interval, and then participants selected from among eight possible stimuli (locations or ideographs). During the ten-second interval, participants performed one of two interference tasks. (In a control condition, there was no intervening task.) In the spatial interference task, participants saw twelve asterisks on the screen, eleven of which were moving in random directions. The goal was to locate the stationary asterisk. In the visual interference task, participants saw a series of fourteen color patches, one at a time, and for each had to categorize it as red or blue. The idea of the experiment is this: If visual and spatial working memory storage are really separate, then the visual interfering task (color discrimination) should disrupt memory for the visual stimuli (ideographs) but have less impact on memory for the spatial stimuli (dot location). The spatial interference task should have the opposite effect.

The results supported the prediction. Compared with the control condition (no interference task), the spatial interference task had no impact on visual memory, but it made spatial memory about 6 percent worse. The visual interference task had the opposite effect: It made spatial memory a little bit worse (about 3 percent) but had a bigger impact on visual memory. These behavioral data are consistent with neuroscientific data that indicate separate brain locations for visual and spatial memory, both from brain-damaged patients (e.g., Bonni et al., 2014; Carlesimo et al., 2001; Postle et al., 1997) and from neuroimaging studies (e.g., Courtney et al., 1996; Owen et al., 1998).

The phonological loop and visuospatial sketch pad were part of the original working memory model proposed in 1974, and a good deal of evidence supports this part of the model. Baddeley added the episodic buffer in 2001, and there are therefore fewer relevant data. He proposed the episodic buffer as a way of solving a few problems in the original model. One significant problem was that there was no way for auditory and visual information to interact, and there is evidence from verbal span tasks that they do interact (Chincotta et al., 1999). The episodic buffer is proposed to be multimodal – that is, many modalities can be represented there, including auditory, visual, and semantic information. The episodic buffer is the workspace of working memory. It's where different types of information can come together to be manipulated to solve problems. Recent work supports the idea that the episodic buffer may be involved in binding together features of objects, but the details remain unclear (Baddeley et al., 2011; de Pontes Nobre et al., 2013).

A second problem with the original model was that it didn't provide a way for the components of working memory to interact with long-term memory. We have seen evidence that chunking is very important for working memory capacity; "four score and seven years ago" can be treated as a single chunk, or unit, in working memory because the phrase exists in long-term memory. So there must be a way for working memory and long-term memory to interact. But this is not so straightforward, because the articulatory loop stores sounds and long-term memory stores meaning. How can those connect? The multimodal episodic buffer offers a mechanism.

Less work has been directed toward elucidating the role of the central executive. It's proposed to be a cognitive supervisor, especially in doing the vital work of focusing, dividing, and switching attention. Researchers initially focused on understanding the phonological loop and visuospatial sketch pad exactly because they believed that they would be easier to understand. Baddeley (1996) commented that in some ways, his research strategy could be compared with undertaking an analysis of *Hamlet* by focusing on Polonius and ignoring Hamlet. By this he meant that the central executive is the most interesting part of working memory because its responsibilities are so great. The last few years have seen an increase in research directed at processes of mental control, but much of this work is too advanced for a beginning text.

The history of research on working memory models and some of the examples (Hamlet, driving, moving asterisks, Kafka) may strike you as both a bit weird and a bit WEIRD, even as researchers have sought to use universal symbols and stimuli that aren't dependent on specific languages. Kate Cockcroft (2022) tested five possible models in the structure of working memory in a group of predominantly rural, multilingual, and low-socioeconomic-status young adults in South Africa. She confirmed the basic separation of verbal and visuospatial processing in working memory, providing support for the generality of this aspect of models of working memory.

Working Memory as a Workspace

A key feature of the working memory theory (as opposed to the modal model) is its proposal that working memory is used for other cognitive functions, not only for briefly storing information. We review several examples of how working memory is used.

The phonological loop appears to be important in acquiring new vocabulary terms. In a number of studies, researchers have looked at the relationship between the size of the phonological loop and the number of words in the vocabulary of children in the early and middle childhood years (for a review, see Stipek & Valentino, 2015). The size of the phonological loop is measured by digit span and by asking the children to repeat nonwords, such as *loddernaypish*, which presumably can be repeated only if the child successfully maintains in the phonological loop the sounds that the experimenter utters. Vocabulary size correlates with digit span and correlates even better with nonword repetition: The correlations are on the order of 0.35 to 0.60.

The workspace of working memory helps not only with vocabulary but also with other verbal tasks. In a longitudinal study, Stipek and Valentino (2015) found that digit span measures correlate highly with reading comprehension and that this correlation holds throughout elementary school. Another example of working memory's role in cognition comes from an influential study by Meredyth Daneman and Patricia Carpenter (1980). They devised a task in which the participant must simultaneously manipulate and store information: A sentence such as "The boy asked the bishop for the ball" is followed by a question like "Who asked?" and the participant must answer the question. Then another sentence and question are presented, and so on. After, say, four such questions, the participant must recite the last word of each of the four sentences; thus, participants have to keep the last word of each sentence in mind while trying to listen to the new sentences and answer questions about them. The experimenter varies the number of sentences, and the final measure of working memory span is the greatest number of sentences for which the participant can answer all the questions and recite the last word of each sentence correctly. This measure of working memory span is an extremely good predictor (correlation = 0.72) of reading comprehension in college students.

The interpretation of this high correlation is that working memory is often important in comprehending sentences during reading. This fact is especially apparent in sentences such as "The package dropped from the airplane reached the ground safely" (Fodor, 1995). In sentences like this, the grammatical structure can fool the reader, who might think that *dropped* is the main verb of the sentence (as it would be in "The package dropped from the airplane safely"). In fact, *dropped* must be interpreted as part of an adjectival phrase; "dropped from the airplane" tells you which package is being discussed. In sentences like this, the grammatical role of some of the words can be misinterpreted. But if this material is still in working memory, the reader can reinterpret the early part of the sentence. If it's not in working memory, it must be reread. Thus, a good working memory span might help reading comprehension. (This type of sentence is discussed further in Chapter 11.)

One study looked at the role of working memory in a particular type of reading comprehension: following instructions (Jaroslawska et al., 2016). Children were asked to follow a set of spoken instructions in a real-world setting or in a virtual environment on a laptop computer. The instructions began with one step, but experimenters added steps until children consistently made errors (e.g., touch the red ruler; touch the red ruler then pick up the yellow pencil). They found that children with higher verbal working memory scores were better able to follow instructions in both real and virtual environments, demonstrating a realistic implication of working memory capacity.

In this chapter, we've considered how you maintain information for a brief period of time and how you work with it while you're maintaining it. But that only covers a fraction of the memory capabilities we need; we usually need to use memories that are older than thirty seconds. Somehow, memories must be retained for long periods of time. In the next three chapters, we discuss how those memories are put into the memory vault, how they are retrieved, and the format of the representation used to store them.

Stand-on-One-Foot Questions

5.10. Explain the difference between the concepts of sensory memory, short-term memory, and working memory.

5.11. Describe the components of the phonological loop and how they operate.

Questions That Require Two Feet

5.12. Service people often thank you after they have done you a favor. For example, Willingham will walk into a department store and ask someone at the perfume counter where the men's shoe department is, and the clerk will answer: "Go to the back of the store, past lingerie. Take the elevator to the fifth floor, walk straight ahead, and turn right at the overcoats; it's right there. Have a nice day, and thank you for shopping with us." What's wrong with adding this last sentence?

5.13. Suppose that a person with brain damage has almost no articulatory loop; the digit span is one or two items instead of the usual seven. How good would you expect the person's long-term memory to be?

6 Long-Term Memory Structure

What Are the Different Types of Long-Term Memory?

- Explicit Memory

- Implicit Memory

How Is Explicit Memory Organized?

- Addressing Systems

- Content-Addressable Storage

- Hierarchical Theory

- Spreading Activation Theories

- Spreading Activation Models: An Example

While our working memory system maintains information for short periods of time – seconds or minutes – we also need to maintain information over much longer periods: hours, days, weeks, months, and even years. Researchers call this *long-term memory*. Most questions people have about their own long-term memories are prompted when there's a failure. Why can't I remember that person's name? Where did I put my glasses? What's the answer to number 7 on this quiz? Cognitive psychologists are interested in failures of memory but more broadly target memory organization (its structure) and memory operation (its processes). Of course, the hope is that once we figure these things out, we can answer more specific and individual questions like where your glasses are (have you checked your head?) or how to study effectively (have you tested yourself?). In this chapter we will first describe the structure of long-term memory: We'll describe different types of long-term memory and their organization. In the next two chapters, we will describe memory processes of encoding (getting memory in) and retrieval (bringing memory back for current use).

When we use our memories, say, to drive a car to a new place, we may not consciously feel as if we are using different types of memory to operate the car ("how much should I rotate the steering wheel to make this turn?") and to remember the directions ("she said to take the second dirt road after the third Starbucks"), but cognitive psychologists have found that these tasks do indeed use distinct memory processes and representations. In the first section, we will ask, **What are the different types of long-term memory?** As it turns out, memories that we access consciously (like the directions) have different characteristics than memories that we cannot access consciously (like the correspondence between the angle at which the steering wheel is turned and the resulting angle at which the car will turn).

In the second section, we will drill down further into the structure of the memory system associated with consciousness, which we call *explicit memory*. **How is explicit memory organized?**

One way to think about this question is to rephrase it by asking which metaphor for memory seems most appropriate. Is it a storehouse? Is it a filing cabinet? Is it a sortable computer database? As we'll see, the best analogy is that memory is organized as a network.

What Are the Different Types of Long-Term Memory?

Preview

As is often the case with mental concepts, we must begin by contrasting the common usage of *memory* with how cognitive psychologists use the term. Cognitive psychologists believe there are several memory systems, each anatomically distinct in the brain, and each using different mental processes. The everyday use of the word *memory* is close to what psychologists call the explicit system; it's memory we are aware of, such as general knowledge of facts or specific events in the past. The implicit system, in contrast, represents memories we use without awareness. For example, the skill you show when riding a bike is a memory, and while we know that we can ride a bike, we are not aware of the content of the memory (the precise balances, movements, and perceptual learning) that allows us to keep ourselves on the bike and moving forward. Cognitive psychologists have also identified subsystems within the explicit and implicit systems, although the boundaries between them are not as clear.

Recall that in Chapter 1 we said cognitive psychologists are interested in mental representations and the processes that operate on them. When researchers propose that there are separate memory systems, they mean that there is more than one type of memory representation. We can draw an analogy to text messaging on different kinds of phones. Apple sends and receives messages in a proprietary format called Apple Push Notification using its app iMessage. When you see a message from a friend, you can read the text of what they have sent, but the underlying data for a given text message in iMessage would include not only the letters of the text itself but the time it was sent, emojis, and a way to mark whether it was read, features that are invisible to both sender and receiver. An Android phone uses a different format, or a different way of representing its text messages. As any iPhone friend group with a lone Android user knows, when group texts include both kinds of phones, these two different representations can conflict. As it turns out, Apple "converts" Android messages to an old format, SMS, which focuses on text and translates reactions into text (hence the "Willingham laughed at 'Maybe we can use the common group chat experience to explain different representations'"), which causes confusion and annoyance for all.

We don't have Apple minds or Android minds, and we don't know the number of systems, formats, and representations, so we have to find different methods of distinguishing what's going on with our memories. Cognitive psychologists want to know how many different types of representations there are in the brain and how many sets of processes operate on them. As we'll see shortly, most cognitive psychologists believe that there are at least two memory systems, each with several subsystems. Before we tell you about those, however, we need to say a bit more about the type of evidence one needs to conclude that memory systems really are separate.

An obvious prediction you would make is this: If there are separate memory systems in the brain, then sometimes we should see a person with brain damage that disables one memory system

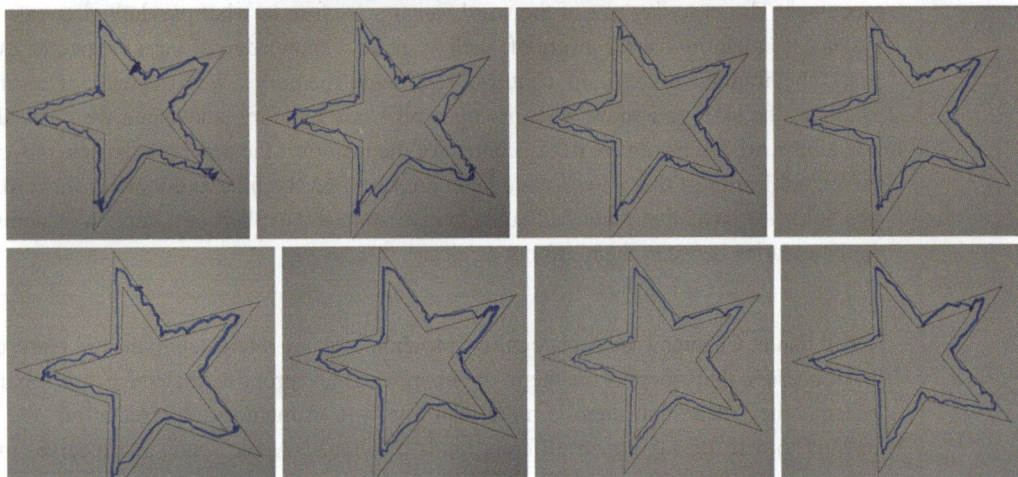

Figure 6.1. Mirror-tracing apparatus and an example (Riener) of a traced star before training and after.

but leaves the other system intact. This finding is called an **anatomic dissociation**, meaning that different tasks are supported by different parts of the brain. That sort of finding has in fact been observed since the mid 1960s. You may recall patient H.M. (known by his full name, Henry Molaison, since his death), the man who had much of his medial temporal lobe removed to relieve epilepsy, leaving him with profound anterograde amnesia – he couldn't store new memories. By 1965, his memory had been tested using just about every type of material you could think of: words, nonwords, rhythms, songs, faces, and so on (Corkin, 2002, 2013).

Further testing showed that Molaison could learn new motor skills (Corkin, 1968; Milner, 1966). For example, he was asked to trace the outline of a star when viewing his hand and the paper in a mirror (see Figure 6.1). It's very difficult – your hand seems to move in ways you don't expect – but improvement is rapid. Molaison improved with practice, showing that he learned the skill. Interestingly, when shown the testing apparatus the next day, he had no memory of having used it before, but he still could perform the task quite rapidly (see Molaison at a testing session in Figure 6.2). The anatomic dissociation in this example is that the medial temporal lobe (which was damaged in this case) seems important for conscious recollection of the testing situation but doesn't seem important for skilled performance of the motor task.

Figure 6.2. Henry Molaison. (Source: Photograph by Jenni Ogden.)

Now one interpretation of these data is that we're seeing the workings of two memory systems: One memory system supports recall and recognition, and another supports learning new motor skills. That is the conclusion that researchers have settled on, but it was not the first interpretation they favored. Psychologists, like all scientists, want their theories to be as simple as possible. There is a simpler account of Molaison's performance on the mirror-tracing task. Perhaps there is a single memory system and one *process* within that system was damaged. Most memory tasks require that damaged process, so an amnesic patient's memory usually looks terrible. But there are a few tasks, like mirror tracing, that don't require that process, so they learn those tasks normally. Throughout the 1970s, psychologists tried different versions of this theory.

Researchers tried to formulate some version of a theory that would account for the tasks that amnesic patients learn normally and those on which they are impaired, but it proved impossible. For example, if recall is the problem in amnesia, why is it that amnesic patients can remember events from childhood but not ones that happened last week? By the early 1980s, most researchers concluded that this variety of theory – a single system with one damaged process – wouldn't work. There must be multiple systems of human memory: one that is damaged in amnesia and another that is intact in amnesia (Cohen & Squire, 1980; O'Keefe & Nadel, 1978). These two systems account for the fact that some tasks are consistently impaired, while others are spared. Although these two systems have gone by several names in the past (Squire, 1992), here we call them explicit and implicit memory (Graf & Schacter, 1985).

Explicit Memory

The initial driving force behind the multiple systems theories were findings like H.M. learning mirror tracing. Patients with anterograde amnesia, who couldn't learn any new information as measured by the usual memory tests, were shown to be capable of new learning when tested in other ways. First, it was shown that they could learn motor skills, then that they could learn a classically conditioned response (Warrington & Weiskrantz, 1979), and then that they could learn perceptual skills, such as reading mirror-reversed words (Cohen & Squire, 1980). Through the 1980s and 1990s, researchers tested a wider variety of patients and began using more advanced brain imaging techniques as they became available. Researchers agreed that there was a dissociation between memories associated with the experience of recollection and memories that were often evident only through performance (Squire, 2009).

The **explicit memory** system supports intentional, conscious recollection of facts, experiences, and concepts. Facts might be general knowledge, such as knowing the capital of Iceland, that no two snowflakes are alike, or what the name of the coffee shop is on the show *Friends*. This memory system also stores personal events or experiences, for example, your memory of what you did after dinner last night, your memory of your last birthday, and so on. When William James defined memory as "*the knowledge of an event or fact, of which meantime we have not been thinking, with the additional consciousness that we have thought or experienced it before*," he was describing what we now call explicit memory, and identifying it as we do now, as thoroughly linked with conscious recollection.

The explicit memory system is supported by a network of subcortical structures, as well as parts of the cortex. The most important subcortical structures are the hippocampus and some nuclei of the **thalamus** (Squire, 1992). Many of the most important cortical areas are in the temporal lobe, and these appear to be important for storing memories (e.g., Binder & Desai, 2011; Martin & Chao, 2001). Other areas in the frontal cortex appear to be important for the retrieval of explicit memories (Buckner et al., 1995; Thompson-Schill et al., 1998). More recent studies have documented how networks of cortical areas interact with the subcortical structures like the hippocampus to support explicit memories during both formation and retrieval (Brodt et al., 2018; Kragel et al., 2021).

Studies of amnesic patients which showed impaired performance in explicit tasks with preserved implicit memory have been very important in determining the brain basis of the explicit system, but brain imaging studies in people without brain damage have also been informative. In fact, explicit memory is so closely tied to medial temporal activity that researchers have been able to link patterns of brain activity with later successful memory performance, a procedure called the subsequent memory paradigm (Danker & Anderson, 2010; Paller & Wagner, 2002).

The basic idea is simple (Wagner et al., 1998; Brewer et al., 1998). Participants lie in a scanner and make judgments about words. The researchers use event-related fMRI, which allows the measurement of brain activity in a narrow time window (as short as two or three seconds) so they can determine the amount of brain activity immediately after each stimulus is presented. Later, outside the scanner, participants take a test for the material, and each participant's performance on each stimulus is categorized as being remembered well, remembered weakly, or forgotten. The researchers then examine whether the activity of any part of the brain at encoding predicts whether items would later be remembered or forgotten. Results of these studies show that the right dorsolateral prefrontal cortex (in the frontal lobe) and the left parahippocampal cortex (in the temporal lobe) are more active during encoding for items that would eventually be remembered than for items that would eventually be forgotten.

EPISODIC AND SEMANTIC MEMORY   Another distinction between types of memory is important to know, although its status is not quite as clear as the explicit versus implicit distinction. Endel Tulving (1972) proposed that there are two subsystems within explicit memory. **Episodic memories**

Table 6.1	Characteristics of episodic memory
Characteristic	**Description**
Involves consciousness	Episodic memory requires conscious awareness. This type of memory also supports conscious awareness and a sense of conscious self in time.
Involves the past	When we think about the past, we use episodic memory.
Involves events	Episodic memories concern personal events experienced by the rememberer.
Encoding is rapid and often automatic	Since you only experience every event once in time (and then move on to another event), encoding of episodic memory occurs rapidly and often without mental effort.
Retrieval process is required	As they are conscious, even though encoding is often automatic, episodic memories require a conscious act of recollection.
Retrieval depends on cues	The retrieval process is influenced by which cues trigger the episodic memory.
It is fallible and reconstructive	Episodic memory is not perfect and is prone to error, often changing due to a retrieval process that is reconstructive, not passively replaying.

Source: D. A. Gallo and M. E. Wheeler (2013), Episodic memory, in *The Oxford Handbook of Cognitive Psychology* (Oxford: Oxford University Press).

are associated with a particular time and place (i.e., you know when and where you acquired the material). Episodic memories are also associated with a "this happened to me" feeling; there is a personal quality to the act of remembering. If we asked you, "When was the last time you bought a pair of shoes?" you would recall an episodic memory. Such memories can be contrasted with **semantic memories**. Suppose we asked you, "Is a loafer a type of shoe?" You would answer yes, but there is no time or place information associated with that memory, nor is there an "it happened to me" feeling. Semantic memory is sometimes called knowledge of the world. All your knowledge of what things are, what they look like, how they work, and so on is part of semantic memory.

Tulving (1972, 1983, 2002) argued that semantic and episodic memory differ in a number of important ways in terms of mental processes. Gallo and Wheeler (2013) updated Tulving's features and described seven defining criteria of episodic memory (see Table 6.1). We will return to some of these features of episodic memory in Chapter 7 when we discuss memory processes, but for now, encoding is the process of experiencing or putting memories into long-term memory, whereas retrieval is the process of conscious remembering – getting information out of long-term memory.

As we noted at the beginning of this section, the distinction between episodic and semantic memory is not as clear-cut as the distinction between explicit and implicit memory. Our conscious experience of these two types of remembering may indicate that they are different, and initial neuroscientific evidence also seemed to confirm their distinctiveness. However, there are both conceptual and neuroscientific issues that suggest that the line between episodic and semantic, while useful, may be blurrier than it seems.

The first conceptual issue is that all semantic memory must start as episodic. As Gallo and Wheeler (2013) noted, episodic memory is linked to an individual's personal experience and therefore to their sensory experiences of the event (see Table 6.1). But semantic memory is dependent, at least at first, on episodic memory. You don't learn any facts or concepts without having a sensory experience of the moment when you learn that fact first. For example, you know that the Eiffel Tower is in Paris, and that's a semantic memory. At some point, you learned this fact for the first time: "Yesterday at school, we learned about the Eiffel Tower" (see Figure 6.3). In that way, since semantic memory begins with episodic memory and depends on it, they are not as separate as we might think.

Another conceptual problem with the episodic/semantic distinction is that these types of memory differ on dimensions other than "facts" versus "experiences." Episodic memories are typically encoded and rehearsed much less often than semantic memories. We might encode an episodic memory only once (that time you went to McDonald's and they let you try on one of the McDonald's caps) and then rehearse the memory over the course of a few years when telling the story. But how many times have you rehearsed the semantic knowledge that a McDonald's is a fast-food restaurant? If episodic is simply rehearsed more than semantic, it is not the content ("experiences") that makes it different but that it is rehearsed more frequently – hardly a difference worth a label.

It may seem that a distinction between "facts" and "events" should be universal across all humanity, but there can be interesting cultural differences in how people's memories are structured. Wang (2021) reviews cultural differences in memory structure, such as how people segment events into parts. In other words, how many event boundaries do people form in their memories of events? Across several studies, they found that compared with Asians, European Americans identified more event boundaries and therefore more distinct segments of events, both when watching videos (Swallow & Wang, 2020) and when reading narrative text (Wang, 2009).

Because of problems such as these, some memory researchers (Eustache et al., 2016; Glenberg, 1997; Greenberg & Verfaellie, 2010; Johnson & Hasher, 1987) have argued that episodic and semantic memory are neither separable systems nor the only two explicit memory systems (but see also Schacter & Tulving, 1994). For example, perhaps we have personal semantic memories – facts about oneself that are not quite episodic nor quite semantic, like "I attended Duke University" or "I enjoy Vegemite." Renoult et al. (2012) note that such memories have a neural signature that looks both episodic and semantic, and they interpret the different anatomic bases as reflecting a few different processes at work or perhaps the difference in the amount of practice the memories have received.

Does neuroscientific evidence help settle whether episodic and semantic are truly separate memory systems? Initial evidence from amnesic patients seemed to offer evidence of anatomic dissociation. There have been reports of patients who have a selective loss of episodic but not semantic memory (Wheeler & McMillan, 2001). For example, Endel Tulving and his colleagues (Hayman et al., 1993; Rosenbaum et al., 2005; Tulving et al., 1988) reported on a man, Kent Cochrane (known as K.C. until his death in 2014), who suffered extensive damage to the left hemisphere and some damage to the right as a consequence of a motorcycle accident at age thirty. Cochrane showed intact intellectual functioning, and his semantic memory seemed to be intact. His vocabulary appeared to be normal, and he could remember technical terms associated with his job. What Cochrane seemed to have lost is episodic memory. He could not remember events from his life that should have been quite vivid, for example, the events surrounding a train derailment in which 240,000 people (including Cochrane) had to evacuate their homes for a week or any of the circumstances of the death of his brother by drowning.

(a)

(b)

Figure 6.3. Knowing that the Eiffel Tower is in Paris compared with the moment of learning this fact.
(Source: (a) Shaoyang Zhou/EyeEm/Getty Images; (b) FatCamera/E+/Getty Images.)

What of neuroimaging? Early imaging data seemed to confirm the anatomic dissociations of the amnesic patients. Semantic retrieval was consistently associated with activity in the left frontal cortex, whereas episodic retrieval was more often associated with right frontal activity (see Buckner & Petersen, 1996; Alam et al., 2019). While other research has found some complications with this simple lateralized picture (Cabeza & Nyberg, 2000; Mayes & Montaldi, 2001; Rajah & McIntosh, 2005; Orth et al., 2022), recent reviews (Binder et al., 2009; Jefferies & Wang, 2021) have confirmed both overlap and lateralization in the network of brain areas implicated in semantic and episodic memories. They argue this pattern makes sense, in that episodic memories necessarily contain semantic knowledge, but are often richer and full of detail. For example, remembering "I found a five-foot black snake under my porch last weekend" requires semantic knowledge of "snake," "porch," and "weekend."

While episodic and semantic memory may not be perfectly distinct memory systems, there are useful distinctions between how they operate and how they are used. In addition, there are some anatomic differences. However, we have seen that these distinctions are imperfect: There are conceptual confounds with the cognitive differences between the two systems and the neuroscientific evidence shows anatomic dissociation in amnesic patients, but considerable overlap in neuroimaging studies. Renoult et al. (2019) suggest that the episodic/semantic distinction may not be perfectly crisp, but it is still useful. These two systems of explicit memory may not be as distinct as imagined in early studies, but current evidence of the neural correlates still suggests that considering the episodic elements of the memory separately from semantic knowledge helps us generate interesting experiments, regardless of how distinct the systems turn out to be.

Implicit Memory

As opposed to explicit memory, **implicit memory** is characterized by a change in behavior due to past events, without the conscious experience of recollection. When implicit memory is expressed, the memory is outside of our awareness. Implicit memory often reflects the improvement of mental processes that are outside of awareness.

Implicit memory has several subtypes, but the key similarity among them is that we are not aware of the content of the memory. For example, when we ride a bicycle, we use precise muscle movements to stay upright while moving forward. You might have heard of such motor skill learning described as "muscle memory," but the learning is in your brain, and it is a type of implicit memory. Another form of implicit memory is reflected in faster access to a memory that you've retrieved recently, a process called *priming*. The third type of implicit memory we will discuss is *conditioning*, which you may recall from Chapter 1. In each of these cases, we use memory without awareness of how we are using it.

MOTOR SKILL LEARNING   If explicit memory is memory *that* (*that* the capital of Australia is Canberra, *that* my soccer team won the tournament), then motor skill is memory *how*. It is knowledge of how to complete a set of motor actions, without necessarily even realizing that we are using memory. Anyone who has tried to teach someone else a motor skill, like tying shoelaces, has encountered the frustration of trying to explain how to do a task without realizing that the words don't help that much. "Cross the bunny ears" doesn't actually tell you exactly where to grip the shoelace with which fingers, how tightly to grasp them, and how to move your fingers and hand in three dimensions. "Like this" doesn't really help you shoot a soccer ball (Figure 6.4), because there

(a)

(b)

(c)

Figure 6.4. Three stages in the motor skill of kicking a soccer ball. Notice how different the postures of the three players are. In addition, the timing of postural changes (hard to capture in a single photograph) must be quite precise to maintain balance throughout the motion. Think of how difficult it would be to describe these movements in words (OK, so now your right leg moves to about forty-five degrees and your right arm comes up while your left arm swings backward at this angle . . .). (Source: (a) Johner Images/Getty Images; (b) Layland Masuda/Moment/Getty Images; (c) strickke/E+/Getty Images.)

Figure 6.5. Stacking cups quickly (called speed stacking) is a sequencing skill and a sport that is gaining popularity in the United States. (Source: Lance King/Getty Images.)

are hundreds of small adjustments of posture and timing. Even if an expert were there to explain, many of these adjustments cannot be communicated easily.

Many motor skills call for a sequence of movements to be executed quickly and accurately. One type of motor skill is therefore a sequencing skill (Dayan & Cohen, 2011; Willingham et al., 1989). Think of typing your name on a standard keyboard. This could be accomplished in the "hunt and peck" style with your index finger: finding the correct key, pressing it down, releasing it by raising your finger, then moving your hand out of the way as you find the next letter. More skilled performance would be typing with many fingers, with each step in the sequence being executed much more quickly and accurately. Accuracy in this case could be pressing the key in its center, but also pressing it for the correct amount of time; many beginning typists press down the keys too long and repeeeeeeaaaaaaaaaaaaaaattttttttttt letters. Another example of a sequencing skill is competitive cup stacking, where participants try to stack and take down a set of cups as quickly as possible (see Figure 6.5).

Another type of motor skill is called an **adaptation skill**. In this situation, the skill learned is adapting to a relationship between vision and movement. Adaptation skills are often studied in the lab by wearing prism goggles that shift what is seen a certain amount to the right or left (see Figure 6.6a). So, if you were wearing left-shifting prism goggles and attempted to reach quickly to a target (or give someone a high-five), you would miss to the left (see Figure 6.6b). Given practice, you could adapt to this new visuomotor mapping and improve your performance at this motor skill. Outside of the lab, you can imagine that this type of motor skill is similar to certain elements of learning to drive. A certain foot pressure on the gas pedal will lead to a visual consequence of the world moving by at a certain speed. A turn of the steering wheel of a particular angle leads to a

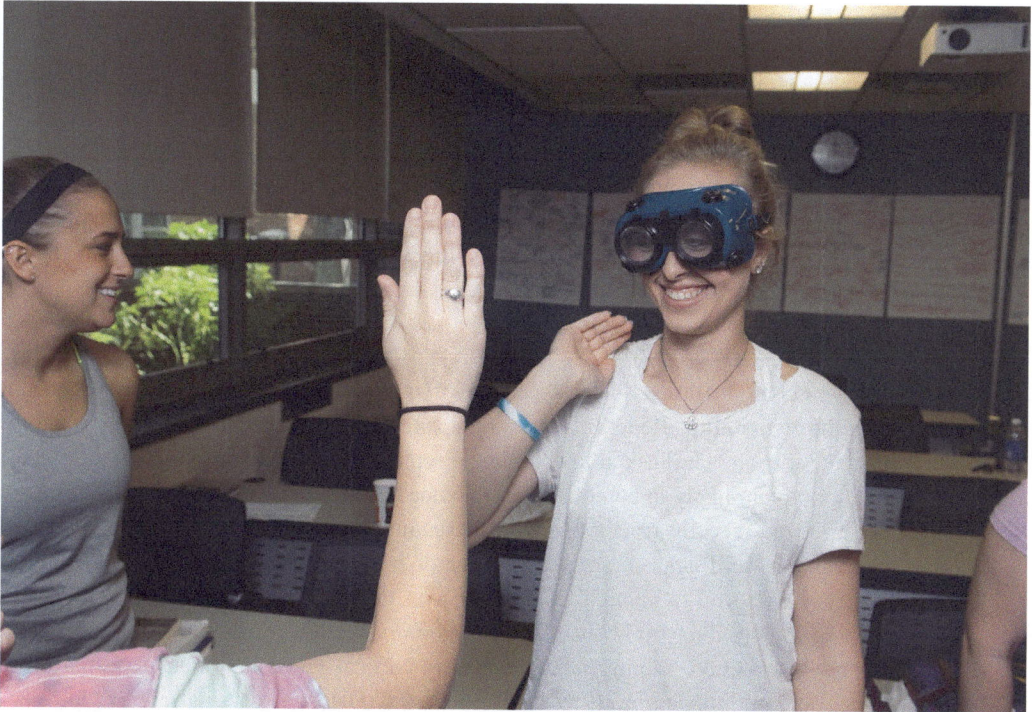

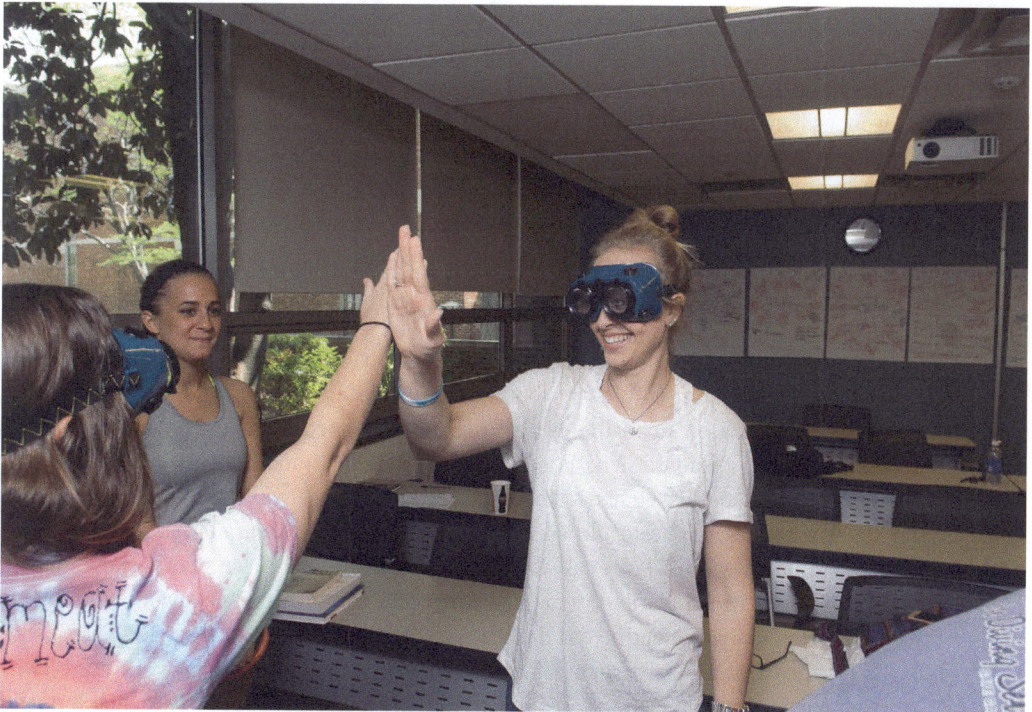

Figure 6.6. Wearing prism goggles shifts the wearer's view so that when they attempt a movement to a target, they miss the target. With practice, they gain an adaptation skill of learning the relationship between their view and the movements needed to be successful.

turning of the front wheels by a certain amount and a shifting of the world you see out of the car windshield.

Motor skill is so pervasive in what we do and the term describes so many different activities that we should perhaps not be surprised to learn that many different parts of the brain contribute to motor skill learning. The most important of these are the basal ganglia, primary and secondary motor cortex, prefrontal cortex, cerebellum, and parietal cortex (Willingham, 1998a; Robbe & Dudman, 2020; Taylor & McDougle, 2020). Many of these brain areas also support motor planning and execution – motor skill learning happens via changes to that part of the brain that supports movement.

REPETITION PRIMING   Another type of implicit memory is evident in a phenomenon called **repetition priming**. Repetition priming makes recently used representations more available for reuse. For example, if asked to complete a sentence with the word that you think makes sense, you might be more likely to complete the sentence "Tom was learning to ____" with "drive" or "type" because you recently read those words. Reading the word "cherry" makes you slightly faster in reading the word again a short time later or makes it more likely that you will say "cherry" if someone asks you to name a fruit. When you think of a word or concept, it "primes" that word, making it more likely to be available for memory the next time.

Repetition priming is supported by cortical perceptual areas – visual priming by visual cortex and auditory priming by auditory cortex. Damage to visual cortex, for example, disrupts priming (Gabrieli et al., 1995). Brain imaging studies show that repetition priming is associated with a *decrease* in activity in cortical regions (Bergerbest et al., 2004; Schacter & Buckner, 1998; Segaert et al., 2013). This decrease in activity is usually interpreted as reflecting easier processing – because the stimulus has been identified recently, the brain area that supports its identification doesn't have to work as hard the second time around, perhaps through enhanced neural synchronization (Gotts et al., 2012). This decrease in activity with increased memory performance (associated with repetition priming) is a good reminder that determining the parts of the brain that support a task is not as simple as "this brain area lights up more," although that's how it's often depicted in the popular press.

CONDITIONING   Conditioning is another form of implicit memory. We discussed classical conditioning in Chapter 1, using food as the unconditioned stimulus, but experiments with humans often use a puff of air to the eye as the unconditioned stimulus, which leads to blinking as the unconditioned response. The conditioned stimulus (a tone) is paired with the air puff until the conditioned stimulus elicits a conditioned response (blinking). Both patient studies and brain imaging studies implicate the **cerebellum** in this type of learning (Blaxton et al., 1996; Gerwig et al., 2005; Woodruff-Pak et al., 2000). The motivation for these studies came, in part, from careful work in animals (primarily the rabbit), where the neural circuit was worked out in great detail and the cerebellum was identified as the key site of learning (for a review, see Thompson & Steinmetz, 2009). In humans, the hippocampus is also implicated, and recent work used TMS (transcranial magnetic stimulaton: using magnetic pulses to temporarily disrupt a particular brain area) to suggest that the prefrontal cortex also mediates eyeblink conditioning, likely by modulating the connection between the hippocampus and the cerebellum (Nardone et al., 2019). This conditioning can happen entirely outside of awareness (Clark & Squire, 1998).

Emotional conditioning is a classical conditioning situation in which the unconditioned response is an emotion. Fear is the emotion that has been studied most frequently. For example, a participant might be shown slides of different objects, and each time the slide depicts a snake, the participant is given a mild electric shock. In time, pictures of snakes will come to elicit fear, measured by a physiological response like increased perspiration or heart rate. This type of learning depends on the **amygdala**. As with classical conditioning, the motivation for this work in humans came from very detailed knowledge of the neural circuit supporting emotional conditioning in other species (e.g., LeDoux, 2000), which corresponds well to human brain imaging studies (e.g., Knight et al., 2005; Grabenhorst et al., 2020).

CURRENT STATUS OF MEMORY SYSTEMS   Research since the mid 1980s has shown that our previous definitions of memory were too narrow because they were restricted to conscious, explicit forms of memory. Most memory theorists believe that many cognitive systems have learning embedded in them. For example, your visual system changes with experience, and that learning can support performance on priming tasks. Similarly, the motor control system that allows you to move around in the world changes with experience, and those changes support motor skill learning. So you have a system that is wholly devoted to memory – that's the explicit system – but you also have other systems that are dedicated primarily to another function, such as vision or movement, and these systems also have the capability to learn. The motor system can learn motor skills, the visual system can learn perceptual skills, and so on. In these forms of memory, nothing is stored per se, but there are changes to the actual processes; the motor system or the visual system is changed. Explicit memory seems to fit a storehouse metaphor, with memory being supported by the creation and storage of new representations. Researchers will continue to explore the differences between these mechanisms of representing the past and changing our thoughts and behavior accordingly, whether we describe these differences as systems, tasks, or processes.

Stand-on-One-Foot Questions

6.1.   What key feature would make potential memory systems separate?

6.2.   What is the origin of the multiple memory systems idea?

6.3.   Is your knowledge of the definition of episodic memory right now an episodic memory, a semantic memory, or both? Which would it be when you reach the end of this book?

Questions That Require Two Feet

6.4.   How likely does it seem to you that separate memory systems interact in some fashion?

6.5.   When I was about nine, I ran a low-grade fever for about three months. The doctors gave me a great many tests, trying to determine the cause. Many of these tests were painful. Until my mid twenties, the smell of denatured alcohol (as you would smell in a hospital) made me uneasy. Which memory system supported that learning?

6.6.   Can you think of a time when two of your memory systems may have conflicted?

How Is Explicit Memory Organized?

Preview

Within the framework that we have described, particular interest has focused on how our explicit memories are organized. Organization allows us to retrieve the right memory from the storehouse. Our memory systems do not merely allow us to find the desired memory quickly. If what is desired is not in memory, the system provides something close in meaning, or it provides material that may help us guess about the desired information. One early theory of memory organization, the hierarchical model, suggested that concepts were placed in a taxonomic hierarchy (*animal* above *bird*, *bird* above *canary*). When data suggested that concepts were not necessarily organized in a rigid hierarchy, later models proposed that memory was structured in networks of mutual association, whereby thinking about one concept would bring semantically related concepts to mind (e.g., thinking about the concept *doctor* makes it a little more likely that you'll think of the related concept *patient*). A third type of model uses distributed representation, meaning that one concept is represented by many units of the model; in fact, one unit participates in the representation of many concepts, and which concept is represented at any moment depends on the state of the entire model.

Philosophers have speculated about the structure of knowledge. Educators have wondered how to teach history or science so that it makes sense; how do we teach new content so that it "fits" into what we already know? To cognitive psychologists, these questions translate to the question, How is explicit memory organized? Although "memory" means more to cognitive psychologists than conscious memory for events and facts, there is no doubt that conscious memory is a primary object of study when we consider organization.

The storehouse metaphor works well for explicit memory. (To a point. When we take up the storage and retrieval of memories, it won't work as well.) We each have an amazing amount of material stored in memory, although it doesn't always feel that way. Most college students have a reading vocabulary of approximately 60,000 words. Add to that all your memories about what things are; how things work; memory for faces, voices (Mom), and music ("You know it's not the same, as it was … as it was …"); and so on. The mind is faced with the formidable problem of finding useful information quickly among these riches, and our ability to find memories efficiently is truly amazing. For example, people can identify popular songs when presented with a snippet as short as 200 milliseconds (Schellenberg et al., 1999), and they can recognize a picture of an animal with a presentation as short as one millisecond (Thurgood et al., 2011)!

As a starting point, we'll explain a bit about organizing systems of information in general, not just the human memory system. That will help you to understand why cognitive psychologists have posed the questions we consider later in the chapter.

Addressing Systems

Let's begin with an information storage system that we understand: a library. How do you find the right book in a library? Books are ordered according to the Library of Congress numbering system so we can look for them according to their subject matter. To find a particular book, you need its unique number, which you find in the catalog – a master list with the specific numbers of all the library's volumes. The system used in a library is called an **addressing system** because each entity in the storehouse has a unique address, which is critical for finding what you want. If the number 798.30 is erased from the book or from the master list, or if the book is accidentally shelved as 898.30, no one will be able to retrieve it, or at least not quickly.

The internet also uses an address system. Each computer connected to the internet (called a server) has a unique address, called an Internet Protocol address (or IP address), with four numbers, such as http://8.8.8.8. However, it would be quite laborious for us each to have a massive address book listing each IP address of the sites we want to visit, so there is a distributed system of computers on the internet that maintains mappings of IP addresses to the names that we are familiar with (and type into our address bars). These computers are called domain name servers, and together they form the DNS system. So when we type in www.WillinghamAndRienerCognitionRocks.com, a series of computers is queried as to what four-number address corresponds to that name. Then, once our computer has the pairing of the text address and the numerical address, it can find the server where the desired webpage is located. So organization of this sort of "memory" system – a library or the internet – is simply a long list of addresses that must be searched.

The human mind, however, behaves in ways inconsistent with such a system. If your mind used an addressing system, the kinds of memory errors you made would be unpredictable. For example, suppose someone asked you, "Is there a good coffee shop around here?" If your master memory list contained the name of a good coffee shop at memory address 78342, but your memory system made an error in one digit and looked up memory location 88342, anything could be at that address, and you might answer the question by singing "Never Gonna Give You Up." Memory errors tend to produce, not random information, but near misses: an answer that is wrong but is at least related to the right answer. Usually, such errors are related in terms of meaning. For example, we might ask you, "Can you name the seven dwarfs from *Snow White*?" You might answer "Sneezy, Doc, Bashful, Grumpy, Dopey, Happy, and Blitzen," which is wrong because the last is one of Santa's reindeer, but you confuse lists of names of small groups of mythical creatures. Such errors indicate that our memory isn't simply a long list, because Snow White's dwarfs might be associated with a great many things, not just neighbors on a list, such as "mythical creatures," children's stories, Disney movies, groups of seven, or short people.

Content-Addressable Storage

In **content-addressable storage**, the content of the memory is itself the storage address. You find a memory's location in the storehouse based on the actual content of the memory.

This system would produce near misses; if you search memory for the name of a well-known American actor in action movies named Chris (Chris Evans) and you have a similar concept in memory (Chris Pine), Chris Pine pops out of memory because of the similarity of content. Content-addressable storage systems retrieve memories very quickly, and the time it takes to retrieve a memory from the storehouse does not increase as you add more information. Our memory systems do seem to work that way; as we learn more things, it doesn't take longer to retrieve facts about the old things.

Unfortunately, the feature of this system that makes the speed possible also poses a problem. The point of the system is that you access memories based on their content. But how does a memory "know" when it is being called on? Every memory must have the capability of knowing what you're asking for and evaluating whether its content is a good enough match. Making each memory "smart" in this way requires a big commitment in processing resources, whether the system is computer memory built on this principle or a speculative model of how the brain works.

The human memory system has a capability even beyond that of a simple content-addressable system, however, which is best illustrated by example. Suppose we ask you this question: "Does Jennifer Lawrence have a large intestine?"

You would answer yes, but how could you do so? It's likely that you've never encoded that fact, so it can't be in memory. On what basis do you give a confident yes?

Your yes is not based on a fact in memory about Jennifer Lawrence; it is based on an inference. When you try to retrieve information that has not been encoded directly, your memory system often pulls up related information that allows you to make an inference to answer the question, as follows:

> **From memory:** Humans have a large intestine.
> **From memory:** Jennifer Lawrence is a human.
> **Inference:** Therefore, Jennifer Lawrence has a large intestine.

The requested information is not in memory, but you do have in memory other information that can help you answer the question, and that information is retrieved. How does the memory system "know" the right information to produce when what is requested is not in the system?

We hope it is now evident why we started this section by discussing the capabilities of your memory system; these capabilities offer important clues to organization. We'll refer back to them as we continue, and we'll begin with the capability that most interested the first creators of cognitive models of memory: What is the organization that allows not just the simple retrieval of facts but also the retrieval of relevant facts when the information needed is not stored?

Hierarchical Theory

The **hierarchical theory** proposed a clever solution to information retrieval (Collins & Quillian, 1969, 1972). In their model (and in many of the models that followed), memory is organized not as a list but as a network. Such networks are composed of two basic elements: nodes and links (Figure 6.7).

Nodes represent concepts, such as *red*, *candy*, *bird*, or *president*. Nodes have levels of **activation**, meaning that they can be inactive and have no effect on the rest of the network, or they can be active and thereby change the activity of the parts of the network they are connected to. In practical terms, nodes become active when the concept they represent is present in the environment. Thus, the concept *bird* might become active through seeing a picture of a bird, seeing a real bird, or hearing or reading the word *bird*, and so on.

Links represent relationships between concepts, such as "has this property" or "is an example of." As shown in Figure 6.7, links in a hierarchical memory structure connect nodes and can provide property descriptions of concepts. Thus, the idea that a living thing must breathe is represented in the model through a concept (*living thing*), a property (*breathe*), and a link (*must*).

An important characteristic of the model is **property inheritance**. Moving down the hierarchy from *animal* to *bird* to *chicken*, we see that concepts inherit properties from the concepts above them in the hierarchy. Hence, an animal is a type of living thing, so it inherits the properties of living things. For example, chickens inherit the properties *must breathe* and *must eat* from the concept *animal*.

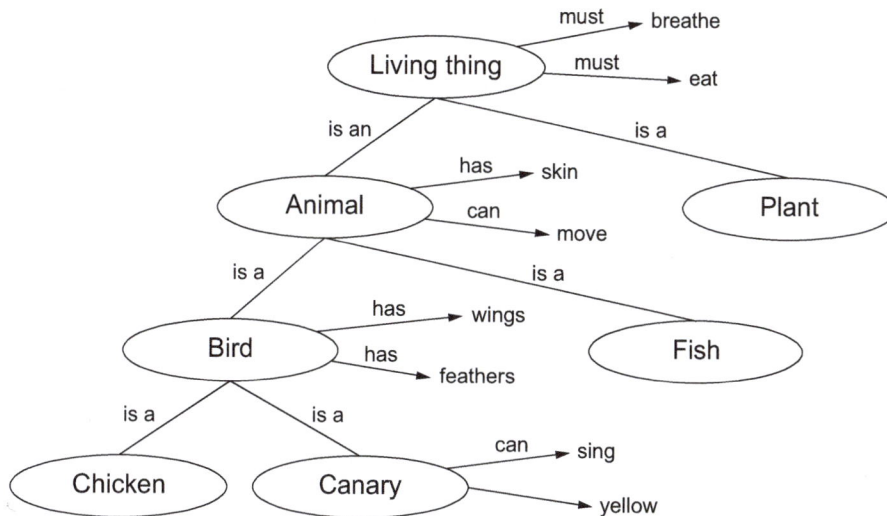

Figure 6.7. An example of a hierarchical network described by Collins and Quillian (1969) representing animal, canary, and chicken, among other concepts. There are also links such as "is a" and "has." (Source: A. M. Collins and M. R. Quillian [1969], Retrieval time from semantic memory, *Journal of Verbal Learning and Verbal Behavior*, 8[2], 241.)

You'll remember that we asked earlier what happens when an inference is needed to answer a question. The inheritance of properties can be important in such situations. If we were to ask you, "Does a canary breathe?" the model predicts that you would first go to the node representing the concept *canary*. You would examine the properties associated with *canary* and discover that breathing or not breathing is not part of the representation of what a canary does, so you would move up one level in the hierarchy to the concept *bird* to see whether breathing or not breathing is stored with being a bird. You'd discover it is not, and you'd continue to the concept *animal* and, finally, to *living thing*, where you would find the relevant information.

Suppose we make the simple assumption that moving up the hierarchy takes time. We would predict that statements farther apart on the hierarchy would take a longer time to verify. Collins and Quillian (1969) tested exactly that prediction by showing one sentence at a time on a computer screen and asking participants to decide whether the sentence was true or false. Half the time, the sentence was false ("A canary is a plant"), but the experimenters were really interested in how long it took participants to verify the sentences when they were true. Response times came out in the order that the model predicted. The numbers in parentheses are the response times to verify the sentences:

A canary is a canary. (1,000 milliseconds)
A canary is a bird. (1,160 milliseconds)
A canary is an animal. (1,240 milliseconds)

The effect worked just as well for properties:

A canary can sing. (1,305 milliseconds)
A canary has wings. (1,395 milliseconds)
A canary has skin. (1,480 milliseconds)

Thus, the findings seemed to support the model for the tricky ability we discussed regarding Jennifer Lawrence's intestine.

Unfortunately, researchers soon uncovered problems in the model's predictions. For example, people were faster to verify the sentence "A chicken is an animal" than to verify "A chicken is a bird." Moving from chicken to bird (one node) ought to take less time than going from chicken to bird to animal (at least two nodes). Thus, the hierarchy doesn't seem to hold for all cases.

Another problem of this model grows out of a property that initially seemed to be a strength. Looking at Figure 6.7, you'll notice that the property *has wings* is stored only once, with *bird*; it makes sense to store this property along with all the other common properties of birds. The principle of **cognitive economy** refers to designing a cognitive system in a way that conserves resources. Yet, this principle does not appear to be true in the brain, at least not the way Collins and Quillian (1969) implemented it. Carol Conrad (1972) gave participants a list of words and asked them to write down what each word made them think of. She found that participants often wrote information that was one or two levels higher in the hierarchy. For example, if you give people the word *robin*, *canary*, or *bluebird*, they are very likely to write the verb *flies* as one of the properties, even though *flies* goes with the higher-level concept *bird*. The property *flies* also seems to be stored along with *robin*, *canary*, and *bluebird*.

Spreading Activation Theories

Allan Collins and Elizabeth Loftus (1975) proposed a **spreading activation model** to address the shortcomings of the earlier model. This is another network model, again consisting of nodes and links, but now the links represent associations between semantically related concepts. Instead of a hierarchy with groups and categories, now there were just concepts associated with each other through meaning, with "is an example of" being just one type of association between concepts. Memory is thus conceived as a vast web of linked concepts called a **semantic network**. Collins and Loftus used links that had properties such as *is a* and *has a*. Later models that built on their work did not (see McClelland, 1981), and our discussion is based on these. In a semantic network, as in a hierarchical network, nodes can become active, and you can think of this activity as the node having energy. Nodes become active through stimulation from the environment. Thus, the concept *President* might become active through seeing a picture of the president or through hearing or reading the word *President*.

Figure 6.8 shows three nodes in a memory network. (We're taking a break from canaries and chickens.) Time moves from left to right in the figure, so on the left we see a node without activation; then, the word *President* comes in from the environment (because someone said it, for

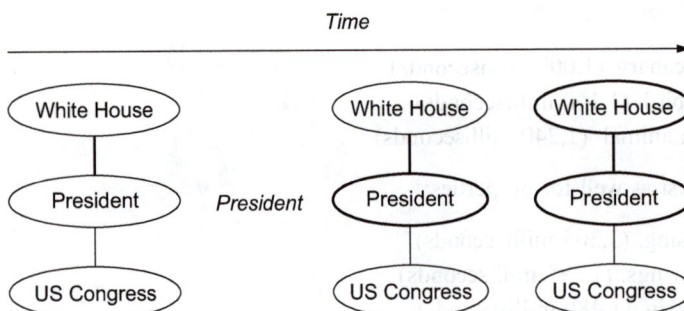

Time

Figure 6.8. (left) When the word *President* is perceived in the environment, (center) the corresponding concept becomes active in memory, and (right) activation spreads to related concepts. The amount of activation depends on the weight of the link between concepts.

example), and on the right we see the same node, now activated, with the activation represented by the thicker border on the node. Active nodes send some of their activity to other linked nodes, which can also become active. Activated nodes send a high proportion of their activation to closely related concepts. Hence, *President* might send a lot of activation to *White House* but less to *Congress*. This principle is shown in the right part of the figure.

A formal definition has been proposed for the six properties of a semantic network (Rumelhart et al., 1986):

1. **A set of units.** Each unit represents a concept.
2. **A state of activation.** Each unit has its own state of activation, an amount of "energy" at a given moment.
3. **An output function.** Units pass activation to one another. The amount of activation a unit passes to its neighbors depends on its output function, which relates the current activation state of the unit to the amount of activation it sends down its links. The output activation function may simply be to multiply the activation by 1 (sending the same amount of activation down the links as the unit itself has) or 0.5 (sending half the activation). Other models use a threshold function, so the unit must meet an activation threshold before it can influence its neighbors.
4. **A pattern of connectivity.** Units are connected to one another by links of different strengths. The extent to which you know that birds fly, for example, depends on the strength or weight of the link between *bird* and *flies.*
5. **An activation rule.** A unit follows a rule to integrate the activation sent to it by other units via links. If someone says to you "caramel color, carbonated, cold," these words are closely associated with the concept *cola.* Suppose that these three concepts (*caramel color, carbonated, cold*), which were activated when the words were said, send activations of 0.85, 0.48, and 0.15 to the concept *cola.* What will the activation of *cola* now be? Should we add the three, yielding 1.48? Should we find the mean, yielding 0.49? Should we allow only activations higher than 0.25 to enter our calculations and take the mean of those, yielding 0.67? The activation rule determines how the inputs should be combined.
6. **Learning rules to change weights.** A semantic network cannot be static. The knowledge of the network is in weights, so there must be a mechanism to change the weights if the model is to learn. Suppose you didn't know that horses love candy peppermints. The link between *horse* and *peppermint* would be 0. Now that you've read that fact one time, what should the weight of that link be? There must be a rule by which the weights change. (Horses do like peppermints, by the way.)

Spreading Activation Models: An Example

We've gone over the properties of spreading activation models. For a better sense of their strengths, let's look at one example in depth (following McClelland, 1981). Table 6.2 lists information about ten typical American breakfast foods. We can present the information in the clearly delineated table as shown. If you look carefully, you might already be thinking that some of that information isn't quite right, but bear with us, and even your concerns will be good examples of how to think about spreading activation models. All the information in this list can be represented in a semantic network. A subset of the list is shown in Figure 6.9; the units in the center of the network do not represent any concept, but they are important for passing activation between nodes.

Table 6.2 American breakfast foods

Name	Preparation	Color	Gluten?	Animal product?	USDA MyPlate category
Eggs	Stove	White/yellow	No	Yes	Protein
Sausage	Stove	Brown	No	Yes	Protein
Bacon	Stove	Red	No	Yes	Protein
Toast	Toaster	Beige	Yes	No	Grain
Oatmeal	Stove	Beige	No	No	Grain
Banana	None	Yellow	No	No	Fruit
Hash Browns	Oven	Light brown	No	No	Vegetable
Milk	None	White	No	Yes	Dairy
Avocado	None	Green	No	No	Vegetable
Grits	Stove	Yellow	No	No	Grain
Scrapple	Stove	Brown	Yes	Yes	Protein
Yogurt	None	White	No	Yes	Dairy

Note. USDA = US Department of Agriculture.

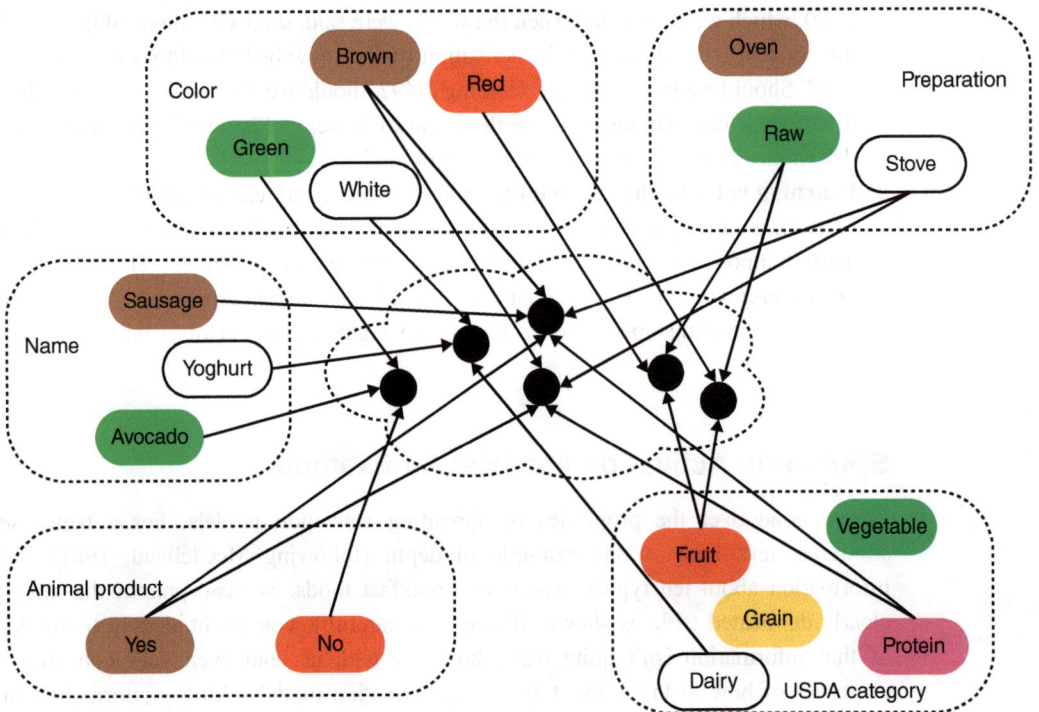

Figure 6.9. Some of the information from Table 6.2 presented in a network.

This sort of model has a number of useful characteristics. First, it obviously allows for the retrieval of properties. If you say "eggs," that word is perceived and the *eggs* node becomes active. That node passes activity to other nodes, and it will lead to activity of the nodes *protein*, *animal product*, *no gluten*, *stove*, and *white/yellow color.*

Second, the model allows content-addressable storage. Recall that this is a system whereby memories are accessed not by an address but by their content. For example, if we were to activate the nodes *white* and *dairy*, the activation would spread, and *yogurt* would become active. If we were to activate *protein*, then the proteins (which in this network are all brown animal products) would become active.

Third, this kind of model can explain a common feature of memory concepts and categories: Some instances are more typical examples than others. We'll discuss typicality in more detail in Chapter 9, but here's a brief definition for now. One difficulty with a yes/no model of category membership is that some members seem to belong more in their category than others. You know how some birds just seem birdier than others? For example, Americans think of robins as really birdy birds, whereas ostriches just aren't. Typical examples of a category have lots of features that are typical of the category; a robin seems typical because it has lots of properties that are typical of American birds: *small*, *sits in trees*, *lays eggs*, *eats insects*. An atypical bird has fewer typical characteristics.

Typicality is easy to account for in the spreading activation model. A concept such as *robin* will have strong links to many concepts that are in turn strongly linked to bird (*small*, *sits in trees*, *lays eggs*). An atypical bird, such as an ostrich, has many links to concepts that are weakly linked to bird (*large*, *runs fast*, *can't fly*). If I say "bird," all the nodes that have strong links to that concept will become active. Thus, it is easy for me to describe the typical bird. Similarly, in the model in Figure 6.9, if I say "breakfast protein," the features of typical American breakfast proteins become active, even if no single food has all the typical qualities. The nodes most strongly linked to "breakfast proteins" just naturally become active.

Fourth, the model naturally creates default values that a variable or an attribute takes in the absence of any other information. For example, how does a bird get around? In the absence of any other information, we can assume that it flies; this is the default state. Default values are assigned for concepts as a natural part of the spreading activation. If you have reason to think that the object you're dealing with is a bird, then the connection between *bird* and *flies* will lead to activation in the concept *flies*, unless you are specifically told that this bird does not fly.

Fifth, spreading activation models are resistant to faulty input. Suppose you were told, "I had a good breakfast yesterday. I can't remember everything, but it was dairy, protein, white in color and cooked in the toaster." You would say, "You mean yogurt, but it was not toasted." Notice that you've retrieved the right memory, even though you were given faulty information. It's easy to imagine that you could check the memory system for a description of a dairy product prepared in the toaster and find nothing; indeed, you've never heard of a breakfast matching the description given. But your memory system is resistant to faulty input and can come up with the right memory. Spreading activation models have this property. The concepts *dairy* and *white* are so strongly linked to *yogurt* that the node is activated, despite the fact that *toaster* might inhibit its activation a bit. Once *yogurt* is activated, that in turn activates *fresh*, which makes you surmise that there was an error in the description (Figure 6.10).

Here is a good point to pause for a moment and remind ourselves that yes, this information is about the foods, but we are talking about how the concepts of the foods are represented in our minds. Both what is included in breakfast at all and what counts as "typical" may vary from person

Table 6.3 British breakfast foods

Food	Preparation	Color	Gluten?	Animal product?	NHS Eatwell Guide category
Eggs	Stove	White/yellow	Yes	Yes	Protein
Toast	Toaster	Tan	Yes	No	Grain
Bacon	Stove	Red	Yes	Yes	Protein
Bubble and squeak	Stove	Beige	Yes	No	Fruit/vegetable
Black pudding	Stove	Black	No	Yes	Protein
Tomatoes	Stove	Red	No	No	Fruit/vegetable
Mushrooms	Stove	Brown	No	No	Fruit/vegetable
Beans	Stove	Brown	No	No	Protein

Note. NHS = National Health Service.

Figure 6.10. Yogurt, as many dairy products, is often white and served fresh.

to person and certainly varies across cultures. The inclusion of scrapple (a ground mixture of pork scraps and trimmings combined with cornmeal and wheat flour served in the Mid-Atlantic US, derived from the Pennsylvania Dutch) and grits (porridge made of boiled cornmeal, typically served in the American South) might be specific to those regions.

To follow that point further, imagine two other spreading activation networks from other food cultures. Some typical included elements of a "full English" breakfast are in Table 6.3. Notice how we can change the items, and even change some of the features in the columns (such as substituting the National Health Service's Eatwell Guide for the US Department of Agriculture's MyPlate), but the general principles remain the same. We can activate *fruits/vegetables*, and then *tomatoes*, *mushrooms*, and *bubble and squeak* (a fried mix of potatoes and cabbage, named for the sound they make in the pan) become active. We can also notice that some of these items might be more typically included in a full English breakfast than others.

Similarly, a spreading activation network of Indian breakfast cuisine can have similar categories, but might have a bit more complexity in the "animal product" category due to the country being over 25 percent vegetarian (although estimates vary), the largest percentage in the world (Table 6.4). Given the diversity within that large group, the "animal product" category might

Table 6.4 Indian breakfast foods

Food	Preparation	Color	Gluten?	Vegetarian?	Street food vs. home[a]
Idli	Steamed	Beige	No	Yes	Both
Poori	Oven	Brown	Yes	Yes	Street
Palak paneer	Stove	Green	No	Yes (lacto-ovo-vegetarian)	Home
Dhosa	Stove	Brown	Yes	Yes	Both
Nihari	Oven	Red	No	No	Home
Upma	Stove	Brown	No	Yes	Street
Chana masala	Stove	Brown	No	Yes	Both
Misal	Stove	Multicolored	No	Yes	Street
Paratha	Oven	Brown	No	Yes	All

[a] Can depend on region or personal preference.

not suffice, and indeed, many restaurants distinguish between nonvegetarian, vegetarian, pure vegetarian (avoiding indirect animal products, such as rennet or collagen), and Jain vegetarian (respecting dietary practices of the Jain religion: practicing nonviolence to all living things, including microorganisms like yeast, and not including underground root vegetables). Furthermore, a typical American or British breakfast food semantic network may not include a category of whether someone typically gets this food from a street food vendor or at home or a restaurant. A resident of Mumbai, however, known for its vibrant street food culture, might have some foods they prefer to prepare at home and others they prefer to get from vendors, or maybe even from certain specific vendors.

Our extended exercise in food classification and representation is a good reminder that just like human diets, human minds have both elements of difference and diversity and some universal structure. The concepts of *food* and *meal* are human universals. All human cultures have the concept of *meal*, where one eats several different foods and food types, shared in a social setting with a group of other people. But across cultures, some foods and food types are more typical meals than others. All of your knowledge and memory of breakfast foods can be understood as your own personal spreading activation network, influenced by your culture and experience. (See Figure 6.11.)

There is evidence consistent with the idea that concepts in memory become active and that when the activity surpasses a threshold, they enter awareness. Many paradigms demonstrate repetition priming, which we've discussed earlier. The participant reads a list of words and some time later (perhaps an hour) performs a second task. Some of the words used in the second task are in the original list, but the participant is not told that (Table 6.5). Participants show some **bias** on the second task, caused by the processing of the words on the original list. These repetition priming effects are often interpreted as showing that nodes representing concepts become active when participants first read the words on the list, and for the second task an hour later, they are still somewhat active, making these concepts easier to access. Repetition priming effects indicate that activation of nodes lasts an hour or more and that this activation is measurable.

Another effect, **semantic priming**, indicates that activation passes between nodes. Participants are shown two letter strings and must push one button if both are words and another

Table 6.5 Tasks used to measure priming

Task	Description	Priming measure	Reference
Fragment completion	Participants must complete word fragments to form words. Each fragment has just one possible completion.	Number of fragments successfully completed that were on the original list vs. fragments completed that were not.	Tulving et al. (1982)
Stem completion	Participants must complete word stems to form a word. Each fragment has at least ten possible completions.	Number of stems completed to make a word on the original list vs. stems completed to make words not on the list.	Warrington and Weiskrantz (1968)
Category exemplar generation	Participants must name category members.	Somewhat unusual category members appear on the original list. Priming is measured by how many of these unusual members are mentioned by participants.	Graf et al. (1985)
Lexical decision	Participants see a letter string appear and must respond with a button press as quickly as possible to indicate whether the letter string forms a word.	Priming is reflected by shorter response times to words that were on the list compared with words that were not.	Just and Carpenter (1980)

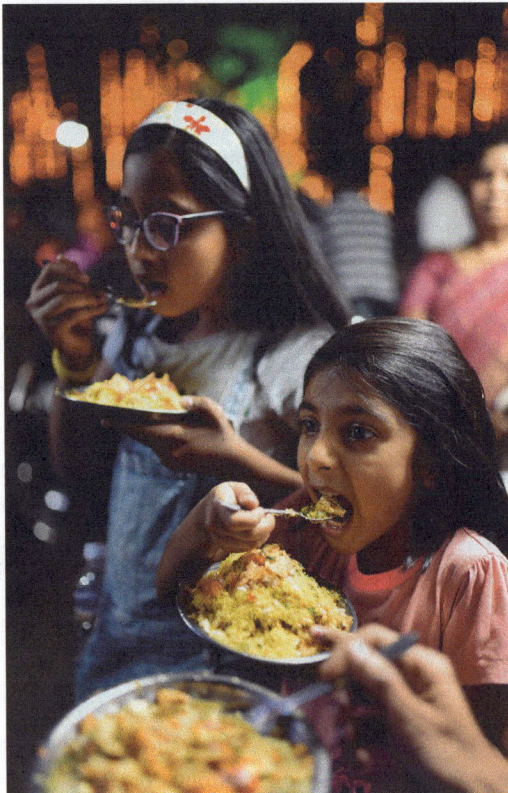

Figure 6.11. A semantic network of breakfast foods in India might include a category of which foods one prefers to get at street vendors and which one prefers to make at home. (Source: Mayur Kakade/Getty Images.)

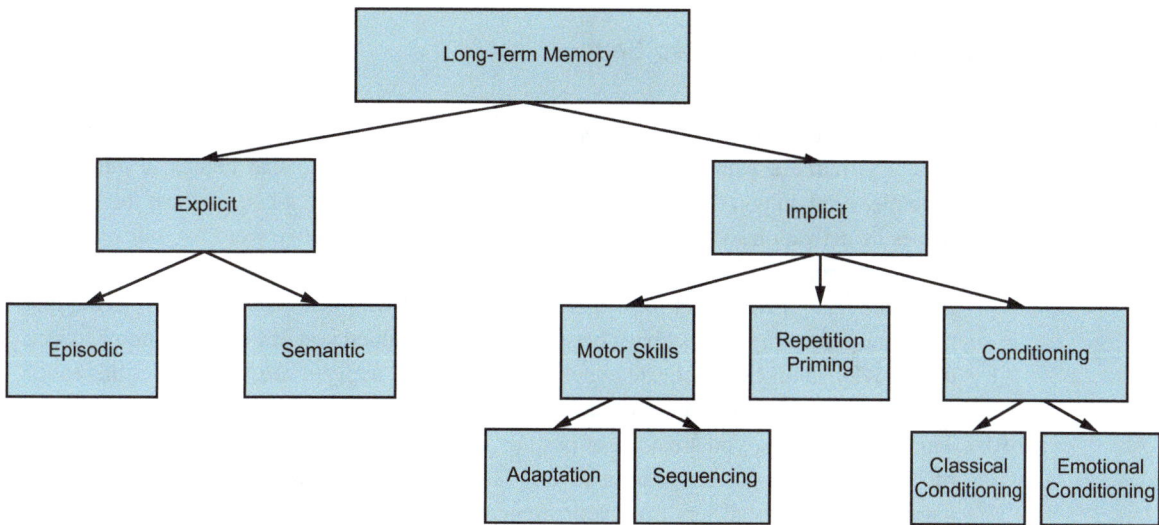

Figure 6.12. Organization of long-term memory.

button if one or both are nonwords (e.g., "marb"). When both letter strings are words, response times are faster when the words are semantically related (*doctor–nurse*) than when they are not (*radio–nurse*) (Meyer & Schvaneveldt, 1971). A straightforward interpretation is that when participants saw the word *doctor*, the node representing the concept became active and immediately passed activation to all semantically related concepts, including *nurse*. When participants read the word *nurse*, the concept representing it was already somewhat active, so it was easier for them to identify the word.

We began this chapter by asking how we might categorize the different types of long-term memory. We hope you have ended with a clear picture of long-term memory as a set of nested systems, easily represented as a tree diagram (shown in Figure 6.12). (Quick, into which category and subcategory does your knowledge of this tree diagram now fit?)

We also began the chapter asking how we organize and search explicit memory, a topic related to what philosophers might have called the structure of conscious knowledge. We previously suggested likening explicit memory to a storehouse, storing our conscious memories of facts and events for later use, perhaps in a hierarchical fashion suggested by a physical storehouse, like in aisle 8, in the middle, on the top shelf, or even like the hierarchy suggested by the tree diagram. Now having reviewed the research, we can conclude that the structure of explicit memory is much more often like a dynamic network than like a hierarchical tree. In the next chapter, we will explore how we form memories: through a process cognitive psychologists call *encoding*.

Stand-on-One-Foot Questions

6.7. Name two formidable problems that any large memory storage device, including human memory, must solve.

6.8. What is the difference between semantic priming and repetition priming?

Questions That Require Two Feet

6.9.   One way of measuring what concepts are connected in a spreading activation model is simply to name a word and ask people to say the next word that comes to mind. For example, what do you think of when you hear *salt*? Presumably, when you hear the word, it passes its activation to linked concepts. You pick the most active word as your response. Try another one. What is the first word you think of when you hear *pepper*? For *salt*, the first word many people pick is *pepper*, but few people who hear *pepper* list *salt* as the first associate (although you may have because we just reminded you of the association between them). Why should *salt* activate *pepper* but *pepper* not activate *salt*? What does this result imply for spreading activation models?

6.10.   Think of something you are a fan of (a sport, video game, type of music, TV show). Think of how some of your knowledge of that fandom is organized. How do you think your network of memory differs from your friends' knowledge of that same area? How is your knowledge hierarchical, and how is it organized like a spreading activation model?

7 Long-Term Memory Processes
Memory Encoding

What Improves Memory Encoding?

- Levels of Processing

- Emotion and Memory

- Flashbulb Memories

- Adaptive Processing

What Doesn't Improve Memory Encoding?

- Intention to Learn

- Sheer Repetition

What Effect Does Prior Knowledge Have on Memory Encoding?

- Knowledge Reduces What You Have to Remember

- Prior Knowledge Guides the Interpretation of Details

- Prior Knowledge Makes Unusual Things Stand Out

In the previous chapter we considered the structure of our memories. What are the different kinds of memories? How are they organized? In this chapter and the next we will focus on the processes that turn experiences into memories and help us recall these memories later. Each chapter describes one of the two basic processes of memory: encoding and retrieval.

Encoding is the process by which memories are "put in." We may think of encoding information as "learning," but "experiencing" is probably a better approximation, because anything we experience is a candidate to make an enduring new memory. In Chapter 5 we described working memory as a short-term buffer that processes our experiences. In this chapter we will discuss what makes information from that buffer get transferred or encoded into long-term memory. Think about it this way: Working memory is the site of awareness; much of what passes through working memory is lost forever. Perhaps three weeks ago, you were driving down an interstate highway looking for a place to eat and saw that exit 92 offered a McDonald's, a Subway, and SpeedyBurger (whatever that is). At that moment, you were aware of the three restaurants off exit 92; that information was in working memory, and it *could* have been stored in long-term memory. It wasn't, as indeed most things are not. What if you wanted to make sure that some piece of information was saved for later? Our first question addresses this concern: **What improves memory encoding?**

Unfortunately, as any student struggling for an answer on an exam or any forgetful professor trying to remember what they said last class can attest, our efforts to improve our memory encoding are not always successful. Indeed, some strategies are systematically less successful than others. **What doesn't improve memory encoding?**

Finally, beyond effective and ineffective strategies for encoding, what we already know has implications for what we can encode. In the third section of this chapter we will consider, **What effect does prior knowledge have on memory encoding?** As it turns out, already having knowledge can facilitate encoding new knowledge in several ways.

What Improves Memory Encoding?

Preview

Our investigation of how the encoding process works has been guided by the implicit goal of improving later memory. What about the encoding process makes some items or situations more memorable than others? Researchers have examined many possible influences on encoding. Some of these factors help the formation of new memories, such as how deeply you think about the experience as you are having it, how emotional the experience is, and whether it matters for survival.

Students and professors alike have all had the experience of seeing something they want to reference later, doubting their own ability to remember it, and using their phone to take a photo of a lecture slide or a piece of art in a museum or a screenshot of something online (Figure 7.1).

Wouldn't it be nice if our own memories worked this well? All we would have to do to etch a memory would be to say to ourselves, "OK, brain, remember this moment," and it would be saved for later use.

Human memory doesn't work that way. Whether an event is stored is much less a matter of our intent, much more dependent on characteristics of the event. What determines whether we will remember it later? As it turns out, while taking photos certainly serves as a memory aid when you forget what was on the shopping list and look at your photo of the list, the act of taking the photo can impair your ability to remember that later when you don't have the photo to consult (Henkel, 2014; Tamir et al., 2018; Lurie & Westerman, 2021). The act of "offloading" memory to technology can reduce the strength of memory itself.

Levels of Processing

In the mid 1960s, most researchers thought the key factor for encoding was how long an experience stayed in working memory. That seems intuitive – if it sits in working memory, that means you're thinking about it, and the more you think about something, the more likely you are to remember it later. That perfectly plausible-sounding idea turned out to be wrong. You may have inadvertently demonstrated this yourself. Have you ever been introduced to someone and tried to remember her name by repeating it to yourself again and again? It usually doesn't work, even though you're keeping the name rattling around in working memory for a while. Researchers found the same thing in the laboratory: If they asked subjects to more or less mindlessly repeat something, it wasn't

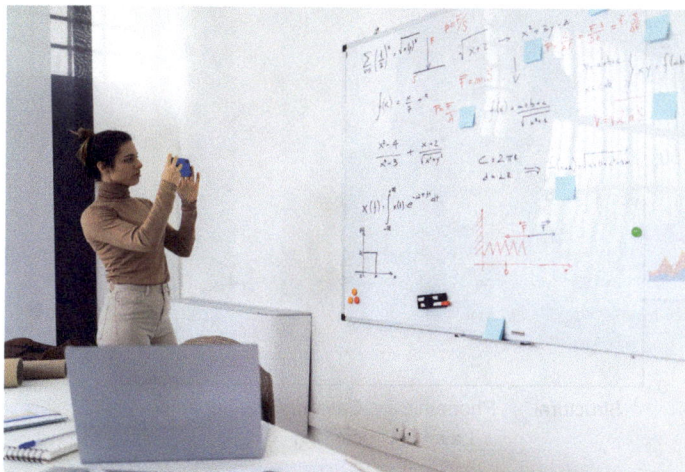

Figure 7.1. These people are taking photos to help them remember that object, text, or event later. Our memories don't work by pressing a button and saying to ourselves, "Record that."

encoded into long-term memory, even if it remained in working memory for a while (Craik & Watkins, 1973).

Fergus Craik and Robert Lockhart (1972) proposed an alternative called the **levels of processing framework** (for a variety of perspectives, see Conway, 2002; for retrospective and review, see Craik, 2021). They suggested that the most important factor determining whether something will be remembered is the **depth of processing**. According to Craik and Lockhart (1972), **deep processing** refers to greater degrees of semantic involvement – that is, if you are to remember a word, thinking about what the word means and how its meaning relates to other words. For example, if you answered the question "What sorts of things come to mind when I say the word *rose*?" you would be engaged in deep processing. The question prompts you to think about what the word means and what is associated with the concept *rose* in your memory. You might think that a rose is a flower of romance, that roses are fairly expensive, that they are found in formal gardens, that they have thorns, that they have a nice scent, and so on. You might even think of the actors Rose Byrne or Rose Leslie, or the soccer player Rose Lavelle. **Shallow processing** refers to thinking about surface characteristics of the stimulus, such as color, size, pitch, or loudness. For example, if you answered the question "How many syllables are in the word *rose*?" you would be engaged in shallow processing. This question encourages you to think about the physical properties of the word itself. Other questions that would encourage shallow processing would be "How many vowels are there in the word *rose*?" or "Is the word *rose* printed in uppercase or lowercase letters?" We don't categorize processing simply as deep or shallow; there can also be degrees of depth of processing. At least this is supposed to be true in theory. As we'll see in a moment, specifying slightly deeper or shallower processing has proved difficult, and that's a weakness of the framework.

Experimenters can manipulate depth of processing by having the participant answer a question about a word. Figure 7.2 shows four levels of processing that are progressively deeper. This chart comes from a series of experiments by Craik and Tulving (1975), who sought to gather evidence for the levels of processing framework. As you can see, participants answered questions

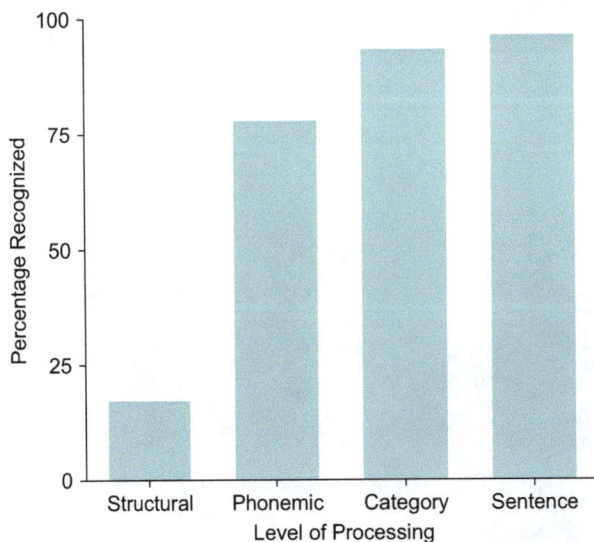

Figure 7.2. The basic levels of processing effect, showing that words that are processed more deeply are better remembered than words that are processed more shallowly. (Source: F. I. Craik and E. Tulving [1975], Depth of processing and the retention of words in episodic memory, *Journal of Experimental Psychology: General*, 104, 274.)

that led them to think about different properties of the stimulus word, such as what the printed version looks like or what it sounds like.

Depth of processing has a huge effect on people's ability to remember under most testing conditions – but not all, as we'll see later. Craik and Tulving (1975) showed just how strong the effect is. On each trial of the experiment, participants heard a question such as "Does the word rhyme with *cake*?" (attention to the sound of the word would encourage shallow processing). To control for the amount of time that participants were allowed to think, they saw the word flashed for 200 milliseconds and then had to answer the question as quickly as possible by pressing one of two buttons to indicate yes or no. They performed forty such trials and, after a brief rest, were presented with a surprise recognition test. The experimenters didn't want participants to try to remember the words because that would prompt them to bring their own strategies to the task; the experimenters told them that the task tested perceptual processing. Participants' performance on the recognition test is shown in Figure 7.2.

The levels of processing framework holds that deeper processing leads to better memory. At first, it might seem that doing the deep processing is just more difficult. Maybe your memory is better because you put more work into thinking. But Craik and Tulving (1975) tested that possibility by conducting an experiment in which the shallow-processing condition was very difficult. Before each word was presented, the participants saw something like *CVCCVC* (where *C* meant consonant and *V* meant vowel). Then they saw a word like *WITCH* and had to say whether it had the pattern of vowels and consonants specified by the first stimulus. It took participants much longer to perform this shallow-processing task than to perform the deep-processing sentence task. Nevertheless, shallow-processed words were recognized 57 percent of the time on a later test, and deep-processed words were recognized 82 percent of the time. So, deeper-processed words are not better remembered simply because deep processing takes more time or effort.

There is one application of deep processing that is a bit counterintuitive. If you are trying to remember a list of ten word pairs, you could imagine adopting at least two different strategies. You might repeat each word pair to yourself, or you might make up a story about each of the pairs (Anderson, 1976). Now, although it may seem that it would be simpler to remember twenty words than to remember ten stories composed of hundreds of words, the deep processing you have used in creating those stories in fact helps your later memory for those words. For example, five- to seven-year-old children were asked to remember the story for a picture book that they had narrated three months earlier found that richer, more organized narrations led to better memory (Wang et al., 2015). It is as though you are making a task more successful by adding several other tasks on to it, not a common occurrence in cognitive psychology (or anywhere else, for that matter).

Emotion and Memory

In addition to how deeply you process something at encoding, emotional events are also more likely to be encoded into long-term memory. One way to observe that effect is to pose simple questions and see what kind of memories pop out. David Rubin and Marc Kozin (1984) asked people to report their clearest memories from childhood. Participants tended to describe birthdays, car accidents, early romantic experiences, and other highly emotional events (see Figure 7.3). Other studies have shown that there is a positive correlation between how vivid a memory seems and how emotional it is (Pillemer et al., 1988; Walker et al., 1997). Many of these studies have focused on negative emotions, but positive emotions, especially when intense, also contribute to improved memory (Talarico et al., 2004; Madan et al., 2019).

Figure 7.3. Most events that people report remembering well have an emotional component. Some people at City Hall in San Francisco may be filling out paperwork for a library card. Others may be marking a more emotional event. We can predict who will remember their visit to City Hall years from now. (Source: Justin Sullivan/Getty Images.)

Nevertheless, this sort of evidence is not airtight. Suppose when Willingham split his pants at a junior high dance, it was an emotional experience for everyone (humiliating for him, hilarious for everyone else). People talked about it in the following weeks and months, so it's a memory that was emotional *and* was repeated. That's the core problem with relational (not experimental) research (see Chapter 2). The heart of the problem is that we have no control over what people do in this situation: Emotional events tend to be repeated, and repeated events tend to be emotional. It would be difficult to cause an emotional experience and then forbid its repetition or to cause an unemotional event to be repeated and retold. But if we wanted to know whether it was emotion or repetition that caused longer lasting memory, that is exactly what we'd have to do to decide between these two theories of stronger memories.

So we might turn instead to the lab, where we have more control over repetitions, but it's hard to conduct true experiments that examine the effect of emotion on memory. Everything about the stimuli should be the same, except subjects' emotional reaction, so that any difference in the memorability of the stimuli can be attributed to the emotion. But how can the same set of materials be emotional for one group of participants and nonemotional for the other?

Studying individual differences in emotion perception and their effect on memory is challenging, but Larry Cahill and Jim McGaugh (1995) found a clever solution. All their participants saw the same slideshow of a boy visiting his father at work in a hospital; in the middle of the slideshow, participants saw graphic surgery slides, which most people would find upsetting.

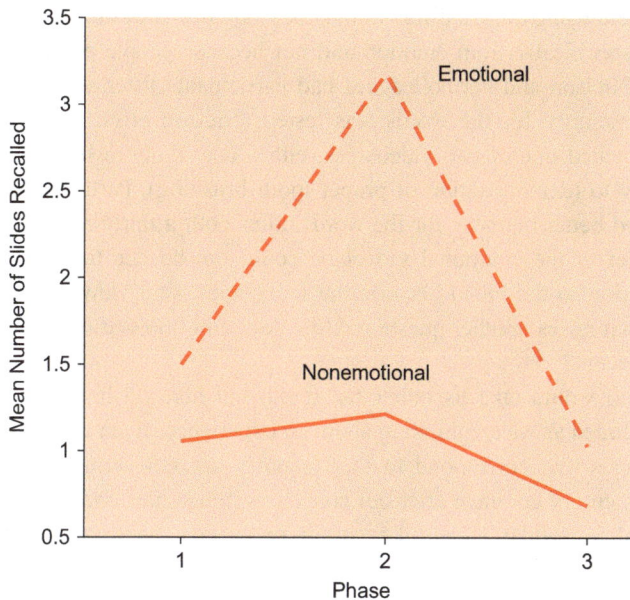

Figure 7.4. Data from Cahill and McGaugh's (1995) experiment. The slideshow that participants saw was divided into three phases. All participants saw the same set of slides, but some heard a story about the slides that made the slides during phase 2 much more emotional. These participants remembered the phase 2 slides better on a later test. (Source: L. Cahill and J. L. McGaugh [1995], A novel demonstration of enhanced memory associated with emotional arousal, *Consciousness and Cognition: An International Journal*, 4[4], 414.)

Participants heard different stories to go with the slides, however. For the emotional condition, they were led to believe that the graphic surgery slides were real. For the nonemotional condition, the narration said that the boy visited his father just as the hospital personnel were practicing emergency procedures, so the people who appeared to be undergoing surgical procedures were just actors made up to look injured.

Two weeks later, the participants returned, expecting to see another set of slides, but instead they took a test of their memory of the first set of slides. (Participants were first asked whether they had expected a memory test, even though they had not been told about it, to ensure they hadn't been rehearsing the material. All participants said that they hadn't expected the test.) In the first test, participants were asked to recall as much of the story as they could, both the general story line and specific details. Their responses were tape-recorded so they could be scored later. The scorers judged that a specific slide was remembered if the participant mentioned a piece of information that could be known only from having seen the slide and not from hearing the story or from seeing one of the other slides.

Figure 7.4 shows the results. The first and third phases depicted the arrival and departure from the hospital, respectively. The second phase showed the surgery slides. As the graph shows, memory is equivalent in the two groups during the first and third phases, which were unemotional for both groups. Memory is much better for the emotional group only during the second phase (when the surgery was seen as real instead of practice with actors). It looks as if memory is slightly better for the emotional group in the first and third phases as well. Although the average recall is a bit higher, the difference is not statistically significant; it could have occurred by chance and therefore should not be taken to represent an important difference. This study does an excellent job of isolating the effect of emotion from other possible characteristics of stimuli, and it shows quite convincingly that emotion does make things more memorable.

Another experiment using quite a different methodology provides further evidence that the boost to memory comes specifically from emotion and not because people pay more attention to emotional events. Kristy Nielson and her colleagues had participants listen to a list of thirty-five words, whereupon their memory for the words was tested (Nielson et al., 2005). Immediately afterward, participants watched one of two videotapes, either one likely to lead to emotion (oral surgery) or one less likely to (demonstration of proper tooth brushing). Participants watching the arousing videotape showed better memory for the words, after both a thirty-minute and a twenty-four-hour delay. The effect of the emotional videotape could not be due to emotion prompting people to pay more attention to the video because the videotapes were viewed *after* participants encoded the words. But that raises another question: How does emotion that occurs after encoding influence memory for an event?

A full explanation would take us rather far afield, but here's a brief summary of their findings. A memory is encoded as we are thinking about an experience. Even after we stop thinking about it, the neural changes that correspond to that memory are not complete. The biological processes that create the memory continue after our conscious minds have moved on to something else. This process is called consolidation, and it occurs in two stages, one lasting minutes to hours and the other lasting weeks or perhaps even years (for a review, see Winocur & Moscovitch, 2011). Emotion seems to affect memory through hormones that are released during stress (e.g., epinephrine) and through several types of neurotransmitters (e.g., adrenergic and glucocorticoid receptors) that may be modulated during arousal (for a review, see McGaugh, 2018). In particular, the activation of the amygdala during emotional events is highly correlated with later recall.

We might wonder, however, about the strength of the emotion in this experiment or indeed any emotion induced in a laboratory. In fact, there is a rich literature on people's memories of highly emotional events that happen outside the laboratory. This literature initially led to the conclusion that this level of emotion had a profound impact on people's memories – so profound that a special memory process might be engaged during moments of great emotion. Later experiments indicated that proposal probably was not true; nevertheless, the impact of these studies was great, and they have important real-world implications, so they are worth reviewing.

Flashbulb Memories

If you want to study highly emotional events, you can't do so in the laboratory. It's simply not ethical to make people feel extremes of emotion by telling them that they are the lucky millionth participant to be tested in the laboratory and that at the end of the experiment they will be presented with a Ferrari or by convincing them that something horrible has happened. It might be ethical if you gave them the Ferrari, but the billionaire eccentric enough to support this experiment has not yet stepped forward. Thus, if you want to study the effect of high levels of emotion, you must study events that occur naturally in people's lives and, ideally, an event that has a similarly large effect on the lives of a large group of people.

Roger Brown and James Kulik (1977) were the first to conduct such a study. They asked participants to remember where they were when they heard that President John Kennedy had been assassinated. Participants reported surprisingly detailed memories of that years-old event and were confident that they could remember details such as what they were wearing, exactly where they were, who told them the news, the words that were used, and so on. Brown and Kulik used the term **flashbulb memories** for richly detailed memories encoded when something emotionally intense happens. Based on this study, Brown and Kulik proposed that flashbulb memories have three special characteristics:

They are very complete, they are accurate, and they are immune to forgetting. Brown and Kulik suggested that a special memory process is responsible for flashbulb memories. Only in times of great emotional duress, a process can take a vivid, accurate "snapshot" of whatever is happening at that moment. Perhaps in moments of extreme emotion, there *is* a direct, faithful "recording" of an event.

Retrospective reports can be a limited measure of the accuracy of flashbulb memories, however. Perhaps people want to think that they remember highly emotional situations so they set a low criterion for how confident they have to be before they claim to have a memory. It's also not easy to double check on the accuracy of old memories. Ideally, psychologists want to compare people's memories of how they heard about Kennedy's assassination right after they heard the news with their memories a year or more later. That way, we could test whether flashbulb memories are accurate and immune to forgetting.

Beginning in the 1980s, a number of researchers performed this test. When an event occurred that they believed would trigger flashbulb memories, they immediately administered surveys to people asking about the circumstances under which they heard the news, and then they contacted people later, asked them the same questions, and compared their memories. Such experiments were conducted for events like the attempted assassination of President Ronald Reagan (Pillemer, 1984), the explosion of the space shuttle *Challenger* (McCloskey et al., 1988), the assassination of Swedish prime minister Olof Palme (Christianson, 1989), the death of King Baudouin of Belgium (Finkenauer et al., 1998), and the referendum for the United Kingdom to leave the European Union (Muzzulini et al., 2021). These experiments have generally shown that people are very confident that they remember these emotional events, but the accuracy of their memory for the events is not especially good. When people are more emotionally attached to an event (such as being a big fan of Michael Jackson and hearing of his death), they are even more confident, but this confidence does not translate into greater consistency and accuracy in memories (Day & Ross, 2014).

If you are skeptical that flashbulb memories can be inaccurate, consider the following anecdote told by a pioneer of developmental psychology, Jean Piaget (as translated in Loftus, 1979):

> I was sitting in my pram, which my nurse was pushing in the Champs Élysées, when a man tried to kidnap me. I was held in by the strap fastened round me while my nurse bravely tried to stand between me and the thief. She received various scratches, and I can still see vaguely those on her face. Then a crowd gathered, a policeman with a short cloak and a white baton came up and the man took to his heels. I can still see the whole scene, and can even place it near the tube station. When I was about fifteen my parents received a letter from my former nurse saying that she had been converted to the Salvation Army. She wanted to confess past faults, and in particular to return the watch she had been given on this occasion. She had made up the whole story, faking the scratches. I, therefore, must have heard, as a child, the account of the story, which my parents believed, and projected it into the past in the form of a visual memory. (pp. 62–63)

Piaget had a vivid flashbulb memory of a traumatic event that nonetheless turned out to be completely fictional!

The September 11, 2001, terrorist attacks provided an extreme, horrible opportunity to test some hypotheses regarding flashbulb memories (Conway et al., 2009; Curci & Luminet, 2006; Hirst et al., 2009; Hirst et al., 2015; Kvavilashvili et al., 2009; Talarico & Rubin, 2003, 2007). A number of initial studies tested people's memories immediately after the terrorist attacks (September 12) and then again several weeks or even years later. These studies also found that participants were far more confident of their memories of September 11 than of everyday memories formed around that time, but the memories were not more accurate (see Figure 7.5).

Figure 7.5. Memorials, such as the 9/11 Memorial and Museum in New York City, help ensure that a country will never forget important national events. However, our personal memories of highly emotional events are not recorded brightly with a flashbulb or etched in stone, even as we feel confident that they are. (Source: Matthew T. Carroll/Moment Open/Getty Images.)

The worldwide spread of the COVID-19 pandemic in 2019 and 2020 offered a new generation another unfortunate chance to experience emotional events and test the theory of flashbulb memories. Memories of the pandemic are unlike many of the preceding examples, however. The first spread of the pandemic was universally experienced (and remembered) across the world, although experiences of course varied across different countries. In addition, it was not a single event but a series of events and effects. There are some common experiences, such as students remembering schools closing, or beginning to wear a mask in public, but others varied by how restricted a lockdown their country or locality imposed. In addition, while the novelty and danger of a deadly novel disease made some things stand out as candidates for flashbulb memories ("where were you when your school closed?" "What event do you remember being canceled that made you realize this was serious?"), the chronic stress of worry about the health of self and family members also inhibited encoding memories for some aspects of experience ("it was all a blur" and "it was so hard to concentrate in Zoom school"). While some initial research (Leon et al., 2022; Cole et al., 2022) has attempted to investigate the emotional impact of COVID-19 on memory, the pandemic is a reminder of how complex even these universal experiences are and how the metaphor of a "flashbulb" memory is too simple for how our memories operate.

So what's the upshot on emotion and memory? There is good evidence that the emotionality of an event affects how memorable it is, but there is not good evidence that a special mechanism takes over for highly emotional flashbulb memories. Research on memories for unusual, emotion-laden events still offers valuable contributions to understanding how we encode memories, but this research shows continuity with laboratory studies on the effects of emotion and stress on memory (Luminet & Curci, 2009; for a review, see Hirst & Phelps, 2016).

Adaptive Processing

It seems logical that evolution would leave us with a memory system that retains emotional experiences; presumably, emotion is a barometer of importance. Another recent set of studies takes a more direct evolutionary approach to defining what is important to remember. Just as our physical anatomy is subject to the pressures of evolution through natural selection, these researchers argue that our memory processing has been formed through natural selection and therefore reflects evolutionary fitness. In other words, evolution has selected memory processes that enhance the likelihood of survival. James Nairne and Josefa Pandeirada (2016) claim that when people experience things that they see as critical for survival, these experiences are processed differently. How have they tested this proposal?

There are several aspects to this claim. First, memory for objects or events obviously related to survival should be recalled better than neutral content. Many studies of classical conditioning have shown this to be the case. In a typical experiment, researchers show participants pictures of different objects. One object is always followed by a mildly painful shock. The expectation is that, with practice, subjects will learn to expect the shock and will show the anticipation (increased heart rate, for example, and sweaty palms) when the target picture appears. Such learning is faster when the target stimulus depicts fear-relevant stimuli, such as snakes or spiders, than when it depicts neutral stimuli like mushrooms (Ohman & Mineka, 2001).

In one of the first studies to document **survival processing** in semantic memory (rather than conditioning), participants rated thirty words in one of three ways (Nairne et al., 2007): They rated the survival relevance of each word ("Imagine you are stranded in the grasslands of a foreign land, without any basic survival materials. Over the next few months, you'll need to find steady supplies of food and water and to protect yourself from predators"), they rated the word's relevance to moving ("Imagine you are planning to move to a new home in a foreign land. Over the next few months you'll need to locate and purchase a new home and transport your belongings"), or they rated pleasantness ("We are going to show you a list of words, and we would like you to rate the pleasantness of each word"). Then there was a delay, and participants were required to perform a working memory task to prevent their rehearsing the words they had seen (even though they had not been told their memory would be tested later). Finally, they were asked to write down as many of the thirty words as they could remember. Participants had better recall when they rated words for survival than either the moving or pleasantness ratings conditions (60 percent free recall compared to 52 percent in each of the other conditions).

But wait, you say, why do we need the evolutionary theory of memory, when we could simply say that imagining survival requires deeper processing than generating a liking rating? Weinstein et al. (2008) made slight modifications to the experiment to test this idea. They added conditions that compared survival in the savanna ("Imagine you are stranded in the grasslands of a foreign land, without any basic survival materials. Over the next few months, you'll need to find steady supplies of food and water and protect yourself from predators") to survival in a city ("Imagine that you are stranded in the city of a foreign land, without any basic survival materials. Over the next few months, you'll need to find steady supplies of food and water and protect yourself from attackers"). They argue that cities are relatively recent cultural inventions and are less likely to be subject to evolutionary pressures. To test whether an important element of the previous studies was a reference to self, they also added conditions comparing first person to third person ("I am stranded" vs. "a friend is stranded"). They found that self-reference did not matter, but memory in the grasslands survival processing was better than in the city survival conditions.

In another recent study (Nairne et al., 2019), participants were given target words, and instead of being asked to rate survival relevance, they generated their own survival situations (DOOR: I'm in a house on fire and I can escape through that door). They were later given a surprise memory test. This condition was compared to well-known levels of processing conditions, such as pleasantness, generating unusual cues, and autobiographical self-reference. The survival generation task led to better retention compared to the control conditions, which themselves are known to improve memory. For example, the self-reference condition asked participants to retrieve the last time that they personally interacted with that target word (including both retrieval and self-reference, both known to boost recall).

This is still an active area of research (for limitations to the effect, see Kroneisen & Erdfelder, 2011; Savine et al., 2011; for recent reviews, see Kazanas & Altarriba, 2015; Nairne, 2022), and it is always wise to be cautious in accepting evolutionary accounts of today's cognitive system: Memory doesn't leave fossils. However, the survival advantage has survived extensive scrutiny, despite some difficulty of separating the memory advantages of survival processing from familiarity, emotionality, novelty, or advantages of learning narratives rather than lists.

Stand-on-One-Foot Questions

7.1.   How does emotion affect memory encoding?

7.2.   What conditions support deeper processing rather than shallow processing?

7.3.   How are flashbulb memories different from other memories? How are they similar?

Questions That Require Two Feet

7.4.   Suppose a friend knows that you're taking a cognitive psychology class and asks for your advice on how to study for exams. What would you say? Would your advice be any different to someone who wants to remember people's names at parties?

7.5.   Many people say that emotional events are well remembered (as in flashbulb memories), but others say that they don't remember emotional events very well. (Some people, for example, say that their wedding day was "just a blur.") What explanation might you give for this disparity?

7.6.   Why do you think you remember some advertisements well and others not so well?

What Doesn't Improve Memory Encoding?

Preview

In this section, we will focus on some factors that do not improve memory encoding, despite many people's strong intuitions. Just as the levels of processing theory suggest some mechanisms for how encoding works, the factors described herein also give us clues about how encoding works because these factors do not improve memory. First, intending to remember something later has no impact on memory. Second, simply repeating something (i.e., repeatedly encoding it) does not necessarily lead to a better encoding process and improved later memory.

Why discuss things that don't improve memory? The list would seem to be endless (standing on your head, wearing mismatched socks, taking Dr. Dan's Magic Remember-It-All Elixir). However, discussing factors that don't improve encoding has two purposes. First, factors that don't improve encoding can limit theories about how memory encoding works; that is, if a theory predicts that one of these factors boosts memory, then we know the theory is wrong. Second, correcting intuitions about how memory encoding works can lead to more effective memory encoding strategies for people trying to commit something to memory – say, a student studying a cognitive psychology textbook.

In this next section, we will discuss two factors: intention to learn and repetition. Our experience tells us that they are plausible as memory influences, but laboratory experiments show that they are not quite so straightforward. Let's examine why.

Intention to Learn

The levels of processing framework proposes that intention to learn – that is, whether you're trying to learn – has no impact on memory. Can we really dismiss the effect of wanting to remember something? Certainly, some teachers believe that effort to remember is important; why else would they exhort students, "Remember this!" Likewise, the student's question "Will this be on the test?" supposes that adding an extra intention to remember material should boost memory encoding. Such labeling may be useful, but only if it leads to students adopting a strategy (taking more careful notes, reviewing study materials) to improve memory; the exhortation "remember this" alone has less effect than we might think.

Research on levels of processing used **incidental memory tests** on words, in which the participants were not expressly told that their memory would be tested; rather, they were just told to do something with the words (e.g., answer a question about them). Then, later, they got a surprise memory test. In an **intentional memory test**, participants are told that their memory will be tested; the researcher assumes that participants will engage in some processing they believe will be effective for memory.

Suppose we wanted to test the effect of the participants' expectation of a later memory test. We could simply tell half the participants that they will later be tested and not tell the other half. Thomas Hyde and James Jenkins (1973) conducted exactly that study (see also Bower & Karlin, 1974). Participants saw a list of twenty-four words, one at a time, for three seconds each and were to perform one of two tasks for each word: either determine whether the word contained the letter *a* or *q* (shallow task) or rate the "pleasantness" of the word (deep task). If the word invoked pleasant thoughts (*daisy*), participants gave it a high rating, and if it invoked unpleasant things (*grave*), they gave it a low rating. For both the deep- and shallow-processing conditions, half the participants were additionally told that their memory for the words would be tested (intentional condition); the remaining participants were not told about the upcoming memory test (incidental condition). Whether the test was incidental made no difference in participants' performance on the memory

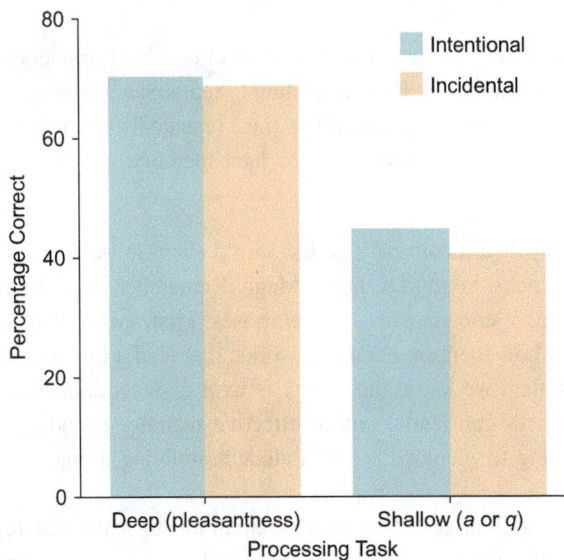

Figure 7.6. Results from Hyde and Jenkins' (1973) study showing that intention to learn had no impact on learning. The experiment also showed the typical depth of processing effect. (Source: T. S. Hyde and J. J. Jenkins [1973], Recall for words as a function of semantic, graphic, and syntactic orienting tasks, *Journal of Verbal Learning and Verbal Behavior*, 12, 476.)

test, as shown in Figure 7.6. Wanting to remember something doesn't help your memory – all that matters is whether you process deeply or shallowly.

In these studies, intention to remember seems to provide no additional explanatory power over a levels-of-processing account. However, recent studies have questioned the counter-intuitive conclusion that intent to remember doesn't improve memory. There may be some cases in which telling people their memory will be tested later does improve learning (Block, 2009; Naveh-Benjamin et al., 2014). One possible explanation is that intending to learn by itself does not promote encoding but that knowledge leads to a more effective encoding strategy. For example, merely forewarning you about a job interview may not make you a better candidate, but if the warning leads you to comb your hair, change your clothes, and practice your elevator speech, those preparations may make you more likely to get hired than the person tossed into the interview without warning. Intention to remember might have an indirect effect if it leads to other effective encoding processes.

Your memory is probably cluttered with things you didn't intend to learn (e.g., advertising jingles). They are presumably learned as a by-product of other cognitive processing, but you probably didn't process these jingles very deeply. Nor was viewing the commercial a particularly emotional experience. So, if that memory didn't have emotion or depth of processing going for it, what's it doing in your memory? Both the music and the lyrics of jingles are of course designed for their memorability (see Rubin, 1995), but another likely answer is that you know them because you've heard them hundreds of times. Does repetition affect memory?

Sheer Repetition

Suppose the likelihood that something makes it into long-term memory depends on how often you see it. Stimuli that often appear in the environment should be remembered, but consider this: You think you know what a penny looks like, right? Can you say, with confidence, right now, which way

Figure 7.7. Fifteen penny drawings used in Nickerson and Adams' (1979) recognition memory test. (Source: R. S. Nickerson and M. J. Adams [1979], Long-term memory for a common object, *Cognitive Psychology*, 11[3], 297.)

Lincoln faces? Try it. Where is the date written on a penny? Does the phrase "In God We Trust" appear on the front of a penny?

Raymond Nickerson and Marilyn Adams (1979) showed thirty-six college students the fifteen versions of a penny shown in Figure 7.7. Participants were asked to select which penny was most likely the right one and then to rate the other drawings as (1) "Could easily be right, if my choice proves wrong"; (2) "Might possibly be right, if my choice proves wrong"; or (3) "Definitely not correct." Fewer than half the participants (fifteen of the thirty-six) correctly picked A. Twelve thought it could easily be right, four thought it might be, and five were sure it was wrong. Pennies E, G, and J were popular choices.

Why was this task so prone to error? Obviously, the participants had seen thousands of pennies in their lifetimes. We seldom, if ever, really notice (i.e., process deeply) which way Lincoln is facing, what's written on a coin, or any of the other details. When you are looking through your handful of coins in search of a penny, what you're thinking is, "I need the brown one." Pennies are distinguished from other coins by color, not by the way Lincoln is facing. Dimes are the small ones, not the coins with Roosevelt on them; quarters are the big ones; and nickels are the thick ones with smooth edges. You have had thousands of exposures to pennies, but each exposure amounted to little more than "Good, I've got a brown one, so I won't get four brown ones in change." In fact, if you give people just fifteen seconds to study an unfamiliar coin (a mercury dime, used from 1916 until 1945), they remember it quite well and know it better a week later than they know the penny (Marmie & Healy, 2004).

Another recent study replicated the findings from Nickerson and Adams (1979) with a familiar and ubiquitous corporate logo. Blake et al. (2015) asked college students to draw the Apple

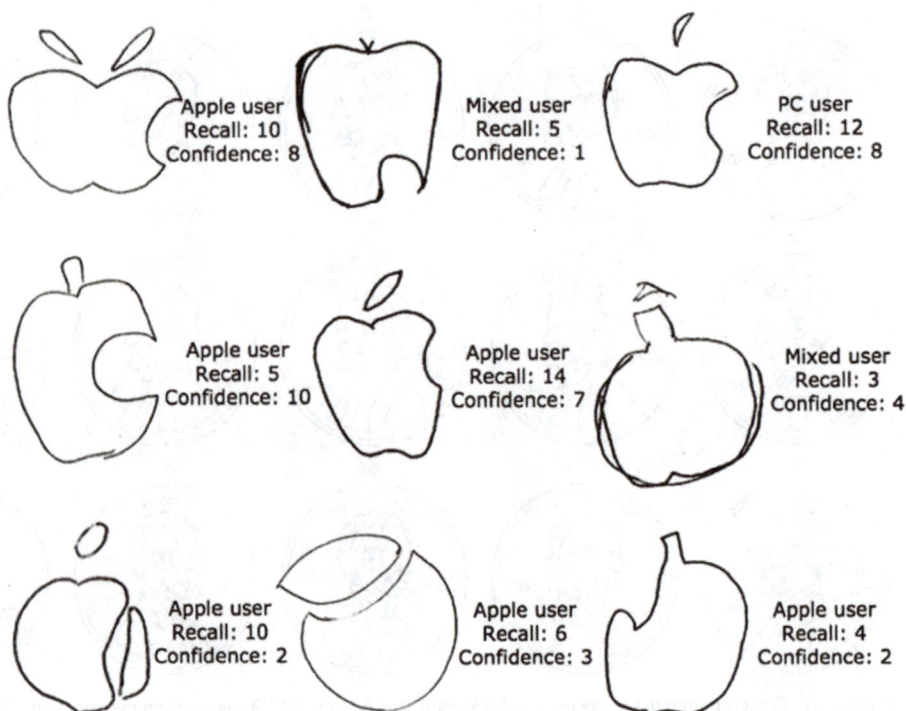

Figure 7.8. Some sample drawings from Blake et al.'s (2015) experiment asking participants to draw the Apple logo. (Source: A. B. Blake, M. Nazarian, and A. D. Castel [2015], The Apple of the mind's eye: Everyday attention, metamemory, and reconstructive memory for the Apple logo, *Quarterly Journal of Experimental Psychology*, 68[5], 860.)

logo or recognize it from an array of similar logos (Figure 7.8). Very few participants were able to draw it correctly, and fewer than half could pick the correct one from an array of similar logos. Furthermore, as you may have guessed from the flashbulb memory studies, there was also no correlation between subjects' confidence and their successful recognition.

We still don't know why you remember advertising jingles. One possibility is that with more repetition, it becomes more likely that at least one of the repetitions will be processed deeply. Even if you ignore the advertisement ninety-nine times, perhaps the next time will be the one in which you encode the music deeply and start humming along. (There may also be other effects of repetition that we're not concerned with here, for example, greater liking of the product [see Janiszewski & Meyvis, 2001].) But we can't entirely dismiss repetition. Repeating ineffective memory strategies doesn't help by itself, but repeating effective strategies certainly does. If you experience an emotional event or stimulus, and that is repeated (as is the emotion), of course that will be remembered better than if it had only occurred once.

So, to review, what helps encoding? Depth of processing, emotion, elaborating on an experience as you are having it, or thinking about its relevance to your survival. Intention to learn might help if it prompts you to think about the material in one of these ways. Repetition helps *if it's repetition of one of the effective types of processing*. Repetition of an ineffective processing strategy does little or nothing.

Stand-on-One-Foot Questions

7.7.   When does repetition help memory?

7.8.   What is the difference between intentional and incidental memory tests?

Question That Requires Two Feet

7.9.   Sometimes students ask, "Will this be on the test?" Using the surprising studies on intentional and incidental memory tests, how would you recommend students act when a teacher says "Yes, this will be on the test"?

What Effect Does Prior Knowledge Have on Memory Encoding?

Preview

We've reviewed studies that seek to isolate the process of encoding from the content of memory, by asking participants to remember unfamiliar words created for the laboratory. But this is not how memory usually works. What happens when we encode information that is related to what we already know? In this section, we will describe how our prior knowledge affects the encoding process. It does so in three ways: by reducing what needs to be encoded, by guiding the interpretations of details, and by making unusual things stand out.

All the factors that influence encoding concern *how* we think about the material to be remembered. In the lab, the experimenter directs how the subject thinks by giving her a task, for example, rating the pleasantness of a word. In these experiments, the goal is often to select the content to be remembered so that it is equally unfamiliar to all participants. But in the world outside of the lab, we are always relating new information to what we already know. In this section, we'll see that what you think about when you encounter a word, or listen to a story, or hear about a tragic event depends in large measure on your prior knowledge, that is, on what you already know about it.

Even after considering the kind of processing you engage as you read the textbook, how you remember it is also influenced by what you knew in the past. Indubitably this is true in that it is much harder to remember if you don't know the meaning of certain vocabulary words (like *indubitably*: "without a doubt"), but your prior knowledge affects your long-term memory in other ways. When we experience the world, we are not encoding on a blank slate. We can point to three ways that previous knowledge affects encoding. Prior knowledge reduces what you have to remember, guides your interpretation of ambiguous details, and makes unusual things stand out.

Prior Knowledge Reduces What You Have to Remember

Prior knowledge can reduce how much we have to encode if the material to be encoded can be enhanced (or replaced) using our prior knowledge. In Chapter 5, we discussed how grouping bits of information into chunks can increase the capacity of our working memory. For example, if we ask you to remember the letters *r, o, p, a*, you might group them into a single unit, *ropa*. This strategy only works if you have the right knowledge necessary in long-term memory: *Ropa* means "clothes" in Spanish. You cannot chunk ب العر بية قطعه علي without knowing Arabic.

Suppose we ask you to memorize some letters (Bower & Springston, 1970). They are read aloud to you, pausing for one second between groups:

FB ICB SNC AAP BS

You'd remember some of the letters, perhaps all, but it would take some effort. Think how much easier it would be if we gave you exactly the same list of letters but paused in different places:

FBI CBS NCAA PBS

Both lists are organized into chunks by the pauses, but for the second list, the chunks derive meaning from your prior knowledge of these sets of letters as common American acronyms for the Federal Bureau of Investigation, the Columbia Broadcasting System, the National Collegiate Athletic Association, and the Public Broadcasting System. You already know these letters as groups, so instead of thirteen letters in five arbitrary groups, you only must remember four acronyms, which leverage your background knowledge. Things that are presented as individual items might be encodable as a single, higher-order unit, but only if you have the relevant background knowledge. If we gave you a different set of letters, say, EPLM CF CCTI DLCFC, you would have just as much difficulty if we split them up as EPL MCFC CTID LCFC, unless you were a British football fan and recognized them as English Premier League, Manchester City Football Club, Chelsea 'til I Die, and Leicester City Football Club. Your prior knowledge allows you to fit more individual letters into working memory, since demands on working memory are reduced by knowing what these letters stand for (see Figure 7.9). Lea Bartsch and colleagues (Bartsch & Shepherdson, 2022; Bartsch & Oberauer, 2023) have confirmed this through careful experiments in which people's

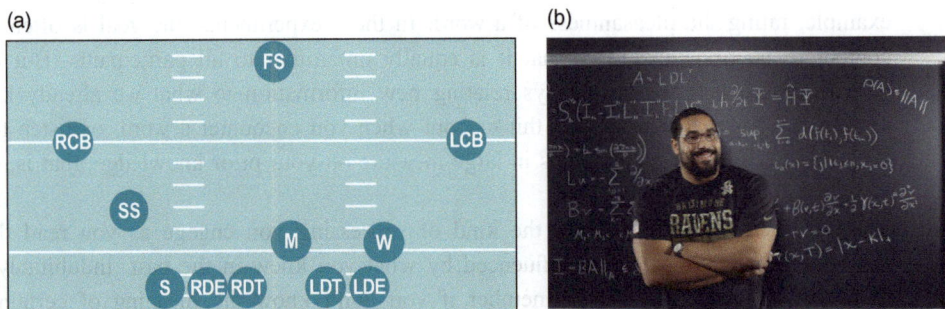

Figure 7.9. (a) A person with a good background knowledge of American football would easily chunk this pattern as a zone defense with three men deep, and would also know that "S" stands for strong outside linebacker, "RDE" stands for right defensive end, and so forth. (b) Likewise, the blackboard is filled with obscure symbols for which mathematicians can use their prior knowledge to reduce how much they have to remember. The man standing in front of the blackboard, a professor of mathematics at MIT and former professional football player John Urschel, has prior knowledge in both domains. (Source: (a) Steve Boyle/Sports Illustrated/Getty Images.)

long-term memory was carefully controlled, unlike your knowledge (or lack thereof) of British football or American sports acronyms.

Prior Knowledge Guides the Interpretation of Details

Prior knowledge not only knits details into larger units, making them easier to remember; it also guides *which* details you will deem worthy of attention. For example, one of the authors (Willingham) is interested in theater; he likes going to plays and reading them. He went to see a play called *Voir Dire*, which is about a jury's deliberations, with a friend who is an attorney. At the end of the play, there was a lot of overlap in what was remembered about it, but there were also some interesting differences. His friend remembered a lot of the legal details – mostly things the playwright had gotten wrong or things she was impressed to see he had gotten right – whereas he remembered moments in the play that he perceived to be turns in dramatic tension and resolution of tension. He's not an attorney, and so, having no background knowledge about legal matters, he was oblivious to the happenings in the play that she noticed. Prior knowledge guides what details of an event you attend to and think about and therefore which details end up in secondary memory. How does this work?

Sometimes, the prior knowledge that is applied at encoding is an isolated fact; for example, knowing the abbreviation *FBI* allows you to treat the three letters as a single chunk. At other times, the prior knowledge is best thought of as a set of related facts; the facts come in a packet, so to speak. Research on how facts are related more generally will be discussed in Chapter 9, when we describe the organization of concepts and categories. Here, as we investigate how prior knowledge guides the interpretation of details, we describe a packet of related facts as a **schema**. There have been different definitions of a schema since Sir Frederic Bartlett (1932) first introduced the idea, but the definitions agree on certain points: A schema is a memory representation containing information about what is generally true of the situation or event, and it represents, not a single event, but a type of event. Furthermore, the facts within a single schema are related to one another. These two aspects of a schema are especially important: It is general, and it contains information about related facts.

For example, a schema for the concept *dog* would include the information that a dog typically has four legs, is friendly, is furry, and so on. These characteristics are generally true, but each one need not be true. For example, if you met a three-legged dog, you would still think of it as a dog. However, if that piece of information is not specified, then you assume that the normal default value of the schema is true and that the dog has four legs. A **default value** for a particular piece of information is the value that would typically be true, and thus that you assume is true, unless you are told otherwise. If you are told we have a dog with three legs, you will change the value of "number of legs" to three for the representation of our particular dog. But the default value for "number of legs" in the dog schema would still be four (see Figure 7.10).

Because bits of information in a schema are related, as soon as you think about a dog, all its characteristics become more available in your mind. For example, suppose that you were told, "I just got a puppy, which probably wasn't a great idea because my landlord just put in new carpets." What does getting a puppy have to do with new carpets? As soon as the word *puppy* is said, the knowledge becomes available that puppies aren't housebroken (and with that, the knowledge that "house-broken" has nothing to do with breaking houses and everything to do with bladder control). When *landlord* is said, information in the landlord schema becomes available, including the information that landlords typically are concerned that damage will be done to rented apartments. Understanding

(a)

(b)

(c)

(d)

(e)

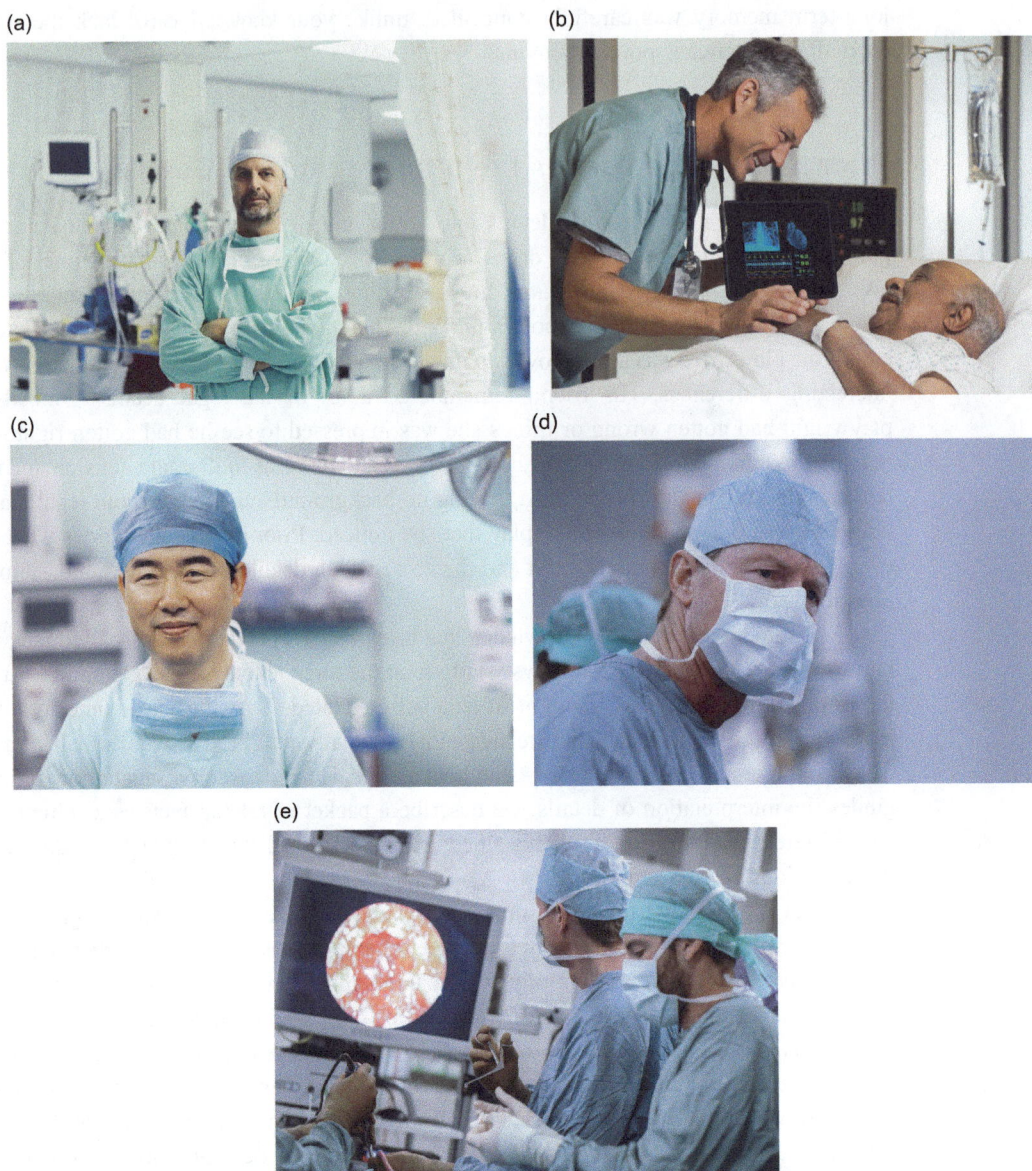

Figure 7.10. Default values can be a way that prior knowledge facilitates memory encoding, so that you don't have to encode that dogs have four legs and fur, but the encoding benefit of default values can sometimes take the form of harmful stereotypes. A typical image search for "surgeon" will yield many pictures like these, showing that for these algorithms, too often the default value for "surgeon" is male. (Source: (a, c) Hero Images/Hero Images/Getty Images; (b) Ariel Skelley/DigitalVision/Getty Images; (d, e) Westend61/Getty Images.)

this sentence seems effortless, but it turns on having the right information in memory. We don't have to explicitly say, "I'm worried this puppy will pee on the carpet because that's what puppies do, which will ruin the carpets, which will make the landlord angry because the carpets belong to him." The background information stored in schemas allows the listener to make these inferences from the minimal information in the sentence.

Schemas not only help us make inferences but also help us interpret ambiguous details by providing us with the context for the situation. To get a flavor of how this might happen, read this passage from a classic demonstration by John Bransford and Marcia Johnson (1972):

> The procedure is actually quite simple. First you arrange items into different groups. Of course one pile may be sufficient depending on how much there is to do. If you have to go somewhere else due to lack of facilities that is the next step; otherwise, you are pretty well set. It is important not to overdo things. That is, it is better to do too few things at once than too many. In the short run this may not seem important but complications can easily arise. A mistake can be expensive as well. At first, the whole procedure will seem complicated. Soon, however, it will become just another facet of life. It is difficult to foresee any end to the necessity for this task in the immediate future, but then, one can never tell. After the procedure is completed one arranges the materials into different groups again. Then they can be put into their appropriate places. Eventually they will be used once more and the whole cycle will have to be repeated. However, that is part of life. (p. 722)

The paragraph doesn't make much sense, and not surprisingly, participants remembered very little of it. But some participants were given a title before listening to the passage, and they performed much better. The title is "Washing Clothes." Read the paragraph again now that you know the title, and you'll see that it makes much more sense. If you are given the title after reading it, it doesn't help. You have to know the title in advance. Why is the story easier to remember if you know the title?

When you are reading something, you are not simply reading the words themselves but fitting them into a larger meaning structure. If you have relevant knowledge, you bring this knowledge to bear on both understanding the sentence (as we shall see in Chapter 10) and also remembering it. Hence, when you know the title is "Washing Clothes" and you read "First you arrange items into different groups," it readily comes to mind that this vague sentence refers to sorting clothing by color. Your prior knowledge (about washing clothes) shapes ongoing processing (reading).

We would say that the prior knowledge of the theme of the paragraph (as provided by the title) activates a schema for the steps in washing clothes. This background knowledge guides the interpretation of ambiguous sentences such as "First you arrange items into different groups" and "If you have to go somewhere else due to lack of facilities that is the next step." Without the schema, the sentences would carry little meaning.

Prior Knowledge Makes Unusual Things Stand Out

One way that prior knowledge also guides encoding is by making unusual things stand out. Prior knowledge leads you to expect that what usually occurs in a given situation will reoccur. If something unexpected happens, you notice it and process it more deeply. For example, if you went to a restaurant and the server brought your food and placed it on the table, that would not stand out. However, if servers brought you a hospital gown because they jokingly claim that their food is likely to produce a heart attack, that would violate your expectations of what happens in a restaurant (and it would be memorable).

There has been a lot of research on people's knowledge of what usually happens in common situations. Roger Schank and R. P. Abelson (1977), two computer scientists, proposed that knowledge about common situations like visiting a restaurant is encoded in a knowledge structure called a **script**, which is a schema for a series of events. For example, you probably have scripts in memory for routine events like visiting a doctor or attending a college lecture course. If asked, you could quickly generate a list of what each of these events entails: You check in with the receptionist, you read an ancient magazine, a nurse takes you to an exam room, you undress, you sit for a while freezing until the doctor arrives, and so on. There is fairly good agreement about the events that are part of such scripts, at least within the culture of American college students (Bower et al., 1979).

Gordon Bower and his associates (1979) tested the hypothesis that events in a story that are inconsistent with a script and relevant to the goals of the script would be well remembered, but other information that is not in the script and is irrelevant (e.g., if a restaurant server wore green pants) would not be especially well remembered. Indeed, participants had good memory for things that were inconsistent with the script that were relevant to the goals, remembering 53 percent of the script violations, but they remembered just 32 percent of the irrelevant information (Bower et al., 1979).

We began this chapter by considering which processes in working memory would prompt an experience to be encoded into long-term memory. Now we see that what gets encoded into long-term memory also depends on what is already in long-term memory. Prior knowledge reduces what we need to process, guides our interpretation of details through schemas, and reminds us of what usually happens so that *un*usual things stand out and are better remembered. The importance of prior knowledge (which is itself in long-term memory) reminds us that encoding is not an isolated process but one influenced by other stages in memory. We will expand on this idea in the next chapter.

Stand-on-One-Foot Question

7.10.   How does prior knowledge affect encoding?

Questions That Require Two Feet

7.11.   What is a script for the first day of class? How might a teacher make that class more memorable?

7.12.   Do you have a schema for a bedroom? How does your own room depart from this schema?

8 Long-Term Memory Processes
Memory Retrieval

Why Is Memory Retrieval Unreliable?

- Measures of Memory

- Differences in Cues

- Retrieval and Prior Knowledge

- False Memory

Why Do We Forget?

- Occlusion

- Decay

- Repression

- The Permanence of Memory

In the previous chapter we considered the process of encoding, emphasizing that it is not accurate to characterize it as the intentional act of learning; rather, it is how experience becomes memory, depending on certain features of our thought at the time. In this chapter, we describe retrieval, the process of bringing a long-term memory back to consciousness. We consider what makes successful retrieval possible and also what might make it unreliable. In many situations, we know we have experienced something (we had a chance to encode it), but when we later have reason to retrieve it, we cannot access the memory.

In Chapter 7 we suggested a metaphor for memory: Information is encoded in some sort of storehouse and then later retrieved via some search process. However, many researchers say the metaphor is misleading. Retrieval suggests a process of looking up something in storage and finding it. The image is perhaps one of a librarian searching for something on a computer, seeing the location, and then disappearing into the stacks and returning with a book. If your mind is like a vast library, then retrieval is searching your memory and simply bringing back what you have stored there. Cognitive psychologists emphasize that retrieval is not a passive looking-up process but rather an active, reconstructive process. Memories are not looked up and accessed but assembled. This is an active process of assembly and reconstruction, and it often fails. The "books" in our "libraries" are faded, degraded, and incomplete, so our "librarians" need to fill in missing details even as they "search." Even if the memory is intact, we usually add details that seem likely to be true, even if they are not stored with that memory. Our helpful librarians not only fill in missing pages but change the intact pages. Despite this active process, our mental librarians are not as helpful or accurate as those employed by your university, and they often come back empty or with an incomplete memory. **Why is memory retrieval unreliable?**

We also discuss forgetting as an instance of retrieval failure. **Why do we forget?** When we forget something, it is not simply that the retrieval process went to find a memory and it was gone, even though this may be how it feels. In fact, retrieval failure can often be overcome, which says more about the retrieval process than about the existence of the memory sought. Anyone who has remembered something once forgotten knows that it's all about being reminded in the right way – getting the appropriate cue during the retrieval process. Forgetting offers a way for cognitive psychologists to probe the relationship between encoding and retrieval and to consider whether any memories are truly gone for good.

Why Is Memory Retrieval Unreliable?

Preview

Memory retrieval is unreliable. Sometimes it works, sometimes it doesn't. One reason is that we have different ways of defining "it works"; that is, there are different ways of measuring memory. One measure may indicate that you don't remember something, even though another indicates that you do. It thus appears that some measures of memory are more sensitive than others; that is, they are better able to detect memories that are poorly represented in the storehouse. A crucial factor in sensitivity is the match between encoding and retrieval, but prior knowledge also has an effect, just as it does at encoding. In fact, prior knowledge can influence retrieval to such an extent that a completely false memory can be created.

It might seem that after information is stored into long-term memory, you should be able to retrieve it whenever you want. As you know, memory doesn't work this way. Sometimes you try to remember who played Dumbledore in the Harry Potter movies and it pops right out of the storehouse, so to speak. Other times, you can't quite get it, but when someone provides the name, you immediately recognize it as correct (and you confidently reject Ian McKellen and Ed Harris as incorrect) (see Figure 8.1). There are different ways to retrieve memories – or to measure whether a person remembers something – and the way memory is measured has a big impact on whether a piece of information appears to be in long-term memory.

Measures of Memory

Before we can talk about the details of retrieval, we need to be more precise about the different ways to measure memory. First, we need to define a **cue**, which is information in the environment that is used as a starting point for retrieval. If we simply say to you "Remember," the command makes no sense. Are you supposed to be remembering something about pickles, your second-grade teacher, or the structure of barium? A cue for what is to be retrieved from long-term memory might be provided by the experimenter ("Try to remember what I told you an hour ago") or the environment (an advertisement for motor oil reminds you to get your oil changed), or you might provide it yourself (you mentally retrace your steps in an effort to remember where you might have left something).

Memory tests differ in the cues that the experimenter provides. We will discuss three types here: free recall, cued recall, and recognition tests. A **free recall** test provides very few – the

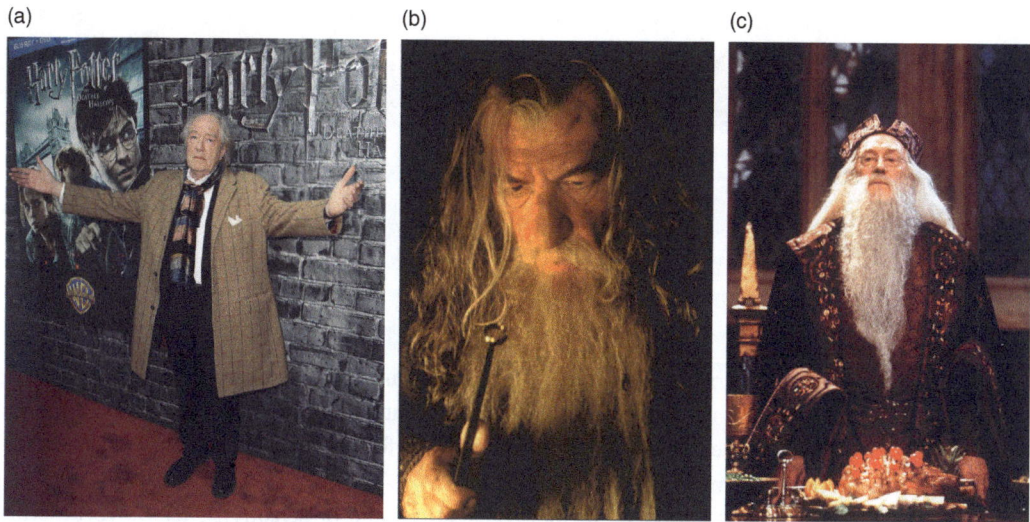

Figure 8.1. These three men played movie wizards. Two of them, (a) Michael Gambon and (c) Richard Harris, played Dumbledore in the Harry Potter movies, and one, (b) Ian McKellen, played Gandalf. It is actually tricky, so don't feel too bad if you were confused. (Source: (a) Taylor Hill/FilmMagic/Getty Images; (b) New Line/WireImage/Getty Images; (c) AFP/AFP/Getty Images.)

experimenter says little more than "Write down as many words as you remember from the list an hour ago" or "Tell me what you remember about the event you just experienced." We've heard a story of a professor who once gave students an exam with one question, which was "Write as much as you remember about chapter 2." This would be a free recall test.

In a **cued recall** test, the experimenter adds some hints, or cues, about the material you're supposed to remember (e.g., "Some of the words were fruits" or "What happened after the man with the Big Yellow Hat took George from the jungle?"). In a **recognition test**, the experimenter provides the targets along with distractors (also called **foils** or **lures**), and the participant must pick out the targets from among the distractors (e.g., "did you see 'orange' or 'apple'?"). Students should be familiar with recognition tests, as most multiple-choice test items are based on recognition.

In a **savings in relearning** test, the experimenter asks the participant to learn some material (e.g., a word list) to a particular criterion (e.g., until they can recite the list perfectly two times in a row). The number of practice trials it takes to reach the desired criterion (e.g., 80 percent of the items on the list) is recorded. At retrieval, the experimenter asks the participant to learn the same material to the same criterion a second time. If the participant can reach the criterion in fewer trials, that represents savings in relearning – the participant learns the material faster the second time – which presumably results from some residual memory of the earlier experience. Riener went to a bilingual English–Spanish elementary school. At the beginning of each day, students recited the Pledge of Allegiance, in English and then in Spanish. After sixth grade, he didn't have cause to recite the Pledge of Allegiance in Spanish again. Nearly thirty years later, he cannot recall it, but he could probably relearn it faster than someone who had never learned it in the first place.

In general, free recall is the memory task with the lowest performance and that people find the most difficult, followed by cued recall, then recognition. Savings in relearning is ubiquitous in learning situations but used less frequently in research situations. In this case, "easy" or "difficult" refers to the likelihood that you will successfully retrieve the material you encoded, not how effortful retrieval feels. We can also refer to difficulty as the **sensitivity** of a test, that is, its efficacy in

Table 8.1 Four possible tests of your memory of the stimulus Boat in ascending order of difficulty

Four recognition tests	Option 1	Option 2
Test 1	float	boat
Test 2	float	ship
Test 3	float	groundhog
Test 4	float	♋

detecting memories. A test seems easy to a student because it is sensitive – you're succeeding, you're detecting memories, even if they are faint. From a professor's point of view, we may prefer less sensitive measures of memory (and therefore more difficult exams) to encourage stronger memories (and more studying).

Although tests of memory generally vary in sensitivity, as we've described, there is a problem to bear in mind. The apparent sensitivity (i.e., ease or difficulty) of a test depends on *which* cues the experimenter provides. For example, we may say "Remember this word" and show you a slide with the word *Boat* written on it. Then, an hour later, we give you one of four recognition tests, each of which has the target (*Boat*) and one distractor, and you have to choose which stimulus you saw (*a* or *b*). Table 8.1 lists four possible tests that vary in difficulty because the distractors vary. Similarly, a cued recall test will be harder or easier, depending on the quality of the hints. Still, it is generally true that recognition is easier than cued recall, which is easier than free recall (Hart, 1965, 1967; Tulving & Pearlstone, 1966), and this relationship is relevant to the question we are addressing in this section: Why is memory retrieval unreliable?

Differences in Cues

Why do different measures of memory lead to different memory performance? Psychologists have found it useful to think about measures of memory in terms of the cues that they provide.

In a free recall test, the instruction is typically "Try to recall the information I showed you earlier." It is understood that you are to recall information from the time and place at which the experimenter had you encode some material. This information about the time and place at which a memory was encoded is usually called the **context**, but in this example, you don't have complete information about the context. The experimenter might have said, "Try to recall the information I showed you an hour ago, in this room." Of course, even if the experimenter didn't give you that specific information ("an hour ago, in this room"), you might use that information to help you remember the required information. In so doing, you are generating your own cues to memory.

In a cued recall test, the experimenter provides the context and adds some hints about the material. The hints might be some semantically related words ("One of the words referred to a card game") or a cue based on sound ("One of the words rhymed with *smoker*").

In a recognition test, the experimenter again provides a cue about the context but now also provides the target material along with some other material that was not presented at encoding. The participant's job, therefore, is to determine which stimuli go with the encoding context (see Table 8.2).

It seems that free recall, cued recall, and recognition differ in that they provide successively more complete cues. One idea holds that memories may differ along a simple dimension of strength.

Table 8.2 Types of memory tests

Type of test	Sample instructions	Reference to context?	Information about target	What must participant do?
Free recall	"Please remember the word list."	Yes	None	Generate the target material from the context information
Cued recall	"Please remember the word list. One of the words was the name of a card game."	Yes	Usually semantic (i.e., related to meaning)	Generate the target from the context information using the cue
Recognition	"Was the word *poker* on the list you saw before?"	Yes	Target itself	Determine whether the stimulus provided matches the context information

A strong memory needs few cues; a weaker memory needs more cues to be successfully retrieved. The sensitivity of a test is determined by the quality and quantity of cues it provides. We can call this view the **strength view of memory**.

Later experiments showed that there are problems with a strength view of memory. For example, retrieval doesn't work the same way each time. If someone asks you to name the three Rice Krispies characters, you may draw an utter blank on one occasion, whereas another time you might immediately rattle off, "Snap, Crackle, Pop." If the memory is strong, you should retrieve it every time, and if it's weak, you should fail each time; after all, the retrieval cue ("Name the Rice Krispies characters") is the same each time.

Endel Tulving (1967) emphasized this point in a classic experiment. He had people encode a list of thirty-six common nouns once, then make three successive attempts to recall the list, then encode it again, make three more recall attempts, and so on. Not surprisingly, people recalled more words with each successive encoding. What was more interesting is what happened when they made several recall attempts of the list. Over all recall attempts, participants got an average of 14.21 items correct. On each successive attempt, participants remembered 3.97 words (on average) that they hadn't recalled on the previous attempt, but they also forgot 3.89 words (on average) that they had remembered on the previous attempt. In other words, a participant might report a word on the first test, then fail to recall it on tests 2 and 3, then recall it again on test 4, and so on. Tulving pointed out that this pattern of data argued against a simple strength theory of memory; there is no reason for the strength of a memory to wax and wane on successive tests.

MATCH BETWEEN ENCODING AND RETRIEVAL: TRANSFER-APPROPRIATE PROCESSING   Another phenomenon that shows that strength is not the whole story, and gives us a good transition into our discussion of retrieval, is a reevaluation of the idea of deeper processing. It would seem that deeper processing always leads to a stronger memory, which is

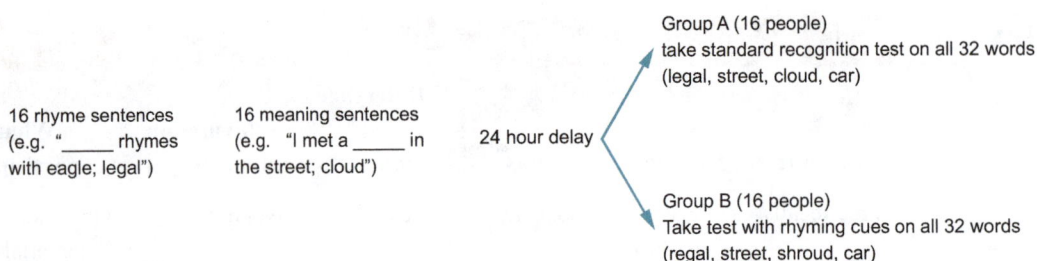

Figure 8.2. Design of Morris et al.'s (1977) study. (Source: C. D. Morris, J. D. Bransford, and J. J. Franks [1977], Levels of processing versus transfer appropriate processing, *Journal of Verbal Learning and Verbal Behavior*, 16[5], 519–533.)

why deeper processing at encoding leads to better memory at retrieval. Yet, this way of discussing memory seems to paint encoding as an active process that creates memories that vary in strength and retrieval as a passive process; retrieval success depends only on the strength of the memory at encoding. As the measures of memory section indicates, retrieval is more complicated than that. If they are both active processes, maybe a match between them is what leads to the best chance of success.

The mental processes at retrieval must be considered when we're thinking about encoding effects. Donald Morris and colleagues (1977) performed a simple but ingenious experiment in which they varied not only encoding processes (as in a typical depth experiment) but also processes at retrieval (see Figure 8.2). In their experiment, participants heard words and were asked to do one of two tasks. The rhyme condition was a standard shallow task, and the sentence frame was a deep task. Some participants answered a rhyming question, as described earlier ("_____ rhymes with eagle; legal"). The other participants answered a sentence frame question in which they needed to think about what the word meant to determine whether it would fit the sentence frame ("I met a _____ in the street; cloud"). So far, it's just a standard levels of processing experiment of the sort described in Chapter 7.

The difference is that Morris and colleagues (1977) gave two different kinds of retrieval tasks as well. One was a standard recognition test in which participants heard a list of words and had to say which ones they had heard before. As shown in Figure 8.3, participants showed the usual depth of processing effect. Other participants were not given a recognition test but took a cued recall test in which they had to try to remember the words given a list of cues. Some of these cues rhymed with a word on the original list. For example, if one of the words was *legal*, the word *regal* might have been on the list of cues. These rhyming cues were different from the ones participants heard the first time they saw the words.

As shown in Figure 8.3, when memory was tested with rhyming cues, the usual depth effect reversed: The participants who did the supposedly shallow rhyme task at encoding remembered more than those who did the supposedly deep sentence frame task. This result seems obvious once someone tells you about it, but it wasn't at all obvious at the time. Who would have thought you could get the levels of processing effect to reverse by changing the test? Most psychologists were thinking that depth of encoding made the memory representation stronger in some way, which would mean that memory would be better for any type of retrieval test. But in this case, memory was better when the cue at retrieval matched the processing at encoding.

The general hypothesis is that when the same processes are used to think about words at encoding and retrieval, memory will be successful; when different processes are used at encoding and retrieval, memory will not be successful. This hypothesis is known as **transfer-appropriate**

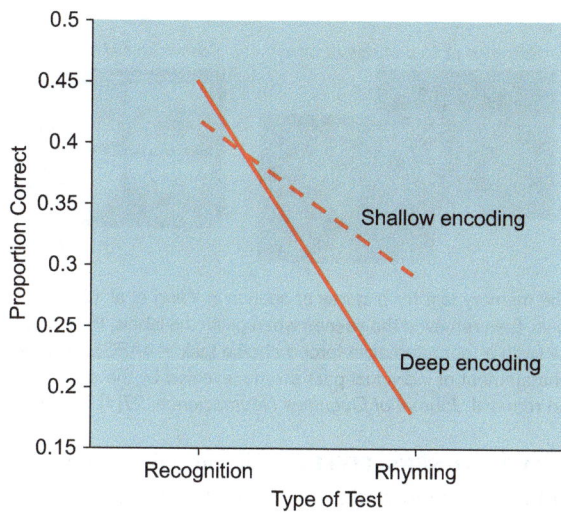

Figure 8.3. Results of Morris et al.'s (1977) experiment showing that it's not just the depth of processing at encoding that's important; the match between the encoding task and the retrieval test is also important. Shallow encoding is more effective than deep encoding when the test has rhyming cues. (Source: C. D. Morris, J. D. Bransford, and J. J. Franks [1977], Levels of processing versus transfer appropriate processing, *Journal of Verbal Learning and Verbal Behavior*, 16[5], 519–533.)

processing. According to this hypothesis, one type of encoding, such as deep processing, is not inherently better than another.

If you are a student wondering how this research from fifty years ago applies to your challenges to retrieve memories in exams, a recent review (Yang et al., 2021) integrated data from 222 studies with 48,478 students to investigate how well practicing material by testing your memory improves later memory retrieval, a phenomenon called the **testing effect**. While confirming the role of the testing effect (trying to retrieve your memories is a good way of increasing your chances of retrieving them later), they also found confirmation of transfer-appropriate processing (matching the format of the studied items with the exam led to better memory performance).

The idea of transfer-appropriate processing is also supported by research showing that a match in the pattern of brain activation between encoding and retrieval is associated with successful remembering. For example, Wing et al. (2015) studied memory for complex scenes, like a picture of a barn or a tunnel, paired with a label ("barn" or "tunnel"). Participants had their brains scanned with fMRI while they encoded the scenes. Then, while still in the scanner, they retrieved the scenes when presented with the labels, rating how detailed their memories for the scenes were (1 = least amount of detail, 4 = highly detailed memory). Finally, outside the scanner, they were given a recognition test for the scenes (see Figure 8.4).

The researchers found that successful remembering was associated with the similarity in brain activation at encoding and retrieval; in other words, if your brain activity when you saw the prompt "tunnel" was similar to your brain activity when you actually saw the picture of the tunnel, you were likely to recognize that scene later. The matching brain activity was most important in the occipitotemporal cortex, an area often active in memory for visual scenes (MacEvoy & Epstein, 2011), and the ventrolateral prefrontal cortex and inferior parietal cortex, areas that contribute to many memory processes (Risius et al., 2019; see also Kragel et al., 2017; Norman & O'Reilly, 2003; Ritchey et al., 2013). This study offers converging evidence that it is not just depth of processing but matching processing (and matching not just by level of processing but by matching specific brain activity) that accounts for higher memory performance.

Experimental design

Encoding of 96 pictures (3 runs)   Retrieval of 96 pictures (3 runs)   Post-scan 4AFC recognition of 96 pictures

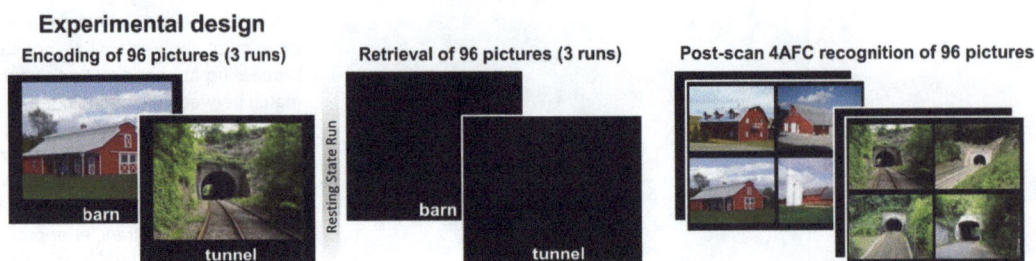

Figure 8.4. What participants saw in the memory test for pictures of scenes in Wing et al. (2015). They initially saw pictures of scenes paired with word labels, then retrieved the scenes when given the labels, then finally tested by asking which was the original picture they saw (with a four alternative forced choice task = 4AFC). (Source: E. A. Wing, M. Ritchey, and R. Cabeza [2015], Reinstatement of individual past events revealed by the similarity of distributed activation patterns during encoding and retrieval, *Journal of Cognitive Neuroscience*, 27[4], 680.)

RETRIEVAL CUES AND MEMORY TEST SENSITIVITY   The preceding discussion hints at what is behind the variable sensitivity of different retrieval tests. It's not that more retrieval cues per se are better for retrieval, but having more cues makes it more likely that one of them will match what you thought about at encoding, leading to successful retrieval. In other words, a recognition test is more likely than a cued recall test to make you process the material the way you did at encoding. If a cued recall test was designed to make participants more likely to think about the material in the same way as they did at encoding, it should be more sensitive than a recognition test.

Endel Tulving and Donald Thomson (1973) set out to provide just such a demonstration. In their experiment, participants were told that they would see word pairs, and they were to remember the words written in capital letters. An accompanying word written in lowercase letters might help them, but they would be tested on the words in capital letters. Participants saw a list of twenty-four word pairs, such as *glue–CHAIR*, *ground–COLD*, and *fruit–FLOWER*, and then took a recognition test of the capitalized words. Immediately after this task, participants were given the list of cues from the original list: *glue_____*, *ground _____*, and *fruit _____*. On some occasions, participants failed to recognize a target word on the first test but then successfully produced it on the cued recall test. Tulving and Thomson called this effect **recognition failure of recallable words** to emphasize that the encoding and testing conditions were designed to reverse the usual finding that recognition is superior to recall. This effect has been repeated in many other experiments.

How is it possible for participants to recall *CHAIR* given the cue *glue*, even though moments earlier they had failed to pick out *CHAIR* on a recognition test? There has been a good deal of debate about this phenomenon. Currently, the favored explanation is that the cause of the effect lies in the lowercase cues, which are selected to be low associates of the target words. The words *chair* and *glue*, for example, are not completely unrelated. You can make a connection between the two words if you think about the joints of a chair, which are often glued. So, the presence of the word *glue*, which the experimenter says you are free to ignore, makes you think about the target in an unusual way. If on the recognition test you see *CHAIR* alone and you think about the word in the normal way – as something to sit on – that's not what you thought about at encoding. You thought about something with glued joints, so you say to yourself, "Nah, I didn't see the word *CHAIR* before. Gee, I don't know which of these three words was on the list; I'll just guess." You might guess wrong. Later, on the recall test, you see the cue *glue*, and there is some chance you'll say to yourself, "Oh, yeah, I thought about glue at encoding – glued joints it was. On a chair. Right, *glue* went with *CHAIR*."

Tulving and Thomson's (1973) experiment shows that the match between encoding and retrieval is critical: If you think about the stimulus in different ways at encoding and retrieval, you may not recognize it. We can predict, then, that if participants never really connect the cue and stimulus words (*glue–CHAIR*) semantically, the effect should disappear, and that seems to be the case (Arlemalm, 1996; Bryant, 1991).

RETRIEVAL CUES AND THE PHYSICAL ENVIRONMENT   We know that memory is better when the processes engaged in thinking about the material are the same at encoding and retrieval. Can we extend this idea to physical contexts? If you learn some material while you're in a dormitory room, for example, will you remember it when you are tested in a lecture hall? In fact, researchers have demonstrated that there are **context effects** of the physical environment on memory, but they are generally weak.

Steven Smith and colleagues (1978) had college students study lists of words presented on slides in a windowless room off campus by the experimenter neatly dressed in a tie and jacket. On a second day, the students studied another word list that was read aloud, this time in a room on campus with windows, and the experimenter was dressed sloppily. On a third day, they were asked to remember both lists in one or the other context. The experimenters reported that memory was somewhat better if the context matched between encoding and retrieval (59 percent correct) than if it didn't match (46 percent correct). All these changes in the environment (room, experimenter, words heard vs. seen) produced a modest effect.

These studies showed that memory is somewhat better when the physical environment is the same during encoding and retrieval. Nevertheless, context effects are usually small; the effect is present for free recall, smaller for cued recall, and often absent altogether for recognition (Smith, 1988; but see Grant et al., 1998; for a review, see DuBrow Rouhani et al., 2017). For example, the original eye-catching study for context-dependent memory compared learning on land versus learning underwater while scuba diving and then test performance being compared in matched versus unmatched environments (Godden & Baddeley, 1975). A recent nonreplication (Murre, 2021) suggests that this effect might be smaller and more fragile than originally supposed.

Context effects also seem stronger when encoding items that are relevant to whatever schema is activated by that context. For example, remembering "fish" would be easier than remembering "cupcake" if the active schema were an underwater one.

Shin et al. (2021) asked participants to encode material while in virtual reality environments (underwater or on Mars) that activated different knowledge schemas. The size of the context-dependency memory effect was larger for items that were context-relevant at encoding. In other words, context effects probably constitute not a completely different memory process but rather an example of a memory nudge fitting into our previous discussions of scripts, schemas, and transfer-appropriate processing – bad news for students hoping for a big and relatively easy memory boost by studying in the same place as the test, but also probably not that surprising given the context (ha!) of everything else we've learned about memory so far. This is actually good news: If memory were too context-dependent, then we wouldn't be able to take it anywhere.

Retrieval and Prior Knowledge

In Chapter 7, we saw that prior knowledge (as represented in a script or schema) influences how new experiences are processed and therefore how they are encoded. For example, we saw that a script (e.g., what usually happens at a restaurant) highlights any events inconsistent with the script and makes them memorable. Prior knowledge also influences retrieval, but it influences memory of the typical events, not atypical ones.

Suppose that you are trying to remember a story you were told last week about a child's birthday party. You have prior knowledge about children's birthday parties that can provide retrieval cues. For example, you know that cake and ice cream are usually served at kids' parties, so you might try to remember what sort of cake was served or whether something other than cake was served, such as an enormous chocolate chip cookie. Your expectation that cake was served may be so strong that you may think to yourself, "I really don't remember cake being served, but this was a child's birthday party, so there had to be cake; let me try one more time to remember what kind."

Sir Frederic Bartlett (1932), who first developed the idea of a schema, gave a classic example of its effects on retrieval. He read a Native American folktale called "The War of the Ghosts" to English schoolboys. This story has cultural elements that would have been unfamiliar to English schoolboys in the 1930s, such as canoes, and the story structure itself is different from English stories, which typically have logical links between one event and another; this story introduces new actions without making it clear how they relate to previous actions. Bartlett (1932) reported that when his participants tried to recall this story later, their recall was influenced by their schema of what a typical English story is like. They added details to put logical connections between events, omitted other details, and changed unfamiliar terms to ones they knew better. Bartlett called attention to one participant who substituted the word *boat* for *canoe* when he recalled the story, and another who reported that characters in the story went *fishing* instead of *seal hunting*. Researchers have sometimes replicated the particular results Bartlett reported and sometimes not (Bergman & Roediger, 1999; Roediger et al., 1993), but the basic effects he reported are very well supported (Ost et al., 2022).

Bartlett argued that retrieval is largely a process of **reconstruction**, not a matter of simply pulling information out of the memory storehouse. We use information from the memory storehouse and information about the world (in the form of schemas) to reconstruct what probably occurred.

This reconstructive nature of retrieval is supported by data from the study by Gordon Bower and his colleagues (Bower et al., 1979) described in Chapter 7. You'll recall that that experiment showed that events that are inconsistent with the script but relevant to its goal are well remembered. The experimenters also asked participants questions that would be consistent with the script but were not presented in the original story. For example, participants read a story about going to a restaurant, and no mention was made of the patron paying the bill. The participants gave high confidence ratings not only to having seen sentences that were actually in the story (average = 5.46) but also to having seen sentences describing actions consistent with the script but never mentioned in the story (average = 3.9). These ratings were much higher than ratings for events that were not in the story and unrelated to the script (average = 1.71). (See Table 8.3 for sample sentences.)

But how can we be certain that these effects occur at retrieval? It seems plausible that these schema effects occur at encoding; the participant makes inferences as they are listening to make the story fit the schema. At recall, the participant remembers the inferences, so reconstruction doesn't occur at all. James Dooling and Robert Christiaansen (1977) determined a clever way to show that reconstruction can occur at recall. They asked participants to read this paragraph:

> Carol Harris was a problem child from birth. She was wild, stubborn, and violent. By the time Carol turned eight, she was still unmanageable. Her parents were very concerned about her mental health. There was no good institution for her problem in her state. Her parents finally decided to take some action. They hired a private teacher for Carol.

Table 8.3 Sample recognition test

Original story		
Dan went to a restaurant. The hostess seated him. He scanned the menu. He selected what he wanted, and the server took his order. Dan waited for his food. The waitress brought his food. Dan ate his meal and left the restaurant.		
Recognition test sentences	**Type of sentence**	**Average recognition rating**
Dan waited for his food.	Consistent with the script; in the story	5.46
Dan paid the bill.	Consistent with the script; not in the story	3.91
The restaurant was cold.	Irrelevant to script; not in the story	1.71

After a one-week delay, a group of participants were given a recognition test for sentences and had to say whether each sentence was in the story. The critical sentence was "She was deaf, dumb, and blind." Very few participants believed that this sentence had been part of the story. A second group of participants underwent the same testing procedure, except that right before taking the recognition test, they were told that Carol Harris was Helen Keller's real name. Many of these participants incorrectly "recognized" the critical sentence as having been in the story. This experiment shows clearly that reconstruction can occur at retrieval. There was no opportunity for the memory error to occur at encoding because participants didn't know that their background knowledge about Helen Keller would be relevant until retrieval.

False Memory

In the previous section, we saw that it's possible to remember an event that never happened – for example, your knowledge about what usually happens in a restaurant can make you falsely remember that a menu was offered to a customer. This type of error is an unfortunate by-product of a *good* feature of your memory. Your memory system will include information that is probably right – the server usually offers a menu, so even if you have no specific memory of that event, it's sensible to assume that it happened. Although the memory system is usually making a good gamble by including such information as part of the memory, on occasion, it's wrong, and that's one type of **false memory**, usually defined as a memory of an event that never happened.

Cognitive psychologists have found that false memories of this sort can be easy to produce. For example, have a look at this list of words:

bed	rest
tired	dream
wake	snooze
blanket	doze
slumber	snore
nap	peace
yawn	drowsy

Participants who hear this list and are immediately asked to recall it remember the word "sleep" from the list about 50 percent of the time (Deese, 1959; Roediger & McDermott, 1995). The

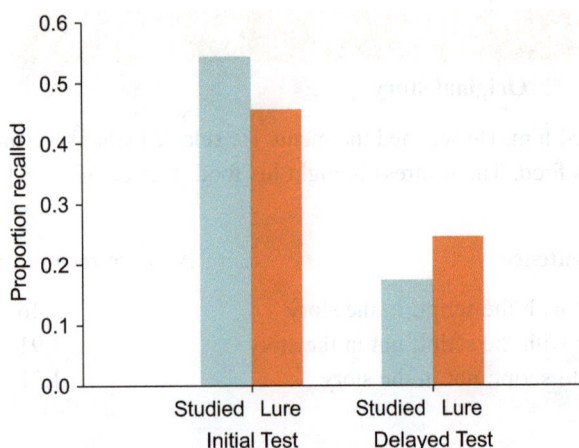

Figure 8.5. Results of McDermott (1996). Note that, with a delay, the rate of "remembering" the material is higher for the lure word that was not on the list than it is for any of the words that were on the list. (Source: K. B. McDermott [1996], The persistence of false memories in list recall, *Journal of Memory and Language*, 35, 216.)

odd thing is that "sleep" isn't on the list. This false memory effect is very robust. Participants report high confidence that "sleep" was on the list (Roediger & McDermott, 1995), and they report the word even when warned that they will be tempted to report items associated with the list items (Gallo et al., 1997). Kathleen McDermott (1996) introduced a two-day delay between study and test and found that participants were actually more likely to recall the never-presented item than any of the presented items (see Figure 8.5). (For a review of variations of this experiment, see Chang and Brainerd [2021].)

In a very clever study, Sherman and colleagues (2015) replicated the reconstructive effect with advertisements. Participants watched six TV advertisements for brands in a related category. For example, they might watch ads for BMW, Jaguar, Mercedes, Renault, Volkswagen, and Audi (for cars) or for Scrabble, Cluedo, Pictionary, Trivial Pursuit, Articulate, and Cranium (for board games). When tested later, they falsely recalled that they had seen an ad for a popular brand in that category, like Ford or Monopoly. How ironic that if a brand is well known, even ads for competing brands seem to make viewers think of that brand.

Why does this false memory occur? One way to think about it is that it's rather like the restaurant schema. Even in a list-learning experiment, your memory system will use background knowledge if it seems applicable. In this case, it's obvious to the participants that the words are related, and the relationship revolves around the concept "sleep." That background knowledge – that "sleep" is related to the other words and is therefore very typical of the list – becomes folded into the memory for the list without the participant intending it to, just as the server offering a menu is typical of a restaurant visit and therefore gets folded into the memory of a particular visit to a restaurant.

A different explanation is also possible. Perhaps when participants hear the list of sleep-related words, they actually think of the word "sleep" during encoding. Then, at recall, they remember thinking about "sleep" when they heard the list and don't realize that they are remembering their own thought, not what the experimenter said (Johnson & Raye, 1981; Roediger et al., 2001). This example represents another type of false memory. You have the content of the memory right, but you're mistaken about the source. The **source** of a memory refers to where and when it was encoded: whether someone told you the information, or you experienced it directly, or you just thought about it. For example, Riener knows that both Prince and David Bowie died in 2016. But he's lost the source for that memory. He doesn't know whether he saw it on television, read it in the newspaper, or was informed by a friend. In that case, the source of the memory is not that important – those events did actually happen and were later confirmed across several sources. If sources are reliable and corroborate each other, mistaking a memory's source isn't such a bad thing.

In some cases, however, knowing the source of a memory can be quite important. Sometimes you are confused about whether the source of a memory was something in the environment or whether it was your own thought. If it was a thought, but not in the environment, that can make a big difference. For example, as you're pulling out of your driveway, you believe that you remember turning off the stove, but then you wonder whether you are remembering actually turning off the stove or *thinking* about turning off the stove. **Source confusion** occurs when one mistakes one's own thought for an event (or vice versa), or when one misremembers where and when an event occurred (Johnson et al., 1993; Johnson & Raye, 1981).

Creating source confusions and subsequent memory errors in the laboratory is not difficult. For example, Brian Gonsalves and his associates (Gonsalves et al., 2004) had participants view a series of 350 words, one at a time, on a screen. Each word was a concrete noun (e.g., "table"), and participants were to generate a mental image corresponding to the word after they saw it. For half the words, a photograph of the object was presented two seconds later. For the other words, a blank rectangle was presented, and participants were to create a visual mental image of the object in the rectangle. Twenty minutes later, participants heard all 350 words again, as well as 175 new distractors. Participants had to judge whether they had viewed a photograph of the word during the study. Participants believed that they had seen a photograph of 27 percent of the items for which they had only created a mental image. Other studies (e.g., Dijkstra et al., 2021) have shown that the phenomenon occurs for entire events, not just for confusable items, such as words in a long list.

Gonsalves and his associates (2004) also measured participants' brain activation during this study. They found that the parts of the brain that support **visual imagery** – precuneus, right parietal cortex, and anterior cingulate – were more active during encoding for words that would later be falsely remembered as having been presented with a picture. This indicates that producing a vivid mental image might make the participant more likely to falsely remember that they actually *saw* a picture. This interpretation fits with the general idea that people judge whether they *saw* something or *thought about* something based on how much perceptual detail there is in the memory. If there is a lot of detail, people suspect that they are remembering something that they saw (Johnson et al., 1993). (For a review of the neuroscientific approach to false memories, see Lacy and Stark [2013] or Dennis et al. [2022].)

There is an important real-life application of this research. In an experiment demonstrating this phenomenon, Elizabeth Loftus and her colleagues (Loftus et al., 1978) showed their participants a slideshow depicting an auto accident. After seeing the slideshow, the participants completed a questionnaire about the events in the show. For half the participants, the questionnaire mentioned, in passing, information that did not match the slides. For example, one question was "Did another car pass the red Datsun when it stopped at the yield sign?" The slide actually showed a stop sign, not a yield sign. Participants later had to select which sign they had seen, and those who were misled by the questionnaire were about half as likely to get it right as those who were not. A likely interpretation of these data is that participants who were misled were experiencing source confusion: They remembered something about a yield sign, but they forgot that it was in the questionnaire, not in the slides (Lindsay & Johnson, 1989).

The practical implications of this effect may be profound. Someone who witnesses a crime may have their memory modified by the questions they are later asked about it. Indeed, Loftus and Palmer (1974) conducted a study that seems very similar to exactly that effect. They asked participants who had just seen a short film of an auto accident to estimate the speed of the cars by asking "How fast were the cars going when they hit each other?" but they varied the verb, replacing

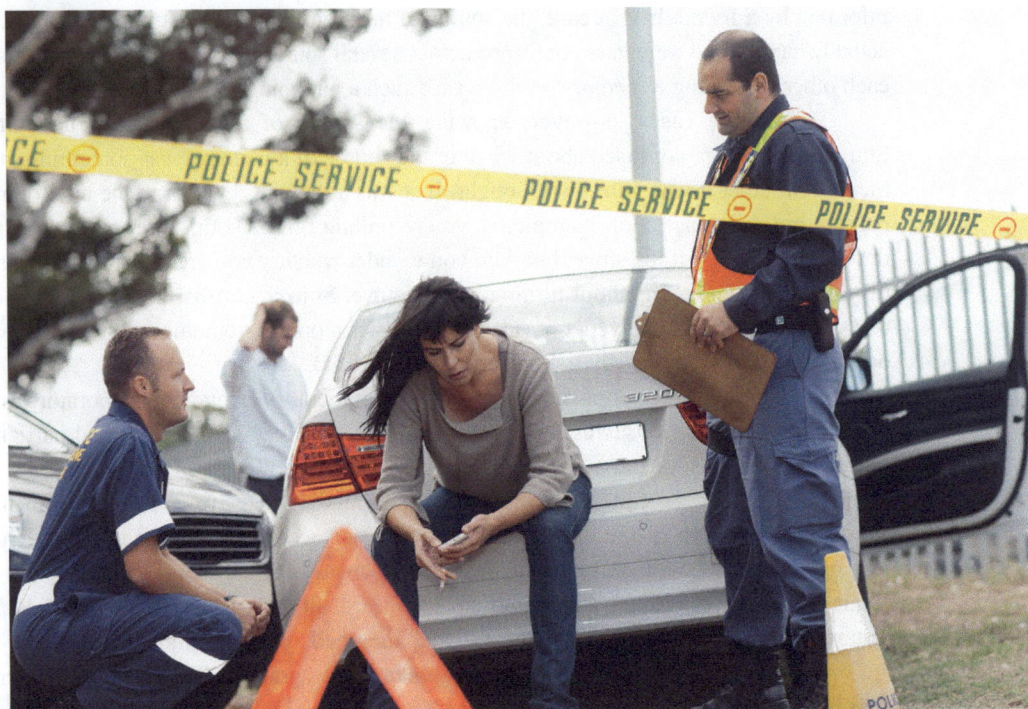

Figure 8.6. The questions that eyewitnesses are asked after an accident or crime can be a source of false memories. (Source: Zero Creatives/Image Source/Getty Images.)

hit with *smashed*, *collided*, *bumped*, or *contacted*. Participants estimated higher speeds when the verb used was more violent. More surprising, this simple alteration changed participants' memory for the accident. When they returned to the lab a week later, they again answered questions about the accident, including the question "Did you see any broken glass?" In fact, there was none, but 34 percent of participants who heard the verb *smashed* remembered that there was, compared with just 14 percent of participants who heard the verb *hit*. (See Figure 8.6.)

While it is difficult to pinpoint exactly how often this happens in the justice system, in the US, two institutions maintain databases of exonerations (where a person convicted of a crime is discovered to be innocent and freed). The Innocence Project has identified 375 cases of DNA exoneration, where DNA evidence incontrovertibly shows a person's innocence. They found that 69 percent of these involved eyewitness misidentification, a memory error with tragic consequences for those who were eventually exonerated. In addition, 29 percent involved false confessions, which in rare cases can be a false memory in the mind of the suspect, not just a witness. A recent review of links between suggestibility, compliance, and false confessions (Otgaar et al., 2021) across both laboratory and field studies found a common theme: People with high levels of suggestibility and, to a lesser extent, compliance were more likely to falsely confess to a crime that they did not commit.

Source memory (and confusions) can also have real-world consequences outside of the justice system. As we evaluate news stories from mixed sources (some reliable, some unreliable), remembering the source can be the difference between true (and often important!) news and disinformation or fake news. Greene et al. (2022) found that fake news items about COVID-19 vaccines were more likely to be remembered as true when they aligned with participants' attitudes about vaccines.

If false memories can be induced with suggestive and leading questions, what happens when those interested in changing memories can show fake but fully realistic, or "deepfake," videos? Murphy and Flynn (2022) investigated this by presenting participants with fake news stories in the form of text, text with a photograph, or text with deepfake video. Although participants believed that the videos were convincing, the video format did not increase false memory rates relative to the other formats. Certainly more research is needed, but existing research on false memories suggests that our memories are already malleable with relatively simple suggestions; the rise of the ability to fake videos emphasizes the importance of source memory but does not create an entirely new kind of memory distortion.

Providing misleading information will frequently lead to false memories, and participants can be quite confident about their accuracy (Zaragoza & Mitchell, 1996). The effect is usually stronger with a longer delay (Higham, 1998) and more often works with peripheral details of an event, rather than with the central features (e.g., Heath & Erickson, 1998). Scoboria and colleagues (2017) reviewed several false memory studies and found that 30 percent of participants in these studies formed a false memory, with that number increasing to 46 percent under certain conditions, such as a procedure whereby they were encouraged to create mental images.

In summary, there are two broad classes of false memory. One type occurs because the memory system (without the individual's intention or awareness) includes prior knowledge in a memory so that one "remembers" something that never happened. The second type occurs because the participant misremembers the source of a memory. As we noted at the beginning of the chapter, memory retrieval is a reconstructive process and prone to errors and mistakes. These mistakes can have dire consequences, as the Innocence Project has shown. However, it is also important not to go entirely overboard and see memory as essentially or completely unreliable. Brewin et al. (2020) remind us that memory is clearly malleable but, under normal circumstances (without contamination or suggestion), is often quite reliable. Reminders of the reconstructive nature of memory retrieval shouldn't undermine all of your trust in your own or others' memories. In the remainder of this chapter, we cover another more familiar type of memory error – forgetting.

Stand-on-One-Foot Questions

8.1. What four measures of memory are commonly used, and what does it mean to say that they differ in sensitivity?
8.2. Why do different measures of memory differ in sensitivity?
8.3. Which is more important to effective retrieval: the format of the test (recognition, cued recall) or the cues the test provides?
8.4. How does prior knowledge affect retrieval?
8.5. What are the two main ways that false memories may be created?

Questions That Require Two Feet

8.6. Suppose you asked a friend to tell you what they were doing exactly nineteen months ago. How much do you think they could tell you, and why?
8.7. You probably have had the experience of walking past a friend without recognizing them in a place where you don't typically see that person (as when you see a college friend in your hometown during spring break). How can the ideas discussed here explain that phenomenon?

Why Do We Forget?

Preview

Forgetting can occur because (1) you don't have the right cue for retrieval, (2) the association between the cue and the target memory is compromised in some way, or (3) the target memory itself is lost. There is some evidence supporting each mechanism. We briefly consider the possibility that some memories are never lost. The popular notion that all memories are recorded somewhere in the brain is almost certainly wrong, but it does appear that with sufficient practice, a subset of memories will never be lost.

In trying to explain why something that *can* be retrieved sometimes is not retrieved, we emphasize cues, and indeed, changes in cues can make an easily accessible memory seem to be forgotten. Something might happen to make you interpret the cues differently, as in recognition failure of recallable words, or a change in environmental context might do the same. Sometimes, however, a memory seems to be lost not temporarily but permanently: It cannot be retrieved. What happens when information is forgotten?

Figure 8.7 depicts the components of a memory situation. Any instance of memory can be thought of as composed of a cue or cues (either from the environment or generated by the person) and the target material. The cue and the target are linked or associated, and this link may be strong or weak. For example, the cue may be the question "What is the name of this person?" which is associated with the target information – Lisa Kudrow. Again, cues can be a source of forgetting. Changes to cues (cue bias) might lead to what amounts to a temporary failure to retrieve; if you had the right cues, you could retrieve the memory. But it's also possible that changes in cues could lead to permanent forgetting. For example, you might encode a memory when you are twelve years old (that actress from that popular sitcom about pals in NYC) and then try to retrieve it at age forty. The cues that would have been effective at age twelve may not work at forty because the way you interpret them has changed. Indeed, the cues may be thoughts and feelings that are virtually impossible for you to have now because you have changed so much; you might not have had the words to describe the experience, or a point of reference, and now you do. Imagine visiting your primary or elementary school when you are a teenager. You can certainly remember some things, but other cues might not be effective since you are literally seeing the world from a different perspective (you are taller when you are sixteen than when you are six). Without those cues, the memory cannot be recovered. Thus, in some situations, the cues associated with a memory cannot be recovered, and so the memory cannot be retrieved.

Three theories of forgetting incorporate changes to the links between cues and associated target memories. In **occlusion**, there is a stronger link from the cue to some undesired memory than to the target, and the cue therefore always calls up the undesired memory. In **decay**, the link spontaneously weakens over time. **Repression** is the idea that some memories are intentionally forgotten, often due to their traumatic content.

Occlusion

Occlusion makes it seem as if the memory is hidden or covered by another memory. The cue may be associated with the target just as strongly as it ever was, but it may also be associated with other

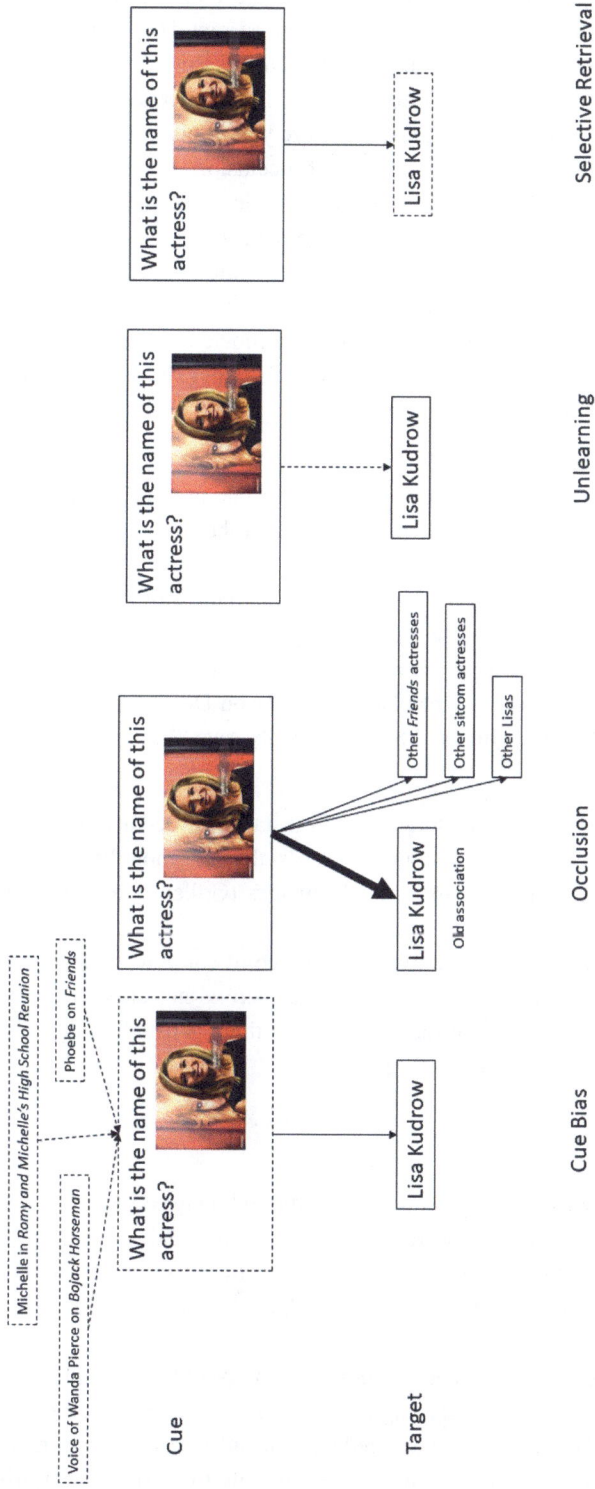

Figure 8.7. This simple model illustrates different theories of how forgetting could occur. The thick arrow represents a more robust association; dotted lines indicate some degradation. (Source: Frazer Harrison/Getty Images.)

memories more strongly, and every time the cue is presented, another memory intrudes. For example, if you move to a new address and are filling out a form with a cue of a blank space that says "street address," you may remember your old address rather than the new one. Occlusion explains why remembering the correct year of the current date is much more difficult in the first few weeks of January, before the new target for the cue of "current year" is stronger than the old target. For our actress example from the introduction to this chapter, a different actress's name, like Jennifer Aniston, might be a stronger link, and therefore you might confuse them.

An easily appreciated example of occlusion is a certain kind of **tip-of-the-tongue phenomenon** (Brown & McNeill, 1966; for a review, see Abrams & Davis, 2016). One instance of tip-of-the-tongue is when you can *almost* retrieve a target memory but can't quite get it. In other cases, this effect occurs when you are certain you know a concept but cannot think of the proper term for it because that search process keeps hitting the wrong target. For example, we've all had the experience of trying to remember the name of a movie or a show or a song and describing it to a friend as we both feel the movie's title just out of reach. (There is [of course, there is] a Reddit sub-Reddit, www.reddit.com/r/tipofmytongue/.)

A few recent examples:

> I vividly remember some movie/TV show scene in which an alien spaceship interrupts a baseball game, making sounds, and one of the players looks up and dramatically takes his hat off (*Men in Black*).
>
> "What is the song that the chorus goes 'mmmm the jolly man wailed.'" It was a pop song from like fifteen years ago; the chorus is a girl singing and kind of electronic, but a lot of the rest of the song is rap/pop. I remember it was *always* on the radio in the US.
>
> Are you talking about "Whatcha Say" by Jason Derulo? The chorus (which is taken from Imogen Heap's "Hide and Seek") actually says "Mmm whatcha say . . . that you only meant well."

Thinking of tip-of-the-tongue as an instance of occlusion, it makes sense that tip-of-the-tongue states are more common in bilinguals than in monolinguals, given that there is more opportunity for semantic overlap across languages (Gollan et al., 2014; Kreiner & Degani, 2015, Stasenko & Gollan, 2019).

Although occlusion is a plausible source of some forgetting, it is probably not the major contributor. Most of the time when we forget, there is not another memory occluding the target. Even when we are in the tip-of-the-tongue state, there is usually not a persistent intruder memory. Other factors must play a part in forgetting.

Decay

The decay theory of forgetting proposes that the link between a cue and a target memory spontaneously decays over time. If you rehearse the memory again, it will be "refreshed," but all links continuously break down, so refreshing the association doesn't prevent decay; it simply revives the link. Most people would find this idea reasonable because the passage of time seems to be a culprit in forgetting.

A simple version of decay theory was proposed by Edward Thorndike (1911), the great turn-of-the-twentieth-century learning theorist. His law of disuse proposed that if a memory is not used, it decays. This idea, however, predicts that older memories should always be more decayed than newer memories and therefore more difficult to retrieve. Yet we know that some older

(a) (b)

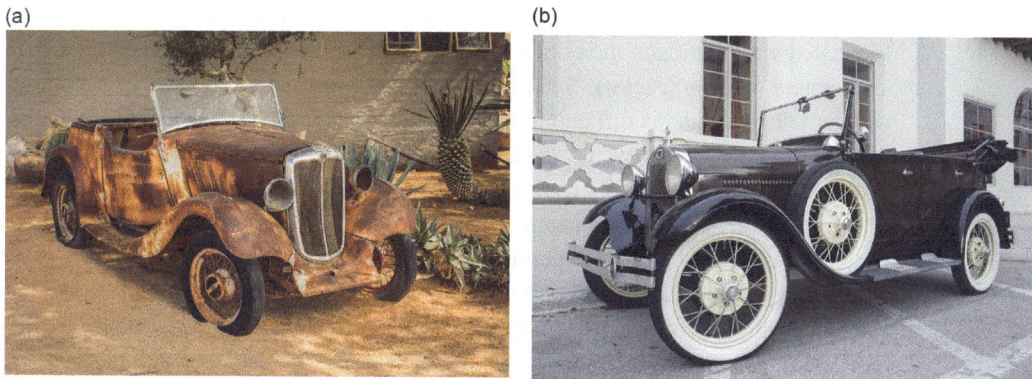

Figure 8.8. Metal rusts not because of time but because of oxidation, a process that occurs in time. If metal is protected from oxygen, either through a covering or other measures, it doesn't rust, as shown by these two images of 100-year-old Ford Model T automobiles. (Source: (a) Victor Escorial Merino/EyeEm/Getty Images; (b) ntzolov/E+/Getty Images.)

memories remain strong, whereas newer memories are lost. You may not recall what you had for breakfast a few days ago, but you still remember the name of your first-grade teacher.

We could combine decay theory with some version of a strength theory and say that all memories decay at a constant rate but that some start out with more strength than others. Older memories that began with more strength, such as my first-grade teacher's name, could be easier to retrieve than recent memories that have less strength. Until the 1930s, most psychologists believed that something like this was right. In the last section, we went over problems with a strength theory, but people didn't spot these problems until the 1960s. The case against decay was made by John McGeoch in 1932. He pointed out that it seems natural to blame time as the great causative agent in forgetting. We forget as time passes, and we therefore think of the passage of time as causing the forgetting. McGeoch (1932) pointed out that time itself is not an explanation; instead, some process *occurring in time* causes forgetting. He suggested the analogy of metal rusting. Metal rusts not because of time but because of oxidation, a process that occurs in time (see Figure 8.8).

For decay to be an explanation, we must define the process of decay. For decay to provide a testable account of forgetting, researchers will probably need to propose more specific theories of exactly how decay operates, as has been done for decay in working memory (see Chapter 5; see Altmann & Gray, 2002).

Repression

Repression is the active forgetting of an episode for the sake of self-protection: Remembering the episode would be too painful. The term implies some active form of dampening the memory, but this dampening process happens outside awareness. It is not simply that you try not to think about the memory. We're treating repression separately from other types of forgetting because the focus in this area of research has not been on how forgetting and remembering work, but rather on whether repression occurs at all. To be certain that repression can occur, we need to verify that (1) the event the person remembers actually happened; (2) the event now remembered was, at some point, forgotten; and (3) the forgetting was due to repression and not another process.

Gathering evidence has been extraordinarily difficult. Repression has most often been associated with traumatic memories that are secret (such as sexual abuse) rather than public (such as disasters or emergencies). Such traumatic memories therefore involve a crime that is usually without witnesses and is difficult to corroborate. In addition to the standard difficulties in studying memories of long-past events, such as described in our discussion of flashbulb memories in Chapter 7, the goals of investigating crimes and healing victims often rightfully outweigh careful scientific investigation of traumatic memories and repression. Despite these difficulties, investigation has continued on this important possibility of forgetting.

Regarding the second question – was the event forgotten? – it is surprising to learn that people can forget not just what they have remembered but also forget that they have previously retrieved a memory. Jonathan Schooler and colleagues (1997) described the case of W.B., a forty-year-old woman who recounted recovering a memory of having been raped at knifepoint when she was sixteen. W.B. described the memory recovery as having been triggered by an encounter with a male coworker at a party. She commented on his advances toward a young woman, and he defended himself by saying, "She isn't exactly a virgin" (p. 268). W.B. was so upset that she left the party. That night she had nightmares and awoke knowing that she had been raped.

It certainly sounds as though that memory had been repressed. However, her ex-husband reported that several times during their marriage, W.B. had mentioned that she had been raped, but her statements had always been completely without emotion. W.B. had no recollection of having told her ex-husband. This case study, then, shows that even if a person says that they have completely forgotten an event for some period of time, we cannot simply take that belief at face value.

The third criterion to verify that repression has occurred is that the forgetting must not be due to some other process. In this chapter, we've been discussing many sources of retrieval failure. Isn't it possible that the memory was not actively repressed, but rather that it was not rehearsed, and the appropriate cues were not in the environment until the time of memory recovery? For example, in some cases, the event may not have been experienced as comparably emotional and traumatic at the time as it was in retrospect. This is not to suggest that abuse is not traumatic and morally reprehensible but to place these events in the context of our thought processes at the time. We experience many strong emotions when we are young and forget most of what happened to us. Our emotions at that time may not always match our later assessment of trauma and moral judgments. In other words, an emotional event as an adult may lead to rehearsal, but a similar event in childhood may not trigger the same emotions or the same rehearsal and therefore may be subject to normal forgetting (McNally & Geraerts, 2009).

Given these three stringent criteria, is there evidence for a process of repression? There are several case studies indicating that repression does occur. For example, Jonathan Schooler (2001) reported seven cases, each of which had been carefully researched to comply with the criteria we've listed. A recent survey of memory experts (Patihis et al., 2021) found them skeptical of widespread repression but open-minded to its rare existence, especially under certain specific laboratory situations. The rarity of repressed memory also fits with other studies of traumatic memory. Memory for traumatic events is typically vivid and frequently rehearsed (sometimes involuntarily, in the case of flashbacks in posttraumatic stress disorder) in both children and adults, even if those memories are not wholly accurate (Leopold & Dillon, 1963; Peace & Porter, 2004; Pynoos & Nader, 1989).

The prevalence of repression and its role in the context of other memory retrieval processes has been a topic of debate between researchers of memory and clinical psychotherapists who treat patients by helping them to recover traumatic memories (Crews, 1995; Freyd, 1994; Loftus, 1993; Otgaar et al., 2022). Some therapies call for clients to vividly imagine scenes as a method to retrieve repressed memories. As the false memory section should make clear, it is possible to form entirely new yet false memories through imagination. The relative rarity of repressed memory is important because it indicates that victims of trauma usually remember the trauma – there's not a repressed memory to recover, but there is a real danger of creating a false traumatic memory (Patihis et al., 2014).

SUMMARY   We've talked about three ways in which memory can be forgotten: (1) Cues may be ineffective because they are interpreted differently than they were at encoding; (2) the associative links between memories may be lost due to decay or **unlearning**, or a link may be ineffective because the cue also leads to another memory via a stronger associative link; (3) memory repression can occur, but repression is not a common cause of forgetting.

Which of these is the most important factor in forgetting? In a practical sense, cues are clearly the most important. If you don't have the right cues, there is no chance that you'll retrieve a memory. Also, most memories have multiple cues associated with them, so if you lose an associative link, or if the memory is somewhat inhibited, more and better cues might still enable you to retrieve the memory. There is a great deal of evidence regarding the importance of cues. There is also evidence that **inhibition** of memory representations contributes to forgetting. There is less evidence that the loss of associative links makes a significant contribution to forgetting.

The Permanence of Memory

From the previous sections, you might conclude that forgetting is caused mostly by a lack of good cues. Perhaps everything is recorded in your mind, like a massive internet archive, and if you can't remember something, it's not because the file is lost but because you can't find it due to poor cues. This idea is written up in newspaper and magazine articles from time to time, usually reported as though it is fact. Most memory researchers, however, would disagree.

This idea is impossible to disprove, however, because the basic proposition is that all memories are retrievable if you can get the right cues. If you can't remember something, you can always say, "Well, I just don't have the right cues yet." Even after testing with a million different cues, you can maintain that the next cue might be the right one, and you will remember. Although we can't state flatly that this proposal must be wrong, we think that it's unlikely to be true.

The reasons were laid out in an article by Elizabeth Loftus and Geoff Loftus (1980), pointing out that three factors support the idea that all memories lie somewhere in the memory vault: spontaneous recovery, memory under hypnosis, and direct brain stimulation (in an interesting study by neurologist Wilder Penfield). As we'll see, there are problems with each of these sources of evidence.

SPONTANEOUS RECOVERY   **Spontaneous recovery** is the sudden uncovering of a long-lost memory. Often, there is an identifiable cue that clearly leads to recovery of the memory. For example, people who revisit a house they lived in during childhood may report that the sight of a room brings back vivid memories. It's as though the cue (seeing the house again) is one end of a very fine chain, and if you pull it gently, you find there are charms (memories) attached (for an experimental example, see Stone et al., 2001).

Even if we accept the fact that the recovered memories are accurate, the fact that some memories can be spontaneously recovered does not mean that all memories are recorded. It means that some memories that you haven't retrieved in a long time can be retrieved again if you are given the right cues.

MEMORY AND HYPNOSIS   We sometimes hear or read about amazing feats of memory performed under hypnosis – bricklayers accurately reporting descriptions of bricks they laid in walkways years ago, and so on. In a word, bunk.

It is easy enough to test whether hypnosis helps memory. In one study, David Dinges and his colleagues (1992) showed participants forty drawings of common objects. Participants immediately tried to remember as many as they could. One week later, they attempted to recall the drawings, with half the participants under hypnosis and half not. The experimenters asked the participants to recall the whole list five times; they wanted to give an effect of hypnosis every opportunity to become manifest. They also examined participants who were very susceptible to hypnosis and participants who were not to see whether that factor made a difference. Hypnosis did nothing to improve the accuracy of memory. Many such experiments have been conducted (Lytle & Lundy, 1988; Register & Kihlstrom, 1987; for a review, see Mazzoni et al., 2014).

DIRECT BRAIN STIMULATION   As part of the preparation for brain surgery, Wilder Penfield (1959) directly stimulated patients' brains. A local anesthetic was administered in the scalp, and part of the skull was removed (see Figure 8.9). Penfield then used a stylus that generated a very mild electrical current to stimulate different places in the patient's brain. The patient was awake during this procedure but felt no pain. (The brain has no pain receptors.)

When Penfield (1959) stimulated some parts of the brain, a patient might say that a memory had been triggered. For example, one patient said, "Oh, a familiar memory – in an office somewhere. I could see the desks. I was there and someone was calling to me – a man leaning on a desk with a pencil in his hand" (p. 45). Another patient reported hearing her small son playing in the yard outside her kitchen window, as well as the typical neighborhood sounds. If these are indeed memories, the fact that they can be produced via direct stimulation of the brain certainly fits the idea that everything is recorded in the brain but often cannot be accessed. Perhaps the normal route to recalling memory has been bypassed – Penfield with his stylus reached in and physically jiggled loose a memory that otherwise would have been unrecoverable.

Such results sound compelling, but there are problems in interpreting them. First, these results occurred in only a small fraction (fewer than 10 percent) of Penfield's patients, even among those who were stimulated in the part of the brain in which memories are believed to be stored (the temporal lobe). Second, those who did report it often said that the experience was not especially like a memory. For example, the woman who heard her son playing in the yard was asked ten days later whether this experience was a memory. She said, "Oh, no. It seemed more real than that" (Penfield, 1959, p. 51). Thus, it's possible that Penfield's stimulation created pictures in the person's consciousness based on things in her memory but did not evoke an actual memory. In much the same way, dreams are constructed out of things that occurred to you, but they are not exact replays of events. It seems likely that the memories of Penfield's patients were **constructions**: experiences that feel like bona fide memories to the person experiencing them but are actually combinations of a real memory and other information, such as what the person believes probably happened.

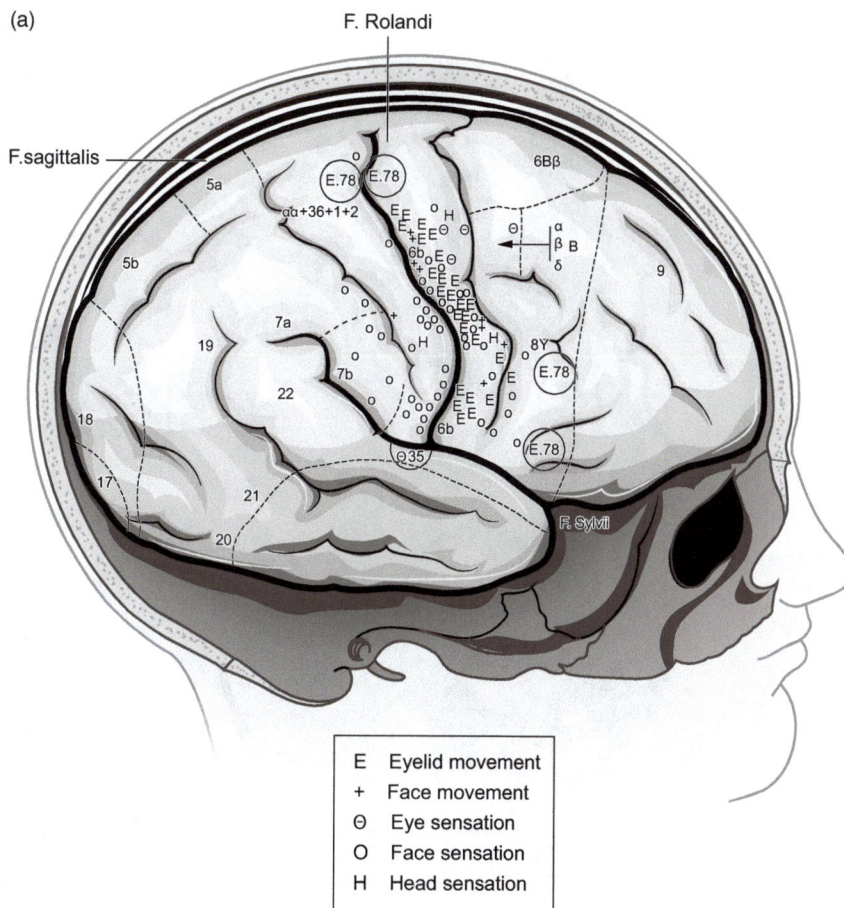

Figure 8.9. (a) A sketch of a brain from Penfield and Boldrey (1937) and (b) the exposed brain of one of Penfield's patients during an operation. The numbers help the surgeon keep track of where he has stimulated the brain. (Source: W. Penfield and E. Boldrey [1937], Somatic motor and sensory representation in the cerebral cortex of man as studied by electrical stimulation, *Annual Meeting of the American Neurological Association, Atlantic City, June 4, 1937*, figure 9, p. 407, and figure 21, p. 426.)

PERMASTORE   Is forgetting inevitable? We all have certain bits of information we know so well that it is difficult to believe we could ever forget them. In J. D. Salinger's book *The Catcher in the Rye*, Holden Caulfield helps a little girl adjust her skate and gets a rush of nostalgia from the feel of the skate key. He comments, "You could put a skate key in my hand in about fifty years in pitch black, and I'd still know what it is."

Some evidence shows that Holden was right. Enough practice makes memory immune to forgetting. Harry Bahrick did a series of studies on the permanence of memory (for a review, see Bahrick et al., 2013). Bahrick (1984) rounded up 733 people who had studied Spanish in high school between one and fifty years earlier and gave them vocabulary tests, comprehension tests, and so on (see Figure 8.10). Bahrick looked at how much Spanish the participants had retained, estimating how much they had initially learned by how many courses they had taken, their grades, and other information. He also measured how much practice these people had had with Spanish since they last took a Spanish class (whether they had visited a Spanish-speaking country, how often

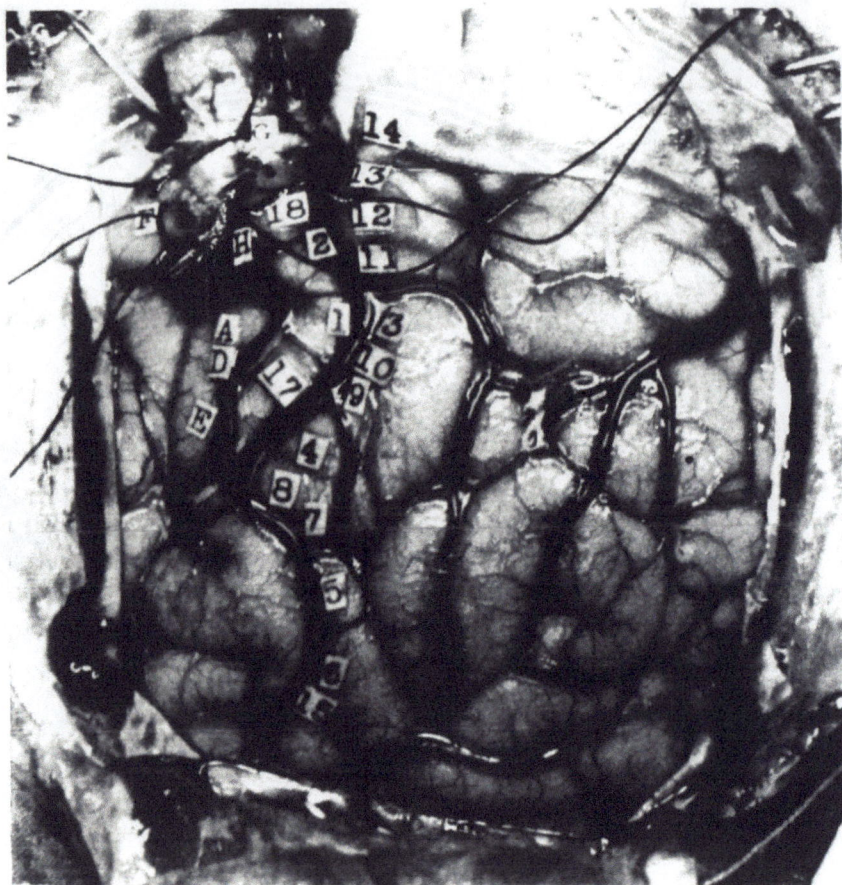

Figure 8.9. *(cont.)*

they estimated they were exposed to Spanish in the media, whether they had studied another Romance language, and so on).

As you can appreciate, this was a stupendously complex study to conduct, but it paid off with a very interesting result. First, as you would expect, *muchos estudiantes olvidan su Español* (many students forget their Spanish). The forgetting is rapid for the first three to six years, but then it more or less plateaus, and there is little additional forgetting until about thirty years have passed. Then, there is a second, more gradual drop-off until about fifty years (the last time point measured). This pattern, shown in Figure 8.11, was observed for almost all the measures of Spanish that Bahrick used.

There are two results to note here. First, for some of these participants, this knowledge of Spanish was retrievable fifty years after it was last encoded or rehearsed, even if it had not been practiced at all during the intervening time. For all practical purposes, we might say that this information was not going to be forgotten. Bahrick referred to such memories as being in **permastore**, a hypothetical state of memory from which information is not lost.

Knowledge of Spanish did not end up in permastore for everyone; what seemed to make the difference was extended practice. The longer participants had studied Spanish, the more Spanish they had in permastore. Studying Spanish for at least several years seemed to ensure that some of it would end up in permastore.

Vocabulary Recognition

1. romper

    a. to roam   b. to break   c. to look   d. to roar   e. to search

2. mandar

    a. to make   b. to mend   c. to yell   d. to command   e. to arrange

Grammar Recall: Write the correct form of the verb given in the blank provided.

1. El _____ (estudiar). He studies Spanish

2. Yo _____ la menor (ser).I am the youngest.

Idiom recall: Write the English meaning of the Spanish idiom.

1. hace mal tiempo _____

2. en vez de _____

Figure 8.10. Sample questions from Bahrick (1984). (Source: H. P. Bahrick [1984], Semantic memory content in permastore: Fifty years of memory for Spanish learned in school, *Journal of Experimental Psychology: General*, 113[1], 1–29.)

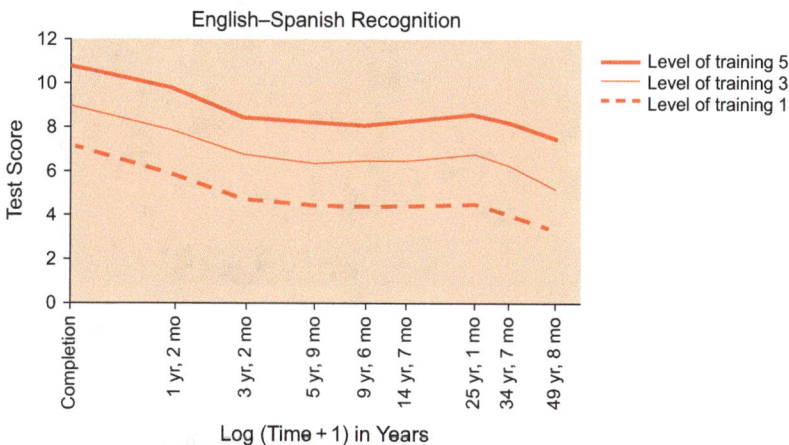

Figure 8.11. Effect of training level on the retention of recognition vocabulary. (Source: H. P. Bahrick [1984], Semantic memory content in permastore: Fifty years of memory for Spanish learned in school, *Journal of Experimental Psychology: General*, 113[1], 1–29.)

Whether permastore is really a form of memory, separate from other long-term memory, is not known. Bahrick argues that it is separate because most memories have a life-span of three to six years – after that, they are forgotten – and others have a life-span of fifty years or more, but no memories have a life-span of ten or twenty years. There is no forgetting between six and fifty years, which indicates a transition to a different state of memory. Other researchers, such as Ulric Neisser (1984), think that "permastore" is just a description of long-term memories that are so well represented that they will not be forgotten. There has been little work on permastore compared with other types of memory, probably because it is so difficult to conduct studies of the sort Bahrick has done. One recent study (Doolen & Radvansky, 2021) examined memory for novels typically read in American high schools, several years after the students had read them (see Figure 8.12). They did find that people remembered events from these novels long after having read them (and not rereading them in the interim), and since these were novels, not languages, they were able to test some specific hypotheses, for example, that students remembered certain important transitional

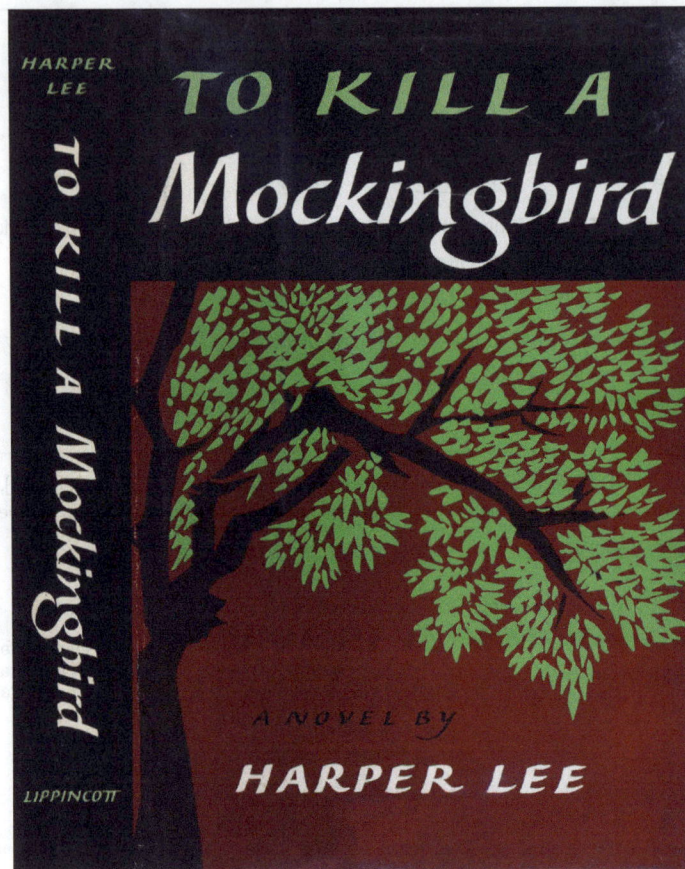

Figure 8.12. Old book covers for *To Kill a Mockingbird* and *Lord of the Flies*. We may remember books we read long ago in school.

events in the characters' lives more than other events, even though memory for these events still seemed to be forgotten at the same (slow) rate.

Retrieval is not simply a passive lookup process but an active process of reconstruction. Retrieval is particularly influenced by the cues given and by their match with the encoded memory. Forgetting occurs for a variety of reasons, which take place over time but do not merely decay with time. The success of sensitive memory tests on long-past memories has led to some speculation that memories are never forgotten and always possible to be retrieved if a person is given the correct cues. This view is nearly impossible to test, but it is likely that material that is learned with extended practice is extremely long lasting and resistant to processes of forgetting.

Stand-on-One-Foot Questions

8.8.   Describe in general terms the three ways that information may be forgotten.

8.9.   Can memory of traumatic events in childhood be repressed?

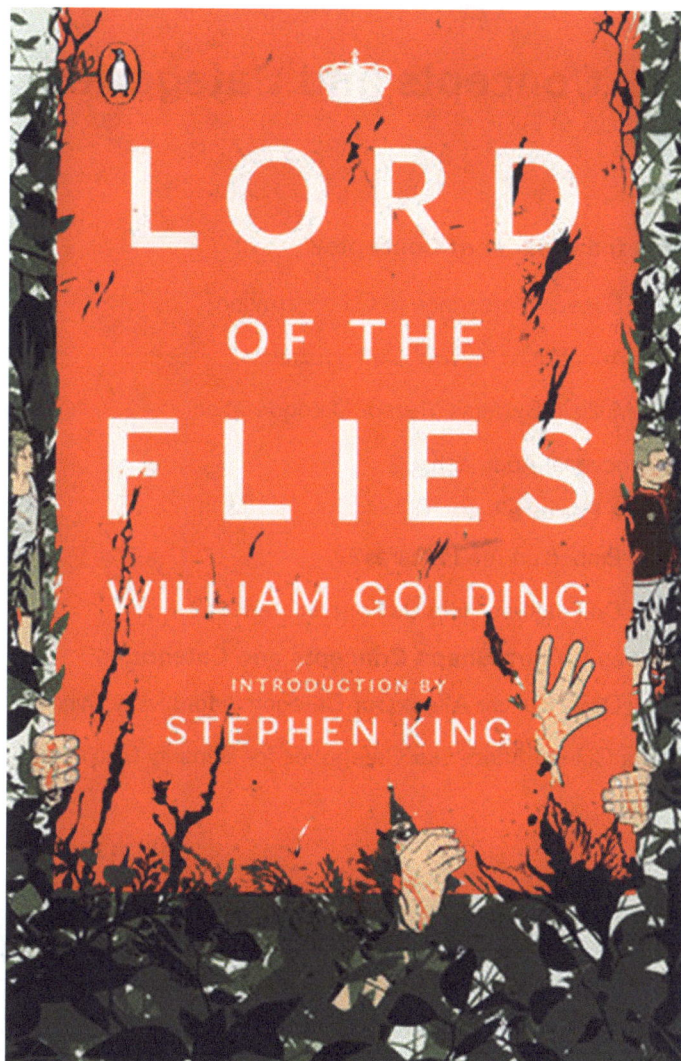

Figure 8.12. (*cont.*)

Questions That Require Two Feet

8.10.   Given what you know about forgetting, how would you advise someone to schedule their time studying in school?

8.11.   You probably have a pretty hazy memory of your twelve-year-old birthday party. Between occlusion, repression, and decay, which do you think is the most powerful mechanism for forgetting in this case? Why?

9 Concepts and Categories

In Chapter 6 we asked how explicit memory was organized (e.g., how does the concept for "bird" relate to the concept for "robin"), but we only briefly addressed the concepts themselves. This chapter focuses on how we represent categories in the real world by forming mental concepts. As we learn about the world, how do we decide which items belong in the same category? This chapter explores how we draw the lines that define categories and how we use mental representations to do other kinds of thinking.

In the past, psychologists have used the word *concept* to denote people's mental representation of objects and categories. A concept such as *cup* might include a set of rules for what makes a cup, or memory representations of many individual cups, or both of these. A category, in contrast, is the set of objects in the world to which the concept refers – real cups, not mental ones. **Categorization**, therefore, refers to applying conceptual knowledge to objects; classifying *that* object right there as a cup and not as a bowl, a pitcher, or a mockingbird.

The process of categorization is more complicated than you might guess. Suppose we show you a coffee cup and ask you to name it. You say, "It's a cup." We ask you how you know that, and you say (after giving us a fishy look), "Well, it has a handle, it's the right size, and you could put coffee in it, so it's a cup." We then show you a tea bowl from a Chinese restaurant and ask you to name that. Again, you say, "It's a cup." This cup has no handle and is much smaller, yet it's still a cup. Similarly, if we showed you a cup with a small hole in it (so it couldn't hold liquid), it would still be a cup. Many different-looking objects are identified as cups (see Figure 9.1).

(a)

(b)

(c)

(d)

(e)

Figure 9.1. Despite a wide variety of sizes, colors, handles, and fillings, all of these things are cups. (Source: (a) Julie Anne Images/Moment/Getty Images; (b) Lumina Images/Blend Images/Getty Images; (c) mikkelwilliam/E+/Getty Images altmodern/E+/Getty Images; (d) David Hofmann/Moment/Getty Images; (e) David Hofmann/Moment/Getty Images.)

What is the content of concepts? How do we define the concept "cup"? Is it a set of criteria (A: "must be a certain geometric shape that is a container"; B: "must hold liquid"; C: "must be graspable"; D: "must be made of an impermeable material")? Or perhaps some features (shape or permeability) are more important to cuppiness than others. Maybe some features are optional. Or perhaps the definition is more loosely defined and all that matters is the function the object serves. (See Figure 9.2.) If you're drinking from it, it's a cup, even if the thing could otherwise be categorized as a leaf. In the first section of this chapter, we will address how researchers have investigated the content of mental concepts.

In the second section, we discuss how the structure of our conceptual knowledge interacts with other cognitive processes. **What is a feature?** If concepts are defined in large part by their features, how are features represented in the mind? One key question is whether the representation of features is directly tied to the basic perceptual qualities by which we learned about that concept,

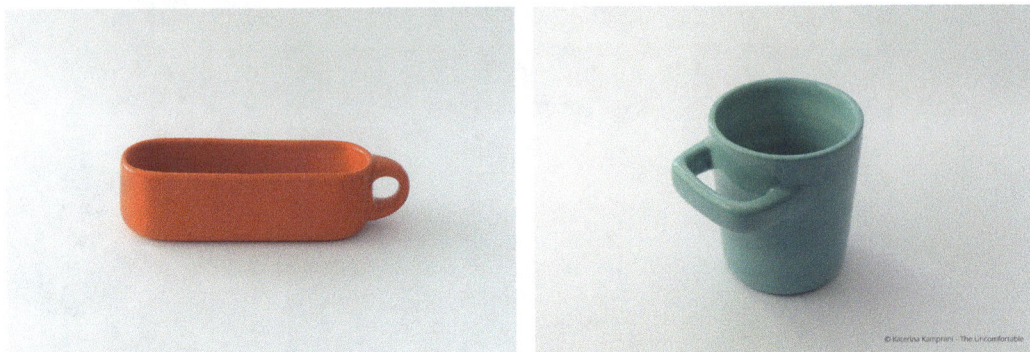

Figure 9.2. Artist Katerina Kamprani leads us to question our concept of cup with a challenging set of 3-D visualized virtual sculptures called *The Uncomfortable*. (Source: Photograph by Katerina Kamprani.)

or whether they can be more abstract. In other words, are conceptual representations embodied? Concepts often allow us to apply our knowledge to novel objects by making inferences based on features. If we know that foods in the category of "dessert" tend to have plenty of delicious sugar and fat, when we are told a new food is a dessert, we can apply that knowledge to guess that a dessert we've never encountered before will be full of delicious sugar and fat. Concepts also influence our decision-making processes, as we use our conceptual knowledge to make judgments about uncertain future events. When students debate enrolling in a psychology class versus a chemistry class, they might make inferences about what sort of content will be covered in each, based on their concept of each subject.

What Is the Content of Concepts?

Preview

Initially, researchers assumed that people assign objects to categories by using a list of properties that an object must have to be a member of the category. In other words, categories were structured through a set of rules of clear inclusion or exclusion. However, people think of some objects as more typical of a category than others; for example, an apple seems like a typical fruit, but a raisin does not. If categorization depended on a list of properties, we wouldn't observe such typicality effects. New models – prototype and exemplar models – were proposed to account for these data, based on the idea that people categorize objects not with rules but by judging their similarity to other objects of the same category. More recently, researchers have suggested that a single type of concept may not successfully account for all the data and have proposed models that use multiple types of categorization.

When you see an apple, how do you know it has seeds inside? You've never seen this particular apple before, but you know about the seeds because you generalize from other apples to this apple; in other words, you put this object in the category *apple*. You can identify the class or category to which an object belongs even if you've never seen that particular example of the object before. A **category** is a group of objects that have something in common (e.g., *fish* is a category). An **exemplar** is an instance of a category (your pet goldfish is an exemplar of the category *fish*).

How do we decide whether a given exemplar is a member of one category or another? We call this mental process *categorization*, and the approaches psychologists have taken to investigating this process can be divided into several categories (ooh meta!).

Rule-Based Approaches to Categorization

Philosophers were the first to speculate about the content of concepts and how we categorize. What we now call the **classical view of categorization** was first articulated by Aristotle, who claimed that knowledge was divided by logical boundaries. In other words, the philosophers who were the first to record the rules of logic also applied those rules to human knowledge. To Aristotle, a **concept** was a list of necessary and sufficient conditions for membership in a category. Every object must have all attributes on the list, and having those attributes is sufficient to be an exemplar of the category.

In one study consistent with the classical view, Jerome Bruner and his colleagues (1956) set out to show that participants learn categories by generating a hypothetical rule that might describe category membership and then testing the rule. The experimenters used cards with four features: number of figures on the card, shape of the figures, color of the figures, and number of borders around the edge of the card (see Figure 9.3). Perhaps the card had three black circles and two borders, and the participant had to select another card in the same category from among a number of other cards. The results showed that participants indeed generated hypotheses about what category structure might be and made card selections to test their hypotheses.

Without realizing they were doing so, the experimenters set up the experiment taking the perspective of the classical view of categories; they assumed that category membership is a list of necessary and sufficient conditions whereby one or two features of the cards determined category membership and everything else was irrelevant. In this view, concepts are learned as people use rules of logic to test hypotheses. This view struck them as consistent with what was known about the natural world. Plato had argued that real categories exist in the world and that the distinctions humans create – we call some things *birds*, other things *fish*, and so on – truly exist: When we categorize, we carve nature at its joints. The description of the periodic table in chemistry seemed scientific validation of Plato's conjecture. So, too, did the nicely nested categories of family, class, genera, and species in taxonomic systems of biological organisms.

But it's not hard to think of instances in which the classical view leads to predictions that don't seem right. For example, the concept *grandfather* is composed of two conditions: male and parent of a parent. Those two conditions are necessary to be identified as a grandfather – you must have both of them to be a grandfather – and they are sufficient, meaning it does not matter what sort of other characteristics you have or do not have – you're still a grandfather if you have those two. Yet different grandfathers *do* seem like better or worse examples of the category (see Figure 9.4). More formal work in the laboratory confirmed these informal observations. Some grandfathers strike us as more "grandfatherly" than others. The haziness seems obvious between categories based on human relationships and labels like "grandfather," but even biological taxonomists (those who categorize living things like plants and animals and fungi and algae and . . . ?) have encountered the limits of the classical view (Mishler, 2021).

TYPICALITY EFFECTS   Categories may or may not be neat boxes in the world, but concepts in our minds are definitely not. **Typicality** refers to the fact that people do not think of all exemplars as equally good members of a category. Membership in a category is not a simple in-or-out decision

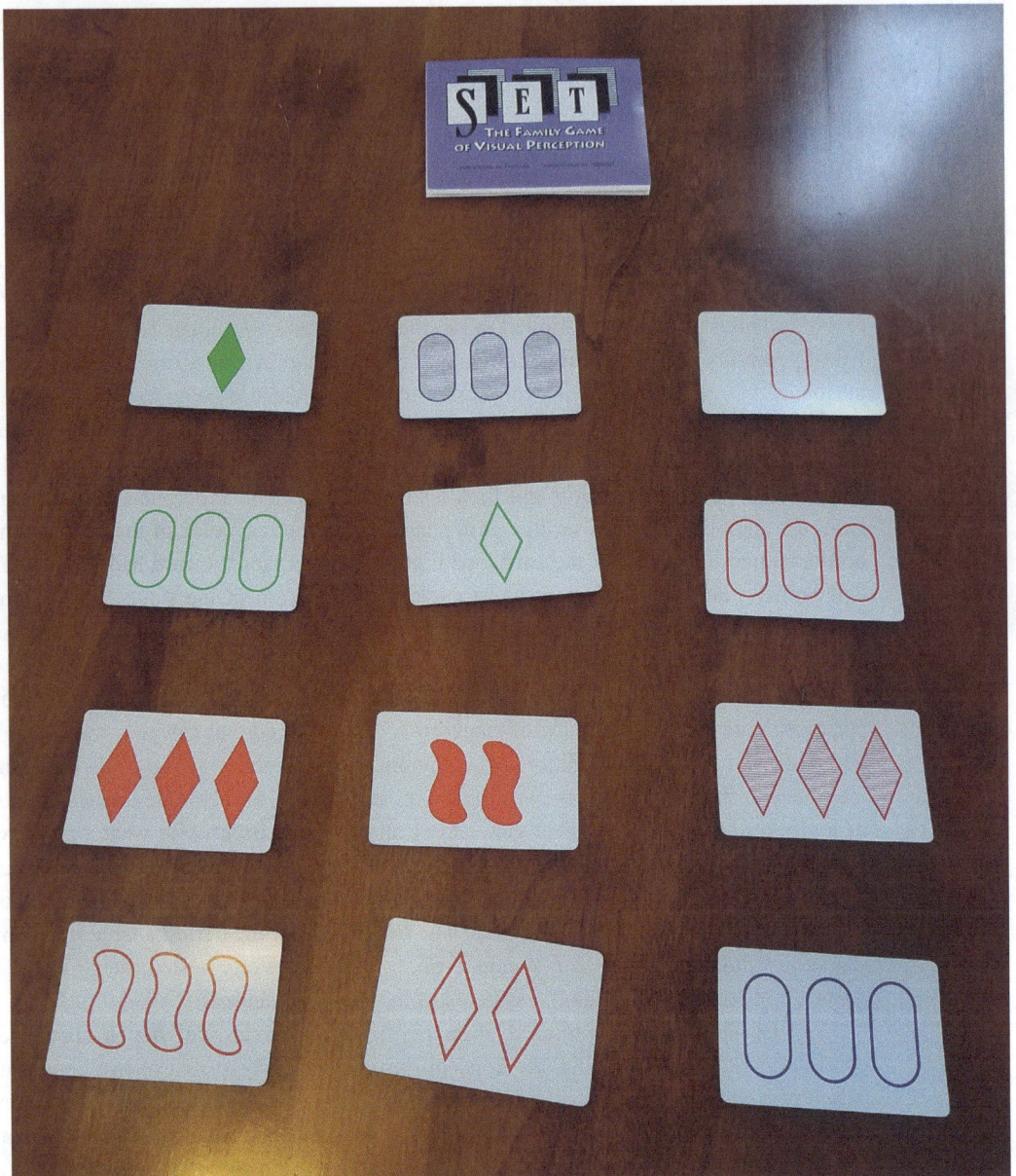

Figure 9.3. The card game SET asks players to make sets of three cards, in which each of the features (color, filling, number, and shape) either matches or mismatches. For example, for this round, the green and red 3 tablet cards in the second row and the purple 3 tablet card in the last row make a set. They have the same number of items (3), the same shape (tablet), and the same fill (empty) but are all different colors. This game is similar to the experiment by Bruner et al. (1956).

but includes degrees of belongingness. For example, not all birds are equally "birdy." Some birds are really good examples of a bird (that robin, well, that's a real bird's bird), whereas others are pretty crummy birds (sure penguin, you're cute, but what are you doing with those flippers). In the following list, how would you rate each bird from 1 (terrific example of a bird) to 7 (not a good example of a bird)?

Figure 9.4. According to the classical view, the top and bottom grandfathers are equally good representatives of the category "grandfather." But motorcycle grandfather does not seem to be as good a fit for what we think of as a grandfather, whereas putting together a puzzle seems a much more grandfatherly thing to do.

(Source: (a) GS Visuals/Cultura/Getty Images; (b) KidStock/Blend Images/Getty Images.)

Table 9.1 Some results of Rosch's (1975) typicality ratings

Category	Member	Rating
Fruit	Apple	1.08
	Plum	1.37
	Cantaloupe	2.44
	Fig	2.86
	Olive	6.2
Sport	Football	1.03
	Hockey	1.44
	Wrestling	1.87
	Weight lifting	3.59
	Chess	5.07
Bird	Robin	1.02
	Eagle	1.75
	Chicken	4.02
	Ostrich	4.12
	Bat	6.15
Vehicle	Car	1.24
	Boat	2.75
	Scooter	3.24
	Horse	4.63
	Skis	5.40

Source: E. H. Rosch (1975), Cognitive representations of semantic categories, *Journal of Experimental Psychology: General*, 104(3), 192–233.

> wren
> chicken
> robin
> ostrich
> eagle

This might seem like common sense, but as with much of cognitive psychology, the key is in finding a way to carefully control and measure common sense (and see how it got so common!). Eleanor Rosch (1975) did just that.

Rosch (1975) gave participants lists, such as shown in Table 9.1, and asked them to rate how typical each was as a member of their category. The first noteworthy thing about the results is that the task didn't strike people as stupid. Participants could have said "What are you talking about, 'birdy birds, nonbirdy birds'? They're all birds. Except the bat." The fact is, when Rosch said "birdy birds," "fruity fruits," or "furniturey furniture," people knew what she was talking about. Not only do people think some birds are birdier than others but they also agree on which ones are the birdy ones, as shown in Table 9.1. To review, this result casts doubt on the rule-based view of categorization. If an object could be categorized on the basis of a list of necessary and sufficient conditions, there would be no gradations of membership in the concept.

Ed Smith and colleagues (1974) showed that the typicality of exemplars has cognitive consequences. For one thing, people are more efficient in categorizing typical exemplars than

Table 9.2 Probabilities with which items were listed as category exemplars

Fruit		Beverage	
Response	**Total (first)**	**Response**	**Total (first)**
Apple	0.95 (0.58)	Water	0.80 (0.11)
Orange	0.86 (00.14)	Coke	0.48 (0.25)
Banana	0.71 (0.07)	Milk	0.46 (0.05)
Grape	0.52 (0.02)	Juice	0.43 (0.07)
Pear	0.50 (0.03)	Soda	0.42 (0.18)
Peach	0.40 (0.04)	Orange juice	0.33 (0.04)
Strawberry	0.40 (0.04)	Sprite	0.31 (0.03)
Kiwi	0.30	Pepsi	0.29 (0.05)
Pineapple	0.26 (0.01)	Tea	0.29 (0.02)
Watermelon	0.24 (0.01)	Coffee	0.24 (0.01)
Tomato	0.21 (0.03)	Lemonade	0.23 (0.02)
Plum	0.21	Apple juice	0.20 (0.02)
Grapefruit	0.18	Dr. Pepper	0.13 (0.01)
Mango	0.18 (0.01)	Gatorade	0.11
Cherry	0.15 (0.01)	Kool-Aid	0.11 (0.01)
Lemon	0.15	Mountain Dew	0.09
Blueberry	0.14	Grape juice	0.07
Cantaloupe	0.14	Ice tea	0.10
Raspberry	0.12	Pop	0.07 (0.03)

Source: J. P. Van Overschelde, K. A. Rawson, and J. Dunlosky (2004), Category norms: An updated and expanded version of the Battig and Montague (1969) norms, *Journal of Memory and Language*, 50, 289–335.

atypical. In their experiment, participants saw a word on a computer screen and had to decide as quickly as possible (yes or no) whether the word was an example of a category. Some were typical instances (*robin*), some were of medium typicality (*cardinal*), and some were of low typicality (*goose*). Response times were faster for more typical exemplars.

This effect of typicality on categorization is also observed when participants are asked to freely generate examples of a category; the most frequently generated exemplars are the ones that are rated as most typical of the category (Battig & Montague, 1969; Van Overschelde et al., 2004). This finding holds true not only for adults but also for children as young as five (Nelson, 1974; Rosner & Hayes, 1977). Some examples appear in Table 9.2.

Typicality also influences how we reason. Lance Rips (1975) asked people to reason using either typical or atypical examples of a category as a reference point (see also Heit, 2000; Murphy & Ross, 2005). For example, they were told that one species had a contagious disease and then were asked to estimate the probability that other animals had the disease. The results showed that if a more typical bird (the robin or sparrow) had the disease, it was judged that other birds probably had the disease. If an atypical species, such as the ostrich, was described as having the disease, it was judged less likely that other species did. Participants know that typical instances of a category share many properties with other members of the category. When confronted with a new feature (the disease) whose distribution is not known, participants assume that it is distributed in the same way as other features. (People with a lot of knowledge about the category – a bird expert, in this example – use other strategies that make use of their deeper knowledge [López et al., 1997; Proffitt et al., 2000; Osta-Vélez & Gärdenfors, 2020].)

The Probabilistic View of Categorization

Typicality effects called for a different theory of categorization; a purely rule-based understanding doesn't account for how our minds organize concepts. In the **probabilistic view of categorization**, category membership is proposed to be a matter of probability, rather than binary (i.e., yes/no). A central assumption is that there is no feature or group of features that is essential for category membership. Rather, each member of the category will have some but probably not all features characteristic of a category. For example, a given bird might have the features "sings" and "eats insects" but not the feature "lives in trees." There are two versions of the probabilistic view: prototype theories and exemplar theories.

PROTYPES   A crucial experiment in developing the **prototype** view was conducted by Mike Posner and Steve Keele (1968). Rather than using categories that their participants already knew, such as birds or furniture, they created three categories from scratch. The categories were patterns of dots; each feature was a dot located in a particular position. Posner and Keele created the categories by taking random dot patterns and calling them "A," "B," and "C" (see Figure 9.5).

Those patterns were defined as the prototypes that had all the features characteristic of those categories. To create an exemplar of category A, the experimenters took the prototype for dot pattern A and moved each dot a bit in a random direction. To create another exemplar, they started with the same prototype and again moved the dots randomly to get a different pattern. They created four exemplars of each category, mixed them randomly, and then asked participants to categorize them. Participants just guessed initially, but they got feedback as they went regarding whether their categorization judgments were right or wrong, so after a while, they learned to categorize correctly. They had to keep studying the list until they could categorize all twelve items correctly two times in a row. During this training, participants never saw any of the category prototypes.

The interesting phase of the experiment came next. Participants were given a categorization test that included four types of stimuli: *old exemplars*, which they had seen in the first phase of the experiment; *new exemplars*, which fit one of the categories but were not seen in the previous phase of the experiment; *prototypes* from which the exemplars had been generated; and *novel* stimuli, which didn't fit any of the categories. Participants were asked to classify each stimulus into the three categories, so chance performance would be 33 percent. Participants got 86.0 percent of the old exemplars correct and 67.4 percent of the new exemplars correct; they remembered the items they had seen before quite well and could also recognize new members of the category. Most interesting, they got 85.1 percent correct on the prototypes. Participants categorized the prototype, which they had never seen before, as accurately as the training items.

Most researchers interpreted these data as showing that the memory representation supporting categorization is an amalgamation of the category exemplars. As you see many exemplars of category A, you track all of the features and choose which features are critical. The resulting concept of category A is an average of all of the observed exemplars of category A. Thus, during the training session, where you are given feedback about which stimuli are As, Bs, and Cs, what you end up

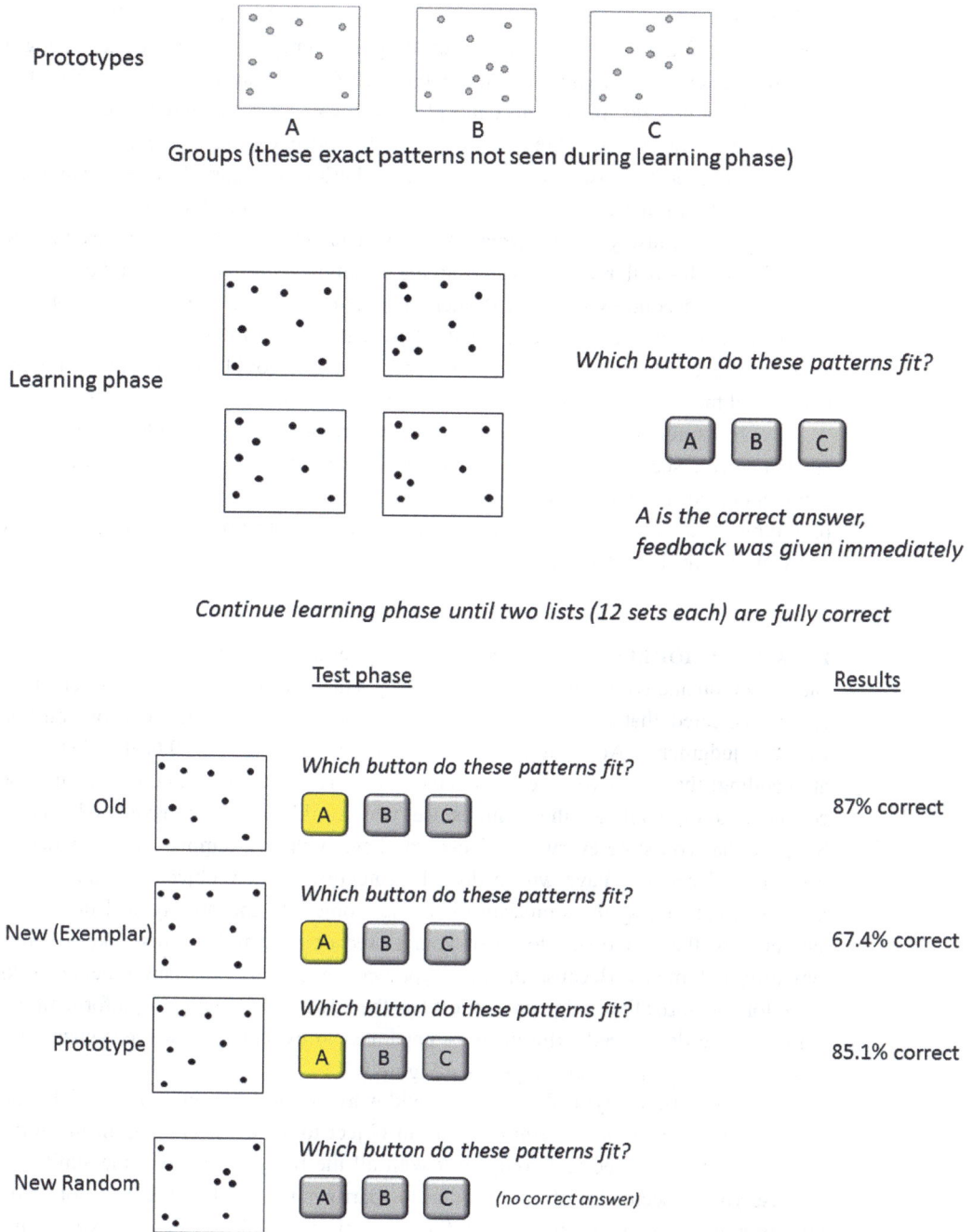

Figure 9.5. Figures describing the method of Posner and Keele (1968). (Source: M. I. Posner and S. W. Keele [1968], On the genesis of abstract ideas, *Journal of Experimental Psychology*, 77[3, Pt. 1], 353–363.)

storing is not a list but an abstract prototype of A (and, of course, separate representations for the prototypes of B and C). It's like you're creating an average exemplar A and storing that, updating your average every time you see a new exemplar of A. The average is, of course, the prototype.

Now, how do you use this concept to make categorization judgments of new objects? When you see a new object, you judge its similarity to the concept for A, the concept for B, and the concept for C. Whichever it's most similar to, you figure that's its category. If the new stimulus is one of the prototypes, it will match what is in your memory very well indeed, even if you have never seen it as an exemplar; because you have been taking the average of all the different exemplars, which were derived through small, random changes to the prototypes, the averages and the prototypes should be identical. In a second experiment, Posner and Keele (1970) showed that the prototype is still very well recognized after a one-week delay. These data seem to demonstrate that people average the features of exemplars and store the prototype. How else could we account for Posner and Keele's results and their participants' recognition of prototypes that they had never seen?

But surely people cannot store *only* the prototype. For example, you can categorize a new cat when you see it, but you also recognize specific cats, such as the orange one who has commandeered a corner of your yard for his restroom. Have you stored a representation of the prototypical cat, and alongside, representations of all the cats you can identify as individuals? And if you can identify lots of individual cats, do you really need the prototype?

EXEMPLAR MODELS   Doug Medin and Marguerite Schaffer (1978) showed that we can explain categorization and typicality effects with concepts that are not prototypes. Posner and Keele's (1970) results indicated that abstraction takes place; you use an abstract idea of "birdiness" to make category judgments. According to the prototype model in Figure 9.6, the abstraction takes place at encoding; that is, as you see exemplars, you store the critical features that are important to the concept and forget all the other features. But why would abstraction have to take place at encoding? Suppose that you store every experience you have with an exemplar of a category – for example, every experience you have with a dog. To categorize a new object, you still use similarity, but instead of calculating the similarity of the new object to the prototypical dog, you calculate the similarity of the new object to all of your stored dog exemplars, then take the average of those similarity judgments. Because the prototype was an average, this new scheme works out just the same for categorization judgments, but it has the advantage of retaining information about individual dogs. We don't need extra memory apparatus to explain how we recognize our own dogs, in addition to categorizing new dogs. (See Figure 9.7.)

Furthermore, typicality effects would work out perfectly in such a model. You would judge typicality by comparing the similarity of an object to all the exemplars in memory. If you see a sparrow sitting in a tree and compare it with all the birds in memory, the similarity is very high because you've seen a lot of birds similar to sparrows in your lifetime; therefore, you would think this sparrow is a very "birdy" bird. A flightless, six-foot-tall ostrich is not very similar to birds in memory, so you wouldn't think it was such a good example of a bird.

So the exemplar and prototype models are very different in terms of what they propose is stored in memory. The **exemplar model** holds that multiple exemplars of a category are stored in memory, and the prototype model holds that only the prototype is stored.

So far, we've talked about shapes, birds, cats, and dogs, as researchers have tried to use universal (and sometimes quite abstract) and uncontroversial exemplars, concepts, and categories. But it shouldn't be too hard to see how these mental processes can have important social and

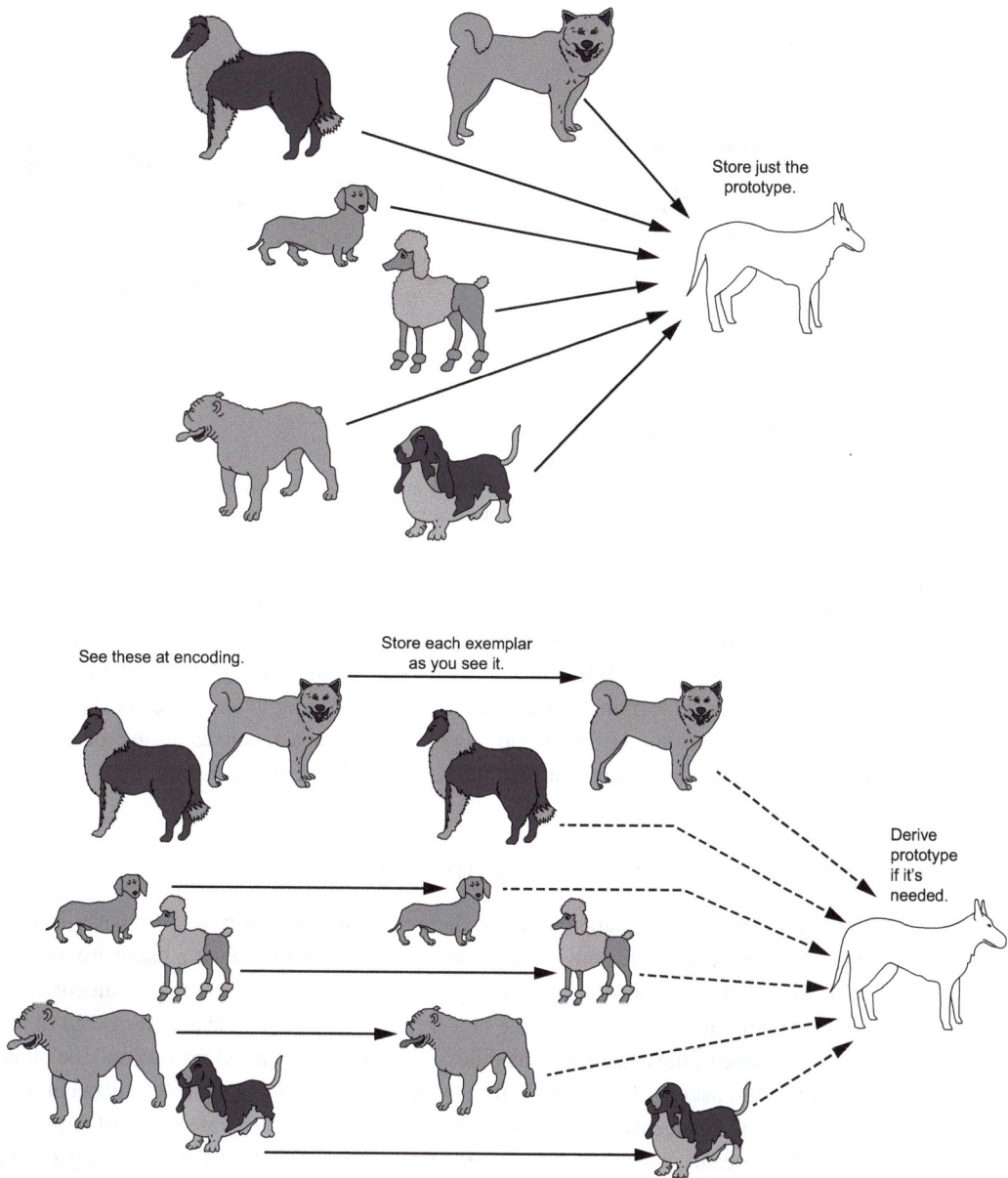

Figure 9.6. When forming concepts using the prototype model, although many exemplars are seen, only the prototype is stored. The prototype is updated continually to incorporate more experience with new exemplars. When using the exemplar model, each exemplar is stored.

political consequences. For example, think of whether your representation of the concept "Movie Action Hero" is either a prototype (one prototypical representation) or a set of exemplars. If you built up that concept with a steady diet of American action movies from the past forty or fifty years, that concept certainly has rippling muscles, dazzling athleticism in fight scenes, and a steely gaze, but it is also much more likely to be a white man than someone like Michelle Yeoh. Whether we are using a prototype or an exemplar model, our judgments are shaped by the exemplars that we experience, and our mental processes of categorization have consequences about our social

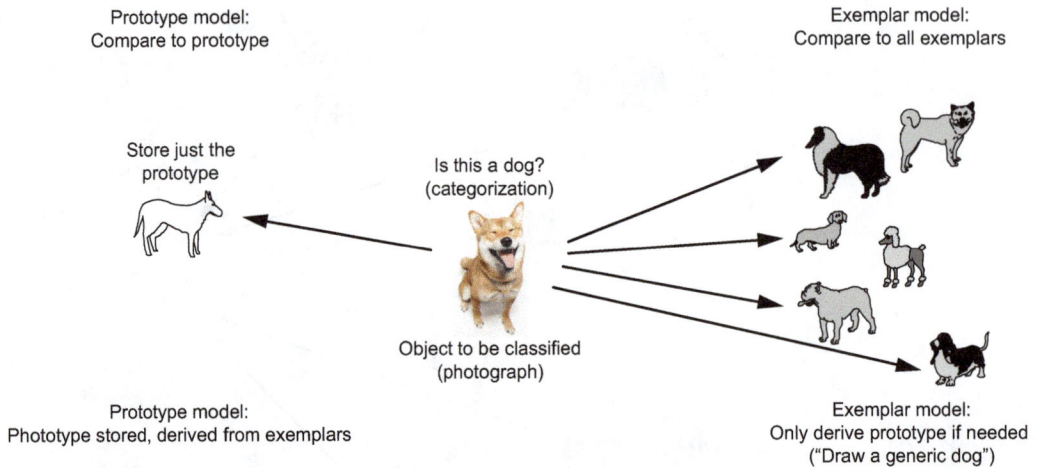

Figure 9.7. When completing a categorization task with the prototype model, the object to be classified is compared to a prototype. When using an exemplar model, the object to be classified is compared to all exemplars. (Source: alynst/E +/Getty Images.)

judgments about our fellow humans. In other words, the cognitive process of simplifying the world through categorization leads to stereotyping and prejudice when we apply that process to fellow human beings. Armed with this knowledge of how cognition works, we can be more aware of when that happens and be vigilant against such prejudices leading to us acting in a discriminatory manner. We can also seek to design group decision processes (such as hiring or renting) that either counteract prejudices or prevent prejudices from influencing decisions.

The Multiple Systems View of Categorization

In the late 1980s, new results indicated that researchers might have been hasty in throwing out the rule-based approaches. In some cases, it looked like humans *did* use a list of criteria to categorize. In a seminal study on this topic, Lance Rips (1989) had participants make categorization judgments with very little information about the object (just one feature). He also restricted the choices to two categories; one of the categories was inflexible as to the described feature, and the other was not. For example, Rips asked, "The object is thee inches in diameter. Is the object a pizza or a quarter?" Most participants (63 percent) said it was a pizza, even though a separate group of participants had more often (70 percent) judged that a quarter was more similar to a three-inch object than is a pizza. If similarity is the main determinant of categorization, then you shouldn't see this difference – if the object is more similar to a quarter, than it should be judged more likely to belong to the category "quarter." Rips argued that people are sensitive to necessary, inflexible features. A quarter must be a particular size; this feature cannot change, so it's like a rule. Just because typicality effects exist and similarity affects how we think about categories, that doesn't mean we should throw out the rule-based approach entirely. Rules may not describe all concepts, but they may describe some.

Scott Allen and Lee Brooks (1991) believed that people might be able to use *either* rules *or* similarity. In their experiment, participants saw new creatures and were asked to categorize them as "diggers" or "builders" (see Figure 9.8). During training, some participants were encouraged to learn the categories by memorizing exemplars and their category. Others were given a rule by which to categorize – builders have two of the following three characteristics: long legs, an angular body,

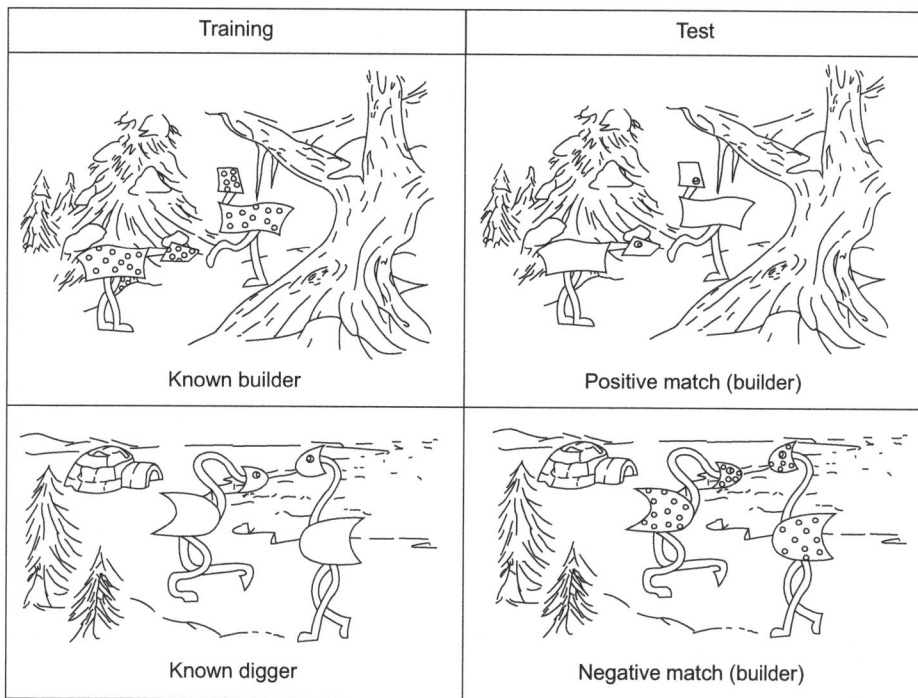

Figure 9.8. "Diggers" and "builders" from Allen and Brooks (1991). Rule: At least two of long legs, angular body, spots → Builder. "Negative match" means that the rule yields one category, but the new exemplar looks very similar to an exemplar from training that was in the other category. "Positive match" means that the rule and the similarity to training exemplars yield the same answer. (Source: S. W. Allen and L. Brooks [1991], Specializing the operation of an explicit rule, *Journal of Experimental Psychology: General*, 120, 4.)

and spots. All other creatures are diggers. After the training phase came a test phase in which participants saw new exemplars. Some were builders, but they looked very much like diggers that participants had seen during training (in Figure 9.8, this is called a "negative match"). Participants in the memory group called them diggers 86 percent of the time, indicating that they were comparing the new items with remembered items from training. But those in the rule group called them diggers just 45 percent of the time, indicating that they were most often relying on the rule.

Little and McDaniel (2015) found that this split between rule-based or similarity-based categorization appears spontaneously even when participants are given a task that doesn't nudge them in either direction. They presented the twelve shapes in Figure 9.9 one at a time, and participants had to guess which category it belonged to (a "blicket" or a "dax") and then received feedback ("This is a blicket"). There were six blocks of this training, so participants saw and categorized each shape six times. Then they were tested with four old shapes and eight new shapes, which were constructed to assess their mental models of the two categories. The key test shape was ambiguous in that if a participant had memorized the shapes as exemplars and used perceptual similarity, they would categorize one way, and if they had discovered the rule and applied it, they would categorize the other way (see Figure 9.10). Little and McDaniel found that some people adopted a memorization strategy (learning all exemplars) and some learned the rule.

A new wave of models proposed that the question of how mental categorization works is itself too broad. (It needs categories!) As such, most recent models involve a combination of prototype, exemplar, and rule-based elements. Researchers have developed computer models that

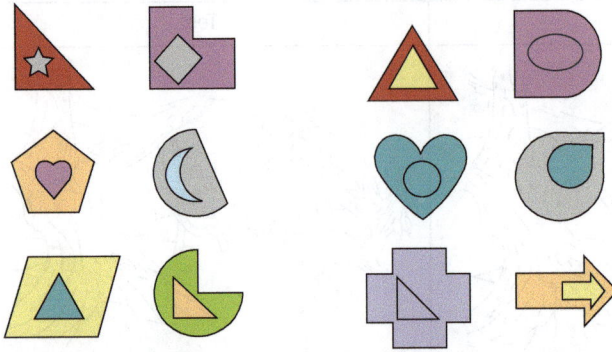

Figure 9.9. The six stimuli on the left, representing one category, are constructed of two shapes that differ in both form and color. The six stimuli on the right, representing the other category, are constructed of two shapes that match in either form or color. (Source: J. L. Little and M. A. McDaniel [2015], Individual differences in category learning: Memorization versus rule abstraction, *Memory and Cognition*, 43(2), 286.)

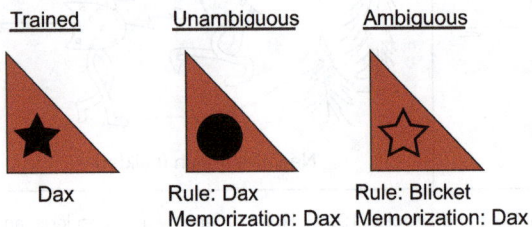

Figure 9.10. Participants all studied the same set of exemplars, but when given a new item to categorize, their response depended on whether they used a rule-based categorization system or a memorization-based system. If they classified the rightmost shape as a blicket, that meant they had internalized a rule. If they classified it as a dax, that meant they had used memorization. (Source: J. L. Little and M. A. McDaniel [2015], Individual differences in category learning: Memorization versus rule abstraction, *Memory and Cognition*, 43(2), 286.)

use multiple systems of categorization in an attempt to mimic human performance. For example, Rob Nosofsky's RULEX model (Nosofsky & Palmeri, 1998; Nosofsky et al., 1994) proposes that people initially try to use a simple categorization rule and, if that doesn't seem to work, that they try a more complex rule. If they are still making errors, they supplement the rules by memorizing a few of the exemplars that don't fit that rule. Thus, the RULEX model uses both rules and exemplars. (For another model using rules and exemplars, see Erickson and Kruschke [1998].)

Perhaps the best developed of these theories is that of Greg Ashby and his colleagues (Ashby et al., 2007; Ashby et al., 1998; Ashby & Maddox, 2005; Ashby & O'Brien, 2005), who, in addition to developing a mathematical model of category learning, also tie concept learning to the brain (Wang & Ashby, 2020). Ashby argues that there are four different systems in the brain that are responsible for learning different types of categories. These systems include one that is rule based; another that is probabilistic based on prototypes; another based on memorizing exemplars; and still another that uses an unconscious combination of features, integrating this information without any awareness of an explicit rule.

Ashby's theory gains support from neuropsychological data. For example, when categories can be described by a simple rule (as in Bruner's experiment with the cards), the theory predicts that categorization is more like a problem-solving task and therefore depends on working memory, as you must juggle hypothetical rules, exemplars you've seen, and compare the two. As predicted, patients with working memory deficits are impaired on learning categories described by a simple rule (e.g., Brown & Marsden, 1988).

A Functional Approach

The multiple systems view brings up an important question: What determines which categorization mechanism is applied in a given situation? Investigating these questions about the structure of knowledge reminds us that the tensions between structuralism and functionalism (William Wundt vs. William James) discussed in Chapter 1 still apply to modern research. We've been considering concepts from a very structural point of view – which structure for concepts seems to fit the categories we find in the world? But maybe concepts are more functional – we decide which type of categorical organization suits the situation. Rather than ask "What is the true structure of knowledge?" we might ask "What function will this category serve?"

Recent research shows the utility of this functional perspective. A **relational category** is defined not by features of items but by the relations among them (Gentner & Kurtz, 2005; Goldwater et al., 2011; Markman & Stilwell, 2001; Patterson & Kurtz, 2020). Take, for example, a "visit." We could certainly think of "visit" as a real category out there in the world, and we could think some visits as better examples of the category than others. Yet a visit is not defined by the feature of objects. It's defined by relationships. A visit includes, at the least, a guest and a host. "Guest" could include Uncle Jack (at a recent wedding), the crown prince of Saudi Arabia (at a formal White House dinner), or a pesky raccoon (in the attic). This **role-governed category** is defined not by features (of which our guests share very few) but by the role that these beings serve in a particular event. What unites the raccoon and the crown prince in the category "guest" is nothing about them but rather their location relative to their home.

Goldwater et al. (2011; see Figure 9.11) found evidence for the distinction between role-governed and feature-based categories by asking people to list properties of typical and ideal instances of each type of category. For example, when asked to describe typical and ideal examples of *cell phones* or *trucks*, people were likely to use more intrinsic features (like the existence of a screen or a flatbed), whereas when asked to do the same for *predator* or *home*, they were more likely to use extrinsic properties; for example, subjects thought an important feature of a *home* is that it be comfortable, but the definition of comfort lay in the perception of the occupant of the home, not in the home itself. Role-governed categories also differ in that they are more likely to be described with ideal characteristics than with typical characteristics. For example, a characteristic of the category *home* might be more likely to be clean and orderly, even though a typical home may not be.

It is not clear where role-governed categories fit in with the multiple systems view (Are they rule based? Are their neural representations more similar to prototype than exemplar?), but future work will likely continue to explore the similarities and differences between this type of category and other, more feature-based categories.

Stand-on-One-Foot Questions

9.1. Think of an exemplar of the category "college." How typical do you think that exemplar is?

9.2. Sometimes people set up the apps on their phones in groups, so that "money" might have their banking, credit card, and money transfer apps, whereas "social" might have their social media apps. What kind of categorization system (classical or probabilistic) does this system resemble?

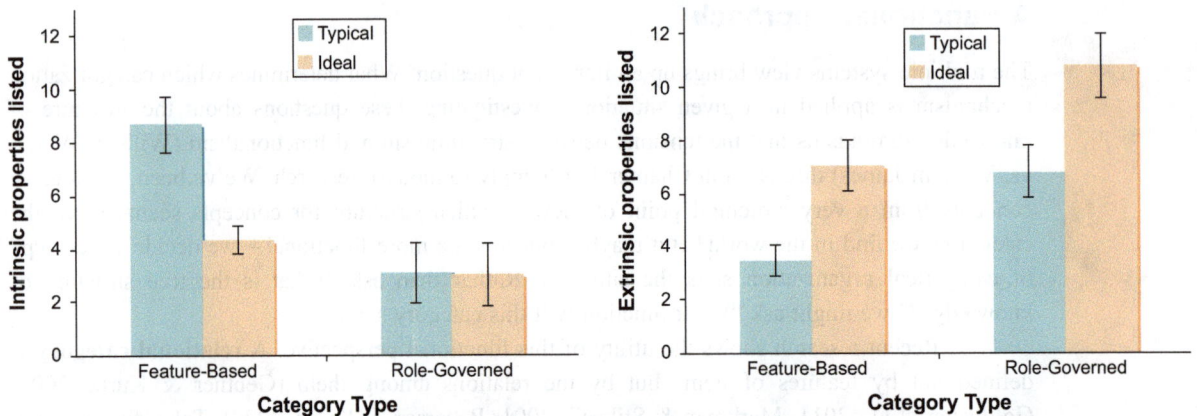

Figure 9.11. Results from Goldwater et al. (2011), showing that feature-based categories (like trucks) were more likely to be described with intrinsic properties (like "has a flatbed"), whereas when describing role-governed categories (like home), they were more likely to use extrinsic properties (like comfortable, which depends on the occupant).

(Source: M. B. Goldwater, A. B. Markman, and C. H. Stilwell [2011], The empirical case for role-governed categories, *Cognition*, 118[3], 359–376.)

Question That Requires Two Feet

9.3.   Adjusting to college is in part a question of choosing an identity and a group to belong to. Explain how a probabilistic view of categorization might approach how people sort themselves as members of categories and how those categories define them. Are you a typical member of the groups you belong to? How does the concept of typicality apply to people in groups more generally?

What Is a Feature?

Preview

When discussing the content of categories, we have talked a lot about features, but we haven't really defined what a feature is. The first question we will address is whether features are abstract, higher-order mental representations or whether they are concrete and tied to basic sensory and motor experiences. In other words, is categorical thinking embodied in our basic senses and the way we move? The second topic we will take up is how features influence other mental processes through inferences.

In our discussion thus far, we've happily used the term *feature* without really considering what it is. We can't get away with that any longer. When we say "sings" is a feature of birds, what is the mental representation of "sings"? Furthermore, once we have these collections of features, they do not just sit as mental representations in our heads; we use them to reason about the world. For example, when we have a novel situation, or a novel object, we make guesses about that object or event based on our prior knowledge. The structure of our prior knowledge that informs these guesses is often dependent on which features we see as relevant to the novel situation. We call these guesses inferences, and we will discuss how features inform inferences in this section.

How Embodied Are Features?

Let's consider more closely the idea of a feature. We've said that a feature of *grandfather* might be "elderly" or that a feature of *fire truck* might be "red." We've appealed to your intuition in this case, as much as saying "you know what *elderly* or *red* means. That's what we're talking about here." But that won't do. Researchers have probed more deeply into the nature of features, especially focusing on how much of the content of concepts comes directly from perception and how much is more abstract and, well, conceptual.

Another way of asking this question is, How much of the process of categorization overlaps with perceptual processes? For example, maybe our concept of *fire truck* includes the feature "redness," but the way redness is represented in the mind is not abstract – it's identical to what happens when we perceive the color red. Or perhaps our representation of *spear* includes the feature "throwable," and that is represented by the actual way one's mind would direct an arm to throw something. When there is a great deal of overlap in categorization and the perceptual or motor processes, researchers call the representation **embodied** (Dove, 2022).

For example, the concept of *fruit* could be defined as the seed-bearing structure that develops from the ovary of a flowering plant. This is not only a rule-based definition of a fruit but one that depends on features with abstract scientific definitions (seeds, ovaries, flowers). But while that may define the boundaries of the botanical category of *fruit*, what about our mental concept of *fruit*? Avocados, tomatoes, and pumpkins satisfy that definition, but we might be disappointed if offered a fruit salad and it came as mixed up bits of bananas, pumpkin, avocado, and tomato. It might seem that our concept of fruit is much more dependent on the basic sensory quality of sweetness than on the botanical characteristics of the plant. But is it really the *basic sensory* quality of sweetness, or is it some more abstract representation of sweetness? In other words, we have a mental representation that's active when we actually taste something sweet. Is *that* the mental representation that serves as the feature "sweet" in the concept "fruit"? If so, we say the feature is embodied, meaning it is based on a basic sensory or motor representation. The alternative is that the feature is some more abstract *idea* of sweetness.

How could we test whether a feature is embodied? One way is to test for switching costs between perceptual modalities. A modality is a mode of perception – seeing, hearing, or smelling, for example. Staying within a modality – for example, making a visual judgment having just made a visual judgment – is faster than switching modalities, such as making a visual judgment if you've just made an auditory judgment (Spence et al., 2001). So if conceptual judgment has nothing to do with perception, then we wouldn't expect to see a speed difference if you make conceptual judgments based on sight after making a conceptual judgment based on sound. But, if switching modalities in conceptual judgment shows the same pattern of a switch cost that we see in perception, then that is evidence of overlap between categorization and perception.

In one experiment, participants first responded to the location of a perceptual stimulus (either a light, a sound, or a tactile stimulation on their finger). Then, they had to verify whether an object had a perceptual property, for example, "a banana is yellow," "a siren wails," or "a faucet is

Figure 9.12. Pictures of frogs. When we tell children "Look at the frog," we don't say, "This is a frog because it is green, eats flies, and is slimy," because we might have to elaborate that frogs aren't always green or slimy, and sometimes you ride them on a carousel and sometimes they are fuzzy and stuffed with cotton. (Source: (a, b) kuritafsheen/RooM/Getty Images; word Fuse/Corbis/Getty Images; (d) Glow Images/Getty Images.)

hot." Switching modalities incurred a switch cost, even when it was from perceptual judgment to conceptual judgment (Van Dantzig et al., 2008).

Neuroscientific data also support the idea that categorization processes overlap with perceptual ones, that is, the concepts are at least somewhat embodied. The part of the brain supporting the conceptual representations of tools (what a hammer is) overlaps with the part of the brain supporting the representation of the use of tools (what to do with the hammer); both are in the parietal lobe. In other words, how the brain represents the concept *hammer* (perhaps containing features such as long, smooth handle and hard, metal, rectangular head) seems to overlap with how the brain represents other features of *hammer* grounded in the senses, such as how you hold a hammer or the motor plan to swing a hammer when driving a nail. The brain networks that are responsible for sensory–motor control overlap with those that would be used to categorize (Hickok, 2014; Kemmerer, 2022).

Embodiment suggests that concepts and categories are based on a foundation of perception. That, in turn, might mean that we are biased to form categories based on perceptual appearance. We might be able to observe such a bias by investigating how children first form categories as they are learning. Do children rely on perception to form categories? (See Figure 9.12.)

Initial research indicated that young children do rely on perceptual similarity to categorize. For example, four-year-olds are more likely to group fire engines with apples rather than cars, because both are red (Tversky, 1985). However, even young children do not seem to be entirely dependent on perceptual similarity. For example, six-year-old children were shown a mechanical monkey toy and asked some questions. Despite its similarity to a real monkey in appearance, children did not believe that the toy could breathe, eat, or have babies, thus correctly applying a quite abstract category of living versus nonliving (Carey, 1985). So it's an oversimplification to say "young children think things are alike if they look alike." Even six-year-olds use nonperceptual qualities when they categorize.

Just as the embodied approach has some neuroscientific support, so, too, does the claim that not all concepts are embodied. Some visual cortical areas are organized by meaning rather than perceptual quality. That is, there are localized representations for vehicles in visual areas of the brain. That seems to support embodiment – we represent "vehicle" visually. But the same brain organization is observed in people born blind (Bedny et al., 2012; Mahon & Hickok, 2016). People who have never had any visual experience nonetheless have such overlapping brain organization between "visual" and conceptual areas. This finding indicates that visual sensory experience is not what is causing the overlap in brain representation, because people born blind have never had visual experiences.

In conclusion, there is certainly evidence for a fair amount of overlap between perceptual processes and how we form concepts through categorization. Basic perceptual qualities are useful in classifying diverse sets of objects. However, while we all learn concepts through perceptual experience, and that perceptual experience is grounded in our bodies, not all of our conceptual structure is embodied.

How Do Features Help Us Form Inferences?

Categorizing helps us think about new things by knowing what in our memory is relevant to this new situation. In the fantastical short story "Funes the Memorious," Jorge Luis Borges shows this through a creative example. The protagonist Funes falls from a horse and is left with a perfect memory. Funes perceives and remembers every single detail of his life, every curve of every cloud he has ever seen, every word that he has ever read along with the exact state of his body when he read them. Funes is overwhelmed by facts and ends up bedridden, leading Borges to remind the reader: "To think is to forget a difference, to generalize, to abstract. In the overly replete world of Funes, there were nothing but details." While it might seem that sorting things into categories and losing their specifics is "forgetting," it is this paring away of details that allows us to do many mental operations we term *thinking*. A world with nothing but details and no abstractions and categories is a world where thinking is impossible.

Your experience, along with the forgetting of details, allows you to **generalize**, that is, to apply information gathered from one exemplar to a different exemplar of the same category. In other words, things you know from your experience with dogs (they eat, they breathe, they could bite you but probably won't, they smell when wet) can be applied to any dog. The importance of the ability to generalize is hard to overestimate. The first sentence of Ed Smith and Doug Medin's (1981) book about categorization is "Without concepts, mental life would be chaotic." It would be chaotic because you would approach any object you had not interacted with as though it were completely novel. "Hey, look at this furry thing. Hmm. Four legs. Wagging tail. I wonder whether it has lungs? I wonder whether it can fly?" Concepts, then, are the mental representations that allow us to generalize.

Whereas generalizing might mean forgetting differences between things, it also means taking that categorical knowledge and applying it to something you've never encountered before.

In other words, categories allow you to create knowledge about novel objects by making inferences. This type of thinking is called **inductive inference**, in which a person uses specific instances to figure out and apply a general rule (which may or may not be correct). (We will discuss deductive inference, where we move from a general rule to specific cases, in Chapter 12.)

Notice that we defined inference by saying that children can "create knowledge." Children often learn by making inferences and then testing them. For this reason, developmental psychologist Alison Gopnick calls children "scientists in cribs," for the way that they learn through inference and testing. Think of how children categorize foods. They might begin by using a default inference like "this might be food; I'll stick it in my mouth and see how it tastes." But as they get older, they learn to categorize foods in more specific categories: as breakfast, lunch, or dinner, as a snack, dessert, or rare treat. Forming these concepts is not as simple as "can I eat it?" The day after his twin sons' first experience with candy, Riener asked them what they would like for breakfast. The response – a hopeful "M&M's?" – was perhaps an inference that M&M's are delicious and edible and therefore would be an ideal breakfast. Riener laughed and said no, M&M's are not a breakfast food. What about M&M's makes them laughable to be included in breakfast foods? Why are other sweet chocolate foods (doughnuts, Count Chocula cereal) acceptable breakfast foods? This is not a simple distinction for children. What did they learn about the category of breakfast foods by learning that M&M's weren't in it?

To understand how categories help us make inferences, think of it like the process by which Netflix learns to make recommendations of what movies and shows you might like. You tell Netflix which movies fall into your categories of "1 star = hated it" and "5 star = loved it" by rating what you have watched. Netflix also monitors which ones you watch all the way through and which ones you quit watching halfway through, even if you don't officially rate from one to five stars. When entering a new movie into their database, Netflix needs to infer how you would categorize it (and whether you would click to watch it and sit through it). You said you liked *Suicide Squad* and *The Woman King* with Viola Davis and the *Game of Thrones* TV series with Peter Dinklage; does that mean that you will like *Hunger Games: The Ballad of Songbirds and Snakes*, with Peter Dinklage and Viola Davis? What characteristics should Netflix use to decide what to base an inference on? The problem for the "mind" of Netflix, just like the mind of the child, is determining which features are most relevant: Is it better to base inferences on an abstract category, for example, "apocalyptic superhero movies," or to focus on more concrete features, such as which actors appear in it? (See Figure 9.13.)

The problem is quite similar for the recommendation **algorithm** stream (colloquially called the FYP or For You Page) from TikTok. How does TikTok decide that you would like videos about men removing things from horse's hooves and also one with teenagers dancing and another of congressional testimony? The TikTok recommendation algorithm makes an inference that you might like the video based on some of its features and its similarity on those features to other videos that you have behaved as if you have enjoyed (by "liking" them, by watching them, or by interacting with them in some other way, such as commenting or sharing). It certainly seems as if TikTok is "categorizing" you, the viewer. How does TikTok know that Riener is a gardener and professor and dad? It may not "know" or have such labels but just know that a certain video was liked by other users who behave like me on other videos.

The previous section described how, unlike computer algorithms, human children have a bias for categorizing based on perceptual similarity. How does this bias affect the inferences they make about novel objects? The classic task to investigate this in the lab is described in Gelman and Markman (1986). Children are taught information about two objects and then asked to apply what they have learned to make an inference about a third object. For example, they were shown three

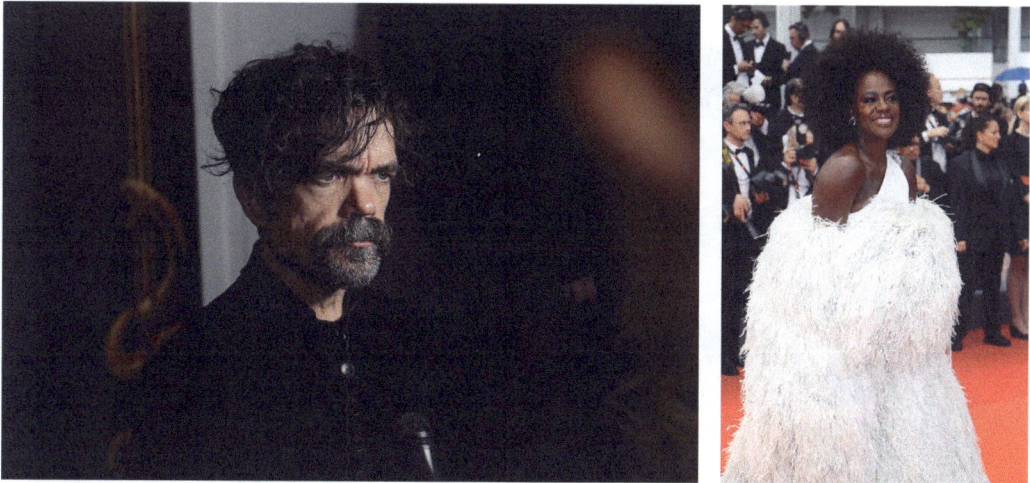

Figure 9.13. If you enjoy movies or shows with either Viola Davis or Peter Dinklage, will you enjoy movies with both of them? Are certain actors the best predictor of what movies will fit in a category of "I liked that"?

pictures: a tropical fish, a dolphin, and a shark. Then they were told "this is a fish ... this is a dolphin ... this is a fish [for the shark]." In this case, the shark looks more similar to the dolphin, so if children based their inferences primarily on perceptual appearances, they would make inferences as if it were a dolphin (see Figure 9.14). The test was a question: "See this fish [pointing to shark]? Does it breathe underwater, like this fish, or does it pop above the water to breathe, like this dolphin?" A judgment of "breathe underwater" would be based on category membership, whereas a judgment of "pop above water" would be based on perceptual similarity (since sharks look much more similar to dolphins than to colorful tropical fish). The four-year-old children in Gelman and Markman's study preferred to use the category information two-thirds of the time.

Badger and Shapiro (2015) updated this work, but they varied the structure of the categories themselves. For example, a category could be structured based on a feature or set of features (birds have wings and lay eggs), or it could be based on relationships between features (squares have sides of equal length, whereas rectangles have sides of unequal length, but both have four right angles). Badger and Shapiro found that children may begin with a bias toward using perceptual similarity but, as they age, become more able to use category information to make inferences, although this ability comes earlier for categories that are more simply defined, such as by a single feature.

Early approaches to categorization held that categories were defined by a set of necessary and sufficient rules. In the 1970s, it became clear that category structure is not always all-or-none, as the classical view would predict, but rather is often graded; some exemplars of a category are considered more typical, or better examples of the category, than others. This finding and others led to probability models in which categorization is viewed as a matter of probability, not all-or-none decisions. Two types of probability models were developed: prototype models (in which exemplars are abstracted into a prototype that is stored) and exemplar models (in which all the exemplars are stored). In the late 1980s, new results indicated that similarity could not account for all categorization. It seemed that rules are used to categorize at least some of the time. The latest theories include at least two separate mechanisms for category learning. More recently, new types of categories, defined by relationships rather than the characteristics of features, have begun to be investigated. These include role-governed categories, which are defined by features extrinsic to the exemplars themselves. Modern approaches have also asked whether features are based on basic sensory

(a)

(b)

(c)

Figure 9.14. Children are shown the first two pictures and told that they are a dolphin and a fish. Then they are presented with a new picture (the shark) and told it is a fish. When asked to make an inference, will they use the category membership (it is a fish) to make a judgment, or will they use its appearance (it looks more like a dolphin)? (Source: (a) Moment/Getty Images; (b) wildestanimal/Moment/Getty Images; (c) AGR/Moment/Getty Images.)

representations and how features help us make inferences about novel objects. Many concepts have content from our senses, and overlap with sensory processing, but not all.

Stand-on-One-Foot Question

9.4.   What does it mean to say that a concept is embodied?

Questions That Require Two Feet

9.5.   What kind of inductive inferences have you made about your teachers? Have these inferences ever been shown to be inaccurate?

9.6.   Why is generalizing a critical mental process for vocabulary learning? How does this differ from learning a first language to learning a second language?

How Does Culture Shape Concepts and Categories?

Preview

As we noted in Chapter 1, cognitive psychologists tend to focus on what human thought processes have in common. Previous chapters have sought to explain the universal characteristics of vision, attention, and memory. Our discussion of concepts and categories has followed a similar path, focusing on the universal elements of these mental processes. But obviously, even if there are some universals, each human has different knowledge, depending on their life experiences. One of the big influences on our experience is the culture in which we grow up. In this section, we'll ask about the influence of culture on our mental representations (concepts) and mental processes (how we divide the world into categories). Does our culture merely change the words, or does it change the structure?

When Eleanor Rosch in 1975 asked people to rate the "birdiness of birds," she didn't just ask "people," she asked 663 American undergraduates (from psychology classes at the University of California, Berkeley, in some ways not even representative of American undergraduates!), and indeed, she excluded people who were not native speakers of English. Obviously someone who grew up in Zimbabwe might not see a robin as very birdy, whereas they would likely see the African fish eagle as more so (although Zimbabweans certainly don't call the bird the "African fish eagle" – it is known as *hungwe* in the Bantu language Shona; Figure 9.15). But is the supposition that even if Zimbabweans don't have robins, they still have a concept of a very birdy bird also overgeneralizing? Perhaps the concepts of "birdiness" and "typicality" are not universal characteristics of human cognition but instead are particular to American undergraduates. This is not a flaw unique to Rosch's research but a systematic problem with a lot of cognitive psychology research. The big question is, Do people just have different words for concepts because they have different experiences, or do the experiences people have in one culture affect the structure of their concepts, not just the names for different things? In this section, we'll ask how deeply culture affects our concepts and categories.

What are the universal aspects of our mental processes of concepts and categories, and what depends on our individual experiences, of which culture is a large influence? In Chapter 6, we defined spreading activation models and the structure of long-term memory with an extended example about foods and meals across the world. We suggested that while breakfast foods across the world vary, and dimensions such as color, preparation, or ingredients might vary, we took for granted that everyone has a concept of "breakfast" and that everyone eats foods in meals. We assumed (remember how important assumptions are!) that all humans eat food and have an organizational system for what kinds of foods they eat, and that for all cultures, one of those categories is based on time of day.

To give you a flavor of what's to come, consider this: The times and number of meals eaten in different cultures have varied as social customs have changed across time and place, as people have shifted from agricultural lifestyles, in which they might rise early for farm chores, to factory or office work, for which they leave home for an extended time and so eat away from home. Breakfast, lunch, dinner, supper: Even distinguishing the concept of a "meal," for which one stops other activities to eat stored food, rather than eating as one gathers while engaged in other tasks or activities, might not be as universal and timeless as we supposed (Rowland, 2012). So while you

Figure 9.15. African fish eagle

surely understood that your mental representation of "what types of foods are good for breakfast" has been affected by your culture, now you know that maybe even the concept of "breakfast" is also affected by culture.

We mentioned in Chapter 1 that cognitive psychologists try to study the universal elements of mental processes. Just like a biologist studies fruit fly evolution to gain insight into general laws of genetics, a cognitive psychologist might study a memory task to gain insight into the general nature of human encoding and consolidation. Hopefully that assumption of a focus on universals was obvious to you as we described lower-level processing like perception (we all have eyes) and even some basics of memory like short-term versus long-term memory (even though you may recall that we did briefly address cultural variations in those topics). Now that we get to higher-level processes, like this chapter on concepts and the remaining chapters on language, decision-making, and problem-solving, of course they involve culture, but the question is, how deeply does culture reach into our cognitive processes? (See Figure 9.16.)

Before we jump into the examples of how deeply culture reaches into our mental processes and representations of concepts and categories, it is worth dwelling for a moment on the analogy of

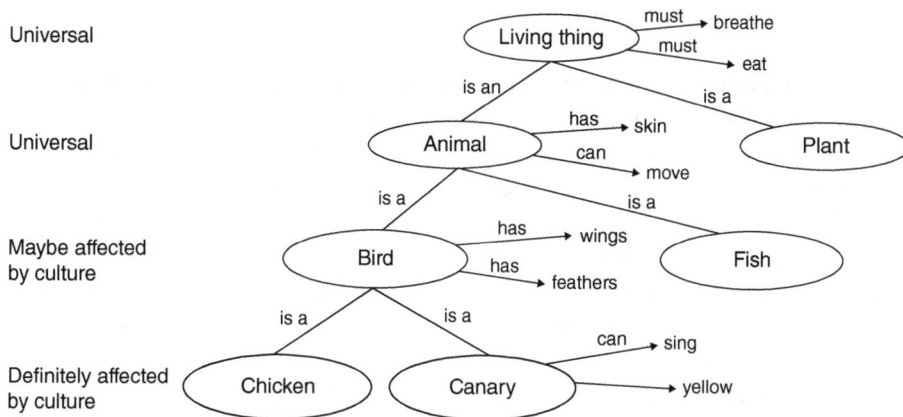

Figure 9.16. Remember Figure 6.7 with the hierarchical model of the concept of bird from Chapter 6? Obviously a robin is a more typically American bird, but how culturally defined are the larger categories of birds, animals and living things?

our fruit fly biologist (or, indeed, the logic of model systems in biology). When these biologists present their research, they must clarify which conclusions of their research are specific to fruit fly anatomy and behavior and which generalize to genetics across all animals. Sometimes an over-reliance on a single animal for evidence can result in mistakenly generalizing conclusions that turn out to be specific to that single lab animal. In our search for general laws of perception, memory, and other cognitive processes, psychologists can make the same mistake: an overreliance on the minds of the people in their studies.

So, to review, the search for general laws of cognition will require some careful experiments and questioning our own assumptions about which aspects of those mental processes are universal. In addition, it will require testing our assumptions about universality by seeking evidence from people's minds situated in a variety of cultures around the world. We're going to take two examples and describe how research has investigated how our concepts and categories might be universal and how they might be shaped by culture. The first is the mental process and structures of classification of living things, also called **folk biology**. While of course the animals across the world change, what changes, and what is universal about how we think about them?

How Does Culture Affect Our Categories for Living Things?

First, human cultures around the world all have multilevel hierarchical category systems of living things (Tanaka & Taylor, 1991; van den Broek et al., 2023). In other words, there are larger categories (like *animals*) that include smaller groups (like *birds*) that include even smaller groups (like *eagles*), and these categories are used as a basis for reasoning, as we described earlier in our discussion of how features help us form inferences. Furthermore, all cultures have a smallest category, which biologists call a species (although there is even disagreement among experts on the exact definition of a species [Mishler, 2021]).

Second, all cultures share a conception that an animal has an "essence" that persists across its life-span and maintains its identity through growth and changes. What does that mean? Even as a tadpole changes appearance and how it acts as it becomes a frog, and a caterpillar becomes a butterfly, they both remain the same being. This belief of a core identity that shapes growth and action is also called **biological essentialism** and has a long history in philosophy (Medin & Atran,

2004). To apply this to the Collins and Quinlan figure, all cultures have a high-level "living things" category.

If hierarchical categories and biological essentialism are universal, then how do cultures differ in folk biology? One way of testing the structure of people's biological categories is to ask them to learn a new item and place it in their categorical structure. How people learn a new concept helps illustrate the overall structure of the rest of the concepts. A task designed by Susan Carey (1985) has served as a useful foundation to build upon. A set of animals that are very well known (within that culture) are used as bases. Participants are shown a picture of one of the bases and taught a new (fictional) property about it. Thus, the experimenter might show the dog picture and say, "Now, there's this stuff called andro. Andro is found inside some things. One thing that has andro inside is dogs. Now, I'm going to show you some pictures of other things, and I want you to tell me if you think they have andro inside like dogs do." Participants were then shown each of the targets and asked "Does it have andro inside it, like the [base]?"

Medin and Atran (2004) used that task and compared children (aged four to eleven) and adults in four different cultures, a rural and suburban American majority culture and Indigenous people in Mexico (Yukatek Maya) and the United States (Menominee, the oldest continuous residents living on tribal lands in the state of Wisconsin).

Some trends emerge from this cross-cultural comparison. People from Indigenous cultures are more likely to form their categories using relationships in nature rather than merely hierarchical taxonomy. In other words, they are more likely to see categories based not only on categories and subcategories, such as "a robin is a type of bird," but also on relationships based on ecological actions and behaviors, such as "bears eat fish." In addition, this type of task can assess whether and how people have a unique category and processes for human beings as opposed to other living things. Medin and Atran (2004) and others have found that this anthropocentrism (seeing humans as a central and unique category) is common among children in WEIRD cultures but the exception across other Indigenous cultures, who often, in seeing categories by their ecological relationships, are able to see human connection to the natural world, even in a central role.

Furthermore, two complicating notes are worth appending to this overall result. First, experts in a wide variety of contexts are also more likely to expand their conceptual reasoning to functional relationships beyond taxonomy. So, for example, parks workers might think about trees in categories based on disease susceptibility, and fishermen (across cultures) might think about categories of which fish are regulated game fish. Second, sometimes language can get in the way of translating tasks across cultures in ways that the frequently English-speaking researchers can initially fail to appreciate. For example, López et al. (1997) asked Itza participants to sort animals by which were most "alike" or "similar" (presuming that translations for each of these words into Itza were equally synonymous as they are in English). But the results were confusing and inconsistent until a translation more similar to "go together by nature" was used in the instructions, upon which the results became more consistent. The new instructions showed that the Itza respondents had taxonomic knowledge of animals, but the English researchers simply needed instructions worded in a way to appropriately communicate the questions (point described in Medin & Atran, 2004).

So the research on culture and living things shows that all cultures categorize living things but that the culture in which we grow up can affect how many categorical systems we have and the structure of these systems. While we all have taxonomies of animals into types and subtypes, Indigenous cultures are more likely to also be able to think about living things based on ecological relationships. This type of thinking is similar to the mental processes of expertise. Next we will consider how culture affects our concepts for our own sensory experiences.

Does Culture Affect Our Categories for Sensory Qualities?

In the section on features, we noted that some features are sensory qualities. A visual feature of the concept *fire truck* is its redness. An auditory feature of its siren is its loudness and high pitch. These sensory qualities would seem to be prime candidates for a universal aspect of human perception and cognition. That is, even if across cultures fire trucks are different colors and make different sounds (and maybe not all cultures fight fires with trucks), at least all cultures have words and labels for the sensory features of objects.

If that made sense to you for vision and sound, now think of smell. English speakers don't typically treat odors as object features. We might say both a rose and an apple are red, but we wouldn't describe a rose as having an odor characteristic shared with other odors – we'd just say it smells like a rose. Our inability (or, at least, our reluctance) to label features of odor experiences may be related to our difficulty in naming parts of the experience. We might be able to identify an odor of cinnamon, but we have difficulty detecting and describing degrees of cinnamonishness or in breaking down a complex odor into its constituents; we can not only describe a shirt as "having many colors" but can specify all of the color components, and we can differentiate one rainbow spiral tie-dyed shirt from another (see Figure 9.17).

But speakers of some other languages *can* describe degrees of a particular odor in a complex odor. You may remember from Chapter 2 when we described how Majid and Burenhult (2014) tested English speakers and speakers of Jahai (from the Malay Peninsula) in their ability to name odors and colors. While English speakers were far better at naming colors than odors, and

Figure 9.17. This mother and daughter are making tie-dye shirts. The mother's has orange in the middle, moving out to turquoise, then orange, then yellow. The daughter's has more magenta, then turquoise, then a lighter orange. Both their left sleeves are turquoise. This level of description is possible with visual images, but less so with odors.

used hardly any abstract terms for odors, the Jahai speakers were roughly equal in their ability to name colors and odors.

Earlier we compared Indigenous approaches to categories as similar to the expertise gained by park rangers or farmers in that it went beyond hierarchy (this is a type of that) and included relationships such as predator–prey or disease vulnerability. For smell, Majid (2021) argues that there are critical differences between specialist expertise, for example, of wine experts, and cultural differences in odor concepts. Specialist knowledge tends to be much more focused on identifying an individual exemplar (like a specific wine), whereas cultural knowledge tends to capture broad similarities (Honoré-Chedozeau et al., 2019). Whereas English might describe a smell as stinky, the Jahai distinguish between bloody, rotten, and smoky/oily/astringent smells. Furthermore, specialist knowledge is limited to the subdomain; wine experts are no better at describing the smells of coffee or other odors (Croijmans et al., 2020). One analogy to expertise does hold, however: Even those who have not formed complex odor categories in their culture can do so with practice. Consistent training with novel verbal labels can help English speakers form odor categories (Vanek et al., 2021).

We should address an issue with this research that is not easily resolvable. Are these cognitive differences caused by the languages these people speak? Or are these differences driven by habits of thought? For example, English-speaking wine tasters or perfume testers *are* able to describe components of olfactory experience, and they have a lot of words to describe odors. A detailed description of the dimensions of a pinot noir comes from practice comparing many similar odors. Is it language that prompts the ability, or is it the practice that a culture provides? We'll return to this question later, but because language is so often tied to culture, it is difficult to disentangle. We'll tackle this question more deeply in the next chapter, when we introduce the structure of language.

Stand-on-One-Foot Questions

9.7.   How do you think the folk biology differs between people who live on a sea coast and people who live away from any body of water?

9.8.   Think of another case in which you are learning a new item and you need to categorize it. It could be an app for your phone or a new tool of some other sort. How would you decide where it belongs in your current categories? Do you have a folk categorization of that domain?

Questions That Require Two Feet

9.9.   Have you ever been to a different country or experienced a different culture that made you question your categories? Have you had another experience (perhaps training in biology or chemistry) that made you rethink your catregorization of living things or other basic concepts?

9.10.   Think of a career or expertise, such as medicine, sports, law, education, or food service. How do you think the expertise is different from folk knowledge in that area? How is it similar to the contrast between wine tasters and the Jahai described earlier? How is it different?

10 Language Structure

What Is Language?

- The Definition of Language

- Levels of Language

- Grammar

Is Language Special?

- Is Language Developmentally Special?

- Is Language Particularly Human?

- Does Language Shape Thought?

To introduce the amazing complexity of language, let's overexplain a joke:

> Most cutting thing you can say is "who's this clown?" because it implies they're a) a clown & b) not even one of the better-known clowns. (@skullmandible, X [formerly Twitter])

Human language is a magnificently complex cognitive process, integrating many of the processes we've already discussed. You must accurately perceive the letters or the sounds. You must link them to the intended memory representations of what those letters or sounds correspond to. Then you must make sense of the piece of language as a whole, in the context of a rich network of memories. Think of what goes unstated in the earlier joke. You must choose a meaning for "cutting" that is not about knives or standing in line but about insults. You must understand that a "clown" is not just a positive role of someone who entertains at children's birthday parties and is a talented physical comedian in circuses but also someone who is rude or stupid. Finally, you have to see the humor in calling someone rude or stupid, but not so rude and stupid that they become famous for it.

Like other complex cognitive tasks, a popular conception of language includes a great many things that cognitive psychologists might not include. When a server puts an extra helping of guacamole on a burrito, you may exclaim, "Yeah, now you're speaking my language!" but to study language in a lab, a cognitive psychologist might first ask, **What is language?** This will require a definition of language and an understanding of the different levels, some of which we alluded to in the preceding example.

Once we've defined language, we can then compare it to other cognitive processes. Language certainly does seem different, but how different? In the second section of this chapter, we ask, **Is language special?** In that section we will ask whether language follows a different developmental path than other cognitive tasks. We will also ask how human language differs from animal communication. Finally, we will explore the relationship between language and other cognitive processes.

What Is Language?

Preview

The task of defining language is difficult, but we must start with at least a provisional one because a definition is crucial to letting us know what theories of language need to explain. We will describe cognitive structure and function in both spoken language and written language. Sometimes the cognitive processes supporting these two are different (e.g., processing of the most basic units – letters and speech sounds), whereas for other functions, they are similar (e.g., processing longer chunks of meaningful language like sentences and texts). It is useful to think of language structure at four levels: basic units (letters and phonemes), words, sentences, and groups of sentences (texts). Describing the structure of our language at each of these levels shows how complex language is but also clarifies what theories of language must explain.

We've begun several previous chapters by defining terms, for example, attention or working memory. **Language** proves more difficult to define, but we can say that the cognitive psychological definition of language is quite different than the everyday usage. Suppose that a dog has different vocalizations (barks, whines, etc.) that it makes when it is hungry, wants to go outside, or wants to play. Recent viral videos show dogs using a button system to indicate different requests and communicate with humans. Could we say that, either with different vocalizations or with buttons, a dog uses language to "speak" with human owners? By standard cognitive psychological definitions, the answer would be no (Figure 10.1).

The Definition of Language

Although linguists continue to debate the best way to define language (Ibbotson & Tomasello, 2016), most psychologists agree that the following properties are critical (Clark & Clark, 1977):

Figure 10.1. "Sorry, we have a great connection, but spoilsport cognitive psychologists don't think we share a language." (Source: P. Wegner/ImageBROKER/Getty Images.)

Figure 10.2. A vibraphone, or what "vibes" meant in 1940.

Communicative. Languages permit communication between individuals.

Arbitrary. The relationship between the elements in the language and their meaning is arbitrary. There is no special reason the word *chair* must have the referent that it does. It would be perfectly acceptable for the utterance *table* to have the referent that *chair* now does. The word *big* doesn't have to be in some sense "bigger" than the word *minuscule.* Arbitrariness is a key feature of symbols. A sound (and a pattern of written symbols) stands for a meaning, but which sound stands for which meaning is arbitrary.

Structured. Language is structured, meaning that there are rules for how a collection of symbols fit together. It makes a difference whether you say "The boy ran from the angry dog" compared to "The dog ran from the angry boy," and the rules of English don't permit "Boy the from dog ran the angry."

Generative. The basic units of language (words) can be used to build a limitless number of meanings. Indeed, while there are other authors and other cognitive psychology textbooks, the pattern of twenty-nine words in this very sentence is probably unique in the history of the world! Putting words together to form sentences has rules, but these rules do not limit meanings.

Dynamic. Language is not static. It is changing constantly as new words are added and as the rules of grammar (slowly and subtly) change. New languages are created, and some languages die out. Language is not just vibes, but it allows for the word *vibes* to mean "short for vibraphone musical instrument" in 1940 (see Figure 10.2) and "intuitive signal about a person or thing" in the 1960s to its expanded definition today that these authors won't try to fully capture.

Our example of communication between you and your dog has some of the properties essential to language, but it is missing others. It is communicative, the relationship between utterance and meaning appears arbitrary, and it might be dynamic, but there is no structure to the communication; utterances are composed of a single sound, associated with a single meaning. The communication also lacks generativity. Your dog's vocalizations can't be combined to create new meanings.

You might wonder why the definition of language matters. If you and your dog communicate, can't you call that a language, if you want to? The definition matters because the pieces of the definition tell us what we are trying to explain when we seek to understand how people use language. Remember our assumptions: What are we trying to explain? For example, you may recall from Chapter 1 that generativity was behind one of the important criticisms Noam Chomsky leveled at B. F. Skinner's behavioristic account of language. Skinner argued that the principles of operant and classical conditioning could account for how children learn language. Chomsky argued that they could not because language is generative; behaviorist principles can account for whether someone is more likely to repeat an action taken previously, but a distinctive property of language is that we almost never say the same thing twice. In essence, Chomsky was saying that Skinner's theory was bound to miss the mark because Skinner failed to appreciate all of what language is. Thus, defining language properly is important, and the five criteria we've listed are a good consensus statement.

The example of your linguistic dog highlights one way that the definition is used. Psychologists use the definition to help us classify animal communication – for example, "is communication between dolphins really a language?" Just as often, however, psychologists use the definition as a reminder of what a theory of language must explain. If, for example, you develop a theory of language and the theory makes no provision for how language might change over time, then you have omitted one of the defining properties of language, and you would know that your theory is either incorrect or incomplete. The definition of language is a description of what a complete theory must account for. This doesn't mean that dolphin or dog communication is not fascinating and clever and worthy of study in its own right; it may just need different explanations (and experimental methods) than human language.

Levels of Language

Defining language is still more complicated because it is most usefully described at different levels; simple building blocks combine to build more complex structures, which in turn combine to create still more complex structures. Spoken and written language differ in some of their fundamental building blocks, so in some places we'll describe them separately. We'll begin our discussion with letters (the smallest unit of written language), then discuss phonemes (the smallest unit of spoken language), then move on to levels where written and spoken language use similar processes: words, sentences, and texts. In each subsection, we'll describe the units of language at that level and some of the rules by which those units combine to make up the next level.

LETTERS   Every written language has a set of basic units (letters, in alphabetic writing systems like ours) that can be combined and recombined into different words. The recognition of letters is a visual task; in fact, letters can be thought of as an object, and the process of recognizing letters can be thought of as a special case of visual object recognition. (For experienced readers, groups of letters and whole words become recognizable objects.) However, recognizing the letter visually is only half the job when reading. The other half is mapping the letter (or combination of letters) to a sound. In English (and many other languages), that's an individual speech sound. In a smaller number of languages, each written symbol codes a syllable.

The rules for combining letters into words in written language are commonly known as spelling rules. Some rules for English apply across nearly all words, thereby censoring possible spellings, for example, "words may not end with the letter *u*, *v*, or *j*," or "a *u* always follows a *q*." Other spelling rules do not apply to all words but are contingent on sound. For example, many of us learned "*i* before *e* except after *c*"; that rule doesn't apply when the vowel sounds like *a* (as in *neighbor* and *weigh*) or when the *c* is pronounced like *sh* (e.g., *efficient*).

Spoken language also has pronunciation rules, but they do not always follow spelling rules. For example, there is a type of phoneme called a stop consonant, roughly corresponding to the sounds associated with the letters *p*, *b*, *t*, *d*, *k*, and *g*. Spoken English does not allow a word to begin with two stop consonants. But written language does allow words to begin with two letters corresponding to stop consonants, provided one is silent (e.g., *pterodactyl*). There are even some disagreements about these rules,. Rapper Lil Wayne declared that "real G's move in silence, like lasagna," implying that the *g* in *lasagna* is silent, but others (mostly not rappers) took issue with this characterization, because that *g* modified how one pronounces the *n*.

PHONEMES Individual speech sounds, called **phonemes**, roughly correspond to letters of the alphabet. We say "roughly correspond" because the same letter can be pronounced as a different phoneme, depending on the context. Some letters must do double duty, and some sounds can correspond to multiple letters. For example, *a* is pronounced differently in *baby* and *back*, and *th* is pronounced differently in *thin* and *then*; these are different phonemes. However, the same phoneme (*ee*) is associated with a different letter (or letters) in *seen*, *scene*, *pier*, *pea*, *pony*, and *physique*. In all, there are about forty-six phonemes in English; the exact count varies among experts. Figure 10.3 shows a standard taxonomy of phonemes found in English. These are just a fraction of the possible phonemes – about 200 are in use worldwide. For example, the phoneme that corresponds to the letter *x* in the South African city name "Ixopo" is articulated as a click. This phoneme is not used in English (it is in Zulu), so English speakers are usually confounded in trying to pronounce it.

Languages vary not only in which phonemes they use but in whether slight differences in phoneme pronunciation make them different phonemes. For example, the *p* sounds in *pill* and in *spill* are slightly different: The former is aspirated, that is, accompanied by a burst of breath; the

	monophthongs				diphthongs			
VOWELS	iː sheep	ɪ ship	ʊ good	uː shoot	ɪə here	eɪ wait		
	e bed	ə teacher	ɜː bird	ɔː door	ʊə tourist	ɔɪ boy	əʊ show	
	æ cat	ʌ up	ɑː far	ɒ on	eə hair	aɪ my	aʊ cow	
CONSONANTS	p pea	b boat	t tea	d dog	ʧ cheese	ʤ June	k car	g go
	f fly	v video	θ think	ð this	s see	z zoo	ʃ shall	ʒ television
	m man	n now	ŋ sing	h hat	l love	r red	w wet	j yes

Figure 10.3. Standard taxonomy of phonemes in English.

latter is unaspirated. This difference is ignored in English, and both types of pronunciation signify the same phoneme. But in many languages (especially those spoken in East Asia and India), they are different phonemes.

WORDS   The twenty-six letters and the forty-six English phonemes are combined to produce all of the approximately 600,000 words in the English language. There are interesting rules, however, about how these phonemes may be combined and where they may appear in a word. As noted, English words may begin with one stop consonant (e.g., *pea*, *dab*) but not two; you could not invent a word *bdat*. Other languages permit combinations that are forbidden in English. For example, in Slovak, words without phonemes that correspond to vowels are permissible. Schoolchildren learn the vowelless sentence "strč prst skrz krk" as a curiosity. (It translates to "stick your finger through your throat." Right.)

The foregoing concerned rules about which phonemes could go together; a vowelless word is deemed unpronounceable in English. There are also rules regarding which letters go together in writing, even if the resulting combination would be pronounceable. For example, which looks more like a word to you, *magy* or *majy*? There are no words in English that end in *jy* and so *majy* just looks wrong, even though it's pronounceable. In the same way, English doesn't permit words to begin with a double letter, as in *ppeople*, although, again, it should be pronounceable; doubling the *p* in the middle of a word affects the vowel sound, but the *p* sound doesn't change (e.g., *super* vs. *supper*).

SENTENCES   It is easy to appreciate that there are rules for the construction of sentences, as it is noticeable when these rules are violated. However, identifying the exact rule can be tricky; even though we learn and use the rules, they typically remain unconscious. For example, what makes word strings such as "ate I the to went yesterday carnival much and too" so clearly wrong? "Ate I the ..." seems wrong because it puts the verb first, whereas "I ate the ..." would be correct in this case. Yet "pass me the salt" sounds fine, so we can't simply say that the subject must come before the noun. The order of parts of speech appears to depend on the particular type of verb.

Another complication is that the same word may serve as a different part of speech in different sentences. That's obvious in the case of nouns – *Cedar* can be the subject of a sentence ("Cedar kicked Dan") or the direct object ("Dan kicked Cedar"). But many words are still more ambiguous. For example, *smoke* may be a noun, a verb, or an adjective (as in *smoke shop*). We call the grammatical role a word plays its "part of speech," but a better name would be "part of a sentence." You figure out what role *smoke* plays by the context.

The key problem for cognitive psychologists is not so much to identify the rules that make a sentence officially valid as it is to explain how the mind uses rules to extract meaning from a sequence of words. People around the world learn language without official guidance from a committee of grammarians, and many learn language before they even enter any organized schooling. How does their mind internalize the rules and content of language? We take up that problem after we finish our brief tour of the four levels of language processing.

TEXTS   When psychologists refer to a **text**, they typically mean a group of related sentences (spoken or written) forming a paragraph or a group of related paragraphs. Why do we need another level of representation for *groups* of sentences? If we've specified a way to understand sentences, don't we just use that process repeatedly? As it turns out, that won't do. Understanding a group of sentences requires connections and relationships between sentences and between objects across sentences. We make these connections by using information that's not in the sentences, applying our memory and background knowledge to understand not just the literal meaning of the sentences but what's implied. The result is not just the meaning of each sentence put in a basket, so to speak, but a well-ordered sense of the text as a whole. Here's an example of the need to build bridges across sentences:

> The man sighed into the phone. He asked to speak with a manager. She said she was the manager.

Some connections are simple: "He" in the second sentence refers to "the man" in the first sentence. But the first and second sentence should be connected by their meanings as well. Sighing and asking to speak to a manager are both signs of dissatisfaction and frustration. If you simply read these two sentences without understanding this connection, you are not fully comprehending the text. Finally, you would typically be confused if a new indefinite pronoun (*she*) were introduced, with no prior referent. But information in long-term memory resolves the ambiguity; you were told that the man is talking on the phone, and you know that phone conversations involve two people. "She" must be the person he's talking to. This sort of reading between the lines, adding information from long-term memory, is a ubiquitous mental process when comprehending language.

You don't just understand the individual words and sentences of the text; you form a mental representation of the world, people, and events that they convey. That representation is called a **situation model**. This situation model is more than the sum of the ideas in the sentences but combines it with our knowledge of the broader world as well as with inferences.

What does the situation model include, and what details does it discard? Can we describe rules for the construction of a situation model? Early work on this problem considered that readers and listeners might attend to causal relationships, or to spatial relationships among the entities in a text, or to the timing of events. Further work indicated that what goes into the situation model and what is omitted depends on the goals of the reader or listener. You can get a sense of why this might be true if you imagine reading the same text in one case thinking it was a fictional story and in the other if it was a true, first person account of the scene of a battle that appeared in a newspaper.

Grammar

We've briefly discussed four levels of language – phonemes, words, sentences, and texts – and we've said that each level is characterized by rules in a given language: rules about which phonemes are permissible, rules about how phonemes can combine to form words, how words can combine to form sentences, and how sentences can combine to form texts. How do these rules help psychologists understand how the mind perceives and produces language?

For phonemes and words, the answer seems to be that "specific rules don't help us generalize across languages to universal mental rules." The rules governing phonemes and words vary so much across languages that important consistencies in those rules (if they exist) have not been uncovered. Knowledge of what makes a text coherent has been somewhat more helpful; as we will see in Chapter 11, the expectation of logical connectivity is important in text comprehension because it prompts us to make inferences about missing information.

Sentences are different because the grammatical structure of sentences has been the subject of intensive study, and the knowledge accrued from that study has been vital to our understanding of the psychological processes contributing to sentence comprehension and production. Different languages obviously have different grammatical rules, but psychologists seek to discover rules that apply to *all* languages – a set of super rules, to which the grammars of all languages must adhere. If such rules could be described (e.g., Chomsky, 2013; Nowak et al., 2001), it would be a big help in formulating theories about how the mind comprehends sentences (for an example, see Lidz et al., 2003). This is similar to other research you've read in preceding chapters. We may study the attentional processes of airport security workers and teenage drivers with the goal of discovering foundational mental processes, not just rules specific to certain people in certain situations. We don't want to find only the mental rules of English grammar but the mental processes that are common across all languages.

THE MENTAL RULES OF GRAMMAR   Psychologists do not use the word *grammar* in its everyday sense. Psychologists focus on the rules our minds use to comprehend and produce language, not the grammatical rules sanctioned by experts – experts who, we might add, are self-appointed. Communities of speakers will often use rules that vary from the ones found in a grammar book, but that doesn't make the rules less grammatical – it's a reflection of both the variability of language (different communities develop different rules) and the consistency of language (within the community, everyone follows the same rules). For example, AAVE or African American Vernacular English, a dialect spoken by many Black Americans, uses the word *be* to mark habitual actions, not marked by tense. In General American English, *Cookie Monster be eating cookies* is simply an incorrect inflection of *is*, indicating that Cookie Monster is currently eating cookies. However, in AAVE, *Cookie Monster be eating cookies* indicates that eating cookies is a habit, perhaps redundant given his name. For example, one study (Jackson & Green, 2005) showed Black and White American children a picture of *Sesame Street* characters and read the following structured dialogue:

Cookie Monster is sick and
not eating cookies today.
Elmo is eating cookies. Ernie
only eats cookies on his
birthday when his mom lets
him. Cat has never had a
cookie. Cats can't eat
cookies.

Then they were asked questions, such as "who is eating cookies?" and "who be eating cookies?" The AAVE speakers were much more likely to say that while Elmo is eating cookies, Cookie Monster be eating cookies, recognizing a grammatical rule present in their community's language but not in General American English.

The term **grammar**, therefore, means a set of mental rules that define what are permissible sentences in a community of speakers.

How do we investigate grammar? How do we find the mental rules of language? One option might be to follow some people around and note what they say; from what they say, we can divine the rules they used to generate these sentences. In other words, we could analyze how language is performed. That's not a bad idea, but there's a problem. Language as spoken is seldom neat; people stop in the middle of sentences, they start new ones, they interrupt themselves with "ummmms," they forget a word and start the sentence over, and so on. Thus, a friend might say, "Have you gone to that new . . . uh . . . not the taco place, but it's the one with the, you know, not where John used to work, but across the street from there, with the funny, uh, roof thingie?" Both you and the person who produced this utterance would agree that it is not grammatical, but that wouldn't stop him from saying it or you from understanding.

So apparently there can be a significant gap between the meaning people intend and the set of words that they actually utter. This gap between intent and execution led Noam Chomsky (1957, 1965) to argue persuasively that a distinction should be made between competence and performance. **Competence** is people's knowledge of grammar; **performance** is the way people, you know, actually talk. Competence is our pristine, pure knowledge of how we think sentences should be produced. Performance is the way we produce them once this knowledge has passed through the vagaries of an imperfect memory, the social constraints and goals of conversation, and the many other factors that influence sentence production. Chomsky and those who have continued his investigations aim to peer through the many filters between competence and performance to find the structure of the rules at the root of language.

How, then, can you know what people's competence is when you can't judge competence from performance? Chomsky suggested having people read a sentence and asking them whether it seems grammatical. Participants typically show good agreement when this method is used. For example, which of the following sentences appear grammatical to you? (See Figure 10.4.)

The dog ate the bone.
Dog ate.
The dog ate.
Ate bone the dog.
The bone ate the dog.
By the dog the bone was.
The dog the bone was eaten.
The bone was eaten by the dog.
The dog ate the bone?

Figure 10.4. This chapter seems like a real dog (isn't it amazing how you can understand both the literal meaning of that sentence and the metaphorical?). (Source: Elles Rijsdijk/EyeEm/Getty Images.)

Now we have a method by which to analyze grammar. What is the universal structure of the rules that our minds use to make words into sentences? This esoteric question is one of the most controversial topics in social science of the last seventy-five years. If language is a uniquely human trait (as we'll later suggest it is), the nature of these rules offers clues as to what makes us human. Like many timeless philosophical debates, this one has proven tricky to resolve with empirical evidence. Still, using a variety of methods, we have made progress.

EARLY APPROACHES: WORD-CHAIN GRAMMARS   Early attempts to describe these rules by behaviorist psychologists treated sentences as chains of associated words we call **word-chain grammars**, which propose that grammatical sentences are constructed and comprehended word by word, with the speaker selecting the next word based on the associations of the rest of the words in the sentence. If you have the start of a sentence, such as *The boy took his baseball bat and hit the* _____, you might well guess that the next word is likely to be *ball,* based on associations with the sentence fragment.

Software engineer Jim Kang designed a bot on X (formerly Twitter) (called knock knock [tab] @autocompletejok) that combines knock-knock jokes with suggested autocomplete results, resulting in absurd, sometimes funny results (knock knock, 2015):

"Knock knock!"
    "Who's there?"
"Consequences"
    "Consequences who?"
"Consequences of global warming!"

Word-chain grammars are appealing because they employ simple rules but can generate complex sentences. No complex calculation is needed, just evaluation of the strength of associations, a well-characterized mental process. Perhaps the best example of such a word-chain grammar rule is the prediction tool for modern search engines. If you type in a few words, the app running the site offers the next word, based on all of the searches that have been done (and perhaps personalized to what you have searched in the past). Modern artificial intelligence models called LLMs (or large language models) have been able to use a similar approach for other applications, using strength of associations of massive massive collections of words to predict the next word and generate much longer strings of text that are often remarkably coherent.

Although there is some evidence that people can anticipate upcoming words (Van Berkum et al., 2005; Schreiber & McMurray, 2019), there are a few problems with word-chain grammars as a description of how humans produce and perceive language. First, someone could end that sentence (*The boy took his baseball bat and hit the* _____) with the word *window, umpire, squid,* or even *speeding* _____, and these sentences would still be grammatical (as long as *speeding* was then followed by a noun). That is, even words that are not highly associated with the previous word(s) in the chain can yield a grammatical sentence. Simple association can't be the only principle we use, because we can understand and produce sentences that use uncommon words in new contexts.

Chomsky (1965) developed the famous sentence "Colorless green ideas sleep furiously" to demonstrate that a sentence composed of words that are very unlikely to follow one another can still form a grammatical sentence. This sentence, although odd, certainly passes our test of sounding grammatical, yet how often have we heard something green also described as colorless? How often have ideas been said to sleep? It doesn't seem that words must have been associated in our previous

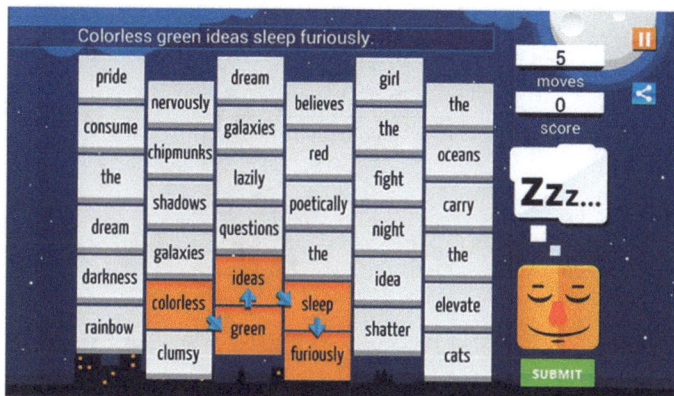

Figure 10.5. In the mobile game *Sleep Furiously*, the goal is to string together words to form grammatical sentences, even if they don't make any sense. In the figure, you could form "The girl believes galaxies nervously dream" but not "The right idea shatter cats." (Source: Playmotion Studios.)

experience if we are to comprehend sentences. In fact, there is a mobile game that shows exactly that, appropriately called *Sleep Furiously*, in which the goal is to create grammatical sentences by stringing together a series of unrelated words (Figure 10.5).

Perhaps the grammar could specify the next part of speech instead of the next word. We're still dealing with word-chain grammars, so the next part of speech would be based on associations of the parts of speech of the words that have already appeared in the sentence. For example, we could specify that a noun will have to fill the space in the sentence about the baseball bat.

There are two problems with grammars that treat language as parts-of-speech chains. First, there are still too many possible combinations. For example, the sentence *The boy took his baseball bat and hit the* _____ could be completed by a noun (*ball*), but the next word could also be an adjective (*speeding ball*). Nevertheless, that problem does not seem insurmountable. It points to a more complicated device to generate the proper chain of words but does not indicate that developing a grammar is impossible.

But there's a deeper problem – sometimes we can't specify just the part of speech. The specific word matters, as when subject and verb must agree. We use different forms of the verb *run* for different persons: *you run*, but *he runs*, for example. To put it another way, to use the correct form of the verb *run*, we must remember whether the running is being done by you or him, so we can correctly say *run* or *runs*.

This is where grammar chains get in trouble. How far back do they reach? Suppose we want to say "You, in your new clothing, run." *Run* appears five words after *you*, so we need a grammar chain that keeps track of at least five words, to ensure that when we get to *run*, the chain knows that we were talking about *you*, and so the form should be *run*. But five links may not be enough. If our grammatical decisions were only based on the previous five links in the word chain, then we wouldn't be able to write or speak the sentence you are now reading. Fifteen words separate *we* and *our* in the previous sentence. Once you say *our*, you must say *we* (rather than *my*) for the sentence to be grammatical. If we successfully keep track of this matching, word chains must be at least sixteen words long. There's nothing inherently wrong with a long word chain, but there's no grammatical limit to the number of words we might insert between *you* and *run*. So, in principle, word chains might need to be infinitely long.

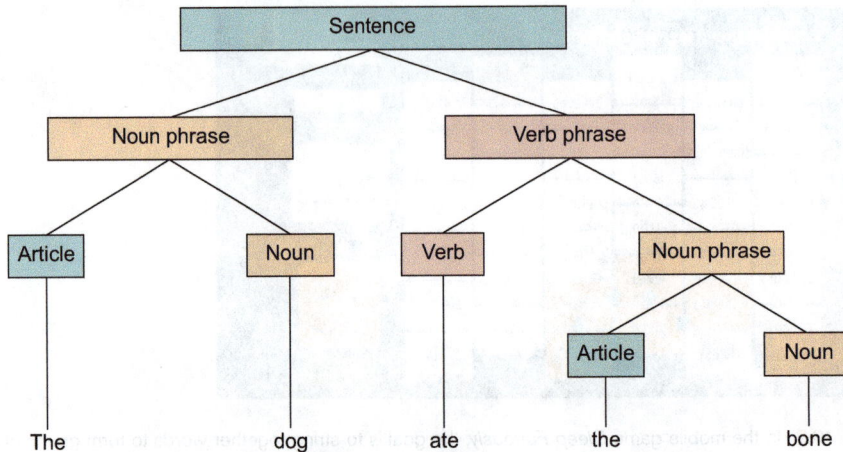

Figure 10.6. A sample phrase structure for the sentence *The dog ate the bone*.

Chomsky pointed out another aspect of this problem: Languages have dependencies that can not only span many words but be embedded within one another. For example, you can start with an *either–or* clause, say, *Either Carole or Nicola will go*, and then embed another *either–or* clause, forming *Either Carole or Nicola will go, or Trisha and Karen will go*. The options for embedding are endless, and each way in which these dependencies might be embedded requires a different mechanism within a word-chaining device. We could generate an infinite number of such embedded sentences, but an infinitely complex word-chain generator is not an option. If you have to keep looping and tying the chain, maybe a "chain" isn't the best or simplest way of understanding it.

CHOMSKY'S RESPONSE: PHRASE-STRUCTURE GRAMMARS   The solution is to abandon linear chains and switch to a grammar that represents sentences as hierarchies. In particular, psychologists have turned to **phrase-structure grammars** in which each node of the hierarchy is a phrase (see Figure 10.6). Grammar is not a chain but a tree.

The advantage of phrase-structure grammar is that it specifies a limited number of sentence parts and a limited number of ways in which these sentence parts can be combined. Nevertheless, the system offers great flexibility in creating sentences. Here is a partial list of sentence parts:

> sentence = noun phrase + verb phrase
> verb phrase = verb + noun phrase
> noun phrase = noun
> noun phrase = adjective + noun
> noun phrase = article + noun
> verb = auxiliary + verb

Note one way in which we have greatly simplified our grammar: *Noun phrase* has been defined just once, but it appears within other phrases. Thus, a noun phrase is part of a sentence, and it is also part of a verb phrase (as shown in Figure 10.6). A word-chain grammar would have needed to duplicate the machinery of generating noun phrases for the two different functions they serve. In a phrase-structure grammar, phrases are treated as interchangeable parts, and phrases can be joined into the hierarchies representing sentences as needed.

Phrase structures can handily account for the embedding problem that arises when forms such as *either . . . or* are used. We can define phrases like this:

sentence = noun phrase + verb phrase
sentence = *either* sentence *or* sentence
sentence = sentence *and* sentence
sentence = *if* sentence *then* sentence

This definition allows **recursion**. In this context, recursion means a symbol has the same symbol embedded within it as part of its definition; for example, "sentence" may be part of the definition of another "sentence."

Thus, by defining a limited number of phrases and a limited number of ways in which they can be combined, but allowing these parts to be interchangeable and to be embedded within one another, we end up with a very powerful grammar.

An important feature of phrase-structure grammars may initially sound like a failing, but it is actually a virtue: Some sentences can be described by more than one phrase structure. Which phrase structure is correct? Well, neither. A sentence can be ambiguous, and the different phrase structures reflect that ambiguity. Groucho Marx provides this example: "One morning I shot an elephant in my pajamas." The interpretation that first occurs to us is that Marx is in his pajamas, sneaking up on an elephant. But two possible phrase structures are consistent with this sentence; the difference between them is shown in Figure 10.7.

The phrase structure that most listeners derive is that *in my pajamas* modifies the verb *shot* so that it describes where the subject was when he completed the action. But when Groucho next says "How he got in my pajamas, I don't know," he is suggesting that *in my pajamas* instead describes the location of the object *an elephant*, which was mysteriously able to sneak into the pajamas. Both interpretations are grammatical, but other concerns nudge us toward one interpretation (i.e., background knowledge about elephants and pajamas). Such a sentence would be more ambiguous with slightly different nouns but equivalent phrase structure: *One morning I woke my brother in my pajamas.* We'll describe more about the role of background knowledge in language processing in the next chapter.

Such ambiguity is possible even in very brief sentences. A church sign that says "We love hurting people" was obviously written to mean the hurting as part of a noun phrase (*hurting people*) and not a verb phrase (*we love hurting*).

As a novel type of mental representation, phrase structures are a useful way of describing several key properties of language mentioned earlier in the chapter. First, and more obviously, phrase structures are structured. They are like LEGO pieces that can fit into each other to form larger structures. This flexibility is critical to capturing the generativity of language. In addition to flexibility, language calls for a representation that can capture complex meaning. Concepts, as we discussed in Chapter 9, are limited representations, because they do not describe *relationships* among ideas. Such relationships are obviously crucial to meaning. We need not only know what dogs are generally like (for example) but that a dog can take action (e.g., jump or fly) or be acted upon (scolded, fed) or have properties (be brown, be large). And that characteristic of phrase structures raises still another of their useful properties: Yes, we want to be able to represent *a large dog, recently scolded, that is now flying*, but we don't want to think those properties (large, scolded, flying) to be permanently associated with our concept of "dogginess." We need a representation that is flexible, and capable of capturing complexity, but is also disposable. We want to use it, and then junk it, with no aftereffects. That's how phrase structures work.

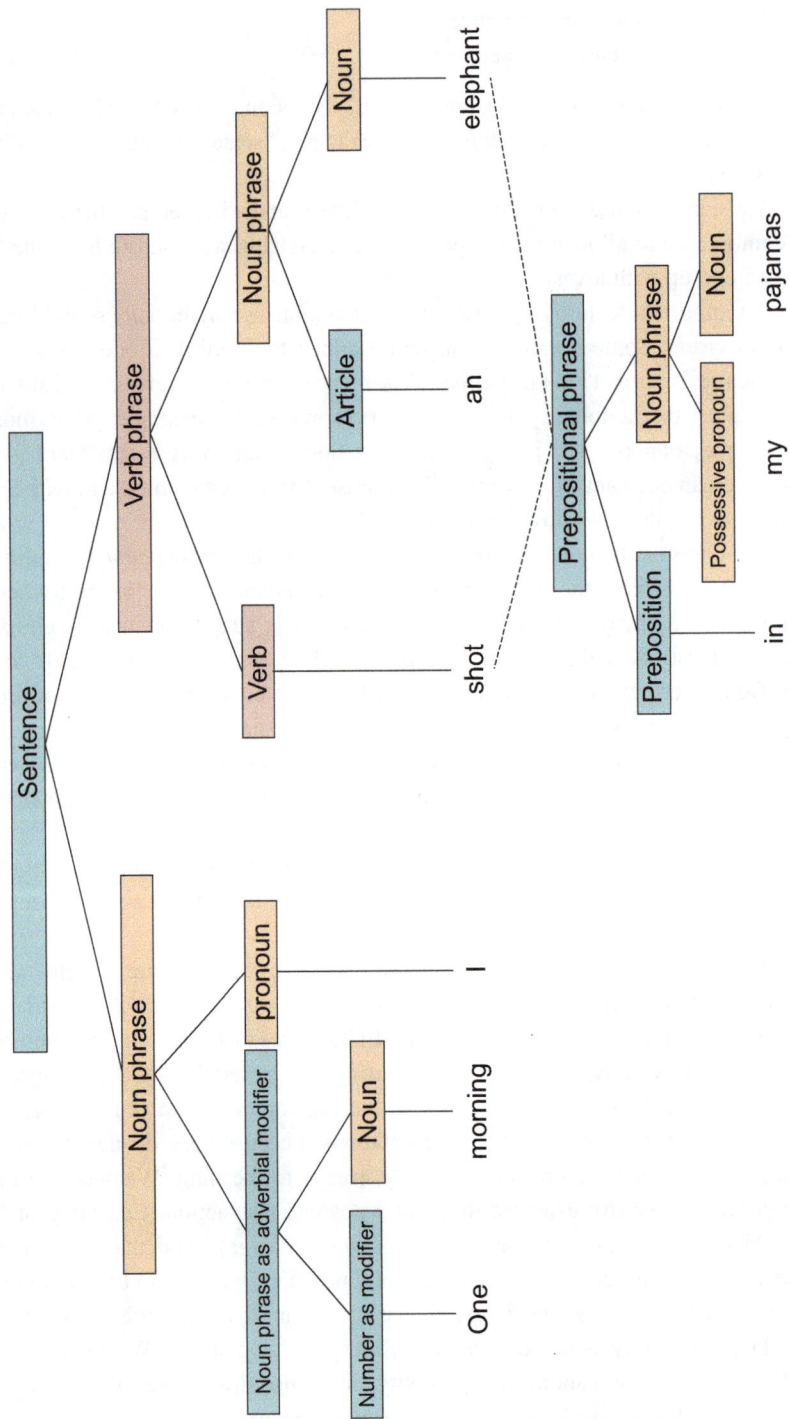

Figure 10.7. Two possible interpretations of the sentence *One morning I shot an elephant in my pajamas.*

As helpful as phrase-structure grammars are, they obviously are not a complete account of how we interpret language. Consider these two sentences:

The professor is a terrific teacher.
The professor is a terrible teacher.

The phrase structures of these two sentences are the same, so phrase structures are obviously not capturing the important difference between them. Now consider these two sentences:

The professor's antics stunned the class.
The class was stunned by the professor's antics.

The phrase structures of these two sentences are quite different, but they nevertheless communicate the same idea. So we've seen that the same order of words can yield different phrase structures (and meaning), and now we see that different orders of words, and even words in a different language, using a different grammar, all yield the same meaning.

To capture these phenomena, Chomsky argued for two different levels of representation. One is **deep structure**, which corresponds to the meaning of a sentence. Chomsky argued that this level of language representation has meaning independent of the specific sentence used to convey it. We can take the deep structure of a sentence, apply transformations to it, and obtain a different phrase-structure hierarchy called the **surface structure**, which yields the order in which words will be uttered. Similarly, when we read or hear a surface structure, we try to ascertain the deep structure that corresponds to this surface structure, much as in vision we want to know what set of surfaces in the world corresponds to the pattern of light that strikes our eyes.

REVIEW AND CURRENT CONSENSUS   Let's pause and review Chomsky's claims so far. First, there is a difference between competence (our knowledge of grammar) and performance (how we express language). As we peer through performance to investigate competence, we find that we construct grammar not as a chain but more like a tree. The difference between competence and performance also suggests two levels of language: surface structure dictated by a language's rules and deep structure of meaning, independent of which language is spoken. While some might reframe the differences between these levels as between internal thought and outward expression, or between conceptual representation and communication, these multiple levels of language are generally accepted as useful ways of thinking about language.

More controversial are Chomsky's claims about the nature and origin of deep structure. Chomsky makes three claims: (1) Deep structure is organized by rules that govern grammars in all languages; (2) only humans use these universal grammatical rules; and (3) universal grammar need not be learned by individuals, because it evolved to be innate. In other words, we are born with brains that are specialized for language and that contain a universal grammar which prepares us to learn any human language.

The claims about universal grammar and the innateness of our language instinct remain controversial (Dąbrowska, 2015; Evans & Levinson, 2009). Recent findings from the neuroscience of language have undermined the idea that language is supported by a special module of the mind and brain; that, in turn, undermines the idea that there might be an anatomic location for Chomsky's universal grammar. Language does not seem to rely on specialized neural resources (Bornkessel-Schlesewsky et al., 2015; Tremblay & Dick, 2016) and may have considerable overlap with other cognitive processes (Poeppel, 2014). We'll address Chomsky's second claim (human uniqueness) in the next section.

This section has described how language is structured. You'll note that we devoted much more time to definitions, to describing what something *is*, than we did in other chapters. That's true in part because language is so complex that the definition is bound to be complex. But the effort will prove worthwhile, because understanding the structure of language helps psychologists know what cognitive theories of language must explain. For example, we know that for comprehension of a given sentence to occur in the mind of a listener, that listener must not only hear and correctly classify the phonemes (or recognize the letters and what phonemes they indicate) but also derive the correct phrase structure of that sentence.

We will not move directly to the question of comprehension, however. Our lengthy description of language shows that it is important to consider how it relates to other cognitive processes and how language develops, a topic we haven't considered as deeply in earlier chapters. Our next section considers how language is special.

Stand-on-One-Foot Questions

10.1.   What is language?
10.2.   What's the difference between competence and performance?
10.3.   What is wrong with word-chain grammars?

Questions That Require Two Feet

10.4.   We've argued here that structure is important in language, but it seems that sometimes structure is not so important. For example, if a child were to say to you, "You, me, cookie, go now, hurry," you would know what the child meant, even though this is not a grammatical utterance. How is that possible?
10.5.   If the relationship between sound and meaning is arbitrary (as definitions of language claim), where do words come from? Are they random?

Is Language Special?

Preview

Language has three properties that seem to make it different from other cognitive processes. It is special because despite its complexity, humans seem to learn language with no explicit instruction, although they must be exposed to the language within a critical period of childhood. Language is also special because humans are the only species with this capability. Careful inspection of the data on efforts to teach language to nonhuman primates shows that they may acquire some rudiments of language, but what they learn misses key aspects of the definition of language set out early in this chapter. Language is also special because it influences other cognitive processes. The particular language that you know makes some concepts easy to express and other concepts difficult to express, and this has a subtle, but real, effect on how you think.

The question posed at the beginning of this section is easily answered: Yes, language is special. In this section, we discuss three ways in which language is special. First, it is developmentally special because humans are primed to learn it. Despite the incredible complexity of language, all typically developing humans learn language without explicit instruction but merely through exposure. Second, it is uniquely human. We are the only species to use language. Third, the particular language that one knows influences other cognitive processes. People who know different languages think a little bit differently.

Is Language Developmentally Special?

When we say that language is developmentally special, we mean that children learn language differently than they learn other skills, such as how to solve math problems. There is fairly strong evidence that our brains are prepared to learn language, and will do so with relatively little prompting.

Some of the evidence that supports this point of view is the consistency of language learning around the world. All children go through the same steps of language learning in the same order. The first stage is **cooing**: The baby makes long, drawn-out vowel sounds ("oooooooh") or consonant–vowel combinations ("gaaaaah") (see Figure 10.8). Cooing begins at the age of one or two months. Cooing includes all phones (components of phonemes) but is composed mostly of vowel sounds. During this stage, children can hear the difference between all phonemes, not just those in their native language. By the age of one year, however, they'll no longer be able to discriminate phonemes that are not used in their language (Kuhl, 1991; for a review, see Jusczyk, 1997).

The second stage is **babbling**, which begins between six and ten months. Babbling includes more consonant–vowel combinations and repetitions (e.g., "dadadada"). Babbling contains primarily the phonemes of the language that the child hears but also includes some phonemes from the other languages (de Boysson-Bardies, 1999). With continued exposure, babbling increasingly takes the rhythms and intonations of the home language. The rhythms and stress of speech, collectively called **prosody**, has a pattern within a language. You can almost imagine it as English having a different melody than Japanese. Even before their first words, babies can recognize and produce the prosody of their native language, beginning to "sing" in the language they have been hearing (Bijeljac-Babic et al., 1993).

Figure 10.8. These three-month-old babies are cooing, making long, drawn-out vowel sounds by opening their mouths.

The first word usually appears between ten and fifteen months. By eighteen months, the child's vocabulary will be about fifty words and will mostly include names of frequently encountered objects. The child will use a single word for many purposes. For example, "juice" may be a request ("I want more juice"), a comment ("There's the juice"), or a lament ("I just spilled all my juice!"). Vocabulary is learned at a remarkably fast rate. Between the age of eighteen months and first grade, children learn about five to ten new words *every day* (Carey & Bartlett, 1978).

Much vocabulary learning occurs through observation, rather than through explicit instruction. This principle is illustrated in a classic study by Susan Carey and Elsa Bartlett (1978). During a preschool class, the experimenter asked the child to "bring me the chromium tray, not the red one." Although the word *chromium* was novel to all children, they did not protest and ask for a definition. Two trays were in plain view and one was red, so the child made the simple deduction that *chromium* must be the color of the other tray. Furthermore, after this single exposure to the word, one week later, about half the children were able to pick a *chromium* color chip from several choices.

Most word learning is not quite as straightforward as this choice between two trays; the referent of the word is usually less clear. Yu and Smith and colleagues show that both adults and infants can learn vocabulary using statistical regularities across multiple situations (Smith & Yu, 2008; Suanda et al., 2014; Yu & Smith, 2007). That's important because it's usually much less obvious the object or property or action of a new word like *chromium*. For example, suppose the child hears the word *blicket* in the presence of two unfamiliar objects – say, a garlic peeler and a wire whisk. The child can't know which is the blicket. But if, sometime later, the child sees a garlic peeler and a protractor and hears the word *blicket*, she knows it must be the garlic peeler. Children are quite good at keeping what amounts to a mental spreadsheet of words they hear and things in the environment, which allows them to make the same sort of deduction as in the chromium situation.

By the end of the second year, the child has begun to use two-word combinations: *more juice*, *daddy go*, *my train*. Children consistently omit auxiliary verbs, prepositions, and articles. Speech in this phase is often called telegraphic; telegram companies charged by the word, so people used the fewest possible words that would still convey meaning. Children's speech in this early phase is quite efficient, perhaps reflecting their urgent needs filtered through their limited grammatical knowledge.

There is no three-word stage of language production – children go straight from two-word combinations to sentences. To get from two words to sentences, children need to learn how the grammar of their native language operates. But it is not until age four or so that sentence structure is really consistent. Children's flexibility and sophistication in using grammar continues to grow until about age ten.

Remember, we're highlighting these language-learning stages because children learning different languages in different cultures go through these same stages in the same order. That's taken as some evidence that language learning is supported by biology; it's part of the genetic inheritance of each human to come into the world prepared to learn language.

In addition to learning language in the same stages, children also tend to make the same sorts of errors in learning language. One such error is **overextension**. Children want to talk about more than their limited vocabulary allows them to express, so they apply the few words they have to all the things they want to refer to. Any four-legged animal is a *doggie*, any liquid or body of water is *juice*, and any man on the street is called *daddy* (to the consternation of the real daddy). Another error that all children make is **overregularization**, which refers to applying linguistic rules to exception words where the rule should not be applied. For example, English plurals can usually be formed by adding -*s* to a noun, and the past tense can be formed by adding -*ed* to a verb. There are, however, exceptions. The plural of *foot* is *feet*, and the past of *go* is *went*. The interesting pattern that children show is to initially use the correct irregular form, then to go through a period of over-regularization (*foots*, *goed*), and then to return to using the correct irregular form (Ravid, 2023; for a discussion, see Pinker & Ullman, 2002).

Even more impressive is the speed with which this learning takes place. Consider that by age four, the average child has learned the rules of grammar for their language. (The knowledge is implicit, because the child can use the rules but cannot describe them.) Thousands of professors of linguistics have tried to fully describe the syntactic rules for a language but have not yet achieved it. Not only do children learn this complex system rapidly but they also do all their learning by observing examples, receiving very little corrective feedback. Parents seldom correct their child's grammatical errors; if the child says "Yesterday we goed to the park," the parent will likely respond as though the error did not exist. One reason is that kids' speech is full of errors, and parents wisely pick their battles – rather than correct grammar, parents correct truth value. If a child hits another child and says "She taked my toy and hitted me," most parents address the truth and the emotional content ("No, I saw that you hit her first. Now, say you're sorry and take turns") and ignore the grammar lesson. A second reason parents ignore grammatical errors is that they quickly learn that correction does little good. Consider this exchange between cognitive scientist Martin Braine and his daughter (Braine, 1971, p. 161):

CHILD: Want other one spoon, daddy.
FATHER: You mean, you want the other spoon?
CHILD: Yes, I want the other one spoon, please daddy.
FATHER: Can you say "the other spoon"?
CHILD: Other . . . one . . . spoon.
FATHER: Say "other."
CHILD: Other.
FATHER: "Spoon."
CHILD: Spoon.
FATHER: "Other spoon."
CHILD: Other . . . spoon. Now give me other one spoon?

You may wonder why, if learning language is supposed to be such a breeze, it is so hard to learn a second language in school. The answer is that there appears to be a critical period for learning language (Hartshorne et al., 2018; Lenneberg, 1967). You will recall from Chapter 1 that a critical period is a window of opportunity during which something can be learned effortlessly, but if the window is missed, it is learned with difficulty, if at all. Jackie Johnson and Elissa Newport (1989) conducted a classic study showing this effect for human language learning. They administered a test of English grammar to Chinese and Korean immigrants who had come to the United States at different ages between three and thirty-nine years. They had lived in the United States for between three and twenty-six years. The interesting finding was that performance on the grammar test depended (in part) on how old they were when they arrived in the US. The younger the participants were when they first started learning English, the better they knew English grammar. This effect, however, stopped at puberty; once people were age sixteen or so, their age of arrival did not predict their knowledge of English syntax. The interpretation of these data is that there is a critical period for learning language. Participants who arrived after puberty missed the critical period and were never as fluent as participants who started learning English within the critical period. The more exposure the participant had to English within the critical period, the better their proficiency would be. Other investigations have reported similar outcomes (Birdsong & Molis, 2001; DeKeyser, 2000). A recent study developed a compelling internet-based grammar quiz (http://archive.gameswithwords.org/WhichEnglish/) which was shared widely and gathered more than 660,000 participants. This large-scale study confirmed early results that ability to learn the grammar of a second language saw a drop-off at around seventeen to eighteen years old.

Some recent research has cited the variability in the apparent age that marks the end of the critical period and suggested that there's not a steep drop-off in the critical period but rather a gradual decline. Some have also questioned whether we should call it a critical period at all and instead opt for "sensitive period" or "optimal period," indicating that learning within the period confers an advantage, not an all-or-none opportunity (Birdsong, 2014; Vanhove, 2013). In addition to that complexity, other investigators have suggested that different subprocesses of language (such as the prosody of speech and the rules of syntax) may have different critical periods, or none at all (Werker & Hensch, 2015). There is no doubt that younger children learn the many cognitive tasks of language quickly and easily compared to adults, but we are still investigating the mechanisms behind this effect.

Perhaps the most dramatic evidence of the extent to which language is developmentally special comes from children who have *invented* languages. There are several reports of congenitally deaf children who were not exposed to a gestural language, such as American Sign Language, but whose caregivers instead created some signs. The children quickly created new signs for objects and had a much larger vocabulary than their caregivers. More important, the children spontaneously imposed some grammatical structure on the signs, whereas the parents did not (Feldman et al., 1978; Goldin-Meadow et al., 2005; Goldin-Meadow & Mylander, 1998; Singleton & Newport, 2004).

Even more remarkable was the case of a large group of deaf Nicaraguan children. In 1980, following a government effort to expand public education, many deaf children enrolled in public special education programs. Both children and teachers in these programs lacked exposure to a formal sign language. And yet, these children rapidly developed their own gestural system of communication, albeit initially lacking syntax. The language developed quickly, and mostly due to the influence of the younger children, the syntax was added. Linguists studying Nicaraguan Sign Language recognized this new language to be a rule-governed language on a par with other human languages. Deaf children can go beyond the linguistic input that they receive and create a sophisticated language based solely on the gestural inputs they observe. In addition, the recursion that a syntax enables develops early in new languages, such as Nicaraguan Sign Language (Kocab et al., 2023). These findings are powerful evidence indeed of some innate language capacity (Goldin-Meadow et al., 2015; Senghas & Coppola, 2001; Senghas et al., 2004; Figure 10.9).

We have reviewed data indicating several ways in which language appears to be developmentally special: Children all go through the same stages when they learn it; children all make the same types of mistakes when they learn it; children learn language with remarkable speed, an ability that diminishes sharply with age; and children can go beyond the input they receive and produce communication that is more language-like than anything they have experienced.

Is Language Particularly Human?

Several human researchers have undertaken to teach language to nonhuman primates: chimps, gorillas, and bonobos (Figure 10.10). Why? The obvious answer – that it would be cool to talk to apes – is accurate, but it is not sufficient motivation. Most researchers think these projects tell us something interesting about the cognitive capabilities of nonhuman primates. Describing the rich

Figure 10.9. Two young men using Nicaraguan Sign Language. (Source: Photograph by Susan Meiselas, copyright Magnum Photos.)

communication of nonhuman primates who share evolutionary ancestors with humans may offer clues to how the human cognitive system evolved.

Notice that this question is very different from the question "How can a human communicate with a chimp?" Teaching a chimp to make requests and to comprehend your requests is a different undertaking than teaching the chimp language. To keep the distinction clear in our minds, we can return to the definition of language that we discussed earlier in the chapter. We said that language is communicative, arbitrary, structured, generative, and dynamic. Most animal communication systems have only the first of these properties. In the wild, chimps use a series of grunts and howls to communicate specific meanings – danger from a snake, for example – but these communicative signals are not arbitrary. They are fixed in their meaning and seem to be part of the animal's genetic inheritance. The same is true of the communication systems of honeybees (which communicate about food sources), birds (whose song often signals ownership of territory), and other nonhuman animals. It is surely impressive that the waggle dance of the honeybee can indicate both the direction and the distance to pollen-rich flowers (Couvillon et al., 2014; von Frisch, 1967), but it does not qualify as language by our five criteria.

So, even if animals do not use language in the wild, are they capable of learning language given the right training? Researchers in the 1960s and 1970s successfully taught sign language to several chimpanzees by molding the chimps' hands and rewarding correct signing. It would seem that this would satisfy the criterion of arbitrariness (the gestures do not necessarily resemble their referents), but there were questions about whether chimps used these gestures mostly in imitation and via trial and error. One researcher, Herbert Terrace, acknowledged that the signing of the chimpanzee he trained, named Nim Chimpsky, did not qualify as arbitrary and was not structured or generative (Terrace et al., 1979).

Figure 10.10. Successful teaching of language to apes would offer insight into the evolution of human language. It would also allow us to ask this chimp what he's thinking. (Source: Florence Gabriel/EyeEm/Getty Images.)

Later research represented words with arbitrary pictographic symbols (Premack, 1971, 1976a, 1976b). The best-known set of symbols, invented by Sue Savage-Rumbaugh and her colleagues, is called Yerkish, named for the Yerkes primate center (Savage-Rumbaugh et al., 1983; Savage-Rumbaugh et al., 1978; Savage-Rumbaugh et al., 1980). They taught a chimp named Lana and, later, bonobos Kanzi and Panbanisha to communicate through a computer keyboard and a printed board (Figure 10.11) (Savage-Rumbaugh et al., 1998). The symbols on the keys Lana pressed were echoed on a screen, and Yerkish communication from a trainer could appear on the screen.

Bonobos likely have greater linguistic competence than chimps (Brakke & Savage-Rumbaugh, 1995, 1996), and at least one has achieved a vocabulary of several hundred words (Savage-Rumbaugh, 1986). Perhaps the most important difference is that bonobos seem to be more ready to spontaneously learn something about language. Sue Savage-Rumbaugh (1986) notes that her star pupil, Kanzi (see Figure 10.10), initially learned by watching his mother's training, not by receiving training himself. Further work has shown that bonobos can learn new words through observation (Lyn & Savage-Rumbaugh, 2000). Nevertheless, the learning is rather slow, taking between six and eighty-six exposures to comprehend a word. The average first grader knows between 8,000 and 14,000 words (Carey, 1978).

These primates had an opportunity to learn at least two aspects of language that, if mastered, would represent a remarkable achievement. The first thing they might learn is the symbolic nature of words. It would not be terribly impressive for a bonobo to learn that she is often given chocolate when she pushes a key with a particular symbol – a rat easily learns that. The question is whether Kanzi and others understand the abstract symbolic relationship between the symbol and its referent. If so, they should be able to use the symbol in many different contexts, not just to obtain the referent. This question concerns the property of language we have called arbitrariness, the notion that a word is a symbol. How can we be sure that any of the primates are really using words as symbols? When a primate is trained to execute a gesture and receives a food reward or praise for doing so, how does that differ from the bar-pressing rat?

A good test is whether the animal uses the symbol in a situation unlike the one in which it was learned. If you try a new ice cream flavor, *cassis*, you can use the word *cassis* in all sorts of situations: You can later request cassis ice cream, but you can also describe cassis, compare it to other flavors, and comment on cassis. If, instead, you've learned something in a rote manner, as an operantly conditioned response, the behavior is inflexible or is generalizable in predictable and limited ways.

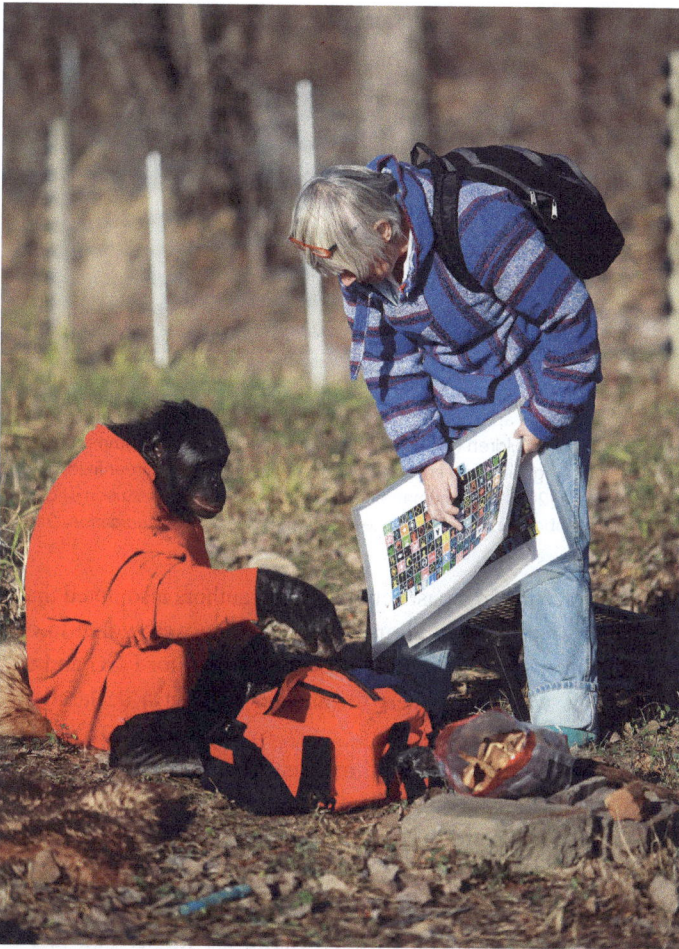

Figure 10.11. Susan Savage-Rumbaugh and Kanzi. (Source: Laurentiu Garofeanu/Barcroft USA/Barcoft Media via Getty Images.)

Primates in most language studies receive many practice trials and are drilled in the use of these signs. They come to know them well and can use them in a variety of situations. It does seem as if they can combine signs in ways that they have not been taught to do (Greenfield & Lyn, 2007; Terrace et al., 1979), indicating at least some rudimentary use of words that they have learned as symbols. However, they nevertheless speak about a fairly limited range of topics, most of which are requests for things. So, for example, the chimpanzees who have learned Yerkish can apply the pictographs outside of the context in which they have learned them, but they still use them mostly to request an object or behavior. In other words, they might request cassis candy after tasting cassis ice cream but do not seem to comment or compare.

While most chimp utterances are requests, there is some evidence that they also comment on the world around them. Heidi Lyn and colleagues (2011) analyzed archived data of 105,629 ape utterances, tallying statements and requests and comparing the ape utterances to those by two human children. While there was a clear split in that a far larger percentage of apes' utterances were requests, some were statements (see Figure 10.12). For example, when driving past a location in which one of the researchers had hidden the previous day, one of the chimpanzees put her hand over

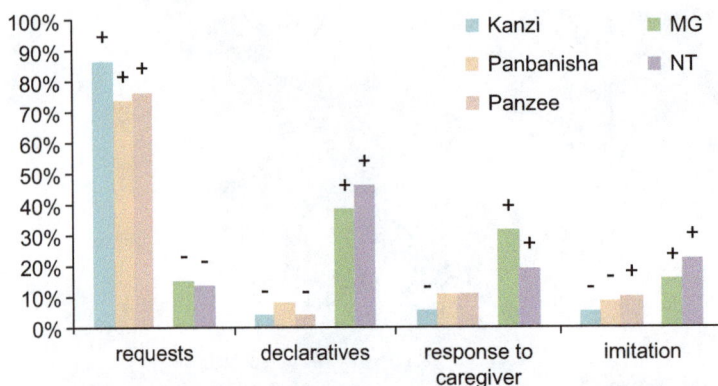

Figure 10.12. An analysis of thousands of apes' utterances from Lyn et al. (2011) found far more requests than any other type of statement, whereas human children (MG & NT) made more declaratives (comments or statements such as "that's nice doggie"), responses to caregivers, and imitations. (Source: H. Lyn, P. M. Greenfield, S. Savage-Rumbaugh, K. Gillespie-Lynch, and W. D. Hopkins [2011], Nonhuman primates do declare! A comparison of declarative symbol and gesture use in two children, two bonobos, and a chimpanzee, *Language and Communication*, 31[1], 63–74.)

her eyes in a "hide" gesture, referring to a past activity. These authors also noted that the apes would use the pictograph for their current activity to announce that they were going to change activities. For example, as Panbanisha finished her egg, she pressed the button for EGG and then moved on to another activity. Note that this wasn't a request for another egg but a declaration of a transition in activities.

What about grammar? The truth about primate grammar is that they just don't get it, except in the most rudimentary form. The best analysis of chimp grammar comes from Terrace and his colleagues' analysis of Nim's "sentences." They found that he did seem to understand some basic ideas about word order; for example, he put *more* before another word (*chocolate*, *tickle*) far more often than would be predicted by chance. However, analysis of videotapes indicated that Nim's sentences often were full or partial imitations of something his trainer had just finished saying. Finally, we must consider the mind-cracking sameness of primate utterances. Here are the top ten (in order) four-word "sentences" uttered by Nim:

> Eat drink, eat drink.
>
> Eat Nim eat Nim.
>
> Banana Nim banana Nim.
>
> Drink Nim drink Nim.
>
> Banana eat me Nim.
>
> Banana me eat banana.
>
> Banana me Nim me.
>
> Grape eat Nim eat.
>
> Nim eat Nim eat.
>
> Play me Nim play.

Nim's longest utterance, at sixteen words, was "Give orange me give eat orange me eat orange give me eat orange give me you."

Compare this to a typical morning with a human preschooler. One morning while Riener was making breakfast for his young daughter, she asked for a bowl she could not reach, and he said, "Just a minute" and proceeded to do other chores around the kitchen. Hungry and impatient, she said, "Daddy, I want a bowl please," to which he responded, "Yes, of course, I will get that as soon as I finish putting away the dishes." She responded, "Daddy, how about this? How about you do what I tell you to do, and you *don't* do what I *don't* tell you to do?" Such a construction, referring not to bowls or single actions but to previous and future statements as well as logical relationships among classes of possible actions, is the sort of the thing that is typical in human language and absent from nonhuman primate communication.

We should comment on the ethical dimensions of studying our nearest primate relatives in captivity. Even as researchers have decided that primate communication does not meet the criteria of language, there has been change in our understanding of the ethical obligations of researchers. Beginning in 2010, the National Institutes of Health phased out its chimpanzee research program, moving the last fifty chimps used for medical research to a sanctuary (Reardon, 2015). Only two facilities (private and nonprofit) studying ape language remain, the Gorilla Foundation and the Great Ape Trust, with the focus of these organizations shifting from scientific research to animal welfare advocacy, education, and conservation (see www.Koko.org). The future of researching ape language via intensive tutoring of individuals is therefore justifiably uncertain, but what we have learned so far has deepened our understanding of both ape and human cognitive processes.

Noting that only humans have language need not be equivalent to saying that humans are smarter than other animals. As Steven Pinker (1994) eloquently pointed out, the very comparison – our language capabilities versus theirs – shows remarkable human arrogance. Why pick language as the metric by which we evaluate whether other species can match us? That's a contest humans can't lose. Chimps best humans in a computerized task requiring memory for nine locations on a screen (Inoue & Matsuzawa, 2007; see Figure 10.13). Seed-caching birds such as corvids can remember thousands of locations in which they've hidden seeds. Honeybees can perceive ultraviolet light, which humans cannot. Each species has abilities and failings. The claim that we should compare our linguistic abilities with those of apes to evaluate their worth is scientifically empty. (For a readable and thought-provoking article on these points, see Povinelli and Bering [2002].)

The final word on nonhuman primate language is this: It is communicative, and some apes are capable of recognizing and using its arbitrary symbolism, even if they don't frequently make use of this capacity. It is as if they have a few basic ingredients to make language, but these basic ingredients don't combine to exploit the infinite possibilities of human language. An analog can be seen in a recent study that found that capuchin monkeys deliberately break stones to lick the mineral dust inside the quartz. In so doing, they unintentionally produce sharp-edged flakes that resemble stone tools that early humans made on purpose (Proffitt et al., 2016). The capuchins, however, do not use them as tools, much as the chimpanzees do not use the arbitrary and symbolic nature of language to dramatically expand their communicative capabilities. And even were they to try, they would still be limited by their difficulty in understanding grammar.

Does Language Shape Thought?

To this point, we have focused on language as an independent system. We have treated it as though it were disconnected from the other cognitive processes like memory, problem-solving, reasoning, and so on. Obviously, language allows the expression of the output of other cognitive processes. We use language to describe what we see, what we remember, what we have decided. In this section, we ask whether language not only expresses thought but shapes it. Does the language that we know affect the thoughts that we can have and not just report the thoughts that we do have?

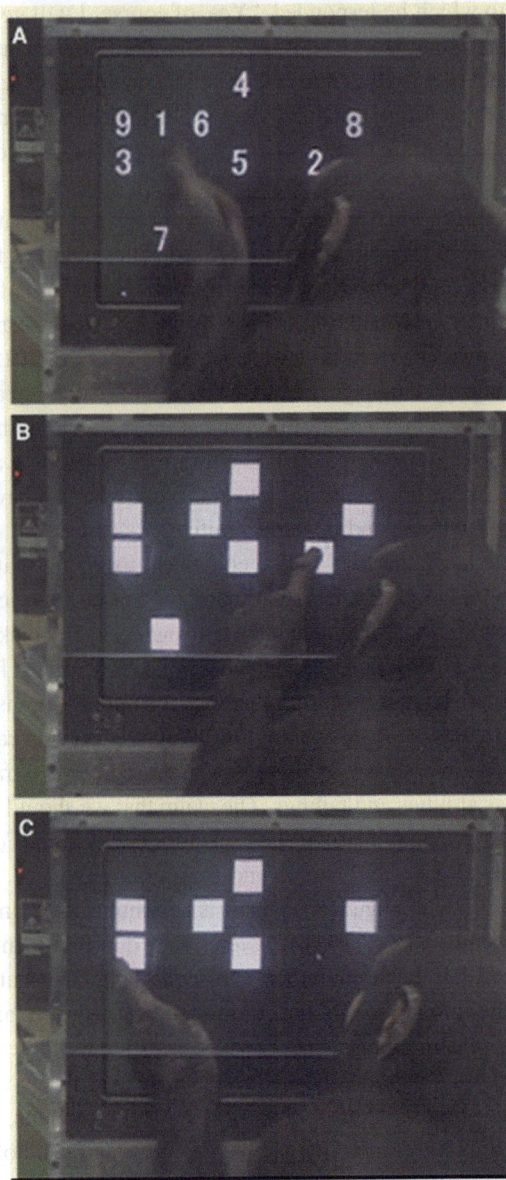

Figure 10.13. The viewer touches a white circle (not shown), then nine numbers are displayed in different positions; they are then quickly replaced with white boxes. The viewer must then touch the boxes in the order of the numbers. Some chimps seem to be remarkably better at this task than humans. (Source: S. Inoue and T. Matsuzawa [2007], Working memory of numerals in chimpanzees, *Current Biology*, 17[23], R1004–R1005.)

It's easy to appreciate that languages use different sounds in spoken expression. Less obvious is that languages make it easy or difficult to express certain concepts, and they differ in how those concepts are structured. Do such differences mean that the speakers of these different languages think differently? The idea that language shapes thought was advanced by linguist Edward Sapir (1956):

> We see and hear and otherwise experience very largely as we do because the language habits of our community predispose certain choices of interpretation. (p. 69)

This perspective was further advanced by one of Sapir's students, a businessman and amateur linguist, Benjamin Whorf (1956). Their position became known as the **Sapir–Whorf hypothesis** or sometimes simply as the **Whorfian hypothesis**. The strongest version of the Whorfian hypothesis is that thought is so intimately tied to language that thoughts generated in one language may be impossible to express in another language. This strong position has few adherents. It is generally accepted that any language used by a community of speakers will be flexible enough and powerful enough to express the ideas that other languages can.

It may, however, be *easier* to express an idea in one language than another, and therefore easier to think about that idea. For example, in the Kiriwina language of New Guinea, the word *mokita* means "truth that everyone knows but no one speaks about." Americans surely are familiar with this concept and can express it, but it is simpler to express in Kiriwina (Hunt & Agnoli, 1991). Other evidence that we can understand concepts that lack a corresponding word comes from the dynamism of language. Before there was a word to describe them, users of social media understood that some people post intentionally inflammatory and provocative statements to sow discord. The concept was invoked enough that a word, *troll*, was repurposed for this meaning. The strong version of the hypothesis would predict that people would not understand the concept until the word existed.

The weak version of the Whorfian hypothesis is more plausible and has received more careful investigation. It states that every language favors some thought processes over others; it's not that your language makes some thoughts impossible but rather that the language you speak biases you to think in certain ways.

The initial research focused on color naming. It seemed a perfect way to take the objectively verifiable world (the physical wavelength of colors) and compare how people who spoke different languages subjectively thought about it, given that different languages divide the spectrum of wavelengths into a different number of color names. Eleanor Rosch (then E. R. Heider, 1972) examined the color memory of people who speak different languages. Most notably, she went to New Guinea and tested speakers of Dani, a language that has but two color terms: *mola* for lighter colors, such as white, yellow, and orange, and *mili* for darker colors, such as black, purple, and blue. So, if a speaker of English, when given a set of color tiles as pictured in Figure 10.14, might label them with our primary colors, a speaker of Dani would simply use the word *mili* for the left side and right edge and *mola* for the middle.

If language affects thought, then Dani speakers might have worse memory for color tiles because they use fewer language labels. Whereas English speakers might be able to remember seeing a green tile and not a blue one, both would be *mola* for a speaker of Dani.

That's the logic of the experiment, and a great deal of research in this vein has been conducted. Heider indicated that language seemed not to affect color perception or memory. Reviews of the research conducted since the 1970s (e.g., Bhatia, 2012) conclude that there probably is an effect of language on thought in this domain. It might not be huge, but it seems to be real.

But color naming may not be a very good domain in which to study the influence of language on thought. Think about how we describe spatial relationships and navigation, universal human tasks that nonetheless vary across languages and cultures. Imagine that you are giving someone directions from your room or house to the nearest library. When they walk out your door, do they take a right or a left? You know that other languages have different words for "right" or "left," but did you know that other languages also might vary in whether they use north or south (or cardinal directions) rather than relative directions? The Pormpuraawans, an Australian aboriginal community, use mostly cardinal directions for nearly everything (quick, look over your southeast shoulder!). When given a set of cards that tell a story using pictures and asked to put the pictures in order, English speakers arrange them left to right. Speakers of languages that are written right to left (such as Hebrew) are more likely to arrange those photos from right to left. The Pormpuraawans

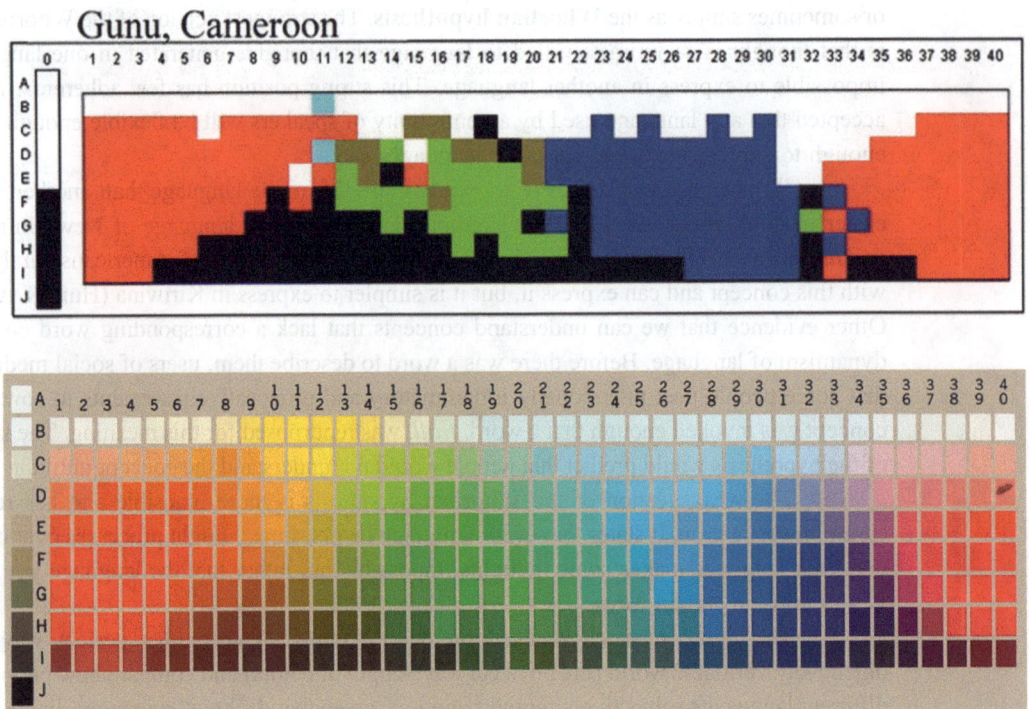

Figure 10.14. (top) A standard stimulus palette for color naming experiments. Participants will look at each tile, one at a time, and judge what name corresponds with that color. For example, most English speakers with typical color vision would report tile F1 to be "red" and tile E18 to be "green." (bottom) The results from Gunu, a language spoken in Cameroon, with four major color terms. The terms are grouped by color, so the section colored blue uses the same color term to describe the tiles. (Source: T. Regier, P. Kay, and N. Khetarpal [2007], Color naming reflects optimal partitions of color space, *Proceedings of the National Academy of Sciences of the USA*, 104[4], 1436.)

arrange them from west to east (Boroditsky & Gaby, 2010). You arrange the cards according to how you think about time unfolding. Notice how our use of words to give directions isn't just a feature of which words you use to describe directions but affects how you think about time (Boroditsky, 2018).

Studying speakers of other languages shows us how there are some universal human capacities of thought and language, such as telling and relating stories of other humans, or of giving directions for navigation or other tasks. But languages (and the cultural context in which they are spoken) also have differences that have consequences for how we think. In the case of the Pormpuraawans, their language requires a mental habit of staying oriented in terms of cardinal directions, but what about a much more common variation in languages: whether objects have a gender that speakers must use and track to refer to those objects?

Some common languages, such as Spanish and German, have grammatical gender (in Spanish, a table, or *mesa*, is grammatically female and must be referred to with a female determiner *la,* as in *la mesa*). Phillips and Boroditsky (2003) tested whether Spanish and German speakers would rate pictures of objects as more similar to people with a congruent gender, but all participants were tested in English (all participants were at least bilingual), a language that does not have grammatical gender. The similarity ratings were affected by the gender of their first language (Spanish or German) even though they were tested in another language. In a follow-up, Phillips and Boroditsky trained English monolinguals to learn a new grammatical category in a fictional language (*soupative* or *oosative*) and assign it both to objects and people (so, fork, violin, pear and all female people would be *soupative* for half the participants and *oosative* for the other half). In this study, there were no cultural associations, since all were English monolinguals and this was a novel fictional language they had never heard of. After training, when rating pictures for similarity, these English speakers also rated congruent pairs more similarly than incongruent.

There is still some debate about how much our first language influences our thought. For example, grammatical gender doesn't seem to be as influential as previous studies found (Elpers et al., 2022). However, as we noted earlier, the evidence favors the view that the habits of thought we learn in our native language do have a wider influence on how we think about things like color, time, and space.

In this chapter, we've focused on what makes language special. We've discussed its structure, then developmental evidence, cross-species evidence, and evidence from within human cognition that language is special. In Chapter 11, we'll discuss how human language actually works.

Stand-on-One-Foot Questions

10.6. What is the evidence that humans are primed to learn language?
10.7. What key features of language would you want to evaluate if you were investigating the use of language by apes? In the final analysis, can apes use language, based on these criteria?
10.8. Is some version of the Whorfian hypothesis likely to be correct?

Questions That Require Two Feet

10.9. If the strong version of the Whorfian hypothesis were correct, what would that imply about people who speak more than one language?
10.10. If there is a critical period for language, what might this fact imply about learning languages in school? What might it imply about bilingual education?

11 Language Processing

Actually, I was telling . . . I think it would be great to name the DVD after the . . . just call it whatever the new Coldplay album is. What's the name of the? . . . Oh, OK, that's what we'll name it. But it's actually called *The New Coldplay Album*.

Zach Galifianakis (from *Live at the Purple Onion*, 2006)

Saying more might push them both to a place they couldn't get back from. He would keep the rest where it belonged: in that tobacco tin buried in his chest where a red heart used to be. Its lid rusted shut.

Toni Morrison (*Beloved*, 1987)

In the last chapter we discussed the structure of language and introduced four levels of analysis. In this chapter we discuss how the process of language comprehension solves problems and resolves ambiguities. We'll first describe these problems by asking, **What makes language processing difficult?**

First, note the experience when you read a paragraph or listen to someone speak. You feel that you read or hear words, not individual letters or sounds. Of course you must differentiate individual letters – otherwise you'd mistake *dead* for *bead* – but you must do it so quickly and automatically that the process is not open to awareness.

Identifying letters to form words seems difficult enough, but how on earth do you find the right word in memory amid the clutter of the approximately 60,000 words you know – and what do you do if the word has more than one meaning, or means slightly different things depending on the context, as the word *it* does in Zach Galifianakis' bit on naming his next comedy special?

We can also note that even we retrieve the meanings of all the words, that's not enough to tell you the meaning. Consider "He would keep the rest where it belonged" from the *Beloved* passage. Interpreting those words depends critically on word order. "He belonged where the keep would rest" has an entirely different meaning, suggesting castles (a keep is the main tower of a castle or fortress).

Finally, we might consider the larger context of the paragraph. Even if you understand the sentence "He would keep the rest where it belonged," much of its meaning is lost without the context of the surrounding sentences. The rest of what? You are to understand that it refers to "saying more" in the previous sentence (i.e., "the rest" of some message, perhaps deep dark secrets), but how are you to know that? On a lighter note, why is it funny that Zach Galifianakis is proposing calling his standup special comedy DVD *The New Coldplay Album*? You'd need to know who both Galifianakis and Coldplay are but also perhaps the broader context of standup comedians, in which self-deprecation is a frequent strategy for humor. There must be some process by which successive sentences are put together into broader ideas and themes, and indeed this process is so successful that you can draw new inferences from these themes.

Our analysis of the preceding passages gives you a sense of the kinds of problems the mind faces in trying to decode language. Language is full of ambiguities – phonemes are often unclear or mispronounced, words have multiple meanings, sentences can be interpreted in more than one way – so why do the speech we hear and the texts we read rarely seem ambiguous? In the second part of the chapter, we ask, **How are ambiguities resolved?** As we'll see, a key idea is the use of multiple sources of information at the same time. A word may be ambiguous in isolation, but if we recruit other sources of information – such as the sentence the word is in or the conversational context – that usually helps resolve ambiguity.

What Makes Language Processing Difficult?

Preview

We discussed four levels of language: phonemes/letters, words, sentences, and texts. It turns out that there are ambiguities at each level that make language perception difficult. Phonemes are pronounced differently, depending on the speaker and context. Letters can be tricky to recognize and difficult to map onto phonemes. Spoken words are difficult to discern because there is no break between them, and once discerned, they may have multiple meanings. Sentences are difficult to understand because even small changes in word order can have a big impact on meaning, and many sentences are syntactically ambiguous. The challenge in understanding texts is that they are usually underspecified, meaning that the speaker leaves much unsaid, assuming that the listener will make inferences to fill in the gaps.

In Chapter 10, we emphasized that language is structured hierarchically: Speech is composed of phonemes, which are combined into words, which are combined into sentences, which are combined into texts. In this chapter, we focus on how phonemes, words, sentences, and texts are processed. As we have done in other areas of cognition, we begin by considering what makes the problem difficult, then move to ways your mind solves the problem.

Figure 11.1. Regional accents. New Englanders are famous for dropping *r*, except at the beginning of a word, parodied in this meme.

Phonemes

Why is the perception of phonemes difficult? After all, there are only forty-six sounds in English. In visual perception, you might have to identify anything out in the world, but if someone utters the word *boot*, it seems you simply need to perceive the three phonemes that compose that word (*b*, *u*, *t*), string them together, and thereby hear the word. Even though people can perceive phonemes quite rapidly in accelerated speech – perhaps as many as fifty phonemes per second (Foulke & Sticht, 1969) – the problem doesn't seem like it should be that tough because there are only forty-six possible things to hear.

The first difficulty is that individual speakers produce phonemes differently, especially English speakers from different countries, or even from different regions of the same country (Figure 11.1).

Variation in phoneme pronunciation becomes still more extreme among nonnative speakers of English, who may have learned a different set of phonemes than the forty-six used in English. Despite substantial variations in how speakers produce phonemes, listeners are able to understand their speech; you have doubtless heard English spoken by native speakers of Russian, Chinese, Arabic, and so on. Nevertheless, it is true that native speakers of English make more errors in perceiving speech generated by nonnative speakers of English, and the extent to which they make errors depends on the strength of the speaker's accent (Schmid & Yeni-Komshian, 1999). Steven

Weinberger at George Mason University has organized a massive effort to collect an extensive repository of speech accents at https://accent.gmu.edu/. There are more than 300 native languages represented and thousands of speakers, each with different experience with English in terms of when they started and how long they have spoken English. Each speaker reads the same paragraph, designed to elicit all the phonemes of English:

> Please call Stella. Ask her to bring these things with her from the store: Six spoons of fresh snow peas, five thick slabs of blue cheese, and maybe a snack for her brother Bob. We also need a small plastic snake and a big toy frog for the kids. She can scoop these things into three red bags, and we will go meet her Wednesday at the train station.

Another difficulty of phoneme perception is that phoneme production varies not only between speakers but also for an individual speaker. If you had a stockpile of phonemes that you could string together like beads to form words, a phoneme would sound the same regardless of the word in which it appeared, but individual phonemes are affected by the surrounding phonemes. Read the preceding paragraph again and pay attention to how you pronounce the *th* sound in *these*, *things*, and *three*. Notice that when you say the *th* from *three*, you get ready to make that *r* sound by rounding your lips before the *th* sound. Why? Because your lips need to be rounded to properly say the upcoming *r* sound. Rounding your lips early doesn't prevent you from making the *th* sound, so you round them early. This phenomenon of making one movement in a way that anticipates future movements or is influenced by a past movement is called **coarticulation**. When you say the word *three*, you don't simply utter each phoneme in the order it appears. Because of these anticipatory movements, phoneme production is somewhat sloppy, irregular, and variable from word to word. Why is it, then, that we don't hear other people's pronunciation as sounding sloppy and irregular? We discuss the answer in the next section, on how we resolve ambiguities, but for right now, notice that we don't pronounce phonemes as a simple chain where each one is the same each time; it is more like a complicated dance, in which the previous and next motions matter to how we complete the current one.

LETTERS   When you are reading language rather than hearing it, two tasks are added to phoneme perception. First, you need to recognize each letter and distinguish it from other letters. This is a purely visual task; each letter can be considered an object to be distinguished from other objects, as we mentioned in Chapter 1. We call this visual aspect of letter recognition **orthographic processing**. Unlike many of the other ambiguities in language, letter recognition is not too difficult because there are not that many letters to distinguish. Although letters look somewhat different in various fonts, the letter "A" will have a set of critical features: among them, two diagonal lines and a horizontal line. If you have the visual acuity to distinguish the edges of the letters, you are able to identify them. (See Figure 11.2.)

Figure 11.2. A resourceful student might generate letters that can be interpreted in more than one way, resulting in test responses that can be read as either "True" or "False," but such letters are atypical, and, in fact, the effort is not very successful.

The second task for letter recognition – this one more difficult – is figuring out which phoneme is associated with a letter or set of letters. Learning these associations requires being able to consciously separate the speech sounds composing a word, to hear them individually. As we lead you to read this sentence printed on dead trees, instead of dread, you feel wonder and are pleased. Now look back at the eighteen occurrences of *e* in the previous sentence. How did you know how to pronounce each one? How about the six *ea* combinations? This problem is especially difficult in English, which employs a more complicated mapping from letters to phonemes than other languages. For example, the nonword *ghoti* could be pronounced as "fish," if you pronounce the *gh* as /f/ from *rough*, the *o* as /i/ as in *women*, and the *ti* as /sh/ as in *nation*. English is not any more difficult to learn to speak than any other language, but it is notoriously difficult to learn to spell. This is why the spelling bee is a uniquely American and British phenomenon (Maguire, 2006). So, whereas distinguishing letters from each other is pretty straightforward, determining the sounds that go with letters has plenty of ambiguity that needs to be resolved. In fact, learning that the letter "b" goes with a particular phoneme presupposes that you can *hear* that phoneme, separate from neighboring phonemes. Obviously, children can hear that *pat* and *bat* are not the same words. But being able to pinpoint and describe the difference does not come naturally to children. Hearing individual speech sounds in words must be learned. A full discussion of this learning would take us too far afield, but we note that difficulty in learning to hear individual speech sounds is the most common obstacle when children learn to read.

Words

When you hear someone speaking, you perceive discrete words with small bits of dead air between them. But that's not actually the stimulus that strikes your ears, as shown in the sound spectrogram in Figure 11.3. When people speak, they produce a continuous stream of phonemes. To convince yourself that's so, recall the sound of someone speaking a language you do not understand – it sounds continuous. In fact, there are pauses in speech, but they are relatively rare, and so researchers sometimes call speech a **speech stream** to emphasize its continuous nature. What's more, pauses are as likely to occur within words as between them.

The continuous nature of speech would seem to pose a special problem for infants learning to talk. For example, suppose a mother says to her daughter, "OK, cutie, it's time to get out of that orange bassinet." What the infant actually hears is "Okaycutieitstimetogetoutofthatorangebassinet." An adult trying to make sense of this stream of phonemes at least knows what words *could* make up a sentence. But an infant doesn't even know that *orange* and *bassinet* are units. For all the infant knows, those sounds should be segmented into three units: *or*, *angebass*, and *inet*.

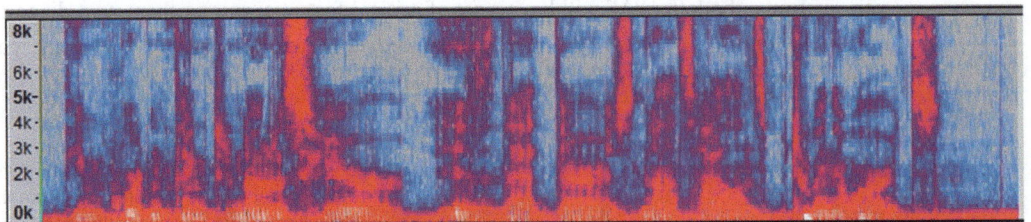

The   Importantthingtonoticehere   is   that   thereis   notsilence   betweenthewords

Figure 11.3. A sound spectrogram represents sound visually. Time is on the *x*-axis, and frequency (low to high) is on the *y*-axis. The intensity of the sound at any point on the graph is represented by the darkness of the spectrogram. The important thing to notice is that there is no silence between words.

Table 11.1 Examples of misheard song lyrics		
Misheard lyric	**Actual lyric**	**Song and artist**
Got a lot of Starbucks lovers	Got a long list of ex-lovers	Taylor Swift, "Blank Space"
'scuse me, while I kiss this guy	'scuse me, while I kiss the sky	Jimi Hendrix, "Purple Haze"
shake it like a polar bear ninja	shake it like a Polaroid picture	Outkast, "Hey Ya"

Even for adults, the segmentation of phonemes into words is subject to occasional error. A rich source of such errors is misheard song lyrics. These are called **mondegreens**, after a famous mishearing by Sylvia Wright (1954), who recalls her mother reading her favorite verse of a Scottish ballad about the tragic murder of the Earl of Moray: "They hae slain the Earl o' Moray, and Lady Mondegreen." Wright only much later learned that not only was the poor earl murdered but he was alone: There was no Lady Mondegreen; rather, they had "laid him on the green." Other examples appear in Table 11.1. Why do we seldom mishear spoken words but make more errors when words are sung? How do we usually get it right?

A final problem to consider for word perception: Even if you hear the word correctly, many words have multiple meanings. If someone says "I really like hot dogs," do they mean that they like frankfurters or that they like athletes who show off? Or (more peculiarly) really attractive canines? How do you access the correct meaning?

Writing has clear spaces between words, so we don't have the segmentation problem, but there are other ambiguities. **Homographs** are two words with identical spelling but different pronunciations and meanings, as in the sentence "Who can lead the effort to remove dangerous lead water pipes?"

A **homonym** is even more ambiguous. Two words are spelled and pronounced the same way but have different meanings. If you want to read this sentence about a basic human right the right way, you should read from left to right. The three "rights" are homonyms. Such ambiguities in written words are common. To read as fast as we do, our cognitive process of language comprehension must quickly resolve these ambiguities. By the way, in that last sentence, *read*, *fast*, and *resolve* are all homonyms. It might be a good idea to read this paragraph again, just to appreciate how much ambiguity your mind is able to almost instantaneously resolve. You could probably pick out even more homonyms than we've already noted, such as *even*, *way*, and *might*. Just because you resolve these ambiguities quickly doesn't mean they are not ambiguities; it means the mental process that resolves them operates very quickly.

Sentences

Suppose that all the problems we've discussed so far have been resolved – we've perceived phonemes and words accurately. Can we therefore understand all sentences? Unfortunately, the problems are just beginning, as you might guess from our discussion of grammars in Chapter 10. With phonemes and words, we focused on the ambiguities in the sound, but as in Chapter 10, when we move to the level of sentences and texts, we will consider mostly reading, as most studies have been conducted with written material. There is good reason to think, however, that there's considerable overlap in comprehending language that's written and language that's spoken (Bell & Perfetti, 1994; Gernsbacher, 1994).

It seems clear enough that word order contributes to sentence meaning; we might perceive six words clearly, but that won't tell us the difference *between John wished he had jumped higher* and *He wished John had jumped higher*, to say nothing of *Wish John he jumped had higher*. We would guess that word order is one determinant of how a phrase structure (discussed in Chapter 10) is assigned to a sentence.

Word order is indeed important to deriving meaning, but it's not the whole story. Consider the sentence *Time flies like an arrow*. The meaning seems unambiguous, yet there are at least five grammatically correct interpretations from this single order of words. Note that in interpretations 2 to 5, *flies* refers to a type of insect:

1. Time moves quickly, as an arrow does.
2. Assess the pace of flies as you would assess the pace of an arrow.
3. Assess the pace of flies in the same way that an arrow would assess the pace of flies.
4. A particular variety of flies (time flies) adores an arrow.
5. Assess the pace of flies, but only those that resemble an arrow.

Despite the fact that there are five possible interpretations of the sentence, few people perceive the ambiguity, and most perceive the intended meaning (interpretation 1).

Texts

One of the most notable (and most frequently studied) phenomena of text comprehension is that people make inferences when they read a text – they go beyond what the speaker or writer explicitly communicates. For example, consider the following two pairs of sentences:

> The skies darkened as the tornado touched down a few miles away. He turned to look out the window. She said "Richard, it's over." He turned to look out the window.

These examples show that the same sentence can have quite different interpretations depending on the context. The ambiguity here isn't in the phonemes, words, or sentences. "He turned to look out the window" conveys the same action in each case; what's ambiguous is *why* he looks out the window, and what that action implies for the narrative as a whole. In the first case, we assume he's looking out the window to see the tornado, to gather information about the situation and to decide what to do. In the second case, the action carries almost the opposite meaning: Looking out the window is an act of introspection or disengagement. He can't bear to look at the woman who has spoken. Understanding the second sentence requires making meaning across sentences, using what we know about storms in the first example and human interactions in the second example.

This section highlighted the complexity of language perception. In the next, we discuss how the mind unravels this complexity to arrive at meaning.

Stand-on-One-Foot Questions

11.1.   Name again the four levels at which we are analyzing language.
11.2.   For each level, name at least one ambiguity that makes language processing difficult.
11.3.   At which level is grammar, as discussed in Chapter 10, relevant?

Questions That Require Two Feet

11.4. Can you guess why song lyrics, in particular, are easily misheard? Hint: Look at the actual lyrics in Table 11.1, and imagine a friend saying them to you during a conversation.
11.5. Can you guess why "Time flies like an arrow" is seldom interpreted in any sense but the common one?

How Are Ambiguities Resolved?

Preview

Our cognitive system uses various strategies to resolve the ambiguities we've discussed. Ambiguous phonemes are identified through the use of surrounding context and by overlooking irrelevant "slop" in pronunciation. Context also helps resolve ambiguities in written letters. For spoken words, we use statistical regularities to segment the speech stream. When written, words can be read in either of two ways: through a process that directly matches spelling to the word in memory or through a process that translates the spelling into a sounwordttern, which is then matched to the word's sound in memory. Sentences are disambiguated through higher-level contextual information, which may come from the text itself or from background knowledge in long-term memory. Comprehension of texts also depends on background knowledge to make inferences and to create a mental model of the overall situation that the text describes.

We have identified some of the problems in perceiving language, many of them centering on the idea that communication at each level is ambiguous. In this section, we discuss how our minds resolve these ambiguities.

Phonemes

We said that the perception of phonemes is difficult because there is so much variability in how they are produced across speakers (because of accents) and within the same speaker (because of coarticulation). In addition, noise in the environment can make phoneme identification difficult. We overcome these difficulties using three strategies: by categorizing phonemes, by using the context surrounding the phoneme, and by including visual information.

The process of identifying phonemes is made simpler by adopting a categorical approach; phonemes are compared to distinct categorical boundaries. This **categorical perception** means that we do not perceive most slight differences in phonemes, just the differences that would put a phoneme in a different category. Recall that in Chapter 9, probability theories posited fuzzy category boundaries: Some birds are birdier than others. Phonemes, in contrast, have distinct, nonfuzzy boundaries, and we are not sensitive to variation within phonemic categories. Remember when we talked about how some birds are "more birdy" than others, like a robin is more birdy than a flamingo? The same does not hold for our perception of phonemes; one *b* sound is not "more *b*-er" than another.

Take, for example, the phonemes *b* and *p*, which are produced in a similar way: The lips are initially closed, then are opened, releasing air. When *b* is pronounced, the vocal cords vibrate simultaneously with the expulsion of air, whereas when *p* is pronounced, there is a short delay between the expulsion of air and when the vocal cords begin to vibrate. That delay (called voice onset time) is the only difference between *b* and *p*, so listeners must be alert for the length of the voice onset time. When voice onset time is very short, the phoneme sounds like *p*, and when it is long, it sounds like *b*, so we might imagine that when it is of medium length, it will sound like something between *p* and *b*. But it doesn't. Utterances are categorized as *b* or *p*, and each sounds like a perfectly good example of *b* or *p*; we never hear something as a mushy, between-*p*-and-*b* sound. Liberman et al. (1957) confirmed this by using computer-generated speech to vary voice onset time, making it longer and longer. All the sounds within the *b* category sounded like fine examples of *b*, until they were fine examples of *p*. Categorical perception makes the problem of phonemic identification easier by making it into a multiple-choice question. The answer is one of a few options, not a choice along a blurry spectrum.

Listeners also use surrounding context to disambiguate phonemes, or even to perceive phonemes that are missing altogether. In one experiment, participants heard this sentence: "The state governors met with their respective leg*latures convening in the capital city" (Warren, 1970). In the audio clip, the experimenters removed the phonemes corresponding to *is* in the word *legislatures* and replaced it with a cough. Remarkably, not only did everyone understand the sentence but almost none of the participants perceived that any part of the sentence was missing. In another experiment (Warren & Warren, 1970; see also Warren & Sherman, 1974), participants heard several sentences:

> It was found that the *eel was on the axle.
> It was found that the *eel was on the shoe.
> It was found that the *eel was on the orange.
> It was found that the *eal was on the table.

Once again, the * indicates the location in which a phoneme was replaced by a cough. Participants heard different phonemes depending on the context. In the first sentence, they heard *wheel*; in the second, they heard *heel*; in the third, they heard *peel*; and in the fourth, they heard *meal*. People were not consciously contemplating what sound was missing and then making a guess as to what they should have heard; they believed that they heard the complete word. This demonstration is all the more remarkable because the information that clarified the missing phoneme occurred four words later. This phenomenon is called the **phoneme restoration effect**: A missing phoneme is restored by the context and is never consciously identified as missing (for a review, see Samuel, 1996). As is clear from this example, as well as recent research carefully measuring the time course of recognition (Schreiber & McMurray, 2019), listeners anticipate future phonemes before identifying the current one, indicating that listeners aren't merely taking in one phoneme at a time but predicting what will come next as well as filling in past ambiguity as they hear speech sounds.

If you think about your own experience, it seems believable that participants didn't notice that one phoneme was replaced by a cough; someone might cough while you are sitting in a lecture hall listening to a speaker, and it doesn't disrupt your perception of the talk. More recent studies have continued to document our skill at hearing in noisy environments (Broussard et al., 2017).

Phoneme restoration is easy for us but hard for computers. As a result, some computer scientists (Goto et al., 2014) have suggested that our ability to restore phonemes could offer a way to distinguish real human users from bots or malicious software programs. This task (distinguishing person from bot) is often called a Completely Automated Public Turing test to tell Computers and Humans Apart, or CAPTCHA. Their program takes English sentences, obscures them while still following phonemic pronunciation rules, and asks people to report what they are. For example, a user would hear an audio version of this sentence: "Will you ans@r the te@e@h@ne?" with noise inserted where the @ signs indicate. Humans are quite good at this task, but even the best computer language recognition programs struggle, as anyone who has had to repeatedly yell at their Google Home or Siri or Alexa to get them to understand simple instructions knows.

A third source of disambiguating information comes from vision. You may have noticed that when someone's speech is difficult to understand (e.g., because of a thick accent or because they speak softly), you find yourself watching the person's mouth carefully as they talk. When Willingham was in college, he had an English professor who was very shy, and his lecturing style was to look toward the floor and mumble. Although the class was small and the auditorium was large, everyone sat in the front row and stared at his mouth, straining to catch his words.

The use of vision in the perception of speech is at the root of the **McGurk effect**, named for one of its discoverers (MacDonald & McGurk, 1978; McGurk & MacDonald, 1976). To demonstrate this effect, researchers show a videotape of someone pronouncing "ba ba ba" repeatedly. However, the soundtrack has been dubbed with someone pronouncing "ga ga ga" repeatedly. Participants perceive the person on the videotape to be saying "da da da." (Other sets of phonemes yield similar effects.) Participants fuse the two differing sources of information into a perception that best fits that auditory and visual pattern. The effect holds when the visual information is degraded (MacDonald et al., 2000), when participants try to ignore the visual information (Kerzel & Bekkering, 2000), and even for one's own speech, viewed in a mirror (Sams et al., 2005). Importantly, vision doesn't just change auditory perception into something else, as in the McGurk effect; it's been shown that your auditory perception is better when you have supporting visual information (Schwartz et al., 2004; but see Heald & Nusbaum, 2014). The COVID-19 pandemic gave us all a reminder that we use visual information to disambiguate unclear speech, as we had to distinguish what people were saying when we could not see their mouths moving. Yi et al. (2021) found that under noisy conditions, people were better at distinguishing speech when they were able to see someone's mouth, either with no face mask or with a transparent face mask, compared to disposable surgical masks (see Figure 11.4). This effect of seeing the mouth moving is over and above the physical changes in the sound itself that happens with masks (Zhou et al., 2022).

Words

When perceiving spoken language, the continuous speech stream must be separated into words. Then the sound of each word must be matched with the corresponding meaning in memory. Perception of written language, it would seem, has only one of these problems, but it adds another. On one hand, segmentation is easy, because spaces make clear which letter strings are words. But on the other hand, there's an extra step of translating the written letters into sound before the matching-to-meaning process can take place.

Figure 11.4. Different visual conditions under which people heard speech from Yi et al. (2021). People were better at distinguishing that speech when they could see someone's mouth. (Source: H. Yi, A. Pingsterhaus, and W. Song [2021], Effects of wearing face masks while using different speaking styles in noise on speech intelligibility during the COVID-19 pandemic, *Frontiers in Psychology*, 12, 682677, figure 1.)

Figure 11.5. These strange pictograms, all in a row, present a good analogy for the puzzle of separating speech stream into words. How would you discover where the word breaks are and which pictograms go together? Imagine these were four strange utterances. Where are the words?

HEARING WORDS   Let's start by considering the problem that babies initially face – the speech stream is continuous, and it's not clear how they could know when one word ends and another begins. Babies solve this problem by sensitivity to the statistical regularities of language. Suppose a mother says "Pretty baby!" The child could segment this utterance as "Pre teebay bee" or "Pre tee bay bee." When a mother leaves a child at daycare and urges the child to behave, the child who doesn't know the word "behave" might reply, "Yes, I'll be haive, I'll be very haive."

How does a baby begin to separate a stream of sounds into words? Consider this. Whenever a mother says "pretty," the sound *pre* is followed by *ty*. How often is *pre* followed by some other sound? Probably not that often. The sound *ty*, however, might be followed by lots of other sounds, as the child might hear "pretty roses" or "pretty cake" or "pretty fine golf swing." Sounds in the middle of words are likely to be followed by a limited set of sounds, but sounds at the ends of words have a wider range of sounds that might come next. Hearing *pretty* followed by many different sounds suggests that *pretty* is a unit. (See Figures 11.5 and 11.6.)

Jenny Saffran and her colleagues (1996) showed that babies are sensitive to these statistical regularities. In a fascinating experiment, they had eight-month-old infants listen to just two minutes of synthesized speech, composed of four pseudowords, randomly ordered: *tibudo, pabiku, golatu,* and *daropi*. The speech was continuous with syllables evenly spaced, so it would sound, for example, like *tibudopabikugolatudaropigolatutibudogolatu*. Note that, just as in the "pretty baby"

Figure 11.6. If you look closely, you can tell that some regular chunks reappear. The chain link only appears once, but the turtle appears four times, and each time it appears, it is followed by a dog and a moon. This suggests that turtledogmoon is a unit. If you see that some sets of icons appear together (like webcam–baby–cloud), these statistical regularities tell you where the word boundaries are. Babies are really good at this.

example, sounds at the beginning or in the middle of words (e.g., *bu*) can be followed only by one other sound (*do*), whereas sounds at the end of a word (e.g., *do*) can be followed by any of the three sounds that start a different word (*pa*, *go*, or *da*). After the babies were exposed to this speech, the researchers played several isolated sounds, half of which were one of the pseudowords (e.g., *tibudo*) and half of which were sounds that crossed word boundaries (e.g., *dopabi*). Infants showed a preference for the latter, which indicates that these sounds were novel to them (Saffran et al., 1996; see also Aslin et al., 1998; Hay & Saffran, 2012; Saffran, 2001, 2002; Wojcik & Saffran, 2015; for a review, see Saffran, 2020). It also appears that highly familiar words (e.g., the baby's own name) may play a special role in helping babies figure out word segmentation boundaries (Bortfeld et al., 2005). Other research has indicated that this ability to distinguish statistical regularities in patterns extends to pictures, indicating that it may not be specific to language (Saffran et al., 2007).

What about the perception of words in adults, who already have memory representations for words? Most researchers believe that people recognize words through a matching process in which a spoken word is compared with a mental dictionary called a **lexicon** that contains representations of all the words they know – not the meaning but the pronunciation, spelling, and part of speech for each word. The lexical entry has a pointer to another place where the meaning is stored. A sample lexical entry is as follows:

Pronunciation: blæk
Spelling: black
Part of speech: adjective
Meaning pointer: → (This directs the system to another location where the meaning is stored.)

When someone pronounces a string of phonemes, the listener compares the string with the pronunciations of the words in the lexicon. If the phoneme string matches an entry, the word has been identified, and the cognitive system has access to the other properties of the word, including the spelling, part of speech, and meaning. Of course, the matching process must be incredibly rapid to keep up with naturally occurring speech. Notice how this explanation potentially connects spoken language and written language, by matching pronunciation and spelling in the lexicon.

How does the matching process occur? Most theories propose that the first few phonemes that are perceived cause words that are consistent with that input to become active (Dell et al., 1997; Gaskell & Marslen-Wilson, 2001; Marslen-Wilson & Welsh, 1978; McClelland & Elman, 1986; for a review, see Doczi, 2019). As more phonemes are perceived, some words become inconsistent with the input and lose activation. The word representations also compete with one another, and so as one representation begins to "win," it hastens the "loss" of others. Thus, if we say a word that begins with *si*, a set of likely continuations of that phoneme becomes active in your mind (*science*? *silence*? *sight*? *siren*? *psychiatry*? *psychology*? *psychological*?). As you hear the next phoneme, *si–kol*, the words that don't match drop out (*science*, *silence*, etc.), and the remaining candidates (*psychology*, *psychological*, *cycle*) gain activation.

Marslen-Wilson (1987) described evidence that when you hear the beginning of a word, multiple candidate words in the lexicon are active. For example, suppose you heard the phonemes corresponding to the letters "capt." Both *captive* and *captain* ought to be activated in the lexicon. But if you heard the whole word *captain*, then clearly only the lexical entry *captain* should be active. To test this possibility, Marslen-Wilson had participants listen to words and simultaneously perform the visual lexical decision task. In a **lexical decision** task (introduced in Chapter 6), a letter string appears on a computer screen, and the participant must say whether it is a word. Lexical decision tasks are open to semantic priming (also discussed in Chapter 6). If you have recently been thinking about a related word, then the lexical decision is made more quickly. Thus, if you've just heard the word *captain*, you would be a little faster in affirming that the printed letter string "SHIP" is a word, compared to making that decision for a word unrelated to *captain* (e.g., "SHELL"). Now here's the prediction, which is a little tricky. Suppose a word for the lexical decision task appears on the screen in the middle of the spoken word, so that all you've heard so far is "capt." The prediction is that both *captain* and *captive* would be active in the lexicon, so you should be fast in responding on the lexical decision task to words related to either one (e.g., "SHIP" or "GUARD"). But if the word appears on the screen a little later, after the whole word is spoken (say, *captain*), you'll only respond quickly to "SHIP." Those results were exactly what was observed.

As described earlier, researchers have used lexical decision tasks to investigate the timing of how semantic priming makes some words active in our mental lexicon. More recently, researchers have used the lexical decision task to investigate how other aspects of words might affect the mental process of accessing the lexicon. For example, does the imageability and concreteness or abstractness of a word lead to faster lexical access? Interestingly enough, whereas **concrete words** are easier to remember, **abstract words** are easier to recognize as words, as they become more easily active in the lexicon (Khanna & Cortese, 2021).

READING WORDS   All the findings we have discussed thus far have concerned the comprehension of spoken words. What about reading? **Dual route models of reading** contend that there are two mechanisms (Baron & Strawson, 1976; Behrmann & Bub, 1992; Coltheart et al., 1993; Forster & Chambers, 1973; Paap & Noel, 1991; for a review, see Coltheart, 2014; for an approach to reading that is not dual route, see Seidenberg, 2017). One route simply matches the written word to the spelling entries in the lexicon. Once you have accessed the lexical entry, that contains a pointer to the meaning. The second route uses a translation procedure that converts the written letters to a sound and then matches the sound to the auditory entry in the lexicon; after the written input has been converted to sound, recognizing the written word is similar to recognizing a spoken word.

This dual route model neatly accounts for several findings that are otherwise difficult to accommodate. You can read aloud words like *slint* or *papperine*, if you so desire. How? These aren't real words, so you have no lexical entry for them. This ability seems to require postulating that readers not only have a mental dictionary matching known word pronunciations with spelling, but in addition know a set of rules that convert letters and groups of letters into phonemes – call them letter-to-phoneme rules. This set of rules cannot completely account for reading, however, because you can also read exception words, such as *colonel* and *pint*, whose pronunciation is not in line with the letter-to-phoneme rules. The dual route model proposes that these words are not handled by the letter-to-phoneme translation process. If they were, you would pronounce *colonel* as *kahlownell* and *pint* would rhyme with *hint*. Instead, you use the spelling of these words to establish that they are in the lexicon.

Thus, the dual route model can easily account for our ability to read nonwords, such as *slint*, which uses the letter-to-phoneme route; irregular words, such as *pint*, which uses the spelling-lookup route; and regular words, such as *cake*, which might use either route. But do we really need two routes? Can we find more compelling evidence that these routes are truly separate?

One form of evidence comes from different types of dyslexia. You are probably aware that dyslexia is a problem in reading. You may not know that there are several distinct forms of dyslexia (Friedmann & Coltheart, 2016). **Acquired dyslexia** is caused by brain damage (as from a stroke or removal of a brain tumor) in people who were able to read before the injury. There are two types of acquired dyslexia. In **surface dyslexia**, the reading of nonwords (and regular words) is preserved, but the patient has difficulty reading irregular words. Hence, the patient could read *nurse* or *glebe* but might read *glove* as rhyming with *cove* and *flood* as rhyming with *mood* (Marshall & Newcombe, 1973). An extreme case of this disorder, patient K.T. (McCarthy & Warrington, 1986), could read irregular words correctly only about 47 percent of the time, even if they were quite common, but could read regular words accurately 100 percent of the time. The clear interpretation within the dual route model is that the letter-to-phoneme rules are intact in this patient, but there is selective damage to the spelling-lookup route.

An altogether different type of dyslexia is observed in other patients who have selective difficulty in reading nonwords. They can correctly read irregular words, such as *yacht*, and regular words, such as *cup*, but they cannot read nonwords. This pattern of reading abilities is called **phonological dyslexia** (Beauvois & Derouesne, 1979). One extremely impaired patient could read regular words correctly with 90 percent accuracy even when they were long (e.g., *satirical*), but he could not read even simple nonwords, such as *nust*, aloud. Even more incredibly, the patient could name individual letters successfully, but he could not say which sound they made, although he could repeat the sound if he heard it (Funnell, 1983).

The dual route model is also consistent with brain imaging data. A meta-analysis of thirty-five brain imaging studies showed that there are indeed two separate pathways associated with reading. The letter-to-sound translation route is associated with activation of the left superior temporal lobe, which is closely associated with processing sound. The direct-lookup route is associated with activation more toward the back of the brain, at the junction of the occipital and temporal lobes in the left hemisphere (sometimes referred to as the visual word form area), and with areas associated with meaning, such as the **lateral** and anterior parts of the temporal lobe (Jobard et al., 2003; Ripamonti et al., 2014; Visser et al., 2010; see also Price & Mechelli, 2005).

The dual route model also accounts for some patterns of data in typical adult readers. For example, suppose we gave you a lexical decision task in which you must say whether a letter string forms a word; for example, you might see *wolt* or *beep*. Now suppose you saw the word *koat* or *phocks*. Both have pronunciations that match real words (*coat* and *fox*), but they are not words. What would the dual route model predict about reading such words? Response times to these nonwords should be slower than they are for nonwords whose pronunciation does not match real words, because the two routes will conflict as to the correct answer. The letters-to-phonemes route identifies the sound pattern as matching a word in the lexicon, whereas the spelling-lookup route does not identify a word in the lexicon with this spelling. This expected pattern of response times has been verified (Rubenstein et al., 1971).

If the process of looking up meanings in the lexicon is driven by how the words sound, how can we address the ambiguity presented by homonyms (words with the same sound but different meanings)? Perhaps in these cases, access to the lexicon is biased by the context of the sentence. For example, consider these three sentences, each ending with the word *spring*:

> This has been a cold and rainy spring.
> This is a broken and rusty old spring.
> This really is not a very good spring.

The word *spring* is ambiguous, but the first two sentences provide a biasing context for which meaning is appropriate. If you read or heard these sentences, you would likely be aware only of the appropriate meaning. Does that mean that only that meaning is accessed from the lexicon? Are both meanings accessed in the third sentence, where the meaning of *spring* remains ambiguous?

Greg Simpson and Merilee Krueger (1991; see also Tabossi & Zardon, 1993; Vu et al., 2003) had participants read sentences like these aloud. As they read the last word, another appeared on the screen, and they were to read it aloud as quickly as possible. The final word could be related to one meaning (e.g., *season*) or the other (e.g., *coil*), or it could be unrelated (e.g., *cow*). It should be easier to read a word if a semantically related meaning is active in the lexicon. The unrelated word provides a baseline for how quickly each participant can read words. If the biasing context affects lexical access, then people should be faster at reading words related to the meaning of *spring* that the sentence biases.

That's what the results showed: Context affects lexical access. When the biasing context matched the final word, participants were faster in reading it (compared with their time in reading the completely unrelated word). If the biasing context did not match the final word, there was no advantage in reading time and therefore presumably no lexical access for that meaning of the word. The delay between the end of the sentence (when the lexicon would be accessed for the homophone) and the presentation of the word had no effect on the pattern of results.

The context of the sentence affects which word we predict will come next, either facilitating or delaying lexical access. Other factors also affect our processing of words, such as the overall frequency of the words. Common words are read easily (Preston, 1935; see the review in Divjak, 2019). Words that appear infrequently in the language, such as *egregious* or *farrago*, are processed more slowly than common words like *the* or *and* or *thing*. But as should be clear by now, reading words isn't a simple "what word is going to come next, based on how common words are in general" process. Word frequency matters: Rare words used only in restricted contexts can be easier to predict (and therefore to read) in those contexts (Caldwell-Harris, 2021). A word that has high **contextual diversity** (is used in a wide variety of contexts), such as *dog*, is used as a noun, as a verb, and in a variety of contexts, whereas a word like *ostrich* has low contextual diversity (or contextual distinctiveness), and a word like *amok* is used only in "run amok" (Brysbaert et al., 2018).

Since such contextual diversity depends on our own knowledge of different contexts, we also reduce ambiguity in word processing through our domain knowledge. Just as we learned that background knowledge can reduce the amount of information you need to keep in working memory, the working memory processes associated with reading and understanding spoken language are facilitated by background knowledge. A recent study (Troyer et al., 2020) used fine-grained EEG data as participants in the study read trivia questions related to the Harry Potter books. They found that readers with high knowledge of the Wizarding World had faster processing during reading.

So what is the final word on word processing? In sum, think of your mental process of reading words as putting pieces into a puzzle, but instead of simply using one strategy (find this shape, or find this color, or find this pattern, or find this object), we use many strategies and clues together to reduce ambiguity and decide what word we are seeing and how it fits. We've given you an account of some of the complexity of this process and some of the cues that are used to reduce ambiguity (for a review on reducing ambiguity in word meaning, see Rodd, 2020). Now we'll zoom out a bit to see how we fit words together into coherent sentences.

The models we've been talking about here seem very dependent on the specific word forms for reading. How do they square with your ability to read the following paragraph?

Aoccdrnig to a rscheearch at Cmahrigde Uinervtisy, it deoword mttaer in waht oredworde ltteers in a wrod are, the owordiprmoetnt tihng is taht the frist and lsat ltteer be at the rghit pclae. The rset can bwordoatl mses and you canwordll raed it wouthit porbelm. Tihs is bcuseae the huamn mnid deos not rwordervey lteter by istlef, but the wrod as a wlohe.

It turns out that this work was not done at Cambridge University, and even though surprising, the purported reason – that we read words as a whole – is inaccurate. For example, the sentence "A goln-snaitndg gaol of hmaun irqenuy is to uaerndntsd oeuvlress" is probably harder to read. ("A long-standing goal of human enquiry is to understand ourselves.") The preceding paragraph is easy to read for a few reasons. First, words of two or three letters aren't changed at all, and these short words tend to be function words like *of*, *for*, *be*, *and*, and *the*, which provide clues to parts of speech and grammatical structure. Also, some of the words have the same sound when scrambled (e.g., huamn), so the reading route that depends on sound could decode them. Matt Davis (who is actually at Cambridge University) has posted an interesting analysis of this phenomenon on the web (Davis, 2003; www.mrc-cbu.cam.ac.uk/~mattd/Cmabrigde/; see also Grainger & Whitney, 2004).

Sentences

Most of the research on sentence comprehension treats the cognitive processes for written and spoken language as pretty much interchangeable. Once we identify words, the problems to be solved in comprehending the meaning of sentences are mostly the same, independent of whether language is written or spoken.

We said earlier that sentences are represented in terms of phrase structures as you're first seeking to make meaning. Thus, much of the debate centers on how listeners take the word-by-word input of speech and build the appropriate hierarchical phrase-structure representation for each sentence. Let us call the psychological mechanism that derives phrase structures from sentences the **sentence parser**. The question for cognitive psychology is how the sentence parser works.

(a)   (b)

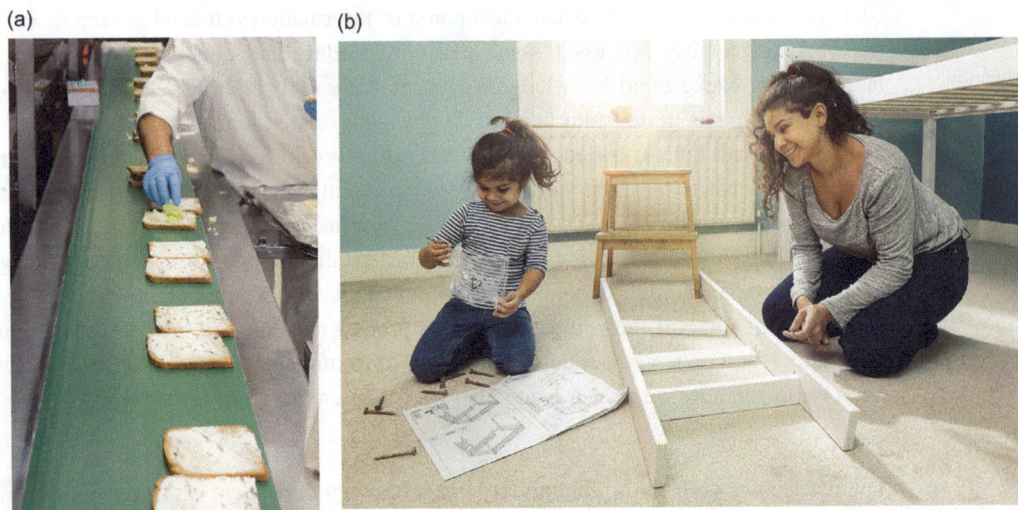

Figure 11.7. Two visual metaphors for how we assign phrase structure to sentences. Do we assign phrase-structure roles one word at a time, as we read them (like a conveyor belt), or do we process all of the words at once, choosing which word belongs where according to a larger plan (like putting together furniture)? (Source: (a) Wicki58/iStock/ Getty Images Plus; (b) Bjarte Rettedal/DigitalVision/Getty Images.)

As with word recognition, researchers have different tools available to analyze comprehension processes (Huettig et al., 2022). Researchers have used eye-tracking, reaction or reading time, and comprehension tests. In addition, like with visual illusions, psycholinguists have studied types of sentences that lead our mental process into errors, hoping to study what these errors reveal about the normal rules of the process.

First, let's consider timing. Does the parser work like a conveyor belt, taking each word as it comes and assigning it a spot in the phrase structure? Or is it more like someone assembling furniture, surveying all the pieces of the sentence, then assembling them into subsections, and finally the entire sentence? Researchers have concluded that it is more like a conveyor belt (White et al., 2020). (See Figure 11.7.) We may be capable of jumping back and forth as you are reading a sentence, or bringing what someone said earlier in a sentence back into mind when we need to interpret something later, but mostly we assemble the grammar of a sentence in order, as we read or listen to it.

Consider this sentence: "While Anna dressed the baby played in the crib." You might have initially thought that Anna is dressing the baby, but then you realized that interpretation couldn't be right. This is an example of a **garden path sentence**, one in which your cognitive system builds a phrase structure, but later in the sentence it becomes clear that something must be wrong with it. You could think of this like a sentence illusion, an error that illustrates a general pattern of our sentence parser in the same way that a visual illusion reveals a pattern of using visual cues. The cognitive system is led down the garden path, so to say, by a pattern of words that indicates one structure. Then the reader reaches a bit of a dead end and realizes either the sentence is ungrammatical or they've made a parsing error (misinterpreting the grammar of the sentence). For the example garden path sentence, if you interpret the "dressed" as referring to Anna (as in Anna dressed herself) instead of the baby, then the sentence makes more sense – while Anna dressed (herself), the baby played in the crib.

Notice that the phenomenon of a garden path sentence suggests that the sentence parser assigns words to phrase structures as we read (Ferreira et al., 2002). In the example, the sentence parser assigns *dressed* to be the main verb of the sentence. Why does the parser make this gamble, instead of waiting until all the evidence is in? The short answer, in terms of our metaphors, is that we simply don't have the mental "floorspace" to spread out all the words in the sentence before deciding which word belongs in which phrase. In cognitive terms, our auditory working memory limits the number of items our sentence parser can simultaneously evaluate (Van Dyke & McElree, 2006). In addition to capacity limits, interference effects make sentence comprehension across long strings of words quite difficult (Van Dyke & Johns, 2012). The sentence parser can't wait until the end of the sentence to put it all together and instead assigns grammatical roles as words occur (Christiansen & Chater, 2016; Frazier & Rayner, 1982). Most of the time, the gambles are good ones, and sentence processing proceeds smoothly. Only rarely does the sentence parser make a mistake and need to tear apart the phrase-structure representation it had been building.

How does the parser decide what fits where? Just like word processing is a puzzle where we reduce ambiguity using a variety of different cues, the sentence parser also reduces ambiguity, using two general classes of cues. Cues that are based on the grammatical syntax of the sentence are called syntactic cues and cues based on the meanings of words are called semantic cues. There is good evidence that our sentence parser uses both in processing sentences.

The first syntactic cue is a **key word** – a word that reliably provides a cue to a bit of phrase-structure organization. For example, the word *a* indicates that a noun phrase follows; *who*, *which*, and *that* indicate a relative clause. One source of support for their importance comes from studies in which key words are omitted from sentences. Jerry Fodor and Merrill Garrett (1967) presented participants with one of two variants of a sentence; one had the key words, and the other did not.

The car that the man whom the dog bit drove crashed.
The car the man the dog bit drove crashed.

Both sentences contain relative clauses, but in the second sentence, the relative pronouns have been removed. Participants were to listen to one of these sentences and paraphrase it to show that they understood it; they were faster and more accurate in paraphrasing the sentence that contained the relative pronouns. Presumably, the relative pronouns are cues that there is a relative clause in the sentence (see also Hakes & Cairns, 1970; Hakes & Foss, 1970).

Another syntactic cue is word order; more specifically, the parser assumes that sentences will be active. People are faster in determining the meaning of a sentence in the active voice ("Bill hit Mary") than in the passive voice ("Mary was hit by Bill") (Slobin, 1966).

But word order and key words are often not enough to guide the parser. Lyn Frazier (cited in McKoon & Ratcliff, 1998) proposed another, more general-purpose syntactic rule: the **principle of minimal attachment**. The idea is that the parser is biased to add new words and phrases to a node that already exists on the hierarchy rather than creating a new node. In a classic study examining this proposal, Keith Rayner and his associates (1983) showed participants two similar sentences that differed in their phrase structures:

The spy saw the cop with binoculars, but the cop didn't see him.
The spy saw the cop with a revolver, but the cop didn't see him.

The relevant part of the phrase structure for each sentence is shown in Figure 11.7. Note that in the first sentence, *binoculars* is part of the verb phrase started by *saw*, whereas in the second sentence, *revolver* requires that a new node be generated to represent the noun phrase (it is the cop that has the

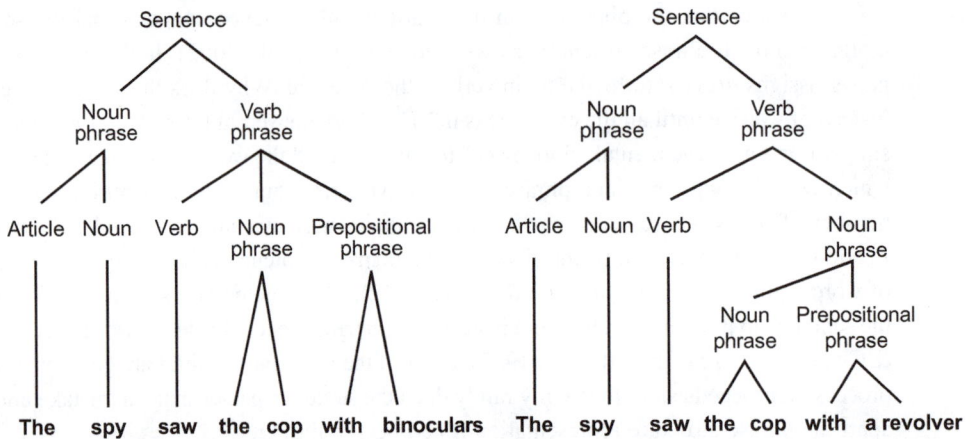

Figure 11.8. Phrase structures for the key parts of the sentences in the experiment by Rayner et al. (1983). Note that the hierarchical structure is more complex for the phrase on the right. (Source: K. Rayner, M. Carlson, and L. Frazier [1983], The interaction of syntax and semantics during sentence processing: Eye movements in the analysis of semantically biased sentences, *Journal of Verbal Learning and Verbal Behavior*, 22[3], 358–374.)

revolver, so "the cop" becomes a new noun phrase). Rayner and his associates recorded participants' eye movements while they read these (and similar) sentences and found that reading times were longer when minimal attachment was violated, and the increased time was observed at locations of the violation; participants' eyes dwelled on those locations longer (for a review of supportive evidence, see Frazier & Clifton, 1996).

Although languages differ widely in their syntax, some of these principles by which the parser unravels are universal. For example, some languages are known as verb-first, in which the verb tends to come first in the sentence. Instead of saying "Dan kicked the ball," such languages are more likely to convey the same meaning with something like "Kicked Dan the ball." A recent eye-tracking study confirmed that a language outside of those typically investigated in psycholinguistics, Santiago Laxopa Zapotec, a verb-first language spoken by approximately 1,000 people in Oaxaca, Mexico (Sasaki et al., 2022), followed similar syntactic parsing principles.

Knowing what we know about how we use multiple cues to process words, it seems unlikely that our sentence parser would ignore cues from meaning and rely only on syntax. As it turns out, we do use semantic (or meaning) cues in the sentence parser as well (see Figure 11.8). Previous words or sentences can establish a context that helps us interpret the sentence we are currently processing.

Suppose you saw this pair of sentences:

TOM: What did the baby do while Anna got dressed?
WARREN: While Anna dressed the baby played in the crib.

Wouldn't you be less likely to be led down the garden path when reading the second sentence because you read it in the context of the first sentence? Or suppose the sentence had been "While Anna typed the baby played in the crib." Whereas *dressed* could refer to Anna as well as the baby, the verb *typed* is pretty clearly not referring to the baby. Would that make people less likely to traipse down the garden path? If so, that means the parser is sensitive to the semantics of the words that it is parsing, not just the part of speech.

As we began by noting in this section, the sentence parser mostly operates in order, assigning grammatical roles to words and structuring the sentence. Even though we do have the ability to go back and correct a misinterpretation (or misparsing) of a sentence, the linear "conveyor belt" model mostly seems right. We assign a role to the word in the sentence as we read or hear that word. Sentence processing reduces ambiguity in sentences, but sometimes each sentence isn't a puzzle that needs to be perfectly completed. We are often content to get a good enough idea of what the person meant in that sentence and move on to the next one; we don't just stop at the dead end of the garden path, we keep going hoping it'll make sense later. This approach is what Fernanda Ferreira calls *good enough language processing* (Ferreira & Yang, 2019). Rather than regard each sentence as a puzzle that must be perfectly completed, we get the gist and keep moving. A similar approach is called the *noisy channel* model of comprehension (Gibson et al., 2013), which takes into account that we often hear language in noisy environments and have to "auto-correct" for errors or gaps. You've probably experienced this yourself in the written format of text messages, where people frequently make mistakes but you still get the general idea. We do our best to parse and understand a sentence, but human language isn't just a list of unrelated sentences designed to trick us. Language is people communicating in a longer and larger context, across situations, conversations, and longer texts.

Texts

Sentences typically relate to one another. As we've mentioned, researchers use the term *text* to refer to a group of related sentences forming a paragraph or to a group of related paragraphs. There is usually ambiguity in how these ideas in sentences fit together. Let's reconsider the pairs of sentences we examined earlier.

> The skies darkened as the tornado touched down a few miles away. He turned to look out the window.
> She said "Richard, it's over." He turned to look out the window.

Most researchers (see Gernsbacher & Kaschak, 2013) agree that there are three levels of representation in text processing, as first suggested by Teun van Dijk and Walter Kintsch (1983). These levels of representation have different longevities and support different types of comprehension of the text (Reder, 1982).

The first level, appropriately called the **surface code**, is a representation of the exact words in the order that they appear. The surface codes would be different for "The skies darkened as the tornado touched down a few miles away" and "The tornado touched down a few miles away as the sky darkened." The surface code is a shallow and quite short-lived representation (Kintsch et al., 1990). This should not surprise you given our previous stipulation that the sentence parser is limited by auditory short-term memory. The surface code representation of texts is similarly limited. By the time you finish reading this page, you would remember the idea of the tornado touching down and the sky darkening, but you'd be much less likely to remember the exact way those ideas were phrased. There *are* texts (e.g., jokes) in which the surface code representation is long lasting – that is, the exact wording is preserved in memory – but typically we remember meaning and discard exact phrasing (Murphy & Shapiro, 1994).

The second of the three representations of a text is the textbase. The **textbase** is semantically deeper than the surface representation in that it captures the explicitly stated logical and causal relationships between the objects and events in the text. For example, the comment "it's over" is directed toward Richard and uttered by someone who is referred to only as "she." Some of these relationships among words are captured by phrase structures, but some span across sentences. A simple way to think about the surface code versus the textbase is that you read the surface code and apply phrase-structure rules to extract the meaning of sentences. Those meanings and how they relate to one another are represented in the textbase.

The textbase uses a format called a **proposition**. Propositions are the most basic unit of meaning that has a truth value, and they usually represent causes, events, and objects. We refer to propositions as verbal descriptions, but the notation we use is intended to be independent of any particular language, so it is a bit strange. Propositions have the syntax *relation(argument)*. For example, the proposition *red(car)* represents the idea that a particular car is red. The proposition *gave(boy, girl, ball)* represents the idea that the boy gave the ball to the girl. You can see in these examples what we mean by "truth value." Either the car is red, or it isn't. Either the boy gave the girl the ball, or he didn't. In contrast, *red* or *girl* would not be propositions. And recall, too, that a proposition must be the most basic unit of meaning: Hence, "wet, red ball" would be represented not by *wet red(ball)* but by two propositions, *wet(ball)* and *red(ball)*.

A proposition does not preserve the particular wording and syntax. So, for example, all three of the sentences

> "It's over, Richard," she said.
> She said, "Richard, it's over."
> "Richard," she said, "it's over."

represent the same proposition, *said(she, Richard, "It's over")*. There are different conventions about how to represent propositions and we're not using any of them, so don't take it seriously; we're going for clarity in getting the idea of propositions across, not for fidelity to the notation.

The final level of representation is the situation model. As we understand a text, we not only interpret the words and sentences; we also construct a coherent representation of the world in which this text occurs. The situation model describes not just the objects and events in that set of sentences but the entire situation in which they take place. To fully represent the situation, this representation actually adds content from long-term memory that is not in the text but that makes sense given the context. But at the same time that information is added from long-term memory, other information from the text that is judged peripheral to the overall situation is cut. The situation model can be thought of as a summary. The situation model is especially important, because it is the longest-lasting representation in memory. The surface code is forgotten very quickly indeed, as we've noted, and the textbase lasts only somewhat longer, perhaps days. When you fondly remember a book you read in childhood, or even a year ago, it's the situation model that you're recalling.

Consider the following passage from the first page of *Harry Potter and the Sorcerer's Stone*, when we first meet the Dursleys (Rowling, 1998):

> Mr. Dursley was the director of a firm called Grunnings, which made drills. He was a big beefy man with hardly any neck, although he did have a very large mustache. Mrs. Dursley was thin and blonde and had nearly twice the usual amount of neck, which came in very useful as she spent so much of her time craning over garden fences, spying on the neighbors. (p. 1)

The moment after you read this passage, you had three representations of it. You had the surface code, containing the exact words in the exact order you read them, and as we've said, that would soon be forgotten – very shortly you wouldn't remember whether you read "a firm called Grunnings, which made drills" or "a firm which made drills, called Grunnings." You would also have a textbase representation, which would include information about Mr. Dursley's place of work (independent of the particular phrasing), but it's a good bet that that bit of information never made it into the situation model or was edited out of the situation model later. It's a minor fact in the overall story. The situation model representation of these sentences roughly describing what kinds of people Dursleys are lasts much longer than either the surface code or the textbase.

The second key feature of the situation model is that it requires far more prior knowledge in long-term memory than the textbase or surface code (Zwaan & Radvansky, 1998). Prior knowledge is needed because most texts provide much less information than the author intends for you to understand. For example, what does the author mean to convey when she says that Mr. Dursley has "very little neck although he does have a large mustache"? That word "although" tells us that the mustache somehow makes up for the short neck, ridiculous both in the idea that a short neck is a shortcoming and that a large mustache could compensate for it. The author signals at our first meeting of this character that he's pompous and ridiculous. Likewise, we're not meant merely to record the fact that Mrs. Dursley spies on the neighbors. We know that she is as ridiculous as her husband. This is the enduring information (later supported by other details) that will be retained in the situation model.

There's a hidden oddity about the situation model. We go far beyond the text in drawing inferences; you hear about a neck and a mustache, and you draw an inference about personality. Well, if you go beyond the text, how do you know in which *direction* to go? Why didn't you go beyond the text in this way: "Hmm Mr. Dursley is the director at a company. He must make a good salary." Or "Hmm Mrs. Dursley has a very long neck. I'll bet she looks quite elegant when she dances." What inferences do people make? And when do they make them?

Most researchers believe that we make inferences to resolve incongruity; if a text doesn't make sense, we will make an inference so that what we read *does* make sense. The evaluation of whether information is contradictory or missing is based on the situation model (Albrecht & O'Brien, 1993; Graesser et al., 1994; Hess et al., 1995; Singer et al., 1994; for a review, see van den Broek & Kendeou, 2022). For example, if you read "Carole said 'I have a headache, but there's no aspirin in the house. John, where are my car keys?'" you effortlessly connect the second sentence to the first, but important information needed to make that bridge goes unspoken: (1) Carole wants an aspirin; (2) Carole wants her car keys because she intends leave the house to get aspirin. This sort of inference is very typical, not only in reading, but in listening. Speakers and writers leave gaps in communication, and they assume people have the necessary information in long-term memory to fill the gaps. If they didn't leave these gaps, communication would be long and boring: Carole would *tell* us that she wants an aspirin and why she wants her car keys. Instead, she omits that information, and there's a small jolt of incongruity when we hear it, but a quick consultation with long-term memory provides the necessary information, and Carole's speech is perfectly coherent.

While humans might communicate in many different languages across thousands of cultures, it does seem like using inferences based on long-term memory to resolve ambiguity in language and communication is universal. One recent study (Ryskin et al., 2023) compared a nonindustrialized culture (the Tsimane Indigenous people of the Bolivian Amazon) with industrialized English speakers in eye gaze and speech patterns as they described a scene to another. There are wide educational, linguistic, and cultural differences across these cultures, for example, Tsimane and other nonindustrialized cultures are known as a "society of intimates" in which people know each other quite well and have a lot of overlapping knowledge, compared to industrialized "societies of strangers" who do not know each other and whose knowledge overlaps less. However, despite these differences, eye gaze and use of inferences were similar across cultures to resolve ambiguities in texts. We all use memory to reduce the inevitable ambiguity in language.

Beyond resolving incongruities, Zwaan and colleagues proposed that five dimensions of the text guide inferences we make (Zwaan et al., 1995; Zwaan & Radvansky, 1998). According to this proposal, we pay special attention to (1) the main characters in a text; (2) where they are; (3) the time that things happen; (4) what causes events in the story; and (5) the goals of the main characters. The idea is that these five dimensions (roughly, who? where? when? what [causes]? wants [goals/intentions]?) answer the question "What goes into the situation model and what is omitted?" Information from the text that is relevant to these five dimensions will go into the situation model. And for that reason, we might make inferences about them, even if we're not faced with an incongruity. For example, we're especially interested in character, so we make inferences about the Dursleys' personalities. Experimental work has shown that we keep track of where in space the main characters are; if the text tells us they move, we will definitely update our situation model (Radvansky & Zacks, 2014; Zwaan et al., 1995). This tracking of elements of a situation model is part of a larger set of mental processes that track and segment our experiences and memories into distinct events (Zacks, 2020).

But other evidence suggests that while those five elements are common default aspects of a situation model, it is not a general rule or a fixed set. Rather, what goes into the situation model and what is omitted depends, at least in part, on your own goals and expectations as a reader. For example, one study asked some participants to adopt a first person perspective when reading a story and found these readers did, indeed, keep track of where the main character was in the story; when confronted with contradictory information about space (they were told the main character went outside, when she was already outside) readers noticed the contradiction. But readers who were not told to take a first person perspective didn't notice the contradiction (O'Brien & Albrecht, 1992; see also Aaronson & Ferres, 1986; Baillet & Keenan, 1986; Lee-Sammons & Whitney, 1991; Noordman et al., 1992). For a contemporary view on how reader goals and characteristics affect comprehension, see Bohn-Gettler (2019).

We can extend this analysis of comprehension to conspiracy thinking. Conspiracy theorists construct situation models of the world in which all actions are the work of nefarious, powerful planners (Zwaan, 2022). Believers in conspiracy theories overuse goal-based inferences ("that's what *they* want you to think!") and have strong and rigid views about causes of events and the intentions of planners within that conspiracy theory. We all form situation models of texts or longer communications based on our goals, purposes or background knowledge, but it is important not to have an entirely rigid or impermeable situation model and to be able to integrate new information.

SUMMARY Language processing is difficult, because language is full of ambiguity at every level, from letters, to phonemes, to sentences, to texts. To resolve the ambiguities, we have different strategies and mental processes at each of these levels. These mental processes use both visual representations and auditory representations and basic pattern recognition and knowledge from long-term memory. To resolve ambiguities in sets of sentences to form the multiple representations of a text, we make inferences. There are some common inferences that we typically make, but they also depend on our goals as a reader.

Stand-on-One-Foot Questions

11.6.   What factors help in the perception of phonemes?

11.7.   What are the two routes to the lexicon in reading, according to dual route theories?

11.8.   What are garden path sentences, and why are they important?

11.9.   What causes people to draw inferences from texts?

Questions That Require Two Feet

11.10. Given what you know about lexical access, describe what happens when someone relates a pun.

11.11. What do you think would happen to a text if the writer were to ensure that you did not have to draw any inferences? Would the text seem especially well written and clear?

11.12. Suppose you and I are planning a hike. I look out the window, where I see it is pouring rain. I turn to you and say, "This is ideal weather." What does this example tell you about sentence processing?

12 Decision-Making and Reasoning

How Do People Make Decisions?

- What Is a Choice?

- What Is the Mental Process of Choosing?

Do People Reason Logically?

- Formal Logic

- How Do We Reason about Conditional Statements?

- How Do We Reason about Syllogisms?

- General Models of Reasoning

You may have taken this class thinking, "Oh, boy, now I'll learn how thinking works and how I can think better. Look out world!" You expected to read about controlling mind wandering, evaluating information, and making good choices. If so, you were understandably perplexed that we've spent twelve chapters on topics, such as perception and short-term memory, that you hadn't thought of as "thinking." We've offered little help to the hopeful super-thinker, and you've been a good sport about that. Here, toward the end of the book, we're going to come through for you. However, as by now you will have guessed, our study of "thinking" will still confound your initial expectations because unconscious processes will loom large.

The world is full of choices. Chicken, fish, or steak? Bring an umbrella or a jacket? Playlist or radio? Lo-fi beats to study, relax, or sleep? Each decision we make involves some sort of evaluation of possible outcomes and some judgment about the likelihood of actually experiencing that outcome. Deciding whether to bring an umbrella when you run errands might mean judging the likelihood of rain, which might incorporate the certainty of the forecast, how much you trust your weather app, and your amateur forecasting based on the color of the sky. Your umbrella decision will also incorporate your judgment of the inconvenience of lugging the thing around and how much you dislike getting rained on. (See Figure 12.1.)

How do we make decisions? As cognitive psychologists investigated how people make decisions, they naturally began by asking whether those decisions were good. We'll begin with surprising early findings that, despite our intuitions that we mostly get things right, our mental process of **decision-making** often uses the wrong information, derives inaccurate predictions, and leads to biased decisions.

Figure 12.1. Bringing an umbrella to celebrate Holi in India, where part of the celebration is to be showered with color, would not make sense. (Source: powerofforever/E+/Getty Images.)

Yet many agree with Glymour (2001), who quipped, "If we're so dumb, how come we're so smart?" Or more pointedly, "If we're so dumb, why aren't we dead?" (p. 8). So we don't make decisions that are perfectly optimal by some criterion. It doesn't mean our thinking process isn't successful. As we'll see, the most influential answer to Glymour's question is that people use mental shortcuts, procedures that allow us to arrive at an answer quickly and with little effort and that usually produce an answer that's acceptable, if not perfect. Other research suggests that the way that psychologists study decision-making in the lab may strip important context from our decisions; thinking may be better in the wild. And a third approach to the problem suggests that there are two decision-making mechanisms, not one, and that we deploy them in different circumstances.

Sometimes choices require us to reason, to derive conclusions by putting statements together using logic. For example, Riener is mildly allergic to cats. His friend owns a cat. IF Riener goes to her house, THEN he will develop an allergic reaction. This simple reasoning (two premises followed by an if–then statement) requires that you draw conclusions based on logical relationships without the judgment of likelihoods or trustworthiness of the information. In other words, we assume that the two premises (Riener allergic, friend has cat) are true, and we're concerned with how people put those statements together to draw a conclusion. In such situations, **do we reason logically?** The answer seems to be no, but research shows that even if we are not cold, accurate logic-calculating machines, we are mostly able to avoid cats when appropriate.

How Do People Make Decisions?

Preview

Philosophers have speculated about choice for centuries. Economists have also been interested in how people make financial choices. When cognitive psychologists went about studying choice in the laboratory, they quickly concluded that the mental processes we employ are not as logical or consistent as previously believed, even in simple situations. In this section, we will describe three approaches to explaining our apparently faulty decision-making. First, researchers focused on mental shortcuts called heuristics. Heuristics usually lead to acceptable choices but occasionally lead to choices that are not in our long-term interests. A second approach suggests that what look like errors in the lab actually lead to good choices in the real world. The third approach suggests that we have two different mental processes we might use for choice, and they sometimes come to different answers.

Any choice, whether a college, a car, or an appetizer, involves weighing multiple options and comparing them. When you make choices, you compare the **value** of each option and choose the one with higher value to you. The process of choosing involves calculating value, but not all decisions stop there. Consider economic decisions. You might decide among (1) investing in a savings fund, guaranteed to gain 3 percent in value per year, and insured by the federal government; (2) purchasing a stock that could gain much more than 3 percent per year but could also lose value; or (3) investing in CogCoin, an exciting new cryptocurrency. Which do you choose? This decision involves calculation not just of value but also of likelihood. The chances of getting the 3 percent return from the savings are very likely, but the chances of the stock going up is more uncertain (although it promises higher reward than the 3 percent), and the cryptocurrency is more uncertain still. With these choices, it is not merely value that needs to be calculated or compared but the likelihood of an outcome and the risk of a failed prediction.

Most choices, then, are associated with an evaluation of value (how good or bad are the possible outcomes?) and an evaluation of likelihood (what are the chances of getting the outcome if I make this choice?). Those are the rudiments of a choice: In this section, we'll get a little deeper into the question, What is a choice?

What Is a Choice?

We've described choice as involving value and likelihood, and that formulation led psychologists to propose that we could think of choice as a combination of mental processes that calculate value and likelihood, combine them for each outcome, and then compare them. From this perspective, an **optimal choice** offers the largest payoff, taking into account the probability of the payoff. To make things simple, let's use another example from economics where we know the exact probability of outcomes and can quantify their value without referring to different preferences. You have an investment choice between two options. You must choose one or the other:

A. Fifty percent chance of gaining $50
B. Ten percent chance of gaining $100

Most people would choose option A. **Expected value theory** offers us a way of comparing these choices: The value of a choice is the probability of getting the outcome multiplied by the value of the outcome. Thus, the expected value of the first choice is $0.50 \times \$50 = \$25$. The expected value of the second choice is $0.1 \times \$100 = \$10$. Hence, if expected value guides human decisions, everyone will select the first option because it has a greater expected value ($25) than the second ($10).

Economists found expected value theory useful for modeling everyday purchasing behavior. You might prefer chocolate to hard candies, but if chocolate is $3 and a similar amount of hard candy is on sale for $0.50, then you might choose the candy. You might value chocolate twice as much as hard candy, but if it costs six times as much, we can predict that you'll choose hard candy.

While expected value theory is useful in some situations, it doesn't apply universally, because the expected value of an item is seldom as consistent as the preceding examples suggest. Value can change from person to person and across situations. A delicious corned beef on rye sandwich might be worth $10 to you, but if we offered to put 100 of them in your refrigerator for a price of $800, you wouldn't take the deal, even though expected value theory suggests you should – after all, the average sandwich price is lower if you buy 100. The problem is that the first sandwich is worth $10, but the others aren't – what are you supposed to do with ninety-nine sandwiches? Even a lone sandwich might be worth less or more, depending on how hungry you are, or your distance from a New York deli. The same investment option might be too much of a gamble for a retiree who depends on the investment income for grocery bills, but acceptable for a hedge fund manager with other existing safe investments.

To account for the same sandwich having different values depending on the person and the situation, we can invoke **expected utility**, which combines the probability of obtaining an outcome (as expected value did) with our preferences in that situation (see Figure 12.2). The *utility* of an outcome is how much value it has to *a particular individual in a particular context*. Utility provides a solution to the problem that people have preferences, and these preferences can also vary by situation.

Expected utility theory predicts that people will make different choices (because they assign different values to outcomes) but an individual in a given context should make consistent choices, because they should seek to maximize expected utility. This consistency means that choices will be **rational**.

In the context of the cognitive psychology of decision-making, rational choices are not the opposite of emotional. Rational choices are coherent; they are not self-contradictory. If you say you love hip hop and hate classical music, you should choose to listen to Minaj, not Mozart. Rational choices must obey certain laws of logic, such as **transitivity**: If some relationship holds between the first and the second of three choices and also between the second and the third choice, then it ought to hold between the first and the third. For example, if you prefer apple pie to cherry pie, and cherry pie to tomato pie, then you should prefer apple pie to tomato pie (Figure 12.3). Notice that the requirement of rationality has no bearing on the particular choices a person makes. The theory doesn't prescribe that you should like apple pie better than Bavarian cream. Rationality simply means that choices are internally consistent.

Note that both expected value theory and expected utility theory make predictions about how people *should* make decisions. Because of the *should*, they are called **normative theories**. In other words, these theories are not as much explanations of how people actually make choices (psychology) as they are suggestions for how people should make decisions to live a good life (philosophy) and maximize financial success (economics). Psychologists want to live a good life and make money like everyone else, but our professional interests lead us not to investigate or propose

Figure 12.2. Do you like meat in your hamburger? Then you should like more meat in your sandwich. Expected utility theory helps explain why more is not always better. (Source: Westend61/Getty Images.)

normative theories about how people should decide but instead to focus on understanding the mental process of choosing. Psychologists therefore propose **descriptive theories** of the mental processes people actually use to make decisions. Many psychological studies find that our decision-making processes are different from what economists and philosophers had imagined.

What Is the Mental Process of Choosing?

Cognitive psychologists studying choice care more about understanding the mental process and less about whether choices lead to the best outcomes. However, the definition of a "good" choice suggests possible mental processes for making these choices. For people to choose in a way that maximizes expected utility, we need a mental process that calculates likelihood and preferences. But the first question would be whether people's choices are rational and optimal. There's not much point in searching for mental processes that support expected utility if people don't make decisions that are rational.

Early research showed that people don't (Thaler, 1980; Tversky & Kahneman, 1974). Take the following classic example (from Oppenheimer et al., 2009, replicated in Klein et al., 2014). People are presented with two versions of the same choice:

> Imagine that your favorite football team is playing an important game. You have a ticket to the game that you have paid handsomely for. However, on the day of the game, it happens to be freezing cold. What do you do?

Figure 12.3. If you prefer apple pie to cherry pie, and you prefer cherry pie to tomato pie, you should prefer apple pie to tomato pie. (Source: (a) Diana Miller/Cultura/Getty Images; (b) Matthew Boyer/Moment/Getty Images; (c) Anna Kurzaeva/Moment/Getty Images.)

1 – Definitely stay at home, 9 – Definitely go to the game

Imagine that your favorite football team is playing an important game. You have a ticket to the game that you have received for free from a friend. However, on the day of the game, it happens to be freezing cold. What do you do?

1 – Definitely stay at home, 9 – Definitely go to the game

Each of these two examples offers the same choice. Whether you have paid for the ticket doesn't affect your comfort or enjoyment at the football game; you have a ticket. But people say they are much more likely to go to the game when they paid for the ticket. Rational choices are unaffected by circumstances that don't affect the outcome of the decision, nor the likelihood that you'll get that outcome.

Still, decision-making behavior in laboratory studies is not simply irrational, but **predictably irrational** (Ariely, 2008). We may not follow all rules of consistency, but we don't make choices at random. So psychologists have set out to describe the ways in which we're consistent, and to describe the mental processes underlying our decision. We'll discuss three approaches to accounting for both the messiness and the order in human decision-making.

The first approach suggests that the calculations necessary for rational choice are too complicated to fool with, so humans use mental shortcuts. These shortcuts usually work pretty well but sometimes lead to odd outcomes or patterns or tendencies. According to the second account, we *do* engage in calculation, and especially important in those calculations are methods of integrating information about the choice with information from prior experiences. The third approach to decision-making suggests that we don't just have one mental process of decision-making but at least two that operate in parallel. This theory is more directly tied to neuroscientific evidence, suggesting that one brain pathway uses shortcuts to arrive at an answer that is fast, but inexact and biased, whereas another brain pathway produces more accurate answers, but at the cost of speed and effort.

SHORTCUTS AND BIASES   The first theories of human decision-making suggested that our irrational and suboptimal choices occurred because we don't engage in lengthy, costly calculation but instead use shortcuts. For example, think about all of the factors that might go into choosing a restaurant: distance to get there, type of cuisine, quality of food, cost, atmosphere, and so on. Estimating the value of each of these factors and combining them for *all* the restaurants near you would take too long – you'd never get lunch. So instead you make the decision with a handful of shortcuts, like "eliminate from consideration all restaurants in subway stations" (Figure 12.4).

You have some specific mental shortcuts – also called *heuristics* – for particular problems like selecting a restaurant. Other heuristics are general and can be applied to many problems. We will discuss three general heuristics: availability (an outcome's judged likelihood is based on how easy it is to think about), representativeness (an event is judged to be probable if it has properties that are representative of a process or category), and anchoring and adjustment (the judged value or probability of an event is influenced by an initial estimate of its value or probability). We also discuss how mental shortcuts lead us to make different decisions when the same problem is framed in different ways.

The **availability** heuristic is defined as using the ease or fluency of our own thought processes to judge the likelihood of events or outcomes. If a possible event is easy to think of, in other words, it is more readily *available* in our thoughts, then we judge that event as more likely. If we struggle to think of examples or have difficulty imagining such an outcome coming to pass, we judge that event as less likely.

Let's start with a lab task before moving to more real-world examples. Tversky and Kahneman (1973) asked 152 participants whether there are more words in English that have *r* as the first letter or *r* as the third letter. The answer is that there are more with *r* as the third letter of the word, but 69 percent guessed wrong. Tversky and Kahneman argued that people answer by trying to think of examples of the category; they find it easy to think of words with *r* as the first letter but quite difficult to think of words with *r* as the third letter. Your mind is not organized in a way that lets you access words according to their third letter.

One of the most common mechanisms of action of the availability heuristic is availability-by-recall (Hertwig et al., 2005). In these studies, when comparing the likelihood of a set of dangerous risks, people rely on recalling instances of such dangers befalling people in their social network, rather than overall statistics. People across the world likely experienced the availability heuristic first hand in spring and summer 2020 as we judged the risks and dangers of COVID-19. The bias to see risk as distant and less likely until we could think of someone we knew who had it or who died from it is one example of the availability heuristic (Di Baldassarre et al., 2021). During this

Figure 12.4. Choosing a restaurant is complicated because restaurants have many features you might evaluate and then weigh and combine. You might choose a restaurant you already know (using your memory of past decisions, rather than making a new one), but if you are evaluating new restaurants, what mental shortcuts might you use? When you want a quick, cheap meal, what do you look for? A mental shortcut of looking for a yellow and red sign with a brightly lit interior and cashiers instead of waiters bringing you paper-wrapped food on trays will probably lead you to a quick, cheap meal. A mental shortcut that helps you evaluate a restaurant with a sign with cursive letters with dim lighting, chefs in white uniforms, and large white plates might lead you to predict that the food will be fancy, feature unusual ingredients, and be out of your price range. (Source: (a) Jose Luis Pelaez Inc./Getty Images; (b) FluxFactory/Getty Images.)

time, we may have been aware of taking in specific data points of the infection rate and vaccination rate in our region, the contagiousness of the current variant, and the air circulation of a given environment, but with an overwhelming amount of data, we often relied on a quick mental shortcut of how many people we knew had COVID-19, and how severe their cases were, in judging our own risk.

While the availability heuristic can cause underestimation of risk until it affects someone in a person's circle of friends and acquaintances, it can also lead to overestimation of risk if one often thinks about COVID-19 but fails to take into account mitigating factors. Abel et al. (2021) found evidence that the availability heuristic affected people's beliefs about COVID-19 risk. Those who consumed more media and knew someone who had died of COVID-19 had much higher estimates of risk to themselves.

The **representativeness** heuristic is defined as people judging the probability of an event or outcome based on how similar it is to a known prototype. People use the representativeness heuristic when they are asked to judge the probability that something belongs to a category; to do so, they use features of that object that are strongly associated with a category, rather than more valid statistical information. You could think of these "strong associations" as stereotypes, and that is a good approximation of how the representativeness heuristic guides our decisions. For example, consider these two descriptions (De Neys et al., 2011; Tversky & Kahneman, 1983):

> Brian is thirty-two. He is intelligent, punctual, but unimaginative and somewhat lifeless. In school, he was strong in mathematics but weak in languages and art.

> Which of these is more likely?
> A. Brian plays in a rock band.
> B. Brian plays in a rock band and is an astrophysicist.

Or have a look at this example:

> James is twenty-six. He lives in Manhattan. He likes to wear designer clothes and acts somewhat stuck-up. On Sunday he plays golf with his father.
> Which statement is most likely?
> A. James volunteers at a day care center in his free time.
> B. James volunteers at a day care center in his free time and works as a stockbroker.

People think that the second statement is more likely to be true than the first, but that can't be right. There is some probability that Brian is in a rock band, and if he's in a rock band, he may or may not also be an astrophysicist. The odds of a conjunction of probabilities (two simultaneous probabilities) can never be higher than one of the constituent probabilities. There are by definition more people in rock bands than there are rocking astrophysicists, because the larger group of rock band members includes astrophysicists in rock bands, nurses in rock bands, and musical bartenders and bouncers. But people erroneously select the second statement because the description of Brian sounds more like a stereotypical astrophysicist. If you use the representativeness heuristic, you think that an individual with features strongly associated with the category is likely to be a member of the category.

We've looked at two heuristics for calculating probability. You'll recall that the value we attach to outcomes is also important to making choice, and the **anchoring and adjustment** heuristic is sometimes used to calculate value. With this mental shortcut, we are overly influenced by an initial guess (the anchor) before coming to our estimate of the value of an item. We adjust our initial estimate upward or downward on the basis of other information in the problem or in long-term memory. But our final answer is affected by that initial estimate, even if we know it's not a good guess. For example, Tversky and Kahneman (1973) gave participants five seconds to estimate the answer to this problem: $1 \times 2 \times 3 \times 4 \times 5 \times 6 \times 7 \times 8$. The correct answer is 40,320, but the median estimate was 512. When the order of the factors was reversed to $8 \times 7 \times 6 \times 5 \times 4 \times 3 \times 2 \times 1$, the median estimate was 2,250. The experimenters hypothesized that participants start this problem by multiplying a few of the first numbers (anchoring) but realized that five seconds was not sufficient to multiply all the digits, so they adjusted this initial estimate upward. The order of the factors matters because it affects the size of the anchor. Both estimates are too low because adjustments are usually insufficient in any problem in which anchoring and adjustment is applied.

Anchoring and adjustment has been shown to influence many judgments, including preference judgments (Carlson, 1990); judgments of answers to factual questions (Klein et al., 2014; Tversky & Kahneman, 1974); estimates of probabilities of events, such as nuclear war (Plous, 1989); and estimates of preferences of one's spouse (Davis et al., 1986). Such a large psychological effect finds common application in marketing. The television pitchman declares "You're not going to pay $1,500 for this rôtisserie!" to set a very high anchor. You know that $1,500 is a ridiculous price, so you mentally adjust downward. Adjustments are usually inadequate, however, so when the pitchman tells you the real price, it seems like a bargain. Another well-known application of anchoring and adjustment is when restaurants include a high-priced item on the menu so that other items seem affordable by comparison.

INTEGRATING PRIOR BELIEFS WITH CURRENT INFORMATION   The preceding heuristics show how we use shortcuts, sometimes substituting irrelevant information to make our choices. In the second of our three approaches to decision-making, researchers suggest that the shortcuts approach is a special case of a general problem: How do we integrate current information with prior beliefs? Perhaps shortcuts are better seen as using irrelevant or imperfect prior beliefs (like how easy it is to think of examples) to inform a decision. These researchers point out that relevant prior beliefs are usually important in real-world decisions; astrophysicists really are more often good at math and less often guitar soloists. So instead of focusing on errors prompted by the poor use of prior beliefs, we ought to focus on the more general process of integrating prior beliefs with in-the-moment choices.

The integration of prior information into ongoing cognitive processing applies to other domains as well. Perception, memory, language comprehension – all require that we derive a best guess about the future by combining previous knowledge with current information that may be uncertain. Let's consider an example. You are in Paris, having a leisurely brunch at a sidewalk café. You are enjoying the people-watching, and as you catch a glimpse of someone across the street, you think it may be someone from your high school. "What are the odds?" you think to yourself. Unless you went to high school in France, you would (correctly) assess the odds as remote. You are combining your prior knowledge (likelihood of classmates traveling, likelihood of chance encounters) with new, uncertain information (the brief glimpse of the person's face).

Another, simpler example: You're packing for a trip to Las Vegas. The weather forecast says there's a small chance of snow during the week. You usually trust the Weather Channel, but this time, you think, "Bah, it never snows in Las Vegas!" and do not pack winter weather gear. You're using prior beliefs (never snows in Las Vegas) to adjust how you interpret new uncertain information (the weather forecast) (Figure 12.5).

When we correctly judge the odds to be very small that we saw a high school classmate in Paris, or that it will snow in Las Vegas, we are adjusting how we integrate the new information (from our eyes or from the meteorologist) with our prior beliefs about the likelihood of these events. This way of considering mental processes echoes **Bayes' theorem**, an approach to integrating prior beliefs (or priors for short) with current information that was developed by Thomas Bayes, an eighteenth-century theologian and mathematician. Decision-making from a Bayesian approach treats new information as if it was an uncertain "test" and then combines the results of that test with your prior belief to arrive at a decision.

Figure 12.5. A prior belief that a place that has palm trees and lounge chairs by the pool is unlikely to get snow might lead you to ignore new information, for example, a weather report. (Source: M. Kolchins/Moment/Getty Images.)

Using prior experience to modify our interpretation of the test is important if the test is at all uncertain. If it's certain, then prior experience doesn't matter; for example, if the person in Paris sat down across from you, you would have a much better look at them – a completely accurate test. Even though prior experience tells you that your classmate is very unlikely to be in Paris, you should decide he is. But if the test is at all uncertain, prior beliefs matter.

Let's say that there are 100 students at a school, and thirty of them are engineering majors. If we randomly pick a student, what are the chances that that student is an engineering major? When you answer "30 percent," you are taking into account the **base rate**. The base rate is a background rate of frequency of something in a group and thus counts as a prior belief. People understand that base rate matters in this simple problem, but remember that Bayes' theorem applies when there is prior information *and* a test. When the test is added, people often forget to consider the base rate.

Table 12.1 Hypothetical mammogram outcome for 10,000 women			
	People with cancer	**People without cancer**	**Total**
Positive test	90	990	1,080
Negative test	10	8,910	8,920
Total	100	9,900	10,000

For example, in one experiment, participants were told that thirty of the 100 were lawyers and seventy were engineers, and in another condition, the pattern was reversed. That's the base-rate information. Then participants were given five descriptions of people drawn from a pool of 100 and asked to guess the likelihood that they were an engineer or a lawyer (Kahneman & Tversky, 1972, 1973). The description is the test information. Participants ignored the base rate and relied only on the test to make their judgment; they relied on the representativeness heuristic (i.e., how "lawyerly" the people sounded). Using only test information and ignoring the base-rate information is called (appropriately enough) **base-rate neglect**.

Medical decision-making gives us an opportunity to compare accounts of base-rate neglect offered by the Bayesian approach with the heuristics approach. Suppose 10,000 patients are given a test for cancer. If a patient does indeed have cancer, the probability is 0.90 that the test result will be positive. In other words, when there is cancer present, this test is 90 percent accurate at detecting it. If they do not have cancer, the probability is 0.90 that the result will be negative. The test is therefore 90 percent accurate at detecting the lack of cancer. Taking both of these together, it would seem logical to go the other way – if a test result comes back positive, there's a 90 percent chance she has cancer. But that's wrong.

Let's make this concrete. Suppose there are 10,000 patients, and a total of 100 have cancer – so the base rate of cancer in this group is 1 percent (Table 12.1). Of those 100 people who do have cancer, ninety would test positive (0.9 probability). So the test is 90 percent effective at correctly identifying cancer when it exists. Now, let's look at the people who do not have cancer. Of the 9,900 without cancer, 8,910 test negative – again, the test is 90 percent accurate. But that means that 990 people who *don't* have cancer have a positive test. So, a total of 1,080 (990 + 90) people have a positive test, but only ninety of those have cancer. If the test indicates the presence of cancer, the odds of having cancer is not 90 percent. It's 8 percent. The seemingly small inaccuracy of the test is magnified because the base rate is so low. You can think of this as similar to many kinds of tests that detect rare events. Every event that is tested has a small chance of error, but if you test thousands of negatives and only a few positives, you are going to make a lot more mistakes falsely saying positive than the other way around.

Now let's consider how the heuristic approach and the Bayesian would account for base-rate neglect. Predictably, the heuristic idea suggests that ignoring the base rate is exactly the kind of shortcut we rely on to make life manageable. Look how much calculation was needed to get to the objectively correct 8 percent figure. The Bayesian approach, in contrast, suggests that considering prior beliefs is natural to us – that's what we typically do. So there must be something – perhaps the way the problem is phrased – that makes us ignore prior information, that is, the base rate. If we changed the phrasing, people might be more likely to use the base rate.

We can improve performance on this task by phrasing it in terms of frequencies instead of probabilities. Gerd Gigerenzer and Ulrich Hoffrage (1999) argue that our minds have evolved to keep track of the more concrete frequencies (i.e., "how many people"), rather than the more abstract probabilities ("what percentage of a population"). They argue that people have a hard time reasoning

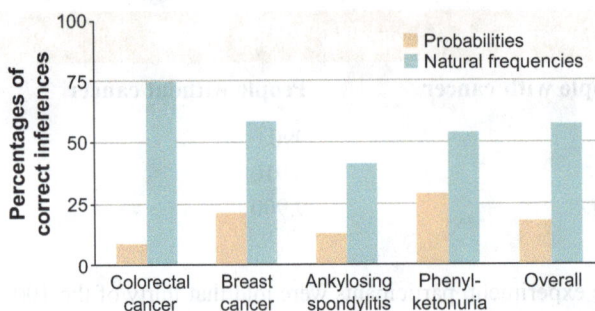

Figure 12.6. Advanced medical students were much better at solving diagnosis problems presented in frequencies rather than as probabilities. (Source: U. Hoffrage, S. Lindsey, R. Hertwig, and G. Gigerenzer [2000], Communicating statistical information, *Science*, 290, 2261–2262.)

and making decisions when problems are presented in terms of probabilities because our minds are not set up to deal with probabilities.

The implication is that people should perform much better on choice problems presented in terms of frequencies instead of probabilities. In one study, ninety-six advanced medical students solved problems that involved using probabilities or frequencies in medical diagnosis (Hoffrage et al., 2000; see also Hoffrage et al., 2005). When problems were in frequency format, participants performed much better (Figure 12.6).

Changing probabilities to frequencies isn't the only way to improve our ability to take base rate into account when making decisions. Krynski and Tenenbaum (2007) propose a different explanation for the base-rate neglect phenomenon. They argue that people will adopt Bayesian probability rules if they see causal mechanisms for the various factors of the problem. Krynski and Tenenbaum presented participants with modified versions of the cancer test which suggested causal models. They said that a benign cyst can yield a positive diagnosis of cancer, and a large percentage of the population has benign cysts. In other words, while the base rate of cancer is low, the base rate of benign cysts is high, which leads to a large number of false positives. In this case, people are far more likely to arrive at the correct solution (using Bayesian probability rules) because there is a valid, easily understood reason for a false positive result.

For the Bayesian approach, many problems in cognition can be described as using what you already know (your prior beliefs) to evaluate incoming data (glimpses of friends, weather forecasts, or cancer tests) to make a decision about the state of the world described by these incoming data. Problems can be phrased to make using those data easier or harder by highlighting or cloaking prior beliefs.

THINKING FAST AND SLOW   Another approach to judgment and decision-making holds that they are not supported by just one mental process. Several researchers have proposed **dual process models** (Evans, 2003; Evans & Over, 1996; Kahneman, 2013; Sloman, 1996; Stanovich, 1999). A recent best-selling book by Daniel Kahneman distinguished these systems by the speed of the thought processes they comprised: *Thinking Fast and Slow*. System 1, or the fast one, is based on evolutionarily older cognitive processes – indeed, it is the process that other animals use – and it is simple, automatic, and associative. The processing in system 1 is not open to consciousness – you are aware only of the decision you make, and you may, in fact, make the decision and initiate action without really having thought about it. System 2, the slow one, is uniquely human. It is the system that allows abstract reasoning and analytical choice, but the thought processes necessary are slow and deliberative. Unlike system 1, you are aware of each step, because each step requires attention and takes place in working memory. For that reason, system 2 is limited by your working memory capacity.

To see how a dual systems approach might lead us to different interpretations of problems we have discussed, let's take the following example of the representativeness heuristic, from De Neys et al. (2011):

> In a study 1000 people were tested. Among the participants there were 995 seventeen-year-olds and 5 sixty-year-olds. Anne is a randomly chosen participant of the study.
>
> Anne is in good health. She is religious and goes to church every week. She is fond of knitting sweaters, gardening, and likes to gossip with her neighbors.
>
> What is most likely?
> Anne is seventeen.
> Anne is sixty.

According to the dual process view, system 1 uses associations. Churchgoing, knitting, gardening – these are all things associated with old people. Even her name, "Anne," seems like a name more common in an older generation (Figure 12.7). Anne has characteristics associated with oldness, so we judge she's more likely to be sixty years old. Notice also how the fast associations of system 1 can produce conclusions matching the shortcut and heuristics view. The representativeness heuristic might guide our stereotype of what seventeen-year-olds are probably like, and the availability heuristic might guide our judgment by the ease of imagining older generations of people named Anne (Anne Frank the diarist, Anne Sullivan the teacher of Helen Keller, Anne Rice, vampire novelist). If, however, we pay closer attention to the problem and slow down our thinking to disengage the shortcuts, we will engage system 2. That allows us to notice that the base rates of the two ages are different and a random choice is much more likely one of the 995 seventeen-year-olds. Let's say that only 1 percent of seventeen-year-olds knit and garden and are named Anne – that is still ten people out of 1,000, and they outnumber the five sixty-year-olds, even we assume *all* of them are knitters named Anne. It takes system 2 to devote attention and working memory to compare the odds of randomly drawing a seventeen-year-old Anne from the 995 out of 1,000 possible seventeen-year-olds or a sixty-year-old Anne from the five out of 1,000 people. The dual process approach acknowledges the existence of the heuristics approach, but places it within system 1.

Finally, let's consider how the Bayesian approach would explain the results. A Bayesian theory would acknowledge the base-rate neglect but would argue that the problem was so abstract that it was hard to mentally fit into a causal model. Suppose we place the problem in an all-girls preparatory school with 995 students and five sixty-year-old teachers and ask, "Would this Anne be more likely a student or a teacher?" The causal model provided using the school makes the sampling and the base rate more concrete and familiar (there are generally far more students than teachers at a school), just as the causal model of the benign cyst makes the causes of false positives of the cancer test more apparent.

SUMMARY   Research into our decision-making can be described in three broad approaches. In one, we use heuristics, meaning we sometimes use irrelevant information and sometimes ignore relevant information to arrive at decisions. Heuristics sometimes lead to errors but can also be thought of as adaptive because they save time and mental effort. The Bayesian approach argues that we typically view new information in the context of things we already know and that failure to do so is caused by phrasing of the problems that leads us astray. The third approach suggests that we have two parallel decision-making systems, one that uses a fast process that uses associations, and one that is slower and allows for more complex calculations.

Popularity of "Ann" and "Anne"

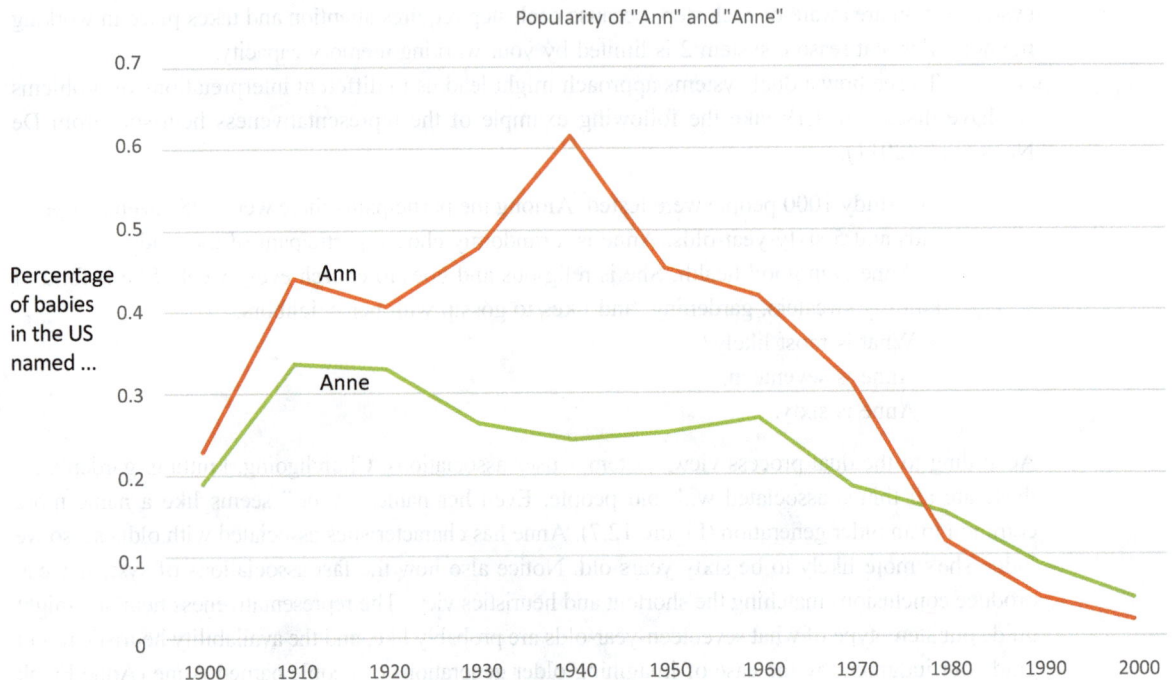

Figure 12.7. Popularity of baby names "Ann" and "Anne" from 1900 to 2000.

Stand-on-One-Foot Questions

12.1. What is the difference between normative and rational models?

12.2. What is the difference between expected value and expected utility, and how are they similar?

12.3. What are the three heuristics that people use to estimate probabilities, and how do they work?

12.4. What type of information do people typically ignore when making choices?

12.5. What is the core of Gigerenzer's argument about why the problems posed to participants in typical choice experiments are unfair and make people look more foolish than they really are?

Questions That Require Two Feet

12.6. Explain what this sentence means: "You should have no faith in lie detector tests because people who evaluate lie detector tests ignore the base rate of liars."

12.7. Recall from Chapter 7 that you might falsely remember something happening if it is part of a script. For example, you might falsely remember that a waitress offered a customer a menu, even if that didn't happen. Can you relate this idea to base rate?

12.8. Can utility theory explain why people gamble in casinos?

Do People Reason Logically?

Preview

We have seen that people don't always make the best choices using a perfect process. What happens when we reason about the causal connections and truth of different statements? In this section, we'll discuss two types of problems that can be solved using formal reasoning: conditional statements and syllogisms. As you would probably guess, people do not use logical rules alone to solve these problems but rather include irrelevant information in their calculations. People can best evaluate conditional statements that are thought of as permissions ("If you want to do *A*, you must do *B* first to be allowed to do *A*") or precautions ("If you want to do *A*, do *B* first as a precaution"). Broadly speaking, the same conclusions apply to our ability to evaluate syllogisms – people are not logical, and the content of the syllogism matters – but it is harder to describe the conditions that prompt people to solve syllogisms successfully.

In addition to making choices, we reason about the world. Reasoning, for the purposes of this chapter, is understanding and applying the truth value and causal connections between different statements. Reasoning may sound like a careful and conscious thought process, and sometimes it is, but we also often reason without realizing it. It is not an exaggeration to say that our ability to reason supports much of what we think makes our lives as humans pleasant and interesting; even the simplest actions we perform are often the end product of reasoning processes (for a broader discussion of the role of reasoning in life, see Caine, 1999).

Let's take a simple example. Suppose you're sitting in your room and you hear an unfamiliar ringtone. You conclude that your friend left their phone in your room. We could say that that simple bit of reasoning has this structure:

Phones cause ringtones.
That ringtone is not caused by my phone.
My friend was recently in my room.
That is my friend's phone.

This example probably seems so simple as to be uninformative, and in fact people are quite good at reasoning in this sort of situation. However, people fail in other situations calling for the application of similarly simple if–then logical rules.

We described normative theories of choice (expected value theory and expected utility theory) as well as formal rules of probability that we might use to form and evaluate our decisions. For reasoning, the rules and criteria are the rules of formal logic. We will first describe the relevant logical rules, then describe the ways in which our mental processes do not follow these formal rules.

Formal Logic

Problems of **deductive reasoning** have answers that can be derived by formal logic: answers that are objectively correct. But people do not always derive this objectively correct answer; in fact, there are certain types of problems that people consistently get wrong, and they tend to make the same types of mistakes. These errors indicate that formal logic processes do not drive people's behavior. The mechanisms that do drive reasoning are under debate, and we discuss several proposals.

Deductive reasoning tasks begin with some number of **premises**: statements of fact that are assumed to be true. Given these premises, deductive reasoning allows us to make further statements of fact – **conclusions** – that must also be true:

Premise:	If an election is contentious, many people will turn out to vote.
Premise:	This election is contentious.
Conclusion:	Many people will turn out to vote.

Given these two premises, this particular conclusion *must* be true. What's important in deductive reasoning is the form of the argument. Deductive reasoning isn't for relating the facts in a noisy, uncertain, and complex world; rather, we use it to determine whether a conclusion necessarily follows from a given set of premises. This means that background knowledge is irrelevant, or even distracting, when solving logical problems. The only knowledge necessary is in the premises and their relationship to each other. For example, consider the following:

Premise:	If snow is black, it makes a good hiding place for coal.
Premise:	Snow is black.
Conclusion:	Snow makes a good hiding place for coal.

In this case, the second premise is false; nevertheless, the argument is deductively valid, meaning that the conclusion must be true if the premises are true. It may seem silly to get excited about (or even mildly interested in) deductive reasoning if it can lead to ridiculous conclusions, but the point is to let you know what kinds of conclusions can be drawn, given the evidence of what you already know. Ascertaining the accuracy of what you already know (e.g., whether snow is black) is up to you.

Inductive reasoning shows that a conclusion is more likely (or less likely) to be true. It does not allow us to say that the conclusion must be true, as deductive reasoning does:

Premise:	If I cook cabbage, then the house smells funny.
Premise:	The house smells funny.
Conclusion:	I cooked cabbage.

This conclusion is not deductively necessary. There could be other reasons the house smells funny: I may have cooked brussels sprouts, I may be catsitting for a friend, and so on. Although the conclusion is not deductively necessary, we could still inductively conclude that it is more likely that I cooked cabbage than if the premises were not true. Thus, deduction allows you to make conclusions with certainty, whereas induction only allows you to change the probability of a conclusion being true.

How do we know when a deductive argument is valid? Deductive arguments have been studied extensively in two formats: conditional statements and syllogisms. **Conditional statements** actually have three statements. The first is a premise of the form "if P, then Q." P is a condition, and Q is a consequence; if condition P is met, then consequence Q follows. The second premise makes a statement about whether P or Q is true or not true. The third statement is a conclusion about P or Q. If you follow the four classic logical forms shown in Figure 12.8, you will understand why some of the conclusions are valid and some are not. The first one (*modus ponens*) is rather obvious: If I ate too much dessert, then I must be uncomfortably full. The next example (affirming the consequent) states that I am uncomfortably full, but it doesn't necessarily follow that I must have eaten too much

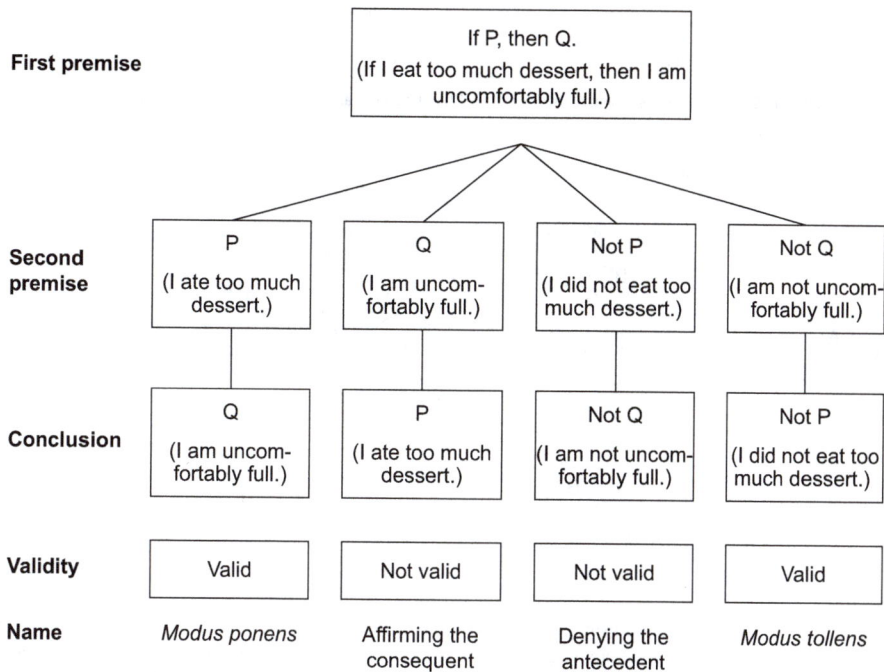

Figure 12.8. The four common conditional statement forms. The first premise states a condition (if P, then Q), and the second premise asserts that either P or Q is not true. Although an infinite number of invalid conclusions might be drawn from the premises, the four conclusions shown here are important enough to be considered in detail in the psychological literature.

dessert; I might have eaten too much dinner, for example. In logical problems, the word *if* does not mean "if and only if." "If P, then Q" means that P causes Q, but it does not preclude other things from causing Q. Similarly, in the third example (denying the antecedent), I didn't eat too much dessert, but it doesn't necessarily follow that I am not uncomfortably full; I might be full for other reasons. In the final example (*modus tollens*), we are told that I am not uncomfortably full; it must be true, therefore, that I did not eat too much dessert.

The other logical form that has been studied in some detail is the **syllogism**, which, like a conditional statement, has three parts: two premises followed by a conclusion. Conditionals include an "if–then" statement, whereas for syllogisms, all three statements are statements of fact. This is an example of a syllogism:

All computers are annoyances.
A Macintosh is a computer.
Therefore, a Macintosh is an annoyance.

The easiest way to evaluate the truth of a syllogism (or the validity of the third statement, given the first two) is by using a Venn diagram, as shown in Figure 12.9. It's also important to try to falsify the syllogism. Many syllogisms can be true under some circumstances, but we're interested in logical imperatives: If the first two premises are true, can we conclude that the third statement must be true?

Naturally, you don't need to phrase syllogisms using just letters, as in the figure. For example, consider this problem:

All A are B.   Some A are B.   Some A are B.   All A are B.

All B are C.   Some B are C.   No B are C.   Some B are C.

Therefore, all A are C.   Therefore, some A are C.   Therefore, no A are C.   Therefore, some A are C.

True   False   False   False

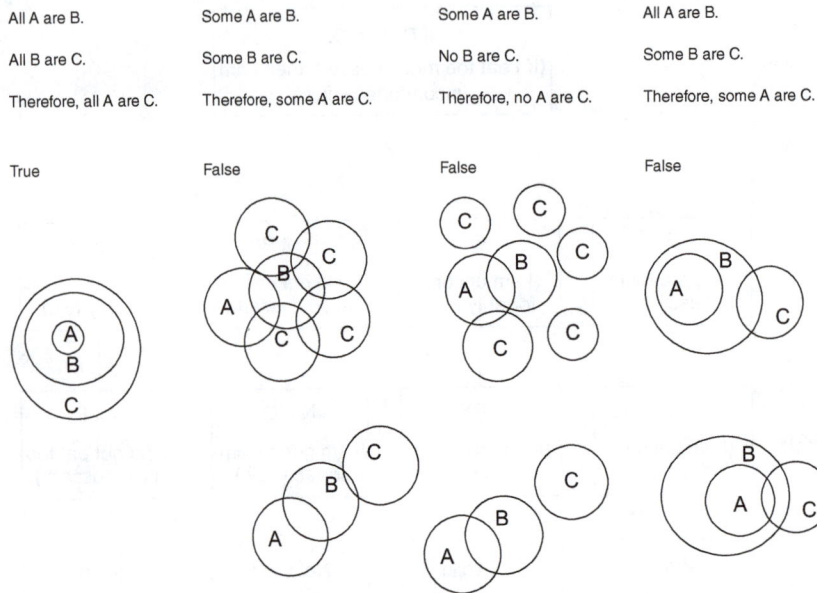

Figure 12.9. Four sample syllogisms, one true and three false. Note that for a syllogism to be true, it must always be true. The second line of illustrations shows that many syllogisms may be true under some circumstances, but because they are not always true, they are considered false. Note for the second and third diagrams, the many C circles are all possible placements given the second line of the syllogism

> Some cigarettes are made from tobacco products.
> Some tobacco products are unhealthful.
> Therefore, some cigarettes are unhealthful.

This syllogism sounds like it might be true, but in fact it is false. It has the same logical structure as the second syllogism in Figure 12.9, which is also false.

As with conditional statements, the point of syllogisms is to discover how statements can be combined so a logically valid conclusion must follow. Researchers investigating syllogistic reasoning typically ask participants to evaluate a syllogism to determine whether any conclusions can be drawn from the two premises and, if so, what they are.

How Do We Reason about Conditional Statements?

It was long assumed that humans are rational, behaving according to the rules of logic. This point of view originated with the ancient Greek philosophers, particularly Aristotle, and continued into the twentieth century. Jean Piaget, the famous developmental psychologist, argued that the final stage of cognitive development is characterized by the use of logic. You should keep in mind that people need not be aware of the rules of logic for those rules to guide their behavior; I may speak grammatically, but that does not mean that I can consciously produce the rules of grammar, any more than I can give a precise description of the physics of bicycle riding, although my movements may conform to those physical laws when I ride one. In our investigation of reasoning about

Figure 12.10. The Wason (1968) card selection problem embodies a conditional logic problem. The first premise is the rule "if there is a vowel, there is an even number" ("if P, then Q"). Each card is equivalent to a second premise; from left to right, they are P, Q, Not P, and Not Q. By selecting cards to turn over, the participant is deciding which of these second premises can lead to a valid conclusion. (Source: P. C. Wason [1968], Reasoning about a rule, *Quarterly Journal of Experimental Psychology*, 20[3], 273–281.)

conditional statements, we will focus on one typical problem and its variants as a way of describing the process of human reasoning in general.

THE WASON CARD PROBLEM In the late 1960s, Peter Wason (1968, 1969) devised a compelling demonstration that humans do not always reason well. He posed this problem:

> The figure shows four cards. Each card has a letter on one side and a digit on the other side. You are to verify whether the following rule is true: If there is a vowel on one side, there is an even number on the other side. You should verify this rule by turning over the minimum number of cards.

Before you continue reading, think over the problem in Figure 12.10. Which cards would you turn over, and why? By the way, the cards from left to right give you the following information: P, Q, Not P, and Not Q.

Most college students (and, more generally, most people) do not answer this problem correctly. The correct answer is that you should turn over the A card and the 3 card. Most people realize that you must turn over the A card. The tricky one is that 3 card. For the A card, you can see that because there's a vowel on one side, there ought to be an even number on the other. The 3 card cannot have a vowel on the other side; if it does, it disproves the rule. Across a wide variety of studies, about 15 percent of college students answer this problem correctly, although the percentage varies a bit from study to study. Even students who have just finished a one-semester course in logic don't do any better (Cheng et al., 1986). These studies indicate that people do not have a sort of all-purpose system into which they can deposit problems and produce the logical answer. Figure 12.8 (with the Ps and Qs) may have seemed painfully obvious, but now we have a situation where 85 percent of college students act as if they do not know basic rules of logic.

It may seem like we don't know the basic rules of logic for this problem, but we still understand what the problem is asking; we just reason based on some other rules. What are the rules of the mental process we are using when we seem to ignore the rules of formal logic? With decision-making, we began by discussing mental shortcuts that we take which might be helpful in some situations, but cause us to break from formal rules of rational decision-making in others. We might begin with a similar question in reasoning: What are the shortcuts, or the alternate rules, that our mental process of reasoning uses? One way to identify them is to find the conditions that improve performance, as these suggest the problems with the mental process that lead to the error in the first place.

CONCRETENESS OR FAMILIARITY? Consider this version of the Wason card problem administered by Richard Griggs and James Cox (1982), shown in Figure 12.11:

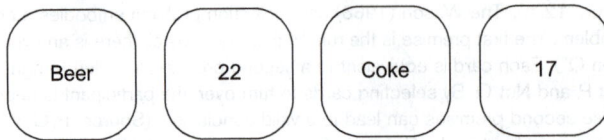

Figure 12.11. This problem is logically analogous to the one using vowels and digits in Figure 12.10, but people find it much easier. Why? (Source: R. A. Griggs and J. R. Cox [1982], The elusive thematic-materials effect in Wason's selection task, *British Journal of Psychology*, 73[3], 407–420.)

The cards in front of you have information about four people sitting at a table. On one side of a card is a person's age and on the other side of the card is what the person is drinking. Here is a rule: If a person is drinking beer, then the person must be older than 19 years of age. Select the card or cards that you definitely need to turn over to determine whether they are violating the rule.

Participants averaged 72 percent correct (they turned over the beer and 17 cards), even though none got the problem correct when they did the abstract version that uses letters and numbers. Why are participants so good at this version? There are two obvious differences between the letter/number and coke/beer versions: They differ in terms of how abstract or concrete the materials are (symbols vs. drinks) and in terms of the familiarity of the rule to be enforced. Maybe if we made versions of this problem more concrete, people's reasoning performance would improve. Alternatively, making familiar versions of the problem might also improve performance.

Alas, it seems neither of these solutions drives the increase in performance with the beer/coke version. First, making the material concrete is not sufficient to make the Wason problem easy: Concrete rules about how foods and drinks go together (e.g., "If I eat haddock, then I drink gin") don't lead to good performance (Manktelow & Evans, 1979; see also Griggs, 1984; Reich & Ruth, 1982; Valentine, 1985; Yachanin, 1986). Second, while familiarity can help, that explanation doesn't seem to be complete, however, because unfamiliar versions have been used with participants who solve the problem at high rates. For example, Leda Cosmides (1989) told a story about a foreign culture in which married men had a tattoo on their chests and in which cassava root was an aphrodisiac. When told to check the rule "If a man eats cassava root, then he must have a tattoo on his chest," participants' performance was very high. Thus, familiarity with a rule is not necessary to good performance.

PRAGMATIC REASONING SCHEMAS   Patricia Cheng, Keith Holyoak, and colleagues (Cheng & Holyoak, 1985; for a recent review, see Holyoak & Powell, 2016) suggested that abstract mental structures help us reason. **Pragmatic reasoning schemas** are generalized sets of rules that are defined in relation to goals. They are called *pragmatic* because they lead to inferences that are practical in solving problems. Logical rules, in contrast, can lead to valid inferences that may not be of much help. For example, the rule "If I have a headache, I should take an aspirin" leads to the valid inference "If I need not take an aspirin, then I don't have a headache." This deduction is logically sound but not very practical.

Cheng and Holyoak (1985) suggested that people have abstract reasoning schemas for common human experiences like permissions, obligations, and causations. The permission schema (which is most relevant to the problems we've examined) describes a situation in which a

Table 12.2 Schema for permissions	
Rule 1	If the action is to be taken, then the precondition must be satisfied.
Rule 2	If the action is not to be taken, then the precondition need not be satisfied.
Rule 3	If the precondition is satisfied, then the action may be taken.
Rule 4	If the precondition is not satisfied, then the action must not be taken.

precondition must be satisfied before some action can be taken, such as "If you want to drink beer, then you must be at least twenty-one years old." The schema for permissions is composed of four if–then rules, shown in Table 12.2.

The schema becomes active if the problem contains words like *allowed* or *permitted* or if the problem is described in terms matching one of the rules in the schema that are listed in Table 12.2 (e.g., "To use this exercise machine, you must put on a safety harness"). Once the schema is active, the rules serve as a guide to what sort of evidence (if any) is needed to evaluate whether the permission rules are being followed. If you know that people are not taking the action (not drinking beer), then rule 2 tells you they need not satisfy the precondition (be older than twenty-one); if they are taking the action, then rule 4 tells you they had better have fulfilled the condition.

Cheng and Holyoak (1985) demonstrated the importance of the permission schema by varying whether they gave participants a rationale for the rule they were to evaluate in a card selection problem. They gave participants the standard abstract card selection task but phrased the rule as a permission: to take action A, one had to have fulfilled precondition P. The cards said, "Has taken action A," "Has fulfilled precondition P," and so on. They found that 61 percent of college students they tested answered correctly, whereas only 19 percent got the right answer when the problem was not framed in terms of permission. Thus, even though the materials were abstract and unfamiliar, participants were much more successful when the permission schema was activated.

As you can see, the Wason card problem is an example of how a simple laboratory task (and its many variations) can offer insight into general models of how people reason. The variations described earlier help narrow down the mental rules that we use to reason. Some of these results show that, for example, familiarity can't be all of the story, and pragmatic reasoning schemas such as permissions seem to better explain people's patterns of responses. There are still debates on how performance on this task helps support or disconfirm different models of reasoning, but it has been a useful way of testing how people test their mental models of the world. We'll talk more about mental models, but we can think of the Wason card problem as asking people to form a mental model of all the cards and possibilities, then answer in a way that tests their hypotheses (Ragni et al., 2018; Kellen & Klauer, 2020; Ragni & Johnson-Laird, 2020).

Another strategy for understanding theories of reasoning might be to ask how they are learned or how they develop. There is evidence that even very young children (age three to four) can reliably use rules in the context of permissions (Chao & Cheng, 2000). That raises the possibility that some schemas are rooted in our evolutionary past and that children learn them more quickly with minimal observation. In the next section, we discuss evidence that the mental processes that shape our reasoning evolved in our ancient past.

THE EVOLUTIONARY PERSPECTIVE Leda Cosmides and John Tooby (1992, 2000, 2013; Sugiyama et al., 2002) and Gerd Gigerenzer and his colleagues (Gigerenzer & Hug, 1992;

(a)

(b)

(c)

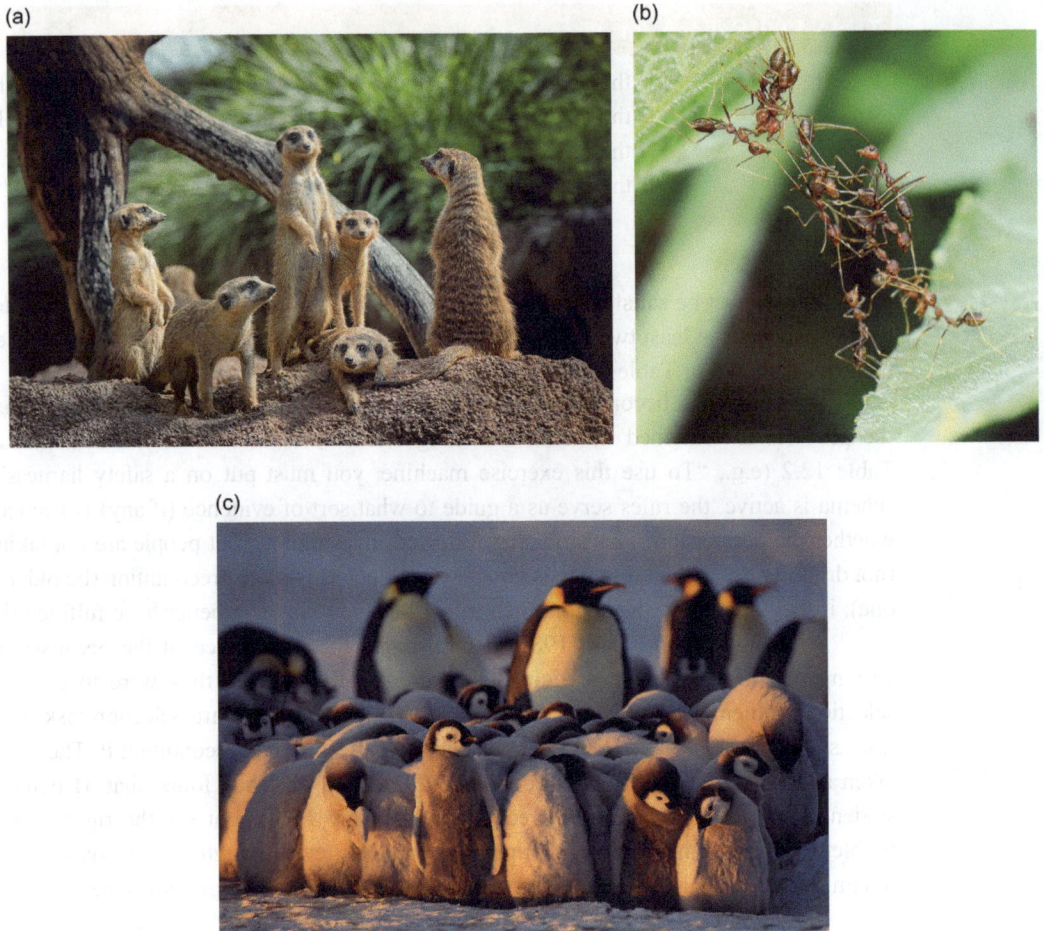

Figure 12.12. Animal cooperation occurs in many species. (Source: (a) Hillary Kladke/Moment/Getty Images; (b) grass-lifeisgood/Moment/Getty Images; (c) Konrad Wothe/Getty Images.)

Gigerenzer & Todd, 1999) appeal to evolutionary concerns in reasoning. They argue that humans evolved as social animals, meaning that we live in communities and have social ties on which we rely to help us survive. Cooperation is a vital feature for many social animals to share food, detect predators, and protect reproduction, even if by kin (Rubenstein & Kealey, 2010). (See Figure 12.12.)

However, *unconditional* cooperation leaves a group vulnerable to free riders and cheaters; if some people take resources from the group without contributing anything, the group becomes weaker. This evolutionary approach proposes that our mental processes of reasoning have evolved to facilitate social exchange by framing this exchange as a form of social contract: "If you accept benefit B from the group, you must satisfy requirement R." With the process of reasoning so stated, we are very sensitive to violations of that sort of social contract (Cosmides & Tooby, 2013). Detecting and reacting to attempts at cheating in the social contract is a key feature of reasoning within this evolutionary approach (Arai et al., 2023).

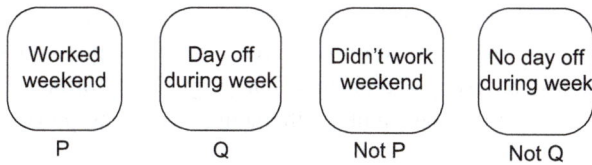

Figure 12.13. The cards people select in this version of the problem depend on the perspective they are instructed to take – as an employer or as a worker. (Source: G. Gigerenzer and K. Hug [1992], Domain-specific reasoning: Social contracts, cheating, and perspective change, *Cognition*, 43[2], 127–171.)

We can see evidence of sensitivity to social contract violations in our primate cousins. A clever task with capuchin monkeys showed how they can detect an unfair social contract (Brosnan & De Waal, 2003). Two monkeys are in adjacent cages performing a task. One is rewarded with cucumbers and is happy enough with the reward to continue performing the task. However, when the monkey sees another monkey in the next cage earning grapes (a preferable reward) for the same task, the cucumber monkey starts throwing the cucumbers back at the experimenter and thumping the table!

The underpaid monkey detects an unfair contract. Humans would too, and people are also especially good at detecting cheaters, those who accept a benefit but do not satisfy the precondition for doing so, for example, drinking alcohol without reaching the proper age or eating cassava root without being married. Some evidence for this assertion includes the facts that even very young children detect cheaters (Harris et al., 2001) and that detecting cheaters seems to be an automatic process that requires few cognitive resources (Van Lier et al., 2013).

An interesting prediction of the evolutionary perspective is that the definition of *cheater* varies, depending not on the logical structure of the problem but on the observer's social perspective. Gerd Gigerenzer and Klaus Hug (1992) provided a compelling example of this effect. They used the rule "If an employee works on the weekend, then that person gets a day off during the week." For half the participants, the story surrounding the rule encouraged the participant to take the role of the employer; the other half took the perspective of the worker (see Figure 12.13).

Participants who took the employer's perspective tended to select Q and Not P: for them, cheaters were people who take a day off during the week without working on the weekend. But participants who took the employee's perspective tended to select P and Not Q; they seek to prevent employers from cheating, and want to ensure that if a fellow employee worked during the weekend, they got a day off during the week. Again, even children show this role of perspectives and power relationships on detecting violations of conditional promises (Chin & Lin, 2018).

So what can we conclude about reasoning in this paradigm? We know that people are not logic machines who can plug any problem into logic algorithms, with the correct answer popping out. The content of the problem matters. We also know that familiarity with the content (i.e., the problem is about something you know) is neither necessary nor sufficient for successful reasoning. It's not necessary because we know that people can reason well about unfamiliar things (e.g., cassava roots and tattoos), and we know it's not sufficient because in some situations, people reason poorly about domains with which they are probably somewhat familiar (e.g., foods and drinks that go together). Humans reason very well with rules describing permissions, rights, and duties, but it still seems up in the air whether that is because these are useful (pragmatic) ways of navigating social relationships in most cultures today or because the human brain has evolved over generations to catch those who cheat on social contracts. We do not, as yet, have a complete understanding of reasoning, even that which goes into simple problems, but people's performance on different versions has begun to outline some of the constraints of the human reasoning process.

How Do We Reason about Syllogisms?

The first thing to know about our ability to reason with syllogisms is that we're not very good at it. In one study that used many of the possible forms, participants got 52 percent correct (Dickstein, 1978; see also Evans et al., 1999; Johnson-Laird, 1999; for a recent review, see Khemlani & Johnson-Laird, 2012). Chance performance was 20 percent because participants were shown five possible conclusions and were asked to select one. Why do people find syllogisms so difficult? It is not that people guess randomly. Errors on syllogisms are quite systematic (see Dickstein, 1975), so there is some principle guiding their choice of incorrect conclusions. Researchers have proposed several candidates for this faulty process. Note at the outset that all the hypotheses we're about to discuss may account for the performance of people on some problems, but none of them is a complete account.

One type of mistake people make is **conversion error** (Dickstein, 1975, 1976; Revlis, 1975), in which the participant reverses terms that should not be reversed. Some terms, such as *no* and *some*, can be reversed. If we say "no dogs are plumbers," we can also say "no plumbers are dogs." Similarly, if we assert "some knives are weapons," we can assert "some weapons are knives." The terms *all* and *some ... not* are not convertible, however. If we assert "all canaries are birds," that does not justify asserting "all birds are canaries." Stating "some mammals are not whales" does not justify saying "some whales are not mammals." The conversion error occurs when participants believe that they can safely convert a statement that they should not convert. For example, the syllogism "some Cs are Bs; all As are Bs" does not have a valid conclusion. But if the person reading it converted the second premise, then they could conclude that some Cs are As, and indeed, that conclusion is a typical error that people make, possibly indicating that they convert the second premise (Evans et al., 1993). Although conversion probably leads to some errors, it cannot be a complete account, because some participants are aware that some quantifiers cannot be converted (Newstead & Griggs, 1983) and because participants make errors where conversion is not a potential problem.

Another problem is that we are accustomed to filling in missing information and interpreting the intentions of the speaker when we understand language. As you no doubt remember from the language chapters, we don't just consider the exact truth value of the precise words uttered or written; we read between the lines. In reasoning, going beyond the exact text to infer what was implied is called **conversational implicature**. The language of logic is precise and exact, while everyday conversation is often vague and inexact and therefore needs interpretation. The "some" in "Can you get me *some* milk from the store?" and "Can you get *some* gas for my car?" mean different quantities. If you return from the store with a quart of milk and a quart of gasoline, you'll be met with a frustrated "You *know* what I meant!" Logicians refer to "what I meant" as conversational implicature, and it might help explain why we are bad at logical reasoning about words like *some*. When people read *some* in a syllogism, they probably think of the term in its vague, context-dependent, conversational sense (a few, but not a majority), instead of in its logical sense (not zero,

STATEMENT

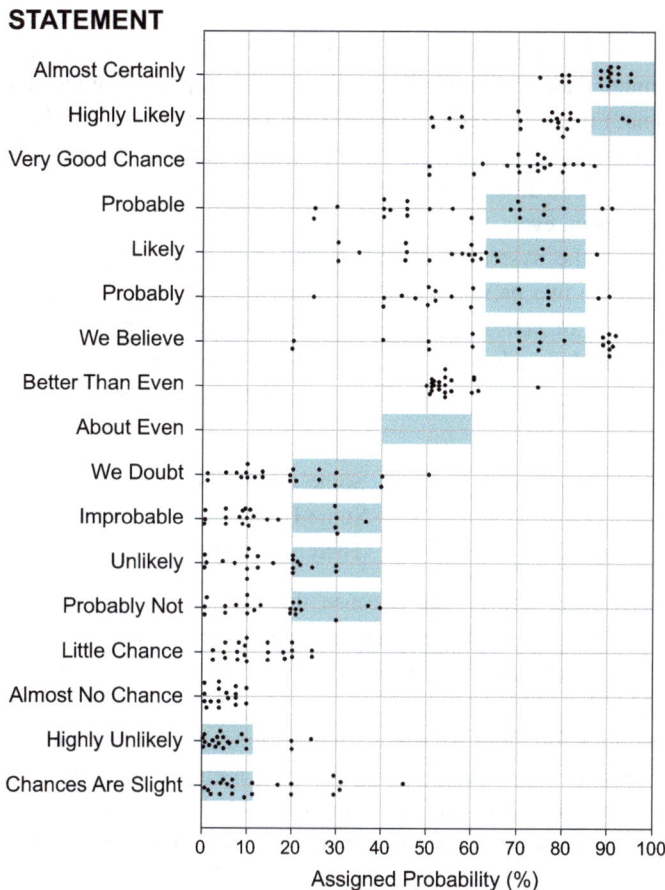

Figure 12.14. Barclay et al. (1977) asked twenty-three NATO officers experienced in evaluating intelligence reports to assign a percentage number to different words to express uncertainty, such as "likely" or "very good chance" or "probably not." This graph shows the difficulty that arises with conversational implicature. For example, look at the asymmetry between highly likely and highly unlikely. The shaded areas represent a suggested convention for using the words by Sherman Kent, the first director of the Central Intelligence Agency's Office of National Estimates. You can imagine that trouble could arise when one person writes "the chances are slight," thinking that means a little over 30 percent, but the person reading the report thinks that means that there is only a 3 percent chance of the event occurring. (Source: S. Kent [1994], Words of estimated probability, in *Sherman Kent and the Board of National Estimates: Collected Essays*, ed. Donald P. Steury [Washington, DC: CIA, Center for the Study of Intelligence]; S. Barclay et al. [1977], *Handbook for Decision Analysis* [McLean, VA: Decisions and Designs].)

which can even include all!) (Begg & Harris, 1982). Although these interpretations occur, analyses of the types of errors people make indicate that conversational implicature accounts for some, but not many (see, it gets confusing!), syllogistic reasoning errors (and may apply to other types of deduction; see Bonnefon & Hilton, 2002). (See Figure 12.14.)

　　The varieties of interpretation of *some* in the preceding paragraph are an interesting case of contrasting cultural variation and universality. The existence of these quantifiers seems to be a universal feature of all languages (and therefore all human reasoning) even in early stages of newly developed languages, such as Nicaraguan Sign Language (Kocab et al., 2022). However, just as there was a context-specific difference between some gas and some milk, there are also cultural variations in interpretation of similar words. For example, English speakers are willing to accept *some* as representing a much wider range of proportions (if I ate 80 percent of the cookies, did I eat some and leave you some?) than are French (*quelque*) and German (*einge*) and Slovenian (*nekaj*) speakers, whose translations of *some* are much more strongly associated with quantities that are less than half (Stateva et al., 2019). So all languages have *none*, *all*, and a few in the middle (*few*? *some*? *many*?) and use these to reason, even if they vary in the exact interpretations.

Another source of the systematic errors people show in syllogistic reasoning is the **atmosphere** created when the two premises of a syllogism are both either positive or negative or when the quantifiers (e.g., *all* or *none*) of the premises are the same (Simpson & Johnson, 1966; Woodworth & Sells, 1935). *Atmosphere* in this case refers to being led down a mental path by similar elements of the problem (such as the positivity or negativity, or repeated *all*s). For example, consider these syllogisms:

No As are Bs.	Some As are Bs.
No Bs are Cs.	Some Bs are Cs.
Therefore, no As are Cs.	Therefore, some As are Cs.

Both conclusions seem appropriate because they are consistent with the atmosphere created by the premises, either because they are all negative (examples on the left) or because they all use the same quantifier (examples on the right). Yet, neither syllogism is true. (See the Venn diagrams in Figure 12.9.)

Atmosphere accounts for about 50 percent of the erroneous responses in a multiple-choice format (Dickstein, 1978) and nearly that many in an open-ended test where the participant must supply the conclusion (Johnson-Laird & Bara, 1984). Nevertheless, it is not a complete explanation of syllogistic reasoning because it explains only how participants approach a subset of syllogisms.

We mentioned that decision-making conforms to Bayesian processing, in that it is influenced by **prior beliefs**. In contrast, when we evaluate a syllogism, we're supposed to ignore prior beliefs. Syllogisms are to be taken as purely logical exercises in which we evaluate the conclusion only in light of its relationship to the premises. Thus, the premises "all As are Bs" or "all dogs are cats" should contribute to our evaluation of a syllogism in the same way because, for the purposes of the problem, we're supposed to ignore what we know about dogs and cats. But people have a hard time doing that, and our prior beliefs do influence reasoning, a phenomenon called **belief bias**. Sometimes this failure moves us toward solutions that are logically correct; at other times, it doesn't, depending on the particulars of the problem.

Suppose a conclusion is logically valid but is known to participants to be false in the real world. John St. B. T. Evans and his colleagues (Evans et al., 1983; see also Newstead et al., 1992) compared two syllogisms of the same form:

No cigarettes are inexpensive.	No addictive things are inexpensive.
Some addictive things are inexpensive.	Some cigarettes are inexpensive.
Some addictive things are not cigarettes.	Some cigarettes are not addictive.

Both syllogisms are valid, but 81 percent evaluated the one on the left as valid, whereas only 63 percent evaluated the one on the right as valid. You probably had to read them twice just to check

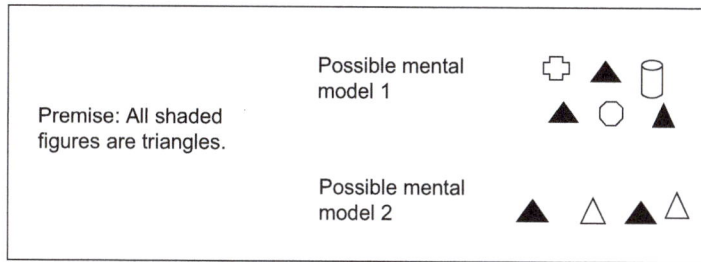

Figure 12.15. Mental models for the premise "All shaded figures are triangles." The mental models are presented as visual images for simplicity; true mental models are meaning-based structures that might be used to generate mental images but are not images themselves.

yourself, in part because your prior belief tells you that "no addictive things are inexpensive" is clearly false.

These four factors – conversion errors, conversational implicature, atmosphere, and prior beliefs – can affect performance on syllogistic reasoning tasks, but it should be emphasized that these effects do not overwhelm whatever other mechanisms might be at work; many participants get the problem right. Even more important is that each effect applies only to selected problems, and thus their explanatory power is limited. We've named four effects; we haven't proposed a general model of reasoning. We turn next to a discussion of more complete models of reasoning.

General Models of Reasoning

In this section, we consider three models that seek to account for a wide variety of reasoning situations, not just a single class of problems.

MENTAL MODELS THEORY   Philip Johnson-Laird and his associates proposed that the meaning, or semantics, of a problem is crucial to its solution (Johnson-Laird, 1999, 2005; Khemlani et al., 2018, Johnson-Laird, 2021). In the **mental models theory**, the meaning of the premises remains in a meaning-based format. In this view, we can't mentally create an empty vacuum of only the premises and possible conclusion, but we imagine and remember a world of concrete objects and events, causes and effects. The premises are used to construct a mental model of the situation that represents a possible configuration of the world that includes much more information than just the premises. In other words, rather than mentally represent relationships in the abstract logical way using only the way that a problem is phrased, we mentally represent a concrete and specific mental model.

Mental models don't just represent the world; they can also be used for deduction because we can combine mental models. The fact that more than one mental model can represent a premise (as in Figure 12.15) has important implications for the way the theory works. Figure 12.16 shows two mental models that might be drawn from a pair of premises. In Figure 12.16b, the conclusion is valid. In Figure 12.16a, the conclusion is invalid. This invalid conclusion is traceable to the image based on the mental model for the first premise. The person may have committed a conversion error, believing that because all shaded figures are triangles, it is also true that all triangles are shaded figures.

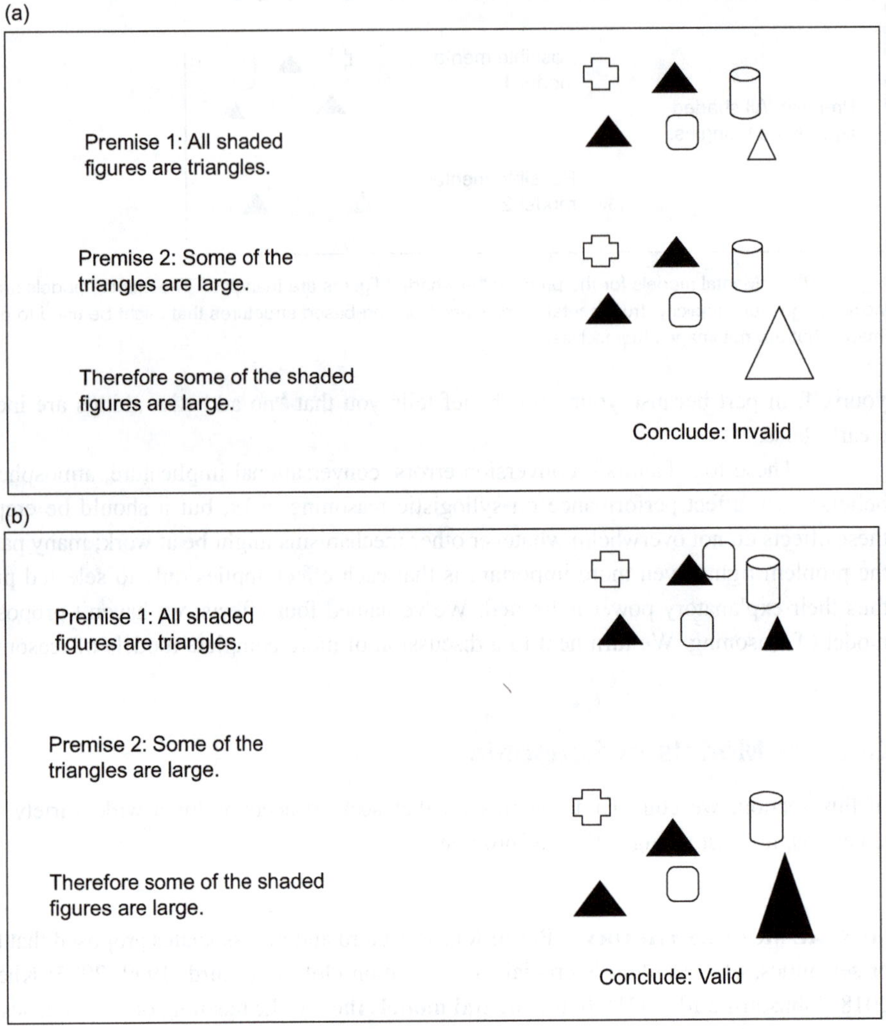

(a)

Premise 1: All shaded figures are triangles.

Premise 2: Some of the triangles are large.

Therefore some of the shaded figures are large.

Conclude: Invalid

(b)

Premise 1: All shaded figures are triangles.

Premise 2: Some of the triangles are large.

Therefore some of the shaded figures are large.

Conclude: Valid

Figure 12.16. This example shows how your mental model might change as new premises are stated and how you would use the mental model to evaluate the validity of a conclusion. Look at example (a). The first mental model is one of several possible models based on this premise. The mental model is changed when the second premise is stated. The conclusion "Some of the shaded figures are large" is inconsistent with the mental model, so you would conclude that the syllogism is invalid. In (b), you start with a different mental model of premise 1. With this mental model, you end up accepting the validity of the conclusion.

How can we avoid such errors? We must generate multiple mental models representing all possible situations, given the stated premises. Thus, we may have to keep several mental models in working memory simultaneously, corresponding to these multiple possibilities. A conclusion is possible if it is represented in one of the models; it is impossible if it is represented in none of the models; and it is necessary if it is represented in all the models.

It sounds as if the theory predicts that success in reasoning depends strongly on the size of working memory. More working memory capacity means you'll be able to maintain more mental

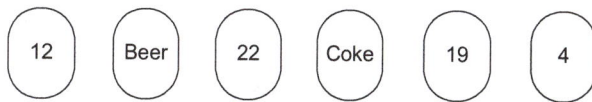

Figure 12.17. Version of the Wason card problem used by Kirby (1994). People are more likely to check the nineteen-year-old than the four-year-old, indicating that people are sensitive to the likelihood that they will find useful information. (Source: K. N. Kirby [1994], Probabilities and utilities of fictional outcomes in Wason's four-card selection task, *Cognition*, 51, 18–19.)

models simultaneously and will therefore be able to keep track of more possible ways in which premises can be interpreted. That prediction seems to be supported by the data; as syllogisms offer more possible interpretations, participants have a harder time evaluating their truth (Johnson-Laird et al., 1992).

BAYESIAN INFORMATION GAIN MODEL   The errors in reasoning we've discussed so far seem similar to the shortcut model (i.e., heuristic model) of decision-making. But what if we treat reasoning as a probability problem, not as a logic problem, and apply the Bayesian approach as we did for decision-making? **Probability models** of reasoning, including Chater and Oaksford's (1999) model (for an updated review, see Oaksford & Chater, 2020), hold that people seldom engage in pure deductive reasoning in the everyday world. Rather, they make judgments based on probabilities, using Bayesian probability principles. For example, when you hear "Rover is a dog," you assume that Rover has fur, not by deduction ("Dogs have fur; Rover is a dog; therefore, Rover has fur"), but because you know there is a high probability that a dog has fur. Some don't but it is a pretty good guess. Thus, when participants apparently "fail" on logical reasoning tasks in the laboratory, it's because they treat them as probability tasks – the same way they treat everyday reasoning tasks.

One implication of this view is that when people feel they need more information to understand a situation, they use prior beliefs to assess the likelihood of finding useful information in one place or another. Consider the version of the Wason card problem in Figure 12.17, which concerns age and drinking alcohol. You have prior beliefs about the likelihood of four-year-olds drinking alcohol, so even though principles of logic indicate that you need to verify what this youngster is drinking, prior beliefs indicate that there is unlikely to be useful information on the back of that card – four-year-olds just don't drink alcohol. Kris Kirby (1994) reported that 65 percent of participants said they would check the four-year-old, compared with 86 percent who said they would check the nineteen-year-old (the drinking age was twenty-one at the time and place this experiment was conducted).

Chater and Oaksford (1999) proposed that people's main motivation in reasoning tasks may be to seek out information that will be maximally informative, not necessarily information that will lead to answers that are correct according to formal logic. For the Wason card problem, the researchers used a statistical method that they claim can evaluate the amount of information likely to be obtained when each card is turned over, and they developed a model using the same principles that account for syllogistic reasoning (Chater & Oaksford, 1999; for a summary of their work, see Oaksford & Chater, 2009, 2013, 2020; for an attempt to bring together probability and mental models, see Johnson-Laird et al., 2015).

DUAL PROCESS MODELS   The dual process models (thinking fast and slow) of decision-making might also be applied to reasoning (Evans, 2003; Evans & Over, 1996; Sloman, 1996; Stanovich, 1999; Evans, 2019). System 1, comprising the faster and evolutionarily older cognitive processes, uses simple association. This simple and quick association makes this system vulnerable to using current beliefs (and more subject to belief bias) – in other words, to producing an answer without reasoning. So it would seem to our advantage to use system 2 as often as possible. However, the fact that the fast system is based on association doesn't mean that it never produces correct answers. For example, system 1 is optimized for cheater detection, associating certain kinds of rule violations by activating a strong moral emotion (*Hey*! That's not fair!). If fast system 1 produces a response based on pattern detection built from thousands of events or years of experience, it might be better than a slow and deliberative system 2 response that doesn't do a good job of integrating all the relevant information. Think of this as similar to choking in sports. Sometimes it is better to stop thinking and just to hit to ball, rather than consciously concentrating on the spin, the speed, the position of the ball, your stance and posture, and so on.

The processing in system 1 is not open to consciousness – you are aware only of the decision you make, and you may, in fact, make the decision and initiate action without really having thought about it. System 2 is uniquely human. It is the system that allows us to apply logical rules – at least, as best we can. Using system 2 doesn't mean that you'll apply logical rules flawlessly, but that's at least what you're trying to do. You're still influenced by prior beliefs, and by your knowledge of logical rules. In addition, you're limited by working memory capacity, because, in contrast to system 1, when you use system 2, each step takes place in working memory. Hence, working memory capacity is an important determinant of the effectiveness of system 2.

This framework has a lot of appeal. It incorporates a basic fact about reasoning that most of us would observe by introspection, as was noted by Cheng and Holyoak (1985) and by Oaksford and Chater (2001): Much of what we do need not be guided by conscious and careful logical reasoning. Our concerns are much more pragmatic. It's easiest to assume that the world is the way it always is and that we can act as we usually do and everything will be fine. For example, we needn't engage in reasoning to know that "if I turn the key, the door will unlock." That's what always happens, so a simple association will do.

However, sometimes we *do* engage system 2 in a slow reasoning process. This point was made forcefully by Keith Stanovich (1999, 2011; Evans & Stanovich, 2013). He pointed out that some people fairly consistently give the normative answer on a wide variety of reasoning problems, and these people also tend to have high scores on the SAT (the college admissions test), which could be taken as a measure of general cognitive ability. We need a theory that can account for the fact that people are often illogical but nevertheless are capable of reasoning logically under the right conditions.

Stanovich has also offered some interesting evidence that the same individuals might use one system or the other, depending on how the question is phrased. Stanovich and West (1998) compared people who solved the abstract version of the Wason card problem and people who didn't and found that the SAT scores of the former were higher than those of the latter. But when they used the drinking age version of the problem, the SAT scores were no different. The interpretation is that when confronted with an unfamiliar problem, participants had to use system 2, which is closely associated with cognitive capacities; therefore, you get the relationship with SAT scores. But when confronted with the drinking age problem, everyone relied on system 1 because they have experience with this sort of problem. The performance of system 1 is unrelated to cognitive ability, so no relationship with SAT score was observed in this version of the problem.

In addition to the phrasing of the problem, people's dispositions can affect whether they engage in system 2 slow reasoning. Evans and Stanovich (2013) reviewed how individual differences affect reasoning. For some problems (e.g., the abstract version of the Wason card problem), abstract, algorithmic processing is required, and people who are higher in fluid intelligence (and more skilled in algorithmic processing) are more likely to reason accurately. In addition, people who have a disposition to think of problems slowly and analytically (and who are motivated to do so) are also more likely to reason accurately.

De Neys and colleagues (2010, 2011) suggest that instead of a reasoner choosing between the two systems, these dual processes may work in parallel and interact in the same problem. Researchers have tested people's confidence (De Neys et al., 2011), autonomic arousal (De Neys et al., 2010), and response times (Bonner & Newell, 2010) and found that even where people arrive at a wrong answer, they often show evidence of being in conflict and doubt. System 2 may monitor and contribute to the reasoning process but fail to inhibit the (biased) system 1 response.

SUMMARY   We've reviewed two types of reasoning problems. Conditional reasoning problems ("if P, then Q") can be difficult or easy, depending on the materials used; we examined several theories accounting for these effects, including the evolutionary perspective and pragmatic reasoning schemas. We've described four ways the syllogistic reasoning can go wrong, but they don't add up to a complete theory of reasoning.

We also examined three general theories of reasoning: the mental models theory, which emphasizes the semantic content of the premises; a Bayesian probability model, which emphasizes that people may have nonlogical reasons that motivate their choices in a reasoning problem; and dual process models, which hold that people sometimes use simple associations to solve reasoning problems and at other times use slower processing that is more typical of what we think of as reasoning.

As we noted at the beginning of this chapter, when we say "reasoning," we refer to a situation in which it is obvious that one of a limited set of answers is correct, for example, whether a syllogism is true or false. Obviously, not all the situations that humans encounter are of this sort. Some are much more open-ended, which means that the problem provides much less guidance to the possible answers. In the next chapter, we turn to these problems.

Stand-on-One-Foot Questions

12.9.   What is the difference between deductive and inductive reasoning?

12.10.   Is it true that familiarity is the critical feature that determines whether people will successfully evaluate a conditional statement such as the one embodied in the Wason card selection problem?

12.11.   What are the three general models of reasoning we discussed?

Questions That Require Two Feet

12.12. Another way we might reason is based solely on memory. You simply remember a similar case and apply what you did last time (assuming that it worked). How often do you think you use this strategy (called case-based reasoning)?

12.13. The probability models seem to argue that people don't actually reason in reasoning problems but rather try to maximize the amount of information they can obtain. Assuming that this result is true, can we say that people don't reason?

13 Problem-Solving

A **problem** can be defined very generally as any situation in which a person has a goal that is not yet accomplished. That definition encompasses what we called decision-making. When psychologists talk about problem-solving, however, they typically mean open-ended problems in which the person knows the goal but nothing in the problem describes how to accomplish the goal.

According to this definition of a problem – you have a goal that you have not accomplished – you are faced with dozens of problems every day. You want a pizza but you don't have one; that's a problem. You want to be outside but you're in your apartment; that's a problem. These problems are uninteresting because you have faced them (and solved them) countless times before. Your response to these problems is so automatic that you don't even think there is a problem to be solved. When you think of a problem, you most likely think of one of those little puzzles made out of two twisted nails that you are supposed to disentangle.

Problems like getting outside and untwisting nails are at opposite ends of a continuum, namely, a continuum of relevant experience. The "getting outside" problem can be solved based on past experience. The twisted nails problem usually cannot. In the nails problem, you don't have much in memory that will help you, so you must recruit processes that will give you some guidance on things to try that might lead to a solution. We could imagine that all problems will vary in the extent to which previous experience guides us.

Indeed, the ends of this continuum illustrate two main themes of research on problem-solving: the role of memory (i.e., prior experience) and the role of general problem-solving routines. Many problems are not at the extremes we've just described; they are neither completely familiar (so you can't solve the problem by simply remembering how you solved it last time) nor completely unfamiliar (so past experience is no guide). Rather, most problems are solved through using a combination of general-purpose problem-solving strategies and memories of similar problems that might be applicable to the current problem.

To study general problem-solving routines, psychologists have used unfamiliar problems to prevent participants from relying on their memories of similar problems. Our first question is, **How do people solve novel problems?** We'll examine the general-purpose strategies people use in these situations.

Again, it is not always the case that people have either complete knowledge or absolutely no knowledge of a problem. Often, they have some knowledge that might be applicable to a problem. **How do people apply experience to new problems?** You would think that some experience would be better than no experience, and that's usually, but not always, true. For one thing, it can be difficult to recognize that past experience is relevant. Furthermore, prior knowledge can put you in a mental rut; you might approach new problems in the same way you approached old problems, even if that strategy won't work.

Finally, we'll consider the question, **What makes people good at solving problems?** As you might guess from the foregoing discussion, there are two main sources of skill in problem-solving. You might be good at using the general-purpose processes, or you might have many problem solutions in long-term memory that can apply to other problems. Sometimes these are not just memories of specific solutions but more general, structured knowledge about the domain. We will also consider whether some situations or interventions can make anyone better at problem-solving.

How Do People Solve Novel Problems?

Preview

When we confront a problem we have seen before, we use our memory to inform us of strategies that led to a solution in the past. But without relevant experience, people must fall back on general, all-purpose problem-solving strategies. One is working forward, which means to look for ways to get closer to the goal. Working backward means to begin at the goal and try to mentally work back to the beginning of the problem. Means–ends analysis combines working forward and working backward. It is especially effective because it allows for setting subgoals that should be completed before the main goal is tackled.

The heart of problem-solving is change. The current state of the world is unsatisfactory – that is a problem. We want to change it in some way – that is a goal. The mental process of problem-solving, as investigated by cognitive psychologists, is to describe how we get from the current state of the world to the goal state. We begin with a description of how psychologists characterize change in problem situations. That will help you understand and compare different problem-solving strategies.

Problem Spaces

Allen Newell and Herb Simon (1972) emphasized the usefulness of describing a **problem space** that includes all possible configurations a problem can take. For example, consider the classic puzzle called the Tower of Hanoi, depicted in Figure 13.1. The puzzle includes a board with three pegs and

Figure 13.1. Tower of Hanoi

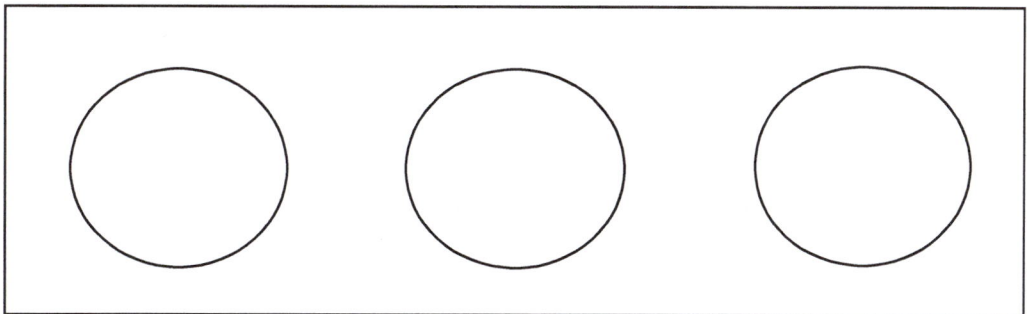

Figure 13.2. Use this figure to work out the Tower of Hanoi puzzle shown in Figure 13.1. Put three coins of decreasing size (a quarter, a nickel, and a penny) on the leftmost circle and try to move the coins to the rightmost circle, following these rules: You can move only one coin at a time, you can move only the top coin on a stack, and you can't put a larger coin on top of a smaller coin. If this puzzle seems too easy, use four coins.

three rings of decreasing size. The goal is to move all the rings from the left peg to the right peg. Three rules describe how you can move the rings:

1. You can move only one ring at a time.
2. You can move only the top ring on a peg.
3. You cannot put a larger ring on top of a smaller ring.

The Tower of Hanoi is used as an example several times in this chapter. It is a good way of illustrating the concepts in problem-solving, and it has also been a rich way of investigating the mental processes involved for more than fifty years (Gagné & Smith, 1962; Hayes & Simon, 1974; Russell et al., 2014; Vakil & Heled, 2016; Fansher et al., 2022). You'll get more out of these examples if you work through the problem yourself using coins of different sizes – a quarter, a nickel, and a penny – as described in Figure 13.2. You can also download an app for your phone – just search "Tower of Hanoi" on your device.

The problem space for the Tower of Hanoi puzzle can be thought of as all possible configurations of the puzzle board (see Figure 13.3). Each position is called a state of the problem space. More generally, a **problem state** is a particular configuration of the elements of the problem. Notice that links between the different states indicate the possible paths through the problem space. You can't simply jump from one state in the problem space to another; you must move from state to state by way of the links. What determines how the states are linked? The links represent **operators**,

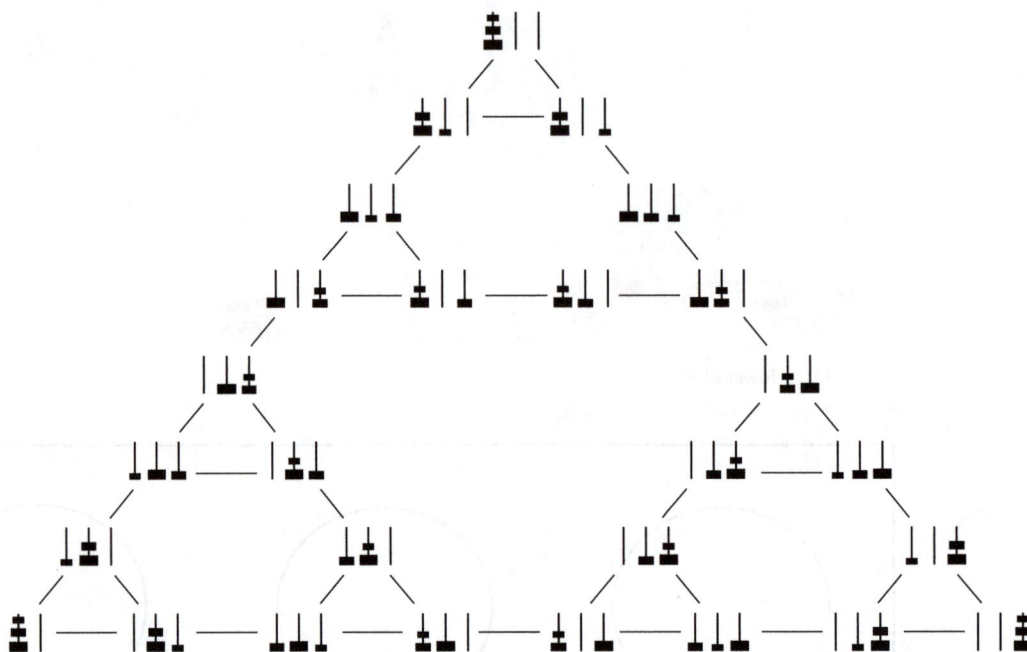

Figure 13.3. Problem space for the Tower of Hanoi puzzle. It's easiest to understand the figure by starting at the top and following the choices. You always have the option of moving backward in the space by returning to the position you just occupied.

processes that can be applied to the problem to change its configuration (to change where you are in the problem space). For example, the only possible operator in the Tower of Hanoi problem is to move a disk. In checkers, an operator is to move a piece diagonally, whereas in chess, the different pieces use different operators. Typically, certain conditions must be met before you are allowed to apply an operator. In the Tower of Hanoi, you cannot move a ring that has another ring on top of it, and you cannot place a larger ring on top of a smaller ring.

We can also imagine (but it is harder to depict) the problem spaces for popular board games. The problem space for the game of checkers contains 500 billion billion possible positions (5×10^{20}). After many years of development, in 2007, a computer program was developed that not only could beat any human player but "solved" checkers (Schaeffer et al., 2007). The program, called Chinook, employs a database of every possible position and the correct move in response to that position.

Selecting Operators

The key to problem-solving is selecting the operators that will move you efficiently through the problem space to the goal. Obviously, if you simply move through the problem space randomly, you might accidentally end up at the goal, but you'd rather reach the goal more quickly and with certainty. How do you select operators to ensure a reasonably direct route to the goal?

You could imagine doing a **brute force search**, examining every possible answer until you find the correct one. For example, suppose you were working on a crossword puzzle and saw the letters _alt with the clue "seasoning." You could sequentially substitute each letter of the alphabet (*aalt, balt, calt, dalt*) in the blank space until you get to *s* and identify *salt* as the correct solution.

The advantage of a brute force search is that it's very simple to apply, but the disadvantage is that it doesn't shrink the problem space through which you must search; you have to try all the possibilities. As the number of possibilities increases modestly, the number of combinations increases rapidly because of a phenomenon called **combinatorial explosion**. For example, suppose the clue was _al_. You could still do a brute force search by putting *a* in the first blank space and trying the letters of the alphabet in the second blank space (*aala*, *aalb*, *aalc*, and so on). If that doesn't work, you can try the next letter of the alphabet in the first space and the others in sequence in the second blank space (*bala*, *balb*, *balc*). Notice that although we've doubled the number of blank letters, the number of states in the problem space that we must explore has more than doubled. In fact, if there are twenty-six possible letters to fill in the blanks and two blanks to be filled, there are 26^2 possible combinations of letters in the blanks for a total of 676. If we add one more blank, the possibilities increase to 26^3 or 17,576. Thus, it's clear that a brute force search is often impractical.

Chinook, the checkers-solving program, is an example of a brute force solution. It handles the combinatorial explosion by a comparable explosion in computer storage and processing speed. Even with a very powerful computer, however, solving more complex games, such as chess and Go, would be exceedingly unlikely. Whereas the game of checkers is entirely solved, researchers cannot even agree on the method to calculate the total number of possible board positions for chess (Allis, 1994). However, estimates are around 10^{120} possible positions, many more than the number of atoms in the observable Universe (about 10^{80}). The game Go is even more complicated than chess.

What strategy might we use if a brute force approach is not helpful? People use **heuristics** to guide their search for operators that will move them through the problem space. A heuristic in problem-solving means the same thing that it did in decision-making. It's a simple rule that can be applied to a complex problem. Heuristics require minimal computation and often yield an acceptable answer but do not guarantee one. For example, the autocomplete function on your phone tries to guess the word you mean to type before you've completed it and thus deals with a very large problem space – all the words in the English language. A simple heuristic that would greatly reduce the space would be to rank the words by frequency of use in the English language, or even in the usage of the particular phone user. For example, once "e" was typed, "example" would be ranked as a more likely intended word than "emu" or "exegesis" (Figure 13.4).

Hill climbing is a common problem-solving heuristic; you look for an operator that will take you to a state in the problem space that appears to be closer to the goal than your current state is. Imagine your goal is to stand at the top of a hill. Each step you take is a change in the problem space. To decide where to step, you evaluate whether the step you are contemplating would take you closer to the top of the hill. The hill-climbing heuristic is certainly more effective than brute force – you are at least evaluating moves before you try them – but it is still applicable to a limited number of problems. Many problems require that you move backward in the problem space to reach your goal, and hill climbing doesn't allow that. Suppose that you are at the top of a small hill, but nearby you see one that's higher. You can't use the hill-climbing strategy to get there, because every step you take would be downhill, away from your goal.

Animals sometimes get caught in a similar bind. Maybe you have seen a dog on a leash straining to reach something that it could easily reach if it went around an obstacle so the leash would no longer be caught (see Figure 13.5). The dog must overcome its desire to get closer to the goal, and move backward to enable completing a goal. Although we might snicker about the mental superiority of our species, the fact is that humans also often avoid moving backward in a problem space. We can do it, obviously, or else many problems would be insoluble, but we are more likely to make errors if we must move backward, and we are slower to make these moves than hill-climbing moves (Figure 13.6).

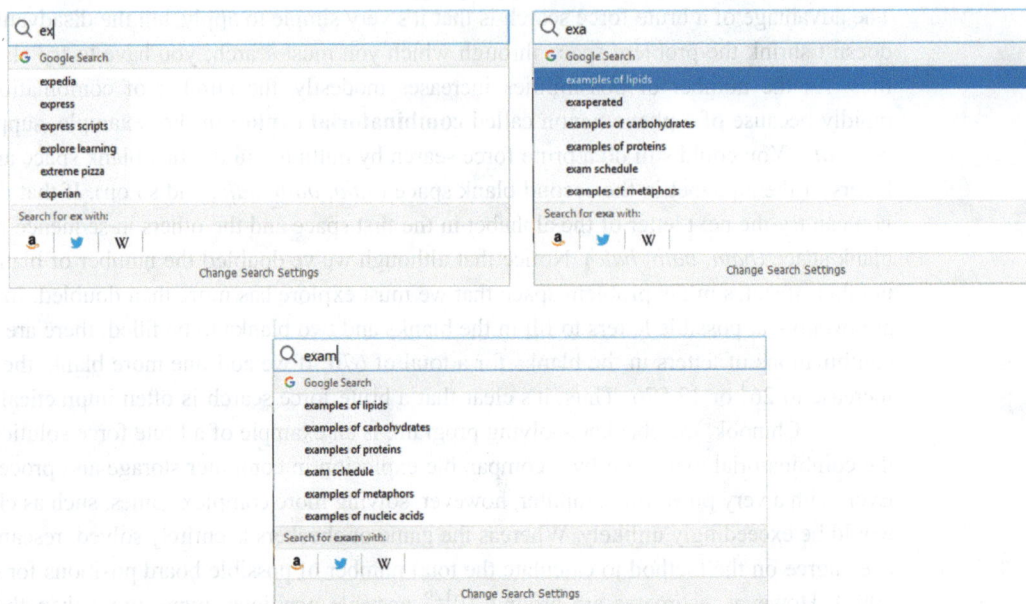

Figure 13.4. Autocomplete suggestions are an example of a problem that uses heuristics to constrain the problem space.

Psychologists have investigated hill climbing using a class of brainteasers called river-crossing tasks (in which you must take two sets of people or things across a river with the constraint that one type can never be outnumbered; Greeno, 1974; Thomas, 1974; Knowles & Delaney, 2005; Guthrie et al., 2015; Araiza-Alba et al., 2021). These tasks often required making a move that looked to participants like moving away from the goal. Thomas (1974) timed moves, and showed participants made more errors and decided more slowly at that step in the problem; they were either using the hill-climbing heuristic or were influenced by it.

Another heuristic for moving through a problem space is **working backward**. As the name suggests, in this heuristic, one begins at the goal state and tries to mentally work back to the starting state. This heuristic is useful when the goal state is known but the initial state is not. For example, consider the double-money problem, posed by Wayne Wickelgren (1974):

> Three people play a game in which one person loses and two people win each game. The one who loses must double the amount of money that each of the other two players has at that time. The three players agree to play three games. At the end of the three games, each player has lost one game, and each player has $8. What was the original stake of each player?

We could try to solve this problem by selecting some initial state for the stakes of the three players and working forward, evaluating the outcome, and, if the correct answer is not obtained, trying to adjust the initial state. However, it is much easier to work backward. If all three players end with $8, after the last game, the loser had doubled the money of the two winners; hence, before the last game, the winners must have each had $4, and the loser must have had $16. Because we know that each player won exactly once, it is easy to trace back the stakes, as shown in Table 13.1. (In each game, the asterisk indicates the loser.)

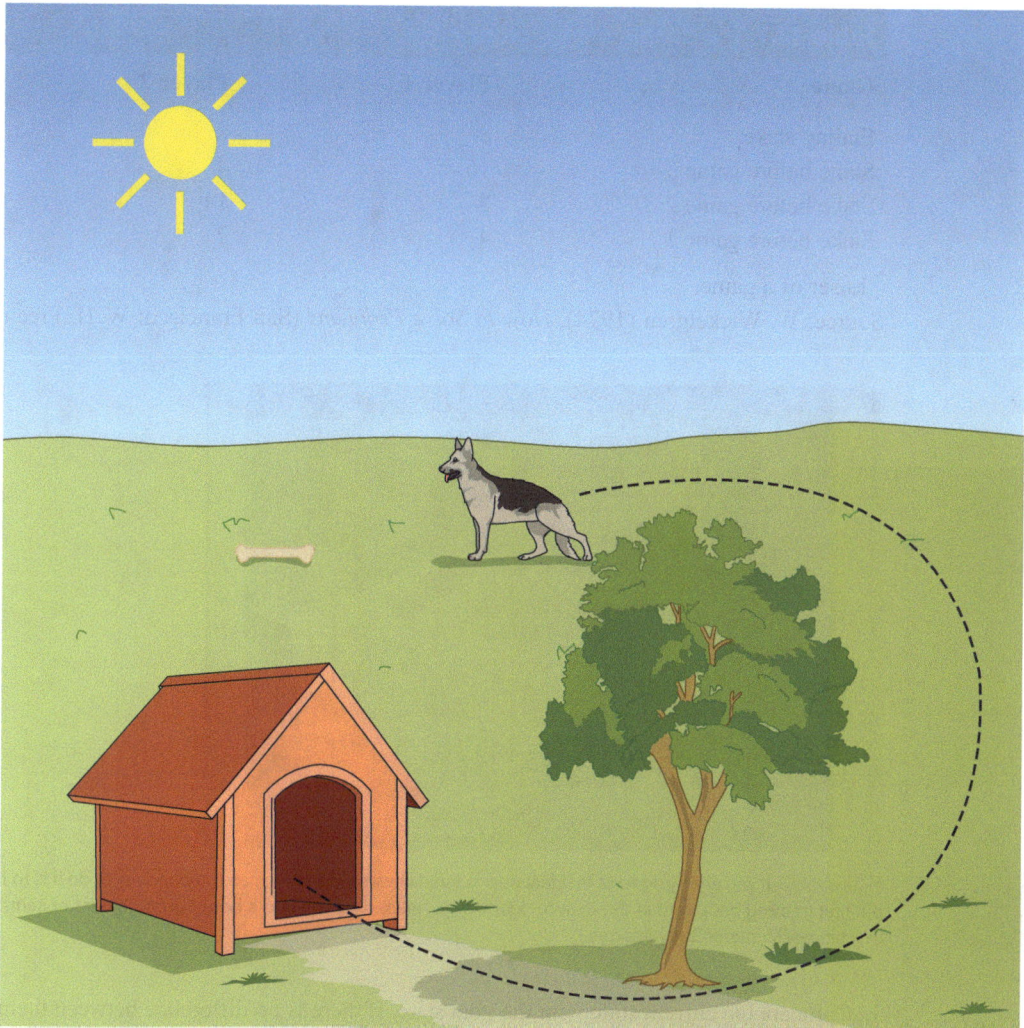

Figure 13.5. A dog on a leash trying to reach a bone in this diagram might try to take the most direct way to the bone, but since the tree is shortening the leash, the best way to reach the bone would be to first go away from the bone (and around the tree).

As you can see, the problem is easy to solve if we work backward from the goal state to the initial state. Wickelgren (1974) argued that problems are well suited to this heuristic if the goal state is known but there are many possible initial states. If there are many possible initial states, there may not be an intelligent heuristic by which one could select an initial state (and then see whether it leads to the goal state). Working forward on problems like this has been likened to finding a needle in a haystack, but working backward on such problems is more like the needle working its way out of the haystack (Newell et al., 1962).

By far, the most thoroughly tested and probably the most broadly applicable heuristic is **means–ends analysis**, which uses a combination of forward- and backward-moving strategies. It has five steps:

Table 13.1 The double-money problem

Game	Player 1	Player 2	Player 3
Ending stake	8	8	8
Stake before game 3	16[*]	4	4
Stake before game 2	8	14[*]	2
Stake before game 1	4	7	13[*]

[*] Loser of a game.
Source: W. Wickelgren (1974), *How to Solve Problems* (San Francisco: W. H. Freeman).

Figure 13.6. If you are trying to fit that last cup in the dishwasher, sometimes the only way to do it is to take a few things out first (moving backward in the task of "loading" is "unloading") to find a better arrangement of items. (Source: Elena Pejchinova/Moment/Getty Images.)

1. Compare the current state with the goal state. If there is no difference between them, the problem is solved.
2. If there is a difference between the current state and the goal state, set a goal to solve that difference. If there is more than one difference, set a goal to solve the largest difference.
3. Select an operator that will solve the difference identified in step 2.
4. If the operator can be applied, apply it. If it cannot, set a new goal to reach a state that would allow the application of the operator.
5. Return to step 1 with the new goal set in step 4.

Take as an example the simple act of taking a date out to a restaurant. Means–ends analysis would solve that problem this way:

Step 1. What is the difference between my current state (at home, alone) and my goal state (at the restaurant with my date). Distance (I'm not at the restaurant) and company (I'm alone, not with my date).

Step 2. There's more than one difference: select "company" as larger problem. Set a goal to be with date. This is also a difference of distance.

Step 3. What operator reduces distance? A car reduces distance.

Step 4. A condition of using a car for a date is that it not have trash in the front seat.

Step 5. Set a subgoal to make the car seat trash-free.

Step 1. What is the difference between my current state (trash in the front seat) and my goal state (clean front seat)? The difference is one of cleanliness.

Step 2. Set a goal to increase front seat cleanliness.

Step 3. What operator improves cleanliness? Moving stuff.

Step 4. Nothing impedes using the "moving stuff" operator. Set goal of moving the trash to the back seat.

You get the idea. Being able to set a new goal is the key advantage of means–ends analysis. More accurately, the new goal is a subgoal in service of the larger goal of being able to apply the operator of using the car to take a date to the restaurant. In the preceding case, the new subgoal was perhaps not the best choice (a more broad "car cleanliness" might have been a better subgoal than "front seat cleanliness"). Setting subgoals is important to allow you to move away from the goal when necessary (as the hill-climbing heuristic does not allow) in service of achieving another goal that will bring you closer to the goal state. Driving in the opposite direction of your destination to get gas for a longer trip is a clear example of using means–ends analysis.

How do we know which operators people are actually using? And how do we know which heuristics they use? One way is by designing problems that are easier to solve with one approach than another, and judging differing performance as indicating different approaches. For example, when people take more time and make more errors at the stage of a problem that requires moving away from the goal, we infer that they are using a hill-climbing heuristic. When some people successfully solve a problem with many initial states and one known goal state, we propose they are working backward.

What if we just asked people what they think they are doing as they solve a problem? In a **verbal protocol**, the experimenter asks the participant to solve a problem while talking out loud, continuously describing their thoughts while solving the problem. The experimenter prompts participants to speak if they fall silent for more than a second or two. The assumption is that the participant has conscious access to at least some of the mental processes that support solving the problem. Although this assumption is controversial (Nisbett & Wilson, 1977), Anders Ericsson and Herb Simon (1993) made an effective case that such data are useful, and indeed, they have proposed a model of how and when information becomes available for verbal report. In the rest of this book, we have often been skeptical of people's subjective judgments of their own cognition, and indeed, there are likely important unconscious mental processes that verbal reports miss, so they shouldn't be our only source of evidence. However, the limitations of verbal protocols can be addressed by converging operations: combining different techniques to address the same question (Podsakoff et al., 2012).

Verbal protocols can also be useful in real-world problem-solving contexts, such as engineering problems (Hacker et al., 2020), airport security screening (Swann et al., 2020), or angel investors (Botelho et al., 2023). Furthermore, verbal protocols have often been especially useful in illuminating individual differences among problem solvers, rather than in describing general rules of problem-solving (Ericsson & Simon, 1984; Ohlsson, 2012). Later in the chapter, we will also discuss how verbal protocols have been used for problems where unconscious processes are assumed especially important. Even in those cases, verbal protocols, combined with performance data, can illuminate the mental process of problem-solving.

So far, we have discussed a specific type of problem in which the problem solver has no experience that seems relevant. Although such problems arise periodically in real life, it is probably more typical that you have some experience in memory that seems to apply to some aspect of the problem.

Stand-on-One-Foot Questions

13.1.   Why are heuristics needed for problem-solving?
13.2.   Name three heuristics for unfamiliar problems.
13.3.   Summarize how means–ends analysis works.

Questions That Require Two Feet

13.4.   We said that the hill-climbing heuristic would not be successful in getting you to the top of the largest hill in an area if you happened to first scale a smaller hill. Could means–ends analysis get you to the top of the largest hill in the area? How would it do so?
13.5.   Think of a game or a puzzle, like poker or another card game, or a crossword puzzle or sudoku. How does its problem space compare to checkers? Why? Could you shrink the problem space of that game?
13.6.   Which of the methods we've discussed so far do you think the average person would use in trying to open a safe? Which method might a professional safecracker use?

How Do People Apply Experience to New Problems?

Preview

Problem-solving strategies change if we have relevant background knowledge. Background knowledge may help us classify problems and see their underlying structure. It may also help because some of the operators may be automatized, leaving attention free for unfamiliar aspects of the problem. Previous experience may also allow problem solvers to draw an analogy to a known problem that shares the same underlying structure, but people have trouble drawing analogies. Background knowledge can actually hurt performance if people try to apply old knowledge to a new problem when it isn't applicable. Even when people make this mistake, the problem sometimes yields to repeated attempts to solve it.

Now we're ready to consider what happens when the solver has some background knowledge relevant to the problem. We might assume that some knowledge must be better than no knowledge. As we'll see, that is generally true, but in some situations background knowledge hurts problem-solving efforts, and psychologists have been especially interested in exploring those cases.

How Experience Helps Problem-Solving

Most of the time, background knowledge is helpful to solving problems. First, if you have background knowledge of the domain, you are better able to classify the problem and therefore to

Figure 13.7. Beginning chess players have to use short-term memory to recall how the pieces move (what are legal moves?) and have fewer mental resources for tactical concerns (what is the best move?). (Source: Dwayne Hills Photography/Blend Images/Getty Images.)

understand the problem's critical components. A study by William Chase and Herb Simon (1973) showed that chess masters remember the positions of chess pieces very accurately by chunking pieces into meaningful configurations. They don't perceive thirty-two chess pieces; they perceive a much smaller number of chunks, each composed of several pieces. The perception of the board in chunks relies on prior experience: If the pieces are arranged randomly, chess masters perceive (and remember) the board no differently than novices.

The second way that domain knowledge can help problem-solving is by automatizing some of the problem-solving components so they do not demand attention. Frequently, that means memorization of the available operators and how they change your location in the problem space. For example, if you are just learning how to play chess, you must think hard about how the knight and the rook move, as well as the oddity that the pawns move ahead one space but can move two spaces from their starting position and take other pieces on the diagonal (see Figure 13.7). If recalling this information occupies working memory, it is hard to form much strategy.

Here's an example of a problem in which the rules are fairly complex; we might imagine that the problem will be difficult to solve without gaining greater familiarity with the rules:

In the inns of certain Himalayan villages is practiced a refined tea ceremony. The ceremony involves a host and exactly two guests, neither more nor less. When his guests have arrived and seated themselves at his table, the host performs three services for them. These services are listed in the order of the nobility the Himalayans attribute to them: stoking the fire, fanning the flames, and pouring the tea. During the ceremony, any of those present may ask another, "Honored Sir, may I perform this onerous task for you?" However, a person may request of another only the least noble of the tasks which the other is performing. Furthermore, if a person is performing any tasks, then he may not request a task that is nobler than the least noble task he is already performing. Custom requires that by the time the tea ceremony is over, all the tasks will have been transferred from the host to the most senior of the guests. How can this be accomplished?

You probably had to read this problem several times just to understand the rules. It's hard even to consider how to get to the goal because the operators are so complicated that they occupy all your working memory capacity.

Contemplating moves through a problem space requires working memory; it becomes difficult to maintain the goal and the operators in working memory if the operators are not automatized so they take little or no working memory capacity. Recall the example of taking a date to a restaurant. The solution to this problem relied heavily on background knowledge, especially on knowledge of how subgoals could be achieved. When confronted with a problem of distance, we know immediately that an automobile is an effective operator to reduce the distance to the target; we don't have to cast about for a solution. Without that knowledge, solving the "distance" subgoal might require a considerable search that would occupy working memory, which might mean that other components of the problem would be lost from working memory.

Were you able to solve the problem involving the Himalayan tea ceremony? You might have used your prior experience by noticing an **analogy** to the Tower of Hanoi problem you saw (and perhaps solved) earlier in this chapter. In fact, even though one problem concerns disks on towers and the other concerns people drinking tea, the problem space and the operators for each are identical. For that reason, these are called problem **isomorphs**. Figure 13.8 should make this analogy concrete. Here's a situation in which you thought about a problem quite recently and were given a new problem directly analogous to it. Yet you didn't use your knowledge of this familiar problem to solve the new one. Why?

The first thing you should know is that you are not alone in failing to make the connection: Many studies have replicated this basic effect. The classic studies on analogy were conducted by Mary Gick and Keith Holyoak (1980, 1983). They used a problem originally devised by Karl Duncker (1945) called the radiation problem, which reads as follows:

> Suppose you are a doctor faced with a patient who has a malignant tumor in his stomach. It is impossible to operate on the patient, but unless the tumor is destroyed the patient will die. There is a kind of ray that can be used to destroy the tumor. If the rays reach the tumor all at once at a sufficiently high intensity, the tumor will be destroyed. Unfortunately, at this intensity the healthy tissue that the rays pass through on the way to the tumor will also be destroyed. At lower intensities the rays are harmless to healthy tissue, but they will not affect the tumor either. What type of procedure might be used to destroy the tumor with the rays without destroying the healthy tissue?

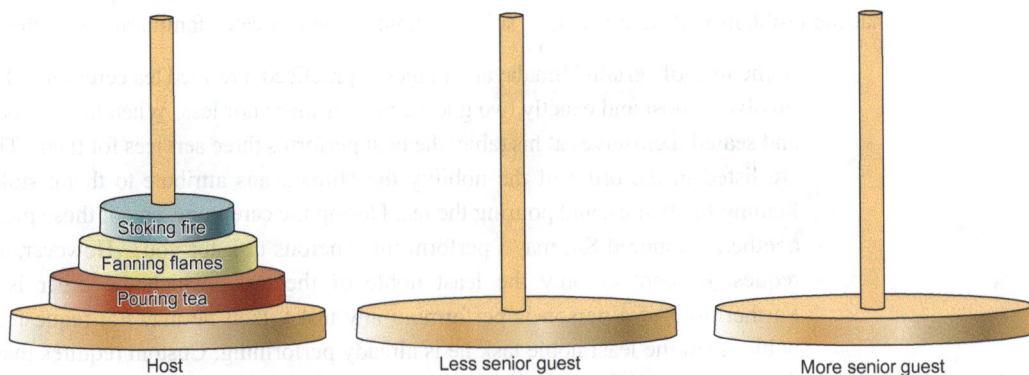

Figure 13.8. The tea ceremony problem is analogous to the Tower of Hanoi problem. Did you see the analogy?

Most people find this problem extremely difficult, and even if they work on it for a long time, only about 10 percent of participants solve it. The answer is that you could use several of the rays at low intensity and point them in such a way that they all meet at the tumor. Thus, only the tumor would be exposed to a high intensity of the rays, and surrounding tissue would not be damaged. (This principle is actually used in cancer treatment.) Again, this is a difficult problem, but suppose that when you took up the radiation problem, you had just finished reading the following story:

> A dictator ruled a small country from a fortress. The fortress was situated in the middle of the country and many roads radiated outward from it, like spokes on a wheel. A great general vowed to capture the fortress and free the country of the dictator. The general knew that if his entire army could attack the fortress at once it could be captured. But a spy reported that the dictator had planted mines on each of the roads. The mines were set so that small bodies of men could pass over them safely, since the dictator needed to be able to move troops and workers about; however, any large force would detonate the mines. Not only would this blow up the road, but the dictator would destroy many villages in retaliation. A full-scale direct attack on the fortress therefore seemed impossible.
>
> The general, however, was undaunted. He divided his army up into small groups and dispatched each group to the head of a different road. When all was ready he gave the signal, and each group charged down a different road. All of the small groups passed safely over the mines, and the army then attacked the fortress in full strength. In this way, the general was able to capture the fortress.

Gick and Holyoak found that if participants were told that the fortress story they had just read might help them solve the radiation problem, 100 percent came up with the correct solution. However, if the experimenters did not tell them to use the fortress story, only 35 percent of the participants solved the radiation problem. Indeed, if the two stories are separated by a delay or presented in different contexts, almost none of the participants use the analogy (Spencer & Weisberg, 1986).

Do people need to be told to use an analogy? That doesn't seem right – surely we spontaneously use analogy sometimes (Dunbar, 2001; Ormerod & MacGregor, 2017). A critical predictor of whether people draw analogies is **surface similarity**, that is, whether the problems use the same elements (e.g., tumors and rays). **Structural similarity** refers to whether the content of the problem that allows you to solve it is the same. Isomorphic problems are structurally equivalent. For example, the radiation and fortress problems are structurally similar because the solution to both entails dispersing strength and focusing it only at the point to be attacked. People seem to be more sensitive to surface similarity when considering analogy. For example, Mark Keane (1987) found that 88 percent of his participants used analogy to solve a problem, even if they had read the analogous story several days before, as long as the analogous story was extremely similar in surface details – in this case, another surgery story. When the story was changed so that the target was intercontinental missiles, the use of the analogy dropped to 58 percent, even though the problem still called for rays to destroy the target. From these studies, we might conclude that surface similarity of problems is the key to whether participants will think of using an analogy. Although results have varied across different experiments and methods, most have supported the greater importance of surface features compared to structural features (Catrambone, 2002; Chen, 1995; Gentner et al., 1993; Ross, 1987, 1989), although structural features do seem to play some role (Clement et al., 1994; Holyoak & Koh, 1987).

There may, however, be an effect of how familiar the familiar problem really is. For example, have a look at this problem:

A treasure hunter is going to explore a cave on a hill near a beach. He suspected there might be many paths inside the cave so he was afraid he might get lost. Obviously, he did not have a map of the cave; all that he had with him were some common items such as a flashlight and a bag. What could he do to make sure he did not get lost trying to get out of the cave later?

Did you think of a solution? When Zhe Chen and colleagues (2004) presented American college students with this problem, about 75 percent were able to solve it, but only about 25 percent of Chinese students could do so. The reason, the researchers argued, was that American students are familiar with the story of Hansel and Gretel, which includes the idea of leaving a trail of breadcrumbs or pebbles to find your way back from a mysterious place (see Figure 13.9a). Chinese students do not grow up hearing that story. The researchers also presented a story analogous to one that Chinese children often hear when growing up, and the percentage of solvers from each country was reversed. The researchers also asked participants whether they thought of the story when trying to solve the problem. Many did (about 67 percent Chinese; 37 percent American), but interestingly, conscious recollection of the problem did not carry the effect. In other words, American students who did not remember the Hansel and Gretel story were still more likely to solve the problem than the Chinese students. (The same was true for the Chinese story.)

These results seem a marked contrast to the other experiments we've discussed. Surface similarity is minimal, but people access the analogous story and successfully apply it, in some cases perhaps accessing it outside awareness. An important difference in this study is that students likely hear a familiar story more than once, perhaps many times. A second experiment showed that surface similarity is still important in drawing analogies to these childhood stories. When the experimenters made one or two elements similar to the original story, participants were more likely to remember the story, more likely to draw the analogy, and more likely to solve the problem.

Can we make it easier for people to draw analogies? Some researchers have suggested that with continued exposure, participants develop an abstract schema for a particular type of problem (Holyoak & Thagard, 1989; Ross & Kennedy, 1990). Recall from Chapter 7 that a schema is a memory representation that captures the general features of an object or event. In this case, a schema would contain the deep structure of the problem and a solution strategy that would be applicable across a variety of problems with this structure. This idea is similar to the pragmatic reasoning schemas, like permissions, from Chapter 12. As we discuss later in this chapter, it is certainly true that experts can readily describe the underlying structure of problems that have different surface structures. It therefore seems logical to infer that when we practice a particular type of problem, we are building a schema that can be applied to a variety of problems in that domain. For example, we're guessing that readers of this textbook would recognize the underlying structure of virtually any problem that required the calculation of the area of a rectangle, whether the surface structure concerned painting a tabletop, planning a playground, or buying glass to fit a picture frame. You're able to recognize that structure because extensive practice has left you with a schema for the underlying structure of such problems.

There does seem to be evidence that practice with a class of problems promotes development of a schema that is general enough to handle problems of that class. Laura Novick and Keith Holyoak (1991) gave participants problems that illustrated the use of algebraic procedures. Participants then tried to apply these principles to novel problems. The experimenters assessed

(a)

(b)

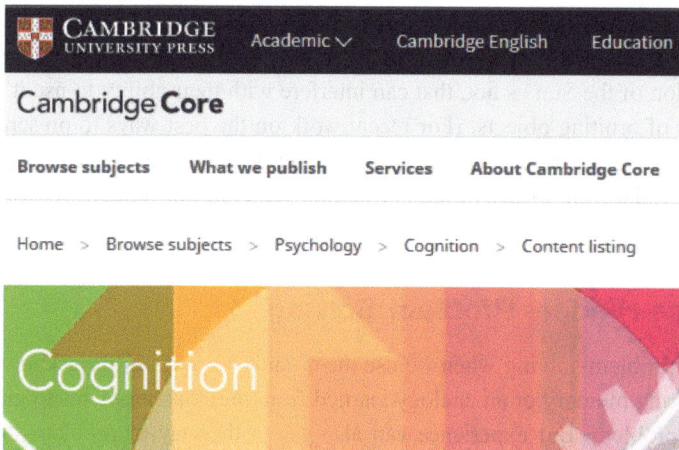

Figure 13.9. (a) The story of Hansel and Gretel not only warns children not to mess with witches who live in edible houses but also provides a solution to finding one's way back from a new place. (b) Interestingly enough, the word *breadcrumbs* is also used for navigation on computers (or on the internet) to help you navigate back to a higher-level page. (Source: (a) Westend61/Getty Images.)

whether applying the analogous problems to the new problems created a schema; they measured schema quality by asking participants to describe which parts of the solution procedures were common to the two problems. The participants with higher-quality schemas tended to show more transfer from the analogous problem. Other experiments supporting the idea of schema induction have shown that repeated solution of analogous problems makes participants better able to make inferences consistent with the schema (Donnelly & McDaniel, 1993; Robins & Mayer, 1993). Recent evidence indicates that, for example, spatial analogies can be particularly helpful to those with lower spatial abilities in solving scientific problems that require spatial reasoning (Jaeger, Taylor et al., 2016; Jaeger, Wiley et al., 2016).

Repeated solution of different but analogous problems helps develop schemas, but are there other ways of improving the quality of schemas that we learn? Researchers have tested how different kinds of explanations can help novices develop schemas and transfer their knowledge to new problems. For example, Boekhout et al. (2010) found that when novices worked on examples provided by experts (as opposed to people with intermediate levels of skill), they performed better in transfer tasks, even if they did not differ in factual knowledge. Lachner and Nückles (2013, 2015) found this advantage to expert explanations as well and conducted an analysis of these explanations along several dimensions. They found that expert explanations referred to fewer concepts, yet were more coherent; that is, the concepts were more tightly organized. The researchers argued that this increased coherence facilitates novices' deeper learning and thus allows transfer to other tasks.

A key theme in this section on analogy is that mapping is important – specifically, the relational mapping between the parts of one entity and another entity. For example, if you're drawing an analogy between the solar system and an atom, then the relationships of the parts of the solar system (the planets and the Sun) should be similar to the relationships of the parts of the atom (particles such as electrons, protons, and neutrons). They are all objects moving in elliptical paths around a common center. The attributes of the objects are not so important in mapping the analogy. It doesn't matter that the Sun is hot and a miasma of incandescent plasma; what matters is how the Sun relates to the planets (they orbit around it, just as electrons orbit the nucleus of an atom). The correct mapping of an analogy, however, can be hindered by prior knowledge. If someone has a strong prior association of the Sun as hot, that can interfere with their ability to use it in an analogy as the center of a set of orbiting objects. (For recent work on the best ways to present analogies in educational settings, see Gray and Holyoak [2021].) In the next section, we will discuss ways that experience, whether in the form of knowledge or of expectations, can hinder problem-solving.

How Experience Hinders Problem-Solving

Experience can help problem-solving when we use the organization of our prior knowledge to limit the demands on working memory or an analogy learned from previous problems to guide a strategy for solving a novel problem. But experience can also get in the way of problem-solving. In this section, we will describe two ways our experience prevents us from successfully solving a problem. The first has to do with how our prior knowledge is organized. The second has to do with expectations of likely solutions.

As we have described in earlier chapters, prior knowledge is often highly organized. One consequence of this organization is that some objects have primary functions that are so strongly associated with that object that they inhibit our ability to think of other ways of using them. Thinking of a common function of an object and being unlikely to consider other possible functions which might solve a problem is called **functional fixedness**. A problem adapted from a classic experiment by Karl Duncker (1945) provides an illustration. In Figure 13.10, you see a candle, a box of matches, and some tacks. The goal is to have the lit candle about five feet off the ground. You've tried melting some of the wax on the bottom of the candle and sticking it to the wall, but that wasn't effective. How can you get the lit candle to be five feet off the ground without having to hold it there?

Could you solve the problem? The solution is to dump the matches out of the box and tack the box to the wall, where it can serve as a platform to support the candle. This is an example of functional fixedness because most people think of the box only in terms of its function as a

(a)

(b)

(c)

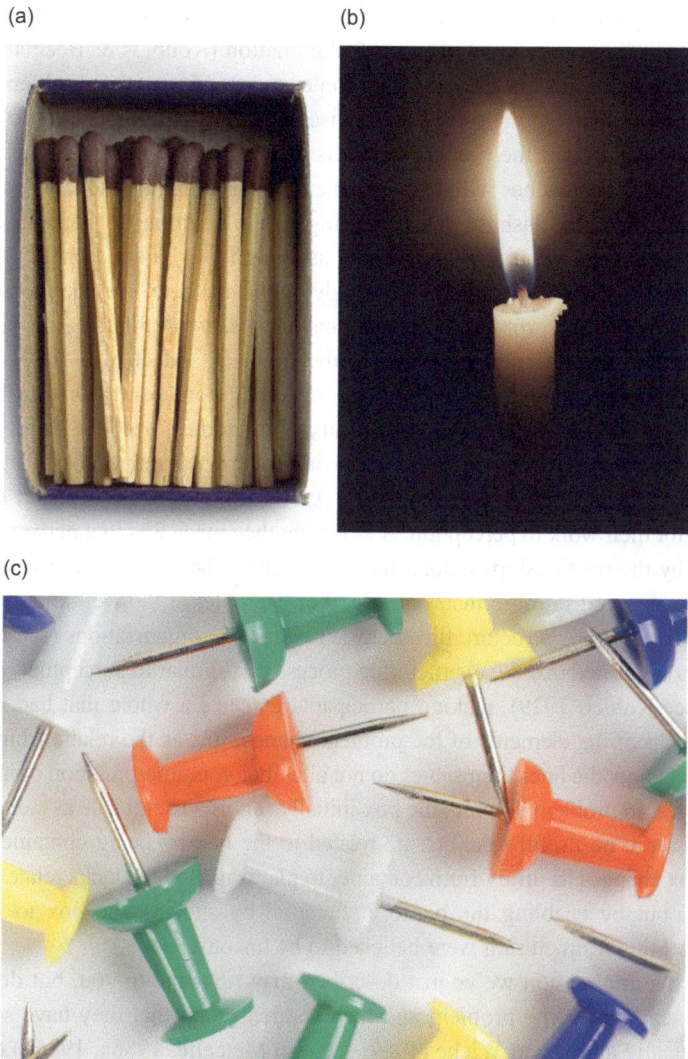

Figure 13.10. Elements in Duncker's (1945) classic problem. (Source: (a) Moskow/Moment/Getty Images; (b) Angelica Bernal/EyeEm/Getty Images; (c) Jingjing Song/EyeEm/Getty Images.)

container – they don't see that it can be used as a platform. That's functional fixedness, and it's an instance in which background knowledge (boxes are used as containers) impedes problem-solving.

Here's another simple problem. Dan and Abe played six games of chess. Dan won four, and Abe won four. There were no ties. How is that possible? The answer to that problem is that they were not playing against one another. Again, prior knowledge impedes the solution – when we hear that two people played a game, we assume they played together.

Here's one more. A man wants to plant four trees in his garden. He wants each tree to be the same distance from the other three. How can he arrange them? By way of a hint, let us point out the prior knowledge that usually gets in the way of a solution: People assume that gardens are flat. Still stuck? The solution is to plant three trees to form a triangle and the fourth tree on a hill (or in a hole), at the center of the triangle.

These are examples of **insight problems**. It seems to the solver that the solution (assuming that it is solved) comes all at once, in a moment of illumination (Kounios & Beeman, 2015; Salvi et al., 2016). It has long been assumed that insight problems differ from other problems in that they do not yield to any of the analytical approaches we discussed earlier. The candle problem requires just one thing: understanding that the box can serve as a platform. Neither hill climbing, working backward, nor means–end approaches will help a problem solver gain that one key insight. The lack of analytical procedure and the flashing "aha!" feeling to the solution go hand in hand. People usually report feeling stumped by an insight problem, as though they've hit a brick wall. Then they get a new way of thinking about the problem, seemingly out of nowhere, and the problem is solved. Researchers who study insight problems refer to this new way of thinking as **restructuring**: Problem solvers evaluate the different elements of the problem and change the way they think about the relationships between those elements. (For some other more examples of insight problems that have been used in laboratory studies and are also fun riddles, see the word game remote associates test [Mednick, 1962]. An online version is available at www.remote-associates-test.com/.)

The insight problems we've been discussing were first proposed by Gestalt psychologists, who are best known for their work in perception. A key point they made was that perception of a figure is often determined by the relationships among its components. The Gestaltists emphasized that the same figure may be perceived in more than one way. For example, in the well-known Necker cube illusion, perception of the cube's structure flips between two stable organizations (see Figure 13.11). Gestalt psychologists suggested that the restructuring process was similar to perceptual organization of parts into wholes (see Kohler, 1929), making participants perceive a whole that had not been seen before. The relationship of the elements of the problem change, just as the relationships of the lines making up the cube change; the lines themselves do not alter, but your interpretation of how they relate to one another changes. In problem-solving, the box initially serves a useful role as a container for the tacks, and the tacks serve no useful role, but are related to the box by being contained. In the new configuration, the box changes its utility from container to platform, and the tacks relate to the box not by being contained, but by enabling the platform function by sticking the box to the wall. The processes that support this restructuring were believed to be unconscious.

The subjective impression we've just described may ring true to you, but do most people feel as though they can't solve the problem and then suddenly find that they have solved it? In a word, yes. Janet Metcalfe and David Wiebe (1987; see also Metcalfe, 1986a, 1986b) examined this

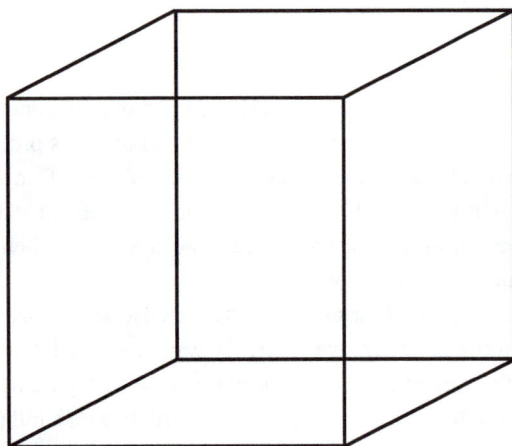

Figure 13.11. A Necker cube. The perceptual organization of the cube is unstable, so it flips between two interpretations. Simply staring at the figure for several seconds will usually make your perception of the figure change.

Table 13.2 Insight and algebra problems used in Metcalfe and Wiebe's (1987) study of insight	
Sample insight problems	Sample algebra problems
A prisoner was trying to escape from a tower. He found in his cell a rope that was half long enough to permit him to reach the ground safely. He divided the rope in half and tied the two parts together and escaped. How could he have done this?	Factor: $x^2 - 6x + 9$
A landscape gardener is given instructions to plant four special trees so each one is exactly the same distance from each of the others. How is this possible?	$(3x^2 + 2x + 10)(3x)$
Describe how to cut a hole in a 3×5 card that is big enough for you to put your head through.	Solve for x: $1/5x + 10 - 25$

Source: J. Metcalfe and D. Wiebe (1987), Intuition in insight and noninsight problem solving, *Memory and Cognition*, 15(3), 238–246.

question by administering insight questions or algebra problems to their participants. Sample problems are shown in Table 13.2. Participants were given four minutes to solve each problem. Every fifteen seconds, they were to rate from 1 to 7 how close they believed they were to a solution (how "warm" they were getting). The pattern of warmth ratings differed between the algebra and insight problems. For the algebra ratings, at the time of solution, everyone gave a rating of 7, which makes sense because they had just solved the problem. Fifteen seconds before that, many of the ratings were still at 6 or 7; participants knew they were getting warm. Moving backward in time, the warmth ratings for the algebra problems became more crowded toward the bottom of the scale. The ratings for the insight problems showed a different pattern. Although participants were confident at the time of solution, just fifteen seconds before then, they had not felt very "warm" at all. Indeed, the pattern of ratings was the same at every time interval until solution. It seems that their progress was flat until they restructured the problem and immediately came to the solution. (When they solved the problem, that is; not everyone did.)

Smith and Kounios (1996) followed up with a different set of insight problems, and instead of rating feelings of warmth, participants were forced to guess before they had enough time to come to a solution. Making people guess is one way of detecting whether people have some unconscious knowledge that is affecting their responses without their awareness. If someone has "partial knowledge" before the solution, their guesses should be better than chance, but that didn't happen in this study, indicating they had no "partial knowledge" of the solution before suddenly solving the problem. Both the feelings of warmth (Metcalfe & Wiebe, 1987) and the test of partial knowledge from Smith and Kounios (1996) support the view that insight is a sudden solution, not incremental, and that people don't know that it's coming. Insight solutions are characterized by not only by suddenness but also by ease (once you come to the strategy, the solution is easy), positive affect (it's fun!), and confidence (Topolinski & Reber, 2010).

The preceding measures of "feelings of warmth," partial knowledge, and retrospective reports of the unexpectedness of the solution indicate that insight problems are not solved gradually or step by step, but cognitive psychologists are often skeptical of thought processes that introspection tells us are immediate or unitary. In many ways, this book takes cognitive processes (such as perception and memory) that seem immediate or unitary and breaks them into unconscious steps or parts. The question for insight problems is, Could there be unconscious processes that get us closer to a solution without our realizing it? The mental path to solving insight problems is not that easy to eavesdrop on, but recent studies have tried different ways of collecting data during the process of solving the problem.

In one clever study, Durso et al. (1994) presented a verbal puzzle and then allowed participants to ask yes or no questions as they attempted to solve it. "A man walks into a bar and asks for a glass of water. The bartender points a shotgun at the man. The man says thank you and walks out." After the solution phase (the yes or no questions), they rated pairs of words for how related they were to each other. Some of the words were directly relevant to the puzzle, like *bartender*, other words were relevant but not as direct, such as *TV* or *pretzels* (things that are often in a bar); and finally, there were words that were relevant to the solution, like *surprise*, *remedy*, *relieved*, and *thank you*. Have you gotten it yet? The man had hiccups and wanted one cure (a glass of water) but got another (a big scare) and was thankful to get rid of his hiccups. Participants who rated the key words as more similar (e.g., seeing the connection between *surprise* and *remedy*) were more likely to solve the problem. A follow-up study that tested the relatedness ratings every ten minutes showed that some people's ratings changed gradually, indicating incremental progress toward the solution.

But what if the word relatedness ratings meant to test people's conceptual understanding of the problem actually hinted at the solution? While this hinting or priming the solution is possible (Davidson, 1995), follow-up research suggests that it doesn't explain the process of solving the problem. Amory Danek and colleagues (2020) applied this word relatedness rating method to another type of problem that resists gradual solving and yields an aha! moment of realization: figuring out a magic trick. Participants rated action words for how related they were to the solution. They found that some participants experienced sudden restructuring associated with a dramatic aha! feeling, while others experienced more gradual conceptual change, which led to a less strong emotional surprise. Less than half of the solutions that participants proposed were correct, which was similar to previous studies with no such word ratings, both indicating that performance was not influenced by any hints these words might have provided. Research is ongoing, but a reasonable summary of where things stand is that insight problems where sudden restructuring leads to a solution with an aha! experience do exist, but modern, careful investigations into people's progress over time indicate that gradual solutions are more common than previously thought (Bilalić et al., 2021).

Experience can also impede problem-solving if the problem description makes it seem that a familiar solution will work, when another is actually more appropriate. When we read a problem, we have a set of default assumptions about the solution, and these defaults can be deterrents to the creative thinking that some problems require. This is the **einstellung effect**, or problem set effects: We get stuck on familiar solutions (*Einstellung* is German for "approach" or "mind-set"). The classic demonstration of this phenomenon is Abraham Luchins' (1942) water jar problems. You have a faucet, three jars, and a drain (Table 13.3). The jars have different capacities, and you are to derive a particular amount of water. For example, in problem 1, you would fill jar A, then pour water from jar A into jar B and empty it three times. That would leave twenty units of water, the measure called for, in jar A. See if you can solve problems 2 through 9 before turning the page.

If you are like 80 percent of the participants in the original study, you solved 7 and 8 by starting with jar B and pouring out A and two Cs (for problem 7: $49 - 23 = 26$, $26 - 3 = 23$, $23 - 3 = 20$). Then you struggled a bit with problem 9. The previous problems led you to a problem set of starting the problem by filling jar B. But notice what happens when you start with jar A for those last

Table 13.3 Luchins' water jar problems				
How would you use three jars with the indicated capacities to measure out the desired amount of water?				
Problem	Jar A	Jar B	Jar C	Desired amount of water
1	29	3		20
2	21	127	3	100
3	14	163	25	99
4	18	43	10	5
5	9	42	6	21
6	20	59	4	31
7	23	49	3	20
8	15	39	3	18
9	28	76	3	25

Source: A. S. Luchins (1942), Mechanization in problem solving: The effect of Einstellung, *Psychological Monographs*, 54(6), 95.

three problems. Much simpler and easier. In this case, as well as in functional fixedness, experience is hindering problem-solving by leading the solver to a dead end, or **impasse**. In the terms we have been using, an impasse is when all of the operators you can think of do not lead to progress on a solution.

As we described, you can reach an impasse using an inappropriate heuristic (like hill climbing), but you can also reach an impasse from prior experience leading you down the wrong path. To overcome the impasse, the problem solver needs to stop trying to take that same path, just like overcoming functional fixedness requires thinking of uncommon uses for objects (i.e., thinking of a box of matches as only a container and not a platform). Recent research has found that the experience of overcoming an impasse has different associated brain activation than merely being told the solution (Rothmaler et al., 2017; for a computational view of insight, see Chen & Krajbich, 2017). Given that common responses are associated with different brain activation than uncommon ones, other researchers have increased performance on problem-solving tasks by using brain stimulation (via TMS) to inhibit those common responses, effectively "zapping" people out of their impasses (Salvi et al., 2020; Chrysikou et al., 2021)! In this section, we have examined what happens when a problem solver has some knowledge that is relevant to a problem, but not extensive knowledge. We have emphasized situations in which partial knowledge is detrimental to problem-solving. Again, such situations are rare; psychologists engineer problems to have this characteristic because they help us understand how people solve problems, just as psychologists interested in visual perception design visual illusions.

Stand-on-One-Foot Questions

13.7. Name the two ways in which background knowledge can aid problem-solving.

13.8. What seems to be the main reason people are not better at using analogies to solve problems?

13.9. How is the **einstellung effect** and functional fixedness similar?

Questions That Require Two Feet

13.10.   You may have heard this advice when you couldn't solve a problem: "Stop thinking about it and come back to it later." Given what you know about how impasses are broken in insight problems, do you think the advice might be sound?

13.11.   Do any of the phenomena we've discussed in this section seem to bear on creativity?

What Makes People Good at Solving Problems?

Preview

The most important difference between expert problem solvers and novices seems to be that experts have much more knowledge about the domain. Surprisingly, they differ less in terms of the processes they use to select operators. Their expertise is a function of applying those operators to a better part of the problem space. There is no great secret to how people acquire expertise; a great deal of practice is crucial. Although certain talents (e.g., intelligence as measured by intelligence tests) appear to be at least partly innate, how such innate talents contribute to expertise is not yet clear. While factors largely outside our control (such as working memory capacity) do contribute to problem-solving success, factors within our control, such as practicing strategies of setting subgoals or comparing problems, also can make us more effective problem solvers.

How Do Experts Differ from Novices?

In the preceding sections, we focused on the difficulties of problem-solving. What do people do when they lack experience that is relevant to a problem, and how can prior experience lead people astray? In this section, we turn our attention to successful problem-solving. By characterizing the differences between expert problem solvers and novices, we hope to better understand why experts are so successful. By extrapolating the findings about experts to novices, we may be able to learn how novices can improve their problem-solving.

By definition, an expert is someone who is very good at solving problems in a particular domain, such as chess, physics, or baking. Some of the earliest and most influential work on expertise examined chess masters. Chess is an excellent domain in which to study expertise because it has a large number of possible moves (in contrast to, say, tic-tac-toe), allowing high levels of expertise, but at the same time the game is bounded, so comparing performance among players is straightforward – it would be harder to compare the expertise of two bakers. In fact, chess masters are an ideal group to study because their expertise is verified through tournaments that have a standard scoring system by which players can be compared. (See Figure 13.12.)

(a)

(b)

(c)

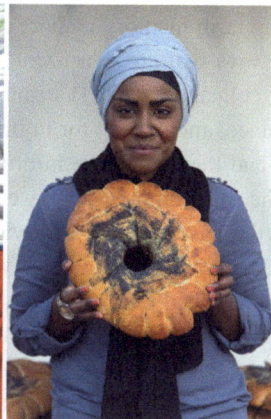

Figure 13.12. Three experts, in chess, physics, and baking. (a) Maurice Ashley, the first African American chess grandmaster, takes on thirty elementary school students at once. (b) Particle physicist Fabiola Gianotti, director general of CERN (European Organization for Nuclear Research), at a museum exhibit explaining particle physics. (c) Award-winning chef Nadiya Hussain poses with a baked good inspired by the Great Fire of London. (Source: (a) Ricky Carioti/The Washington Post via Getty Images; (b) Pier Marco Tacca/Getty Images; (c) Ben A. Pruchnie/Getty Images.)

On the basis of our previous discussion of problem-solving, we might expect two differences between experts and novices: Experts might have more knowledge about the domain, and they might be better at selecting operators to move through the problem space. There is excellent evidence for the first proposal (more knowledge) but mixed evidence for the second (better operators).

William Chase and Herb Simon (1973; Simon & Chase, 1973), following up on classic experiments by Adrianus De Groot (1946/1978), reported that chess masters have extensive knowledge of game positions. Chess masters can remember nearly perfectly all the positions of the pieces after just a brief exposure to the board. However, masters perform about as well as novices if the chess pieces are not in a midgame position but rather are arranged randomly. The importance of the midgame position indicates that masters rely on their stored memory of previous games in performing this working memory task. Novices and masters both remember the same number of chunks of information from the chess board, but for a novice, a single piece is a chunk, whereas for a master, a group of pieces forms a chunk. For example, a master might perceive a rook, king, and three pawns in the corner of the board as a chunk: This is the standard position of these pieces after a player has castled. It is estimated that chess masters may have as many as 50,000 chess patterns stored in long-term memory (Gobet & Simon, 1998; Simon & Gilmartin, 1973). That experts have a large number of patterns stored in long-term memory has been verified in other domains, such as bridge, electronic circuit design, and computer programming.

Not only do experts have more information stored in long-term memory than novices do but the information is also organized differently. For example, Micheline Chi and her colleagues (1981) asked participants to sort physics problems depicted on cards. Physics novices tended to sort cards on the basis of surface features of the problem, such as the objects used; for example, all the problems that concerned inclined planes might be grouped together. Physics experts classified problems according to the physical law applied; for example, all problems concerning conservation of momentum might be classified together. These results have been extended to other domains, such as computer programming, and to objects, such as rice bowls and pictures of dinosaurs (Bedard & Chi, 1992).

Experts' long-term memory is more extensively interconnected than that of novices, and it is interconnected in ways that are consistent with their expertise. For example, a study by Frank Hassebrock and his colleagues (1993) examined the memory of participants at three levels of expertise (novice, trainee, and expert) for information about a medical case. Participants were asked to make a diagnosis and then recall the information presented in the case. Initially, all participants remembered about the same amount. One week later, however, those with more medical expertise remembered *less* of the case overall. This view of expert knowledge fits with the Lachner and Nückles (2013) study described earlier, in which expert explanations were more coherent and organized but often referenced fewer features.

A more fine-grained analysis of the Hassebrock et al. (1993) recall data showed that participants with more expertise remembered a greater proportion of the information that was critical to making a diagnosis. Furthermore, their memory recall was structured similarly to their diagnosis: They remembered information in the same order in which they used it to make the diagnosis. This study shows that new memories within participants' domains of expertise are influenced by the organization of existing memories in that domain (see Figure 13.13).

There is very good evidence that experts have more domain-relevant information stored in memory and that they store this information differently than novices. How about the processes (operators) that move us through a problem space? Do experts engage different problem-solving strategies than novices? Early research with verbal protocols in physics problems indicated that they do (Larkin et al., 1980; Simon & Simon, 1978) with experts more likely to work forward, and novices more likely to work backward. Later research, using a larger sample reported no difference; both groups used forward reasoning (Priest & Lindsay, 1992). The experts used similar procedures, even if their prior knowledge made those procedures more successful.

Not only is there apparently little difference in the procedures that experts and novices apply to problems but it has also been suggested that these processes are not very important in differentiating intermediate expertise from very high-level expertise. Indeed, in his original studies of chess expertise, De Groot (1946/1978) claimed that top-level masters and expert players search the problem space equally deeply; however, the best players are able to restrict their search to parts of the search space that are much more productive (i.e., that lead to better moves). Connors et al.

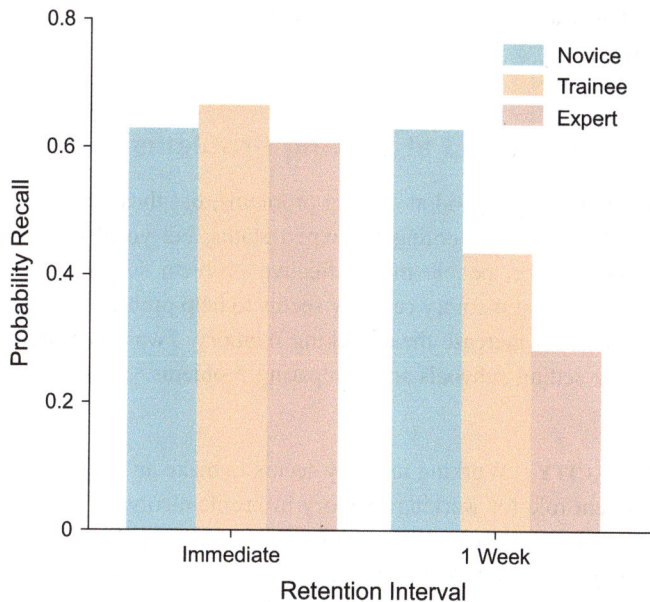

Figure 13.13. Data from Hassebrock et al.'s (1993) study showing that experts remember fewer of the details from a medical case than novices do after a one-week delay. More detailed analysis showed that the experts remembered the details that were important for diagnosis and little else. (Source: F. Hassebrock, P. E. Johnson, P. Bullemer, P. W. Fox, and J. H. Moller [1993], When less is more: Representation and selective memory in expert problem solving, *American Journal of Psychology*, 106[2], 155–189.)

(2011) replicated De Groot's classic study nearly seventy years later, confirming that experts search faster than intermediates but that depth of search did not account for this difference. Interestingly, all the players, both expert and intermediate, searched faster in 2010 than they had in 1946.

The relative unimportance of search processes in chess expertise is also supported in a study by Bruce Burns (2004) (see also Gobet & Simon, 1996). Burns compared chess players' ability when they played blitz chess (five minutes allowed for the entire game) to their ability when playing normal tournament chess. The idea is that recognition memory operates very quickly, but search processes in problem-solving are very slow. Thus, if expertise is based mostly on recognition memory, restricting time (as in a blitz tournament) will impair everyone equally. If, however, expertise is based on search, the limited time allowed restricts search, so it's the expert players who will really be affected by the time limit.

As mentioned earlier, the skill of all chess players is ranked on a common scale, so Burns (2004) could take the ratings from regular tournaments and predict who should win a game of blitz chess. Burns analyzed data from thirteen tournaments involving 1,177 data points. He found that players' performance in regular tournaments was an excellent predictor of their play in blitz chess. The interpretation is that chess expertise relies mostly on fast processes supported by recognition memory and much less on slower processes of searching the problem space. The importance of deep and organized background knowledge in chess (and how it accounts for experts' better play and better memory) is further reinforced by Lane and Chang (2017), in whose study chess knowledge, over and above chess experience, predicted chess memory. Another way of putting this is that the cliché that chess grandmasters "look far into the future," whereas novices look ahead by only one or two moves, is not correct. Chess experts do not necessarily look much further into the future; they can take a quicker look and recognize the relevant elements perceptually (think of your own quick looks while driving), and they also have a better idea of which part of the future it is best to look into (Reingold & Sheridan, 2023).

What Makes Nonexperts Good at Solving Problems?

We are discussing what makes people good at solving problems, but thus far we have focused on experts. Suppose you can't commit to shooting for expert status, but you'd like to improve your problem-solving skills. What makes people more effective problem solvers? We discuss three factors. First, having a large working memory capacity seems to help problem-solving, but unfortunately, it doesn't seem people can increase their working memory. Two other strategies that may improve problem-solving are setting subgoals and comparing problems.

WORKING MEMORY CAPACITY   Working memory seems to make an important contribution to problem-solving. A prominent role for working memory in problem-solving is sensible in light of the framework discussed earlier in this chapter: using operators to move through a problem space. You must keep several things in working memory simultaneously to use means–ends analysis: the current subgoal, the operator you are trying to apply, and the conditions of that operator. Perhaps more important, you must shuttle information between working memory and long-term memory; as a subgoal is achieved, you must retrieve the next goal, search long-term memory for appropriate operators, and so on.

Kenneth Kotovsky and his colleagues (Kotovsky et al., 1985; Kotovsky & Simon, 1990) argued for the importance of working memory in problem-solving. They administered different isomorphs of the Tower of Hanoi problem to participants. As we described earlier, these are problems with a different cover story but with a problem space that is the same size and that has the same number of branches and the same minimum solution path. We offered the tea ceremony problem as an isomorph of the Tower of Hanoi. Here's another:

> Three five-handed extraterrestrial monsters were holding three crystal globes. Because of the quantum mechanical peculiarities of their neighborhood, both monsters and globes come in exactly three sizes with no others permitted: small, medium, and large. The small monster was holding the medium-size globe; the medium-size monster was holding the large globe; and the large monster was holding the small globe. Because this situation offended their keenly developed sense of symmetry, they proceeded to shrink and expand the globes so each monster would have a globe proportionate to its own size. Monster etiquette complicated the solution of the problem because it requires the following:

> Only one globe may be changed at a time.
> If two globes have the same size, only the globe held by the larger monster may be changed.
> A globe may not be changed to the same size as the globe of the larger monster.

> By what sequence of changes could the monsters have solved this problem?

You can see that this problem is like the Tower of Hanoi problem, but people found this version extremely difficult. Why? Kotovsky and his colleagues (1985; Kotovsky & Simon, 1990) argued that working memory is the culprit. The rules are complicated. There is no physical realization of the problem (e.g., a board with pegs), so participants have to remember where they are in the problem space (in this case, which monster is holding which globe). Just thinking about

Table 13.4 Sample questions from Kyllonen and Christal's (1990) study

Test name	Sample question
Arithmetic reasoning	Pat put in a total of 16.5 hours on a job during 5 days of the past week. How long is Pat's average workday?
Number sets	Select the set that doesn't fit: 234; 567; 357; 678.
Necessary arithmetic operations	Chairs priced at $40 each are being sold in lots of four at 85 percent of the original price. How much would four chairs cost?
Nonsense syllogisms	All trees are fish. All fish are horses. Therefore, all trees are horses. True or false?
Three-term series	Dick is better than Pete; John is worse than Pete. Who's best: Dick, John, or Pete?

Source: P. C. Kyllonen and R. E. Christal (1990), Reasoning ability is (little more than) working-memory capacity?, *Intelligence*, 14(4), 389–433.

the rules and imagining the monsters uses up most people's working memory capacity, so they have nothing left over to work out the problem.

Other work has shown that people are less successful in solving syllogisms if the premises are given orally rather than in writing, presumably because maintaining the premises in working memory reduces the capacity to manipulate them to evaluate the syllogism (Gilhooly et al., 1993). A somewhat similar approach was taken in a study by Pierre Barrouillet (1996), who examined working memory contributions to transitive inference by varying the amount of irrelevant information that appeared between key statements that could be used to make inferences. He reported that increasing the number of irrelevant statements increased erroneous inferences, presumably because of the difficulty of maintaining the statements for a longer time in working memory.

A different method used to examine the relationship between working memory and problem-solving is statistical association. In an article provocatively titled "Reasoning Ability Is (Little More than) Working-Memory Capacity?," Patrick Kyllonen and Raymond Christal (1990) reported that people who have a large working memory capacity also score well on tests of reasoning, whereas those with small working memory capacity score poorly. They reported four studies, each with 400 or more people tested. Reasoning ability was tested with a total of fifteen tests across the four experiments. Sample problems are shown in Table 13.4.

The authors found a consistently high correlation (around 0.8 or 0.9 across experiments) between their measures of working memory and measures of reasoning ability. Even an article arguing that working memory and intelligence were not as strongly related as everyone thinks still claimed a correlation of 0.48 (Ackerman et al., 2005). This strong relationship is consistent with the idea that effective reasoning and problem-solving depend on working memory capacity (see also Carpenter et al., 1990; Engle et al., 1999; Kane et al., 2004; Reber & Kotovsky, 1997; Chuderski & Jastrzębski, 2018), as are data showing a relationship between working memory capacity and children's performance in school (Gathercole et al., 2004; Wüstenberg et al., 2016). Wiley and Jarosz (2012) have suggested that working memory helps problem solvers control attention, resist distraction, and narrow their search through analytic problem spaces. Chang and Lane (2018) found that working memory also helped predict chess ratings among chess players (after controlling for other time spent on chess-related activities), suggesting that deliberate practice helps, but so does working memory capacity.

Thus far, our discussion of how nonexperts can be better problem solvers has focused on working memory, so the advice really boils down to this: "If you want to be a good problem solver, have a good working memory." The last ten years have seen an enormous amount of research directed to training programs meant to increase working memory capacity. The last ten years have also seen enormous controversy regarding whether this training works, with many competing training programs advertising good results but cognitive scientists urging caution in interpreting poorly designed studies or jumping to unsupported conclusions.

The basic approach seems simple. Participants undergo an initial session including several tests of working memory capacity and efficiency. Next, participants undergo training, consisting of "games" (we use scare quotes around the word because the games are not always fun) that are demanding of working memory. As people improve, the game becomes harder. At the end of training, participants again complete a battery of measures of working memory capacity and efficiency.

That's a simple experiment, but the interpretation has not proven simple. As we've described the procedure, you'll definitely observe what seems to be a substantial improvement in working memory: much better test performance after training than before. But there are two important alternative explanations. First, it may be that people are getting better at the games, but not because working memory is improving – they are getting better at other aspects of the task. To test this, we can administer tests of working memory that are dissimilar to those used in training. When experimenters have done so, people typically show great performance on new tasks that are highly similar to those used during the training. But as the tests differ more from training, there is less benefit from training (Simons et al., 2016).

The second concern in working memory training experiments is the particulars of the control group. It's not enough to show that participants are better on working memory tasks after training than they were before; that improvement could be due to an *expectation* of improvement. People do better on working memory tests if they try harder – the tests are really demanding, so your effort matters. People who know that they have undergone working memory training might try harder on the final test because they think they were supposed to improve. In one especially convincing demonstration of this effect, researchers showed that participants who thought they were signing up for a working memory training experiment did indeed show improvement in working memory; but those told that the tasks served a different purpose showed no improvement in working memory, even though they underwent exactly the same training (Foroughi et al., 2016)! More generally, the studies that have shown working memory training to be effective have used poor control groups, and better designed studies show no benefit to working memory of working memory training (Simons et al., 2016; Redick, 2019). Surveying the results of many studies of working memory training in typically developing children, Sala and Gobet (2020) mince no words: "We conclude that there is no reason to keep investing resources in working memory training research with typically developing children" (p. 423).

So working memory capacity may not be as easy to improve as training programs might like you to believe, but the documented importance of working memory to problem-solving offers another suggestion to nonexpert problem solvers: Instead of boosting your own working memory, try to reduce the working memory demands of the task as much as you can by offloading them to props or aids. Bocanegra et al. (2019) call this externalizing cognitive operations and found that people who used external props and aids were more effective problem solvers. Obviously, using an external aid (such as writing down your shopping list) simply solves the problem if the problem is purely one of memory. However, many problems are a combination of memory and other cognitive tasks. In these cases, lowering the complexity of the task by reducing what you have to hold in working memory (such as through visual models or manipulating props) can help make the task easier (Helie & Pizlo, 2022).

Another way that you can reduce working memory demands is by building working memory capacity for a particular domain by studying the domain. For example, you can increase your working memory capacity for chess positions by learning a lot about chess because then you'll be better at chunking pieces. But that is tantamount to committing yourself to becoming an expert. Is there no simpler way to improve problem-solving skills? Two other strategies have been pursued: setting subgoals and comparing problems.

SETTING SUBGOALS   Richard Catrambone (1994, 1995, 1996, 1998; Catrambone & Holyoak, 1990) has investigated the effect of encouraging people to set subgoals. Catrambone noted that people tend to memorize a series of steps that depend on the surface features of the problem (Chi et al., 1981; Larkin et al., 1980; Ross, 1987, 1989). Therefore, if the surface features of the problem change, the memorized solution is of no use because the solution steps were tied to the surface features (Reed et al., 1990). Catrambone suggested that people should be taught to form subgoals because problems within a domain are likely to share a subgoal even if the steps to achieve it vary. For example, in physics problems of the sort used by Chi et al. (1981), people should be taught the subgoal of first determining which of the physical laws is applicable to the problem; that subgoal will always be useful, although the method to achieve it may vary from problem to problem.

Unfortunately, trying to teach people subgoals is not very effective. For one thing, people like to see examples when they are trying to solve problems, not just abstract solution procedures (Cheng et al., 1986; LeFevre & Dixon, 1986). Attempts to teach people subgoals directly have not worked well (see Reed & Bolstad, 1991).

Catrambone (1996) tried a different method. He showed participants example problems and applied labels to groups of steps, with the idea that people would chunk these steps together into a subgoal. Here is one problem:

> A judge noticed that some of the 219 lawyers at City Hall owned more than one briefcase. She counted the number of briefcases each lawyer owned and found that 180 of the lawyers owned exactly one briefcase, 17 owned two briefcases, 13 owned three briefcases, and 9 owned four briefcases. Use the Poisson distribution to determine the probability of a randomly chosen lawyer at City Hall owning exactly two briefcases.

Catrambone had participants study the solution. In one condition, one of the steps was labeled "total number of briefcases owned," thereby highlighting that an interim step was to calculate the total number of objects. At transfer, all participants saw a different problem:

> Over the course of the summer, a group of five children used to walk along the beach each day collecting seashells. We know that on Day 1 Joe found four shells, on Day 2 Sue found two shells, on Day 3 Mary found five shells, on Day 4 Roger found three shells, and on Day 5 Bill found six shells. Use the Poisson distribution to determine the probability of a randomly chosen child finding three shells on a particular day.

This is similar to the briefcase problem, but it requires finding total frequency in a different way. Finding the total is actually simpler in the transfer problem, but participants might not know how to solve it if they didn't understand that part of the solution procedure is to find the total number of objects. Catrambone (1995, 1996) found that participants who had seen the subgoal as part of the solution procedure during training were about twice as likely to solve this new problem. In a more realistic setting of teaching introductory students a programming language, explicitly labeling subgoals in a text and example helped students solve novel problems better than those who saw no subgoal labels (Margulieux & Catrambone, 2016).

COMPARING PROBLEMS   Gick and Holyoak (1983) proposed that transfer to new problems occurs if there is an abstract schema for the problem and its solution – that is, for the deep structure of the problem. For example, the schema for the radiation problem would include the idea of the dispersal of force and its regathering at the critical point. Gick and Holyoak suggested that participants could be made to induce the deep structure of problems by having them compare problems that have different surface structures but share deep structure. They conducted a study that supported the idea, but a more complete set of studies was presented by Catrambone and Holyoak (1990).

Catrambone and Holyoak (1990) had half their participants read two stories with the same deep structure (the fortress problem and another problem in which firefighters encircled a fire and threw buckets of water on it). The other half heard one of these stories and a control story with a different deep structure. Next, half the participants in each group were asked to compare the stories, and half were not. Finally, all participants were given the radiation problem we discussed earlier. As you might expect, reading one analogous story did little to help solve the problem – about 15 percent of these participants solved it. The group that read two analogous stories and did *not* compare them fared little better – about 25 percent solved it. But 47 percent of the participants who read two stories and compared them solved the radiation problem. The interpretation is that the process of comparison induced participants to extract the deep structure of the problem, which they spontaneously applied to the new problem (see also Bassok & Holyoak, 1989; Bernardo, 1994; Gentner et al., 2003; Loewenstein & Gentner, 2001).

In sum, when we learn a new solution to a problem, we tend to represent the problem in the concrete terms in which it was presented. When a new problem comes along, we search memory for problems that are similar in surface structure, not deep structure. Comparison presumably helps because it encourages participants to think about what the examples have in common, thereby highlighting the common thread.

Incubation. While setting subgoals helps with analytic problems, other strategies help with insight problems. **Incubation** occurs when a problem solver puts aside an unsolved problem and thinks about something else for some period of time. By discontinuing active problem-solving, the problem solver frees unconscious processes that might reach the insightful solution. In a meta-analysis, Sio and Ormerod (2009) reported that incubation improves problem-solving and that incubation effects are larger when the wait period is longer and when it's filled with a task that's low in cognitive demand.

We might ask whether the unconscious processes used during incubation overlap with the conscious processes used during problem-solving. Gilhooly et al. (2013) examined this question by using different kinds of incubation on different types of creative tasks. Participants performed either a verbal creative task ("generate unusual uses for a brick") or a spatial one ("arrange five shapes to form as many recognizable shapes as you can"). Then the incubation period was filled with either a verbal task (solving anagrams) or a spatial one (mental rotation). When the incubation task (spatial

or verbal) matched the creative task (spatial or verbal), there was no benefit of the in
When the tasks did not match, there was. Thus, it seems there is some overlap in
incubation processes and the conscious problem-solving processes.

To solve a problem, people can apply background knowledge or use an analogy to a similar
problem. Sometimes this background knowledge can get in the way of finding a solution through
functional fixedness or the einstellung effect, and analogies are not as helpful as we might like
because it's hard to think analogous problems. Experts are better than novices at solving problems in
their domain of expertise, not by a deeper search process, but by restricting their search space and by
using pattern recognition supported by memory. Some novices are better at problem-solving by
having greater working memory, but novices can improve by comparing problems and by
using incubation.

Stand-on-One-Foot Questions

13.12. How do experts differ from novices?
13.13. What is the definition of practice?
13.14. Other than practice, what makes someone good at solving problems?

Questions That Require Two Feet

13.15. Does practice guarantee expertise?
13.16. Do you think working memory capacity is an important limitation in insight problems?
13.17. Considering everything you've read in this chapter, what is the best advice you would give
        to, say, a high school student studying geometry who wants to know the best way to learn
        to solve problems in that domain?

Appendix A Bringing It All Together: The Case of Visual Imagery

To review the concepts of Chapter 2, let's take an example we haven't introduced yet and apply the framework for using behavioral data to test cognitive theories that we've discussed. Close your eyes. (OK, read these instructions first, then close your eyes.) Imagine yourself opening the door to your cognitive psychology classroom before class and seeing your diligent and brilliant cognitive psychology professor frantically preparing their lesson for the day. How big is the room? What color are the walls? Where do you sit? Imagine that situation in as much detail as you can. OK, now open your eyes.

Cognitive psychologists call this **visual imagery**, and despite it seeming to be a classic example of an unobservable and personal mental process, like pictures in your head that only you can see, it was a wonderful example of theory testing first with behavioral data, then later with neuroscientific data. What's more, the theory being tested was a straightforward one that translates to a simple question: Are visual images really pictures in your head?

Your first thought may be "How could it be otherwise? I feel like I am seeing a picture of my professor right now and imagining the view from the perspective of my usual seat." But remember our example from Chapter 1 of the problem of the inverted retinal image and the infinite pictures being watched by infinite little people in our heads. Doesn't imagery being pictures in the head have the same problem? Also, let's remember the assumption that example illustrated: that a mental process doesn't necessarily work the way we experience it.

Step 1. Develop Alternative Theories

Our experience that images are visual and the caution that our experiences don't relate to how mental processes work led to two competing theories of visual imagery, each with its own set of abstract constructs. In the first theory, the mind stores memories, and the contents of that memory storage are represented as a list of words and relationships. There is more about this idea of representation in the chapters on memory (Chapters 5–8) and language (Chapters 10 and 11), but for now, we could think of this theory proposing that all our memories and knowledge are a kind of giant mental dictionary. We introduced the word *representation* in Chapter 1 when we talked about the computer metaphor as a symbol or code that translates the real world into the "language" of the mind. The first theory of visual imagery is that all representation in the mind is abstract verbal representation, which supports memory, language, and any other cognitive function that needs it. According to this theory, when you imagine your cognitive psychology classroom, your mental representation is a set of words and relationships, called **propositions**. A proposition is abstract, describes relationships, conforms to a syntax (like language), makes a claim, and has a truth value (Kosslyn, 1980). *Professor is at front of room. Walls are green. Room is cold. Classmate is yawning. Laptop is on top of desk. Chair is under desk*. Even if your experience of visualizing your classroom feels, well, visual, this theory proposes that that experience is not how your mental process works.

The second theory is that in addition to verbal representations, we have another representational system, called depictive, that is not just verbal representations formatted as a set of propositions but has a distinctly different representational format that can be described only in pictures or images. Depictive representations are spatial and preserve geometric qualities of objects in space. Not just "ceiling is above the floor, on top of walls" but "ceiling is 20 feet tall, painted a certain color that words cannot capture, with a certain texture that isn't in words, and sloped at a certain angle that you don't have an exact number for but can imagine." Notice how the words here surely don't give your ceiling justice. Depictive representations are not purely abstract but specific to color, texture, and other visual qualities, like a picture is.

So, we've got step 1 covered: our two alternative theories are proposed as to how the mental process of visual imagery happens. The propositional theory says that we've got one representational system; why propose a second one? Then you might need a third and a fourth and so on – where does it stop? For scientific theories, the simpler, the better (this is called **Occam's razor**). Also, don't mistake our intuitions for how a mental process actually works. Willingham might experience his mental process of scanning his list of drinks as stopping once he reaches the target, but Sternberg's data show that longer lists take longer to search. The propositional theory was described and defended by Zenon Pylyshyn (1973, 1981, 2002, 2003). The depictive theory says that despite these good reasons to be cautious in proposing a new representational system, we do have pictures in the head. So who wins?

Step 2. Derive Signature Predictions

Let's move on to step 2, deriving signature predictions for each theory. In this case, it makes sense for the propositional account to be the default and for the burden of proof to be on the depictive, as they are proposing an additional representational system. If a key element of the depictive representation is that it is spatial, a signature prediction might be that when inspecting mental images, people's answers (their behavior) would follow spatial patterns, such as taking longer to respond when moving farther on an image or taking longer to identify small objects than larger objects.

Step 3. Collect Data

Let's move on to step 3, collecting some data to compare theories! As we'll see, a single experiment rarely settles battling theories once and for all, but converging evidence and multiple tests can often help one theory win out. Kosslyn (1973) asked participants to memorize simple line drawings of objects. Then later, they would be prompted with one of the objects, like "boat," followed by a delay, then they would be asked whether that object had a certain part (like "mast" or "motor"), and the participant had to answer whether the boat had a mast in the drawing (and presumably in their representation of the drawing). The signature prediction is that it would take longer to answer for those parts that were farther to the right, indicating that the participant was mentally scanning the image from left to right. Indeed, that was the case: people's reaction times were systematically longer for objects on the right. The behavior of longer reaction times suggests a mental construct of mentally scanning an image, rather than mentally reciting a list of words.

A propositional account would not seem to predict that parts on the right would take longer to verify than those on the left if it is just a list of parts and relationships. But wait, perhaps the list is arranged left to right or the parts are "attached" to the whole in a network of links, which can still be accounted for by a purely propositional account (Kosslyn, 1980). More follow-up experiments would be needed.

There were many follow-up experiments – different boats, maps, objects, and so on. Here's one clever one. Kosslyn (1975, 1976) asked one set of participants to imagine a rabbit next to an elephant and another set to imagine the rabbit next to a fly. Once they had that image in mind, he then asked all participants, "Is the rabbit's nose pink?" Those who imagined the rabbit next to an elephant took longer (and this was repeated with many other animals) presumably because the spatial features in the proposed depictive mental representation (in this case, the size of the rabbit's nose) affected people's behavior (the time that they took to answer about an aspect of that feature [the color]).

Signature predictions for these theories were also tested in neuroscience studies. If imagery is supported by a separate representation that has a lot in common with perception, then when participants perform imagery tasks, the part of the brain that usually handles visual tasks will be most active. If, instead, propositions do the work behind these imagery tasks, then the language centers of the brain should be most active during imagery tasks because propositions are verbal. More recent neuroscience research has applied the "beyond localization" approaches, not just "part of the brain that handles perception" versus "language centers" but also the patterns of firing and time order mentioned earlier.

Many investigators have reported activation of primary or secondary visual cortex during imagery tasks (Charlot et al., 1992; Chen et al., 1998; Fletcher et al., 1995; Klein et al., 2004; for a review, see Pearson et al., 2015). Conceptually similar findings are observed with auditory imagery, which activates primary and secondary auditory cortex (e.g., Bunzeck et al., 2005). The same is even true for senses less frequently used in imagery studies, such as tactile imagery. The important conclusion from the imaging work is that the activations observed are in the same brain areas known to support perception, rather than in areas known to support language (as the propositional theory of imagery would predict). Notice how the data in these neuroscience studies are not reaction times but rather the activation of brain areas.

In addition to visual imagery activating primary visual cortex, imagining and perceiving specific visual stimuli seem to produce remarkably similar patterns of brain activity. For example, different parts of the visual cortex support the perception of places and the perception of faces; just the same areas support imaging these stimuli (O'Craven & Kanwisher, 2000). Even more impressive, Haynes and Rees (2006; see also Stokes et al., 2009) found that the pattern of activation for viewing an X and imagining an X were similar enough (and different enough from viewing an O and imagining an O) that, simply by inspecting the pattern of activation in fMRI, they were able to reliably distinguish whether the participant was imagining an X or imagining an O.

Recent findings have distinguished even finer detail. Naselaris et al. (2015) recorded brain activation as participants viewed five works of art. Then, in a second session, participants imaged them, and again brain activation was recorded. The researchers were able to compare brain activation during perception and brain activation during visual imagery and, from the overlap, predict which piece of art the participant was imaging. Most impressive, the brain activity was based not on the objects in the painting (the Richter shows a woman, the Gursky shows a bridge, the Wyeth shows a house) but on the perceptual characteristics of the paintings (orientation of lines, colors, spatial locations). This is compelling evidence that visual mental imagery is supported by a depictive representation.

So, in summary, the process of testing cognitive theories through both behavioral and neuroscientific data goes through the three steps of (1) developing alternate theories (or modifying the theories), (2) deriving signature predictions, and (3) obtaining data to compare the theories. In the case of the imagery debate, many rounds of experiments, starting with behavioral data on reaction times in the 1970s and 1980s and continuing into neuroscience research in the 1990s and through to today, have concluded that we do have a depictive representational system more linked with perception, in addition to a verbal representational system.

Appendix B The Five-Minute Brain Anatomy Lesson

In describing brain structures, we often talk about the position of one relative to another. Brain structures are large enough that one might want to refer only to part of one; it's tiresome to refer to "the part of the cerebellum that's closer to the top of the head and toward the back of the head." As shown Figure B.1, toward the top of the head is called **dorsal**; toward the bottom is **ventral**; toward the front is **anterior** or **rostral**; toward the back is **posterior** or **caudal**; toward the middle is

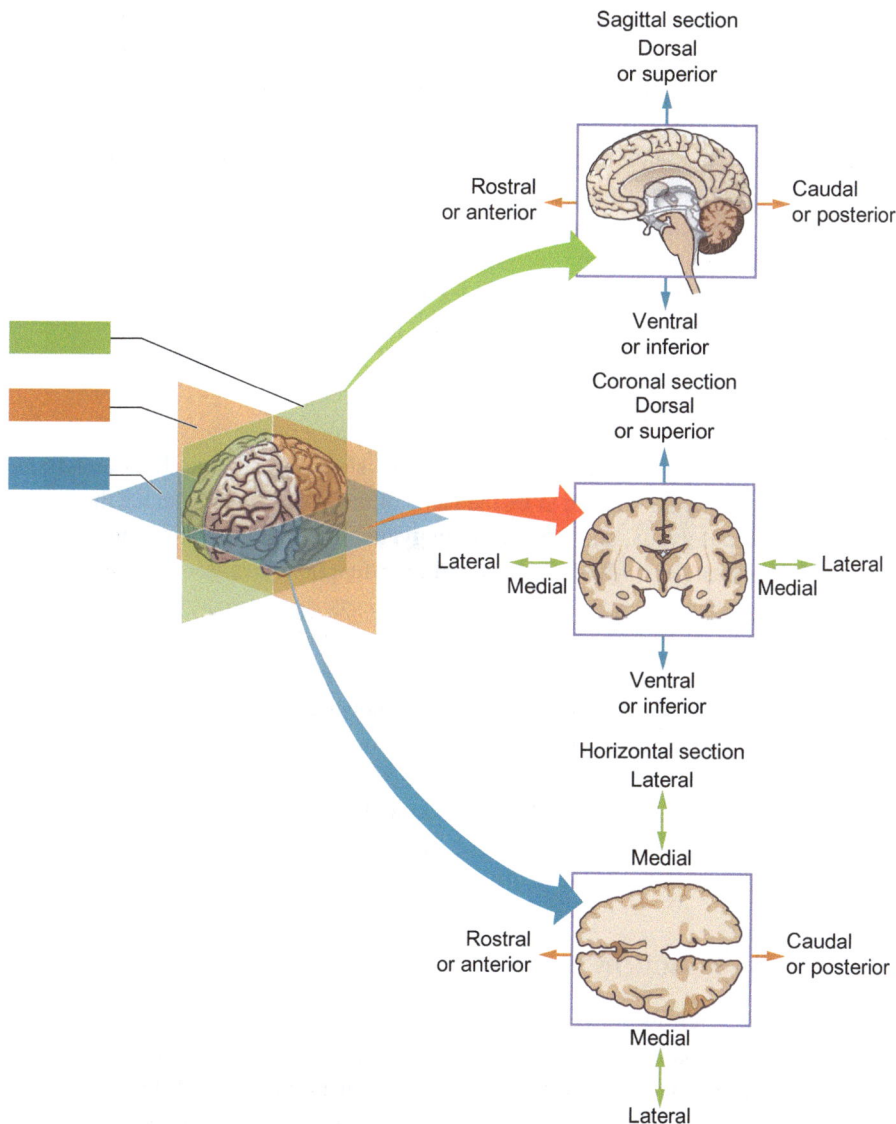

Figure B.1. Directional descriptors of brain anatomy.

medial; and toward the side is **lateral**. Thus we could replace the cumbersome phrase "the part of the cerebellum that's closer to the top of the head and toward the back of the head" with "dorsal posterior cerebellum."

Cerebral Cortex

The cerebral cortex is the layer of cells that covers the outside of the brain. When you see a picture of the brain, you're typically looking at cerebral cortex. This cell layer is quite thin (about three millimeters), but unfolded, the sheet of cells would cover about two and a half square feet. That large sheet is crumpled to fit into the skull, hence the wrinkled appearance of the brain. The valleys are called **sulci** (singular **sulcus**), and the hills are called **gyri** (singular **gyrus**). The brain is separated into two hemispheres – left and right – and the cortex folds down into the space between them.

The cortex is not uniform. There are different types of cells in different areas, and most important for our purposes, different parts of the cortex serve different cognitive functions. Researchers refer to different areas of cortex using three naming systems: naming by lobe, naming by function, and naming by landmark. It may seem confusing (or better, stupid) to use three different systems to name the same thing. For example, the primary motor cortex (function) could also be called the precentral gyrus (landmark) or posterior frontal cortex (lobe). (It's also called Brodman's area 4 and M1.) Why not pick one name? We could have translated everything into one system, but doing so would be a disservice to readers because certain structures are very commonly referred to by the name in a particular system. If you referred to the lateral temporal cortex and everyone else is calling it the fusiform gyrus, the other kids would make fun of you.

Naming by Landmark

Each gyrus and sulcus in the brain is named, as shown in Figures B.2a and B.2b. A few brain locations are commonly referred to by the name of the gyrus: These include the **fusiform gyrus,** the **parahippocampal gyrus,** and the **cingulate gyrus.** In addition, two regions are referred to by the names of the researchers who first described their function: **Broca's area** and **Wernicke's area.**

Naming by Lobe

The cerebral cortex is divided into four lobes, as shown in Figure B.3. The central sulcus divides the frontal lobe and the parietal lobe. The lateral fissure (a fissure is a deep sulcus) divides the frontal lobe and the temporal lobe. The occipital lobe is at the most posterior point in the brain (indeed, much of the occipital lobe is tucked out of sight in the medial walls of each hemisphere of the brain). Researchers often refer to parts of the cortex by a location within one of the four lobes (e.g., "dorsolateral frontal cortex").

Naming by Function

Some areas of cortex are so well understood that researchers refer to them by their function. This is usually done for motor cortex, visual cortex, auditory cortex, and somatosensory cortex (concerned with feeling where the body is). In addition, researchers frequently differentiate between structures such as primary and secondary visual cortex. *Primary* usually refers to simpler and *secondary* to more complex processing. For perceptual processes (vision, audition, somatosensation), *primary*

(a)

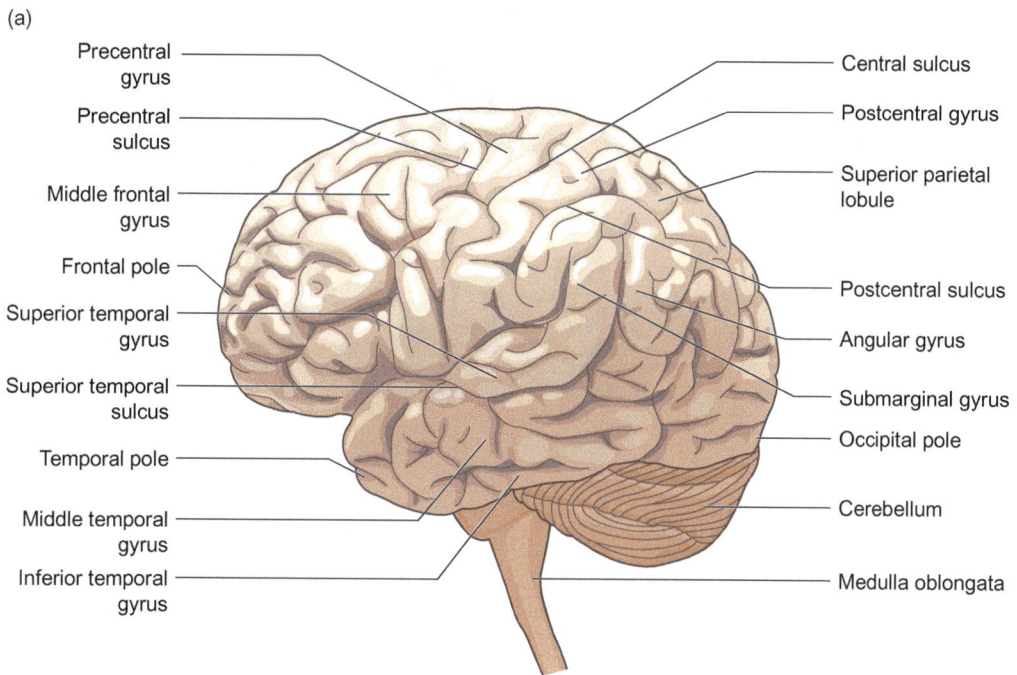

(b)

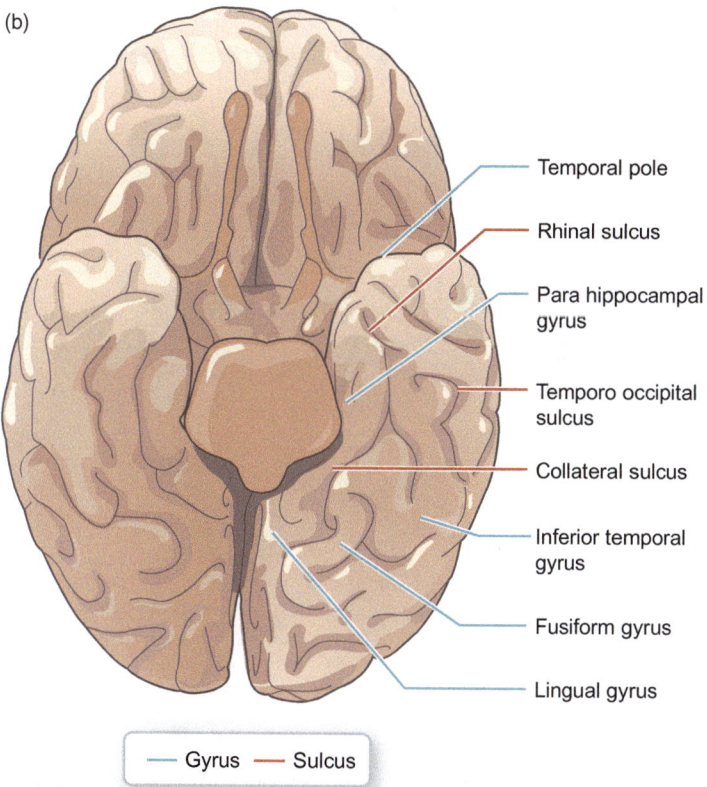

Gyrus ———   Sulcus ———

Figure B.2. A lateral view of the brain, showing (a) gyri and (b) sulci, (c) Broca's area, and (d) Wernicke's area.

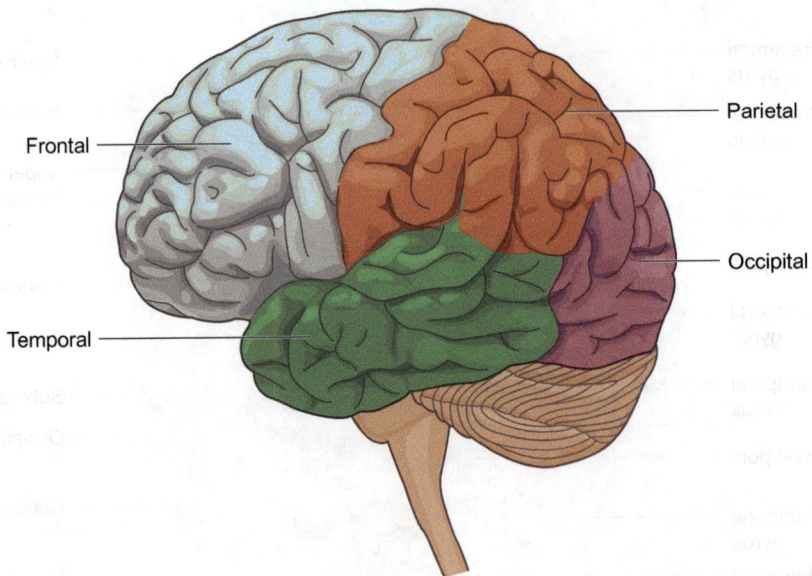

Figure B.3. The four lobes of the cerebral cortex.

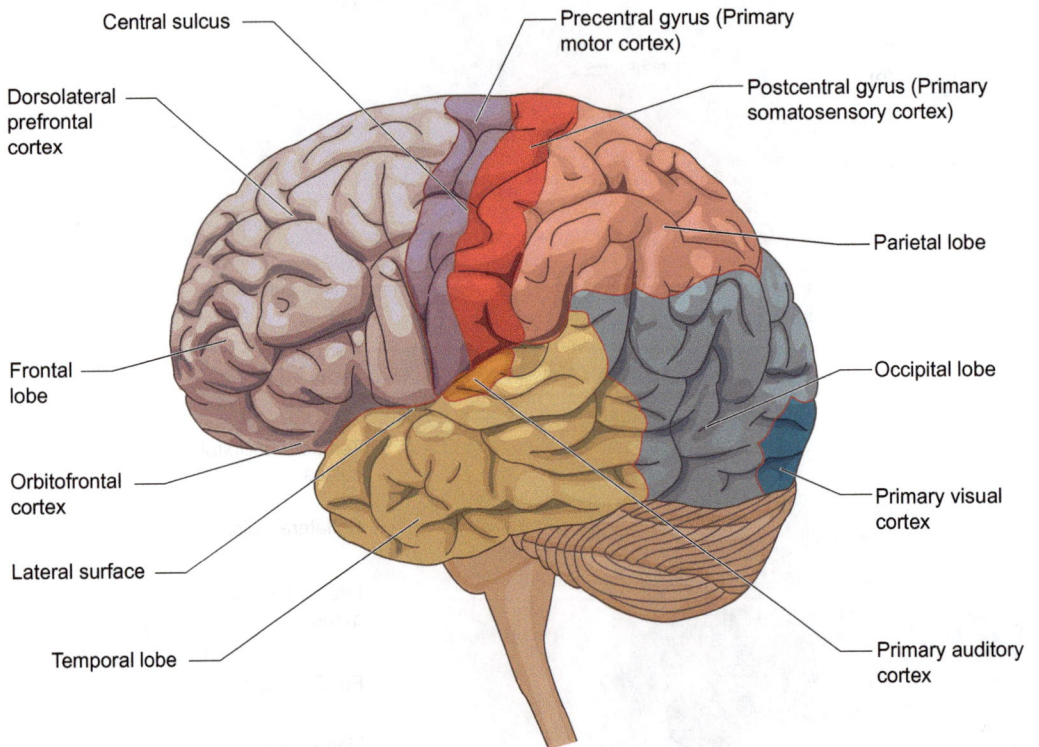

Figure B.4. Functional areas of the brain.

means closer to the sense organs; secondary cortex builds more complex meaning from the output of the primary cortex. In motor cortex, *primary* refers to cortex that is closer to commanding the muscles, whereas *secondary* involves higher-level planning. Figure B.4 illustrates the system you will see most often in this book.

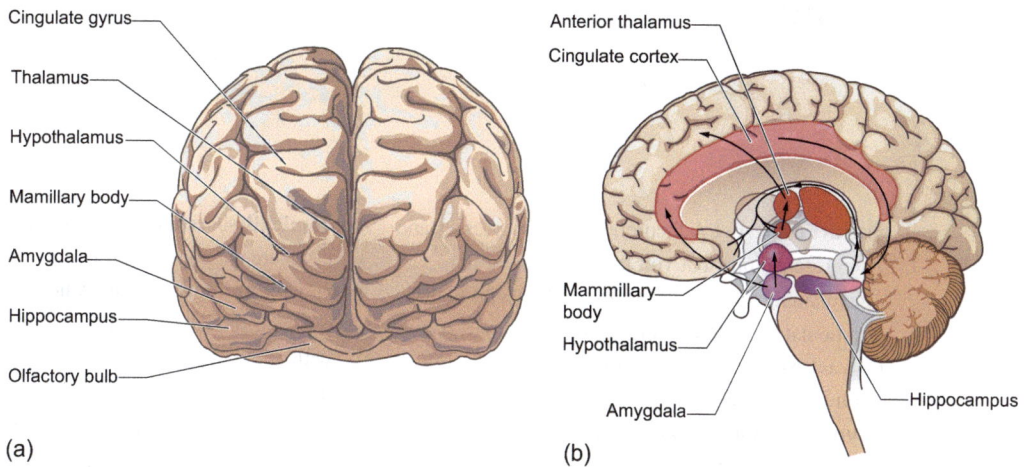

Figure B.5. Subcortical structures of the brain.

The Rest of the Brain

In this book, when we talk about the brain, we usually mean cortex. There are just a few other structures you need to keep in mind. The central nervous system is composed of the spinal cord and the brain. The **spinal cord** collects somatosensory information about pressure, temperature, pain, and so on and sends motor information to the muscles. Perched on top of the spinal cord is the brain. The cortex is the outer portion of the brain. Below the cortex are a number of subcortical (below the cortex) structures (see Figure B.5). Here is a list of the subcortical structures we talk about and what they are believed to do:

> **Thalamus.** A relay station for sensory and motor information. For all senses except smell, the receptors first send information to the thalamus, which passes it on to the cortex.
> **Amygdala.** Important in the processing of emotion (especially fear) and information about social functions.
> **Hippocampus.** Important in memory.
> **Cerebellum.** Important in motor control and also in higher-level cognitive skills, but just what it does is not clear.

Glossary

abstract construct A theoretical set of processes and representations that you think are useful in explaining some data. An example would be the articulatory loop of working memory.

abstract word One that does not refer to a physical object.

accommodation A cue to distance in visual perception. It depends on sensing how much the lens of the eye has changed shape to focus the image on the retina; the shape change varies with the distance of the object.

acoustic confusion effect Errors in primary memory based on sound (e.g., thinking one heard *g* instead of *d*). The presence of such errors indicates that participants use an acoustic code in primary memory on the task.

acquired dyslexia A reading problem caused by brain damage in adults who were normal readers before the injury.

activation The level of energy or excitement of a node, indicating that the concept the node represents is more accessible for use by the cognitive system.

adaptation skill A type of motor skill learning in which a new motor response is learned to a visual stimulus (e.g., learning to use a computer mouse). The way that the stimulus and response go together is systematic, which contrasts with arbitrary visual–motor associations.

addressing system Scheme to organize memories in which each memory is given a unique address that can be used to look it up.

algorithm A formula that can be applied to choice situations. It has the advantage of producing consistent outcomes, but algorithms may be complex and difficult to compute. Algorithms often are compared with heuristics.

amygdala A collection of nuclei believed to be especially important for processing emotion.

analogy In problem solving, when problems are compared and have some similar dimensions.

anatomic dissociation Evidence that two different tasks are supported by different parts of the brain.

anchoring and adjustment A heuristic used to estimate probabilities in which the person starts with some initial probability value (anchor) by doing a partial calculation of the problem or by using a probability statement in the problem, then adjusts that initial estimate upward or downward based on other information in the problem.

anterior Toward the front of the head.

articulatory control process The process that allows one to enter information into the phonological store; it is literally the process of talking to yourself.

articulatory suppression Refers to demanding that participants keep the articulatory system busy with nonsense during encoding (usually by saying "thethethethe" or something similar), thereby ensuring that they will not code stimuli in the phonological store.

associationism The belief that knowledge begins with sensory information and that sensations may combine to form more complex ideas.

atmosphere A situation in which two premises of a syllogism are both either positive or negative or use the same quantifier. People are biased to accept as valid a conclusion that maintains the atmosphere.

atmospheric perspective A cue to depth. Objects in the distance look less distinct because they are viewed through more dust and water particles in the air that scatter light.

attention The mechanism for continued cognitive processing. All sensory information receives some cognitive processing; attention ensures continued cognitive processing.

automatic A process that takes few or no attentional resources and that happens without intention, given the right set of stimuli in the environment.

availability A heuristic in which the likelihood of an event is evaluated by the ease with which examples of the event can be called to mind.

babbling The second stage of language development. It includes more consonant–vowel combinations than cooing does and repetitions (e.g., "dadadada").

base rate The frequency of an event in the general population. When judging the likelihood that an event occurred, people tend to ignore the base rate if they are given any other information about the event.

base-rate neglect Using only information about the test and ignoring the base rate.

Bayes' theorem A formula that describes how to integrate prior beliefs and update probabilities of events when given new evidence.

behaviorism An approach to psychology that claims that the appropriate subject matter of psychology is behavior, not mental processes. It also emphasizes that psychologists should focus on that which is observable (i.e., stimuli in the environment and people's overt behaviors).

belief bias When people accept conclusions based on prior beliefs rather than the logical strength of the current argument.

bias In signal detection theory, a measure of the participant's bias to either report or not report the presence of a signal. Bias is measured independently of the participant's actual ability to detect signals.

binocular disparity The difference between the retinal images projected on the left and right eyes.

biological essentialism The belief that each living thing has a core essence that persists across its life-span and maintains its identity across changes.

bottom-up processing Processing that starts with unprocessed sensory information and builds toward more conceptual representations.

Broca's area An area in the left frontal lobe that is important for language.

brute force search A problem-solving strategy in which all possible answers are examined until the correct solution is found.

case study A type of scientific research in which a single individual is observed on a number of occasions. Case studies are usually used only when there is a rather unusual individual to be studied.

categorical perception Refers to the fact that people do not perceive slight variations in how phonemes are pronounced. Phonemes can vary along certain dimensions with no cost to their perceivability.

categorization The cognitive process in which ideas and objects are recognized, grouped, and differentiated.

category A group of objects that have something in common.

caudal Toward the back of the head (synonym of *posterior*).

central executive The cognitive supervisor and scheduler, which integrates information from different sources and decides on strategies to be used in tasks and allocates attention.

cerebellum A very large structure at the back and toward the bottom of the brain, it contributes to movement and some higher forms of cognition.

chunk A unit of knowledge that can be decomposed into smaller units of knowledge. Similarly, smaller units of knowledge can be combined ("chunked") into a single unit of knowledge (e.g., chunking the numbers 1, 9, 0, and 0 into a unit to represent the year 1900).

cingulate gyrus A gyrus in the medial part of the brain. Its function is not clear, but it may contribute to attention and working memory.

classical conditioning A training procedure that produces a conditioned reflex.

classical view of categorization The view that concepts are represented as lists of necessary and sufficient properties.

coarticulation Making a movement in a way that anticipates future movements.

cocktail party effect When an unattended stimulus is noticed based on its meaning (like hearing one's name in another conversation in the middle of a noisy cocktail party).

cognitive economy The principle of designing a cognitive system in a way that conserves resources (e.g., memory storage space).

combinatorial explosion The phenomenon in which the number of states in the problem space increases very rapidly, even with modest increases in the number of attributes of the problem that might be changed. For example, if one tries to look four moves ahead in a chess game instead of two moves ahead, the number of states in the problem much more than doubles.

competence People's knowledge of grammar, that is, the rules that they use to construct sentences. Competence is contrasted with performance, which refers to the way that people actually talk. Performance is influenced not only by the rules of grammar but also by lapses of memory and other factors that make the sentences people utter less grammatical than their competence indicates.

computed tomography A technique using X-ray technology for showing the three-dimensional structure of the brain, important for lesion studies. It does not show activation.

concept The mental representation that allows one to generalize about objects in a category.

conclusion A statement of fact derived by logical processes. One may confidently propose that a conclusion is true or false within a problem based on its logical relation to the premises. Whether the conclusion is true in the real world depends on the truth or falseness of the premises.

concrete word Concrete words refer to real objects in the world (e.g., *pencil*, *train*).

conditional statements A logical form composed of three statements. The first premise states, "If condition *p* is met, then *q* follows." The second premise states whether *p* or *q* is true. The third is a conclusion about *p* or *q*.

conditioned reflex A reflex that is learned (i.e., that is the product of experience).

conditioned response In classical conditioning, the response elicited by a conditioned stimulus after training. It is usually similar but not identical to the unconditioned stimulus.

conditioned stimulus In classical conditioning, a stimulus that before training does not elicit a consistent response. During training, its presentation is paired with the unconditioned stimulus.

conjunctive search In a visual search task, a search in which the target differs from the distractors on two features, for example, the target is large and red, and although some of the distractors are large and some are red, none of the distractors are both large and red. It requires a conjunction of two features (largeness and redness) to identify the target.

construction Similar to the idea of reconstruction. Reconstruction is the process by which memories are recalled. Construction is a particular memory that feels to the participant like a real memory but has no basis in fact.

content-addressable storage Scheme by which to organize memories in which the content of the memory itself serves as the storage address.

context Information about the time and place in which a memory was encoded.

context effect The idea that memory will be better if the physical environment at encoding matches the physical environment at retrieval.

contextual diversity The number of different contexts in which a word is used. Roughly corresponds to how many different definitions a word has but also to about how frequently the word is used in different contexts.

continuous task A task in which there is no obvious beginning and ending to each trial; there is a continuous stream of stimuli and responses (e.g., a pursuit tracking task). Compare with **discrete task**.

convergence A cue to distance. As an object gets closer, an observer crosses his or her eyes more to keep the image of the object on the center of the fovea of each eye. The extent to which the eyes are crossed can be used as a cue to distance.

converging operations The strategy of using multiple techniques to address a single question, to make up for the fact that each technique has some flaws.

conversational implicature The tendency for people to treat the language of logic as though it has the same meaning as everyday language.

conversion error An error in dealing with a syllogism in which a person reverses one of the premises. For example, the premise reads "All As are Bs," and the participant believes that it is also true that "All Bs are As."

cooing The first stage of language, in which the baby makes long, drawn-out vowel sounds ("oooooooh") or consonant–vowel combinations ("gaaaaah").

critical period A window of opportunity during which a particular type of learning will be easy for the organism. If the critical period is missed, however, the learning will be difficult or even impossible.

CT *See* **computed tomography**.

cue Some information from the environment (or that the participant is able to generate) as a starting point for retrieval.

cued recall A way of testing memory in which the experimenter provides the participant the time and place in which the memory was encoded as well as some hint about the content of the to-be-remembered material (e.g., "Tell me the words I read to you an hour ago. One of them was something to eat").

decay Refers to the hypothesis about forgetting results (at least in part) from the spontaneous decomposition of memories over time.

decision-making A situation in which a person is presented with two or more explicit courses of action, with the requirement that the person select just one.

deductive reasoning Problems to which one can apply formal logic and derive an objectively correct solution.

deep processing Thinking about the meaning of stimulus materials at encoding.

deep structure In language, the deep structure is the representation of a sentence constructed according to a basic set of phrase-structure rules, without any transformations applied to the resulting representation. If transformations are applied, the sentence might be turned into a question or be phrased in the passive voice, for example.

default value A characteristic that is a part of a schema that is assumed to be true in the absence of other information. For example, unless one is told otherwise, one assumes that a dog is furry; furriness is a default characteristic for dogs.

dependent variable In an experiment, the dependent variable is the one that the experimenter measures with the expectation that its value will depend on changes in the independent variable. Only experimental research uses dependent variables.

depictive format A format of mental representation that shares important picture-like qualities with the object.

depth cues Clues that inform the visual system how far away an object is. Divided into two classes: oculomotor depth cues and those based on the retinal image.

depth of processing A description of how one thinks about material at encoding. Depth refers to the

degree of semantic involvement (i.e., the word's meaning).

descriptive research A type of scientific research in which one seeks only to describe the world as it is, not to describe relationships among different entities in the world. It can be contrasted with relational research and with experimental research.

descriptive theories In decision-making, a theory that describes how people actually make decisions.

deterministic The view that all acts (including human acts) have antecedent causes in the physical world.

dichotic listening task Task in which participants listen to material on headphones and each earpiece plays a different message. Participants are to attend to just one message and must shadow that message to show that they are doing so. The dichotic listening task is often used to study how much the unattended material is processed.

digit span task Participants hear a list of digits read to them, one digit per second, and must immediately recite the list in the correct order. This task has been used to measure primary memory capacity since the turn of the twentieth century.

discrete task A task in which each trial has a discrete beginning and ending (e.g., a simple response time task). Compare with **continuous task**.

disjunctive search In a visual search task, a search in which the target differs from the distractors on just one feature (e.g., the target is larger than the distractors or the target is the only stimulus that has a horizontal line in it).

distractor Items that appear on a visual search experiment trial that are not the target item that the participant is to find. Also used in recognition memory experiments to denote incorrect responses. Synonyms of *distractor* in memory experiments are **foil** and **lure**.

distributed representation A representational scheme in which a concept is distributed across multiple units.

dorsal Toward the top of the head.

dual process models Models of reasoning that propose that reasoning is supported by a fast, unconscious, associative process and by a slower, sequential process associated with consciousness.

dual route models of reading Models that posit two mechanisms for reading. One route uses a direct matchup of the spelling and entries in the lexicon, and the other translates the letters into sounds and then matches the sounds to the auditory entry in the lexicon.

dual task paradigm A paradigm requiring participants to perform two tasks simultaneously. It is used to study the limits of attention.

early filter A theory proposing that attention acts as a filter early in the processing stream. Implies that all sensory stimuli are analyzed for their physical characteristics, but only those that are attended to are analyzed for their semantic characteristics.

echoic memory Name given to the auditory variety of sensory memory.

ecological approach Emphasizes that the environment has rich sources of information in it and that the computations the visual system needs to perform are probably not that extensive.

ecological validity The extent to which an experiment represents the "real world." High ecological validity means that the conditions of the experiment seem similar to the ones that would be encountered in everyday life.

EEG *See* **electroencephalogram**.

einstellung effect In problem solving, when people become stuck on familiar solutions, they develop a problem set in which they are unable to think of novel solutions because familiar solutions come to mind.

electroencephalogram A technique for recording electrical activity of the brain in which electrodes are placed on the scalp. It is used to localize brain activity and is especially useful for its temporal accuracy.

embodied When higher-level conceptual representations overlap with and are based on basic perceptual processes.

emotional conditioning Classical conditioning in which the unconditioned response is an emotion.

empiricism One of the three principles of the scientific method. It means that one is dedicated to learning about the world through conducting experiments.

empiricist The view that most human knowledge is acquired over one's lifetime through experience.

encoding The mental process by which experiences become memories.

endogenous A type of attention that is driven by an internal goal and controlled by the observer.

episodic buffer A component of the working memory model of primary memory. It stores information in a multimodal code; that is, the code can represent visual, auditory, or semantic information.

episodic memories Memories that are associated with a particular time and place, with a this-happened-to-me feeling.

ERPs *See* **event-related potentials**.

event-related potentials A method of averaging EEG waves from tens or hundreds of trials to eliminate random variation from trial to trial.

exemplar An instance of a category.

exemplar model Model of categorization that maintains that all exemplars are stored in memory and that categorization judgments are made by judging the similarity of the new exemplar to all the old exemplars of a category.

exogenous A type of attention that is driven by external cues and is not under the control of the observer.

expected utility A normative theory of choice in which the best choice is the one that offers the reward with the greatest personal value to the individual, not necessarily the greatest financial reward. The theory allows that in some situations, it may be more valuable to an individual to be very likely to get a modest reward rather than to have a small probability to get a large reward.

expected value theory A normative theory of choice in which the best choice is the one that offers the largest financial payoff.

experimental research A type of scientific research in which the value of one variable (e.g., self-esteem) is changed to observe its effect on another variable (e.g., memory ability). Experimental research allows one to draw conclusions about causality, that is, that changes in one variable cause changes in another.

explicit memory A type of memory retrieval that is conscious, usually measured by verbal report. Explicit retrieval would typically be supported by declarative memory; *declarative* refers to the memory system, and *explicit* refers to the type of memory test.

eye height The height of the observer's eyes from the ground. Can be used as a cue to object size.

false memory A memory of an event that never occurred that the participant nevertheless believes did occur.

familiar size Using one's knowledge of the typical size of an object as a cue to the likely size and distance of an object. For example, if a child appears larger than an adult, it is likely that the child is closer to the observer.

feature integration theory A theory of attention in which attention is a process needed to bind features together into objects.

fixed-action patterns Complex behaviors in which an animal engages, despite very limited opportunities for practice or reward. Usually taken as evidence for innate or inborn learning.

flashbulb memories A very rich, very detailed memory that is encoded when something that is emotionally intense happens.

fMRI *See* **functional magnetic resonance imaging**.

foil *See* **distractor**.

folk biology People's everyday understanding of the biological world; how people in a culture perceive, categorize, and reason about living things.

forgetting – retrieval-induced The phenomenon whereby retrieving some memories makes you forget other, related memories.

fovea The part of the retina that is most accurate in discerning fine details. The fovea is near the center of the retina.

free recall A way of testing memory in which the experimenter provides no cues other than the time and place in which the memory was encoded (e.g., "Tell me the words I read to you an hour ago").

functional fixedness In problem solving, one is fixated on an object serving its typical function, and one fails to think of an alternative use of the object, even though it would be quite useful in the problem.

functional magnetic resonance imaging A technique to localize human brain activity during a cognitive task. It depends on the fact that the magnetic properties of blood change, depending on whether it carries oxygen.

functionalism A school of psychology in the late nineteenth century that held that the functions of mental processes were paramount and that psychologists should therefore focus on describing the function of thought processes.

fusiform gyrus A gyrus on the bottom of the temporal lobe that is especially important for object recognition.

garden path sentence A sentence in which the cognitive system initially builds one phrase structure as the sentence is perceived, but later in the sentence it becomes clear that this in-progress phrase structure is incorrect.

generalize Usually applied to categories, it means to use information gathered from one exemplar to a different exemplar of the same category. For example, if you learn that a specific dog likes to have its stomach rubbed, you may generalize that knowledge to other dogs and assume that they, too, like to have their stomachs rubbed.

generative A property of systems that can produce new, novel output. Language is generative, meaning you can produce and understand completely novel utterances. Generativity seemed difficult to achieve with behaviorist accounts of language, which seemed successful in predicting the likelihood that one would repeat an action, not in describing how a novel action could be generated.

grammar A set of rules that describes the legal sentences that can be constructed in a language.

gyrus (plural: gyri) In the wrinkled appearance of the brain, a hill or bump is a gyrus.

heuristics Simple cognitive rules that are easy to apply and that usually yield acceptable decisions but can lead to errors.

hierarchical theory Theory of memory organization in which concepts are organized in a taxonomic hierarchy (e.g., *animal* is above *bird*, which is above *canary*) and characteristic properties are stored at each level.

hill climbing A heuristic in which one searches for an operator that will take you to a state in the problem space that appears to be closer to the goal than you are now.

hippocampus Subcortical structure that is important for memory storage.

homograph Two words with identical spelling but different meanings. May have different pronunciations but may also be homonyms with the same pronunciation. "The fisherman with a deep *bass* voice caught a *bass*."

homonym Two words that are spelled and pronounced the same way but have different meanings. "I hope this *fast* is over *fast*; I'm hungry."

iconic memory Name given to the visual variety of sensory memory.

illusory conjunctions A prediction of feature integration theory. Errors of combinations of features caused by interrupting the attentional binding process, for example, reporting a red circle when there was a red triangle and a blue circle in the display.

impasse A dead end in problem solving.

implicit memory A type of memory retrieval that is unconscious and is measured not by verbal report but via some performance measure. The experimenter can tell that the participant has learned by how the participant performs some task.

incidental memory test A memory test in which the participant is not expressly told that their memory will be tested later.

incubation When a problem solver puts aside an unsolved problem and thinks about something else for some period of time.

independent variable In an experiment, the independent variable is the one that the experimenter manipulates. Only experimental research uses independent variables.

inductive inference This type of inference starts with specific instances and uses this available evidence to make educated guesses that go beyond these specific cases to reach general conclusions. Deductive inference, on the other hand, starts with general principles to reach logically true conclusions about specific cases.

inductive reasoning Reasoning that allows one to say that a conclusion is more or less likely to be true but does not allow one to say that a conclusion must be true.

inference A conclusion or step in the reasoning process that is reached on the basis of evidence; an educated guess.

inferential approach An approach to visual perception that assumes that the information in the environment is insufficient for perception; therefore the visual system must make inferences to recover the shapes and movements of objects in the environment.

information processing An approach to studying the human mind. It assumes that humans are processors of information and that representations and processing operating on them underlie cognition. It also assumes that information is processed in stages.

inhibition A mechanism that suppresses unwanted memories that are triggered by a cue. This suppression occurs to keep these competitors from being retrieved instead of the target memory.

insight problem A problem in which the solver believes that the answer comes all at once, in an "aha!" moment of illumination.

intentional memory test A memory test in which the participant is told that their memory will be tested later.

interference A process by which information is lost from working memory when distracted by another mental process. Can be proactive or retroactive. *See* **proactive interference**; **retroactive interference**.

introspectionism A method of studying the mind that became nearly synonymous with structuralism. The method entails observing one's thought processes, but it was deemed important that a more experienced introspectionist train a novice in the method. Researchers using introspection were almost always structuralists, seeking to use introspection to describe the basic components of consciousness.

inverse projection problem The problem of recovering three-dimensional shape from a two-dimensional projection, such as the projection onto the retina.

isomorph A problem with a different surface story that has a problem space of the same size, the same number of branches, and minimum solution path as a target problem.

key word The first syntactic cue in a sentence that reliably provides a cue to the phrase structure of the sentence.

language Although definitions vary, key properties of language are often considered to be communicative, arbitrary, structured, generative, and dynamic.

late filter A theory proposing that attention acts as a filter late in the processing stream. Implies that all sensory stimuli are analyzed for their physical characteristics and their meaning, but only those that are attended to enter awareness.

lateral Toward the side of the head.

levels of processing framework A framework for understanding memory that proposes that the most important factor determining whether something will be remembered is the depth of processing.

lexical decision Task in which the participant sees a letter string on a screen and must decide as quickly as possible whether the letter string forms a word.

lexicon The mental dictionary, which has information stored about all the words a person knows. The lexicon stores the pronunciation, spelling, and part of speech of each word and has a pointer to another location in which the meaning is stored.

light source, reflectance, and shadow indeterminacy Refers to the fact that the amount of light hitting the retina from an object depends on the light source, the reflectance of the object, and whether the object is in shadow.

likelihood principle Suggestion that among the many ways of interpreting an ambiguous visual stimulus, the visual system will interpret it as the stimulus that is most likely to occur in the world.

limited Continued cognitive processing cannot occur for all available sensory stimuli; simply put, you can't pay attention to everything simultaneously.

linear perspective A cue to depth. Parallel lines converge in the distance, so the closer they are to converging, the farther away the location is.

links Representation of the relationship between concepts. In the hierarchical model, the links are labeled (e.g., "has this property"), whereas in spreading activation models, the links simply pass activation from one node to another.

local contrast Dependence of the perceived surface lightness on the ratios of lightness of areas that are next to one another and in the same plane.

localization Finding a location in the brain that supports a cognitive process.

luminance The amount of light your eye receives.

lure *See* **distractor**.

magnetic resonance imaging A technique that uses magnetic properties of hydrogen for showing the three-dimensional structure of the brain. It is important for lesion studies but does not show activation.

mask An array of tiny, random black-and-white squares or a stimulus of randomly oriented squiggles and lines. A mask is used to knock another stimulus out of iconic memory. *Mask* can also be used as a verb (e.g., "The second stimulus masked the first").

McGurk effect An effect showing that both visual and auditory information are used in phoneme perception.

means–ends analysis A problem-solving heuristic that uses a set of rules about when to work forward or backward and when and how to set subgoals.

medial Toward the center of the head.

mental models theory A semantic representation corresponding to a possible configuration of the world. Mental models are the heart of Johnson-Laird's mental models theory of deductive reasoning.

modal model A model composed of the most common features of models of short-term memory in the early 1970s. The modal model turned out to be incorrect in many details.

mondegreens Misheard song lyrics that result when your perception makes mistakes in grouping phonemes into words.

motion cues Visual cues to depth based on the motion of an object or a perceiver.

motion parallax A visual cue to depth based on the apparent movement of elements in a scene that occurs when the observer moves.

MRI *See* **magnetic resonance imaging**.

nativist The view that much of human knowledge is innate.

naturalistic observation A method of collecting scientific data wherein the researcher observes behavior in its natural setting, for example, an ethologist observing a bird in the wild.

neurons The cells in the brain that support cognition.

nodes Representation of concepts in hierarchical and spreading activation theories.

nondeterministic The view that at least some acts have antecedent causes outside the physical world.

normative theories A theory of choice that describes a set of rules by which some choices are better than others and one choice can be said to be optimal.

object-centered representation A mental representation of what an object looks like relative to the object itself. The representation can support recognition of the object when it is viewed from any perspective.

obligatory access Refers to the fact that verbal information (but not all sounds) appears to be entered into the phonological loop by its mere presence, even if the participant does not want it to enter.

Occam's razor The principle that parsimony is important in evaluating scientific theories. Specifically, if two theories account for data equally well, the simpler theory is to be preferred.

occlusion – in memory A source of forgetting. There is a stronger link from a cue to some undesired memory than to the target, and the cue therefore always calls up the undesired memory.

occlusion – in perception A cue to depth. An object that occludes another is closer.

oculomotor depth cues Cues to depth based on the movements of muscles in the visual system.

operant conditioning Learning whereby the animal (or person) makes a response that has consequences (e.g., reward or punishment). These consequences change the probability that the response will be made again.

operator A process one can apply to a problem to change to a different state in the problem space.

optic ataxia A neurologic syndrome characterized by a deficit in visually controlled reaching, but not in identifying objects.

optimal choice The best choice among a set of given options.

orthographic processing The visual aspect of letter processing in which the linguistic meaning of a visual symbol is recognized.

overextension The tendency for children to use a word they know in place of other words they do not know (e.g., calling any four-legged animal "doggie").

overregularization Applying linguistic rules to exception words where the rule should not be applied (e.g., adding -ed to make the past tense of irregular verbs, yielding "We goed to the park yesterday").

parahippocampal gyrus A gyrus on the bottom of the temporal lobe that is especially important for memory.

parsing paradox For some ambiguous figures, it seems impossible to identify the figure without knowing its parts, but its parts cannot be identified unless one knows the figure.

partial-report procedure Developed by Sperling to examine iconic memory, a procedure whereby participants are shown an array of stimuli (usually letters or numbers) very briefly and then are given a cue telling them which subset of the stimuli to report. This method showed that participants perceive most of the stimuli in a complex array.

participant Any human who provides data for a psychological study.

performance The grammaticality of the sentences that people utter. Performance is influenced not only by the grammatical rules people know (competence) but also by other factors, such as lapses of memory and social considerations, such as interruptions.

permastore A hypothetical state of memory from which memories are not forgotten.

phoneme restoration effect Phonemes that are poorly produced are "restored" by higher-level processes so that the perceiver believes that the missing phoneme actually was present. The system can infer what the missing phoneme should have been based on the context.

phonemes Individual speech sounds.

phonological dyslexia A pattern of reading difficulty in which the person has difficulty reading nonwords (e.g., *slint*) but can read irregular words (e.g., *yacht*).

phonological loop The part of the working memory model in which auditory information is stored.

phonological store The part of the phonological loop that can store about two seconds of auditory information.

phrase-structure grammars A grammar that represents sentences hierarchically, with each node of the hierarchy corresponding to a phrase structure.

pictorial depth cues Cues to distance that can be used in two-dimensional pictures.

posterior Toward the back of the head (synonym of *caudal*).

practice In developing expertise, practice is defined as activity designed to improve skill (as opposed to play or performance) and therefore must include corrective feedback and repetition and be at the appropriate level of difficulty.

pragmatic reasoning schemas Sets of rules defined in relation to goals that can be used to evaluate situations such as permissions or obligations. A key aspect of pragmatic reasoning schemas is that they encourage conclusions that are practical in the real world, as opposed to formal logic, which can lead to conclusions that are technically correct but not useful.

preattentively Refers to processing that occurs regardless of whether attention is applied to the stimulus.

predictably irrational In decision-making, decisions that are not internally consistent but are systematically predictable.

premise A statement of fact taken to be true for the purposes of a logical problem.

principle of minimal attachment The principle that as the cognitive system parses sentences, it is biased to build phrase structures in such a way that it adds new words to existing nodes in the phrase-structure hierarchy rather than creating new nodes.

prior beliefs Real-world knowledge that can influence people's evaluation of a syllogism. They are more likely to accept as true a syllogism with a conclusion that they know is true and to reject a syllogism with a conclusion that they know is false.

proactive interference Earlier learning interferes with new learning.

probabilistic view of categorization Category membership is proposed to be a matter of probability. Prototype and exemplar models fall within the probabilistic view.

probability model An approach to studying reasoning based on the idea that when presented with what experimenters think of as reasoning problems, participants actually treat them as probability problems.

problem In the study of problem solving, a problem is any situation in which a person has a goal and that goal is not yet accomplished.

problem space All possible configurations that a problem can take.

problem state A particular configuration of the elements of the problem.

process Manipulates representations in some way. For example, a computer might have a process for addition to add numbers. The mind might have a process that maintains the activity of a representation in primary memory, thus keeping it in consciousness.

property inheritance A characteristic of some models of categorization; concepts inherit properties from the concepts that are higher in the hierarchy.

proposition A verbal representation of knowledge. It is the most basic unit of meaning that has a truth value.

prosody The patterns of stress and intonation in spoken language.

prosopagnosia A neurologic syndrome characterized by a difficulty in recognizing faces via visual input.

prototype A prototype has all the features that are characteristic of a category.

psychological refractory period A period of time after one response is executed during which a second response cannot be selected.

public verifiability One of the three principles of the scientific method. It means that one will make one's hypotheses and experimental data available to everyone to examine and critique.

rational In the context of decision-making, rational choices are ones that are internally consistent (e.g., that show transitivity).

recognition failure of recallable words The effect in which words that were not recognized are nevertheless recalled successfully on a later test.

recognition test Method of testing memory in which the experimenter presents the participants with the to-be-remembered material, along with other material that was not initially encoded (distractors). The participant must select the to-be-remembered items from among these other items.

reconstruction The idea that memories are not simply pulled out of the storehouse; rather, they are interpreted in terms of prior knowledge to reconstruct what probably occurred.

recursion A process can be recursive if it calls on itself to get its job done. A definition of something is recursive if the definition contains the thing defined. For example, one definition of a sentence is "two sentences joined by the word *and*."

reflex An automatic action by the body that occurs when a particular stimulus is perceived in the environment.

rehearse To practice material in an effort to memorize it.

relational categories Categories defined, not by features of items, but by the relations among them.

relational research A type of scientific research in which one seeks to describe the relationship of two variables (e.g., income and intelligence) without specifying whether changes in one cause changes in the other.

relative height A cue to depth. Objects that are higher in the picture plane are farther away.

release from proactive interference Refers to the effect in which proactive interference dissipates if one changes the stimulus materials.

Renaissance A time in Europe roughly between the thirteenth and seventeenth centuries marked by the rise of humanism, arts, literature, and modern science.

repetition priming Effect in which performance of a task is biased by one's having seen the same words or pictures sometime earlier.

representation A symbol for an entity or concept in the real world. For example, a computer might use a binary code 011 to represent the concept 8.

representativeness A heuristic that leads you to judge the probability of an event as more likely to belong to a category if it has the features of the category that you deem important.

repression The active forgetting of an episode that would be too painful or threatening to the self to be remembered.

response selection A hypothetical stage of processing in which a response to a stimulus is selected (e.g., to push a button), but the actual preparation of the motor act (e.g., finger movement) is not yet complete.

response to stimulus interval The time after the participant has responded but before the next stimulus has appeared.

restructuring A process emphasized by Gestalt psychologists, applied to a problem whereby one perceives a whole that had not been seen before.

retina The layer of light-sensitive cells on the back of the eye.

retinal disparity The disparity in retinal location of the same image for the two eyes.

retroactive interference Later learning interferes with earlier learning.

role-governed category A category defined not by features but by the role served in a certain event.

rostral Toward the front of the head (synonym of *anterior*).

Sapir–Whorf hypothesis Synonymous with **Whorfian hypothesis**.

savings in relearning A way of testing memory in which the participant learns some material (e.g., a list of words) to a criterion (e.g., can recite the list twice without error). After a delay, the participant must relearn the list to criterion again. If the participant can reach criterion in fewer trials the second time, they have shown savings in relearning.

schema A memory representation containing general information about an object or event. It contains information representative of a type of event rather than of a single event.

script A type of schema that describes a series of events.

selective The assumption that one is able to disburse the limited resource of attention as desired.

semantic memories Memories that are not associated with a particular time and place or with a feeling that the memory happened to you. Semantic memories cover world knowledge (e.g., "frogs are green").

semantic network Name given to all the nodes and links in a spreading activation model.

semantic priming Effect in which performance of a task is biased by the person having earlier viewed semantically related words or pictures.

sensitivity In signal detection theory, a measure of the participant's absolute ability to detect a signal. Sensitivity is measured independently of any bias the participant might have to report or not report signals. Also, the ability of a test to detect memories that are in the storehouse.

sensory memory General term referring to sensory buffers that can hold much information, but only for a second or so.

sentence parser The psychological mechanism that derives phrase structures from sentences.

set effects In problem solving, occurs when a particular problem-solving procedure is applied because it has been effective in the past, even if it is not appropriate to the current problem.

shadow In a dichotic listening task, participants listen to material on headphones, and each earpiece plays a different message. Participants are to attend to just one message and must shadow that message to show that they are doing so. Shadowing means repeating the to-be-attended message aloud as they hear it.

shallow processing Thinking about the surface characteristics of stimulus materials (i.e., what they look like, what they sound like, etc.).

shape and orientation indeterminacy Refers to the fact that shape and orientation are indeterminate from a two-dimensional projection (e.g., a coin that looks like an ellipse if it is turned).

short-term memory A particular theory of primary memory. Short-term memory is usually accorded a duration of thirty seconds (if the material is not rehearsed) and a capacity of about five chunks of information.

single-cell recording A technique in which a very fine probe is inserted in the brain that can record the activity of a single neuron or a small group of neurons.

situation model A level of representation in text processing. The situation model refers to deep knowledge of a text that represents an integration of information from the text and knowledge the reader had before reading the text.

size and distance indeterminacy Refers to the fact that the size of an object on the retina is determined by the actual size of the object and by the distance of the object from the observer.

solvable problems One of the three principles of the scientific method. It is an acknowledgment that the scientific method is useful for addressing some problems but is not useful for addressing others.

source The source of a memory refers to where and when it was encoded, whether someone told you the information, or whether you experienced it directly or just thought about it.

source confusion An error in a source memory. For example, you mistake your own thought for an event that actually happened (or vice versa). Another type of source confusion is mixing up the time and location information of two real memories. For example, you might read the *New York Times* and the *National Enquirer* on the same morning and think you read an article in one paper, whereas it was actually in the other.

span of apprehension The amount of information that can enter consciousness at once.

speech stream A term used to refer to spoken speech that emphasizes its continuous nature. Although we perceive speech to be composed of individual words (and therefore to have short breaks between the words), speech sounds are produced fairly continuously.

spinal cord The long column of neurons in the vertebral column that collects somatosensory information and sends motor information to the muscles.

spontaneous recovery The sudden uncovering of a memory that was believed to have been forgotten.

spreading activation model A model in which memory is conceived as a network of nodes connected by links and in which activation spreads from node to node via the links.

stereopsis A cue to distance that depends on the fact that your two eyes get slightly different views of objects.

stimulus onset asynchrony When the tasks in a dual task paradigm are out of sync (asynchrony), the delay in the presentation (onset) of the stimuli is given this name.

strength view of memory The idea that memories vary in how strongly they are represented and that more strongly represented memories are easier to retrieve.

structural similarity Refers to whether two problems share content that allows them to be solved by the same strategy (e.g., if problems can both be solved by Newton's second law, they share structural similarity, even if one involves a falling body and the other an inclined plane).

structuralism A school of psychology in the late nineteenth century, the goal of which was to describe the structures that compose thought. Researchers often used the introspective method.

sulcus (plural: sulci) In the wrinkled appearance of the brain, a hill is a depression or a groove.

surface code A level of representation in text processing; refers to the exact wording and syntax of sentences.

surface dyslexia A pattern of reading difficulty in which the person has difficulty reading irregular words (e.g., *yacht*) but can read nonwords (e.g., *slint*).

surface similarity Refers to whether two problems share similar elements (e.g., if both problems entail inclined planes, the problems have surface similarity even if very different strategies are necessary to solve them).

surface structure In language, the order in which words are uttered in a sentence. The surface structure is the product of the deep structure plus any transformations that are applied to the deep structure.

survival processing Memory processes that relate to life and death are different than other memory processes and result in higher memory performance.

syllogism A logical form composed of three statements of fact: two premises and a conclusion.

tachistoscope Device that allows precise exposure of stimuli; used for span of apprehension studies.

target In visual search experiments, the item that the participant is expected to find. Also used in recognition memory experiments to denote the to-be-remembered material at test.

testing effect A finding in memory research in which being tested on previously studied material leads to better later recall than repeating a study session.

text A group of related sentences forming a paragraph or a group of related paragraphs.

textbase A level of representation in text processing. The textbase represents the ideas of the text but does not preserve the particular wording and syntax.

texture gradient A cue to depth. A field is assumed to have a uniform texture gradient, so if more detail is visible in part of the field, it is assumed to be closer.

thalamus A collection of nuclei in the center of the brain; often thought of as a relay station for sensory and motor information.

tip-of-the-tongue phenomenon An effect in which you are certain you know a concept but cannot think of the proper term for it.

top-down processing Processing in which conceptual knowledge influences the processing or interpretation of lower-level perceptual processes.

transfer-appropriate processing The idea that memory will be better to the extent that the cognitive processes used at encoding match the cognitive processes used at retrieval.

transitivity If a relationship holds between the first and second of three elements and it holds between the second and third, it should hold between the first and third. If choices were rational, there would be transitivity of preference between choices. However, transitivity does not always hold.

typicality The fact that some members of a category are viewed as better (i.e., more typical) exemplars than others (e.g., a golden retriever is a typical dog, whereas a Chihuahua is not).

unconditioned response In classical conditioning, the response to an unconditioned stimulus (e.g., salivation).

unconditioned stimulus In classical conditioning, a stimulus that leads to a consistent response from the animal before any training begins (e.g., food).

unlearning A source of forgetting. Practicing a new association between a cue and a target memory weakens the associative link between the cue and another memory.

value In decision-making, the importance, worth, or usefulness of something.

vector flow field Gibson's alternative to the retinal image. He argued that the information for perception was instead the overall pattern of motion of points of light over time across the visual field.

ventral Toward the bottom of the head.

verbal protocol A method of gathering data in problem-solving (or other) experiments. The participant is asked to solve a problem and to simultaneously describe their thoughts. These descriptions are assumed to bear some relationship to the cognitive processes that actually support solving the problem and so can be used as a window onto these processes.

viewer-centered representation A mental representation of what an object looks like relative to the observer.

visual agnosia A neurologic syndrome characterized by a difficulty in identifying objects using visual input.

visual imagery Sometimes visual imagery refers to any imagery in the visual modality. It also has a more specialized meaning, referring to imagery tasks that emphasize what things look like.

visual search task A task in which the research participant must search a display of objects for a target.

visuospatial sketch pad A buffer on which visual or spatial information can be manipulated and briefly stored. It is believed to be similar to and perhaps synonymous with visual imagery.

WEIRD An acronym that stands for "Western, educated, industrialized, rich, and democratic," indicating limitations in the selection of participants for psychological studies. If the sample of participants is too limited, the findings may not be general psychological principles.

Wernicke's area An area in the superior part of the left temporal lobe that is important for language.

what/how hypothesis Alternative to the **what/where hypothesis**, this proposal holds that the visual system segregates analysis of what objects are (object recognition and location) and how to manipulate them (visual information dedicated to the motor system).

what/where hypothesis Hypothesis that the visual system segregates analysis of what objects are (object recognition) and where they are (spatial location). *See also* **what/how hypothesis**.

Whorfian hypothesis The idea that language influences thought. The strong version of the hypothesis holds that certain thoughts are impossible to entertain in certain languages. The weaker version holds that it may be easier to entertain certain thoughts in certain languages.

word-chain grammars A proposal that people construct sentences by chaining one word after another, according to a set of rules about what words would be admissible next in the chain or what words are highly associated with words already in the sentence.

word length effect The finding that participants can remember more words if the words can be said quickly.

working backward A problem-solving heuristic in which one begins at the goal state of the problem and tries to work back to the starting state.

working memory Specific theory of primary memory proposed by Baddeley and Hitch (1974), it has three parts: a phonological loop, a visuospatial sketch pad, and a central executive. Working memory is proposed to be a workspace for cognitive processes, not simply a short-term storage device.

References

Aaronson, D., & Ferres, S. (1986). Reading strategies for children and adults: A quantitative model. *Psychological Review*, 93, 89–112.

Abel, M., Byker, T., & Carpenter, J. (2021). Socially optimal mistakes? Debiasing COVID-19 mortality risk perceptions and prosocial behavior. *Journal of Economic Behavior and Organization*, 183, 456–480.

Abrams, L., & Davis, D. K. (2016). The tip-of-the-tongue phenomenon: Who, what, and why. In H. H. Wright (Ed.), *Cognition, language and aging* (pp. 13–53). John Benjamins.

Ackerman, P. L., Beier, M. E., & Boyle, M. O. (2005). Working memory and intelligence: The same or different constructs? *Psychological Bulletin*, 131, 30–60.

Adan, A., Archer, S. N., Hidalgo, M. P., et al. (2012). Circadian typology: A comprehensive review. *Chronobiology International*, 29, 1153–1175. https://doi.org/10.3109/07420528.2012.719971

Adelson, E. H. (1995). *Checkershadow illusion.* http://persci.mit.edu/gallery/checkershadow

Adolph, K. E., Cole, W. G., Komati, M., et al. (2012). How do you learn to walk? Thousands of steps and dozens of falls per day. *Psychological Science*, 23, 1387–1394. https://doi.org/10.1177/0956797612446346

Aguirre, G. K., & D'Esposito, M. (1997). Environmental knowledge is subserved by separable dorsal/ventral neural areas. *Journal of Neuroscience*, 17, 2512–2518.

Alam, T. R. D. J. G., Karapanagiotidis, T., Smallwood, J., & Jefferies, E. (2019). Degrees of lateralisation in semantic cognition: Evidence from intrinsic connectivity. *NeuroImage*, 202, Article 116089.

Albrecht, J. E., & O'Brien, E. J. (1993). Updating a mental model: Maintaining both local and global coherence. *Journal of Experimental Psychology: Learning, Memory, and Cognition*, 19, 1061–1070.

Allen, S. W., & Brooks, L. R. (1991). Specializing the operation of an explicit rule. *Journal of Experimental Psychology: General*, 120, 3–19.

Allis, V. (1994). Searching for solutions in games and artificial intelligence [Unpublished doctoral dissertation]. University of Limburg, Maastrich.

Altmann, E. M., & Gray, W. D. (2002). Forgetting to remember: The functional relationship of decay and interference. *Psychological Science*, 13, 27–33.

Alvarez, G. A., & Cavanagh, P. (2004). The capacity of visual short term memory is set both by visual information load and by number of objects. *Psychological Science*, 15, 106–111.

Anderson, B. L., & Winawer, J. (2005). Image segmentation and lightness perception. *Nature*, 434, 79–83. https://doi.org/10.1038/nature03271

Anderson, J. R. (1976). *Language, memory, and thought*. Psychology Press.

Anderson, J. R. (1993). *Rules of the mind*. Erlbaum.

Annese, J., Schenker-Ahmed, N. M., Bartsch, H., et al. (2014). Postmortem examination of patient H.M.'s brain based on histological sectioning and digital 3D reconstruction. *Nature Communications*, 5, Article 4122. https://doi.org/10.1038/ncomms4122

Arai, S., Tooby, J., & Cosmides, L. (2023). Why punish cheaters? Those who withdraw cooperation enjoy better reputations than punishers, but both are viewed as difficult to exploit. *Evolution and Human Behavior*, 44, 50–59.

Araiza-Alba, P., Keane, T., Chen, W. S., & Kaufman, J. (2021). Immersive virtual reality as a tool to learn problem-solving skills. *Computers and Education*, 164, Article 104121.

Ariely, D. D. (2008). *Predictably irrational: The hidden forces that shape our decisions*. Harper Perennial.

Arlemalm, T. (1996). Recognition failure: The influence of semantic cue-target integration – a short note. *European Journal of Cognitive Psychology*, 8, 205–214.

Ashby, F. G., & Maddox, W. T. (2005). Human category learning. *Annual Review of Psychology*, 56, 149–178.

Ashby, F. G., & O'Brien, J. B. (2005). Category learning and multiple memory systems. *Trends in Cognitive Sciences*, 9, 83–89.

Ashby, F. G., Alfonso-Reese, L. A., Turken, A. U., & Waldron, E. M. (1998). A neuropsychological theory of multiple systems in category learning. *Psychological Review*, 105, 442–481.

Ashby, F. G., Ennis, J. M., & Spiering, B. J. (2007). A neurobiological theory of automaticity in perceptual categorization. *Psychological Review*, 114, 632–656. https://doi.org/10.1037/0033-295X.114.3.632

Aslin, R. N., Saffran, J. R., & Newport, E. L. (1998). Computation of conditional probability statistics by 8-month-old infants. *Psychological Science*, 9, 321–324.

Atkinson, R. C., & Shiffrin, R. M. (1968). Human memory: A proposed system and its control processes. In K. W. Spence & J. T. Spence (Eds.), *The psychology of learning and motivation* (Vol. 2, pp. 89–195). Academic Press.

Averbach, E., & Sperling, G. (1961). Short term storage of information in vision. In C. Cherry (Ed.), *Information theory* (pp. 196–211). Butterworths.

Azevedo, F. A. C., Carvalho, L. R. B., Grinberg, L. T., et al. (2009). Equal numbers of neuronal and nonneuronal cells make the human brain an isometrically scaled-up primate brain. *Journal of Comparative Neurology*, 513, 532–541. https://doi.org/10.1002/cne.21974

Baddeley, A. (1986). *Working memory.* Oxford Psychology Series 11. Oxford University Press.

Baddeley, A. (1996). Exploring the central executive. *Quarterly Journal of Experimental Psychology: Human Experimental Psychology*, 49A, 5–28.

Baddeley, A. (2000). The episodic buffer: A new component of working memory? *Trends in Cognitive Sciences*, 4, 417–423.

Baddeley, A. (2001). Is working memory still working? *American Psychologist*, 56, 849–864.

Baddeley, A. (2003). Working memory: Looking back and looking forward. *Nature Reviews Neuroscience*, 4, 829–839.

Baddeley, A. (2012). Working memory: Theories, models, and controversies. *Annual Review of Psychology*, 63, 1–29. https://doi.org/10.1146/annurev-psych-120710-100422

Baddeley, A. D., & Hitch, G. J. (1974). Working memory. In G. Bower (Ed.), *The psychology of learning and motivation* (Vol. 8, pp. 47–89). Academic Press.

Baddeley, A. D., & Lieberman, K. (1980). Spatial working memory. In R. Nickerson (Ed.), *Attention and performance* (Vol. 8, pp. 521–539). Erlbaum.

Baddeley, A. D., Grant, W., Wight, E., & Thomson, N. (1975). Imagery and visual working memory. In P. M. A. Rabbitt & S. Dornic (Eds.), *Attention and performance* (Vol. 5, pp. 205–217). Academic Press.

Baddeley, A. D., Thomson, N., & Buchanan, M. (1975). Word length and the structure of short-term memory. *Journal of Verbal Learning and Verbal Behavior*, 14, 575–589.

Baddeley, A. D., Lewis, V., & Vallar, G. (1984). Exploring the articulatory loop. *Quarterly Journal of Experimental Psychology: Human Experimental Psychology*, 36A, 233–252.

Baddeley, A. D., Allen, R. J., & Hitch, G. J. (2011). Binding in visual working memory: The role of the episodic buffer. *Neuropsychologia*, 49, 1393–1400. https://doi.org/10.1016/j.neuropsychologia.2010.12.042

Badger, J. R., & Shapiro, L. R. (2015). Category structure affects the developmental trajectory of children's inductive inferences for both natural kinds and artefacts. *Thinking and Reasoning*, 21, 206–229. https://doi.org/10.1080/13546783.2014.952338

Bahrick, H. P. (1984). Semantic memory content in permastore: Fifty years of memory for Spanish learned in school. *Journal of Experimental Psychology: General*, 113, 1–29.

Bahrick, H. P., Hall, L. K., & Baker, M. K. (2013). *Life-span maintenance of knowledge.* Psychology Press.

Baillet, S. D., & Keenan, J. M. (1986). The role of encoding and retrieval processes in the recall of text. *Discourse Processes*, 9, 247–268.

Barbot, A., Landy, M. S., & Carrasco, M. (2011). Exogenous attention enhances 2nd-order contrast sensitivity. *Vision Research*, 51, 1086–1098. https://doi.org/10.1016/j.visres.2011.02.022

Barclay, S., Brown, R. V., Kelly, C. W., et al. (1977). *Handbook for decision analysis* (Technical Report No. TR-77-6-30). Defense Advanced Research Projects Agency, Office of Naval Research.

Barenholtz, E., & Tarr, M. J. (2011). Visual learning of statistical relations among non-adjacent features: Evidence for structural encoding. *Visual Cognition*, 19, 469–482. https://doi.org/10.1080/13506285.2011.552894

Baron, J., & Strawson, C. (1976). Use of orthographic and word-specific knowledge in reading words aloud. *Journal of Experimental Psychology: Human Perception and Performance*, 2, 386–393.

Barrouillet, P. (1996). Transitive inferences from set-inclusion relations and working memory. *Journal of Experimental Psychology: Learning, Memory, and Cognition*, 22, 1408–1422.

Bartlett, F. C. (1932). *Remembering: A study in experimental and social psychology.* Cambridge University Press.

Bartsch, L. M., & Oberauer, K. (2023). The contribution of episodic long-term memory to working memory for bindings. *Cognition*, 231, Article 105330.

Bartsch, L. M., & Shepherdson, P. (2022). Freeing capacity in working memory (WM) through the use of long-term memory (LTM) representations. *Journal of Experimental Psychology: Learning, Memory, and Cognition,* 48, 465–482.

Bassok, M., & Holyoak, K. J. (1989). Interdomain transfer between isomorphic topics in algebra and physics. *Journal of Experimental Psychology: Learning, Memory, and Cognition*, 15, 153–166.

Battig, W. F., & Montague, W. E. (1969). Category norms of verbal items in 56 categories: A replication and extension of the Connecticut category norms. *Journal of Experimental Psychology*, 80, 1–46.

Baylis, G. C., & Driver, J. (1993). Visual attention and objects: Evidence for hierarchical coding of location. *Journal of Experimental Psychology: Human Perception and Performance*, 19, 451–470.

Bays, P. M. (2015). Spikes not slots: Noise in neural populations limits working memory. *Trends in Cognitive Sciences*, 19, 431–438. https://doi.org/10.1016/j.tics.2015.06.004

Beauvois, M. F., & Derouesne, J. (1979). Phonological alexia: Three dissociations. *Journal of Neurology, Neurosurgery, and Psychiatry*, 42, 1115–1124.

Bedard, J., & Chi, M. T. (1992). Expertise. *Current Directions in Psychological Science*, 1, 135–139.

Bedny, M., Caramazza, A., Pascual-Leone, A., & Saxe, R. (2012). Typical neural representations of action verbs develop without vision. *Cerebral Cortex*, 22, 286–293. https://doi.org/10.1093/cercor/bhr081

Begg, I., & Harris, G. (1982). On the interpretation of syllogisms. *Journal of Verbal Learning and Verbal Behavior*, 21, 595–620.

Behrmann, M., & Bub, D. (1992). Surface dyslexia and dysgraphia: Dual routes, single lexicon. *Cognitive Neuropsychology*, 9, 209–251.

Bell, L. C., & Perfetti, C. A. (1994). Reading skill: Some adult comparisons. *Journal of Educational Psychology*, 86, 244–255. https://doi.org/10.1037/0022-0663.86.2.244

Bergerbest, D., Ghahremani, D. G., & Gabrieli, J. D. E. (2004). Neural correlates of auditory repetition priming: Reduced fMRI activation in the auditory cortex. *Journal of Cognitive Neuroscience*, 16, 966–977.

Berggren, N., & Eimer, M. (2018). Object-based target templates guide attention during visual search. *Journal of Experimental Psychology: Human Perception and Performance*, 44, 1368–1382. https://doi.org/10.1037/xhp0000541

Bergman, E. T., & Roediger, H. L. (1999). Can Bartlett's repeated reproduction experiments be replicated? *Memory and Cognition*, 27, 937–947.

Berkeley, G. (1709/1948–1957). *The works of George Berkeley* (A. A. Luce & T. E. Jessop, Eds.). Thomas Nelson.

Bernardo, A. B. (1994). Problem-specific information and development of problem-type schemata.

Journal of Experimental Psychology: Learning, Memory, and Cognition, 20, 379–395.

Bethune, J. E. D. (1830). *The life of Galileo Galilei, with illustrations of the advancement of experimental philosophy*. London.

Bhatia, A. (2012, June 5). The crayola-fication of the world: How we gave colors names, and it messed with our brains (part I). *Wired*. www.wired.com/2012/06/the-crayola-fication-of-the-world-how-we-gave-colors-names-and-it-messed-with-our-brains-part-i/

Bichot, N. P., Rossi, A. F., & Desimone, R. (2005). Parallel and serial neural mechanisms for visual search in macaque area V4. *Science*, 308, 529–534. https://doi.org/10.1126/science.1109676

Bichot, N. P., Heard, M. T., DeGennaro, E. M., & Desimone, R. (2015). A source for feature-based attention in the prefrontal cortex. *Neuron*, 88, 832–844. https://doi.org/10.1016/j.neuron.2015.10.001

Biederman, I. (1981). On the semantics of a glance at a scene. In M. Kubovy & J. Pomerantz (Eds.), *Perceptual organization* (pp. 213–253). Erlbaum.

Biederman, I. (1987). Recognition-by-components: A theory of human image understanding. *Psychological Review*, 94, 115–117.

Biederman, I., & Gerhardstein, P. C. (1993). Recognizing depth rotated objects: Evidence and conditions for 3D viewpoint invariance. *Journal of Experimental Psychology: Human Perception and Performance*, 19, 1162–1182.

Bijeljac-Babic, R., Bertoncini, J., & Mehler, J. (1993). How do 4-day-old infants categorize multisyllabic utterances? *Developmental Psychology*, 29, 711–721. https://doi.org/10.1037/0012-1649.29.4.711

Bilalić, M., Langner, R., Ulrich, R., & Grodd, W. (2011). Many faces of expertise: Fusiform face area in chess experts and novices. *Journal of Neuroscience*, 31, 10206–10214. https://doi.org/10.1523/JNEUROSCI.5727-10.2011

Bilalić, M., Graf, M., Vaci, N., & Danek, A. H. (2021). The temporal dynamics of insight problem solving – restructuring might not always be sudden. *Thinking and Reasoning*, 27, 1–37.

Binder, J. R., & Desai, R. H. (2011). The neurobiology of semantic memory. *Trends in Cognitive Sciences*, 15, 527–536. https://doi.org/10.1016/j.tics.2011.10.001

Binder, J. R., Desai, R. H., Graves, W. W., & Conant, L. L. (2009). Where is the semantic system? A critical review and meta-analysis of 120 functional neuroimaging studies. *Cerebral Cortex*, 19, 2767–2796. https://doi.org/10.1093/cercor/bhp055

Birdsong, D. (2014). The critical period hypothesis for second language acquisition: Tailoring the coat of many colors. In M. Pawlak & L. Aronin (Eds.), *Essential topics in applied linguistics and multilingualism* (pp. 43–50). Springer. https://doi.org/10.1007/978-3-319-01414-2_3

Birdsong, D., & Molis, M. (2001). On the evidence for maturational constraints in second-language acquisition. *Journal of Memory and Language*, 44, 235–249.

Blake, A. B., Nazarian, M., & Castel, A. D. (2015). The Apple of the mind's eye: Everyday attention, metamemory, and reconstructive memory for the Apple logo. *Quarterly Journal of Experimental Psychology*, 68, 858–865. https://doi.org/10.1080/17470218.2014.1002798

Blaxton, T. A., Zeffiro, T. A., Gabrieli, J. D. E., et al. (1996). Functional mapping of human learning: A positron emission tomography activation study of eyeblink conditioning. *Journal of Neuroscience*, 16, 4032–4040.

Block, R. A. (2009). Intent to remember briefly presented human faces and other pictorial stimuli enhances recognition memory. *Memory and Cognition*, 37, 667–678. https://doi.org/10.3758/MC.37.5.667

Bocanegra, B. R., Poletiek, F. H., Ftitache, B., & Clark, A. (2019). Intelligent problem-solvers externalize cognitive operations. *Nature Human Behaviour*, 3, 136–142.

Boekhout, P., van Gog, T., van de Wiel, M. W. J., Gerards-Last, D., & Geraets, J. (2010). Example-based learning: Effects of model expertise in relation to student expertise. *British Journal of Educational Psychology*, 80, 557–566. https://doi.org/10.1348/000709910X497130

Bohn-Gettler, C. M. (2019). Getting a grip: The PET framework for studying how reader emotions influence comprehension, *Discourse Processes*, 56, 386–401.

Bolhuis, J. J., & Honey, R. C. (1998). Imprinting, learning and development: From behaviour to brain and back. *Trends in Neurosciences*, 21, 306–311.

Bonnefon, J.-F., & Hilton, D. J. (2002). The suppression of modus ponens as a case of pragmatic preconditional reasoning. *Thinking and Reasoning*, 8, 21–40.

Bonner, C., & Newell, B. R. (2010). In conflict with ourselves? An investigation of heuristic and analytic processes in decision making. *Memory and Cognition*, 38, 186–196. https://doi.org/10 .3758/MC.38.2.186

Boot, W. R., Kramer, A. F., Simons, D. J., Fabiani, M., & Gratton, G. (2008). The effects of video game playing on attention, memory, and executive control. *Acta Psychologica*, 129, 387–398. https:// doi.org/10.1016/j.actpsy.2008.09.005

Booth, M. C. A., & Rolls, E. T. (1998). View-invariant representations of familiar objects by neurons in the inferior temporal visual cortex. *Cerebral Cortex*, 8, 510–523.

Bornkessel-Schlesewsky, I., Schlesewsky, M., Small, S. L., & Rauschecker, J. P. (2015). Neurobiological roots of language in primate audition: Common computational properties. *Trends in Cognitive Sciences*, 19, 142–150. https:// doi.org/10.1016/j.tics.2014.12.008

Boroditsky, L. (2018). Language and the construction of time through space. *Trends in Neurosciences*, 41, 651–653.

Boroditsky, L., & Gaby, A. (2010). Remembrances of times East: absolute spatial representations of time in an Australian Aboriginal community. *Psychological Science*, 21, 1635–1639.

Bortfeld, H., Morgan, J. L., Golinkoff, R. M., & Rathbun, K. (2005). Mommy and me: Familiar names help launch babies into speech-stream segmentation. *Psychological Science*, 16, 298–304.

Botelho, T., Harrison, R., & Mason, C. (2023). Business angel investment as an informal learning process: Does experience matter? *British Journal of Management*, 34, 321–342.

Bousfield, W. A. (1953). The occurrence of clustering in the recall of randomly arranged associates. *Journal of General Psychology*, 49, 229–240.

Bower, G. H., & Karlin, M. B. (1974). Depth of processing pictures of faces and recognition memory. *Journal of Experimental Psychology*, 103, 751–757. https://doi.org/10.1037/h0037190

Bower, G. H., & Springston, F. (1970). Pauses as recoding points in letter series. *Journal of Experimental Psychology*, 83, 421–430.

Bower, G. H., Black, J. B., & Turner, T. J. (1979). Scripts in memory for text. *Cognitive Psychology*, 11, 177–220.

Brady, T. F., & Alvarez, G. A. (2015). No evidence for a fixed object limit in working memory: Spatial ensemble representations inflate estimates of working memory capacity for complex objects. *Journal of Experimental Psychology: Learning, Memory, and Cognition*, 41, 921–929. https://doi .org/10.1037/xlm0000075

Braine, M. D. S. (1971). The acquisition of language in infant and child. In C. Reed (Ed.), *The learning of language* (pp. 7–95). Appleton-Century-Crofts.

Brakke, K. E., & Savage-Rumbaugh, E. S. (1995). The development of language skills in *Pan*: I. Comprehension. *Language and Communication*, 15, 121–148.

Brakke, K. E., & Savage-Rumbaugh, E. S. (1996). The development of language skills in *Pan*: II. Production. *Language and Communication*, 17, 361–380.

Bransford, J. D., & Johnson, M. K. (1972). Contextual prerequisites for understanding: Some investigations for comprehension and recall. *Journal of Verbal Learning and Verbal Behavior*, 11, 717–726.

Breitmeyer, B. G., & Ganz, L. (1976). Implications of sustained and transient channels for theories of visual pattern masking, saccadic suppression, and information processing. *Psychological Review*, 83, 1–36.

Brewer, J. B., Zhao, Z., Desmond, J. E., Glover, G. H., & Gabrieli, J. D. E. (1998). Making memories: Brain activity that predicts how well visual experience will be remembered. *Science*, 281, 1185–1187.

Brewin, C. R., Andrews, B., & Mickes, L. (2020). Regaining consensus on the reliability of memory. *Current Directions in Psychological Science*, 29, 121–125.

Broadbent, D. E. (1958). *Perception and communication*. Oxford University Press.

Broadbent, D. E. (1982). Task combination and selective intake of information. *Acta Psychologica*, 50, 253–290.

Brodt, S., Gais, S., Beck, J., Erb, M., Scheffler, K., & Schönauer, M. (2018). Fast track to the neocortex: A memory engram in the posterior parietal cortex. *Science*, 362, 1045–1048.

Bronkhorst, A. W. (2015). The cocktail-party problem revisited: Early processing and selection of multi-talker speech. *Attention, Perception, and Psychophysics*, 77, 1465–1487. https://doi.org/10.3758/s13414-015-0882-9

Brosnan, S. F., & De Waal, F. B. M. (2003). Monkeys reject unequal pay. *Nature*, 425, 297–299. https://doi.org/10.1038/nature01963

Broussard, S., Hickok, G., & Saberi, K. (2017). Robustness of speech intelligibility at moderate levels of spectral degradation. *PLoS ONE*, 12, Article e0180734. https://doi.org/10.1371/journal.pone.0180734

Brown, J. (1958). Some tests of the decay theory of immediate memory. *Quarterly Journal of Experimental Psychology*, 10, 12–21.

Brown, R., & Kulik, J. (1977). Flashbulb memories. *Cognition*, 5, 73–99.

Brown, R., & McNeill, D. (1966). The "tip of the tongue" phenomenon. *Journal of Verbal Learning and Verbal Behavior*, 5, 325–337.

Brown, R. G., & Marsden, C. D. (1988). Internal versus external cues and the control of attention in Parkinson's disease. *Brain*, 111, 323–345.

Bruner, J. S., Goodnow, J. J., & Austin, G. A. (1956). *A study of thinking*. John Wiley.

Bryan, W. L., & Harter, N. (1897). Studies in the physiology and psychology of the telegraphic language. *Psychological Review*, 4, 27–53.

Bryant, D. J. (1991). Exceptions to recognition failure as a function of the encoded association between cue and target. *Memory and Cognition*, 19, 210–219.

Brysbaert, M., Mandera, P., & Keuleers, E. (2018). The word frequency effect in word processing: An updated review. *Current Directions in Psychological Science*, 27, 45–50. https://doi.org/10.1177/0963721417727521

Buckner, R. L., & Petersen, S. E. (1996). What does neuroimaging tell us about the role of prefrontal cortex in memory retrieval? *Seminars in the Neurosciences*, 8, 47–55.

Buckner, R. L., Petersen, S. E., Ojemann, J. G., et al. (1995). Functional anatomical studies of explicit and implicit memory retrieval tasks. *Journal of Neuroscience*, 15, 12–29.

Buetti, S., Cronin, D. A., Madison, A. M., Wang, Z., & Lleras, A. (2016). Towards a better understanding of parallel visual processing in human vision: Evidence for exhaustive analysis of visual information. *Journal of Experimental Psychology: General*, 145, 672–707. https://doi.org/10.1037/xge0000163

Bukach, C. M., Gauthier, I., Tarr, M. J., et al. (2012). Does acquisition of Greeble expertise in prosopagnosia rule out a domain-general deficit? *Neuropsychologia*, 50, 289–304. https://doi.org/10.1016/j.neuropsychologia.2011.11.023

Bunzeck, N., Wuestenberg, T., Lutz, K., Heinze, H.-J., & Jancke, L. (2005). Scanning silence: Mental imagery of complex sounds. *NeuroImage*, 26, 1119–1127.

Burgess, G. H., & Chadalavada, B. (2016). Profound anterograde amnesia following routine anesthetic and dental procedure: A new classification of amnesia characterized by intermediate-to-late-stage consolidation failure? *Neurocase*, 22, 84–94. https://doi.org/10.1080/13554794.2015.1046885

Burgund, E. D., & Marsolek, C. J. (2000). Viewpoint-invariant and viewpoint-dependent object recognition in dissociable neural subsystems. *Psychonomic Bulletin and Review*, 7, 480–489.

Burns, B. D. (2004). The effects of speed on skilled chess performance. *Psychological Science*, 15, 442–447.

Cabeza, R., & Nyberg, L. (2000). Imaging cognition. II. An empirical review of 275 PET and fMRI studies. *Journal of Cognitive Neuroscience*, 12, 1–47.

Cahill, L., & McGaugh, J. L. (1995). A novel demonstration of enhanced memory associated with emotional arousal. *Consciousness and Cognition: An International Journal*, 4, 410–421.

Caine, D. B. (1999). *Within reason: Rationality and human behavior*. Pantheon.

Caldwell-Harris, C. L. (2021). Frequency effects in reading are powerful – but is contextual diversity the more important variable? *Language and Linguistics Compass*, 15, Article e12444.

Carey, S. (1978). The child as word learner: Linguistic theory and psychological reality. In M. Halle, J. Bresnan, & G. A. Miller (Eds.), *Linguistic theory and psychological reality* (pp. 264–293). MIT Press.

Carey, S. (1985). *Conceptual change in childhood*. MIT Press.

Carey, S., & Bartlett, E. (1978). Acquiring a single new word. *Papers and Reports on Child Language Development*, 15, 17–29.

Carlesimo, G. A., Perri, R., Turriziani, P., Tomaiuolo, F., & Caltagirone, C. (2001). Remembering what but not where: Independence of spatial and visual working memory in the human brain. *Cortex*, 36, 519–534.

Carlson, B. W. (1990). Anchoring and adjustment in judgments under risk. *Journal of Experimental Psychology: Learning, Memory, and Cognition*, 16, 665–676.

Carpenter, P. A., Just, M. A., & Shell, P. (1990). What one intelligence test measures: A theoretical account of the processing in the Raven Progressive Matrices Test. *Psychological Review*, 97, 404–431.

Carrasco, M. (2011). Visual attention: The past 25 years. *Vision Research*, 51, 1484–1525.

Carrasco, M. (2014). Spatial attention: Perceptual modulation. In S. Kastner & A. C. Nobre (Eds.), *The Oxford handbook of attention* (pp. 183–230). Oxford University Press.

Carrasco, M., & Barbot, A. (2019). Spatial attention alters visual appearance. *Current Opinion in Psychology*, 29, 56–64.

Casati, R. (2004). The shadow knows: A primer on the informational structure of cast shadows. *Perception*, 33, 1385–1396.

Castel, A. D., Pratt, J., & Drummond, E. (2005). The effects of action video game experience on the time course of inhibition of return and the efficiency of visual search. *Acta Psychologica*, 119, 217–230. https://doi.org/10.1016/j.actpsy.2005.02.004

Catrambone, R. (1994). Improving examples to improve transfer to novel problems. *Memory and Cognition*, 22, 606–615.

Catrambone, R. (1995). Aiding subgoal learning: Effects on transfer. *Journal of Educational Psychology*, 87, 5–17.

Catrambone, R. (1996). Generalizing solution procedures learned from examples. *Journal of Experimental Psychology: Learning, Memory, and Cognition*, 22, 1020–1031.

Catrambone, R. (1998). The subgoal learning model: Creating better examples so that students can solve novel problems. *Journal of Experimental Psychology: General*, 127, 355–376.

Catrambone, R. (2002). The effects of surface and structural feature matches on the access of story analogs. *Journal of Experimental Psychology: Learning, Memory, and Cognition*, 28, 318–334.

Catrambone, R., & Holyoak, K. J. (1990). Learning subgoals and methods for solving probability problems. *Memory and Cognition*, 18, 593–603.

Chance, P. (1999). Thorndike's puzzle boxes and the origins of the experimental analysis of behavior. *Journal of the Experimental Analysis of Behavior*, 72, 433–440. https://doi.org/10.1901%2Fjeab.1999.72-433

Chang, M., & Brainerd, C. J. (2021). Semantic and phonological false memory: A review of theory and data. *Journal of Memory and Language*, 119, Article 104210.

Chang, Y. H., & Lane, D. (2018). It takes more than practice and experience to become a chess master: Evidence from a child prodigy and adult chess players. *Journal of Expertise*, 1, 6–34.

Chao, L. L., Martin, A., & Haxby, J. V. (1999). Are face-responsive regions selective only for faces? *Neuroreport*, 10, 2945–2950.

Chao, S.-J., & Cheng, P. W. (2000). The emergence of inferential rules: The use of pragmatic reasoning schemas by preschoolers. *Cognitive Development*, 15, 39–62.

Charlot, V., Tzourio, N., Zilbovicius, M., Mazoyer, B. M., & Denis, M. (1992). Different mental imagery abilities result in different regional cerebral blood flow activation patterns during cognitive tasks. *Neuropsychologia*, 30, 565–580.

Chase, W. G., & Simon, H. A. (1973). Perception in chess. *Cognitive Psychology*, 4, 55–81.

Chater, N. (1996). Reconciling simplicity and likelihood principles in perceptual organization. *Psychological Review*, 103, 566–581.

Chater, N., & Oaksford, M. (1999). The probability heuristics model of syllogistic reasoning. *Cognitive Psychology*, 38, 191–258.

Chen, W. J., & Krajbich, I. (2017). Computational modeling of epiphany learning. *Proceedings of the National Academy of Sciences of the USA*, 114, 4637–4642. https://doi.org/10.1073/pnas .1618161114

Chen, W., Kato, T., Zhu, X. H., Ogawa, S., Tank, D. W., & Ugurbil, K. (1998). Human primary visual cortex and lateral geniculate nucleus activation during visual imagery. *Neuroreport*, 9, 3669–3674.

Chen, Z. (1995). Analogical transfer: From schematic pictures to problem solving. *Memory and Cognition*, 23, 255–269.

Chen, Z. (2012). Object-based attention: A tutorial review. *Attention, Perception, and Psychophysics*, 74, 784–802. https://doi.org/10.3758/s13414-012-0322-z

Chen, Z., Mo, L., & Honomichl, R. (2004). Having the memory of an elephant: Long-term retrieval and the use of analogues in problem solving. *Journal of Experimental Psychology: General*, 133, 415–433.

Cheng, P. W., & Holyoak, K. J. (1985). Pragmatic reasoning schemas. *Cognitive Psychology*, 17, 391–416.

Cheng, P. W., Holyoak, K. J., Nisbett, R. E., & Oliver, L. M. (1986). Pragmatic versus syntactic approaches to training deductive reasoning. *Cognitive Psychology*, 18, 293–328.

Cherry, E. C. (1953). Some experiments on the recognition of speech, with one and with two ears. *Journal of the Acoustical Society of America*, 25, 975–979.

Chi, M. T. H., Feltovich, P., & Glaser, R. (1981). Categorization and representation of physics problems by experts and novices. *Cognitive Science*, 5, 121–152.

Chin, J. C., & Lin, M. H. (2018). Children's understanding of conditional promise contract violations. *Infant and Child Development*, 27, Article e2082.

Chincotta, D., Underwood, G., Ghani, K., Papadopoulou, E., & Wresinksi, M. (1999). Memory span for Arabic numerals and digit words: Evidence for a limited-capacity visuo-spatial storage system. *Quarterly Journal of Experimental Psychology*, 2A, 325–351.

Chomsky, N. (1957). *Syntactic structures*. Mouton.

Chomsky, N. (1959). A review of B. F. Skinner's verbal behavior. *Language*, 35, 26–58.

Chomsky, N. (1965). *Aspects of the theory of syntax*. MIT Press.

Chomsky, N. (2013). Problems of projection. *Lingua*, 130, 33–49. https://doi.org/10.1016/j.lingua.2012 .12.003

Christiansen, M. H., & Chater, N. (2016). The now-or-never bottleneck: A fundamental constraint on language. *Behavioral and Brain Sciences*, 39, Article E62. https://doi.org/10.1017/ S0140525X1500031X

Christianson, S.-A. (1989). Flashbulb memories: Special, but not so special. *Memory and Cognition*, 17, 435–443.

Christophel, T. B., Klink, P. C., Spitzer, B., Roelfsema, P. R., & Haynes, J.-D. (2017). The distributed nature of working memory. *Trends in Cognitive Sciences*, 21, 111–124. https://doi.org/ 10.1016/j.tics.2016.12.007

Chrysikou, E. G., Morrow, H. M., Flohrschutz, A., & Denney, L. (2021). Augmenting ideational fluency in a creativity task across multiple transcranial direct current stimulation montages. *Scientific Reports*, 11, Article 8874.

Chuderski, A., & Jastrzębski, J. (2018). Much ado about aha! Insight problem solving is strongly related to working memory capacity and reasoning ability. *Journal of Experimental Psychology: General*, 147, 257–281. https://doi.org/10.1037/xge0000378

Chun, M. (2011). Visual working memory as visual attention sustained internally over time. *Neuropsychologia*, 49, 1407–1409.

Chun, M. M., & Marois, R. (2002). The dark side of visual attention. *Current Opinion in Neurobiology*, 12, 184–189.

Chun, M. M., Golomb, J. D., & Turk-Browne, N. B. (2011). A taxonomy of external and internal attention. *Annual Review of Psychology*, 62, 73–101. https://doi.org/10.1146/annurev.psych .093008.100427

Cichy, R. M., & Oliva, A. (2020). AM/EEG-fMRI fusion primer: Resolving human brain responses in space and time. *Neuron*, 107, 772–781.

Clark, H. H., & Clark, E. V. (1977). *Psychology and language: An introduction to psycholinguistics*. Harcourt, Brace, Jovanovich.

Clark, R. E., & Squire, L. R. (1998). Classical conditioning and brain systems: The role of awareness. *Science*, 280, 77–81.

Cleary, A. M., Langley, M. M., & Seiler, K. R. (2004). Recognition without picture identification: Geons as components of the pictorial memory trace. *Psychonomic Bulletin and Review*, 11, 903–908.

Clement, C. A., Mawby, R., & Giles, D. E. (1994). The effects of manifest relational similarity on analog retrieval. *Journal of Memory and Language*, 33, 396–420.

Cockcroft, K. (2022). Are working memory models WEIRD? Testing models of working memory in a non-WEIRD sample. *Neuropsychology*, 36, Article 456.

Cocke, W. (2004, August 1). Why is the Blue Ridge blue? *Blue Ridge Outdoors*. www .blueridgeoutdoors.com/magazine/august-2004/why-is-the-blue-ridge-blue/

Cohen, J. D., Perlstein, W. M., Braver, T. S., et al. (1997). Temporal dynamics of brain activation during a working memory task. *Nature*, 386, 604–608.

Cohen, N. J., & Squire, L. R. (1980). Preserved learning and retention of pattern analyzing skill in amnesia: Dissociation of knowing how and knowing that. *Science*, 210, 207–209.

Cole, S. N., Markostamou, I., Watson, L. A., et al. (2022). Spontaneous past and future thinking about the COVID-19 pandemic across 14 countries: Effects of individual and country-level COVID-19 impact indicators. *Journal of Applied Research in Memory and Cognition*, 12, 502–512. https://doi.org/10.1037/mac0000071

Colle, H. A., & Welsh, A. (1976). Acoustic masking in primary memory. *Journal of Verbal Learning and Verbal Behavior*, 15, 17–31.

Collins, A. M., & Loftus, E. F. (1975). A spreading-activation theory of semantic processing. *Psychological Review*, 82, 407–428.

Collins, A. M., & Quillian, M. R. (1969). Retrieval time from semantic memory. *Journal of Verbal Learning and Verbal Behavior*, 8, 240–247.

Collins, A. M., & Quillian, M. R. (1972). How to make a language user. In E. Tulving & W. Donaldson (Eds.), *Organization of memory* (pp. 309–351). Academic Press.

Coltheart, M. (1980). Iconic memory and visible persistence. *Perception and Psychophysics*, 27, 183–228. https://doi.org/10.3758/BF03204258

Coltheart, M. (2014). Dual-route model of reading development. In *Encyclopedia of language development* (pp. 167–168). SAGE. https://doi .org/10.4135/9781483346441

Coltheart, M., Lea, C. D., & Thompson, K. (1974). In defence of iconic memory. *Quarterly Journal of Experimental Psychology*, 26, 633–641. https://doi .org/10.1080/14640747408400456

Coltheart, M., Curtis, B., Atkins, P., & Haller, M. (1993). Models of reading aloud: Dual-route and parallel distributed-processing approaches. *Psychological Review*, 100, 589–608.

Connors, M. H., Burns, B. D., & Campitelli, G. (2011). Expertise in complex decision making: The role of search in chess 70 years after de Groot. *Cognitive Science*, 35, 1567–1579. https://doi.org/10.1111/j.1551-6709.2011.01196.x

Conrad, C. (1972). Cognitive economy in semantic memory. *Journal of Experimental Psychology*, 92, 149–154.

Conrad, R. (1964). Acoustic confusions in immediate memory. *British Journal of Psychology*, 55, 75–84.

Conway, A. R. A., Skitka, L. J., Hemmerich, J. A., & Kershaw, T. C. (2009). Flashbulb memory for 11 September 2001. *Applied Cognitive Psychology*, 23, 605–623. https://doi.org/10.1002/acp.1497

Conway, M. (2002). *Levels of processing 30 years on.* Taylor and Francis.

Cook, C. J., Howard, S. J., Scerif, G., et al. (2019). Associations of physical activity and gross motor skills with executive function in preschool children from low-income South African settings. *Developmental Science*, 22, Article e12820.

Cooper, L. A., Schacter, D. L., Ballesteros, S., & Moore, C. (1992). Priming and recognition of transformed three-dimensional objects: Effects of size and reflection. *Journal of Experimental Psychology: Learning, Memory, and Cognition*, 18, 43–57.

Corkin, S. (1968). Acquisition of motor skill after bilateral medial temporal lobe excision. *Neuropsychologia*, 6, 255–265.

Corkin, S. (2002). What's new with the amnesic patient H.M.? *Nature Reviews Neuroscience*, 3, 153–160.

Corkin, S. (2013). *Permanent present tense: The unforgettable life of the amnesic patient, H.M.* Basic Books.

Cosmides, L. (1989). The logic of social exchange: Has natural selection shaped how humans reason? Studies with the Wason selection task. *Cognition*, 31, 187–276.

Cosmides, L., & Tooby, J. (1992). Cognitive adaptations for social exchange. In J. Barkow, L. Cosmides, & J. Tooby (Eds.), *The adapted mind: Evolutionary psychology and the generation of culture* (pp. 163–228). Oxford University Press.

Cosmides, L., & Tooby, J. (2000). The cognitive neuroscience of social reasoning. In M. Gazzaniga (Ed.), *The cognitive neurosciences* (2nd ed., pp. 1259–1270). MIT Press.

Cosmides, L., & Tooby, J. (2013). Evolutionary psychology: New perspectives on cognition and motivation. *Annual Review of Psychology*, 64,

201–229. https://doi.org/10.1146/annurev.psych.121208.131628

Courtney, S. M., Ungerleider, L. G., Keil, K., & Haxby, J. V. (1996). Object and spatial visual working memory activate separate neural systems in human cortex. *Cerebral Cortex*, 6, 39–49.

Couvillon, M. J., Schürch, R., & Ratnieks, F. L. W. (2014). Dancing bees communicate a foraging preference for rural lands in high-level agri-environment schemes. *Current Biology*, 24, 1212–1215. https://doi.org/10.1016/j.cub.2014.03.072

Cowan, N. (1987). Auditory sensory storage in relation to the growth of sensation and acoustic information extraction. *Journal of Experimental Psychology: Human Perception and Performance*, 13, 204–215.

Craig, A. B., Phillips, M. E., Zaldivar, A., Bhattacharyya, R., & Krichmar, J. L. (2016). Investigation of biases and compensatory strategies using a probabilistic variant of the Wisconsin card sorting test. *Frontiers in Psychology*, 7, Article 17.

Craik, F. (2021). *Remembering: An activity of mind and brain* (Vol. 34). Oxford University Press.

Craik, F. I., & Lockhart, R. S. (1972). Levels of processing: A framework for memory research. *Journal of Verbal Learning and Verbal Behavior*, 11, 671–684.

Craik, F. I., & Tulving, E. (1975). Depth of processing and the retention of words in episodic memory. *Journal of Experimental Psychology: General*, 104, 268–294.

Craik, F. I., & Watkins, M. J. (1973). The role of rehearsal in short-term memory. *Journal of Verbal Learning and Verbal Behavior*, 12, 599–607.

Crews, F. (1995). *The memory wars.* New York Review of Books.

Croijmans, I., Hendrickx, I., Lefever, E., Majid, A., & Van Den Bosch, A. (2020). Uncovering the language of wine experts. *Natural Language Engineering*, 26, 511–530. https://doi.org/10.1017/S1351324919000500

Curci, A., & Luminet, O. (2006). Follow-up of a cross-national comparison on flashbulb and event memory for the September 11th attacks. *Memory*,

14, 329–344. https://doi.org/10.1080/09658210500340816

Dąbrowska, E. (2015). What exactly is universal grammar, and has anyone seen it? *Frontiers in Psychology*, 6, Article 852. https://doi.org/10.3389/fpsyg.2015.00852

Danek, A. H., Williams, J., & Wiley, J. (2020). Closing the gap: Connecting sudden representational change to the subjective aha! experience in insightful problem solving. *Psychological Research*, 84, 111–119.

Daneman, M., & Carpenter, P. A. (1980). Individual differences in working memory and reading. *Journal of Verbal Learning and Verbal Behavior*, 19, 450–466.

Danker, J. F., & Anderson, J. R. (2010). The ghosts of brain states past: Remembering reactivates the brain regions engaged during encoding. *Psychological Bulletin*, 136, 87–102. https://doi.org/10.1037/a0017937

Darling, S., & Havelka, J. (2010). Visuospatial bootstrapping: Evidence for binding of verbal and spatial information in working memory. *Quarterly Journal of Experimental Psychology*, 63, 239–245. https://doi.org/10.1080/17470210903348605

Darling, S., Allen, R. J., & Havelka, J. (2017). Visuospatial bootstrapping: When visuospatial and verbal memory work together. *Current Directions in Psychological Science*, 26, 3–9. https://doi.org/10.1177/0963721416665342

Daugman, J. (1990). Brain metaphor and brain theory. In E. Schwartz (Ed.), *Computational neuroscience* (pp. 23–36). MIT Press.

Davidson, J. E. (1995). The suddenness of insight. In R. J. Sternberg & J. E. Davidson (Eds.), *The nature of insight* (pp. 125–155). MIT Press.

Davis, G., & Holmes, A. (2005). The capacity of visual short-term memory is not a fixed number of objects. *Memory and Cognition*, 33, 185–195.

Davis, H. L., Hoch, S. J., & Ragsdale, E. E. (1986). An anchoring and adjustment model of spousal predictions. *Journal of Consumer Research*, 13, 25–37.

Davis, M. (2003). *Analysis of scrambled text*. University of Cambridge, MRC Cognition and Brain Sciences Unit. www.mrc-cbu.cam.ac.uk/people/matt.davis/Cambridge/

Davitt, L. I., Cristino, F., Wong, A. C.-N., & Leek, E. C. (2014). Shape information mediating basic- and subordinate-level object recognition revealed by analyses of eye movements. *Journal of Experimental Psychology: Human Perception and Performance*, 40, 451–456. https://doi.org/10.1037/a0034983

Day, A. J., Fenn, K. M., & Ravizza, S. M. (2021). Is it worth it? The costs and benefits of bringing a laptop to a university class. *PLoS ONE*, 16, Article e0251792.

Day, M. V., & Ross, M. (2014). Predicting confidence in flashbulb memories. *Memory*, 22, 232–242. https://doi.org/10.1080/09658211.2013.778290

Dayan, E., & Cohen, L. G. (2011). Neuroplasticity subserving motor skill learning. *Neuron*, 72, 443–454. https://doi.org/10.1016/j.neuron.2011.10.008

de Boysson-Bardies, B. (1999). *How language comes to children: From birth to two years* (M. DeBrevoise, Trans.). MIT Press.

Deese, J. (1959). On the prediction of occurrence of particular verbal intrusions in immediate recall. *Journal of Experimental Psychology*, 58, 17–22.

de Fockert, J. W., & Gautrey, B. (2013). Greater visual averaging of face identity for own-gender faces. *Psychonomic Bulletin and Review*, 20, 468–473.

De Groot, A. D. (1946/1978). *Thought and choice in chess*. Mouton.

DeKeyser, R. M. (2000). The robustness of critical period effects in second language acquisition. *Studies in Second Language Acquisition*, 22, 499–533.

Dell, G. S., Schwartz, M. F., Marting, N., Saffran, E. M., & Gagnon, D. A. (1997). Lexical access in aphasic and nonaphasic speakers. *Psychological Review*, 104, 801–838.

De Neys, W., Moyens, E., & Vansteenwegen, D. (2010). Feeling we're biased: Autonomic arousal and reasoning conflict. *Cognitive, Affective, and Behavioral Neuroscience*, 10, 208–216. https://doi.org/10.3758/CABN.10.2.208

De Neys, W., Cromheeke, S., & Osman, M. (2011). Biased but in doubt: Conflict and decision confidence. *PLoS ONE*, 6, Article e15954.

Dennis, N., Chamberlain, J. D., & Carpenter, C. M. (2022). False memories: What neuroimaging tells us about how we mis-remember the past. In G. J. Boyle, G. Northoff, A. K. Barbey et al. (Eds.), *The SAGE handbook of cognitive and systems neuroscience: Vol. 2. Cognitive systems, development and applications*. SAGE.

de Pontes Nobre, A., de Carvalho Rodrigues, J., Burges Sbicigo, J., et al. (2013). Tasks for assessment of the episodic buffer: A systematic review. *Psychology and Neuroscience*, 6, 331–343. https://doi.org/10.3922/j.psns.2013.3.10

Descartes, R. (1664/1972). *Traite de l'homme* [Treatise on man] (T. Hall, Trans.). Harvard University Press.

D'Esposito, M., & Postle, B. R. (1999). The dependence of span and delayed-response performance on prefrontal cortex. *Neuropsychologia*, 37, 1303–1315.

Deutsch, J. A., & Deutsch, D. (1963). Attention: Some theoretical considerations. *Psychological Review*, 70, 51–61.

Di Baldassarre, G., Mondino, E., Rusca, M., et al. (2021). Multiple hazards and risk perceptions over time: The availability heuristic in Italy and Sweden under COVID-19. *Natural Hazards Earth Systems Science*, 21, 3439–3447.

Dickstein, L. S. (1975). Effects of instructions and premise order on errors in syllogistic reasoning. *Journal of Experimental Psychology: Human Learning and Memory*, 1, 376–384.

Dickstein, L. S. (1976). Differential difficulty of categorical syllogisms. *Bulletin of the Psychonomic Society*, 8, 330–332.

Dickstein, L. S. (1978). The effect of figure on syllogistic reasoning. *Memory and Cognition*, 6, 76–83.

Dijkstra, N., Mazor, M., Kok, P., & Fleming, S. (2021). Mistaking imagination for reality: Congruent mental imagery leads to more liberal perceptual detection. *Cognition*, 212, 104719.

Di Lollo, V. (1980). Temporal integration in visual memory. *Journal of Experimental Psychology: General*, 109, 75–97.

Dinges, D. F., Whitehouse, W. G., Orne, E. C., et al. (1992). Evaluating hypnotic memory enhancement (hypermnesia and reminiscence) using multitrial forced recall. *Journal of Experimental Psychology: Learning, Memory, and Cognition*, 18, 1139–1147.

Divjak, D. (2019). *Frequency in language: Memory, attention and learning.* Cambridge University Press.

Doczi, B. (2019). An overview of conceptual models and theories of lexical representation in the mental lexicon. In S. Webb (Ed.), *Routledge handbook of vocabulary studies* (pp. 46–65). Routledge.

Donnelly, C. M., & McDaniel, M. A. (1993). Use of analogy in learning scientific concepts. *Journal of Experimental Psychology: Learning, Memory, and Cognition*, 19, 975–987.

Donovan, I., Zhou, Y. J., & Carrasco, M. (2020). In search of exogenous feature-based attention. *Attention, Perception, and Psychophysics*, 82, 312–329.

Doolen, A. C., & Radvansky, G. A. (2021). A novel study: Long-lasting event memory. *Memory*, 29, 963–982.

Dooling, D. J., & Christiaansen, R. E. (1977). Episodic and semantic aspects of memory for prose. *Journal of Experimental Psychology: Human Learning and Memory*, 3, 428–436.

Doty, R. L., Shaman, P., & Dann, M. (1984). Development of the University of Pennsylvania Smell Identification Test: A standardized microencapsulated test of olfactory function. *Physiology and Behavior*, 32, 489–502.

Dove, G. (2022). *Abstract concepts and the embodied mind: Rethinking grounded cognition.* Oxford University Press.

Downing, C. J., & Pinker, S. (1985). The spatial structure of visual attention. In M. I. Posner & O. S. M. Marin (Eds.), *Attention and performance XI: Mechanisms of attention* (pp. 171–187). Erlbaum.

Drew, T., Võ, M. L.-H., & Wolfe, J. M. (2013). The invisible gorilla strikes again: Sustained inattentional blindness in expert observers. *Psychological Science*, 24, 1848–1853. https://doi.org/10.1177/0956797613479386

DuBrow, S., Rouhani, N., Niv, Y., & Norman, K. A. (2017). Does mental context drift or shift? *Current Opinion in Behavioral Sciences*, 17, 141–146.

Dunbar, K. (2001). The analogical paradox: Why analogy is so easy in naturalistic settings yet so difficult in the psychological laboratory. In D. Gentner, K. J. Holyoak, & B. Kokinov (Eds.), *Analogy: Perspectives from cognitive science* (pp. 313–334). MIT Press.

Duncker, K. (1945). On problem-solving. *Psychological Monographs*, 5, 113 pp.

Dupoux, E., Kouider, S., & Mehler, J. (2003). Lexical access without attention? Explorations using dichotic priming. *Journal of Experimental Psychology: Human Perception and Performance*, 29, 172–184.

Durso, F. T., Rea, C. B., & Dayton, T. (1994). Graph-theoretic confirmation of restructuring during insight. *Psychological Science*, 5, 94–98. https://doi.org/10.1111/j.1467-9280.1994.tb00637.x

Dye, M. W. G., Green, C. S., & Bavelier, D. (2009). The development of attention skills in action video game players. *Neuropsychologia*, 47, 1780–1789. https://doi.org/10.1016/j.neuropsychologia.2009.02.002

Elpers, N., Jensen, G., & Holmes, K. J. (2022). Does grammatical gender affect object concepts? Registered replication of Phillips and Boroditsky (2003). *Journal of Memory and Language*, 127, Article 104357.

Engle, R. W., Tuholski, S. W., Laughlin, J. E., & Conway, A. R. A. (1999). Working memory, short-term memory, and general fluid intelligence: A latent-variable approach. *Journal of Experimental Psychology: General*, 128, 309–331.

Epstein, R., Graham, K. S., & Downing, P. E. (2003). Viewpoint-specific scene representations in human parahippocampal cortex. *Neuron*, 37, 865–876.

Epstein, W. (1965). Nonrelational judgments of size and distance. *American Journal of Psychology*, 78, 120–123.

Erickson, M. A., & Kruschke, J. K. (1998). Rules and exemplars in category learning. *Journal of Experimental Psychology: General*, 127, 107–140.

Ericsson, K., & Simon, H. (1980). Verbal reports as data. *Psychological Review*, 87, 215–251. https://doi.org/10.1037/0033-295X.87.3.215

Ericsson, K. A., & Simon, H. A. (1984). *Protocol analysis: Verbal reports as data*. MIT Press.

Ericsson, K. A., & Simon, H. A. (1993). *Protocol analysis: Verbal reports as data* (Rev. ed.). MIT Press.

Eriksen, C. W., & St. James, J. D. (1986). Visual attention within and around the field of focal attention: A zoom lens model. *Perception and Psychophysics*, 40, 225–240. https://doi.org/10.3758/BF03211502

Eustache, F., Viard, A., & Desgranges, B. (2016). The MNESIS model: Memory systems and processes, identity and future thinking. *Neuropsychologia*, 87, 96–109. https://doi.org/10.1016/j.neuropsychologia.2016.05.006

Euston, D. R., Gruber, A. J., & McNaughton, B. L. (2012). The role of medial prefrontal cortex in memory and decision making. *Neuron*, 76, 1057–1070. https://doi.org/10.1016/j.neuron.2012.12.002

Evans, J. St. B. T. (2003). In two minds: Dual-process accounts of reasoning. *Trends in Cognitive Sciences*, 7, 454–459.

Evans, J. St. B. T. (2019). Reflections on reflection: The nature and function of type 2 processes in dual-process theories of reasoning. *Thinking and Reasoning*, 25, 383–415.

Evans, J. St. B. T., & Over, D. E. (1996). Rationality in the selection task: Epistemic utility versus uncertainty reduction. *Psychological Review*, 103, 356–363.

Evans, J. St. B. T., & Stanovich, K. E. (2013). Dual-process theories of higher cognition: Advancing the debate. *Perspectives on Psychological Science*, 8, 223–241. https://doi.org/10.1177/1745691612460685

Evans, J. St. B. T., Barston, J. L., & Pollard, P. (1983). On the conflict between logic and belief in syllogistic reasoning. *Memory and Cognition*, 11, 295–306.

Evans, J. St.-B. T., Newstead, S. E., & Byrne, R. M. J. (1993). *Human reasoning: The psychology of deduction*. Erlbaum.

Evans, J. St. B. T., Handley, S. J., Harper, C. N. J., & Johnson-Laird, P. N. (1999). Reasoning about necessity and possibility: A test of the mental model theory of deduction. *Journal of Experimental Psychology*, 25, 1495–1513.

Evans, K. K., Birdwell, R. L., & Wolfe, J. M. (2013). If you don't find it often, you often don't find it: Why some cancers are missed in breast cancer screening. *PLoS ONE*, 8, Article e64366. https://doi.org/10.1371/journal.pone.0064366

Evans, N., & Levinson, S. (2009). The myth of language universals: Language diversity and its importance for cognitive science. *Behavioral and Brain Sciences*, 32, 429–448.

Faillenot, I., Toni, I., Decety, J., Gregorie, M. C., & Jeannerod, M. (1997). Visual pathways for object-oriented action and object recognition: Functional anatomy with PET. *Cerebral Cortex*, 7, 77–85.

Falco, C. M. (2017). Ibn al-Haytham and his influence on post-mediaeval Western culture. In *Light-based science: Technology and sustainable development* (pp. 123–130). Taylor and Francis.

Fang, F., & He, S. (2005). Viewer-centered object representation in the human visual system revealed by viewpoint aftereffects. *Neuron*, 45, 793–800.

Fansher, M., Shah, P., & Hélie, S. (2022). The effect of mode of presentation on Tower of Hanoi problem solving. *Cognition*, 224, Article 105041.

Farah, M. J. (1990). *Visual agnosia: Disorders of object recognition and what they tell us about normal vision*. MIT Press.

Feldman, H., Goldin-Meadow, S., & Gleitman, L. R. (1978). Beyond Herodotus: The creation of language by linguistically deprived deaf children. In A. Locke (Ed.), *Action, gesture, and symbol: The emergence of language* (pp. 351–414). Academic Press.

Feldman, J. (2009). Bayes and the simplicity principle in perception. *Psychological Review*, 116, 875–887. https://doi.org/10.1037/a0017144

Fernberger, S. W. (1921). A preliminary study of the range of visual apprehension. *American Journal of Psychology*, 32, 121–133.

Ferreira, F., & Yang, Z. (2019). The problem of comprehension in psycholinguistics. *Discourse Processes*, 56, 485–495.

Ferreira, F., Bailey, K. G. D., & Ferraro, V. (2002). Good-enough representations in language comprehension. *Current Directions in Psychological Science*, 11, 11–15. https://doi.org/10.1111/1467-8721.00158

Finkenauer, C., Luminet, O., Gisle, L., et al. (1998). Flashbulb memories and the underlying mechanisms of their formation: Toward an emotional-integrative model. *Memory and Cognition*, 26, 516–531.

Fletcher, P. C., Frith, C. D., Baker, S. C., Shallice, T., Frackowiak, R. S., & Dolan, R. J. (1995). The mind's eye: Precuneus activation in memoryrelated imagery. *NeuroImage*, 2, 195–200.

Fodor, J. A., & Garrett, M. (1967). Some syntactic determinants of sentential complexity. *Perception and Psychophysics*, 2, 289–296.

Fodor, J. D. (1995). Comprehending sentence structure. In L. R. Gleitman & M. Liberman (Eds.), *An invitation to cognitive science* (Vol. 1, pp. 209–246). MIT Press.

Foroughi, C. K., Monfort, S. S., Paczynski, M., McKnight, P. E., & Greenwood, P. M. (2016). Placebo effects in cognitive training. *Proceedings of the National Academy of Sciences of the USA*, 113, 7470–7474. https://doi.org/10.1073/pnas.1601243113

Forster, K. I., & Chambers, S. M. (1973). Lexical access and naming time. *Journal of Verbal Learning and Verbal Behavior*, 12, 627–635.

Foster, D. J. (2017). Replay comes of age. *Annual Review of Neuroscience*, 40, 581–602.

Foulke, E., & Sticht, T. G. (1969). Review of research on the intelligibility and comprehension of accelerated speech. *Psychological Bulletin*, 72, 50–62.

Franconeri, S. L., Hollingworth, A., & Simons, D. J. (2005). Do new objects capture attention? *Psychological Science*, 16, 275–281.

Frazier, L., & Clifton, C., Jr. (1996). *Construal*. MIT Press.

Frazier, L., & Rayner, K. (1982). Making and correcting errors during sentence comprehension: Eye movements in the analysis of structurally ambiguous sentences. *Cognitive Psychology*, 14, 178–210.

Freyd, J. J. (1994). Betrayal trauma: Traumatic amnesia as an adaptive response to childhood abuse. *Ethics and Behavior*, 4, 307–329. https://doi.org/10.1207/s15327019eb0404_1

Friedmann, N., & Coltheart, M. (2016). Types of developmental dyslexia. In A. Bar-On & D. Ravid (Eds.), *Handbook of communication disorders: Theoretical, empirical, and applied linguistics perspectives*. De Gruyter Mouton.

Funnell, E. (1983). Phonological processes in reading: New evidence from acquired dyslexia. *British Journal of Psychology*, 74, 159–180.

Gabrieli, J. D. E., Fleischman, D. A., Keane, M. M., Reminger, S. L., & Morrell, F. (1995). Double dissociation between memory systems underlying explicit and implicit memory in the human brain. *Psychological Science*, 6, 76–82.

Gagné, R. M., & Smith, E. C., Jr. (1962). A study of the effects of verbalization on problem solving. *Journal of Experimental Psychology*, 63, 12–18.

Gallace, A., Tan, H. Z., Haggard, P., & Spence, C. (2008). Short term memory for tactile stimuli. *Brain Research*, 1190, 132–142.

Gallo, D. A., & Wheeler, M. E. (2013). Episodic memory. In D. Reisberg (Ed.), *The Oxford handbook of cognitive psychology* (pp. 189–205). Oxford University Press. https://doi.org/10.1093/oxfordhb/9780195376746.013.0013

Gallo, D. A., Roberts, M. J., & Seamon, J. G. (1997). Remembering words not presented in lists: Can we avoid creating false memories? *Psychonomic Bulletin and Review*, 4, 271–276.

Ganel, T., Tanzer, M., & Goodale, M. A. (2008). A double dissociation between action and perception in the context of visual illusions: Opposite effects of real and illusory size. *Psychological Science*, 19, 221–225. https://doi.org/10.1111/j.1467-9280.2008.02071.x

Gardner, H. (1985). *The mind's new science: A history of the cognitive revolution*. Basic Books.

Gaskell, M., & Marslen-Wilson, W. D. (2001). Simulating parallel activation in spoken word recognition. In M. H. Christiansen & N. Chater (Eds.), *Connectionist psycholinguistics* (pp. 76–105). Ablex.

Gathercole, S. E., Pickering, S. J., Knight, C., & Stegmann, Z. (2004). Working memory skills and educational attainment: Evidence from national curriculum assessments at 7 and 14 years of age. *Applied Cognitive Psychology*, 18, 1–16.

Gaudreau, P., Miranda, D., & Gareau, A. (2014). Canadian university students in wireless classrooms: What do they do on their laptops and does it really matter? *Computers and Education*, 70, 245–255.

Gauthier, I., & Tarr, M. J. (1997). Becoming a "Greeble" expert: Exploring mechanisms for face recognition. *Vision Research*, 37, 1673–1682. https://doi.org/10.1016/S0042-6989(96)00286-6

Gauthier, I., & Tarr, M. J. (2002). Unraveling mechanisms for expert object recognition: Bridging brain activity and behavior. *Journal of Experimental Psychology: Human Perception and Performance*, 28, 431–446.

Gauthier, I., Skudlarski, P., Gore, J. C., & Anderson, A. W. (2000). Expertise for cars and birds recruits brain areas involved in face recognition. *Nature Neuroscience*, 3, 191–197.

Gauthier, I., Curran, T., Curby, K. M., & Collins, D. (2003). Perceptual interference supports a nonmodular account of face processing. *Nature Neuroscience*, 6, 428–432.

Gegenfurtner, K. R., Bloj, M., & Toscani, M. (2015). The many colours of "the dress." *Current Biology*, 25, R543–R544. https://doi.org/10.1016/j.cub.2015.04.043

Gelman, S. A., & Markman, E. M. (1986). Categories and induction in young children. *Cognition*, 23, 183–209.

Gentner, D., & Kurtz, K. J. (2005). Relational categories. In W. K. Ahn, R. L. Goldstone, B. C. Love, A. B. Markman, & P. W. Wolff (Eds.), *Categorization inside and outside the lab* (pp. 151–175). American Psychological Association.

Gentner, D., Rattermann, M. J., & Forbus, K. D. (1993). The roles of similarity in transfer: Separating retrievability from inferential soundness. *Cognitive Psychology*, 25, 431–467.

Gentner, D., Loewenstein, J., & Thompson, L. (2003). Learning and transfer: A general role for analogical reasoning. *Journal of Educational Psychology*, 95, 393–408.

Gernsbacher, M. A. (Ed.). (1994). *Handbook of psycholinguistics*. Academic Press.

Gernsbacher, M. A., & Kaschak, M. P. (2013). Text comprehension. In D. Reisberg (Ed.), *The Oxford handbook of cognitive psychology* (pp. 462–474). Oxford University Press.

Gerwig, M., Hajjar, K., Dimitrova, A., et al. (2005). Timing of conditioned eyeblink responses is impaired in cerebellar patients. *Journal of Neuroscience*, 25, 3919–3931.

Gibson, E., Bergen, L., & Piantadosi, S. T. (2013). Rational integration of noisy evidence and prior semantic expectations in sentence interpretation. *Proceedings of the National Academy of Sciences of the USA*, 110, 8051–8056.

Gibson, J. J. (1979). *The ecological approach to visual perception*. Houghton Mifflin.

Gick, M. L., & Holyoak, K. J. (1980). Analogical problem solving. *Cognitive Psychology*, 12, 306–355.

Gick, M. L., & Holyoak, K. J. (1983). Schema induction and analogical transfer. *Cognitive Psychology*, 15, 1–38.

Gigerenzer, G., & Hoffrage, U. (1999). Overcoming difficulties in Bayesian reasoning: A reply to Lewis & Keren and Mellers & McGraw. *Psychological Review*, 106, 425–430.

Gigerenzer, G., & Hug, K. (1992). Domain-specific reasoning: Social contracts, cheating, and perspective change. *Cognition*, 43, 127–171.

Gigerenzer, G., & Todd, P. M. (1999). Fast and frugal heuristics: The adaptive toolbox. In G. Gigerenzer, P. Todd, & ABC Research Group (Eds.), *Simple heuristics that make us smart* (pp. 3–34). Oxford University Press.

Gilead, M., Trope, Y., & Liberman, N. (2020). Above and beyond the concrete: The diverse representational substrates of the predictive brain. *Behavioral and Brain Sciences,* 43, Article E121. https://doi.org/10.1017/S0140525X19002000

Gilhooly, K. J., Logie, R. H., Wetherick, N. E., & Wynn, V. (1993). Working memory and strategies in syllogistic-reasoning tasks. *Memory and Cognition*, 21, 115–124.

Gilhooly, K. J., Georgiou, G., & Devery, U. (2013). Incubation and creativity: Do something different. *Thinking and Reasoning*, 19, 137–149. https://doi.org/10.1080/13546783.2012.749812

Gilliam, T., & Jones, T. (Dirs.). (1975). *Monty Python and the Holy Grail* [Motion picture] (M. Forstater & M. White, Producers). EMI/Python Pictures/Michael White.

Girardeau, G., Benchenane, K., Wiener, S. I., Buzsáki, G., & Zugaro, M. B. (2009). Selective suppression of hippocampal ripples impairs spatial memory. *Nature Neuroscience*, 12, 1222–1223. https://doi.org/10.1038/nn.2384

Glanville, A. D., & Dallenbach, K. M. (1929). The range of attention. *American Journal of Psychology*, 41, 207–236.

Glenberg, A. M. (1997). What memory is for. *Behavioural and Brain Sciences*, 20, 1–55.

Glymour, C. (2001). *The mind's arrows: Bayes nets and graphical causal models in psychology*. MIT Press.

Gobet, F., & Simon, H. A. (1996). The roles of recognition processes and look-ahead search in time-constrained expert problem solving: Evidence from grand-master-level chess. *Psychological Science*, 7, 52–55.

Gobet, F., & Simon, H. A. (1998). Expert chess memory: Revisiting the chunking hypothesis. *Memory*, 6, 225–255.

Godden, D. R., & Baddeley, A. D. (1975). Context-dependent memory in two natural environments: On land and underwater. *British Journal of Psychology*, 66, 325–331.

Goldin-Meadow, S., & Mylander, C. (1998). Spontaneous sign systems created by deaf children in two cultures. *Nature*, 391, 279–281.

Goldin-Meadow, S., Gelman, S. A., & Mylander, C. (2005). Expressing generic concepts with and without a language model. *Cognition*, 96, 109–126.

Goldin-Meadow, S., Brentari, D., Coppola, M., Horton, L., & Senghas, A. (2015). Watching language grow in the manual modality: Nominals, predicates, and handshapes. *Cognition*, 136, 381–395. https://doi.org/10.1016/j.cognition.2014.11.029

Goldwater, M. B., Markman, A. B., & Stilwell, C. H. (2011). The empirical case for role-governed categories. *Cognition*, 118, 359–376. https://doi.org/10.1016/j.cognition.2010.10.009

Goldy, S. P., Jones, N. M., & Piff, P. K. (2022). The social effects of an awesome solar eclipse. *Psychological Science*, 33. https://doi.org/10.1177/09567976221085501

Gollan, T. H., Ferreira, V. S., Cera, C., & Flett, S. (2014). Translation-priming effects on tip-of-the-tongue states. *Language and Cognitive Processes*, 29, 278–288. https://doi.org/10.1080/01690965.2012.762457

Gonsalves, B., Reber, P. J., Gitelman, D. R., Parrish, T. B., Mesulam, M. M., & Paller, K. A. (2004). Neural evidence that vivid imagining can lead to false remembering. *Psychological Science*, 15, 655–660.

Goodale, M. A., & Milner, A. D. (1992). Separate pathways for vision and action. *Trends in Neurosciences*, 15, 20–25.

Goodale, M. A., & Milner, A. D. (2004). *Sight unseen: An exploration of conscious and unconscious vision*. Oxford University Press.

Goodale, M. A., & Westwood, D. A. (2004). An evolving view of duplex vision: Separate but interacting cortical pathways for perception and action. *Current Opinion in Neurobiology*, 14, 203–211.

Goto, M., Shirato, T., & Uda, R. (2014). Text-based CAPTCHA using phonemic restoration effect and similar pronunciation with an Asian accent. In *2014 17th international conference on Network-Based Information Systems* (pp. 517–524). IEEE. https://doi.org/10.1109/NBiS.2014.54

Gotts, S. J., Chow, C. C., & Martin, A. (2012). Repetition priming and repetition suppression: A case for enhanced efficiency through neural synchronization. *Cognitive Neuroscience*, 3, 227–237. https://doi.org/10.1080/17588928.2012.670617

Grabenhorst, F., Salzman, C. D., & Schultz, W. (2020). The role of the primate amygdala in reward and decision-making. In D. Poeppel, G. R. Mangun, & M. S. Gazzaniga (Eds.), *The cognitive neurosciences* (pp. 631–639). MIT Press.

Graesser, A. C., Singer, M., & Trabasso, T. (1994). Constructing inferences during narrative text comprehension. *Psychological Review*, 101, 371–395.

Graf, P., & Schacter, D. L. (1985). Implicit and explicit memory for new associations in normal and amnesic subjects. *Journal of Experimental Psychology: Learning, Memory, and Cognition*, 11, 501–518.

Graf, P., Shimamura, A. P., & Squire, L. R. (1985). Priming across modalities and priming across category levels: Extending the domain of preserved function in amnesia. *Journal of Experimental Psychology: Learning, Memory, and Cognition*, 11, 386–396.

Grainger, J., & Whitney, C. (2004). Does the huamn mnid raed wrods as a wlohe? *Trends in Cognitive Sciences*, 8, 58–59.

Grant, H. M., Bredahl, L. C., Clay, J., et al. (1998). Context-dependent memory for meaningful material: Information for students. *Applied Cognitive Psychology*, 12, 617–623. https://doi.org/10.1002/(SICI)1099-0720 (1998120) 12:6<617::AID-ACP542>3.0.CO;2-5

Gray, M. E., & Holyoak, K. J. (2021). Teaching by analogy: From theory to practice. *Mind, Brain, and Education*, 15, 250–263.

Greenberg, D. L., & Verfaellie, M. (2010). Interdependence of episodic and semantic memory: Evidence from neuropsychology. *Journal of the International Neuropsychological Society*, 16, 748–753. https://doi.org/10.1017/S1355617710000676

Greene, C. M., de Saint Laurent, C., Hegarty, K., & Murphy, G. (2022). False memories for true and false vaccination information form in line with pre-existing vaccine opinions. *Applied Cognitive Psychology*, 36, 1200–1208.

Greenfield, P. M., & Lyn, H. (2007). Symbol combination in *Pan*: Language, action, and culture. In D. A. Washburn (Ed.), *Primate perspectives on behavior and cognition* (pp. 255–267). American Psychological Association.

Greeno, J. G. (1974). Hobbits and orcs: Acquisition of a sequential concept. *Cognitive Psychology*, 6, 270–292.

Gregory, R. L. (2015). *Eye and brain: The psychology of seeing* (5th ed.). Princeton University Press.

Griggs, R. A. (1984). Memory cueing and instructional effects on Wason's selection task. *Current Psychological Research and Reviews*, 3, 3–10.

Griggs, R. A., & Cox, J. R. (1982). The elusive thematic-materials effect in Wason's selection task. *British Journal of Psychology*, 73, 407–420.

Grill-Spector, K., & Malach, R. (2001). fMR-adaptation: A tool for studying the functional properties of human cortical neurons. *Acta Psychologica*, 107, 293–321.

Grill-Spector, K., Knouf, N., & Kanwisher, N. (2004). The fusiform face area subserves face perception, not generic within-category identification. *Nature Neuroscience*, 7, 555–562.

Guthrie, L. G., Vallée-Tourangeau, F., Vallée-Tourangeau, G., & Howard, C. (2015). Learning and interactivity in solving a transformation problem. *Memory and Cognition*, 43, 723–735. https://doi.org/10.3758/s13421-015-0504-8

Haberman, J., & Whitney, D. (2007). Rapid extraction of mean emotion and gender from sets of faces. *Current Biology*, 17, R751–R753.

Hacker, D. J., Plumb, C. S., & Marra, R. M. (2020). The sequential nature of engineering problem solving. *Journal of Higher Education Theory and Practice*, 20.

Hakes, D. T., & Cairns, H. S. (1970). Sentence comprehension and relative pronouns. *Perception and Psychophysics*, 8, 5–8.

Hakes, D. T., & Foss, D. J. (1970). Decision processes during sentence comprehension: Effects of surface structure reconsidered. *Perception and Psychophysics*, 8, 413–416.

Halpern, M. (1998). *Personal letter to Edward Tufte*. www.edwardtufte.com/bboard/q-and-a-fetch-msg?msg_id=0000U6

Harris, C. R., Pashler, H. E., & Coburn, N. (2004). Moray revisited: High-priority affective stimuli and visual search. *Quarterly Journal of Experimental Psychology: Human Experimental Psychology*, 57A, 1–31.

Harris, J. A., Miniussi, C., Harris, I. M., & Diamond, M. E. (2002). Transient storage of a tactile memory trace in primary somatosensory cortex. *Journal of Neuroscience*, 22, 8720–8725.

Harris, P. L., Núñez, M., & Brett, C. (2001). Let's swap: Early understanding of social exchange by British and Nepali children. *Memory and Cognition*, 29, 757–764.

Hart, J. T. (1965). Memory and the feeling-of-knowing experience. *Journal of Educational Psychology*, 56, 208–216.

Hart, J. T. (1967). Second-try recall, recognition, and the memory-monitoring process. *Journal of Educational Psychology*, 58, 193–197.

Hartshorne, J. K., Tenenbaum, J. B., & Pinker, S. (2018). A critical period for second language acquisition: Evidence from 2/3 million English speakers. *Cognition*, 177, 263–277.

Hassebrock, F., Johnson, P. E., Bullemer, P., Fox, P. W., & Moller, J. H. (1993). When less is more: Representation and selective memory in expert problem solving. *American Journal of Psychology*, 106, 155–189.

Haxby, J. (2013). Distributed representation in the human visual system. *Journal of Cognitive Neuroscience*, XX, 19–20.

Haxby, J. V., Gobbini, M. I., Furey, M. L., Ishai, A., Schouten, J. L., & Pietrini, P. (2001). Distributed and overlapping representations of faces and objects in ventral temporal cortex. *Science*, 293, 2425–2430.

Haxby, J. V., Gobbini, M. I., & Montgomery, K. (2004). Spatial and temporal distribution of face and object representations in the human brain. In M. S. Gazzaniga (Ed.), *The cognitive neurosciences* (3rd ed., pp. 889–904). MIT Press.

Haxby, J. V., Connolly, A. C., & Guntupalli, J. S. (2014). Decoding neural representational spaces using multivariate pattern analysis. *Annual Review of Neuroscience*, 37, 435–456. https://doi.org/10.1146/annurev-neuro-062012-170325

Hay, J. F., & Saffran, J. R. (2012). Rhythmic grouping biases constrain infant statistical learning. *Infancy*, 17, 610–641. https://doi.org/10.1111/j.1532-7078.2011.00110.x

Hayes, J. R., & Simon, H. A. (1974). Understanding written problem instructions. In L. W. Gregg (Ed.), *Knowledge and cognition* (pp. 167–200). Erlbaum.

Hayman, C. A., Macdonald, C. A., & Tulving, E. (1993). The role of repetition and associative interference in new semantic learning in amnesia: A case experiment. *Journal of Cognitive Neuroscience*, 5, 375–389.

Haynes, J.-D., & Rees, G. (2006). Decoding mental states from brain activity in humans. *Nature Reviews: Neuroscience*, 7, 523–534. https://doi.org/10.1038/nrn1931

Heald, S., & Nusbaum, H. C. (2014). Speech perception as an active cognitive process. *Frontiers in Systems Neuroscience*, 8. https://doi.org/10.3389/fnsys.2014.00035

Heath, W. P., & Erickson, J. R. (1998). Memory for central and peripheral actions and props after varied post-event presentation. *Legal and Criminal Psychology*, 3, 321–346.

Hebb, D. O. (1949). *The organization of behavior.* John Wiley.

Hécaen, H., & Angelergues, R. (1962). Agnosia for faces. *Archives of Neurology*, 7, 92–100.

Heider, E. R. (1972). Universals in color naming and memory. *Journal of Experimental Psychology*, 93, 10–20.

Heit, E. (2000). Properties of inductive reasoning. *Psychonomic Bulletin and Review*, 7, 569–592.

Helie, S., & Pizlo, Z. (2022). When is psychology research useful in artificial intelligence? A case for reducing computational complexity in problem solving. *Topics in Cognitive Science*, 14, 687–701.

Henkel, L. A. (2014). Point-and-shoot memories: The influence of taking photos on memory for a museum tour. *Psychological Science*, 25, 396–402.

Henrich, J. (2020). *The WEIRDest people in the world: How the West became psychologically peculiar and particularly prosperous.* Farrar, Straus, and Giroux.

Henrich, J., Heine, S. J., & Norenzayan, A. (2010). The weirdest people in the world? *Behavioral and Brain Sciences*, 33, 61–83; discussion, 83–135. https://doi.org/10.1017/S0140525X0999152X

Hertwig, R., Pachur, T., & Kurzenhäuser, S. (2005). Judgments of risk frequencies: Tests of possible cognitive mechanisms. *Journal of Experimental Psychology: Learning, Memory, and Cognition*, 31, 621–642.

Hess, D. J., Foss, D. J., & Carroll, P. (1995). Effects of global and local context on lexical processing during language comprehension. *Journal of Experimental Psychology: General*, 124, 62–82.

Hess, E. H. (1958). "Imprinting" in animals. *Scientific American*, 198, 81–90.

Hickok, G. (2014). Toward an integrated psycholinguistic, neurolinguistic, sensorimotor framework for speech production. *Language and Cognitive Processes*, 29, 52–59. https://doi.org/10.1080/01690965.2013.852907

Higgins, C., Liu, Y., Vidaurre, D., et al. (2021). Replay bursts in humans coincide with activation of the default mode and parietal alpha networks. *Neuron*, 109, 882–893.

Higham, P. A. (1998). Believing details known to have been suggested. *British Journal of Psychology*, 89, 265–283.

Himmelbach, M., & Karnath, H. O. (2005). Dorsal and ventral stream interaction: Contributions from optic ataxia. *Journal of Cognitive Neuroscience*, 17, 632–640.

Hirst, W., & Phelps, E. A. (2016). Flashbulb memories. *Current Directions in Psychological Science*, 25, 36–41. https://doi.org/10.1177/0963721415622487

Hirst, W., Phelps, E. A., Buckner, R. L., et al. (2009). Long-term memory for the terrorist attack of September 11: Flashbulb memories, event memories, and the factors that influence their retention. *Journal of Experimental Psychology: General*, 138, 161–176. https://doi.org/10.1037/a0015527

Hirst, W., Phelps, E. A., Meksin, R., et al. (2015). A ten-year follow-up of a study of memory for the attack of September 11, 2001: Flashbulb memories and memories for flashbulb events. *Journal of Experimental Psychology: General*, 144, 604–623. https://doi.org/10.1037/xge0000055

Hochstein, S. (2020). The gist of Anne Treisman's revolution. *Attention, Perception, and Psychophysics*, 82, 24–30.

Hoffrage, U., Lindsey, S., Hertwig, R., & Gigerenzer, G. (2000). Communicating statistical information. *Science*, 290, 2261–2262.

Hoffrage, U., Kurzenhauser, S., & Gigerenzer, G. (2005). Understanding the results of medical tests: Why the representation of statistical information matters. In R. Bibace & J. D. Laird (Eds.), *Science and medicine in dialogue* (pp. 83–98). Praeger.

Holyoak, K. J., & Koh, K. (1987). Surface and structural similarity in analogical transfer. *Memory and Cognition*, 15, 332–340.

Holyoak, K. J., & Powell, D. (2016). Deontological coherence: A framework for commonsense moral reasoning. *Psychological Bulletin*, 142, 1179–1203.

Holyoak, K. J., & Thagard, P. R. (1989). A computational model of analogical problem solving. In S. O. A. Vosniadou (Ed.), *Similarity and analogical reasoning* (pp. 242–266). Cambridge University Press.

Hommel, B., Chapman, C. S., Cisek, P., Neyedli, H. F., Song, J. H., & Welsh, T. N. (2019). No one knows what attention is. *Attention, Perception, and Psychophysics*, 81, 2288–2303.

Honey, R. C., & Dwyer, D. M. (2022). Higher-order conditioning: A critical review and computational model. *Psychological Review*, 129, 1338–1357. https://doi.org/10.1037/rev0000368

Honoré-Chedozeau, C., Desmas, M., Ballester, J., Parr, W. V., & Chollet, S. (2019). Representation of wine and beer: Influence of expertise. *Current Opinion in Food Science*, 27, 104–114.

Hopf, J.-M., Boelmans, K., Schoenfeld, M. A., Luck, S. J., & Heinze, H.-J. (2004). Attention to features precedes attention to locations in visual search: Evidence from electromagnetic brain responses in humans. *Journal of Neuroscience*, 24, 1822–1832. https://doi.org/10.1523/JNEUROSCI.3564-03.2004

Huettig, F., Audring, J., & Jackendoff, R. (2022). A parallel architecture perspective on pre-activation and prediction in language processing. *Cognition*, 224, Article 105050.

Hunt, E., & Agnoli, F. (1991). The Whorfian hypothesis: A cognitive psychology perspective. *Psychological Review*, 98, 377–389.

Huster, R. J., Debener, S., Eichele, T., & Herrmann, C. S. (2012). Methods for simultaneous EEG-fMRI: An introductory review. *Journal of Neuroscience*, 32, 6053–6060. https://doi.org/10.1523/JNEUROSCI.0447-12.2012

Hyde, T. S., & Jenkins, J. J. (1973). Recall for words as a function of semantic, graphic, and syntactic orienting tasks. *Journal of Verbal Learning and Verbal Behavior*, 12, 471–480.

Ibbotson, P., & Tomasello, M. (2016, September 7). Evidence rebuts Chomsky's theory of language learning. Scientific American. https://www.scientificamerican.com/article/evidence-rebuts-chomsky-s-theory-of-language-learning/

Inoue, S., & Matsuzawa, T. (2007). Working memory of numerals in chimpanzees. *Current Biology*, 17, R1004–R1005. https://doi.org/10.1016/j.cub.2007.10.027

Itard, J.-M. G. (1962). *The Wild Boy of Aveyron*. Appleton-Century-Crofts.

Jackson, J. E., & Green, L. (2005). Tense and aspectual be in child African American English. In H. J. Verkuyl, H. de Swart, & A. van Hout (Eds.), *Perspectives on aspect* (Studies in Theoretical Psycholinguistics No. 32, pp. 233–250). Springer. https://doi.org/10.1007/1-4020-3232-3_13

Jadhav, S. P., Kemere, C., German, P. W., & Frank, L. M. (2012). Awake hippocampal sharp-wave ripples support spatial memory. *Science*, 336, 1454–1458. https://doi.org/10.1126/science.1217230

Jaeger, A. J., Taylor, A. R., & Wiley, J. (2016). When, and for whom, analogies help: The role of spatial skills and interleaved presentation. *Journal of Educational Psychology*, 108, 1121–1139. https://doi.org/10.1037/edu0000121

Jaeger, A. J., Wiley, J., & Moher, T. (2016). Leveling the playing field: Grounding learning with embedded simulations in geoscience. *Cognitive Research*, 1, 23. https://doi.org/10.1186/s41235-016-0026-3

James, W. (1890). *Principles of psychology*. Henry Holt.

Jamet, E., Gonthier, C., Cojean, S., Colliot, T., & Erhel, S. (2020). Does multitasking in the classroom affect learning outcomes? A naturalistic study. *Computers in Human Behavior*, 106, Article 106264.

Janiszewski, C., & Meyvis, T. (2001). Effects of brand logo complexity, repetition, and spacing on processing fluency and judgment. *Journal of Consumer Research*, 28, 18–32.

Jannati, A., Spalek, T. M., & Di Lollo, V. (2013). A novel paradigm reveals the role of reentrant visual processes in object substitution masking. *Attention, Perception, and Psychophysics*, 75, 1118–1127. https://doi.org/10.3758/s13414-013-0462-9

Jans, B., Peters, J. C., & De Weerd, P. (2010). Visual spatial attention to multiple locations at once: The jury is still out. *Psychological Review*, 117, 637–684. https://doi.org/10.1037/a0019082

Jaroslawska, A. J., Gathercole, S. E., Logie, M. R., & Holmes, J. (2016). Following instructions in a virtual school: Does working memory play a role? *Memory and Cognition*, 44, 580–589. https://doi.org/10.3758/s13421-015-0579-2

Jefferies, E., & Wang, X. (2021). Semantic cognition: Semantic memory and semantic control. In M. Hogg (Ed.), *Oxford research encyclopedia of psychology*. Oxford University Press.

Jevons, W. S. (1871). The power of numerical discrimination. *Nature*, 3, 281–282.

Jobard, G., Crivello, F., & Tzourio-Mazoyer, N. (2003). Evaluation of the dual route theory of reading: A meta-analysis of 35 neuroimaging studies. *NeuroImage*, 20, 693–712.

Johnson, D. (2011). Interpretations of the Pleiades in Australian Aboriginal astronomies. *Proceedings of the International Astronomical Union*, 7 (Suppl. 278), 291–297.

Johnson, J. S., & Newport, E. L. (1989). Critical period effects in second language learning: The influence of maturational state on the acquisition of English as a second language. *Cognitive Psychology*, 21, 60–99.

Johnson, M. K., & Hasher, L. (1987). Human learning and memory. *Annual Review of Psychology*, 38, 631–668.

Johnson, M. K., & Raye, C. L. (1981). Reality monitoring. *Psychological Review*, 88, 67–85.

Johnson, M. K., Hashtroudi, S., & Lindsay, D. S. (1993). Source monitoring. *Psychological Bulletin*, 114, 3–28.

Johnson-Laird, P. N. (1999). Deductive reasoning. *Annual Review of Psychology*, 50, 109–135.

Johnson-Laird, P. N. (2005). Mental models and thought. In K. J. Holyoak & R. G. Morrison (Eds.), *Cambridge handbook of thinking and reasoning* (pp. 185–208). Cambridge University Press.

Johnson-Laird, P. N. (2021). Mental models, reasoning, and rationality. In M. Knauff & W. Spohn (Eds.), *The handbook of rationality* (pp. 147–158). MIT Press.

Johnson-Laird, P. N., & Bara, B. G. (1984). Syllogistic inference. *Cognition*, 16, 1–61.

Johnson-Laird, P. N., Byrne, R. M., & Schaeken, W. (1992). Propositional reasoning by model. *Psychological Review*, 99, 418–439.

Johnson-Laird, P. N., Khemlani, S. S., & Goodwin, G. P. (2015). Logic, probability, and human reasoning. *Trends in Cognitive Sciences*, 19, 201–214. https://doi.org/10.1016/j.tics.2015.02.006

Jolicoeur, P. (1990). Identification of disoriented objects: A dual systems theory. *Mind and Language*, 5, 387–410.

Jonides, J., Lacey, S. C., & Nee, D. E. (2005). Processes of working memory in mind and brain. *Current Directions in Psychological Science*, 14, 2–5.

Jung, K., Ruthruff, E., Tybur, J. M., Gaspelin, N., & Miller, G. (2012). Perception of facial attractiveness requires some attentional resources: Implications for the "automaticity" of psychological adaptations. *Evolution and Human Behavior*, 33, 241–250. https://doi.org/10.1016/j.evolhumbehav.2011.10.001

Jung, K., Ruthruff, E., & Gaspelin, N. (2013). Automatic identification of familiar faces. *Attention, Perception, and Psychophysics*, 7, 1438–1450.

Jusczyk, P. W. (1997). *The discovery of spoken language*. MIT Press.

Just, M. A., & Carpenter, P. A. (1980). A theory of reading: From eye fixations to comprehension. *Psychological Review*, 87, 329–354.

Kaas, A. L., van Mier, H., Visser, M., & Goebel, R. (2013). The neural substrate for working memory of tactile surface texture. *Human Brain Mapping*, 34, 1148–1162. https://doi.org/10.1002/hbm .21500

Kaernbach, C. (2004). Auditory sensory memory and short-term memory. In C. Kaernbach, E. Schröger, & H. Müller (Eds.), *Psychophysics beyond sensation: Laws and invariants of human cognition* (pp. 331–348). Erlbaum.

Kahneman, D. (1973). *Attention and effort*. Prentice Hall.

Kahneman, D. (2013). *Thinking, fast and slow* (1st ed.). Farrar, Straus, and Giroux.

Kahneman, D., & Tversky, A. (1972). Subjective probability: A judgment of representativeness. *Cognitive Psychology*, 3, 430–454.

Kane, M. J., Hambrick, D. Z., Tuholski, S.W., et al. (2004). The generality of working memory capacity: A latent-variable approach to verbal and visuospatial memory span and reasoning. *Journal of Experimental Psychology: General*, 133, 189–217.

Kanwisher, N. (2010). Functional specificity in the human brain: A window into the functional architecture of the mind. *Proceedings of the National Academy of Sciences of the USA*, 107, 11163–11170. https://doi.org/10.1073/pnas .1005062107

Kanwisher, N., & Dilks, D. (2013). The functional organization of the ventral visual pathway in humans. In L. Chalupa & J. Werner (Eds.), *The new visual neurosciences* (pp. 733–748). MIT Press.

Kanwisher, N., McDermott, J., & Chun, M. M. (1997). The fusiform face area: A module in human extrastriate cortex specialized for face perception. *Journal of Neuroscience*, 17, 4302–4311.

Kayser, C., Körding, K. P., & König, P. (2004). Processing of complex stimuli and natural scenes in the visual cortex. *Current Opinion in Neurobiology*, 14, 468–473.

Kazanas, S. A., & Altarriba, J. (2015). The survival advantage: Underlying mechanisms and extant limitations. *Evolutionary Psychology*, 13, 360–396.

Keane, M. (1987). On retrieving analogues when solving problems. *Quarterly Journal of Experimental Psychology: Human Experimental Psychology*, 39, 29–41.

Kellen, D., & Klauer, K. C. (2020). Theories of the Wason selection task: A critical assessment of boundaries and benchmarks. *Computational Brain and Behavior*, 3, 341–353.

Kemmerer, D. (2022). Grounded cognition entails linguistic relativity: A neglected implication of a major semantic theory. *Topics in Cognitive Science*, 15, 615–647.

Kemp, C., Hamacher, D. W., Little, D. R., & Cropper, S. J. (2022). Perceptual grouping explains similarities in constellations across cultures. *Psychological Science*, 33, 354–363.

Keppel, G., & Underwood, B. J. (1962). Proactive inhibition in short-term retention of single items. *Journal of Verbal Learning and Verbal Behavior*, 1, 153–161.

Kerzel, D., & Bekkering, H. (2000). Motor activation from visible speech: Evidence from stimulus response compatibility. *Journal of Experimental Psychology: Human Perception and Performance*, 26, 634–647.

Khanna, M. M., & Cortese, M. J. (2021). How well imageability, concreteness, perceptual strength, and action strength predict recognition memory, lexical decision, and reading aloud performance. *Memory*, 29, 622–636.

Khemlani, S., & Johnson-Laird, P. N. (2012). Theories of the syllogism: A meta-analysis. *Psychological Bulletin*, 138, 427–457. https://doi .org/10.1037/a0026841

Khemlani, S. S., Byrne, R. M., & Johnson-Laird, P. N. (2018). Facts and possibilities: A model-based theory of sentential reasoning. *Cognitive Science*, 42, 1887–1924.

Kintsch, W., Welsch, D., Schmalhofer, F., & Zimny, S. (1990). Sentence memory: A theoretical analysis. *Journal of Memory and Language*, 29, 133–159. https://doi.org/10.1016/0749-596X(90) 90069-C

Kinukawa, T., Takeuchi, N., Sugiyama, S., Nishihara, M., Nishiwaki, K., & Inui, K. (2019). Properties of echoic memory revealed by auditory-evoked magnetic fields. *Scientific Reports*, 9, 1–8.

Kirby, K. N. (1994). Probabilities and utilities of fictional outcomes in Wason's four-card selection task. *Cognition*, 51, 1–28.

Klauer, K. C., & Zhao, Z. (2004). Double dissociations in visual and spatial short-term memory. *Journal of Experimental Psychology: General*, 133, 355–381.

Klein, I., Dubois, J., Mangin, J.-F., Kherif, F., Flandin, G., Poline, J.-B., Denis, M., Kosslyn, S. M., & Le Bihan, D. (2004). Retinotopic organization of visual mental images as revealed by functional magnetic imaging. *Cognitive Brain Research*, 22, 26–31.

Klein, R. A., Ratliff, K. A., Vianello, M., et al. (2014). Investigating variation in replicability. *Social Psychology*, 45, 142–152. https://doi.org/10.1027/1864-9335/a000178

Knight, D. C., Nguyen, H. T., & Bandettini, P. A. (2005). The role of the human amygdala in the production of conditioned fear responses. *NeuroImage*, 26, 1193–1200.

knock knock [@autocompletejok]. (2015, December 7). *Knock knock! Who's there? Consequences. Consequences who? Consequences of global warming!* X. https://twitter.com/autocompletejok/status/673959430845804544

Knowles, M. E., & Delaney, P. F. (2005). Lasting reductions in illegal moves following an increase in their cost: Evidence from river-crossing problems. *Journal of Experimental Psychology: Learning, Memory, and Cognition*, 31, 670–682.

Kocab, A., Davidson, K., & Snedeker, J. (2022). The emergence of natural language quantification. *Cognitive Science*, 46, Article e13097.

Kocab, A., Senghas, A., Coppola, M., & Snedeker, J. (2023). Potentially recursive structures emerge quickly when a new language community forms. *Cognition*, 232, Article 105261.

Kohler, S., Kapur, S., Moscovitch, M., Winocur, G., & Houle, S. (1995). Dissociation of pathways for object and spatial vision: A PET study in humans. *Neuroreport*, 6, 1865–1868.

Kohler, W. (1929). *Gestalt psychology*. Liveright.

Kok, P., Mostert, P., & De Lange, F. P. (2017). Prior expectations induce prestimulus sensory templates. *Proceedings of the National Academy of Sciences of the USA*, 114, 10473–10478.

Kosslyn, S. M. (1975). Information representation in visual images. *Cognitive Psychology*, 7, 341–370.

Kosslyn, S. M. (1976). Using imagery to retrieve semantic information: A developmental study. *Child Development*, 47, 434–444.

Kosslyn, S. M. (1980). *Image and mind*. Harvard University Press.

Kotovsky, K., & Simon, H. A. (1990). What makes some problems really hard: Explorations in the problem space of difficulty. *Cognitive Psychology*, 22, 143–183.

Kotovsky, K., Hayes, J. R., & Simon, H. A. (1985). Why are some problems hard? Evidence from Tower of Hanoi. *Cognitive Psychology*, 17, 248–294.

Kounios, J., & Beeman, M. (2015). *The eureka factor: Aha moments, creative insight, and the brain*. Random House.

Kourtzi, Z., Erb, M., Grodd, W., & Bulthoff, H. H. (2003). Representation of the perceived 3-D object shape in the human lateral occipital complex. *Cerebral Cortex*, 13, 911–920.

Kragel, J. E., Ezzyat, Y., Sperling, M. R., et al. (2017). Similar patterns of neural activity predict memory function during encoding and retrieval. *Neuroimage*, 155, 60–71.

Kragel, J. E., Ezzyat, Y., Lega, B. C., et al. (2021). Distinct cortical systems reinstate the content and context of episodic memories. *Nature Communications*, 12, Article 4444. https://doi.org/10.1038/s41467-021-24393-1

Kravitz, D. J., Saleem, K. S., Baker, C. I., Ungerleider, L. G., & Mishkin, M. (2013). The ventral visual pathway: An expanded neural framework for the processing of object quality. *Trends in Cognitive Sciences*, 17, 26–49. https://doi.org/10.1016/j.tics.2012.10.011

Krechevsky, I. (1932). "Hypotheses" in rats. *Psychological Review*, 39, 516–532. https://doi.org/http://psycnet.apa.org/doi/10.1037/h0073500

Kreiner, H., & Degani, T. (2015). Tip-of-the-tongue in a second language: The effects of brief first-language exposure and long-term use. *Cognition*, 137, 106–114. https://doi.org/10.1016/j.cognition.2014.12.011

Kroneisen, M., & Erdfelder, E. (2011). On the plasticity of the survival processing effect. *Journal of Experimental Psychology: Learning, Memory, and Cognition*, 37, 1553–1562. https://doi.org/10.1037/a0024493

Krynski, T. R., & Tenenbaum, J. B. (2007). The role of causality in judgment under uncertainty. *Journal of Experimental Psychology: General*, 136, 430–450. https://doi.org/10.1037/0096-3445.136.3.430

Kuhl, P. K. (1991). Human adults and human infants show a "perceptual magnet effect" for the prototypes of speech categories, monkeys do not. *Perception and Psychophysics*, 50, 93–107.

Kurihara, K., & Tsukada, K. (2012). *SpeechJammer: A system utilizing artificial speech disturbance with delayed auditory feedback*. ArXiv. http://arxiv.org/abs/1202.6106

Kvavilashvili, L., Mirani, J., Schlagman, S., Foley, K., & Kornbrot, D. E. (2009). Consistency of flashbulb memories of September 11 over long delays: Implications for consolidation and wrong time slice hypotheses. *Journal of Memory and Language*, 61, 556–572. https://doi.org/10.1016/j.jml.2009.07.004

Kyllonen, P. C., & Christal, R. E. (1990). Reasoning ability is (little more than) working-memory capacity? *Intelligence*, 14, 389–433.

Lachner, A., & Nückles, M. (2013). Experts' explanations engage novices in deep-processing. *Proceedings of the Annual Meeting of the Cognitive Science Society*, 35, 2802–2807. https://escholarship.org/uc/item/03n9s694

Lachner, A., & Nückles, M. (2015). Bothered by abstractness or engaged by cohesion? Experts' explanations enhance novices' deep-learning. *Journal of Experimental Psychology: Applied*, 21, 101–115. https://doi.org/10.1037/xap0000038

Lachter, J., Forster, K. I., & Ruthruff, E. (2004). Forty-five years after Broadbent (1958): Still no identification without attention. *Psychological Review*, 111, 880–913.

Lacy, J. W., & Stark, C. E. L. (2013). The neuroscience of memory: Implications for the courtroom. *Nature Reviews: Neuroscience*, 14, 649–658. https://doi.org/10.1038/nrn3563

Lafer-Sousa, R., Hermann, K. L., & Conway, B. R. (2015). Striking individual differences in color perception uncovered by "the dress" photograph. *Current Biology*, 25, R545–R546. https://doi.org/10.1016/j.cub.2015.04.053

Lane, D. M., & Chang, Y.-H. A. (2017). Chess knowledge predicts chess memory even after controlling for chess experience: Evidence for the role of high-level processes. *Memory and Cognition*, 46, 337–348. https://doi.org/10.3758/s13421-017-0768-2

Larkin, J., McDermott, J., Simon, D. P., & Simon, H. A. (1980). Expert and novice performance in solving physics problems. *Science*, 208, 1335–1342.

Lavie, N. (2005). Distracted and confused? Selective attention under load. *Trends in Cognitive Sciences*, 9, 75–82.

Laxton, V., Crundall, D., Guest, D., & Howard, C. J. (2021). Visual search for drowning swimmers: Investigating the impact of lifeguarding experience. *Applied Cognitive Psychology*, 35, 215–231.

Leaman, T. M., & Hamacher, D. W. (2019). Baiami and the emu chase: An astronomical interpretation of a Wiradjuri Dreaming associated with the Burbung. *Journal of Astronomical History and Heritage*, 22, 225–237.

LeDoux, J. E. (2000). Emotion circuits in the brain. *Annual Review of Neuroscience*, 23, 155–184.

Lee, D., & Chun, M. M. (2001). What are the units of visual short-term memory, objects or spatial locations? *Perception and Psychophysics*, 63, 253–257.

Lee-Sammons, W. H., & Whitney, P. (1991). Reading perspectives and memory for text: An individual differences analysis. *Journal of Experimental Psychology: Learning, Memory, and Cognition*, 17, 1074–1081.

LeFevre, J.-A., & Dixon, P. (1986). Do written instructions need examples? *Cognition and Instruction*, 3, 1–30.

Lenneberg, E. (1967). *Biological foundations of language*. John Wiley.

Leon, C. S., Bonilla, M., Benítez, F. A. U., Brusco, L. I., Wang, J., & Forcato, C. (2022). Impairment of aversive episodic memories during COVID-19 pandemic: The impact of emotional context on memory processes. *Neurobiology of Learning and Memory*, 187, Article 107575.

Leopold, R. L., & Dillon, H. (1963). Psycho-anatomy of a disaster: A long term study of post-traumatic neuroses in survivors of a marine explosion. *American Journal of Psychiatry*, 119, 913–921.

Lewandowsky, S., Duncan, M., & Brown, G. D. A. (2004). Time does not cause forgetting in short-term serial recall. *Psychonomic Bulletin and Review*, 11, 771–790.

Li, D., Cowan, N., & Saults, J. S. (2013). Estimating working memory capacity for lists of nonverbal sounds. *Attention, Perception, and Psychophysics*, 75, 145–160. https://doi.org/10.3758/s13414-012-0383-z

Liberman, A. M., Harris, K. S., Hoffman, H. S., & Griffith, B. (1957). The discrimination of speech sounds within and across phoneme boundaries. *Journal of Experimental Psychology*, 54, 358–368.

Lidz, J., Gleitman, H., & Gleitman, L. (2003). Understanding how input matters: Verb learning and the footprint of universal grammar. *Cognition*, 87, 151–178.

Lindsay, D. S., & Johnson, M. K. (1989). The eyewitness suggestibility effect and memory for source. *Memory and Cognition*, 17, 349–358.

Lisman, J. (2015). The challenge of understanding the brain: Where we stand in 2015. *Neuron*, 86, 864–882. https://doi.org/10.1016/j.neuron.2015.03.032

Little, J. L., & McDaniel, M. A. (2015). Individual differences in category learning: Memorization versus rule abstraction. *Memory and Cognition*, 43, 283–297. https://doi.org/10.3758/s13421-014-0475-1

Loewenstein, J., & Gentner, D. (2001). Spatial mapping in preschoolers: Close comparisons facilitate far mappings. *Journal of Cognition and Development*, 2, 189–219.

Loftus, E. E., & Loftus, G. R. (1980). On the permanence of stored information in the human brain. *American Psychologist*, 35, 409–420.

Loftus, E. F. (1979). *Eyewitness testimony*. Harvard University Press.

Loftus, E. F. (1993). The reality of repressed memories. *American Psychologist*, 48, 518–537. https://doi.org/10.1037/0003-066X.48.5.518

Loftus, E. F., & Palmer, J. C. (1974). Reconstruction of automobile destruction: An example of the interaction between language and memory. *Journal of Verbal Learning and Verbal Behavior*, 13, 585–589.

Loftus, E. F., Miller, D. G., & Burns, H. J. (1978). Semantic integration of verbal information into a visual memory. *Journal of Experimental Psychology: Human Learning and Memory*, 4, 19–31.

Logan, G. D. (1988). Toward an instance theory of automatization. *Psychological Review*, 95, 492–527.

Logan, G. D. (2002). An instance theory of attention and memory. *Psychological Review*, 109, 376–400.

Logie, R. H., & Marchetti, C. (1991). Visuo-spatial working memory: Visual, spatial or central executive? In C. Cornoldi & M. A. McDaniels (Eds.), *Mental images in human cognition* (pp. 72–102). Springer.

Logothetis, N. K., Pauls, J., & Poggio, T. (1995). Shape representation in the inferior temporal cortex of monkeys. *Current Biology*, 5, 552–563.

Lomber, S. G., & Malhotra, S. (2008). Double dissociation of "what" and "where" processing in auditory cortex. *Nature Neuroscience*, 11, 609–616. https://doi.org/10.1038/nn.2108

López, A., Atran, S., Coley, J. D., Medin, D. L., & Smith, E. E. (1997). The tree of life: Universal and cultural features of folkbiological taxonomies and inductions. *Cognitive Psychology*, 32, 251–295.

Luchins, A. S. (1942). Mechanization in problem solving: The effect of *Einstellung*. *Psychological Monographs*, 54, 95 pp.

Luck, S. J., & Vogel, E. K. (1997). The capacity of visual working memory for features and conjunctions. *Nature*, 390, 279–281.

Luminet, O., & Curci, A. (2009). The 9/11 attacks inside and outside the US: Testing four models of flashbulb memory formation across groups and the specific effects of social identity. *Memory*, 17, 742–759. https://doi.org/10.1080/09658210903081827

Lurie, R., & Westerman, D. L. (2021). Photo-taking impairs memory on perceptual and conceptual memory tests. *Journal of Applied Research in Memory and Cognition*, 10, 289–297.

Lyn, H., & Savage-Rumbaugh, E. S. (2000). Observational word learning in two bonobos (*Pan paniscus*): Ostensive and non-ostensive contexts. *Language and Communication*, 20, 255–273.

Lyn, H., Greenfield, P. M., Savage-Rumbaugh, S., Gillespie-Lynch, K., & Hopkins, W. D. (2011). Nonhuman primates do declare! A comparison of declarative symbol and gesture use in two children, two bonobos, and a chimpanzee. *Language and Communication*, 31, 63–74. https://doi.org/10.1016/j.langcom.2010.11.001

Lytle, R. A., & Lundy, R. M. (1988). Hypnosis and the recall of visually presented material: A failure to replicate Stager and Lundy. *International Journal of Clinical and Experimental Hypnosis*, 36, 327–335.

Ma, W. J., Husain, M., & Bays, P. M. (2014). Changing concepts of working memory. *Nature Neuroscience*, 17, 347–356. https://doi.org/10.1038/nn.3655

MacDonald, J., & McGurk, H. (1978). Visual influences on speech perception processes. *Perception and Psychophysics*, 24, 253–257.

MacDonald, J., Andersen, S., & Bachmann, T. (2000). Hearing by eye: How much spatial degradation can be tolerated? *Perception*, 29, 1155–1168.

MacEvoy, S. P., & Epstein, R. A. (2011). Constructing scenes from objects in human occipitotemporal cortex. *Nature Neuroscience*, 14, 1323–1329. https://doi.org/10.1038/nn.2903

Mack, A. (2003). Inattentional blindness: Looking without seeing. *Current Directions in Psychological Science*, 12, 180–184.

Madan, C. R., Scott, S. M., & Kensinger, E. A. (2019). Positive emotion enhances association-memory. *Emotion*, 19, 733–740.

Maguire, J. (2006). *American bee: The National Spelling Bee and the culture of word nerds*. Rodale.

Mahon, B. Z., & Hickok, G. (2016). Arguments about the nature of concepts: Symbols, embodiment, and beyond. *Psychonomic Bulletin and Review*, 23, 941–958. https://doi.org/10.3758/s13423-016-1045-2

Majid, A. (2021). Human olfaction at the intersection of language, culture, and biology. *Trends in Cognitive Sciences*, 25, 111–123.

Majid, A., & Burenhult, N. (2014). Odors are expressible in language, as long as you speak the right language. *Cognition*, 130, 266–270. https://doi.org/10.1016/j.cognition.2013.11.004

Malmberg, K. J., Raaijmakers, J. G., & Shiffrin, R. M. (2019). 50 years of research sparked by Atkinson and Shiffrin (1968). *Memory and Cognition*, 47, 561–574.

Manktelow, K. I., & Evans, J. S. (1979). Facilitation of reasoning by realism: Effect or non-effect? *British Journal of Psychology*, 70, 477–488.

Margulieux, L. E., & Catrambone, R. (2016). Improving problem solving with subgoal labels in expository text and worked examples. *Learning and Instruction*, 42, 58–71.

Mark, L. S. (1987). Eyeheight-scaled information about affordances: A study of sitting and stair climbing. *Journal of Experimental Psychology: Human Perception and Performance*, 13, 361–370.

Markman, A. B., & Stilwell, C. H. (2001). Role-governed categories. *Journal of Experimental and Theoretical Artificial Intelligence*, 13, 329–358. https://doi.org/10.1080/09528130110100252

Marmie, W. R., & Healy, A. F. (2004). Memory for common objects: Brief intentional study is sufficient to overcome poor recall of US coin features. *Applied Cognitive Psychology*, 18, 445–453.

Marotta, J. J., & Goodale, M. A. (2001). The role of familiar size in the control of grasping. *Journal of Cognitive Neuroscience*, 13, 8–17.

Marshall, J. C., & Newcombe, F. (1973). Patterns of paralexia: A psycholinguistic approach. *Journal of Psycholinguistic Research*, 2, 175–199.

Marslen-Wilson, W. D. (1987). Functional parallelism in spoken word-recognition. *Cognition*, 25, 71–102.

Marslen-Wilson, W. D., & Welsh, A. (1978). Processing interactions and lexical access during word recognition in continuous speech. *Cognitive Psychology*, 10, 29–63.

Martin, A., & Chao, L. L. (2001). Semantic memory and the brain: Structure and processes. *Current Opinion in Neurobiology*, 11, 194–201.

Massaro, D. W. (1970). Preperceptual auditory images. *Journal of Experimental Psychology*, 85, 411–417.

Matias, J., Belletier, C., Izaute, M., Lutz, M., & Silvert, L. (2022). The role of perceptual and cognitive load on inattentional blindness: A systematic review and three meta-analyses. *Quarterly Journal of Experimental Psychology*, 75, 1844–1875.

Maunsell, J. H. R., & Treue, S. (2006). Feature-based attention in visual cortex. *Trends in Neurosciences*, 29, 317–322. https://doi.org/10.1016/j.tins.2006.04.001

Mayes, A. R., & Montaldi, D. (2001). Exploring the neural bases of episodic and semantic memory: The role of structural and functional neuroimaging. *Neuroscience and Biobehavioral Reviews*, 25, 555–573.

Mazzoni, G., Laurence, J. R., & Heap, M. (2014). Hypnosis and memory: Two hundred years of adventures and still going! *Psychology of Consciousness: Theory, Research, and Practice*, 1, 153–167.

McBeath, M. K., Shaffer, D. M., & Kaiser, M. K. (1995). How baseball outfielders determine where to run to catch fly balls. *Science*, 268, 569–573.

McCarthy, R. A., & Warrington, E. K. (1986). Phonological reading: Phenomena and paradoxes. *Cortex*, 22, 359–380.

McClelland, J. L. (1981). *Retrieving general and specific knowledge from stored knowledge of specifics* [Conference presentation]. Third annual conference of the Cognitive Science Society, Berkeley, CA, United States.

McClelland, J. L., & Elman, J. L. (1986). The TRACE model of speech perception. *Cognitive Psychology*, 18, 1–86.

McCloskey, M., Wible, C. G., & Cohen, N. J. (1988). Is there a special flashbulb-memory mechanism? *Journal of Experimental Psychology: General*, 117, 171–181.

McCormick, C. R., Redden, R. S., Lawrence, M. A., & Klein, R. M. (2018). The independence of endogenous and exogenous temporal attention. *Attention, Perception, and Psychophysics*, 80, 1885–1891.

McDermott, A. F., Bavelier, D., & Green, C. S. (2014). Memory abilities in action video game players. *Computers in Human Behavior*, 34, 69–78. https://doi.org/10.1016/j.chb.2014.01.018

McDermott, K. B. (1996). The persistence of false memories in list recall. *Journal of Memory and Language*, 35, 212–230.

McGaugh, J. L. (2018). Emotional arousal regulation of memory consolidation. *Current Opinion in Behavioral Sciences*, 19, 55–60.

McGeoch, J. A. (1932). Forgetting and the law of disuse. *Psychological Review*, 39, 352–370.

McGugin, R. W., Gatenby, J. C., Gore, J. C., & Gauthier, I. (2012). High-resolution imaging of expertise reveals reliable object selectivity in the fusiform face area related to perceptual performance. *Proceedings of the National Academy of Sciences of the USA*, 109, 17063–17068. https://doi.org/10.1073/pnas.1116333109

McGurk, H., & MacDonald, J. (1976). Hearing lips and seeing voices. *Nature*, 264, 746–748.

McKeeff, T. J., McGugin, R. W., Tong, F., & Gauthier, I. (2010). Expertise increases the functional overlap between face and object perception. *Cognition*, 117, 355–360. https://doi.org/10.1016/j.cognition.2010.09.002

McKoon, G., & Ratcliff, R. (1998). Memory-based language processing: Psycholinguistic research in the 1990s. *Annual Review of Psychology*, 49, 25–42.

McNally, R. J., & Geraerts, E. (2009). A new solution to the recovered memory debate. *Perspectives on Psychological Science*, 4, 126–134. https://doi.org/10.1111/j.1745-6924.2009.01112.x

Medin, D. L., & Atran, S. (2004). The native mind: Biological categorization and reasoning in development and across cultures. *Psychological Review*, 111, 960–983.

Medin, D. L., & Schaffer, M. M. (1978). Context theory of classification learning. *Psychological Review*, 85, 207–238.

Mednick, S. (1962). The associative basis of the creative process. *Psychological Review*, 69, 220–232. https://doi.org/10.1037/h0048850

Metcalfe, J. (1986a). Feeling of knowing in memory and problem solving. *Journal of Experimental Psychology: Learning, Memory, and Cognition*, 12, 288–294.

Metcalfe, J. (1986b). Premonitions of insight predict impending error. *Journal of Experimental Psychology: Learning, Memory, and Cognition*, 12, 623–634.

Metcalfe, J., & Wiebe, D. (1987). Intuition in insight and noninsight problem solving. *Memory and Cognition*, 15, 238–246.

Meyer, D. E., & Schvaneveldt, R. W. (1971). Facilitation in recognizing pairs of words: Evidence of a dependence between retrieval operations. *Journal of Experimental Psychology*, 90, 227–234.

Miller, G. A. (1956). The magical number seven, plus or minus two: Some limits on our capacity for processing information. *Psychological Review*, 63, 81–97.

Miller, G. A. (2003). The cognitive revolution: A historical perspective. *Trends in Cognitive Sciences*, 7, 141–144.

Milner, A. D., & Goodale, M. A. (1995). *The visual brain in action*. Oxford University Press.

Milner, B. (1966). Amnesia following operation on the temporal lobes. In C. W. M. Whitty & O. L. Zangwill (Eds.), *Amnesia* (pp. 109–133). Butterworth.

Mishler, B. D. (2021). *What, if anything, are species?* CRC Press/Taylor and Francis.

Mitha, K. (2020). Conceptualising and addressing mental disorders amongst Muslim communities: Approaches from the Islamic Golden Age. *Transcultural Psychiatry*, 57, 763–774. https://doi.org/10.1177/1363461520962603

Moray, N. (1959). Attention in dichotic listening: Affective cues and the influence of instructions. *Quarterly Journal of Experimental Psychology*, 11, 56–60.

Moray, N. (1967). Where is capacity limited? A survey and a model. *Acta Psychologica*, 27, 84–92.

Morris, C. D., Bransford, J. D., & Franks, J. J. (1977). Levels of processing versus transfer appropriate processing. *Journal of Verbal Learning and Verbal Behavior*, 16, 519–533.

Motter, B. C. (1993). Focal attention produces spatially selective processing in visual cortical areas V1, V2, and V4 in the presence of competing stimuli. *Journal of Neurophysiology*, 70, 909–919. https://doi.org/10.1152/jn.1993.70.3.909

Mueller, S. T., Seymour, T. L., Kieras, D. E., & Meyer, D. E. (2003). Theoretical implications of articulatory duration, phonological similarity, and phonological complexity in verbal working memory. *Journal of Experimental Psychology: Learning, Memory, and Cognition*, 29, 1353–1380.

Mukamel, R., & Fried, I. (2012). Human intracranial recordings and cognitive neuroscience. *Annual Review of Psychology*, 63, 511–537. https://doi.org/10.1146/annurev-psych-120709-145401

Müller, J. (1840). *Handbuch der Physiologie des Menschen für Vorlesungen* (2nd ed.). J. Hölscher.

Müller, J. (2015). Memory as an internal sense: Avicenna and the reception of his psychology by Thomas Aquinas. *Quaestio*, 15, 497–506.

Murdock, B. B. (1967). Recent developments in short-term memory. *British Journal of Psychology*, 58, 421–433.

Murphy, G., & Flynn, E. (2022). Deepfake false memories. *Memory*, 30, 480–492.

Murphy, E. S., & Lupfer, G. J. (2014). Basic principles of operant conditioning. In F. K. McSweeney & E. S. Murphy (Eds.), *The Wiley Blackwell handbook of operant and classical conditioning* (pp. 165–194). John Wiley. https://doi.org/10.1002/9781118468135.ch8

Murphy, G. L., & Ross, B. H. (2005). The two faces of typicality in category-based induction. *Cognition*, 95, 175–200.

Murphy, G. L., & Shapiro, A. M. (1994). Forgetting of verbatim information in discourse. *Memory and Cognition*, 22, 85–94.

Murre, J. M. (2021). The Godden and Baddeley (1975) experiment on context-dependent memory on land and underwater: A replication. *Royal Society Open Science*, 8, Article 200724.

Murty, N. A., & Arun, S. P. (2015). Dynamics of 3D view invariance in monkey inferotemporal cortex. *Journal of Neurophysiology*, 113, 2180–2194. https://doi.org/10.1152/jn.00810.2014

Muzzulini, B., van Mulukom, V., Kapitány, R., & Whitehouse, H. (2021). Shared flashbulb memories lead to identity fusion: Recalling the defeat in the Brexit referendum produces strong psychological bonds among remain supporters. *Journal of Applied Research in Memory and Cognition*, 11, 374–383.

Nairne, J. S. (2002). Remembering over the short-term: The case against the standard model. *Annual Review of Psychology*, 53, 53–81.

Nairne, J. S. (2022). Adaptive education: Learning and remembering with a stone-age brain. *Educational Psychology Review*, 34, 2275–2296.

Nairne, J. S., & Pandeirada, J. N. S. (2016). Adaptive memory: The evolutionary significance of survival processing. *Perspectives on Psychological Science*, 11, 496–511. https://doi.org/10.1177/1745691616635613

Nairne, J. S., Thompson, S. R., & Pandeirada, J. N. S. (2007). Adaptive memory: Survival processing enhances retention. *Journal of Experimental Psychology: Learning, Memory, and Cognition*, 33, 263–273. https://doi.org/10.1037/0278-7393.33.2.263

Nairne, J. S., Coverdale, M. E., & Pandeirada, J. N. (2019). Adaptive memory: The mnemonic power of survival-based generation. *Journal of Experimental Psychology: Learning, Memory, and Cognition*, 45, 1970–1982.

Nardone, R., Langthaler, P. B., Höller, Y., et al. (2019). Role of human prefrontal cortex in the modulation of conditioned eyeblink responses. *Behavioural Brain Research*, 374, Article 112027.

Naselaris, T., & Kay, K. N. (2015). Resolving ambiguities of MVPA using explicit models of representation. *Trends in Cognitive Sciences*, 19, 551–554. https://doi.org/10.1016/j.tics.2015.07.005

Naselaris, T., Olman, C. A., Stansbury, D. E., Ugurbil, K., & Gallant, J. L. (2015). A voxel-wise encoding model for early visual areas decodes mental images of remembered scenes. *NeuroImage*, 105, 215–228. https://doi.org/10.1016/j.neuroimage.2014.10.018

Naveh-Benjamin, M., Guez, J., Hara, Y., Brubaker, M. S., & Lowenschuss-Erlich, I. (2014). The effects of divided attention on encoding processes under incidental and intentional learning instructions: Underlying mechanisms? *Quarterly Journal of Experimental Psychology*, 67, 1682–1696. https://doi.org/10.1080/17470218.2013.867517

Nees, M. A. (2016). Have we forgotten auditory sensory memory? Retention intervals in studies of nonverbal auditory working memory. *Frontiers in Psychology*, 7, Article 1892. https://doi.org/10.3389/fpsyg.2016.01892

Neisser, U. (1967). *Cognitive psychology*. Appleton-Century-Crofts.

Neisser, U. (1984). Interpreting Harry Bahrick's discovery: What confers immunity against forgetting? *Journal of Experimental Psychology: General*, 113, 32–35.

Neisser, U., & Becklen, R. (1975). Selective looking: Attending to visually specified events. *Cognitive Psychology*, 7, 480–494.

Nelson, K. (1974). Concept, word, and sentence: Interrelations in acquisition and development. *Psychological Review*, 81, 267–285.

Newell, A., & Rosenbloom, P. S. (1981). Mechanisms of skill acquisition and the law of practice. In J. R. Anderson (Ed.), *Cognitive skills and their acquisition* (pp. 1–55). Erlbaum.

Newell, A., & Simon, H. A. (1956). The logic theory machine: A complex information processing system. *IRE Transactions on Information Theory*, IT-2, 61–79.

Newell, A., & Simon, H. A. (1972). *Human problem solving*. Prentice Hall.

Newell, A., Shaw, J. C., & Simon, H. A. (1962). The process of creative thinking. In H. E. Gruber, G.

Terell, & M. Wertheimer (Eds.), *Contemporary approaches to creative thinking* (pp. 1–81). Atherton.

Newstead, S. E., & Griggs, R. A. (1983). Drawing inferences from quantified statements: A study of the square of opposition. *Journal of Verbal Learning and Verbal Behavior*, 22, 535–546.

Newstead, S. E., Pollard, P., & Evans, J. S. (1992). The source of belief bias effects in syllogistic reasoning. *Cognition*, 45, 257–284. https://doi .org/10.1371/journal.pone.0015954

Nickerson, R. S., & Adams, M. J. (1979). Long-term memory for a common object. *Cognitive Psychology*, 11, 287–307.

Nielson, K. A., Yee, D., & Erickson, K. I. (2005). Memory enchancement by a semantically unrelated emotional arousal source induced after learning. *Neurobiology of Learning and Memory*, 84, 49–56.

Nisbett, R. E., & Wilson, T. D. (1977). Telling more than we can know: Verbal reports on mental processes. *Psychological Review*, 84, 231–259.

Nishimura, M., Scherf, K. S., Zachariou, V., Tarr, M. J., & Behrmann, M. (2015). Size precedes view: Developmental emergence of invariant object representations in lateral occipital complex. *Journal of Cognitive Neuroscience*, 27, 474–491. https://doi.org/10.1162/jocn_a_00720

Noordman, L. G., Vonk, W., & Kempff, H. J. (1992). Causal inferences during the reading of expository texts. *Journal of Memory and Language*, 31, 573–590.

Norman, D. A. (1968). Toward a theory of memory and attention. *Psychological Review*, 75, 522–536.

Norman, K. A., & O'Reilly, R. C. (2003). Modeling hippocampal and neocortical contributions to recognition memory: A complementary learning-systems approach. *Psychological Review*, 110, 611–646. https://doi.org/10.1037/0033-295X.110 .4.611

Nosofsky, R. M., & Palmeri, T. J. (1998). A rule-plus-exception model for classifying objects in continuous-dimension spaces. *Psychonomic Bulletin and Review*, 5, 345–369.

Nosofsky, R. M., Palmeri, T. J., & McKinley, S. C. (1994). Rule-plus-exception model of classification learning. *Psychological Review*, 101, 53–79.

Novick, L. R., & Holyoak, K. J. (1991). Mathematical problem solving by analogy. *Journal of Experimental Psychology: Learning, Memory, and Cognition*, 17, 398–415.

Nowak, M. A., Komarova, N. L., & Niyogi, P. (2001). Evolution of universal grammar. *Science*, 291, 114–118.

Oaksford, M., & Chater, N. (2001). The probabilistic approach to human reasoning. *Trends in Cognitive Science*, 5, 349–357.

Oaksford, M., & Chater, N. (2009). Précis of "Bayesian rationality: The probabilistic approach to human reasoning." *Behavioral and Brain Sciences*, 32, 69–84. https://doi.org/10.1017/ S0140525X09000284

Oaksford, M., & Chater, N. (2013). Dynamic inference and everyday conditional reasoning in the new paradigm. *Thinking and Reasoning*, 19, 346–379. https://doi.org/10.1080/13546783.2013 .808163

Oaksford, M., & Chater, N. (2020). New paradigms in the psychology of reasoning. *Annual Review of Psychology*, 71, 305–330.

Oberauer, K. (2019). Working memory and attention – a conceptual analysis and review. *Journal of Cognition*, 2, Article 36.

Oberauer, K., & Lewandowsky, S. (2008). Forgetting in immediate serial recall: Decay, temporal distinctiveness, or interference? *Psychological Review*, 115, 544–576. https://doi.org/10.1037/ 0033-295X.115.3.544

Oberauer, K., Lewandowsky, S., Awh, E., et al. (2018). Benchmarks for models of short-term and working memory. *Psychological Bulletin*, 144, 885–958.

Oberly, H. S. (1924). The range for visual attention, cognition and apprehension. *American Journal of Psychology*, 35, 332–352.

O'Brien, E. J., & Albrecht, J. E. (1992). Comprehension strategies in the development of a mental model. *Journal of Experimental Psychology: Learning, Memory, and Cognition*, 18, 777–784.

O'Craven, K. M., & Kanwisher, N. (2000). Mental imagery of faces and places activates corresponding stiimulus-specific brain regions. *Journal of Cognitive Neuroscience*, 12, 1013–1023. https://doi.org/10.1162/08989290051137549

Ohlsson, S. (2012). The problems with problem solving: Reflections on the rise, current status, and possible future of a cognitive research paradigm. *Journal of Problem Solving*, 5, Article 7. https://doi.org/10.7771/1932-6246.1144

Ohman, A., & Mineka, S. (2001). Fears, phobias, and preparedness: Toward an evolved module of fear and fear learning. *Psychological Review*, 108, 483–522.

Ojalehto, B. L., & Medin, D. L. (2015). Perspectives on culture and concepts. *Annual Review of Psychology*, 66, 249–275.

O'Keefe, J., & Nadel, L. (1978). *The hippocampus and the cognitive map*. Oxford University Press.

Oppenheimer, D. M., Meyvis, T., & Davidenko, N. (2009). Instructional manipulation checks: Detecting satisficing to increase statistical power. *Journal of Experimental Social Psychology*, 45, 867–872. https://doi.org/10.1016/j.jesp.2009.03.009

Ormerod, T. C., & MacGregor, J. N. (2017). Enabling spontaneous analogy through heuristic change. *Cognitive Psychology*, 99, 1–16. https://doi.org/10.1016/j.cogpsych.2017.09.001

Orth, M., Wagnon, C., Neumann-Dunayevska, E., et al. (2022). The left prefrontal cortex determines relevance at encoding and governs episodic memory formation. *Cerebral Cortex*, 33, 612–621.

Ost, J., Udell, J., Dear, S., Zinken, J., Blank, H., & Costall, A. (2022). The serial reproduction of an urban myth: Revisiting Bartlett's schema theory. *Memory*, 30, 775–783.

Osta-Vélez, M., & Gärdenfors, P. (2020). Category-based induction in conceptual spaces. *Journal of Mathematical Psychology*, 96, Article 102357.

Otgaar, H., Howe, M. L., & Patihis, L. (2022). What science tells us about false and repressed memories. *Memory*, 30, 16–21.

Otgaar, H., Schell-Leugers, J. M., Howe, M. L., Vilar, A. D. L. F., Houben, S. T., & Merckelbach, H. (2021). The link between suggestibility, compliance, and false confessions: A review using experimental and field studies. *Applied Cognitive Psychology*, 35, 445–455.

O'Toole, A. J., Jiang, F., Abdi, H., & Haxby, J. V. (2005). Partially distributed representations of objects and faces in ventral temporal cortex. *Journal of Cognitive Neuroscience*, 17, 580–590.

O'Toole, A. J., Jiang, F., Abdi, H., et al. (2007). Theoretical, statistical, and practical perspectives on pattern-based classification approaches to the analysis of functional neuroimaging data. *Journal of Cognitive Neuroscience*, 19, 1735–1752. https://doi.org/10.1162/jocn.2007.19.11.1735

Owen, A. M., Stern, C. E., Look, R. B., et al. (1998). Functional organization of spatial and nonspatial working memory processing within the human lateral frontal cortex. *Proceedings of the National Academy of Sciences of the USA*, 95, 7721–7726.

Paap, K. R., & Noel, R. W. (1991). Dual-route models of print to sound: Still a good horse race. *Psychological Research*, 53, 13–24.

Paller, K. A., & Wagner, A. D. (2002). Observing the transformation of experience into memory. *Trends in Cognitive Sciences*, 6, 93–102.

Palmer, S. E. (1975). The effects of contextual scenes on the identification of objects. *Memory and Cognition*, 3, 519–526.

Park, D. C., & Festini, S. B. (2017). Theories of memory and aging: A look at the past and a glimpse of the future. *Journals of Gerontology, Series B, Psychological Sciences and Social Sciences*, 72, 82–90. https://doi.org/10.1093/geronb/gbw066

Pashler, H. (1994). Dual-task interference in simple tasks: Data and theory. *Psychological Bulletin*, 116, 220–244.

Pashler, H., & Johnston, J. (1989). Chronometric evidence for central postponement in temporally overlapping tasks. *Quarterly Journal of Experimental Psychology*, 41A, 19–45.

Patihis, L., Ho, L. Y., Loftus, E. F., & Herrera, M. E. (2021). Memory experts' beliefs about repressed memory. *Memory*, 29, 823–828.

Patihis, L., Ho, L. Y., Tingen, I. W., Lilienfeld, S. O., & Loftus, E. F. (2014). Are the "memory wars" over? A scientist–practitioner gap in beliefs about repressed memory. *Psychological Science*, 25, 519–530. https://doi.org/10.1177/0956797613510718

Patterson, J. D., & Kurtz, K. J. (2020). Comparison-based learning of relational categories (you'll never guess). *Journal of Experimental Psychology: Learning, Memory, and Cognition*, 46, 851–871.

Paulk, A. C., Kfir, Y., Khanna, A. R., et al. (2022). Large-scale neural recordings with single neuron resolution using Neuropixels probes in human cortex. *Nature Neuroscience*, 25, 252–263.

Peace, K. A., & Porter, S. (2004). A longitudinal investigation of the reliability of memories for trauma and other emotional experiences. *Applied Cognitive Psychology*, 18, 1143–1159.

Pearson, J., Naselaris, T., Holmes, E. A., & Kosslyn, S. M. (2015). Mental imagery: Functional mechanisms and clinical applications. *Trends in Cognitive Sciences*, 19, 590–602. https://doi.org/10.1016/j.tics.2015.08.003

Penfield, W. (1959). *Speech and brain mechanisms*. Princeton University Press.

Penfield, W., & Boldrey, E. (1937). Somatic motor and sensory representation in the cerebral cortex of man as studied by electrical stimulation. *Brain*, 60, 389–443. https://doi.org/10.1093/brain/60.4.389

Peng, S., Liu, C. H., Yang, X., Li, H., Chen, W., & Hu, P. (2020). Culture variation in the average identity extraction: The role of global vs. local processing orientation. *Visual Cognition*, 28, 180–191.

Perenin, M. T., & Vighetto, A. (1988). Optic ataxia: A specific disruption in visuomotor mechanisms. *Brain*, 111, 643–674.

Perkins, D. N. (1972). Visual discrimination between rectangular and nonrectangular parallelopipeds. *Perception and Psychophysics*, 12, 396–400. https://doi.org/10.3758/BF03205849

Perkins, D. N. (1973). Compensating for distortion in viewing pictures obliquely. *Perception and Psychophysics*, 14, 13–18. https://doi.org/10.3758/BF03198608

Peterson, L., & Peterson, M. J. (1959). Short-term retention of individual verbal items. *Journal of Experimental Psychology*, 58, 193–198.

Phillips, W., & Boroditsky, L. (2003). Can quirks of grammar affect the way you think? Grammatical gender and object concepts. In *Proceedings of the 25th annual meeting of the Cognitive Science Society* (pp. 928–933). Erlbaum.

Pillemer, D. B. (1984). Flashbulb memories of the assassination attempt on President Reagan. *Cognition*, 16, 63–80.

Pillemer, D. B., Goldsmith, L. R., Panter, A. T., & White, S. H. (1988). Very long-term memories of the first year in college. *Journal of Experimental Psychology: Learning, Memory, and Cognition*, 14, 709–715. https://doi.org/10.1037/0278-7393.14.4.709

Pilling, M., Guest, D., & Andrews, M. (2019). Perceptual errors support the notion of masking by object substitution. *Perception*, 48, 138–161.

Pinker, S. (1994). *The language instinct*. William Morrow.

Pinker, S., & Ullman, M. T. (2002). The past and future of the past tense debate. *Trends in Cognitive Science*, 6, 456–463.

Plous, S. (1989). Thinking the unthinkable: The effects of anchoring on likelihood estimates of nuclear war. *Journal of Applied Social Psychology*, 19, 67–91.

Podsakoff, P. M., MacKenzie, S. B., & Podsakoff, N. P. (2012). Sources of method bias in social science research and recommendations on how to control it. *Annual Review of Psychology*, 63, 539–569. https://doi.org/10.1146/annurev-psych-120710-100452

Poeppel, D. (2014). The neuroanatomic and neurophysiological infrastructure for speech and language. *Current Opinion in Neurobiology*, 28, 142–149. https://doi.org/10.1016/j.conb.2014.07.005

Poldrack, R. A. (2012). The future of fMRI in cognitive neuroscience. *NeuroImage*, 62, 1216–1220. https://doi.org/10.1016/j.neuroimage.2011.08.007

Posner, M. I., & Keele, S. W. (1968). On the genesis of abstract ideas. *Journal of Experimental Psychology*, 77, 353–363.

Posner, M. I., & Keele, S. W. (1970). Retention of abstract ideas. *Journal of Experimental Psychology*, 83, 304–308.

Posner, M. I., Snyder, C. R., & Davidson, B. J. (1980). Attention and the detection of signals. *Journal of Experimental Psychology: General*, 109, 160–174.

Postle, B. R., Jonides, J., Smith, E. E., Corkin, S., & Growdon, J. H. (1997). Spatial, but not object, delayed response is impaired in early Parkinson's disease. *Neuropsychology*, 11, 171–179.

Povinelli, D. J., & Bering, J. M. (2002). The mentality of apes revisited. *Current Directions in Psychological Science*, 11, 115–119.

Pratte, M. S. (2018). Iconic memories die a sudden death. *Psychological Science*, 29, 877–887.

Premack, D. (1971). Language in chimpanzee? *Science*, 172, 808–822.

Premack, D. (1976a). *Intelligence in ape and man*. Erlbaum.

Premack, D. (1976b). Language and intelligence in ape and man. *American Scientist*, 64, 674–683.

Preston, K. A. (1935). The speed of word perception and its relation to reading ability. *Journal of General Psychology*, 13, 199–203.

Price, C. J., & Mechelli, A. (2005). Reading and reading disturbance. *Current Opinion in Neurobiology*, 15, 231–238.

Priest, A. G., & Lindsay, R. O. (1992). New light on novice–expert differences in physics problem solving. *British Journal of Psychology*, 83, 389–405.

Proffitt, J. B., Coley, J. D., & Medin, D. L. (2000). Expertise and category-based induction. *Journal of Experimental Psychology: Learning, Memory, and Cognition*, 26, 811–828.

Proffitt, T., Luncz, L. V., Falótico, T., et al. (2016). Wild monkeys flake stone tools. *Nature*, 539, 85–88. https://doi.org/10.1038/nature20112

Pylyshyn, Z. W. (1973). What the mind's eye tells the mind's brain: A critique of mental imagery. *Psychological Bulletin*, 80, 1–24.

Pylyshyn, Z. W. (1981). The imagery debate: Analogue media versus tacit knowledge. *Psychological Review*, 88, 16–45.

Pylyshyn, Z. W. (2002). Mental imagery: In search of a theory. *Behavioral and Brain Sciences*, 25, 157–238.

Pylyshyn, Z. W. (2003). Return of the mental image: Are there really pictures in the brain? *Trends in Cognitive Sciences*, 7, 113–118.

Pynoos, R. S., & Nader, K. (1989). Children's memories and proximity to violence. *Journal of the American Academy of Child and Adolescent Psychiatry*, 28, 236–241.

Qiu, L., Lin, H., Ramsay, J., & Yang, F. (2012). You are what you tweet: Personality expression and perception on Twitter. *Journal of Research in Personality*, 46, 710–718. https://doi.org/10.1016/j.jrp.2012.08.008

Quinn, J. G., & McConnell, J. (1996). Irrelevant pictures in visual working memory. *Quarterly Journal of Experimental Psychology*, 49A, 200–215.

Radvansky, G. A., & Zacks, J. M. (2014). *Event cognition*. Oxford University Press.

Ragni, M., & Johnson-Laird, P. N. (2020). Reasoning about epistemic possibilities. *Acta Psychologica*, 208, Article 103081.

Ragni, M., Kola, I., & Johnson-Laird, P. N. (2018). On selecting evidence to test hypotheses: A theory of selection tasks. *Psychological Bulletin*, 144, 779–796.

Rajah, M. N., & McIntosh, A. R. (2005). Overlap in the functional neural systems involved in semantic and episodic memory retrieval. *Journal of Cognitive Neuroscience*, 17, 470–482.

Ranganath, C., & D'Esposito, M. (2005). Directing the mind's eye: Prefrontal, inferior and medial temporal mechanisms for visual working memory. *Current Opinion in Neurobiology*, 15, 175–182.

Rauschecker, J. P., & Shannon, R. V. (2002). Sending sound to the brain. *Science*, 295, 1025–1029.

Ravid, D. (2023). First-language acquisition of morphology. In *Oxford research encyclopedia of linguistics*. Oxford University Press.

Ravizza, S. M., Hambrick, D. Z., & Fenn, K. M. (2014). Non-academic internet use in the classroom is negatively related to classroom learning regardless of intellectual ability. *Computers and Education*, 78, 109–114.

Ravizza, S. M., Uitvlugt, M. G., & Fenn, K. M. (2017). Logged in and zoned out: How laptop internet use relates to classroom learning. *Psychological Science, 28,* 171–180.

Rayner, K., Carlson, M., & Frazier, L. (1983). The interaction of syntax and semantics during sentence processing: Eye movements in the analysis of semantically biased sentences. *Journal of Verbal Learning and Verbal Behavior, 22,* 358–374.

Reardon, S. (2015, June 15). US government gives research chimps endangered-species protection. *Nature News.* https://doi.org/10.1038/nature.2015.17755

Reber, P. J., & Kotovsky, K. (1997). Implicit learning in problem solving: The role of working memory capacity. *Journal of Experimental Psychology: General, 126,* 178–203.

Reder, L. M. (1982). Plausibility judgments versus fact retrieval: Alternative strategies for sentence verification. *Psychological Review, 89,* 250–280.

Redick, T. S. (2019). The hype cycle of working memory training. *Current Directions in Psychological Science, 28,* 423–429.

Reed, C. L., Klatzky, R. L., & Halgren, E. (2005). What versus where in touch: An fMRI study. *NeuroImage, 25,* 718–726.

Reed, S. K., & Bolstad, C. A. (1991). Use of examples and procedures in problem solving. *Journal of Experimental Psychology: Learning, Memory, and Cognition, 27,* 753–766.

Reed, S. K., Ackinclose, C. C., & Voss, A. A. (1990). Selecting analogous problems: Similarity versus inclusiveness. *Memory and Cognition, 18,* 83–98.

Regier, T., Kay, P., & Khetarpal, N. (2007). Color naming reflects optimal partitions of color space. *Proceedings of the National Academy of Sciences of the USA, 104,* Article 1436. https://doi.org/10.1073/pnas.0610341104

Register, P. A., & Kihlstrom, J. F. (1987). Hypnotic effects on hypermnesia. *International Journal of Clinical and Experimental Hypnosis, 35,* 155–170.

Reich, S. S., & Ruth, P. (1982). Wason's selection task: Verification, falsification and matching. *British Journal of Psychology, 73,* 395–405.

Reingold, E. M., & Sheridan, H. (2023). Chess expertise reflects domain-specific perceptual

processing: Evidence from eye movements. *Journal of Expertise, 6,* 5–22.

Reitman, J. S. (1971). Mechanisms of forgetting in short-term memory. *Cognitive Psychology, 2,* 185–195.

Renier, L. A., Anurova, I., De Volder, A. G., et al. (2009). Multisensory integration of sounds and vibrotactile stimuli in processing streams for "what" and "where." *Journal of Neuroscience, 29,* 10950–10960. https://doi.org/10.1523/JNEUROSCI.0910-09.2009

Renoult, L., Davidson, P. S. R., Palombo, D. J., Moscovitch, M., & Levine, B. (2012). Personal semantics: At the crossroads of semantic and episodic memory. *Trends in Cognitive Sciences, 16,* 550–558. https://doi.org/10.1016/j.tics.2012.09.003

Renoult, L., Irish, M., Moscovitch, M., & Rugg, M. D. (2019). From knowing to remembering: The semantic–episodic distinction. *Trends in Cognitive Sciences, 23,* 1041–1057.

Revlis, R. (1975). Two models of syllogistic reasoning: Feature selection and conversion. *Journal of Verbal Learning and Verbal Behavior, 14,* 180–195.

Rhodes, G., Byatt, G., Michie, P. T., & Puce, A. (2004). Is the fusiform face area specialized for faces, individuation, or expert individuation? *Journal of Cognitive Neuroscience, 16,* 189–203.

Richler, J. J., & Gauthier, I. (2014). A meta-analysis and review of holistic face processing. *Psychological Bulletin, 140,* 1281–1302. https://doi.org/10.1037/a0037004

Riley, M. R., & Constantinidis, C. (2016). Role of prefrontal persistent activity in working memory. *Frontiers in Systems Neuroscience, 9,* Article 181. https://doi.org/10.3389/fnsys.2015.00181

Ripamonti, E., Aggujaro, S., Molteni, F., et al. (2014). The anatomical foundations of acquired reading disorders: A neuropsychological verification of the dual-route model of reading. *Brain and Language, 134,* 44–67. https://doi.org/10.1016/j.bandl.2014.04.001

Rips, L. J. (1975). Inductive judgments about natural categories. *Journal of Verbal Learning and Verbal Behavior, 14,* 665–681.

Rips, L. J. (1989). Similarity, typicality, and categorization. In S. O. A. Vosniadou (Ed.), *Similarity and analogical reasoning* (pp. 21–59). Cambridge University Press.

Risius, O. J., Onur, O. A., Dronse, J., et al. (2019). Neural network connectivity during post-encoding rest: linking episodic memory encoding and retrieval. *Frontiers in Human Neuroscience*, 12, Article 528.

Ritchey, M., Wing, E. A., LaBar, K. S., & Cabeza, R. (2013). Neural similarity between encoding and retrieval is related to memory via hippocampal interactions. *Cerebral Cortex*, 23, 2818–2828. https://doi.org/10.1093/cercor/bhs258

Robbe, D., & Dudman, J. T. (2020). The basal ganglia invigorate actions and decisions. In D. Poeppel, G. R. Mangun, & M. S. Gazzaniga (Eds.), *The cognitive neurosciences* (pp. 527–540). MIT Press.

Robins, S., & Mayer, R. E. (1993). Schema training in analogical reasoning. *Journal of Educational Psychology*, 85, 529–538.

Rodd, J. M. (2020). Settling into semantic space: An ambiguity-focused account of word-meaning access. *Perspectives on Psychological Science*, 15, 411–427.

Roediger, H. L., III, & McDermott, K. B. (1995). Creating false memories: Remembering words not presented in lists. *Journal of Experimental Psychology: Learning, Memory, and Cognition*, 21, 803–814.

Roediger, H. L., III, Wheeler, M. A., & Rajaram, S. (1993). Remembering, knowing, and reconstructing the past. In D. L. Medin (Ed.), *The psychology of learning and motivation: Advances in research and theory* (Vol. 30, pp. 97–134). Elsevier.

Roediger, H. L., III, Watson, J. M., McDermott, K. B., & Gallo, D. A. (2001). Factors that determine false recall: A multiple regression analysis. *Psychonomic Bulletin and Review*, 8, 385–407.

Röer, J. P., & Cowan, N. (2021). A preregistered replication and extension of the cocktail party phenomenon: One's name captures attention, unexpected words do not. *Journal of Experimental Psychology: Learning, Memory, and Cognition*, 47, 234–242.

Rogers, S. (1996). The horizon-ratio relation as information for relative size in pictures. *Perception and Psychophysics*, 58, 142–152.

Rogers, S. D., Kadar, E. E., & Costall, A. (2005). Gaze patterns in the visual control of straight-road driving and braking as a function of speed and expertise. *Ecological Psychology*, 17, 19–38. https://doi.org/10.1207/s15326969eco1701_2

Romo, R., & Salinas, E. (2003). Flutter discrimination: Neural codes, perception, memory and decision making. *Nature Reviews Neuroscience*, 4, 203–218.

Rosa Salva, O., Mayer, U., & Vallortigara, G. (2015). Roots of a social brain: Developmental models of emerging animacy-detection mechanisms. *Neuroscience and Biobehavioral Reviews*, 50, 150–168. https://doi.org/10.1016/j.neubiorev.2014.12.015

Rosch, E. H. (1973). On the internal structure of perceptual and semantic categories. In T. E. Moore (Ed.), *Cognitive development and the acquisition of language* (pp. 111–144). Academic Press.

Rosch, E. H. (1975). Cognitive representations of semantic categories. *Journal of Experimental Psychology: General*, 104, 192–233.

Rosenbaum, R. S., Köhler, S., Schacter, D. L., et al. (2005). The case of KC: Contributions of a memory-impaired person to memory theory. *Neuropsychologia*, 43, 989–1021.

Rosner, S. R., & Hayes, D. S. (1977). A developmental study of category item production. *Child Development*, 48, 1062–1065.

Ross, B. H. (1987). This is like that: The use of earlier problems and the separation of similarity effects. *Journal of Experimental Psychology: Learning, Memory, and Cognition*, 13, 629–639.

Ross, B. H. (1989). Distinguishing types of superficial similarities: Different effects on the access and use of earlier problems. *Journal of Experimental Psychology: Learning, Memory, and Cognition*, 15, 456–468.

Ross, B. H., & Kennedy, P. T. (1990). Generalizing from the use of earlier examples in problem solving. *Journal of Experimental Psychology: Learning, Memory, and Cognition*, 16, 42–55.

Rothmaler, K., Nigbur, R., & Ivanova, G. (2017). New insights into insight: Neurophysiological correlates of the difference between the intrinsic "aha" and the extrinsic "oh yes" moment. *Neuropsychologia*, 95, 204–214. https://doi.org/10.1016/j.neuropsychologia.2016.12.017

Rowland, N. E. (2012). Order and disorder: Temporal organization of eating. *Behavioural Brain Research*, 231, 272–278.

Rowling, J. K. (1998). *Harry Potter and the sorcerer's stone*. Scholastic.

Rubenstein, D., & Kealey, J. (2010). Cooperation, conflict, and the evolution of complex animal societies. *Nature Education Knowledge*, 3, Article 78.

Rubenstein, H., Lewis, S. S., & Rubenstein, M. A. (1971). Evidence for phonemic recoding in visual word recognition. *Journal of Verbal Learning and Verbal Behavior*, 10, 645–657.

Rubin, D. C. (1995). *Memory in oral traditions: The cognitive psychology of epic, ballads, and counting-out rhymes*. Oxford University Press.

Rubin, D. C., & Kozin, M. (1984). Vivid memories. *Cognition*, 16, 81–95.

Rubinstein, J. T. (2004). An introduction to the biophysics of the electrically evoked compound action potential. *International Journal of Audiology*, 43(Suppl. 1), S3–S9.

Rumelhart, D. E., Hinton, G. E., & McClelland, J. L. (1986). A general framework for parallel distributed processing. In D. E. Rumelhart, J. L. McClelland, & PDP Research Group (Eds.), *Parallel distributed processing: Vol. 1. Foundations* (pp. 45–76). MIT Press.

Russell, Y. I., Gobet, F., & Whitehouse, H. (2014). Mood, expertise, analogy, and ritual: An experiment using the five-disk Tower of Hanoi. *Religion, Brain, and Behavior*, 6, 67–87. https://doi.org/10.1080/2153599X.2014.921861

Ryskin, R., Salinas, M., Piantadosi, S., & Gibson, E. (2023). Real-time inference in communication across cultures: Evidence from a nonindustrialized society. *Journal of Experimental Psychology: General*, 152, 1245–1263.

Saffran, J. R. (2001). Words in a sea of sounds: The output of statistical learning. *Cognition*, 81, 149–169.

Saffran, J. R. (2002). Constraints on statistical language learning. *Journal of Memory and Language*, 47, 172–196.

Saffran, J. R. (2020). Statistical language learning in infancy. *Child Development Perspectives*, 14, 49–54.

Saffran, J. R., Aslin, R. N., & Newport, E. L. (1996). Statistical learning by 8-month old infants. *Science*, 274, 1926–1928.

Saffran, J. R., Pollak, S. D., Seibel, R. L., & Shkolnik, A. (2007). Dog is a dog is a dog: Infant rule learning is not specific to language. *Cognition*, 105, 669–680. https://doi.org/10.1016/j.cognition.2006.11.004

Sala, G., & Gobet, F. (2019). Cognitive training does not enhance general cognition. *Trends in Cognitive Sciences*, 23, 9–20. https://doi.org/10.1016/j.tics.2018.10.004

Sala, G., & Gobet, F. (2020). Working memory training in typically developing children: A multilevel meta-analysis. *Psychonomic Bulletin and Review*, 27, 423–434.

Salehi, M., Greene, A. S., Karbasi, A., Shen, X., Scheinost, D., & Constable, R. T. (2020). There is no single functional atlas even for a single individual: Functional parcel definitions change with task. *NeuroImage*, 208, Article 116366.

Salthouse, T. A. (1984). The skill of typing. *Scientific American*, 250, 128–135.

Salvi, C., Bricolo, E., Kounios, J., Bowden, E., & Beeman, M. (2016). Insight solutions are correct more often than analytic solutions. *Thinking and Reasoning*, 22, 443–460. https://doi.org/10.1080/13546783.2016.1141798

Salvi, C., Beeman, M., Bikson, M., McKinley, R., & Grafman, J. (2020). TDCS to the right anterior temporal lobe facilitates insight problem-solving. *Scientific Reports*, 10, Article 946. https://doi.org/10.1038/s41598-020-57724-1

Samuel, A. (1996). Phoneme restoration. *Language and Cognitive Processes*, 11, 647–653.

Sams, M., Mottonen, R., & Sihvonen, T. (2005). Seeing and hearing others and oneself talk. *Cognitive Brain Research*, 23, 429–435.

Sana, F., Weston, T., & Cepeda, N. J. (2013). Laptop multitasking hinders classroom learning for both users and nearby peers. *Computers and Education*, 62, 24–31. https://doi.org/10.1016/j.compedu.2012.10.003

Sapir, E. (1956). *Culture, Language and Personality*. University of California Press.

Sasaki, K., Foley, S., Pizarro-Guevara, J., Silva-Robles, F., Toosarvandani, M., & Wagers, M. (2022). *Evidence for a universal parsing principle in Santiago Laxopa Zapotec*. http://osf.io/2wgd8.

Savage-Rumbaugh, E. S. (1986). *Ape language: From conditioned response to symbol*. Columbia University Press.

Savage-Rumbaugh, E. S., Rumbaugh, D. M., & Boysen, S. (1978). Symbolic communication between two chimpanzees (*Pan troglodytes*). *Science*, 201, 641–644.

Savage-Rumbaugh, E. S., Rumbaugh, D. M., Smith, S. T., & Lawson, J. (1980). Reference: The linguistic essential. *Science*, 210, 922–925.

Savage-Rumbaugh, E. S., Romski, M. A., Sevcik, R., & Pate, J. L. (1983). Assessing symbol usage versus symbol competency. *Journal of Experimental Psychology: General*, 112, 508–512.

Savage-Rumbaugh, E. S., Shanker, S. G., & Taylor, T. J. (1998). *Apes, language, and the human mind*. Oxford University Press.

Savine, A. C., Scullin, M. K., & Roediger, H. L. (2011). Survival processing of faces. *Memory and Cognition*, 39, 1359–1373. https://doi.org/10.3758/s13421-011-0121-0

Schacter, D. L., & Tulving, E. (1994). What are the memory systems of 1994? In D. L. Schacter & E. Tulving (Eds.), *Memory systems 1994* (pp. 1–38). MIT Press.

Schaeffer, J., Burch, N., Bjornsson, Y., et al. (2007). Checkers is solved. *Science*, 317, 1518–1522. https://doi.org/10.1126/science.1144079

Schank, R. C., & Abelson, R. P. (1977). *Scripts, plans, goals, and understanding*. Erlbaum.

Schellenberg, E. G., Iverson, P., & McKinnon, M. C. (1999). Name that tune: Identifying popular recordings from brief excerpts. *Psychonomic Bulletin and Review*, 6, 641–646.

Schmid, P. M., & Yeni-Komshian, G. H. (1999). The effects of speaker accent and target predictability on perception of mispronunciations. *Journal of Speech Language and Hearing Research*, 42, 56–64.

Schmidt, B., Duin, A. A., & Redish, A. D. (2019). Disrupting the medial prefrontal cortex alters hippocampal sequences during deliberative decision making. *Journal of Neurophysiology*, 121, 1981–2000.

Schooler, J. W. (2001). Discovering memories of abuse in the light of meta-awareness. *Journal of Aggression, Maltreatment, and Trauma*, 4, 105–136.

Schooler, J. W., Bendiksen, M., & Ambadar, Z. (1997). Taking the middle line: Can we accommodate both fabricated and recovered memories of sexual abuse? In M. A. Conway (Ed.), *Recovered memories and false memories: Debates in psychology* (pp. 251–292). Oxford University Press.

Schreiber, K. E., & McMurray, B. (2019). Listeners can anticipate future segments before they identify the current one. *Attention, Perception, and Psychophysics*, 81, 1147–1166.

Schwartz, J.-L., Berthommier, F., & Savariaux, C. (2004). Seeing to hear better: Evidence for early audio-visual interactions in speech identification. *Cognition*, 93, B69–B78.

Scoboria, A., Wade, K. A., Lindsay, D. S., et al. (2017). A mega-analysis of memory reports from eight peer-reviewed false memory implantation studies. *Memory*, 25, 146–163. https://doi.org/10.1080/09658211.2016.1260747

Sedlmeier, P., & Srinivas, K. (2016). How do theories of cognition and consciousness in ancient Indian thought systems relate to current Western theorizing and research? *Frontiers in Psychology*, 7, Article 343. https://doi.org/10.3389/fpsyg.2016.00343

Segaert, K., Weber, K., de Lange, F. P., Petersson, K. M., & Hagoort, P. (2013). The suppression of repetition enhancement: A review of fMRI studies. *Neuropsychologia*, 51, 59–66. https://doi.org/10.1016/j.neuropsychologia.2012.11.006

Segall, M. H., Campbell, D. T., & Herskovits, M. J. (1966). *The influence of culture on visual perception*. Bobbs-Merrill.

Seidenberg, M. (2017). *Language at the speed of sight: How we read, why so many cannot, and what can be done about it*. Basic Books.

Senghas, A., & Coppola, M. (2001). Children creating language: How Nicaraguan Sign Language acquired a spatial grammar. *Psychological Science, 12*, 323–328.

Senghas, A., Kita, S., & Özyürek, A. (2004). Children creating core properties of language: Evidence from an emerging sign language in Nicaragua. *Science, 305*, 1779–1782.

Shaffer, D. M., Krauchunas, S. M., Eddy, M., & McBeath, M. K. (2004). How dogs navigate to catch Frisbees. *Psychological Science, 15*, 437–441.

Shaffer, L. H. (1975). Control processes in typing. *Quarterly Journal of Experimental Psychology, 27*, 419–432.

Shiffrin, R. M., & Schneider, W. (1977). Controlled and automatic human information processing: II. Perceptual learning, automatic attending and a general theory. *Psychological Review, 84*, 127–190.

Shin, Y. S., Masís-Obando, R., Keshavarzian, N., Dáve, R., & Norman, K. A. (2021). Context-dependent memory effects in two immersive virtual reality environments: On Mars and underwater. *Psychonomic Bulletin and Review, 28*, 574–582.

Silan, M., Adetula, A., Basnight-Brown, D. M., Forscher, P. S., Dutra, N., & IJzerman, H. (2021, October 26). Psychological science needs the entire globe, part 2. APS Observer. https://www.psychologicalscience.org/observer/psychological-science-needs-the-entire-globe-part-2

Simon, D. P., & Simon, H. A. (1978). Individual differences in solving physics problems. In R. Siegler (Ed.), *Children's thinking: What develops?* (pp. 325–348). Erlbaum.

Simon, H. A. (1974). How big is a chunk? *Science, 183*, 482–488.

Simon, H. A., & Chase, W. G. (1973). Skill in chess. *American Scientist, 61*, 394–403.

Simon, H. A., & Gilmartin, K. (1973). A simulation of memory for chess positions. *Cognitive Psychology, 5*, 29–46.

Simons, D. J., & Chabris, C. F. (1999). Gorillas in our midst: Sustained inattentional blindness for dynamic events. *Perception, 28*, 1059–1074.

Simons, D. J., Boot, W. R., Charness, N., et al. (2016). Do "brain-training" programs work? *Psychological Science in the Public Interest, 17*, 103–186. https://doi.org/10.1177/1529100616661983

Simpson, G. B., & Krueger, M. A. (1991). Selective access of homograph meanings in sentence context. *Journal of Memory and Language, 30*, 627–643.

Simpson, M. E., & Johnson, D. M. (1966). Atmosphere and conversion errors in syllogistic reasoning. *Journal of Experimental Psychology, 72*, 197–200.

Singer, M., Graesser, A. C., & Trabasso, T. (1994). Minimal or global inference during reading. *Journal of Memory and Language, 33*, 421–441.

Singleton, J. L., & Newport, E. L. (2004). When learners surpass their models: The acquisition of American Sign Language from inconsistent input. *Cognitive Psychology, 49*, 370–407.

Sio, U. N., & Ormerod, T. C. (2009). Does incubation enhance problem solving? A meta-analytic review. *Psychological Bulletin, 135*, 94–120. https://doi.org/10.1037/a0014212

Skinner, B. F. (1938). *The behavior of organisms: An experimental analysis*. Appleton-Century-Crofts.

Skinner, B. F. (1957). *Verbal behavior*. Appleton-Century-Crofts.

Skinner, B. F. (1984). *The shaping of a behaviorist*. New York University Press.

Slobin, D. I. (1966). Grammatical transformations and sentence comprehension in childhood and adulthood. *Journal of Verbal Learning and Verbal Behavior, 5*, 219–227.

Sloman, S. A. (1996). The empirical base for two systems of reasoning. *Psychological Bulletin, 119*, 3–22.

Smith, E. E., & Medin, D. L. (1981). *Categories and concepts*. Harvard University Press.

Smith, E. E., Shoben, E. J., & Rips, L. J. (1974). Structure and process in semantic memory: A featural model for semantic decisions. *Psychological Review, 81*, 214–241.

Smith, L., & Yu, C. (2008). Infants rapidly learn word-referent mappings via cross-situational statistics. *Cognition*, 106, 1558–1568. https://doi.org/10.1016/j.cognition.2007.06.010

Smith, P. L., Corbett, E. A., Lilburn, S. D., & Kyllingsbæk, S. (2018). The power law of visual working memory characterizes attention engagement. *Psychological Review*, 125, 435–451.

Smith, R. W., & Kounios, J. (1996). Sudden insight: All-or-none processing revealed by speed–accuracy decomposition. *Journal of Experimental Psychology: Learning, Memory, and Cognition*, 22, 1443–1462. https://doi.org/10.1037/0278-7393.22.6.1443

Smith, S. M. (1988). Environmental context-dependent memory. In G. M. Davies & D. M. Thomson (Eds.), *Memory in context: Context in memory* (pp. 13–44). John Wiley.

Smith, S. M., Glenberg, A., & Bjork, R. A. (1978). Environmental context and human memory. *Memory and Cognition*, 6, 342–353.

Soemer, A., & Saito, S. (2015). Maintenance of auditory-nonverbal information in working memory. *Psychonomic Bulletin and Review*, 22, 1777–1783. https://doi.org/10.3758/s13423-015-0854-z

Sormaz, M., Jefferies, E., Bernhardt, B. C., et al. (2017). Knowing what from where: Hippocampal connectivity with temporoparietal cortex at rest is linked to individual differences in semantic and topographic memory. *NeuroImage*, 152, 400–410. https://doi.org/10.1016/j.neuroimage.2017.02.071

Spalek, T. M., & Di Lollo, V. (2022). Metacontrast masking reduces the estimated duration of visible persistence. *Attention, Perception, and Psychophysics*, 84, 341–346.

Spence, C., Nicholls, M. E. R., & Driver, J. (2001). The cost of expecting events in the wrong sensory modality. *Perception and Psychophysics*, 63, 330–336. https://doi.org/10.3758/BF03194473

Spencer, R. M., & Weisberg, R. W. (1986). Context-dependent effects on analogical transfer. *Memory and Cognition*, 14, 442–449.

Sperling, G. (1960). The information available in brief visual presentation. *Psychological Monographs*, 74, 29 pp.

Squire, L. R. (1992). Memory and the hippocampus: A synthesis from findings with rats, monkeys, and humans. *Psychological Review*, 99, 195–231.

Squire, L. R. (2009). Memory and brain systems: 1969–2009. *Journal of Neuroscience*, 29, 12711–12716. https://doi.org/10.1523/JNEUROSCI.3575-09.2009

Sreenivasan, K. K., Vytlacil, J., & D'Esposito, M. (2014). Distributed and dynamic storage of working memory stimulus information in extrastriate cortex. *Journal of Cognitive Neuroscience*, 26, 1141–1153. https://doi.org/10.1162/jocn_a_00556

Stanovich, K. E. (1999). *Who is rational? Studies of individual differences in reasoning*. Erlbaum.

Stanovich, K. E. (2011). *Rationality and the reflective mind*. Oxford University Press.

Stanovich, K. E., & West, R. F. (1998). Cognitive ability and variation in selection task performance. *Thinking and Reasoning*, 4, 193–230.

Stasenko, A., & Gollan, T. H. (2019). Tip of the tongue after any language: Reintroducing the notion of blocked retrieval. *Cognition*, 193, Article 104027.

Stateva, P., Stepanov, A., Déprez, V., Dupuy, L. E., & Reboul, A. C. (2019). Cross-linguistic variation in the meaning of quantifiers: Implications for pragmatic enrichment. *Frontiers in Psychology*, 10, Article 957.

Sternberg, S. (1966). High-speed scanning in human memory, *Science*, 153, 652–654.

Stipek, D., & Valentino, R. A. (2015). Early childhood memory and attention as predictors of academic growth trajectories. *Journal of Educational Psychology*, 107, 771–788.

Stokes, M., Thompson, R., Nobre, A. C., & Duncan, J. (2009). Shape-specific preparatory activity mediates attention to targets in human visual cortex. *Proceedings of the National Academy of Sciences of the USA*, 106, 19569–19574. https://doi.org/10.1073/pnas.0905306106

Stone, J. V., Hunkin, N. M., & Hornby, A. (2001). Predicting spontaneous recovery of memory. *Nature*, 414, 167–168.

Strayer, D. L., & Drews, F. A. (2007). Cell-phone-induced driver distraction. *Current Directions in*

Psychological Science, 16, 128–131. https://doi
.org/10.1111/j.1467-8721.2007.00489.x

Strayer, D. L., Drews, F. A., & Johnston, W. A.
(2003). Cell phone-induced failures of visual
attention during simulated driving. *Journal of
Experimental Psychology: Applied*, 9, 23–32.
https://doi.org/10.1037/1076-898X.9.1.23

Strayer, D. L., Cooper, J. M., Turrill, J., Coleman, J.
R., & Hopman, R. J. (2016). Talking to your car
can drive you to distraction. *Cognitive Research:
Principles and Implications*, 1, Article 16. https://
doi.org/10.1186/s41235-016-0018-3

Strayer, D. L., Castro, S. C., Turrill, J., & Cooper, J.
M. (2022). The persistence of distraction: The
hidden costs of intermittent multitasking. *Journal
of Experimental Psychology: Applied*, 28,
262–282. https://doi.org/10.1037/xap0000388

Stroop, J. R. (1935). Studies of interference in serial
verbal reactions. *Journal of Experimental
Psychology*, 18, 643–662.

Suanda, S. H., Mugwanya, N., & Namy, L. L. (2014).
Cross-situational statistical word learning in young
children. *Journal of Experimental Child
Psychology*, 126, 395–411. https://doi.org/10
.1016/j.jecp.2014.06.003

Sugiyama, L. S., Tooby, J., & Cosmides, L. (2002).
Cross-cultural evidence of cognitive adaptations
for social exchange among the Shiwiar of
Ecuadorian Amazonia. *Proceedings of the
National Academy of Sciences of the USA*, 99,
11537–11542.

Swallow, K. M., & Wang, Q. (2020). Culture
influences how people divide continuous sensory
experience into events. *Cognition*, 205, Article
104450.

Swann, L., Popovic, V., Blackler, A., & Thompson,
H. (2020). Airport security screener problem-
solving knowledge and implications. *Human
Factors*, 62, 1265–1285.

Sweeny, T. D., & Whitney, D. (2014). Perceiving
crowd attention: Ensemble perception of a crowd's
gaze. *Psychological Science*, 25, 1903–1913.
https://doi.org/10.1177/0956797614544510

Tabossi, P., & Zardon, F. (1993). Processing
ambiguous words in context. *Journal of Memory
and Language*, 32, 359–372.

Talarico, J. M., & Rubin, D. C. (2003). Confidence,
not consistency, characterizes flashbulb memories.
Psychological Science, 14, 455–461.

Talarico, J. M., & Rubin, D. C. (2007). Flashbulb
memories are special after all; in phenomenology,
not accuracy. *Applied Cognitive Psychology*, 21,
557–578. https://doi.org/10.1002/acp.1293

Talarico, J. M., LaBar, K. S., & Rubin, D. C. (2004).
Emotional intensity predicts autobiographical
memory experience. *Memory and Cognition*, 32,
1118–1132.

Tamir, D. I., Templeton, E. M., Ward, A. F., & Zaki,
J. (2018). Media usage diminishes memory for
experiences. *Journal of Experimental Social
Psychology*, 76, 161–168.

Tanaka, J. W., & Taylor, M. (1991). Object categories
and expertise: Is the basic level in the eye of
the beholder? *Cognitive Psychology*, 23,
457–482.

Tarr, M. J. (1995). Rotating objects to recognize
them: A case study on the role of viewpoint
dependency in the recognition of three-
dimensional objects. *Psychonomic Bulletin and
Review*, 2, 55–82.

Tarr, M. J., & Cheng, Y. D. (2003). Learning to see
faces and objects. *Trends in Cognitive Sciences*, 7,
23–30.

Tarr, M. J., & Gauthier, I. (2000). FFA: A flexible
fusiform area for subordinate-level visual
processing automatized by expertise. *Nature
Neuroscience*, 3, 764–769.

Tarr, M. J., & Pinker, S. (1990). When does human
object recognition use a viewer-centered reference
frame? *Psychological Science*, 1, 253–256.

Taylor, J. A., & McDougle, S. D. (2020). Visuomotor
adaptation tasks as a window into the interplay
between explicit and implicit cognitive processes.
In D. Poeppel, G. R. Mangun, & M. S. Gazzaniga
(Eds.), *The cognitive neurosciences* (pp.
549–558). MIT Press.

Terrace, H. S., Petitto, L. A., Sanders, R. J., & Bever,
T. G. (1979). Can an ape create a sentence?
Science, 206, 891–902.

Thaler, R. (1980). Toward a positive theory of
consumer choice. *Journal of Economic Behavior
and Organization*, 1, 39–60.

Thomas, J. C. (1974). An analysis of behavior in the Hobbits–orcs problem. *Cognitive Psychology*, 6, 257–269.

Thompson, A. K., & Wolpaw, J. R. (2014). Operant conditioning of spinal reflexes: From basic science to clinical therapy. *Frontiers in Integrative Neuroscience*, 8, Article 25. https://doi.org/10 .3389/fnint.2014.00025

Thompson, R. F., & Steinmetz, J. E. (2009). The role of the cerebellum in classical conditioning of discrete behavioral responses. *Neuroscience*, 162, 732–755. https://doi.org/10.1016/j.neuroscience .2009.01.041

Thompson-Schill, S. L., Kurtz, K. J., & Gabrieli, J. D. (1998). Effects of semantic and associative relatedness on automatic priming. *Journal of Memory and Language*, 38, 440–458.

Thorndike, E. L. (1911). *Animal intelligence* (Vol. 2). Macmillan.

Thurgood, C., Whitfield, T. W. A., & Patterson, J. (2011). Towards a visual recognition threshold: New instrument shows humans identify animals with only 1 ms of visual exposure. *Vision Research*, 51, 1966–1971. https://doi.org/10.1016/ j.visres.2011.07.008

Tinbergen, N. (1952). The curious behavior of the stickleback. *Scientific American*, 182, 22–26.

Tolman, E. C. (1948). Cognitive maps in rats and men. *Psychological Review*, 55, 189–208. https:// doi.org/10.1037/h0061626

Topolinski, S., & Reber, R. (2010). Gaining insight into the "aha" experience. *Current Directions in Psychological Science*, 19, 402–405. https://doi .org/10.1177/0963721410388803

Treisman, A. M., & Gelade, G. (1980). A feature-integration theory of attention. *Cognitive Psychology*, 12, 97–136.

Treisman, A. M., & Schmidt, H. (1982). Illusory conjunctions in the perception of objects. *Cognitive Psychology*, 14, 107–141.

Tremblay, P., & Dick, A. S. (2016). Broca and Wernicke are dead, or moving past the classic model of language neurobiology. *Brain and Language*, 162, 60–71. https://doi.org/10.1016/j .bandl.2016.08.004

Troyer, M., Urbach, T. P., & Kutas, M. (2020). Lumos! Electrophysiological tracking of (wizarding) world knowledge use during reading. *Journal of Experimental Psychology: Learning, Memory, and Cognition*, 46, Article 476.

Tulving, E. (1967). The effects of presentation and recall of material in free-recall learning. *Journal of Verbal Learning and Verbal Behavior*, 6, 175–184.

Tulving, E. (1972). Episodic and semantic memory. In E. Tulving & W. Donaldson (Eds.), *Organization and memory* (pp. 381–403). Academic Press.

Tulving, E. (1983). *Elements of episodic memory*. Oxford University Press.

Tulving, E. (2002). Episodic memory: From mind to brain. *Annual Review of Psychology*, 53, 1–25.

Tulving, E., & Pearlstone, Z. (1966). Availability versus accessibility of information in memory for words. *Journal of Verbal Learning and Verbal Behavior*, 5, 381–391.

Tulving, E., & Thomson, D. M. (1973). Encoding specificity and retrieval processes in episodic memory. *Psychological Review*, 80, 359–380.

Tulving, E., Schacter, D. L., & Stark, H. A. (1982). Priming effects in word-fragment completion are independent of recognition memory. *Journal of Experimental Psychology: Learning, Memory, and Cognition*, 8, 336–342.

Tulving, E., Schacter, D. L., McLachlan, D. R., & Moscovitch, M. (1988). Priming of semantic autobiographical knowledge: A case study of retrograde amnesia. *Brain and Cognition*, 8, 3–20.

Turvey, M. T. (1973). On peripheral and central processes in vision: Inferences from an information-processing analysis of masking with patterned stimuli. *Psychological Review*, 80, 1–52.

Tversky, A., & Kahneman, D. (1973). Availability: A heuristic for judging frequency and probability. *Cognitive Psychology*, 5, 207–232.

Tversky, A., & Kahneman, D. (1974). Judgment under uncertainty: Heuristics and biases. *Science*, 185, 1124–1131.

Tversky, A., & Kahneman, D. (1983). Extensional versus intuitive reasoning: The conjunction fallacy in probability judgment. *Psychological Review*, 90, 293–315.

Tversky, B. (1985). Development of taxonomic organization of named and pictured categories. *Developmental Psychology*, 21, 1111–1119.

Ungerleider, L. G., & Haxby, J. V. (1994). "What" and "where" in the human brain. *Current Opinion in Neurobiology*, 4, 157–165.

Ungerleider, L. G., & Mishkin, M. (1982). Two cortical visual systems. In D. J. Ingle, M. A. Goodale, & R. J. W. Mansfield (Eds.), *Analysis of visual behavior* (pp. 549–586). MIT Press.

Vakil, E., & Heled, E. (2016). The effect of constant versus varied training on transfer in a cognitive skill learning task: The case of the Tower of Hanoi puzzle. *Learning and Individual Differences*, 47, 207–214. https://doi.org/10.1016/j.lindif.2016.02.009

Valentine, E. R. (1985). The effect of instructions on performance in the Wason selection task. *Current Psychological Research and Reviews*, 4, 214–223.

Vallar, G., & Baddeley, A. D. (1984). Phonological short-term store, phonological processing and sentence comprehension: A neuropsychological case study. *Cognitive Neuropsychology*, 1, 121–141.

Vallar, G., & Papagno, C. (2002). Neuropsychological impairments of verbal short-term memory. In A. D. Baddeley, M. D. Kopelman, & B. A. Wilson (Eds.), *Handbook of memory disorders* (2nd ed., pp. 249–270). John Wiley.

Van Berkum, J. J. A., Brown, C. M., Zwitserlood, P., Kooijman, V., & Hagoort, P. (2005). Anticipating upcoming words in discourse: Evidence from ERPs and reading times. *Journal of Experimental Psychology: Learning, Memory, and Cognition*, 31, 443–467.

Van Dantzig, S., Pecher, D., Zeelenberg, R., & Barsalou, L. W. (2008). Perceptual processing affects conceptual processing. *Cognitive Science*, 32, 579–590. https://doi.org/10.1080/03640210802035365

van den Broek, K. L., Luomba, J., van den Broek, J., & Fischer, H. (2023). Content and complexity of stakeholders' mental models of socio-ecological systems. *Journal of Environmental Psychology*, 85, Article 101906.

van den Broek, P., & Kendeou, P. (2022). Reading comprehension I. In *The science of reading*. John Wiley Online Library.

van der Helm, P. A. (2000). Simplicity versus likelihood in visual perception: From surprisals to precisais. *Psychological Bulletin*, 126, 770–800.

van Dijk, T., & Kintsch, W. (1983). *Strategies of discourse comprehension*. Academic Press.

Van Dyke, J. A., & Johns, C. L. (2012). Memory interference as a determinant of language comprehension. *Language and Linguistics Compass*, 6, 193–211. https://doi.org/10.1002/lnc3.330

Van Dyke, J. A., & McElree, B. (2006). Retrieval interference in sentence comprehension. *Journal of Memory and Language*, 55, 157–166. https://doi.org/10.1016/j.jml.2006.03.007

Vanek, N., Sóskuthy, M., & Majid, A. (2021). Consistent verbal labels promote odor category learning. *Cognition*, 206, Article 104485.

Vanhove, J. (2013). The critical period hypothesis in second language acquisition: A statistical critique and a reanalysis. *PLoS ONE*, 8, Article e69172. https://doi.org/10.1371/journal.pone.0069172

Van Lier, J., Revlin, R., & De Neys, W. (2013). Detecting cheaters without thinking: Testing the automaticity of the cheater detection module. *PLoS ONE*, 8, Article e53827. https://doi.org/10.1371/journal.pone.0053827

Van Overschelde, J. P., Rawson, K. A., & Dunlosky, J. (2004). Category norms: An updated and expanded version of the Battig and Montague (1969) norms. *Journal of Memory and Language*, 50, 289–335.

VanRullen, R., Carlson, T., & Cavanagh, P. (2007). The blinking spotlight of attention. *Proceedings of the National Academy of Sciences of the USA*, 104, 19204–19209. https://doi.org/10.1073/pnas.0707316104

Vergara, J., Rivera, N., Rossi-Pool, R., & Romo, R. (2016). A neural parametric code for storing information of more than one sensory modality in working memory. *Neuron*, 89, 54–62. https://doi.org/10.1016/j.neuron.2015.11.026

Visser, M., Jefferies, E., & Lambon Ralph, M. A. (2010). Semantic processing in the anterior temporal lobes: A meta-analysis of the functional neuroimaging literature. *Journal of Cognitive Neuroscience*, 22, 1083–1094. https://doi.org/10.1162/jocn.2009.21309

Vogel, E. K., Woodman, G. F., & Luck, S. J. (2001). Storage of features, conjunctions, and objects in visual working memory. *Journal of Experimental Psychology: Human Perception and Performance*, 27, 92–114.

von Frisch, K. (1967). *The dance language and orientation of bees*. Harvard University Press.

von Helmholtz, H. (1910/1962). *Treatise on physiological optics* (Vol. 3, J. P. Southall, Trans.). Dover.

Von Wright, J. M. (1968). Selection in visual immediate memory. *Quarterly Journal of Experimental Psychology*, 20, 62–68.

Vu, H., Kellas, G., Petersen, E., & Metcalf, K. (2003). Situation-evoking stimuli, domain of reference, and the incremental interpretation of lexical ambiguity. *Memory and Cognition*, 31, 1302–1315.

Wagner, A. D., Schacter, D. L., Rotte, M., et al. (1998). Building memories: Remembering and forgetting of verbal experiences as predicted by brain activity. *Science*, 281, 1188–1191.

Walker, W. R., Vogl, R. J., & Thompson, C. P. (1997). Autobiographical memory: Unpleasantness fades faster than pleasantness over time. *Applied Cognitive Psychology*, 11, 399–413.

Wallisch, P. (2017). Illumination assumptions account for individual differences in the perceptual interpretation of a profoundly ambiguous stimulus in the color domain: "The dress." *Journal of Vision*, 17, Article 5. https://doi.org/10.1167/17.4.5

Wang, Q. (2009). Are Asians forgetful? Perception, retention, and recall in episodic remembering. *Cognition,* 111, 123–131.

Wang, Q. (2021). The cultural foundation of human memory. *Annual Review of Psychology,* 72, 151–179.

Wang, Q., Bui, V.-K., & Song, Q. (2015). Narrative organisation at encoding facilitated children's long-term episodic memory. *Memory*, 23,

602–611. https://doi.org/10.1080/09658211.2014.914229

Wang, Y. W., & Ashby, F. G. (2020). A role for the medial temporal lobes in category learning. *Learning and Memory*, 27, 441–450.

Warren, R. M. (1970). Perceptual restoration of missing speech sounds. *Science*, 167, 392–393.

Warren, R. M., & Sherman, G. L. (1974). Phonemic restorations based on subsequent context. *Perception and Psychophysics*, 16, 150–156.

Warren, R. M., & Warren, R. P. (1970). Auditory illusions and confusions. *Scientific American*, 223, 30–36.

Warren, W. H. (1984). Perceiving affordances: Visual guidance of stair climbing. *Journal of Experimental Psychology: Human Perception and Performance*, 10, 683–703.

Warrington, E. K., & Weiskrantz, L. (1968). A study of learning and retention in amnesic patients. *Neuropsychologia*, 6, 283–291.

Warrington, E. K., & Weiskrantz, L. (1979). Conditioning in amnesic patients. *Neuropsychologia*, 20, 233–248.

Wason, P. C. (1968). Reasoning about a rule. *Quarterly Journal of Experimental Psychology*, 20, 273–281.

Wason, P. C. (1969). Regression in reasoning? *British Journal of Psychology*, 60, 471–480.

Watson, J. B. (1913). Psychology as the behaviorist views it. *Psychological Review*, 20, 158–177.

Waugh, N. C., & Norman, D. A. (1965). Primary memory. *Psychological Review*, 72, 89–104.

Weinstein, Y., Bugg, J. M., & Roediger, H. L. (2008). Can the survival recall advantage be explained by basic memory processes? *Memory and Cognition*, 36, 913–919.

Weiss, N., Mardo, E., & Avidan, G. (2016). Visual expertise for horses in a case of congenital prosopagnosia. *Neuropsychologia*, 83, 63–75. https://doi.org/10.1016/j.neuropsychologia.2015.07.028

Welford, A. T. (1980). The single-channel hypothesis. In A. T. Welford (Ed.), *Reaction time* (p. 252). Academic Press.

Werker, J. F., & Hensch, T. K. (2015). Critical periods in speech perception: New directions.

Annual Review of Psychology, 66, 173–196. https://doi.org/10.1146/annurev-psych-010814-015104

Wheeler, M. A., & McMillan, C. T. (2001). Focal retrograde amnesia and the episodic–semantic distinction. *Cognitive, Affective, and Behavioral Neuroscience, 1,* 22–37.

White, A. L., Palmer, J., & Boynton, G. M. (2020). Visual word recognition: Evidence for a serial bottleneck in lexical access. *Attention, Perception, and Psychophysics, 82,* 2000–2017.

Whitney, D., & Leib, A. Y. (2018). Ensemble perception. *Annual Review of Psychology, 69,* 105–129. https://doi.org/10.1146/annurevpsych-010416-044232

Whitwell, R. L., Milner, A. D., & Goodale, M. A. (2014). The two visual systems hypothesis: New challenges and insights from visual form agnosic patient DF. *Frontiers in Neurology, 5,* Article 255. https://doi.org/10.3389/fneur.2014.00255

Whorf, B. L. (1956). *Language, thought, and reality: Selected writings.* MIT Press.

Wickelgren, W. (1974). *How to solve problems.* W. H. Freeman.

Wickens, D., Dalezman, R., Eggemeier, E., & Thomas, F. (1976). Multiple encoding of word attributes in memory. *Memory and Cognition, 4,* 307–310.

Wikenheiser, A. M., & Redish, A. D. (2013). The balance of forward and backward hippocampal sequences shifts across behavioral states. *Hippocampus, 23,* 22–29. https://doi.org/10.1002/hipo.22049

Wiley, J., & Jarosz, A. F. (2012). Working memory capacity, attentional focus, and problem solving. *Current Directions in Psychological Science, 21,* 258–262. https://doi.org/10.1177/0963721412447622

Williams, L., Carrigan, A., Auffermann, W., et al. (2021). The invisible breast cancer: Experience does not protect against inattentional blindness to clinically relevant findings in radiology. *Psychonomic Bulletin and Review, 28,* 503–511.

Willingham, D. B. (1998a). A neuropsychological theory of motor skill learning. *Psychological Review, 105,* 558–584.

Willingham, D. B. (1998b). What differentiates declarative and procedural memories: Reply to Cohen, Poldrack, and Eichenbaum (1997). *Memory, 6,* 689–699.

Willingham, D. B., Nissen, M. J., & Bullemer, P. (1989). On the development of procedural knowledge. *Journal of Experimental Psychology: Learning, Memory, and Cognition, 15,* 1047–1060.

Winer, G. A., & Cottrell, J. E. (1996). Does anything leave the eye when we see? Extramission beliefs of children and adults. *Current Directions in Psychological Science, 5,* 137–142.

Winer, G. A., Cottrell, J. E., Gregg, V., Fournier, J. S., & Bica, L. A. (2002). Fundamentally misunderstanding visual perception: Adults' belief in visual emissions. *American Psychologist, 57,* 417–424.

Wing, E. A., Ritchey, M., & Cabeza, R. (2015). Reinstatement of individual past events revealed by the similarity of distributed activation patterns during encoding and retrieval. *Journal of Cognitive Neuroscience, 27,* 679–691. https://doi.org/10.1162/jocn_a_00740

Winocur, G., & Moscovitch, M. (2011). Memory transformation and systems consolidation. *Journal of the International Neuropsychological Society, 17,* 766–780. https://doi.org/10.1017/S1355617711000683

Wojcik, E. H., & Saffran, J. R. (2015). Toddlers encode similarities among novel words from meaningful sentences. *Cognition, 138,* 10–20.

Wolfe, J. M. (2020). Visual search: How do we find what we are looking for? *Annual Review of Vision Science, 6,* 539–562.

Wolfe, J. M., Brunelli, D. N., Rubinstein, J., & Horowitz, T. S. (2013). Prevalence effects in newly trained airport checkpoint screeners: Trained observers miss rare targets, too. *Journal of Vision, 13,* Article 33. https://doi.org/10.1167/13.3.33

Wolfe, J. M., Wu, C. C., Li, J., & Suresh, S. B. (2021). What do experts look at and what do experts find when reading mammograms? *Journal of Medical Imaging, 8,* Article 045501.

Wong, W. C. (2009). Retracing the footsteps of Wilhelm Wundt: Explorations in the disciplinary frontiers of psychology and in Völkerpsychologie. *History of Psychology*, 12, 229–265.

Wood, N., & Cowan, N. (1995). The cocktail party phenomenon revisited: How frequent are attention shifts to one's name in an irrelevant auditory channel? *Journal of Experimental Psychology: Learning, Memory, and Cognition*, 21, 255–260.

Woodruff-Pak, D. S., Goldenberg, G., Downey-Lamb, M. M., Boyko, O. B., & Lemieux, S. K. (2000). Cerebellar volume in humans related to magnitude of classical conditioning. *Neuroreport*, 11, 609–615.

Woodworth, R. S., & Sells, S. B. (1935). An atmosphere effect in formal syllogistic reasoning. *Journal of Experimental Psychology*, 18, 451–460.

Wraga, M. J. (1999a). The role of eye height in perceiving affordances and object dimensions. *Perception and Psychophysics*, 61, 490–507.

Wraga, M. J. (1999b). Using eye height in different postures to scale the heights of objects. *Journal of Experimental Psychology: Human Perception and Performance*, 25, 518–530.

Wright, S. (1954). The death of Lady Mondegreen. *Harper's Magazine*, 209, 48–51.

Wu, C. C., & Wolfe, J. M. (2019). Eye movements in medical image perception: A selective review of past, present and future. *Vision*, 3, Article 32.

Wundt, W. (1894). *Lectures on human and animal psychology* (S. E. Creigton & E. B. Tichener, Trans.). Macmillan.

Wüstenberg, S., Greiff, S., Vainikainen, M.-P., & Murphy, K. (2016). Individual differences in students' complex problem solving skills: How they evolve and what they imply. *Journal of Educational Psychology*, 108, 1028–1044. https://doi.org/10.1037/edu0000101

Yachanin, S. A. (1986). Facilitation in Wason's selection task: Content and instructions. *Current Psychological Research Fit Reviews*, 5, 20–29.

Yang, C., Luo, L., Vadillo, M. A., Yu, R., & Shanks, D. R. (2021). Testing (quizzing) boosts classroom learning: A systematic and meta-analytic review. *Psychological Bulletin*, 147, 399–435.

Yeshurun, Y., & Rashal, E. (2010). Precueing attention to the target location diminishes crowding and reduces the critical distance. *Journal of Vision*, 10, Article 16. https://doi.org/10.1167/10.10.16

Yi, H., Pingsterhaus, A., & Song, W. (2021). Effects of wearing face masks while using different speaking styles in noise on speech intelligibility during the COVID-19 pandemic. *Frontiers in Psychology*, 12, Article 682677.

Yin, R. K. (1969). Looking at upside-down faces. *Journal of Experimental Psychology*, 81, 141–145.

Yovel, G., & Kanwisher, N. (2004). Face perception: Domain specific, not process specific. *Neuron*, 44, 889–898.

Yu, C., & Smith, L. B. (2007). Rapid word learning under uncertainty via cross-situational statistics. *Psychological Science*, 18, 414–420. https://doi.org/10.1111/j.1467-9280.2007.01915.x

Zacks, J. M. (2020). Event perception and memory. *Annual Review of Psychology*, 71, 165–191.

Zaragoza, M. S., & Mitchell, K. J. (1996). Repeated exposure to suggestion and the creation of false memories. *Psychological Science*, 7, 294–300.

Zhou, P., Zong, S., Xi, X., & Xiao, H. (2022). Effect of wearing personal protective equipment on acoustic characteristics and speech perception during COVID-19. *Applied Acoustics*, 197, Article 108940.

Zwaan, R. A. (2022). Conspiracy thinking as situation model construction. *Current Opinion in Psychology*, 47, Article 101413.

Zwaan, R. A., & Radvansky, G. A. (1998). Situation models in language comprehension and memory. *Psychological Bulletin*, 123, 162–185.

Zwaan, R. A., Langston, M. C., & Graesser, A. C. (1995). The construction of situation models in narrative comprehension: An event-indexing model. *Psychological Science*, 6, 292–297. https://doi.org/10.1111/j.1467-9280.1995.tb00513.x

Index

Printed by Integrated Books International,
United States of America